SOMETHING BIGGER
THAN OVERTHROWING SMALL GOVERNMENTS

Chapter	Table Of Contents	
P	Preface	Page 3
1	Anointed	Page 5
2	God's Work	Page 25
3	Send Me	Page 42
4	Operation Restore Hope	Page 58
5	A Stone's Throw Away	Page 91
6	An Ounce of Prevention	Page 121
7	If We Do Not ... Who Will?	Page 137
8	Heading Home	Page 150
9	The War on Children	Page 157
10	Getting Started	Page 170
11	Operation Cinco De Mayo	Page 183
12	Operation Lily Pad	Page 203
13	Operation Kimchi	Page 252
14	Operation Salix	Page 273
15	Operation Iceberg	Page 302
16	Operation Pinwheel	Page 332
17	Operation Van Helsing	Page 356
18	Married To Al Qaeda	Page 401
19	Operation Dagger	Page 420
20	By What Authority?	Page 473
21	How To Murder A Child Without Killing Them	Page 485
22	What Hides In The Darkness	Page 502
23	If We Do Not ... Who Will?	Page 519
A	Addendums	Page 529
B	Bibliography	Page 553
T	Tribute	Page 557

Copyright © 2020 by Bazzel Baz

All rights reserved. No part of this publication may be reproduced, distributed, or transmitted in any form or by any means, including photocopying, recording, or other electronic or mechanical methods, without the prior written permission of the publisher, except in the case of brief quotations embodied in critical reviews and certain other noncommercial uses permitted by copyright law.

Published by Pen, Cloak, & Dagger Inc.
Manhattan Beach, CA 90266
United States of America

Author Website: BazBooks.com

Hardback ISBN 978-1-949280-06-7
Paperback ISBN 978-1-949280-08-1
eBook ISBN 978-1-949280-07-4

Printed in the United States of America

SOMETHING BIGGER

THAN OVERTHROWING SMALL GOVERNMENTS

BY BAZZEL BAZ
FORMER CIA SPECIAL OPERATOR
TURNED EXTREME HUMANITARIAN

PREFACE

In order to understand how I got where I am now, it's imperative to understand where I came from, the peculiar events, and the political, historical, philosophical and spiritual influences that set in motion a life dedicated to the rescue of missing and exploited American children. When people are chosen by God it is because their heart is not set upon the things of this world nor do they aspire after the honors of men. If they are people after God's own heart, then they are an open and willing vessel to serve God's purposes on this earth.

In the Bible God spoke to leaders when they were in a crisis of belief (Abraham, Isaac, Moses, Daniel, David, Gideon, and the list goes on). It is in their crisis of belief that God spoke to them about their calling. They knew it was God who called them, and they didn't question their calling.

I would hope that nothing written in this book would be taken as self-righteous, but understood as the viewpoint of a strongly opinionated man who has seen and experienced things that have made me confident in my calling ... despite my many shortcomings.

I encourage you, the reader, to mentally put on tennis shoes and leave your slippers by the lazy boy. The pay-off will enrich your life,

Something Bigger Than Overthrowing Small Governments

your world view and personal vitality by gaining perspective from a CIA-Special-Operator-turned-extreme-humanitarian.

Cultivate the journey by being in the moment — the sights, smells, reliving the sequence of events — while looking down on the scene from the perspective of history, realizing its significance, its relevance to the now, and its impact on the future.

Common life experiences result in common viewpoints based on common knowledge. Extraordinary life experiences result in extraordinary viewpoints based on extraordinary knowledge. The viewpoints in this book tend to be neither common, nor popular, but might be wiser and more accurate, allowing the reader to gain perspective.

The dramatic narrative of flashbacks and tangents are far from aimless if the reader is interested in this journey. The structure of this book is multi-dimensional and demands that the reader think, pay attention to details, analyze and navigate fault lines in order to follow the direction and flow of the manuscript ... no different than life itself. Seeking to view this book one-dimensionally means you'll miss the redeeming qualities of people and events that make the book interesting.

It is a book that much like life will take you in multiple directions but in the end, will come full circle. If you have never stepped out of your comfort zone, let me encourage you to take up the challenge of reading a book that defies the odds in so many ways ... a book that will send you on a journey that will inspire and empower you to make a difference in this world.

Bazzel Baz

CHAPTER 1
ANOINTED

Heading into any war zone can make a man come to grips with eternity. You evaluate life and try to figure out what motivates you to charge into the dragon's den, just so you know for sure that what you are about to do is worth it all, whether you survive or die in the process. As I tried to make sense of it all I could not help but take myself back to the beginning of my childhood, with an evidentiary process that set in concrete my right thinking. My life would be riddled with miraculous events that would convince me that the finger print of God was not just there to identify me as one of His own, but that he had sent me here to this earth for a purpose ... to glorify Him in what would become a calling to save children, and with that calling His angels would serve as my invisible army of protection.

In 1958 as a young lad of 2 ½ years, I was fearlessly compelled or even led by the spirit of adventure to run off to unknown parts of the neighborhood of Westover Air Force base where we lived ... against my mother's instructions to stay put and play next to the back door of the apartment. One block away I found a manhole under construction and that is where I played until the APs (Air Police) discovered me there and decided to take me down to the station for a little interrogation.

Actually, they were very nice, handing me a Coke and some cookies which as a child probably jump started my memory bank which

5

Something Bigger Than Overthrowing Small Governments

led to me disclosing the name and rank of my father. Not bad for a 2 ½ year old having just perfected the English language ... as my mother would tell it in years to follow. Both my parents arrived at the station to retrieve their son, and home we went. My mother was grateful for my return and at the same time baffled at how I could have gotten that far in such a short time. I recall her telling me afterwards in a very loving manner that it was important for me to obey her like she had asked the first time and never do this again. And I'm sure she was confident at the time that I would do exactly that ... but it wasn't the case.

Six months later at the age of 3 while sitting in the back seat of a Chevy, my mother drove us from my grandmother's house in Cayce, South Carolina. I would study the trees, the roads, the houses and intersections, plotting my fearless adventure to retrace that same three-mile trek as soon as we arrived home on Abbott Rd. It all landed in my favor once we got there, my mother telling me to go outside and play. I set out on foot through my neighborhood, crossing railroad tracks, calculating my dart through traffic over a major two-lane highway and eventually arriving back at my grandmother's house. My uncle Derwin stepped outside when he saw me and asked, "Where is your mother?" to which I replied, "At home." He laughed as if I were joking, until he exhausted his search, my mother nowhere to be found, and then picked up the phone and made the call.

"Maybelle, do you know where your son is?"

"Of course." Her response was typical of a mother who knew exactly where her son was. "He's playing in the yard."

Bazzel Baz

My uncle handed me the phone. "Hi Mommy, I'm at Grand Mama's."

In about ten minutes my mother rolled up in the car and approached me with a sense of curiosity, totally baffled at how I had managed to achieve such a feat. Then she smiled, relieved that I was okay, and we went home. I don't remember her ever speaking of it again except to my father ... neither of them was angered ... simply amazed ... just perhaps knowing that something not of this world was happening in my life.

I would push the envelope again while at that tender age by sneaking away again on two occasions and sitting myself next to the train track, watching as the train barreled towards me, listening to the engineer sound the warning horn and facing my fears as the exhilaration of the wind and power of the mighty locomotive sped by just one foot away. I was compelled to do so, understanding the danger of getting too close but all the while having no spirit of fear. It was as if I were facing a giant dragon, refusing to allow it to shake my fortitude. The acceleration of the wind and power that engulfed my tiny being when the train roared by had set something in motion in my soul that would later prove worthy of tackling bigger giants.

As I look back at all of it, how crazy was that as a child? It wasn't as if I was tempting God, but it was as if God was in some unexplainable way teaching me. I knew enough to not get on the track ... I wasn't stupid, but at those moments I also knew it was important for me to be there.

Something Bigger Than Overthrowing Small Governments

Even my dreams were influenced. My flying dreams were the best. I dreamed in color and I interacted with people that I had never met in real life. When I would awake from sleep in my growing years, I would see events unfold just as I had dreamed of them nights before. It wasn't as if I knew they were coming, it was just recall as they unfolded, a type of déjà vu. The very first time it occurred I was about seven years old. My father and mother and sister and I were driving to Georgetown, South Carolina to visit my grandfather. My sister and I were asleep in the back seat. I dreamed of a car with three young men in it heading in the opposite direction on the two-lane highway. Moments later I woke and leaned forward across the front seat and was talking with my mother, when suddenly the car being driven by the boys in my dream passed us going the opposite direction.

"I swear I just saw that car and boys in my dream," I blurted.

My mother reacted with, "I don't want you to ever use the word 'swear' again. Where did you learn that?"

"But I did," I remarked, "they were just in my dream."

My mom and dad gave a look to one another as if they knew something I didn't know but was quickly finding out. I can see it to this day the way they communicated with just their eyes ... the silence was deafening. I will never forget it. I sat back in my seat really thinking about the weirdness of what had just happened in my head.

I could not let it go and later at my grandfather's house in Georgetown spoke with my mother about what had occurred in my head. She told me it was a gift from God and not to make a big deal about it ... just like when the thunder from a storm would shake the foundation of the house and we sat quietly huddled in a corner with my Mom's arms wrapped around my sister and me. She would reassure us that this was the work of God and to respect them but fear them not, for

He loved us and would protect us. It made those moments more acceptable for a boy like me who felt as if I could call up the wind by invoking the name of Jehovah ... which to my surprise seemed to be the case when I would sit high in the trees and have my conversations with God.

Trees aren't always seen as the place a parent wants their kid to hang out because most of the time no good can come of it, or so parents would think. But on one such occasion in Augusta, Georgia, some good did come from my tree climbing. When the limb I was standing on broke and sent me to the ground, my head missed the pup tent line stake by a few inches.

Since it was a metal stake, I am pretty sure it would have split my head open like a ripe melon, and I would have made an early entry into the gates of Heaven. Or if I had survived, I would have spent the rest of my life looking like a freak explaining why I had a metal stake sticking out of my head. I doubt that medical technology in those days was advanced enough to safely remove it, so they would have just left it there. Okay, maybe that's not the case, but thanks to God neither happened.

The fall knocked the wind out of my lungs and when they filled back up, the exhale was a cry to bring every mother in the neighborhood to my rescue. But on this day it was just my mother, the only person I trusted and needed ... with an Avon lady in tow, wearing a pink dress, heels and funny round hat that looked more like a larger version of those hats you see on monkeys next to the blind man standing with a tin cup than anything that should be worn on a human head ... of big hair. I know she used White Rain for hairspray because you could smell it even in the open air of our back yard. God showed great favor that day in two ways ... He saved my life and He provided an excuse for my mother to get rid of a rather pushy makeup salesperson who just had no intention of leaving until she had sold my mother a ton of product.

This lady was so relentless in her mission that she said to my mother, "Oh, he'll be okay, bring him in the house and I can show you the Avon Kitty Cat Decanter and Charisma Cream Vanity Jar."

I was looking up at my mother's eyes while she held me in her arms, and I swear — wait ... I'm not supposed to use that word. Okay, I promise I saw fire in her eyes.

Something Bigger Than Overthrowing Small Governments

She turned to the Avon lady and said, "I think we're done here. You need to leave."

And with that the Avon lady in her pink dress and funny hat huffed and puffed and departed. My Mother held me close and then stood me to my feet.

"You stepped on a limb that was smaller than the size of your leg, didn't you?" she asked.

Some good always comes out of injury if you live to talk about it, and as I continued down the path that seemed more chosen for me than me choosing it, I made it a point to pay very close attention to other folk's stories of survival in my family ... like my father for example.

My father, strangely enough, has on multiple occasions been spared from death. Like the time his entire flight crew in Alaska were setting off on a mission and another airman begged my dad to allow him to take his place so he could visit his girlfriend. My father said yes, the flight took off, and moments later, crashed into a mountain killing all on board. My father, safely on the ground, realized his life had been spared ... and he would go on in life to encounter other similar events, making him take notice of God's favor.

I believe he was chosen by God because his heart was not set upon the things of this world, nor did he aspire the honors of men. He, like my mother and my sister, was a person after God's own heart, which made him an open and willing vessel to serve God's purposes on this earth.

Matthew 22:14 in the Bible tells us that "Many are called but few are chosen." We stop being chosen people when we cover our sins, gratify our pride, have vain ambitions or stop doing God's work. That is not my father and that is why he had favor.

Bazzel Baz

AIR CRASH KILLS 8 IN ALASKA
Albuquerque Journal New Mexico 1956-12-28

    Anchorage, Alaska (AP) - An Air Force tanker plane carried its eight-man crew to death Wednesday night on a snow-covered mountainside northwest of here. The Air Force reported a ground party and two helicopters had reached the spot where the four-engine plane struck, exploded and burned. There were no survivors. The Pentagon announced the plane's home base was Turner Air Force Base at Albany, Ga.

The crew members were:
LT. THOMAS H. PATTON, 28, Corvalis, Ore.
2nd LT. JAMES D. DELLINGER, 22, Charlotte, N.C.
1st LT. LEON E. REID, 23, Hicksville, N.Y.
1st LT. LUTHER G. LAMM, 26, Lucama, N.C.
M-SGT. OTTO D. McADAMS, JR., 32, Braddock, Pa.
T-SGT. THERMAN C. RAINER, 31, Raville, La.
S-SGT. JOHN B. PYLAND, 25, Ozark, Ala.
A2-C WILLIAM P. HUDGSON, 20, Redwood City, Calif.

    The air officials also declined to say whether the KB29, a tanker version of the World War II B29, was loaded with gasoline for aerial refueling at the time of the crash. The disaster came shortly after the plane's takeoff from the big Elmendorf base near here. The plane struck Bald Mountain, about 50 miles northwest, in the rugged Talkeetna range. The terrific explosion was heard, and the fire seen many miles away.
    One radio message was received from it after the take-off. An air force spokesman said there was no indication of any trouble.

Something Bigger Than Overthrowing Small Governments

Baz' father was spared from death on multiple occasions.

    The mystery of my life mirrored that of my father almost to the exact set of circumstances while I was stationed in Guantanamo Bay, Cuba from May 1982-83.

"The base defenses included extensive minefields, a fence topped with barbed wire and an innovation, hundreds of large buoys that were originally built to anchor underwater submarine nets and are now intended to block the base's roads should the Cubans ever attack." Our Commander Col. George Navadel was enthusiastic about our defense preparations.

American response to violation of the base, however, was likely to take other forms than instant reinforcement.

Senior officers at Roosevelt Roads in Puerto Rico made it clear that the United States would strike elsewhere in Cuba in the event of attack. The base was a relic of that first burst of American overseas expansion that began with the Spanish-American War. The Navy, recognizing Guantanamo's value as a coaling station, accepted the 45 square miles of land and water from the newly established Republic of Cuba in 1903. Americans have been there ever since. [1]

I was a fresh First Lieutenant taking over a real command, Leeward Guard. The Naval Base is divided into three main geographical sections: Leeward Point, Windward Point, and Guantanamo Bay. Guantanamo Bay physically divides the Naval Station into sections. The bay extends past the boundaries of the base into Cuba, where the bay is then referred to as Bahía de Guantanamo. Guantanamo Bay contains several cays, which are identified as Hospital Cay, Medico Cay, North Toro Cay, and South Toro Cay.

Leeward Point of the Naval Station is the site of the active airfield. Major geographical features on Leeward Point include Mohomilla Bay and the Guantanamo River. Three beaches exist on the Leeward side. Windward Point contains most of the activities on the Naval Station. There are nine beaches available to base personnel. The highest point on the base is John Paul Jones hill at a total of 495 feet. The geography of Windward Point is such that there are many coves and peninsulas along the bay shoreline providing ideal areas for mooring ships.

Something Bigger Than Overthrowing Small Governments

First Lieutenant Bazzel Baz, Guantanamo Bay, Cuba | 1982-1983

Upon my arrival at the barracks I was met by SSgt. Fink as four or five Enlisted Marines in war paint and weapons passed me by.

"Where are they headed?" I asked.

"Just on patrol ... it's part of the assignment," Fink replied.

I didn't think much about it at the time as we headed to my office where I would spend the next tour of duty relying on SSgt. (Staff Sergeant) Fink to keep me ahead of the game when it came to the needs of my Marines.

Within one week of that arrival I found myself standing in front of Col. George Navadel having to explain why there were U.S. Mine Field signs and an American flag in front of Cuban machine gun bunkers on Cuban soil. I didn't have an explanation ... I had no idea what he was talking about ... no one had reported it on our side of the base. Of course not ... why would they ... since it was highly likely my men were the ones who had done it. I immediately took a ride to the fence line and sure enough, there they were, just as he had said. Evidently the Cubans had reported it to the U.S. State Department, who

Bazzel Baz

fired off some pretty nasty inquiries to the United States Marine Corps, who in turn fired off some curious inquiries to GTMO and Col. Navadel.

An international incident was brewing, and I found myself having to think fast and act appropriately. I called SSgt. Fink into my office, looked him square in the eye and said, "Okay, tell me that the Marines with war paint on the day I arrived did not go across the fence line and do this."

He looked at me and smiled. "Sir, could have been anyone."

The fact that my Marines were doing what they had been trained to do, be fearless, and that they were actually exercising their skills to get to the Cuban bunkers and pull this off, was in my opinion admirable, and to some degree deserved a commendation. I actually relayed this in private to Col. Navadel and he did not put up much of an argument. He was such a Marine's Marine and he loved his men. He'd sacrifice for them if need be.

I returned the smile to SSgt. Fink and said, "Not sure what's going to happen with this, but I know that ultimately Col. Navadel will pay the price." The smile on SSgt. Fink's face dissolved.

Right then a call from Post 3 came in requesting my presence. I alerted my driver and made my way there, up the tower and grabbed the binoculars from the PFC on duty. And wouldn't you know it ... there stood Fidel Castro himself in all his glory with some Anglo

Something Bigger Than Overthrowing Small Governments

news reporter interviewing him about the incident. He was no more than 300 yards from our Post and a tempting delight to any would-be assassin. The CIA had for years made attempts on Castro's life and now he was being served up to me, a regular Marine, on a silver platter.

"You can probably make that shot sir," the young PFC said.

"You're probably right," I replied, still peering through the binoculars. "How far do you think that is?" I asked.

"Two ... two fifty," he said. Something told me that the shot that would echo around the world would also put me behind bars the rest of my life and so I pocketed the thought, only to pull it out from time to time and think how I would have changed history. Discretion is the greatest part of valor, and on that day, I don't know if it was a good judgment call or not ... having an opportunity to rid the world of evil. But what I did know is the last thing Col. Navadel needed was another international incident. We had come to love him as much as he loved us, and it was that respect and admiration that made me think of what would honor him rather than make me famous.

As I handed back the binoculars, I placed my hand on the shoulder of the PFC, "God will have His way with Castro."

I looked out over the land and smiled with the thought of my Marines actually outsmarting the Cubans and making it to their bunkers and back undetected. Three weeks later those Marines responsible for crossing the fence line would turn themselves in to Col. Navadel. They would be officially reprimanded and shipped off the island. Col. George Navadel gained my eternal admiration as one of the most impressive and gracious Marine Corps Officers I served under, for I am certain he stood in defiance of liberal politicians who would have wanted a stiffer penalty for my good Marines.

U.S. and Cuban troops placed some 55,000 land mines across the "no man's land" around the perimeter of the naval base creating the second largest minefield in the world, and the largest in the Western Hemisphere. My job wasn't to shoot Castro ... my job ... defend the base.

Bazzel Baz

The Second Largest Minefield in the World

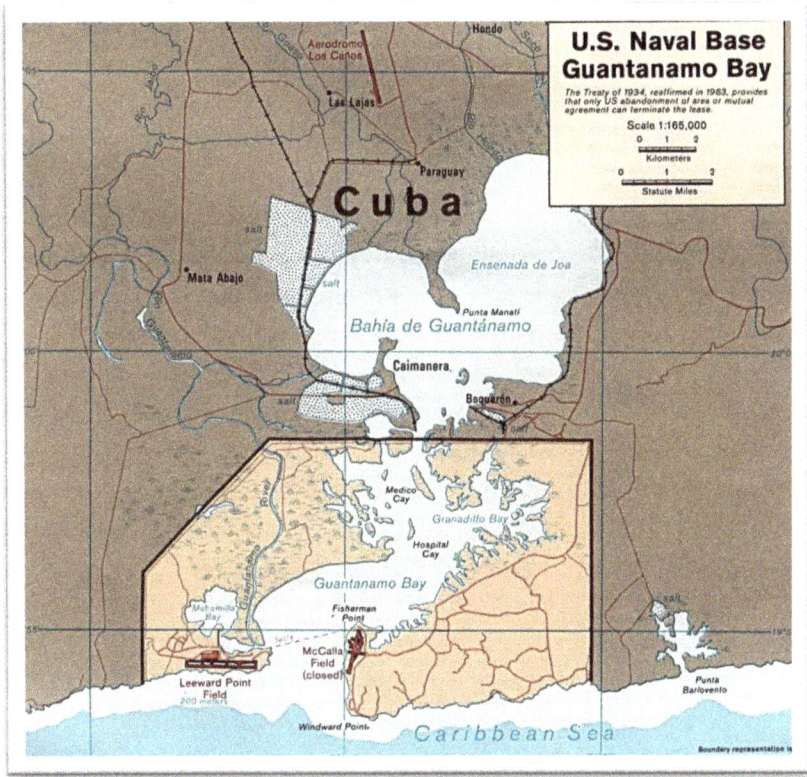

    The coral dust flared from underneath the wheels of three USMC jeeps, more like smoke than debris, as they came to a sudden stop in front of my barracks. It was a Tuesday morning in March. As dynamic as their entry, the men in each vehicle wore bare-chested toughness covered only with flak jackets and dirt, as if they had been running from the enemy with no time to shower or even catch a breath. They remained silent, just looking at me and my Staff Sergeant ... just looking at them. There was a touch of rogue permeating the stench of sweat that beaded their faces, as if cheating death was more serious than I in my inexperience had tasted. It made me proud to be standing there in the company of such fine Marines, even though I hadn't any idea who they were.

    They reminded me of The Rat Patrol, the American action and adventure television series that aired on ABC between 1966 and 1968.

Something Bigger Than Overthrowing Small Governments

It was a series that followed the exploits of four Allied soldiers — three Americans and one Englishman — who were part of a long-range desert patrol group in the North African campaign during World War II. Their mission was to attack, harass and wreak havoc on Field Marshal Rommel's vaunted Afrika Korps. If I did not know better, I would have thought this was them reincarnated, minus the Englishman of course.

The Marine to the right of the driver in the first jeep slowly swung his feet out of the not-so-well-designed M151 to find his place on the very unforgiving geography of Cuba — especially if you wanted to low crawl your way to a defensive position. He stepped front and center, jovial and impressive, with just enough weight to warrant caution for his next PFT (physical fitness test). His motto — at least in my mind — if walking was good for your health the postman would be immortal. "I'm Ed Polocz, welcome to GTMO."

I couldn't help but smile. He was the most undemanding and yet straightest Marine outside of Col Navadel I had met thus far, making no bones about the fact that we were all stationed in the armpit of Cuba, and that maintaining a clean uniform was an uphill battle and frankly dumb as far as he was concerned ... especially polished boots.

We went inside to my office and he offered an amazing description of himself and his team, who were responsible for maintaining the very minefield, a portion of those 55,000 land mines across the "no man's land" around the perimeter of the naval base. That meant stepping into the minefield in a calculated fashion almost every day with no room for error, and moving, replacing and shifting both anti-tank and anti-personnel mines around, making sure you recorded their new hiding place. It was nuts as far as I was concerned, but Ed felt rather comfortable with it all as a Combat Engineer. He spoke of his family living on the Windward side and how he and they were ready to leave the dust bowl in a few months, a permanent change of duty. You couldn't help but like him more than most, not cavalier by any means but just fun to be around, giving hope for anyone having island fever.

He concluded by asking me to join him and his team in the minefield to see firsthand what it was all about. I felt it was worth accepting since these were the mines that were pretty much the first line of defense for me and my men at the barracks. I certainly did not want to unappreciative.

Mine field, Guantanamo Bay, Cuba

His SSgt. stepped into the office, "Skipper, we gotta go before the sun gets too hot."

Ed shook my hand and I grabbed my flak jacket, 45 cal. and canteens, stepping out the door when ... the phone rang. "Wait one, I'll be right there," pretty excited about joining the Rat Patrol.

Headquarters on Windward had a call for me from Col. Navadel and put me on hold. I sat there at my desk waiting for about four minutes when Ed walked back in my office. "Holding for the C.O.," I blurted.

Ed, pointed at his watch and said, "We'll meet you out there," and told me which area of the minefields and off what track of road, but honestly, I can't remember exactly where it was ... I just knew I'd find it with the help of my men.

The conversation with the boss lasted about twenty minutes. I hung up the phone and started out the door when ... KABOOM!!! ... the sound of an explosion to the west of my position, in the mine fields of course. The combat engineers were doing their thing, clearing mines as they did day in and day out. A bit of excitement flushed through my

Something Bigger Than Overthrowing Small Governments

system as I thought of the education, I was about to receive at the hands of some very competent war fighters. I could see the dirty plume billow skyward as I had seen on multiple occasions when a mine would be tripped by a deer navigating the deadly fault lines not so well. And then, I could hear ... WOP, WOP, WOP, the blades of a UH1 Huey quickly approaching from Windward. Something wasn't right and I summoned my driver immediately.

My instincts told me what I did not want to hear ... and I did my best to close the ears of my mind with positive thoughts and calmness reserved for those who come from a place of logic rather than emotion, but as hard as I tried, the thought of someone killed bled through the cracks of my virgin character the closer we came to the site of the incident. When we arrived the UH1 was departing, and with it was Ed Polocz, blown in half and barely hanging on for dear life. His team of combat engineers were in shock but holding it together as would be expected of Marines, not trying to predict the outcome but knowing there was little hope.

His second in command, a Gunnery Sgt., whose name I cannot recall, told me that they had properly marked off the safe zone with engineer tape but that Ed had mistakenly stepped over a few inches on top of a M16 bounding anti-personnel mine also known as a bouncing betty.

BOUNCING BETTY M16 MINE

When emplaced, most of an M16 mine is buried underground so it can be extremely difficult to spot them visually, particularly in areas of long grass, heavy undergrowth or other debris. The M16 contains large amounts of metal, so it is very easy to detect using a mine detector. However, it is important to note that the act of moving the detection head over the ground may strike the prongs and trigger the mine. The mine consists of a cast iron body in a thin steel sleeve. A central fuse well on the top of the mine is normally fitted with a pronged M605 pressure and tilt fuse. Sufficient pressure on the prongs or tension on an attached tripwire causes the release of a striker.

The freed striker is forced into a percussion cap which ignites a short pyrotechnic delay. The purpose of this delay is to allow the victim to move off the top of the mine, to prevent its upward movement from being blocked. Once the delay has burned through, a 4.5-gram black powder charge is ignited, which launches the inner iron body of the mine up into the air (leaving behind the steel outer sleeve). The charge also ignites a second pair of pyrotechnic delays.

The mine rises to a height of 0.3 to 1.7 meters before one or both of the pyrotechnic delays detonate the main charge of the mine, which sprays high-velocity steel fragments 360° around the point of detonation. These metal fragments have an expected casualty radius of 27 meters. [2]

The Gunnery Sgt. said that in the flash of a moment when their eyes met, Ed broke a quirky smile as if he knew the fatal mistake was more than he bargained for on that day. It would be reported by the Navy that Captain Edward S. Polocz Jr., a Marine from Pitman in Southern New Jersey, died of injuries suffered in an accidental mine explosion at the Naval Base at Guantanamo Bay in Cuba. It would be recorded in my mind that on that very day, had I been alongside him, I too would have probably died.

There were not many days that I traveled the fence line that paralleled the minefields that I did not think of Ed or the rest of his kind who continued day in and day out to perform their duties. But life would go on and the mission would keep us occupied enough to think less of death and more of life ... or at least until I was reminded of it again.

I made a policy of taking the ferry to the Windward side every Friday morning to attend a staff briefing. Afterwards I would take that same ferry back to my headquarters on Leeward. More often than not, even if the ferry was pulling away, it would stop and push back in to shore to let us board. I always knew I could count on the ferry captain to be kind that way.

In April 1983 another Friday staff briefing on Windward would run long and my jeep driver and I were late getting to the docks, the

Something Bigger Than Overthrowing Small Governments

ferry pulling away to make the return trip to Leeward side. I had not seen my parents and sister in about six months and was eager to get back to my side of the island so I could catch a C131-F flight up to Naval Air Station (NAS) Jacksonville, Florida, and then bring me back that Saturday. We waited for the ferry to return to shore like it normally did, but on this day the courtesy was not extended, and you guessed it ... I missed my flight.

I was pretty disappointed when I got back to my side of the island that Thursday only to watch the C-131-F take off from the runway with about 1/3 of the passengers being friends or acquaintances from the island. I also knew they were happy to get off the island, a bit of R & R needed by all of us, and for just a moment I felt left out of the celebration. I made the call home to my family in the U.S. explaining that I would not be arriving, and my sister said, "Don't worry, we love you, God has a reason for everything. We'll see you for Christmas in December."

That Saturday in April 1983, at NAS Jacksonville was the scene of the second worst airplane crash in the stations' history. Of the 14 personnel on board their home bound C-131 flight to Guantanamo Bay, Cuba, the very flight I was supposed to be on, only one survived the crash. The disaster occurred shortly after takeoff from NAS Jacksonville around noon on Saturday, April 30.

Naval Air Station Ferry, Jacksonville, Florida

C-131-F Crash Naval Air Station
Jacksonville, FL, April 30, 1983

The plane had just crossed the St. Johns River, heading east over San Jose Blvd, when the pilot radioed that his left engine was on fire and he was returning to the base. One minute later, debris from the ill-fated aircraft struck a car on Old King's Road. Then as the aircraft was over the St. Johns River about ¼ mile from the start of the runway and approximately 200 feet up, the left wing separated from the aircraft. When the fuselage hit the water the plane exploded, killing 13 of those on board. The sole survivor, AT2 Melissa Kelly, suddenly finding herself in the St. Johns River grabbed onto the first floating object she could reach; her own suitcase. [3]

Something Bigger Than Overthrowing Small Governments

    For all of us at Gitmo, the tragedy shook us as a military community and I would spend years remembering my sister's words "God has a reason for everything," playing it against the memory of how annoyed I was at the ferry captain for not coming back to shore ... like smacking a tennis ball against the backboard over and over, the swing not quite polished enough to get it right.

    The dust of this tragic event would settle on top of the loss of Ed Polocz, something I had tried to keep in the duffle bag of my mind ... but now, both were too amplified, and I was too fragile to ignore them. Two times God had saved my life in Cuba to let me know I had His favor, His anointing, for *something bigger in life than overthrowing small governments.* And such words like "favor" and "anointing" would never even dawn on me if people of faith, who would be there to see a multitude of other miraculous events in my life, hadn't mentioned it. It didn't matter what the rest of the world would think. The rest of the world hadn't been in my shoes, seen what I had seen or heard what I was hearing from God in more ways than just in my head and my heart ... a voice distinguishable from other voices. My prayer as a child to make my life the biggest adventure of all was about to come true ... and God wasn't finished with me ... or the world.

Chapter 2
GOD'S WORK

I was recruited by the CIA in 1985. As a Captain in the United States Marine Corps at that time I was responsible for developing one of the first Counter Terrorism Curriculums for the USMC. It would find its home at the Staff NCO Academy with the help of more experienced Officers than myself, Col. Patty Collins of the USMC Command and Staff College at Quantico Va., Color Sergeant Shanks of the Royal British Marines, Sergeant Major Beck, Col. Jim Williams and Medal of Honor recipient Col. Wesley Fox , both who commanded the Staff NCO (Non Commissioned Officer) Academy also in Quantico Va. on separate occasions. The Marine Corps was responding to the 1983 attack by a suicide bomber who detonated a truck bomb in the building serving as a barracks for the 1st Battalion 8th Marines in Beirut, Lebanon. The death toll was 241 American servicemen: 220 Marines, 18 sailors, and three soldiers. Our dead were beyond the count of grief and I was ready to lead the charge of retribution in any way I could. When men looked at me, I wanted them to say, "There is one that I can follow."

It was a typical day in Quantico as I headed out the gates to attend a Counter Terrorism Conference at the National War College ... sweltering humidity that would turn my well-starched uniform into a wrinkled laundry bag by the time I drove my jeep with no air conditioner through the D.C. traffic. Exciting as it was to think that I would be for the first time sitting with some of the highest-ranking officers in all departments of the military — who by the way, had been down range in Vietnam and other conflicts — I was a bit apprehensive.

I was young, no combat experience and only had the knowledge of guerrilla warfare that I acquired from the stories of my grandfather fighting against the Ottoman Empire in the 1900s and the never-told stories of my Green Beret father, who graciously tolerated my curiosity of war and offered advice that would encourage me to follow my heart

Something Bigger Than Overthrowing Small Governments

but to never love war. He made it clear that duty was different from desire and that discretion was the greatest part of valor.

My journey to the National War College wasn't as bad as I thought it would be. I looked relatively intact, enough to be presentable if I seated myself more towards the back of whatever the room offered. I made it a habit to stay as sharp in uniform as possible at all hours, not unlike every Marine I know. We take pride in everything we do, and attention to detail serves us well beyond threads that may unravel on a button. It literally keeps us alive while others are dying around us in combat. I believe it started for me at The Citadel as a cadet, so it was effortless to live this way in the Marine Corps and I am grateful for it.

As I walked towards this institution of strategic warfare, I stopped at the main entrance to take it all in, trying to decide whether this building was a replica of the Smithsonian Institution or The National Cathedral or a combination of both. I wondered if I would depart that day from this institute of higher learning with as much tactical knowledge as General Patton, ready to destroy every terrorist that was a threat to my country.

Its two giant Roman or Corinthian columns skyrocketed to the statue of an eagle perched looking to the right. It brought back memories of how Ken Bowman and I as freshman cadets at The Citadel one night decided to scale a building to place an inscribed belt with buckle around the neck of a similar statue on campus. Our mission failed miserably after Ken decided that he could not finish the monkey climb up the drainpipe and chose to let go and take his chances with the 30-foot fall. There was no amount

Baz' Graduation from the Citadel

of encouragement from my position already on the top of the building that could convince him otherwise and it ended with him breaking his ankle, busting his head, crushing his spleen and wrist if I recall. I found my way through a window, down the stairs inside the building and to Ken, who I fireman-carried to the infirmary.

We were scared as any freshman would be and held allegiance to one another and our cover story ... a procedure that had been drilled in our heads from day one. We suffered the consequences of our actions ... me receiving 100 tours and Ken never coming back to The Citadel because his recovery time was too extensive. He was an amazing classmate and to this day I will never forget him. But as I closed the memory of that event gazing up at that eagle, I put it all behind me and marched up the stairs of The National War College to carry out my duties. I decided not to climb this building.

As you can imagine, the day was filled with good speakers and not so good speakers, subject matter that begs for comedic content but that is all so difficult to do because we're talking about bad guys doing bad things to innocent people. So you take it all in with great patience and cipher what you can to make you more intelligent than those at that time who pretended to know a lot about terrorism but had never set foot in an undercover capacity in a terrorists' camp to actually learn the truth. I know this to be true because years later I would find myself and other operators doing just that, cautiously infiltrating a former PLO camp in Tunisia to collect intelligence. I myself believed it was not enough to just dance with the devil ... I believed it best to poke him in the eye as well.

And so, my thoughts drifted to more clandestine strategies as the voice of various speakers echoed in the cobwebs of my brain. It wasn't enough for me to learn about all the stats and terrorist operations that seemed to be the bulk of each speaker's presentation ... I wanted to know what I personally could do to stop the evil.

As the day continued, there was a wealth of knowledge and indeed I was sitting among some of the finest officers in our military. But as mentioned, I was in the back of the room pretty much hidden as best I could, just to keep a low profile, which is where I felt most comfortable ... not because I lacked confidence but because I felt comfortable flying under the radar.

Something Bigger Than Overthrowing Small Governments

Humility has its benefits. It allows you to stay quiet in a meeting while everyone else pontificates. When you're finally called upon, you can button up the meeting with an all-inclusive statement that either enhances what everyone else said or points out the flaws in what was said. Either way you're not shooting in the dark and you appear much wiser.

I was happy where I was, but I was only fooling myself because there were two gentlemen happy where they were as well and probably where they were for the same reason. I caught a glimpse of a name tag on one gentleman's civilian suit coat that said, "John Cham Roué, CIA." What ... CIA? Wait a minute, I thought those guys were undercover, in the shadows, invisible, ghost, spooks, secret squirrels that NEVER appeared in public. It actually took me by surprise and was creepy in a way ... not that they were CIA, but that they were CIA and sitting right behind me. Knowing what I know now from my own training in the clandestine service, I wasn't hiding much of my unease from them and for certain they could tell that the eyes in back of my head were wide open. I didn't squirm nor did I even breathe at that point ... or so it seemed. I wanted so badly to turn around and take another look at that name tag just to make sure I wasn't delusional, but I never made that move. It wasn't because I was afraid. In fact it was thrilling that I had encountered "big foot" when others were still trying to determine if he or its breed even existed. No, I just sat there knowing that when I turned around, they would have disappeared, just like in every espionage movie I had seen. And you know what ... I was right.

The last speaker concluded and told everyone to take a 15-minute coffee break. I stood up, looked behind me and POOF! No spooks. A bit disappointed I made my way to the daunting halls of history to find the nearest head (bathroom). I finished at the watering hole and collected my thoughts before heading for a cup of Joe (coffee). There was no line in front of the silver stallion dispenser ... giant size of course because as most know ... the military uses coffee to not only fuel war fighters, but they use it to run tanks ... well at least in theory. And since most Marines are built like tanks it just stands to reason that the coffee dispenser would be "ginormous." See how that works?

Anyway, I grabbed a cup of Joe and leaned gently against the bulkhead (wall) when suddenly a voice from heaven said, "Captain Baz how would you like to do God's work?" I thought I would spit my coffee out as I choked off-guard seeing John Chamroué standing behind me. His comrade wasn't trailing far from his side, with a slight smile breaking the wrinkles on his face ... I think they were pleased with their sniper-like approach of sorts. Even though I realized it wasn't a voice from heaven, or at least not yet, it didn't water down my curiosity or my manners, and I extended my hand for an introduction. Right off the bat I asked about his overt identification and stated how unusual I found that to be. He smiled and told me he was a recruiter and that his job required him to travel the U.S. and the world in search of men and women who might make good candidates for the Clandestine Service.

I later came to understand that "doing God's work" was a term frequently used by most of us in the CIA to quietly initiate discussion about clandestine operations. I don't recall ever having a secret handshake or a wink of the eye or any of that stuff you find in organizations like the Masons, Moose, Elks, Rabbits, Birds or whatever you may think is a secret society. No, they were simply quiet professionals who just knew one another as if they could smell it. And for some reason on that day, John Chamroué could smell my enthusiasm and interest ... as if he actually knew that the letter I wrote to the "Counter Intelligence Agency" when I was ten years old was on file all these years. Yes, it is true that even as a kid, and even before I knew it was actually the "Central" rather than "Counter" Intelligence Agency, I had fired off my request to come aboard. And believe it or not, they actually responded and said basically, "Come see us when you grow up." I had thought little to nothing more about it until now.

Wow, who would have guessed, real spies standing in front of me asking if I am interested in working for them. John shook my hand and said, "We'll be in touch." And with that he and his trusted sidekick departed, but not too far before he looked back, pointing his finger and said, "Let's just keep this between you and me, okay?"

A little beside myself with joy of course, I returned to my seat to finish listening to whomever else was on the "I-know-more-about-terrorists-than-you" list but honestly wasn't even hearing a word. I kept playing the conversation between me and "big foot" over and over, and then suddenly I realized ... I had not even given him my contact information. I was screwed. My big moment to be a part of "The

Something Bigger Than Overthrowing Small Governments

Gentlemen of the Shade" had come and gone and I was so caught up in the events that I failed to provide the most critical of information, my number, my address, my post office box, my shoe size, my everything and anything that would ensure they did in fact reach back out. And worst of all, they probably noticed my lack of mindfulness and had made their decision right then and there that I wasn't sharp enough to catch flies.

The day was a little longer on the drive back to Quantico and frankly I didn't care whether my uniform looked like a wrinkled laundry bag. I was preoccupied with what I thought was a little devastating, my failure to provide my contact information, but as I drew closer to the Staff NCO Academy, I shook it off and like every good Marine, marched forward with the next assignment in mind. Everything happens for a reason and sometimes I don't understand it all but I'm okay with not understanding it all.

The week and in fact the month to follow would see nothing but the printed pages of a book that GySgt. Hartsel and I were working on titled *Terrorism Survival Handbook for Families*. It was a rather skinny but highly explosive volume of all the right things to do and not do in order to survive being the target of a terrorist attack. We hoped to sell and distribute the much-needed advice as a means of pocketing a little cash ourselves, but it took a backseat to the plethora of work thrown at us by the Academy, which was not only training up noncommissioned officers to lead Marines, but now lead them against an enemy of Islamic fighters who declared Jihad on America. I was certain we would be at war within the year against the "rag heads," a name used within the ranks to describe any middle easterner taking up arms against the U.S. So I braced myself hoping to be one of the first to go should that happen.

Congress delayed commitments to not only the Marine Corps but to all the services until they could come to grips with how the war would be fought. So we cooled our jets and settled back into academia, itching for a fight but seeing none on the horizon. It was on such a day after lengthy discussions with Col. Williams about the political handcuffs placed on the armed forces that I entered my office to find a yellow sticky on my desk that read, "Report to Col. Dorman in Bld. ▓▓▓ at 1500 hrs. tomorrow."

Bazzel Baz

      I approached my immediate supervisor Maj. Allard to inquire about the note, which he knew nothing about. In fact, no one in the office that I asked seemed to know anything about the note or where it came from or in fact, who Col. Dorman was. The only thing they did know was where Bld. ▇ was located, down on the Potomac River across from the Naval Hospital somewhere ... somewhere.

      So the next day I took a walk, longer than I expected to find Bld. ▇. Sure enough, there it stood not far off the banks of the Potomac River in all its dilapidated glory, unusual for any building on a spit and polish Marine Corps base. An eyesore at best, the white paint flaked from the wooden trim like the body of a snake shedding its skin. Truth be known, snakes do not shed their skin. They shed a layer of ... well ... shed. They retain their skin after shedding (obviously), and their skin is usually much more vibrant immediately after the shed. But I wasn't expecting anything about this building to be vibrant, especially inside by the looks of what was staring me in the face on the exterior. The grass was uncut with enough growth to hide a sniper in a ghillie suit, the red brick old enough to have been used by Moses to throw at Pharaohs' Army, and mildewed concrete steps leading to a bristled screen door doing its best to protect an even thicker hardwood door that needed a good coat of paint itself ... it had seen better days. I double and triple checked my yellow sticky to make sure I was at Bld. ▇ which the more I think about it, appeared empty and ready for a demolition team. I had heard that the Naval Hospital was soon to be abandoned and demolished so why not this building? I turned to walk away and then thought, "What does it hurt, knock on the door," and so I did.

      I knocked once, twice, three times ... nothing. I turned to depart and then, the door opened. A distinguished female in her late 50s, a well-dressed civilian smiled and said, "Captain Baz, Col. Dorman is expecting you." She held the door as I entered and nodded in the direction to my right, down the hall. I glanced back to see her closing the door behind me and then I noticed where I was standing. The interior of the building had an elaborate decor of dark hardwood, polished floors, with something historically romantic about its formal surroundings. It was completely devoted to serious undertakings that I would not understand until my departure in the next hour.

Something Bigger Than Overthrowing Small Governments

    I knocked on the door to my right and entered only to find another room decorated in a fashion to bring dramatic style to the space that was anything but Marine Corps. From the custom oak-front cabinets to the gold button trim on the chairs, this room was rooted in sleek sophistication. Overhead, a chandelier crafted from fine glass anchored the center of the room, where a solid, yet sleek couch stood grandly. Dark brown upholstery with gold trellis design on the chairs brought dignified color to the space. The wallpaper bridged the gap between the light and dark tones. "Captain Baz reporting as ordered sir," in commanding fashion, I voiced. Silence blanketed the air with a thickness that could have choked an elephant.

    Sitting in front of me was a mahogany desk with the brown leather chair turned with its back to me. All I could see was the top of silver crew cut head and a trail of cigar smoke dancing upward. It felt like I stood there for ages. The leather chair finally rotated 180 degrees to reveal a Marine's Marine ... piercing eyes, square jawed, tanned. Looking me right in the face was a man who meant business. He pulled the cigar from his mouth and studied it like an artifact, saying nothing and yet saying everything with a tint of silence indicative of the same cold steel of a bayonet. He placed the fire stick in the ashtray and fixed his attention on the other Marine in the room ... me.

    "I understand the CIA has been in touch with you." Now you can imagine what I was thinking. I hadn't mentioned my meeting with John Cham roué to anyone, especially anyone in the Marine Corps. My lips were as tight as the anus on a man preparing for the proctologist. I didn't know how to respond and so I didn't. Col. Dorman glared at me as if he was pleased with how I reacted. He eased back into his chair and began to tell me a story. "Do you remember hearing about the Naval Attaché who was shot by terrorist from a speeding vehicle in the streets of Beirut as he was leaving the Hilton Hotel?"

    "I recall hearing something like that, Sir," I replied.

    "Yes, but did you hear the rest of the story about how he picked himself up and pulled his trusted Uzi from his briefcase and as the terrorist turned their car back to run him over, he gunned them all down?"

    "No, Sir, I did not hear that part," wondering where this was all going.

"Well that was me, Captain, and after killing those bastards I took a seat in the Hilton and said, "Get me a doctor" ... which they did, and that's why I love the Hilton."

I just stood there taking it all in and finally said, "I'm not sure what this has to do with me being here, Sir."

"It has everything to do with you being here, Captain. You see, I was that Naval Attaché, but I wasn't a Naval Attaché, I was CIA and I'm here to ask you, boy ... do you want to join the CIA?"

Evidently the long arms of the CIA were longer than I suspected, and I relished the idea that they had people undercover on loan from the Marine Corps. It was all pretty intriguing and evermore enticing as I stood there still not knowing what to say. "You're a Citadel grad, a fine Marine Corps Officer and if you stay the course, you'll probably pick up a star or two down the road ... if being a General is what you want. Or you can join the CIA and see the world ... it's just a matter of what you want out of life."

"I need a little time to think about this, Sir," finally escaped my lips, solemn at best, but nevertheless understood by both of us that this was a big decision. "You do that, Captain," he ordered and then, "You're dismissed."

I took a step back, did an about face and clutched the brass door handle when my mind jumped into gear with one very important question. I looked over my shoulder and asked, "Sir, what would you do if you were me?"

He picked up his cigar and once again studied it more intensely than before, as if figuring what words of wisdom would be appropriate. He leaned back in the chair and rotated it 180 degrees to no longer expose himself. I was now looking at the identical posture of things when I first entered the room, the top of a silver crew cut head and a trail of cigar smoke dancing upward. "Why, I would join the CIA, boy ... I'd join the CIA."

Two weeks later in 1985 my Honorable Discharge was being processed, no questions asked by my superiors. I was about to enter the most exciting and most dangerous time of my life in the world of espionage.

I would later come to know Col. Dorman as "Two Dogs," as was so eloquently put by those in the CIA that knew of him and his

Something Bigger Than Overthrowing Small Governments

exploits, particularly an Intelligence Star recipient by the name of Jim Monroe. He was the first face I saw when I arrived at an out-of-the-way covert office. Jim was a Crimson Tide patriot from Alabama who sported a southern accent that took the edge off his rock-hard demeanor when I first met him. He had a good smile, but not to be underestimated since his time down range flourished in the days when MACSOGV and the Phoenix Program ruled the darkness in the Vietnam Conflict.

In 1968 during the Tet Offensive, he, along with Drew Dix United States Army military adviser to the Army of the Republic of Vietnam commandeered a jeep with a 50 caliber machine gun. They repeatedly entered Chau Phuon and rescued a number of stranded Army Nurses and other civilians who would surely have died at the hands of the invading North Vietnamese Army. For this Jim Monroe would receive the CIA's highest recognition, the Intelligence Star, and Drew Dix, the Medal of Honor.

Evidently, I had passed the gauntlet of psychological testing, medical approvals, polygraphs and interviews in order to be put on a three-year probationary status, or I would not be standing in front of Monroe, welcoming me to the small but elite enclave known as Ground Branch, Special Operations Group.

Buck Ashby, his second in command entered the room and stood tall to my right, informally observing the conversation. He then slid some paperwork on Jim's desk and escorted me to another office for my introduction to John Herms. John was one of two men who would oversee my assignments as my team leaders for the next seven years until I transferred to Maritime Branch for waterborne operations. The other team leader would be Ron Franklin.

John was a Citadel grad as well, recruited to the CIA from Delta Force, and went by the name of Pencil Neck. Yes, Pencil Neck. To this day I have absolutely no idea where he got that name. He was a rather lean individual, more like a stick than a boulder, but I noticed nothing odd about his neck at all.

John Herms, "Pencil Neck," team leader in Somalia with 106RR Vehicle

    John would go on to retire from the CIA and contract in Afghanistan in 2015 teaching Afghan pilots how to maneuver Hind Helicopters. He dressed his upper lip with a rather bushy mustache and laughed at some of the strangest things ... like when I had parachute malfunctions back to back on the same jump day. It was the type of laugh that resonates from college roommates when someone puts peanut butter in your shoes as a practical joke, as long as no one is hurt in the process. Well I survived the potentially fatal skydiving episode, so I think he felt relieved to know that he could spend the rest of his life telling that story and laughing just as hard as he did immediately after the event.

    He still laughs about it even to this day. When I really think about it, it made me laugh too. And in the future when things would get hot and we were staring death in the face ... weirdly enough ... I would laugh at even moments like those.

Something Bigger Than Overthrowing Small Governments

Ron Franklin, "Popeye," team leader, and Baz at Sturgis, South Dakota

    Ron Franklin was former Sgt.Maj. for Delta Force, lived with the Hmong in Vietnam, was beat up, shot up, broken up all in the name of special operations, and managed to more than survive as a pillar of muscular strength in his enormous biceps and forearms ... thus the name "Popeye." Even his laugh was that of Popeye, and his Tabasco flavor concoctions in an ammo can brought new meaning to fine dining in Angola. But he didn't always find humor in things, like the time Greg Vogel and I put a live chicken in his footlocker hoping for it to spring out and scare the dickens out of the tough guy when he opened it. I'm sure that the exhaustion of training Contra Rebels day in and day out did not make for the best of relaxed vacations, and tensions could have been running a little high, but hey, we thought it would take the edge off a bit. But we were wrong ... really wrong.

    One thing about Ron was the fact that he maintained his tie to civilization by the way he kept his clean, pressed, nicely folded underwear and white T-shirts in the footlocker, rank and filed like men in a platoon. Greg and I waited in the hooch with the anticipation of children eager to open Christmas presents. I could see we were both holding our breath so we could blurt out our laughter like two opera singers.

Ron came in out of his shower, opened the lid to his footlocker and just stood there looking down. There was nothing for us to react to ... nothing was happening except the silence of men soon to be walking dead ... should Ron react with the fury he had unleashed against the worst of his enemies in combat. "Crap ... chicken crap," was all he said. He looked at Greg and I and we knew it wasn't as funny as we hoped for. We immediately jumped up and started apologizing. Greg and I looked down in the locker and sure enough ... chicken crap, all over Ron's army of white underwear — the green kind that I recall used to get stuck on the bottom of my shoes when I was a boy at my grandfather's ... the kind that you scrape off but it doesn't scrape off, it just smears more.

Greg looked at me, I looked at Greg and we sort of started laughing but managed to hold it in long enough for Ron to exit the hooch with, "Clean my clothes." It wasn't that the chicken crap was funny as much as it was the poor chicken who had decided that this was her new home and just sat there looking up at Ron, defying him to remove her. He eventually forgave Greg and me after he ran us and a troop of Contra Rebels up and down the runway with our AK-47s extended over our head for what felt like three hours ... which wasn't funny. But hey, when you're seeking forgiveness from those who mean the world to you, three hours is nothing, right? Some days you're the dog and some days you're the hydrant.

I guess I could go on and on about not only these heroes but a dozen more that I served with who influenced my life for the better and who did the most incredible deeds for the nation. But then this would turn out to be a book about my CIA career rather than certain events in the CIA being the springboard to my life with *The Association for the Recovery of Children* (ARC). I can say, however, that I am the least of these great men of the CIA, and my admiration for them is indescribable. They know who they are. And when I salute them with a toast, I do so repeating the famous words of Col. Nick Pratt now deceased, "Here's to us, not many like us, in fact very few ... and most of them are dead." To this day I regard most of them with the highest

Something Bigger Than Overthrowing Small Governments

esteem ... a few, and very few I would never want to serve with again. And they as well know exactly who they are.

Over the course of the next ten years I would find myself engaged in just about every history-changing event one could hear about in the media, Angola with UNITA, Russian invasion of Afghanistan, Iran Contra, drug wars in South America, building hostage rescue forces, training anti-terrorists units, civil war in Somalia, airline hijackings, the fall of the Soviet Union and the list goes on. It would alter the way I saw life more than I could imagine, sharpen me beyond expectations and allow me to learn from some of the finest operators to ever set foot on this planet. With much thanks and gratitude to all of them for what I learned from them, by the end of my time with the CIA my resume would come to read as follows:

RESUME - BAZZEL BAZ

Operative supporting the Central Intelligence Agency and other U.S. Government agencies in field intelligence collection operations throughout the Far East, Middle East, Northern Europe, Central/South America, Mediterranean and Africa.

- Recipient of the Intelligence Commendation Medal for the performance of especially commendable service or for an act or achievement significantly above normal duties which results in an important contribution to the mission of the Agency.
- Directly responsible for running clandestine operations that resulted in new political and economic initiatives ending the Cold War.
- As a member of SAD, directly involved in President Reagan's Covert Action program that is given credit for assisting in ending the Soviet occupation of Afghanistan.
- As the hostage negotiator for a major airline hijacking on foreign soil, successfully coerced a leading terrorist

organization into letting its guard down long enough for Special Operations units to launch.
- Brokered matters of national and international interest between fighting factions and successfully influenced military and political leadership in accepting and implementing policy and programs.
- Trained foreign Presidential Security Forces, Special Forces and Combat Police for the 1988 Olympic Games in Seoul South Korea.
- Trained Polish Counter-terrorism units in oil platform takedowns.
- Was relentless in persuading a disenchanted U.S. Congress to apply new technologies, the deployment of anti-aircraft systems under life-threatening conditions to support a U.S. Government 20-billion-dollar covert initiative which resulted in defeat of one of the most powerful communist military forces on the planet.
- Officer in charge of 30 million dollars of valued CIA Maritime assets for collection missions in support of Presidential Findings in addition to Secretary of Defense and National Security Agency signal intelligence operations.
- Attached to the first team deployed to the Civil War in Somalia 1991 tasked to provide intelligence to U.S. Forces
- As part of a team, performed covert actions including, but not limited to, planning, infiltration, exfiltration, unconventional warfare, anti-smuggling, small unit tactics, aerial delivery, cost analysis and instructing foreign assets.
- Supervised operational training in support of internal and field requirements responsible for National Security Planning Group mandated programs.
- Managed a 17.3 million-dollar CIA contingency ordinance program and personnel to include acquisition, transportation, maintenance, research and development.
- Liaison with U.S. Joint Task Military units and foreign political leaders for clandestine operations involving

planning and coordination with Senior U.S. Officials that budgeted $1.7 billion to fund the War on Drugs.

1978-1985 Captain -United States Marine Corps

Naval oriented expeditionary warrior of final resort providing maximum versatility in chaotic and uncertain conditions of crisis and conflict; trained in core competencies of gunnery on infantry weapons, combat operations, and battlefield awareness; employing a variety of weapons, and through communications links, supporting arms including artillery, naval gunfire, and close air support; sea-based, projecting onto vital littorals in any climate or place, capable of the full spectrum of combat, day or night, against opposing forces with a full spectrum of capabilities, including NBC; using maneuver warfare to locate, close with, and destroy the enemy by fire and maneuver; either on foot or mounted on trucks, assault vehicles, assault craft, or vertical assault aircraft; able to secure and defend self and vital terrain by repelling the enemy's assault by fire, maneuver, and close combat; cultivated in a leadership continuum that develops the basic warrior through experience and coaching into a fully qualified noncommissioned officer and staff noncommissioned officer, a combat leader of Marines who trains and directs the actions of Marines in teams, sections, squads, and platoons, while coordinating with higher and adjacent units and supporting units.

- Director of Resident Instruction Teams responsible for providing enlisted Marines progressive and career-level educational opportunities to improve their leadership, critical thinking capability, and sound tactical skills in an increasingly distributed and joint environment.
- In response to the 1983 Beirut Barracks Bombing, Baz was selected as one of four members of an elite team of Officers tasked to develop the first counter-terrorism curriculum for the Marine Corps.
- Ground Defense Force Commander Leeward Guard Guantanamo Bay, Cuba, tasked to protect the U.S. Naval

Base from potential military aggression/invasion from Communist Cuba. The area of responsibility included miles of barbed wire fence lines, guard and observation towers, along with thousands of active landmines, making it the second heaviest fortified border in the world, only surpassed by the Korean DMZ.
- Naval Flight Student.

CHAPTER 3
SEND ME

It was the seventh year of my baptism by fire in an organization of secrecy that has been responsible for preserving the freedom of the United States since its conception. More often than not, this comes at the criticism of members of Congress and civilians who have no idea the depth of evil that continually knocks on the door of the Republic. It was a time in my life where selfless deeds of heroism were performed daily by the men and women who took an oath to defend our nation. They never ever asked to be thanked for it, but to always remain in the shadows so that some small margin of normalcy could remind them of what is was to be human, have a family, have friends, enjoy a barbeque and a bike race or just have a moment to laugh at the ludicrous presentations of those in media and the Senate who thought they knew what was happening in the world but actually had no idea. I suppose had those spokespeople been the type of people who could be trusted with a secret, all of that may have been different. But I can't remember a time when something confidential wasn't leaked from The Hill for personal or political gain with absolutely no regard for the safety of the very men and women I now speak of ... the CIA.

I made every attempt to stay out of CIA Headquarters (Langley) as much as possible, as did every other Ground Branch Officer. If for any reason you were ever assigned a stent there, it was like a death sentence. As paramilitary case officers, we had not grown accustomed to the political two-step most suits in Headquarters prided themselves in. Their privilege came mostly at the expense of we who were in the field risking our lives. And even more grievously, those suits climbed to the top on the back of our good deeds. Not all were that way, but certainly many who had grown up with us seemed to forget the true spirit of patriotism. Too easily they traded it in for favors and promotions. Most of us swore we would quit "The Outfit" if they forced us to move to an office near the flagpole and abandon our covert facility. It made absolutely no sense to us as to why the CIA would stress the importance of undercover officers adhering to their tradecraft — and actually reprimand them for not doing so strictly — and yet still require them to either report openly to the biggest CIA target in Virginia for meetings or actually work there from day to day in a vaulted office. They played it hypocritically, never answering the one question that ran through our minds, "Don't you think that the bad guys can actually photograph every car entering the gate and put a name to a tag and tell who is working there?"

The only people who seemed to get it right were NOCs (Non-Official Cover). They lived a deniable life for the entire time serving the Clandestine Service and made sure their meetings with other CIA officials followed the same strict protocol as with their assets or recruited agents. And perhaps there were a few who got their arms twisted to report to the "puzzle palace" just as we were, but I never met them.

Well, that isn't exactly true. There was this one time when someone walked up to me at Headquarters and said, "I served with your father in Vietnam."

I replied, "You must be mistaken; my father was in the Army in Vietnam."

He smiled and walked away ... never to be seen again by myself until much later. His name ... Harry Pugh. I would later be surprised at the fact that my father was more familiar with the CIA than I was, evidently working either for them or hand-in-hand while he was in Vietnam. And later in 2014 Jim McGinnis, retired from the CIA would say something similar, "I knew your father in Panama." As I would discover later, Jim and my father had run a joint CIA/Special Forces operation in 1967 near a sugar mill called "La Esperanza" that was located on the road between Santa Cruz and Montero, Bolivia. I've heard it said, there are no coincidences with God.

Walking the halls of Headquarters meant seeing real people, women and men of all shapes and sizes, all ages rushing back and forth like ants in Johnston Murphy shoes that gripped the highly buffed floors with such precision that they could disappear through combination-clad doors in the blink of an eye, never to be seen again.

It was intriguing but certainly not as fun as walking the halls of our off-the-grid covert office at Ground Branch in tennis shoes and T-

Something Bigger Than Overthrowing Small Governments

shirts where the only combination-clad door was the one that got you into the building in the first place. We had Johnston Murphy shoes and suits as well, but they hung on the back of our individual office doors and only were worn when we did find ourselves at Headquarters, which was within its own right, a spectacle. We never fit in and we never went unnoticed by the locals. We walked differently, we were physically fit, we carried a sense of purpose higher than most, and we were on a mission.

I can remember frequently being called "knuckle dragger" by Case Officers of one or two of the Divisions in the Directorate of Operations (D.O.) or Analysts from the Directorate of Intelligence (D.I.) or Instructors at "The Farm." The Farm is a facility run by the CIA for the purpose of training CIA's clandestine officers as well as officers of other organizations specializing in clandestine activities. They never called you a "knuckle dragger" to your face for fear of losing their life, but it was common knowledge that they spoke it amongst themselves. We found it rather amusing because, truth be known, they couldn't fight their way out of a wet paper bag and most of them and their Divisions depended on us to collect intelligence in war zones so they wouldn't have to risk their own lives. If I sound biased, it's because I am — I loved the paramilitary lifestyle.

I can assure you that my opinions of our Agency's elite were shared by more people than just myself. I remember on a given day walking out of a meeting of SIS (Senior Intelligence Service) officers and passing the desk of one of my favorite secretaries, Carol. She habitually voiced her discontent with higher ranking personnel overburdening those below them with sicky nonsense. Because of her outspoken nature, Carol was oftentimes reprimanded by her bosses and was basically told to keep her mouth shut. Because she was a determined, 76-year-old patriot, that was virtually impossible. On this day on which Carol chose to engage my presence, she launched into a 15-minute dissertation expressing her disgruntled sentiments. After getting an earful, I came to realize that she was pretty much justified in her viewpoint. Toward the end she explained that she was working for nothing more than a bunch of "needle-dicked bird rapers." The term itself was something so foreign to me that I literally stood there in silence as did Carol waiting for my reaction. Look, I have no idea what a "needle-dicked bird raper" is, but I believed her and they sounded pretty dangerous.

1988 and 1991 would bring more than just cloak and dagger activities, they would bring tragedy on the home front involving both sets of my grandparents. My grandfather on my father's side (Ralph Abbes Baz) will have passed away while I was in Africa on assignment. Prior to boarding my departing flight from Dulles International airport, I received a call over the loudspeaker directing me to an airline information center. They informed me that I needed to call my Uncle Doug in Florida. Uncle Doug informed me that my grandfather's health was failing. My father was on a flight but would be making his way to the care home to join my Uncle once he landed. I think my Uncle had some idea of my association with "The Outfit" since he himself was a former FBI Agent, but he never let on to such knowledge. He encouraged me to head out on my assignment and said that he would keep me in the loop. I had spent good times with my grandfather in my younger days growing up and had no regrets. I headed to Africa and two weeks later I was informed by the U.S. Embassy in Nairobi that my grandfather had passed. The funeral would be in a few days, which made things a little complicated from where I was, as far as getting back on time to help with arrangements. I convinced myself there was nothing I could do and that I had paid my respects by the way I honored my grandfather all the years I had spent with him.

What I failed to realize, and what I would come to regret all of my life is that it wasn't about paying my respects, it was about being there for my parents, to support them, something that never crossed my mind. Too wrapped up in my duties, too selfish, too immature, too — whatever it was that prevented me from going home was all wrong. It should never be about us, it's about the ones we love and putting them first, being a good servant to them and meeting their needs. In this unselfish duty, we are raised up to be wiser men. I would visit the grave of my grandfather once I returned to the U.S. The fresh, red sand advertised his burial site, which stood out among the many other sites of gray sand in Georgetown S.C. I would collapse at the headstone in tears for more than an hour, my amazing sister and my wife at the time hovering in silence, respectfully allowing me the time for my heart to

Something Bigger Than Overthrowing Small Governments

bleed. I remembered loving my grandfather so much that as a young boy I prayed that God would take my life before He took his, so I would never have to see this day. But that didn't happen.

Later I would tell my father and mother how sorry I was for not being there, and they would say, "You were there son, in spirit ... you are always there for us." They were too kind to me and too loving, beyond what any average father and mother could be to a son seeking his own adventures. Perhaps they understood, perhaps they were no different, perhaps they had the heart of God and forgiveness was part of what they learned from the man we would always miss ... my grandfather.

In 1991 my grandparents on my mother's side would be assaulted in their own home by a young man who had broken and entered with intent to steal and possibly kill. They were barely able to fight him off but not without sustaining serious injury. He was later found by the local South Carolina law enforcement and imprisoned.

It was in 1992 that I made a decision that would alter my life forever. John Herms called me into his office on a late November 1992 evening when the cold, frost-bitten ground of Northern Virginia was not welcomed at all by we who righteously enjoyed warmer climates even if they were malaria infested. He pushed an intelligence report on the unrest in Somalia in front of me. "Digest this," he said, disturbed by the circumstances and yet mistakenly allowing a smile to sneak from underneath his bushy mustache. It read like the predecessor of a Wikipedia report. The Somali Civil War was an ongoing civil war taking place in Somalia. It grew out of resistance to the Siad Barre regime during the 1980s. By 1988-90 the Somali Armed Forces had begun engaging various armed rebel groups, including the Somali Salvation Democratic Front in the northeast, the Somali National Movement in the northwest, and the United Somali Congress in the south.

In December 1990 United Somali Congress (USC) rebels entered Mogadishu. Four weeks of battle between Barre's remaining troops and the USC ensued, over the course of which the USC brought in more forces into the city. By January 1991, USC rebels had managed to defeat the Red Berets, in the process toppling Barre's. The remainder of the regime's forces then finally collapsed. Some became irregular regional forces and clan militias. After the USC's victory over Barre's troops, the other rebel groups declined to cooperate with it, as each instead drew primary support from their own constituencies. Among these other opposition movements were the Somali Patriotic Movement (SPM) and Somali Democratic Alliance (SDA), a Gadabuursi group which had been formed in the northwest to counter the Somali National Movement Isaaq militia. For its part, the SNM initially refused to accept the legitimacy of the provisional government that the USC had established. However, the SNM's former leader Ahmed Mohamed Silanyo later proposed a power-sharing framework in March 1991 between the SNM and USC under a new transitional government.

Various armed factions began competing for influence in the power vacuum and turmoil that followed, particularly in the south. Many of the opposition groups subsequently began competing for influence in the power vacuum that followed the ouster of Barre's regime. In the south, armed factions led by USC commanders General Mohamed Farah Aidid and Ali Mahdi Mohamed, in particular, clashed as each sought to exert authority over the capital. In the northwest, at the Burao conference of April-May 1991, SNM secessionists proclaimed independence for the region under the name Somaliland. They concurrently selected the SNM's leader Abdirahman Ahmed Ali Tuur as president.

In Somalia armed factions competed for power | 1991-1992

Something Bigger Than Overthrowing Small Governments

In August 1992 Operation Provide Relief (UNOSOM–I) officially began to provide humanitarian relief for the people of Somalia. This mission was unsuccessful due to the UN's inability to deliver food and supplies. Relief flights into Somalia were often looted as soon as they landed. The resulting inter-clan warfare led to the destruction of the agriculture of Somalia, which then led to starvation for many of its people. One of the main sources of power in Somalia has been the control of food supplies. Hijacked food was used to secure the loyalty of clan leaders, and food was routinely exchanged with other countries for weapons.

Among the effects of the 1990 fighting was the temporary collapse of customary law. As I continued to the report, it became clear that this would precipitate the arrival of UNITAF and UNOSOM peacekeeping forces in December 1992.

The U.N. asked its member nations for assistance. In December 1992, in one of his last acts as President, George Bush proposed to the U.N. that United States combat troops lead the intervention force. The U.N. accepted this offer and 25,000 U.S. troops were deployed to Somalia. A joint and multinational operation, Restore Hope — called UNITAF (Unified Task Force) — was a US-led, UN-sanctioned operation that included protection of humanitarian assistance and other peace-enforcement operations. President Bush stated that this would not be an "open-ended commitment." The objective of Operation Restore Hope was to rapidly secure the trade routes in Somalia so that food could get to the people. President Bush stated that U.S. troops would be home in time for Bill Clinton's inauguration in January.

Someone had to be on the ground ahead of the game to provide intelligence to the U.S Military prior to their arrival and SOG was picking up the tab. "The head shed is requesting two operators from Ground Branch. We'll split into two teams supplemented by Delta and our pick of Somali mercenaries. A gulf stream is being prepped to depart in four days. It's show time," John barked ... the smile from underneath his bushy mustache now brazenly undeniable.

I could not have been more excited myself. As silly as it may sound, two Citadel men carrying on the traditions of "The Long Gray Line" (see Addendums) in covert fashion added some comfort to the unpredictable fog of war we would be facing. I walked out of his office and down the hallway to my own and I smiled at the thought of one day addressing a graduating class at The Citadel and touching upon our exploits just enough to encourage them to stay on the razors edge if they wanted to be different. I could see it now ... pushing up to the microphone with the Corps of Cadets expecting a forty-five-minute speech I would surprise them with a burst transmission of wisdom, "Life is not a journey to the grave with the intention of arriving safely in a pretty and well-preserved body, but rather to skid in broadside, thoroughly used up, totally worn out, and proclaiming, 'Wow, what a ride!'" [4]

If you knew anything about this military institution of higher learning in South Carolina (The Citadel) you would grasp the fullness of my words. Great people have distinguished themselves and created a standard of honor and performance that we who underwent the rigors of discipline understood and intended to emulate. It was often referred to as The Long Gray Line ... the names of Citadel graduates and how they served and how some died. I've never been certain that my name would ever be on that list, but for those who are, they are certainly worth mentioning because it is the culmination of their exploits that inspired graduates like me to make a difference in this world. It is well worth your read in the Addendum section.

There is nothing like the feeling of being overwhelmed and against all odds in a country at war. It's how David must have felt when he went up against Goliath and his army. I carried a greater power with me and had no fear as to where I was headed ... which ironically began at Headquarters. Yes, the place we tried to stay away from. I needed to meet a few people at Africa Division (AF) for a quick briefing and then to Alias Docs to pick up my credentials and pocket litter. There was a sense of jealously in the air from other Ground Branch Officers who would have loved to have been chosen for this assignment but there was only room for two and I was glad to have been one of those. By the end of the day everything was in place and all I needed to do was go home and pack my gear.

I woke the next morning to a light blanket of snow on the ground, the kind that resonates with ugliness after the sun peeks its head through the clouds to melt it away ... slushy streets that make the sound of faucet water underneath the tires of your car while heading to work.

Something Bigger Than Overthrowing Small Governments

The phone rang and it was my mother. All was well at home, but she needed to ask me for a favor. The man that had assaulted my grandparents the year before in 1991 was due to arrive in court in Columbia S.C. for a hearing and if there were no one to represent my grandparents, who were too elderly to attend, the man would go free, or at least that is the way my grandparents' attorney explained it. My mother and father were dealing with their own crisis with the family business and asked if I would be the one to be there in court for my grandparents. My mother had no idea at the time what she was asking of me ... she had no knowledge of my affiliation with the CIA nor the fact that I had just volunteered to go to Somalia, nor the fact that Somalia was the brass ring in my career.

Opportunities like this did not come all the time, foolishly I thought. If I had been in my right mind, I would have realized that the conditions of the world would only get worse over time and there would be hundreds of opportunities like this in the future ... but that wasn't where my head was.

I grew noticeably silent and my mother on the other end asked, "Son are you okay?" I had to be quick on my feet with just the right response to cover my secret life.

"Just looking at the schedule Mom" was my reply but in reality, I suddenly found myself revisiting the events surrounding my time in Africa and the death of my other grandfather when I could have been home but was not, when I could have supported my parents but I did not, when I could have been unselfish and I was not. All of this played out on the battlefield of my skull like two fighting factions of consciousness and subconsciousness. I did not even allow time for the battle to end before I said, "No problem at all Mom, I will be there ... love you."

I hung up the phone and sat in my big leather chair sipping tea as the fireplace roared with a flame that somehow warmed not just my body from the cold seeping through the cracks of my historical home, but my soul from the cold seeping through the cracks in my personality that would have even considered saying anything but "yes" to the people who had sacrificed and loved me all of my life.

I dressed myself and headed to my covert office, playing out the opening words I would use to tell John Hermes that I would have to bail on the assignment and the reasons why. Would he understand? Would he be mad? Would he think I was dishonorable? I had no idea what he would think, but I knew that it mattered to me what he would think. Despite my hardness for maintaining my individuality and caring less about what most people think, I have come to realize that it does matter to me, to some extent, what people think, especially those whom I admire. I do want them to think the best of me, but not for me, but to honor those who have come before me.

    I always honored my family by the way I lived my life. Yes, I made mistakes along the way, not many, but enough to make me wake up and smell the coffee and never do them again. And yes, I did compromise twice in my life ... yes twice, and no more than that, I can promise. I myself, and not with the encouragement or threat of anyone else, burned the details of those events into my mind forever so I would never allow anyone to influence me or would never want something so bad that I compromised ... even if others did.

    The drive into work that morning was challenging. John had not yet arrived at the office, and just when I thought I had breathing room to rehearse my speech, he did arrive. Before he could hang his coat behind the door I entered and shut the door behind me. He was generous enough to let me explain my dilemma and, surprisingly enough, to put his hand on my shoulder and tell me that he totally understood the situation and that there would be more opportunities down the line. And then he asked, "Who do you think is qualified to take your place?"

    To which I replied, "Who do you want covering your six?" He smiled and said he would have to think about that.

    I departed the office for Headquarters in order to inform AF Division and Special Operations Group (SOG) that I would not be taking the assignment. I will never forget this moment as long as I live. I was coming down the hall and Larry Freedman commonly known as "Superjew" to we who loved him so much, stopped me and said, "I hear you won't be heading to Somalia, so I'm going to be taking your place." I looked at Larry. For a moment he spoke to me with no words, just a kind look, smiled and gave me a hug. I wouldn't know what all that was about until later. Larry always had the kindest smile and the best

Something Bigger Than Overthrowing Small Governments

sense of humor, and I considered him a dear friend. He was more than suited for this assignment.

Days later John and Larry launched to Somalia and I handled family matters to ensure that the man who had attacked my grandparents remained behind bars. From the sidelines I and other Ground Branch Officers monitored the intelligence reports from John and Larry because we knew we were soon to follow. And then, all of that changed ... for all of us. Larry had been killed near Bardera when the vehicle he was riding struck an anti-tank mine.

Michael Robert Patterson on his Arlington National Cemetery Website as well as the article by Ted Gup in the Addendums section sum up the events that I believe needed to be included in this book to properly bring honor to a "secret warrior who tested all who came in contact with him, taking their measure and weeding out the squeamish."

Larry Freedman "Superjew" with Delta Team and Vehicles

ARLINGTON NATIONAL CEMETERY WEBSITE
by Michael Robert Patterson

GREENSBURG, Pennsylvania-Friends of the only American to be killed so far during the U.S. military relief mission to Somalia say the Fayetteville, North Carolina, man may have had covert responsibilities along with his civilian duties.

Friends of former Green Beret Lawrence N. Freedman said Freedman had kept in touch with the Special Forces in the years since he left active duty to become a civilian employee of the Army, the Greensburg Tribune-Review reported Tuesday.

Freedman, 51, was buried Tuesday at Arlington National Cemetery in Virginia following a funeral service at the Army chapel at nearby Fort Meyer.

He was killed last Wednesday near Bardera when the vehicle he was riding struck an anti-tank mine. Three State Department officials were injured.

"He was a soldier's soldier," said longtime friend Arthur Lacey. "He had a lot of influence over a lot of men -- all positive."

Some of those interviewed by the newspaper spoke only on the condition that they not be identified by name. "He was always someplace where nobody knew where he was," a childhood friend told the newspaper. "He was always in the forefront of what was happening."

Freedman grew up in Philadelphia and at the time of his death lived near Fort Bragg, North Carolina, headquarters of Army Special Forces.

He enlisted in the Army on September 30, 1965, and served for 25 years, said Joyce Wiesner, a spokesman at the Army Reserve Personnel Center in St. Louis. A medical specialist, Freedman retired December 31, 1990, with the rank of sergeant major. Freedman served in Vietnam for two years and earned two Bronze Stars and a Purple Heart, Wiesner said.

After participating in six campaigns in Vietnam, Freedman was stationed for several years in Okinawa, Wiesner said. Acquaintances said Freedman was involved in intelligence work in connection with the U.S. dispute with Libya and also during the Falklands war, in which the United States backed Great Britain's effort against Argentina.

Something Bigger Than Overthrowing Small Governments

They said Freedman was secretive about his military duties. They said they thought he was a member of the Delta Force, a rapid-deployment unit, and that he probably had covert responsibilities in Somalia.

State Department officials referred questions about Freedman to the Defense Department, which said such information could not be released without the permission of Freedman's family, the Tribune-Review said.

ARLINGTON NATIONAL CEMETERY WEBSITE
by Ted Gup

Sergeant Major Freedman was not a Department of Defense employee when he was killed in Somalia in 1992 but was in fact a CIA operative. The Department of Defense job was just his cover while inside Somalia. His nickname was "Superjew" and he relished the moniker. A complete story of him is in Chapter 14 of The Book Of Honor by Ted Gup.

On a tip from a CIA employee, Prof. Gup knew only that the fallen CIA operator was the first American casualty in Somalia. He followed a trail of clues through newspaper clippings, obituaries, records at Arlington National Cemetery, Mr. Freedman's family's rabbi, and a list of survivors, who talked about the life of the man.

"I still had not confirmed that it was Larry Freedman until I contacted his widow and learned about his involvement in the agency," says Prof. Gup. [5]

I sat there at my desk quietly pondering the death of Larry, the guy that had taken my place and the events surrounding my family obligations that had prevented what could have been me instead of Larry. I looked at sacrifice in the purest sense of the word and thought about how Jesus Christ had sacrificed his life for me, and strangely it felt as if Larry had either done the same or as if he knew that he had been called to do the same. I know it doesn't make sense reading it in my book but if you could have seen the exchange between Larry and me the day he said, "I'm taking your place," you would understand. My life had been spared again.

Something drew me to go to Larry's office, just to look in one more time like the days I would look in and see him at his desk, smiling. It was vacant and sterile, his desk as he had left it, orderly. Then a piece of 8 ½ x 11 paper taped to the front of the steel cabinet where he kept his training manuals grabbed my attention ... not just the paper, but what was yellow highlighted on the paper. As I moved in closer to get a better look, I was overwhelmed with that same feeling you get when you are on sacred ground worthy of reverence. And then ... there it was in big bold print, "Principles of War" in bullet point format. Highlighted in yellow was, "Never take the road, it is always mined."

I just stood there, wondering if Larry had highlighted that before he departed or if someone else had highlighted it after his death. Either way, it was one of the principles to adhere to if you were going to increase your chances of survival down range and it reinforced my feeling that perhaps Larry knew God would be calling him home. In months to follow I would find myself trying to boil it down to dry ingredients and blow it away ... denying the fact that Larry Freedman had died, thinking perhaps it was all some magnificent plot by the CIA to hide Larry so he could go deeper undercover for some incredible assignments against terrorists.

Larry and John's mission ushered in the United States Marines coming ashore in Mogadishu on 09 December 1992 and quickly establishing an expeditionary infrastructure to facilitate security and the delivery of food to the starving Somalis. On December 11th, the Marines established a Civil Military Operations Center (CMOC) and co-located it with the U.N.'s Humanitarian Operations Center (HOC). The CMOC quickly became the national focus point for NGO/U.S. military coordination, which unbeknownst to them, added great cover for a bunch of paramilitary officers running around in blue jeans, tennis shoes, bulletproof vests and M4 Carbines. The commander of the 1st Marine Expeditionary Force (I MEF) commanded a JTF/CTF composed of air, naval, Marine, Army, and special operations forces (SOF) components, who I would work hand in hand with in collecting intelligence.

Something Bigger Than Overthrowing Small Governments

I wanted to prepare myself for the worst-case scenario ... a humanitarian mission turned sour. I really didn't want to end up in a shooting war and from what I was hearing it was a real possibility. I found it rather puzzling during my lifetime the number of people that ask the one question I never seemed to have the answer for ... the one question that not even I would ask another person that had experienced the ugliness of war. "How many people have you killed?" Perhaps it isn't really the question as much as it is the caviler manner in which they asked ... as if they were asking for the time of the day, or directions, with little to no consideration to the severity of the whole experience and how it may impact a warrior's life. I think people have watched too many movies, walking away at the end of the 90-minute review leaving all the bloody death and destruction on the screen, and not on their hands.

It was not until Christmas Day of 1992 before I would ship out to Somalia, that I finally found a way to answer that question, sitting with my father and talking about Mogadishu, Larry's death and the death of many warriors we both had known.

He spoke of a time in Vietnam when he was approached by a young Army PFC and asked, "Sir, how many gukes have you killed?"

Much to his surprise, my father said, "None."

The young PFC was confused because surely the man who stood before him, the legendary Green Beret who men followed into battle, his commander and soul saving confidant had to have taken the life of the enemy or he would not be standing.

My father noted his confusion and stated, "You never go into battle to take a life ... you're just trying to defend your own. Do you remember when you went to boot camp? They taught you to become a rifleman and then you went to advance training and learned to shoot targets. That's what you shot ... targets, all day and all night until you could hit anything that moved or popped up in front of you in the woods."

The PFC followed with curious eyes, wondering where all of this was leading. Finally, my father capped the conversation with this.

"What I shoot in this war are targets. The enemy is nothing but a target. If he ever becomes a man, you'll never leave here being able to live with yourself. If he's a target ... you will."

My thoughts slowly returned to where I was, Christmas 1992 and where I was heading ... Mogadishu, Somalia. I embraced my father, "Thanks dad," and we headed to the dining room table to join everyone for Christmas dinner.

I looked down at the end of the table as he began to offer the blessing ... everyone's head bowed, and eyes shut except mine. I was still taking in his words.

My father was the only man I knew in my lifetime that was forced to yell out the one command men shy away from ... "Fix bayonets." I would never experience that type of hand to hand combat where the sweat and blood of the enemy stuck to you like glue when the sun came up the following day. But he had, as never revealed by himself but by others who served with him. I think he knew what he was talking about. His words were taken to heart and served me well the rest of my life in every conflict in the CIA or outside as a Contractor.

I left Florida and headed back to Virginia to throw myself back into developing situations in Africa. John Hermes would remain in Somalia until the end of January 1993 and then return home. He would make it very clear that Larry was dead. I would see it in his eyes as he told the sequence of events and how it all unfolded. Enough was said. I packed my gear to enter one of the world's most dangerous cities ... Mogadishu.

Something Bigger Than Overthrowing Small Governments

CHAPTER 4
OPERATION RESTORE HOPE

Once President Clinton was inaugurated, he stated his desire to scale down the U.S. presence in Somalia, and to let the U.N. Forces take over. In March 1993, the U.N. officially took over the operation, naming this mission UNOSOM–II. The objective of this mission was to promote "nation building" within Somalia. Everyone has a right to be stupid ... some politicians just abuse the privilege.

I caught a commercial flight to Nairobi Kenya and met up with a CIA contact once I cleared customs who would carefully guide me to a nondescript hanger where I boarded another airplane that would take me into Mogadishu Somalia.

There are two rainy seasons in Kenya, the first is from March to the end of May and the second shorter season runs from October to the end of November. I missed both of them. The props of the DC3 turned once, choked and stopped. Turned twice, choked and stopped. Turned the third time and found their life, ordered to dance to the sounds of the Pratt & Whitney R-2000 Twin Wasps engines and the smell of exhaust bellowing from beneath.

I imagined Air Branch, the '90s relative of Air America having about 20 of these birds staged in various remote airfields around the world and even some biplanes because the budget wasn't that great in house. Those poor fly boy friends of mine were always scrambling to find the next penny just to keep oil in these things and meet all the operational demands of the 7th floor at CIA Headquarters in Langley, VA. It was as if whoever was running the show expected things to stay in the air, on the water and in the jungle by magic.

Many of the Intelligence Officers who had risen to the ranks of management in SAS (Special Activities Service) had little experience with Special Operations. In order to manage special operations, they needed to be familiar with how such operations were planned and executed. The current system of managers was selected based on PCS foreign intelligence assignments and, in my opinion, was unacceptable for running special operations. They had no idea of the challenges of things like traveling the world in alias. They should have, but for some reason it was as if they had forgotten simple tradecraft and protocol like backstopping addresses and identifications, as if they didn't care if your cover got blown or not ... directly opposite of everything I learned at The Farm. They did not know when to guide and when to direct and often had their fingers in the pie without having a clue as to the damage that was being done by their interference.

As a result, things like per diem were taken away from us in Ground Branch because they considered having a government issued sleeping bag as "government quarters provided." I kid you not. The idea of a hotel along the way was out of the question. So if you think that was ridiculous then you can now imagine how ridiculous things must have been in Air Branch. Corners seemed to be getting cut just to carry out the missions. And with that, I had my doubts about this DC3 on its way to Mogadishu Somalia that choked a few times.

The last time I remembered being in a DC3, which by the way was built in the 40s, was in 1986 out of Nairobi Kenya heading south to Kamina Air Base, the secret staging area for the CIA in support of UNITA and Jonas Savimbi in Angola. In a highly secret operation, the Central Intelligence Agency had used an abandoned air base here to airlift arms to guerrillas in Angola. Landing largely at night, C-130 and Boeing 707 cargo jets with the markings "Santa Lucia Airways" arrived there with arms deliveries on three occasions. Historically it had the footprints of famous mercenaries like Major Mike Hoare.

ARMED FORCES VS. REBELS IN CONGO | 1964

In early 1964, a new crisis broke out as Congolese rebels calling themselves 'Simba' (Swahili for 'Lion') rebelled against the government. They were led by Pierre Mulele, Gaston Soumialot and Christophe Gbenye who were former members of Gizenga's Parti Solidaire Africain (PSA). The rebellion affected Kivu and Eastern (Orientale) provinces.

Something Bigger Than Overthrowing Small Governments

By August they had captured Stanleyville and set up a rebel government there. As the rebel movement spread, discipline became more difficult to maintain, and acts of violence and terror increased. Thousands of Congolese were executed, including government officials, political leaders of opposition parties, provincial and local police, schoolteachers, and others believed to have been Westernized. Many of the executions were carried out with extreme cruelty, in front of a monument to Lumumba in Stanleyville. Tshombe decided to use foreign mercenaries as well as the ANC to suppress the rebellion.

Mike Hoare was employed to create the English-speaking 5 Commando ANC at <u>Kamina</u>, with the assistance of a Belgian officer, Colonel Frederic Vanderwalle, while <u>6 Commando ANC</u> was French-speaking and originally under the command of a Belgian Army Colonel, Lamouline. By August 1964, the mercenaries, with the assistance of other ANC troops, were making headway against the Simba rebellion.

Fearing defeat, the rebels started taking hostages of the local white population in areas under their control. These hostages were rescued in Belgian airdrops (Dragon Rouge and Dragon Noir) over Stanleyville and Paulis with U.S. airlift support. The operation coincided with the arrival of mercenary units (seemingly including the hurriedly formed 5th Mechanized Brigade) at Stanleyville which was quickly captured. It took until the end of the year to completely put down the remaining areas of rebellion. [6]

Jump back to 1986 where President Mobutu Sese Seko of Zaire had repeatedly denied accusations by other African leaders that American aid to the Angolan rebels led by Jonas Savimbi passed through Zaire. Largely supplied by South Africa, the guerrillas of the Union for the Total Independence of Angola, or UNITA, were fighting to overthrow Angola's Marxist Government.

American aid to UNITA was budgeted at $15 million in late 1985. United States officials had refused to disclose the supply route. Transfer through South Africa would violate an American embargo on arms shipments to South Africa. Diplomats at the United States Embassy in Kinshasa and at the American Consulate in Lubumbashi, 250 miles southeast of here, declined to discuss the military aid to UNITA. [In Washington, a spokesman for the Central Intelligence Agency, Sharon Foster, said that the agency would not confirm or deny any allegation of covert activities, but that "any covert activity we might be conducting would be in support of U.S. policy and under appropriate authority."] The issue was highly sensitive in Zaire because two years earlier, Zaire and Angola had signed a mutual nonaggression pact. But according to Western diplomats, aid workers and businessmen in Kinshasa and Lubumbashi, most of the aid has been funneled through there.

The Kamina air base was built in the 1950's by Belgium, which administered Zaire at the time as the Belgian Congo. The base, once the largest between the Sahara and South Africa, had since fallen into ruin ... except for the tiny 12' x 12' swimming pool, with a single tiny palm tree that we had built to add some comfort for those who stayed there around the clock. I mean think about it, you're stranded on an abandoned base with shattered windows, lions roaming the bush, unpredictable natives not far away and literally no way back to civilization unless you fly out.

In typical Air America style, I think the boys deserved a little relaxation from the tormenting heat of the day and the loneliness that so often accompanied this type of clandestine assignment ... hiding in plain sight. Thus, from time to time you would see one or two of them, or us in Hawaiian shirts, shorts and sunglasses sitting in lawn chairs — as if the watering hole was the Roman inspired pool built by the newspaper

Something Bigger Than Overthrowing Small Governments

magnate who inspired "Citizen Kane," William Randolph Hearst, and that Kamina Base was part of his fairytale castle in the hills. I don't think we ever expected Charlie Chaplin, Clark Gable and other legendary figures to come splash in our version of the outdoor Neptune Pool. But for we who held up at the secret base from time to time, it was a bit of paradise that could only be appreciated by men who weren't looking to give an autograph to anyone except the admin officer when they turned in their alias documentation after arriving stateside.

From the air, the two landing strips measuring about 7,000 feet each and in good repair as well as the dozens of support buildings spread out across a flat plain of wooded savannah. The base was closed to unauthorized visitors, whether by air or from Kamina, a railroad junction town of 100,000. Roads from Kamina to Angola-200 miles west of here-were largely impassable. There was a railroad line from there to Angola, but I don't recall it being used for shipping the arms. We always flew arms to Jamba, UNITA headquarters in southeastern Angola.

Baz on UNITA Soccer Team

Baz firing 106RR

Something Bigger Than Overthrowing Small Governments

In one of the better articles written by James Brooke for the *NY Times* in 1987, it appeared that our little secret wasn't really a secret.

U.S. ARMS AIRLIFT TO ANGOLA REBELS IS SAID TO GO ON
By James Brooke, *The New York Times*, July 27, 1987

ABIDJAN, Ivory Coast, July 26- A secret airlift of American arms to Angolan guerrillas continues through southern Zaire, two Western diplomats stationed in Zaire said today. One of the diplomats said the flights were as frequent as four to five a week. The arms are flown from Kinshasa's international airport in a C-141 cargo plane marked Santa Lucia Airways to an abandoned Belgian air base near Kamina, in Zaire's Shaba province, he said. From there, a light blue C-130 cargo plane shuttles the weapons to areas in Angola, the diplomat said. Coping With the Heat A team of Americans, led by a colonel, coordinates the operation in Kamina, the diplomat said. To cope with Central Africa's heat, the Americans have built a small swimming pool at the base, he added.

Also at the base is a detachment of about 12 guerrillas of the Union for the Total Independence of Angola, he said. The rebels, led by Jonas Savimbi, are fighting to overthrow Angola's Marxist Government. Zaire's President, Mobutu Sese Seko, has repeatedly denied that his country allows any American aid for UNITA to pass through his country. The rebel movement is criticized by many African leaders for receiving most of its arms from South Africa. 'It Is Better to Talk' In a fresh reminder of the insurgents' South African link, Mr. Savimbi visited Johannesburg last month and counseled local black leaders, "It is better to talk than to fight so that you can identify the common problems and differences." This correspondent visited Kamina in late January and wrote about the arms shipments. He has since been barred from returning to Zaire, but last week two diplomats reached there by telephone said the shipments were continuing.

American aid to the guerrillas has in the past included automatic weapons, ammunition and shoulder-held anti-aircraft missiles, like Stingers. It is not clear how the arms get to Zaire. Supply operations at Kamina were reportedly suspended for two weeks in mid-April when about 65 United

States soldiers of the Rapid Deployment Force, based at Fort Bragg, N.C., conducted counterinsurgency training for Zairian troops at Kamina. United States aid to the insurgents has been legal since August 1985, when the United States Senate revoked an amendment that had barred assistance to Angola's warring factions since June 1976.

Last year, the Reagan Administration said it gave $15 million of aid to the rebels. Last month, Administration officials said they planned to give another $15 million. The money comes out of the Central Intelligence Agency budget and does not need formal Congressional approval. Reference by North in Washington, the Senate hearings on the covert supply of weapons to anti-Marxist guerrillas in Nicaragua has not investigated possible illegal arms shipments to the rebels in the early 1980's. Earlier this month, Sam Joseph Bamieh, a California businessman, testified under oath before a House subcommittee that Saudi Arabia's royal family provided millions of dollars to the rebels in the early 1980's at the behest of William J. Casey, who was then Director of Central Intelligence. In February 1986, Leut. Col. Oliver L. North told a group of United Methodist Church leaders in Washington that he had taken part in two wars-in Vietnam and Angola. It is unclear whether his Angola assignment took place before, during or after the nine-year arms embargo.

No buildup at Kamina last Wednesday, Chester A. Crocker, Assistant Secretary of State for African Affairs, declined to say how American aid reaches the insurgents. Transfer through South Africa would violate an international embargo on arms shipments to South Africa. "There is no buildup at Kamina," Mr. Crocker said in an interview conducted by satellite with journalists in Lisbon and London. "It is a Soviet line that is being echoed around the free world for reasons that I cannot quite understand." State Department officials have said that the United States aid to the rebels is small when compared with an estimated one billion dollars of aid sent by the Soviet Union to Angola in the last year. Crocker Goes to Angola Two weeks ago, Mr. Crocker spent two days in Angola's capital, Luanda, seeking to negotiate a withdrawal of an estimated 37,000 Cuban troops from Angola and an end to hostilities between the Government and Unita, as the rebel group is known. "It was a waste of time," the diplomat said. Mr. Crocker said he left Luanda convinced that the Angolan Government is "still

Something Bigger Than Overthrowing Small Governments

preoccupied and focused on military solutions in the south and hoping that they can, in just one more dry season, perhaps, crush the forces of Unita."

On July 17, two days after Mr. Crocker left Luanda, the United States Senate voted to repeal Angola's most-favored nation trading status. The bill, which would affect the sizable level of American oil imports from Angola, needs House approval before becoming law. Earlier this month, the Senate voted against a proposed embargo of all American investment and trade with Angola.

Last month, *The New York Times* received copies of two typewritten memorandums that refer to the arms supply operation. Both seem to be written by Zairian intelligence services to President Mobutu in the wake of the Feb. 1 Times story about the arms airlift. Times Obtains Memos Last week, a Western diplomat stationed in Zaire examined the documents, written in French. The diplomat, who declined to be identified, said he believed them to be genuine. "The operation is directed by a white C.I.A. officer with the rank of major," said one memorandum, written under the heading "Information note to the President." The second document, dated Feb. 10, 1987, and headed "Security Measures," said: "The C.I.A. will regularly furnish information on all the journalists who ask for visas for Zaire." [Kathy Pherson, a Central Intelligence Agency spokeswoman in Washington, asked about the assertions in the document, declined to comment. "There is no way I can respond to that," she said late Sunday night.]

Under the heading, "The airports used for this operation: Kamina," the memorandum recommended: "Replace Colonel Munga, current head of this air base because he drinks a lot and regularly steals fuel stocked for this operation." According to one diplomat in Zaire, Colonel Munga has not been replaced. A second diplomat who visited Kamina base last year added another detail in a recent interview.

American technicians installed runway lights to allow the supply flights to land at night. Last January, a large number of American military cargo planes could be seen landing and taking off from Kinshasa's airport at Ndjili. American Embassy officials said the planes were carrying arms to Chad. [7]

And thus, plausible deniability was the flavor of the day. Admit nothing, deny everything, and make counter accusations even if very smart reporters like James Brooke had found the treasure.

A tap on my shoulder brought me back to 1993. "On the ground in ten," shouted the co-pilot as he made his way back to the rear of the fuselage to piss in a white plastic painter's bucket tied down with some green military webbing. It wasn't anything new to me that CIA pilots make-shifted a lot of things like this flying toilet because Headquarters never seemed to give Air Branch a decent budget to go first class on anything. The suits expected flying and water machines to simply run forever without needing repair and there were the constant arguments back at Langley between Special Activities Service and the Seventh Floor regarding these types of expenses. It was a war I certainly wasn't going to win because it was way beyond my pay grade. But it certainly didn't prevent me from wanting to join in and fight for guys who always managed to fly in and out of dangerous places to pick us up, and usually at the most inopportune times — i.e. bad weather, war zones, low on fuel, no sleep.

I glanced out the window. The topography looked so much different heading north over Somalia than it did south to Angola. There was no dense green jungle to speak of. The country as a whole is mostly barren desert, but there are two Monsoon seasons. When the northeastern monsoon is in effect (December to February) the weather is moderately hot in the north, and hot in the south. When the southwest monsoon is in effect (May to October) the south is still very hot, but the north is even hotter.

Add civil strife, land mines, and angry people, sprinkled with an Islamic taste for revenge and "hot" becomes an understatement. However, I must say that the beaches were impressive enough to make me think for a second that should Somalia ever get its act together, this would be a prime location for resorts. Blue water, hot sun, clean sand and sharks ... lots of sharks. Okay, maybe it wouldn't be ideal for water activities but hey, if they can make it happen in a country like Mexico, why not here? If I recall, the Mexican drug cartels dominated the wholesale illicit drug market and controlled 90% of the cocaine entering the United States. And along the way the official death toll of the Mexican Drug War was at least 60,000. Let's see, Somalia had clans

Something Bigger Than Overthrowing Small Governments

that exported a drug called Chat and the death toll of the Somali Civil War would be 500,000. Yep, prime real estate.

Further down the coast as I got closer to Mogadishu, I spotted the U.S. Naval Fleet offshore. The airfield was blanketed with cargo containers, green tents and oddly enough a chain linked fence compound with a few Winnebago style campers owned by the CIA ... of course. An American flag flew proudly alone on a twenty-foot radio pole atop a sandy hill overlooking the Indian Ocean, rather appropriately if I may say so myself.

The vast bulk of UNITAF's total personnel strength was provided by the United States (some 25,000 out of a total of 37,000 personnel) and sitting on that airfield. Other countries that contributed to UNITAF were Australia, Bangladesh, Belgium, Botswana, Canada, Egypt, Ethiopia, France, Germany, Greece, India, Republic of Ireland, Italy, Kuwait, Morocco, New Zealand, Nigeria, Norway, Pakistan, Saudi Arabia, Spain, Sweden, Tunisia, Turkey, United Arab Emirates, the United Kingdom and Zimbabwe.

Bazzel Baz

    The brown dust blanketed green canvas tents housing military forces but paid no attention to the six abandoned Russian MIG fighter jets resting on the side of a hill.

Something Bigger Than Overthrowing Small Governments

The concrete tarmac housed its own variety of aircraft and support vehicles ... C130s, Sea Stallion helicopters and foreign flying machines belonging to folks of a different language. And although we wouldn't share a common language, we would share a common purpose which expressed itself in the smiles from almost every UNITAF soldier in their big white U.N. armored vehicles we would pass from time to time. It made you want to like them right off the bat. However, I would be lying if I did not point out that the Nigerian and Pakistani forces turned out to be worthless on a day when Aidid would decide to flex his clan muscle at K4 Circle ... a place we would have preferred not be but, as it would turn out, needed to be in order to provide intelligence. You know that tingly little feeling you get when you really like someone you've just met? That's common sense leaving your body, especially in Mogadishu.

The lower our approach to Mogadishu the lower my mind sunk to thoughts of enemy fire and the fact that leaving Nairobi, Kenya was like leaving paradise. Intelligence reported that many of the Somali Clans had close ties with terrorist organizations and Mujahideen from Afghanistan, and that many of the weapons they procured came from those sources. The thought of a Stinger Missile, British Blow Pipe or even small arms fire hitting this transport did not sit any better with me than it did with the volumes of cargo and supplies refusing to give an inch of space for a traveler like myself. The cargo became my next best friend, and I knew it was just as concerned as I was. How silly ... to let your imagination get away with you ... talking to boxes in my mind, like Tom Hanks talked to Wilson the Volleyball in his 2000 movie "Cast Away." I could have played it out a different way if I could turn reality into imagination ... a different place and a different time just to make my mind laugh a bit more at the make-believe report being read back at Langley by the 7th floor.

> "Baz and a Naval Intel Officer by the name of Einsel heard the Cartel was using a cave earlier used by OSS. They mounted out. At 12:00 noon they both jumped from our high-altitude weather balloons (at 102,000 ft), without oxygen or clothes, armed only with plastic forks from McDonalds. They were free falling HANO (high altitude no-opening) directly onto the sentries. Feeling bad about taking life, they decided to impact 100 feet from the sentries, run up to them, and cut their own wrists ... thereby proving they were Baaaaaaaaaad Dudes. Obviously, those who did not pass out, fled, and the women climbed trees."

If only it were that easy. A slap of rough air, a pitch of the left wing and me falling off a box coming face to face with the fuselage meant fun time was over. I was pretty sure from that negative gravity feeling in my stomach that we were descending, oddly enough, in a manner customary to Air America types who did not take pleasure in having OMS (Office of Medical Service) pull lead out of their hind end — you know, those tiny fragments of metal we call shrapnel that make their way from the muzzle of a gun pointed skyward by, in this case, uneducated and highly angered Islamic Dusty Nuts.

The DC3 touched down with little to no bump, and broke slow enough for me to not feel it much. The heat of the day was upon me like an instant sauna and I could not wait for us to come to a stop and open the cargo door. As we taxied down the runway, sometimes I would go forward a bit, like when someone decides to stop at a light at the last minute when they first thought they could make it through.

Something Bigger Than Overthrowing Small Governments

The cargo door opened, and sunshine appeared like a blinding light, so pronounced that it was difficult at first to see the two men greeting me. Once I put on my sunglasses, I could see their faces but to this day cannot recall their names. One was a burley fellow with a dark mustache, the CIA logistics officer for the base, and the other a slim, kind-hearted officer who was sure to meet his maker if he did not toughen up a bit. He was scared of everything that was happening around him, and just being outside the protection of the CIA base, which was located in the old U.S. Embassy compound, was cutting it close as far as he was concerned.

Everyone was armed with something ... a Browning or shotgun or M4. Their civilian attire properly disguised them as State Department employees to the rest of the world, but their mannerisms betrayed them. There is just something about CIA people on foreign soil. They move differently, see with more than their eyes and hear with more than their ears, especially if they've been trained by paramilitary officers at The Farm. If that's not the case, then they're an accident waiting to happen.

We carried on the normal get-to-know-you conversations and loaded into an Isuzu Trooper. Off the tarmac and past a gate guarded by non-impressive Pakistani soldiers we exited the point of no return. We drove rather quickly along the pot-holed roads and war-torn buildings that seriously painted their own history with more bullet holes than you could shake a stick at. This was a war zone unlike any I had seen thus far in my career and it smelled of death and destruction, uncompromised by any U.N. efforts and there was no law. Driving fast was a good thing because it gave less chance of someone getting a bead on you with their weapons. I liked that strategy ... it made sense. And then all of that got tossed out the window when we hit the marketplace not far from the safety of the U.S. Embassy. The Trooper was now moving at five miles per hour simply to avoid running over the sea of people. The driver honked the horn to no avail.

The streets were loaded like ants moving at a snail's pace. They appeared more similar to Arab or Caucasoid than to African populations I had known. Almost everyone carried an Ak47, or RPG, or machetes or sticks with nails protruding like porcupines. Perhaps if they changed the Trooper horn to gunshot sounds the people would get out of the way much faster. It was Dodge City at its best.

Something Bigger Than Overthrowing Small Governments

"Keep your windows up unless you want to have someone stick their hand in and grab your shades," blurted the logistics officer.

"Everyone looks stoned, what's up with that?" I inquired.

"They chew Chat ... see that green stain on their teeth. It induces manic behaviors and hyperactivity, similar in effects to those produced by amphetamine. What sucks are the withdrawal symptoms, when they are coming down, depression, irritability and the occasional psychotic episode resembling a hypomanic state."

All eyes were upon the foreigners traveling in the Isuzu Trooper and I mean all eyes. As much as I wanted to go unnoticed, it just wasn't happening, and my level of comfort was diminishing quickly. The vehicle came to a stop, the driver unwilling to push through the crowd. He honked the horn again, but the crowd ignored him. "You know what else sucks," he commented, "the fact that we're stuck in the middle of this while they are coming down."

Something to my right caught my attention ... a young Somali boy seeking his rite of passage, angry eyes that telegraphed his intent and then WHAM!! He slammed an AK-47 up against my window, barrel pointed directly at my head and his finger clearly on the trigger. I knew enough about the region and the culture to complete my understanding of what a rite of passage in Somalia entailed. Killing an American was more than enough to elevate this boy to manhood in the eyes of fellow clansmen and give him a story to tell his grandchildren.

I was unarmed and about to die. My life flashed in front of me like a helpless child, and then back to my viewpoint as a man who had no intention of allowing this ten-year-old to live long enough to be a grandfather. His look had given me permission to think this way. If he was going to embark on a journey of revenge, he'd better have dug two graves. I looked him square in the eye, grabbed the door handle preparing to jam his weapon backwards and beat the living snot out of him with any end of that weapon I could get my hands on. And then the Trooper moved forward, just enough and just fast enough to leave him behind.

I turned my head and starred him down until he was swallowed up by the crowd. Strangely my eyes caught sight of a trash-filled drainage channel or rut that paralleled the street we were on. I thought to myself ... the only difference between a rut and a grave is the depth.

At that moment I made the decision that I and every member of my team were going home when this was all over. I would later give the order to shoot anyone — man, woman, or child — who pointed a weapon at us. This brief encounter was surreal and took me to the story of my father cheating death once more in Vietnam when a small boy tossed a hand grenade in his jeep. It lodged itself under the seat where no one could reach it in time. Fortunately, the pin was never pulled. But I am certain that he gave the same command to his men when it came to rules of engagement.

Being in Mogadishu wasn't about diplomacy, nor was it about listening to some Department of State candy ass who was sitting in Washington ordering us to maintain a defensive posture. We had seen the results of such orders from State when the Beirut Barracks Bombings (October 23, 1983, in Beirut, Lebanon) occurred during the Lebanese Civil War. Two truck bombs struck separate buildings housing United States and French military forces — members of the Multinational Force (MNF) in Lebanon — killing 299 American and French servicemen. The sentries at the gate were operating under Department of State rules of engagement which made it very difficult to respond quickly to the truck. Sentries were ordered to keep their weapons at condition four (no magazine inserted and no rounds in the chamber). As soon as I could reach the CIA base, I intended to find a weapon and insert a magazine. I was not going home in a body bag.

We rolled up to the U.S. Embassy, the 80-acre compound along Afghoy Road in the local K-7 district, recently reopened and being guarded by U.S. Marines, everywhere. Snipers occupied the top of every building with sandbag positions for the grunts, armed and ready for a fight. Its rather ghostly appearance was no more than a reflection of its inhabitants two years before.

This is a photo of the Embassy compound viewed from left in 1992, after it was re-occupied to serve as headquarters for Operation Restore Hope. The walled chancery (foreground) is most prominent, but it was located within an outer-walled Embassy compound (note wall in upper left, top). The administrative office building (top right) and Marine House (top, right of center) are visible. The helicopter landing zone was between the chancery and Marine House, above the round-about.

Something Bigger Than Overthrowing Small Governments

OPERATION EASTERN EXIT

On 30 December 1991, violence escalated 'an order of magnitude' as militants entered Mogadishu, which was quickly enveloped by a general state of lawlessness. On 30-31 December, diplomats, including many stationed in offices elsewhere in the city, were collected and housed in the Embassy compound, except two volunteers who remained in the Embassy's K-7 residential apartments located across Afghoy Road from the Embassy. The volunteers in the K-7 building would be needed as look-outs for the Embassy compound's main gate. On the morning of 31 December, the defense attaché was nearly killed when his vehicle was sprayed with bullets and that evening, a soldier at a roadblock shot the tires of a vehicle carrying another defense official. Attempts by the U.S. and other nations' diplomats, in particular the Italian Embassy, to negotiate a ceasefire for foreigners to leave were unsuccessful. Afghoy Road became a 'shooting gallery,' preventing those in safe havens outside the Embassy from reaching it. On New Year's Day, the first American civilians began to seek refuge at the Embassy.

Ambassador Bishop requested an evacuation of the American community on 1 January, indicating that the evacuation could be with the planned Italian, French, or German evacuation efforts, but preferred an evacuation by the U.S. military. The State Department authorized the evacuation on 2 January and on that day Ambassador Bishop specifically requested an evacuation by the U.S. military, thereby initiating Operation Eastern Exit. Ambassador Bishop had spent a considerable amount of time discussing contingency plans for evacuation with other diplomatic posts. Ultimately, ten heads of missions — eight ambassadors and two chargés d'affaires — along with their staff sought refuge in the U.S. Embassy compound and were evacuated.

Ambassador Bishop had visited Central Command in August 1990, where he worked with military experts to update the Embassy's E & E plan. The first notice that an evacuation of the Mogadishu Embassy would be needed came on the morning of 1 January, when the top naval commander at Central Command sent a message to his naval operations staff: "Better have Amphib crowd take a look at a helo NEO of Mogadishu! time/distance to get there from Masirah OP area." Following the ambassador's 2 January evacuation request, the commander of Central Command ordered Air Force aircraft to the region, the movement of amphibious ships to Mogadishu, and requested United States Special Operations Command to prepare for a noncombatant evacuation operation.

The initial plan was to evacuate via Mogadishu International Airport. Soon after the evacuation request, the United States Air Force deployed C-130 transport planes and an AC-130, for gunfire support, to Nairobi, Kenya, awaiting clearances to enter Somalia and the ability to safely transfer evacuees from the Embassy to the airport. However, the U.S. and other foreign embassies were unable to contact anyone within the government to obtain clearances. It also became apparent that the rebels had an ineffective command-and-control structure, making it impossible to negotiate any ceasefire or guarantee of safe passage. Likewise, government troops faced a command-and-control problem; reports indicated that army units were separating along clan lines, in some cases soldiers shot officers of a different clan when given orders they disagreed with. Thus, it became clear that safe passage to the airport would not be possible. Several other nations also had aircraft mobilized to reach Mogadishu, but faced the same problems of landing and transit of evacuees to the airport.

On 4 January, several incidents, including a couple exchanges of gunfire, suggested that the Embassy's security detail was insufficient to hold off armed Somalis until the USS Guam and USS Trenton arrived with their helicopters and soldiers, at that time scheduled to arrive on 7 January. The Embassy had just six Marine guards, whose job was limited to protecting the chancery. Ambassador Bishop made an urgent request to Washington for two platoons of soldiers to parachute into the Embassy to defend it until the ships arrived. The request was denied, but the Ambassador was told that an advance element from the vessels would reach the Embassy the following morning.

The USS Guam

The USS Guam and USS Trenton began transit from the coast of Oman towards Mogadishu at 2230 hrs. (2330 hrs. Oman time) on 2 January. The commander of Amphibious Group Two had initially proposed a seven-ship Amphibious Task Group, composed of vessels anchored at Masirah Island (off Oman) and Dubai and including four amphibious ships so that the full range of amphibious capabilities would be available for the operation. However, intervention in Kuwait seemed imminent and the commander of naval forces at Central Command did not want to divert that many ships from the Persian Gulf, thus the decision to send two of the closest ships. Although the two vessels were selected by mid-afternoon on 2 January, the transfer of some personnel from Dubai to Masirah caused a delay of eight to ten hours. The USS Guam and USS Trenton carried forces from the 4th Marine Expeditionary Brigade, including a detachment of CH-53E Super Stallion helicopters — the largest helicopters operated by the U.S. military — and two squadrons of CH-46 Sea Knight helicopters.

The USS Trenton

Planning began in earnest as the ships got underway, with a combined command center on the USS Guam. On the morning of 3 January, the task force's command questioned why they were not given the option of an amphibious landing and requested a tank landing ship be added to the task force; the request was denied. A warrant officer who had previously served as a Marine Security Guard (MSG) at the Mogadishu Embassy during the mid-1980s was found who could identify the location of the Embassy. Despite Ambassador Bishop's planning with Central Command, the task force had been provided outdated information. The former MSG told planners that a new Embassy had been planned and was under construction several years prior. In fact, the new Embassy was located further inland and, after receiving updated information, task force commanders determined that a beach landing, requiring troops to fight their way across the city, was too risky. Initial plans had the ships launch their helicopters at 0100 on 7 January. However, in response to indications from Ambassador Bishop that conditions in Mogadishu were deteriorating, planners considered 1,050-nautical-mile (1,940 km; 1,210 mi) and, later, 890-nautical-mile (1,650 km; 1,020 mi) flights with the CH-53Es while the ships were still located in the northern Arabian Sea. The situation in Mogadishu stabilized somewhat and the mission was delayed until 5 January.

On the evening of 4 January, the final execute order was issued for a 0245 launch of two CH-53E Super Stallions to arrive at the Embassy at dawn. The 60 soldiers selected for the security detail were issued weapons and ammunition. Two Marine Corps KC-130 refueling tankers were mobilized closer to the operation, from Bahrain to Oman, to refuel the helicopters in route to Mogadishu and the two helicopters transferred from the USS Trenton to the USS Guam.

Two CH-53E Super Stallions carrying a 60-man security detail — 51 Marines and nine Navy SEALs — departed the USS Guam at 0247, 466 nautical miles (863 km; 536 mi) from the Embassy, and were expected to arrive at 0620. They performed two aerial refuelings. During the first refueling, a

Something Bigger Than Overthrowing Small Governments

pipe burst on one of the helicopters, dousing soldiers in fuel and nearly forcing a return to the Guam; problems with the helicopters' navigation system also complicated the refueling rendezvous. The helicopters arrived in Mogadishu at dawn, crossing the coast just south of the harbor at just 25-50 feet (7.6-15.2 m) in altitude on a route that was planned to avoid areas of more intense violence reported in the northern parts of the city. On their arrival in Mogadishu, the crew of the helicopters were using an outdated 1969 map, which showed the Embassy in an isolated area. Furthermore, they had been told the Embassy could be discerned by its white stucco perimeter wall and golf course. The Embassy was, in fact, surrounded by new development and the crew saw white stucco walls around many buildings in the city. The helicopters were flying too low to spot a strobe light which was placed atop the Embassy's water tower (the highest point within the Embassy compound) and the golf course in the Embassy compound had a black, oil-coated surface — not the familiar green grass that the helicopter crew would recognize. After breaking radio silence (their only direct communication with the Embassy was unencrypted) to contact the Embassy, they were able to discern it and land at 07:10. As they arrived, a group of about 100 to 150 Somalis were attempting to enter the Embassy compound via ladders on the wall, but promptly scattered as the helicopters arrived.

The security detail quickly moved to establish a perimeter around the Embassy compound and the Air Force's AC-130 arrived to provide overhead support. Ambassador Bishop gave the security detail clear instructions on the rules of engagement: they could only use deadly force if people came over the Embassy compound's walls with obvious hostile intent. He also identified three zones of defense, stating a preference to retreat to the third zone before the use of deadly force:

- The entire Embassy Compound
- The Chancery, Joint Administrative Office (JAO) building, Marine House, and the helicopter landing zone (HLZ)
- The Chancery and JAO buildings (the two "safe haven" buildings where the evacuees were held)

Ambassador Bishop clearly explained his rationale to the security detail, which was to avoid any impression that they were intervening in the violence in Mogadishu. He feared that the Embassy would be targeted by organized attacks if any group involved in the clashes got the impression that the U.S. was intervening in the conflict. To this effect, he requested the Voice of America and BBC broadcast announcements that the forces were present only to evacuate the Embassy and would not interfere in the conflict. The Marines who had been doused in fuel during the refueling were able to take a shower and wash their clothes. Marines board two CH-53E Super Stallion helicopters (with refueling probes attached) on the USS Bataan, a ship similar to the USS Guam).

After an hour on the ground, the helicopters left with the first 61 evacuees, including all American civilians and four heads of mission. Evacuees were provided blankets on one of the flights to remain warm. Complications with the only in-flight refueling on the return nearly prevented refueling, which would have forced the helicopters to divert to the Somali desert and await a rescue. At 0940, the helicopters arrived on the Guam and unloaded the evacuees.

No threats came upon the Embassy during the day, although truckloads of armed Somalis frequently drove by the Embassy along Afghoy Road. Only one incident seemed to directly target the Embassy. A sniper and a spotter were positioned on the Embassy's water tower (the highest structure in the compound) and came under fire; they were ordered to not return fire and soon thereafter ordered to leave their position on the water tower.

The Office of Military Cooperation, just one and a half blocks from the Embassy, required evacuation. Despite its proximity to the Embassy, an armed convoy was needed to evacuate persons trapped there by the unrest. A convoy of vehicles with several Marines and SEALs left the Embassy at 0847 and returned ten minutes later with 22 persons from

Something Bigger Than Overthrowing Small Governments

the OMC (four Americans, a Filipino, and 17 Kenyans). This was the only excursion outside the Embassy by the security detail. Throughout the day, foreign diplomats contacted the Embassy desiring to be evacuated; the U.S. welcomed these requests but required all of them to find their own transportation to the Embassy. A Somali officer who had a previous relationship with the Embassy, Major Siad, agreed to travel to rescue the German chargé d'affaires and British ambassador (junior staff from the British Embassy had previously come to the U.S. Embassy).

The Soviet Union was unable to land a plane in Mogadishu the previous day and the Soviet ambassador asked Ambassador Bishop if he and his staff could be rescued; Ambassador Bishop, a tennis partner of his Soviet counterpart, agreed but only if they found their own way to the Embassy. Seeing the helicopters on the morning of 5 January, they realized the Americans would not remain in the city much longer. At the request of Ambassador Bishop, Major Siad agreed to transport the Soviets, but only if he was paid enough; the U.S. Embassy paid Major Siad, who returned with the Soviet ambassador and 38 of his staff. The brother of President Barre, who was also a Major General and Chief of Police, showed up at the Embassy in the afternoon with 25 members of his family requesting to be evacuated, but was turned away after a vocal conversation with the ambassador.

The operation did not include soldiers to handle the evacuation control center (ECC), which was set up in the JAO. A 44-person force consisting primarily of soldiers to handle the ECC was planned for insertion with the CH-53E Super Stallions after they had returned to the Guam. However, this was cancelled over objections from the commander of the security detail. The deficit was partially handled by Embassy staff that assisted a few soldiers from the security detail. The evacuees were grouped into 15-person "sticks" to be loaded onto the helicopters and were limited to one piece of luggage apiece. Some attempted to bring more, resulting in problems coordinating their evacuation. Furthermore, many evacuees had pets they wanted to bring, which were not allowed. Most pets were killed by their owners; some were given poison. Meanwhile, the soldiers were allowed to consume anything they wanted from the Embassy's commissary, such as candy, sodas, and souvenirs (most had been stationed on ships for several months). They were also allowed use or take anything they needed from the Embassy;

the medic filled several bags with medical supplies to return to the ship.

As evening approached, work began to prepare the HLZ for the main evacuation. The area was used as a parking lot and several vehicles were left without keys by staff that had already been evacuated. Some cars had to be broken into to be moved. Chemical lights were placed in the HLZ in a NATO "Y" pattern. The entire mission would be conducted with night vision goggles, which required all lights in the Embassy compound to be turned off.

The main evacuation occurred in the early morning hours of 6 January and consisted of four waves of five CH-46 helicopters. The timing of this phase was determined by range of the CH-46 Sea Knight, which lack aerial refueling capability; the ships were about 350-380 nautical miles (650-700 km; 400-440 mi) away during this phase. An AC-130 was sent from Saudi Arabia to provide gunfire support during the evacuation and two UH-1 Iroquois helicopters were on standby to provide gunfire support, but were not deployed.

The first wave departed the Guam at 2343 hrs. As the second wave landed, Major Siad arrived at the Embassy gate accompanied by two truckloads of soldiers and held a grenade in one hand and a radio in the other. His request to speak with the ambassador was granted. Major Siad demanded that the evacuation cease immediately because the Somali government had not granted the U.S. permission to carry out such a military operation. He claimed that he would radio soldiers to shoot down the helicopters if the operation continued.

The second and third waves were able to depart without incident as the ambassador negotiated with the Major, who finally agreed to settle the matter for several thousand dollars in cash and keys to the ambassador's armored car. Ambassador Bishop remained engaged in conversation with the Major until he reached the helicopter landing zone to depart with the final wave to prevent the Major from reneging on the deal. The final wave departed the Embassy at 0149 and landed on the Guam at 0223; twenty minutes later, Ambassador Bishop declared the evacuation complete.

Armed looters were observed entering the Embassy compound as the final wave departed. The doors of the chancery — the main building of the Embassy — were reportedly blown open by RPGs within two hours of the Embassy's evacuation. Somali employees of the Embassy —

Something Bigger Than Overthrowing Small Governments

known as foreign service nationals (FSNs) — could not be evacuated. Ambassador Bishop tried unsuccessfully to have these employees airlifted to safer parts of Somalia. Many of the FSNs had sought refuge in the Embassy with their families and about 30 were hired as guards and protected the Embassy throughout the ordeal. Local banks had been closed for some time and the Embassy was unable to pay the FSNs. The Ambassador left the FSNs with keys to the commissary and warehouse on the Embassy compound and they were permitted to take anything they needed. [8]

I seriously doubt the FSNs had an opportunity to reap the benefits before the vulture club arrived on the scene. The vulture club was what I called anyone who would steal food from a baby, kill the elderly and rape women in Mogadishu, which was more common than I cared to accept.

The 1993 version of U.S. soil in Somalia spoke volumes of the havoc that had occurred ... bullet holes, burnt out buildings, debris all interwoven between U.S. Marine Corps defensive positions.

Our vehicle passed through the check point and somewhat ornate main gate, decorated with three makeshift signs ... one white cardboard sign written in black, "MAIN GATE," one brown cardboard sign written in black, "REAR GATE" with a large black arrow pointing

84

to the right and another brown cardboard sign written in red with a red cross and a red arrow pointing to the right, "MEDICAL EMERGENCY USE REAR GATE."

    A few Somali children sat outside observing the actions of the two Marine guards who opened the gate for us to enter. I could not help but wonder if these kids were put there to report back to the enemy, whoever the enemy was. They had a bird's eye view of everything that was going on in the compound, and it just didn't seem right to let them sit there — or anyone who was not part of the operation. You would be better off standing next to a wolverine with a "pet me" sign.

Something Bigger Than Overthrowing Small Governments

    Just inside about thirty feet was the first green sandbag bunker with desert camo netting overhead harboring a 60-caliber machine gun and trigger puller. And another 100 feet from that, in the roundabout, a heavily fortified circle of those same green sandbags and desert camo netting, perhaps a fallback position should the compound be overrun again. We came to a stop in front of the Embassy.

    I dismounted and immediately noticed two Americans standing next to another Isuzu Trooper eyeing me ... the Isuzu Trooper with the steering wheel on the right side instead of the left. These were the codenamed ... "Centra Spike" boys also known as the United States Army Intelligence Support Activity (USAISA), frequently shortened to Intelligence Support Activity or ISA, and nicknamed "The Activity." They were part of the United States Army Special Operations unit originally subordinated to the U.S. Army Intelligence and Security Command (INSCOM), and tasked to collect actionable intelligence in advance of missions by other U.S. special operations forces. One wore a "Restore Hope" T-shirt, blue jeans and tennis shoes, while the other had a safari vest, pink shirt, shorts and, of all things, ... sandals. Little did I know at the time that these guys would be escorting me back to the safe house where we would be running our operation.

I followed my CIA associates into the building. Clearly abandoned at one time, the visible remains within the concrete halls of the old citadel spoke volumes of a once thriving center of U.S. diplomacy in Somalia.

Something Bigger Than Overthrowing Small Governments

Its lifeblood was slowly pumping in the movements and conversations between Marines of the 15 Marine Expeditionary Unit, (elements of the 1st Battalion 7th Marine and 3rd Battalion, 11th Marines, 9th Marines) who secured the entire compound. The dusty hallways offered their own charming Somalia experience.

You never forget the smell of Somalia once you have your nose rubbed in it. It isn't a bad smell ... just distinctive. This was going to be an interesting tour of duty. I found it comforting to be among Marines even though they had no idea who I was or what I would be doing. It felt like family, and I set my sights on meeting the man in charge when I got the first chance ... Colonel Anthony Zinni, the Director of Operations for the Unified Task Force for Operation Restore Hope. Building a relationship on the ground with my Marine brothers would come in handy later down the line, and I knew that if I were planning on running around armed in civilian attire that I wanted them to know who I was ... or to as much of a degree as I could without blowing my cover. I really didn't know at this stage what the SOP (standard operating procedure) would be for working operatives on the ground in Mogadishu, but one thing I did know was that this was no place for civilians.

The door opened at the western end of the hallway and what do you think I saw ... civilians. Okay, they weren't exactly civilians, but they weren't exactly paramilitary case officers either. Most of the time when I had seen CIA personnel from the Divisions working in country it was in a nice building somewhere in the main city, and they wouldn't think about putting themselves in harm's way. But I have to give it to these folks ... that is exactly where they were, in harm's way and busy as a bunch of bees doing what they did best, disseminating intelligence and running the station. They were focused, brave and diligent with a slight twinge of apprehension — rightfully so because there was nothing stopping this compound from being attacked. They had families like everyone else, and I am sure they wanted to see them again as soon as their time in country was over. How to make it to departure date was something that must have been on the forefront of their minds each day they woke.

I was ushered into the office of the Chief of Station (COS). She stood about five foot five, short dark hair, black eyeglasses and beige safari pants and shirt ... the kind you get at REI. She wore them as a commander should and made certain I knew she was in charge ... a stiff handshake with a cunning smile.

"Welcome to Mogadishu. I need paramilitary case officers that can run agents, not just blow things up. Can you do that?"

"I can," was my reply.

She literally got in my face and held a beat, sniffing me out. "That guy Ground Branch sent me down in Kismayo right now is worthless. Let me ask you again ... can you do the job?"

I leaned in a few inches unintimidated, a slight smile creasing my face ... "I can," was my second reply.

"Good, then we won't have any problems," she barked. "It's still dangerous around here so watch your back. You can grab a weapon from the armory. For now, here's where we are and here is Lido Base where you'll be operating out of," pointing to a map on the wall. "There aren't any updated maps of Mog (Mogadishu) ... the last we had was handed down from the '60s, so mapping operations are in order if we're going to stay here long term. Armed factions led by United Somali Congress (USC) commanders Ali Mahdi Muhammad and General Mohamed Farah Aidid, in particular, have been clashing as each seeks to exert authority over the capital. We have an agreement with Ali Mahdi Mohamed to offer some protection of Lido Base, and although he's pro-democratic and probably the good guy in all of this, it's no guarantee."

At that moment, a handsome fellow with a boyish smile stepped into the office ... his name was Rich. Rich was the Africa Division case officer manning the safe house on the other side of the Green Line.

> Along the epicenter of the fight between two clan militias for control of the Somali capital, the line dividing Mogadishu was also a microcosm of Somalia's past and future. Its streets were littered with the fallen monuments of both colonial and indigenous masters; its bombed and ransacked buildings standing as testimony to the latest blood rivalry for control. [9]

His Hawaiian shirt, white shorts and tennis shoes did not set him that far apart from the Centra Spike boys I saw eyeing me earlier in

Something Bigger Than Overthrowing Small Governments

the round about. He offered his hand, "I'm Rich, and I'll be taking you to Lido Base as soon as the COS is finished briefing you."

"We're good here, Rich," she trumped. "Make sure Baz gets a full briefing on the current situation, and I'll see you guys here on Friday for the staff meeting. Keep your head down." And with that she sat back and buried herself in paperwork.

I headed to the armory, signed out an M4, five mags with ammo, thanked my CIA associates and followed Rich out the front doors to ... you guessed it, the two Centra Spike boys waiting at the other Isuzu Trooper.

For the sake of security let's just call them Jake and Bud. Jake wore the shorts and pink T-shirt and Bud wore the Restore Hope T-shirt. I got introduced to two of the finest Centra Spike operators I had ever met. Their sense of humor surpassed their fear of war, and it was indeed a pleasure riding through the streets of Mogadishu at 60 miles an hour when we could, just to avoid being shot at. It was very apparent that getting across the green line to Ali Mahdi Mohamed's side of town was what everyone in the Trooper wanted, but that driving back across it on Friday to attend the upcoming "staff meeting" was not.

Chapter 5
A STONE'S THROW AWAY

"This is K4 circle," Rich said as we drove through the roundabout. "Last week they were burning tires here and preventing people from using this road ... problem is, it's the only way for us to get to the Embassy without going ten miles out of our way in more dangerous territory."

I tapped Rich on the shoulder, "I think it's okay to drive through burning tires," I said.

Jake looked at me, "I like how you think."

The remnants of what must have been at one time a playground for those interested in archeology and cultural history was in no way as rich in appearance as it once was before the civil war. Bullet holes

Something Bigger Than Overthrowing Small Governments

peppered almost every ancient building I saw, only surpassed by the even larger craters and half-standing walls, a testimony to the intense fighting that had taken place. I did my best to see through it all and recapture the images of what it used to be, wanting to appreciate the historical value of what once was ... but it was difficult.

If you know anything of the history in this region, the maritime trade in the 1st century CE that connected the inhabitants in Mogadishu area (known to the Greeks as Sarapion) with other communities along the Indian Ocean coast as well as the Persian influences made this an important place in the world. With Muslim traders from the Arabian Peninsula arriving around 900 CE, Mogadishu became a regional center for commerce. On the archaeological side of the house coins from China, Sri Lanka and Vietnam dating back to the Song, Ming and Qing Dynasty could be found, giving even more proof of its importance.

I imagined a very sophisticated society in those days and wondered where it all went wrong for them to go from that to where they were now, almost an uneducated, unsophisticated, barbaric display of irreverence for all that their ancestors had accomplished. It actually angered me to think that they would be so foolish to erase any evidence of their past that, frankly, if I were a Somali, I would have been proud of. And I was not alone in my thinking. Those Somali friends I would acquire while on the ground shared my concerns. They had not forgotten that the war was caused by political turmoil with a people acting out of desperation, but that was never in their opinion a hall pass for destruction of their rich history. They, like myself were familiar with this display of eradication from other warmongers like Stalin in the former Soviet Union. He burned Bibles, books, closed churches, tore down statues of anyone and anything that reminded the people of freedom or their rich past of Mother Russia.

Cut to the future and we would see it again when the Taliban in March 2001 destroyed the Great Buddha statues by dynamite on orders from leader Mullah Mohammed. And with ISIS in Iraq and, yes, even again in the United States when the Confederate Flag in South Carolina would no longer fly over the capital, and Confederate Memorials honoring veterans across America would be torn down. And the political excuse for this occurring would make no more sense than what had happened in Somalia.

Something Bigger Than Overthrowing Small Governments

CHARLESTON CHURCH SHOOTING

On the evening of June 17, 2015, a mass shooting took place at Emanuel African Methodist Episcopal Church in downtown Charleston, South Carolina, United States. The church is one of the United States' oldest black churches and has long been a site for community organization around civil rights. Nine people were killed, including the senior pastor and state senator, Clementa C. Pinckney. A tenth person was shot and survived.

Police arrested a white suspect, later identified as 21-year-old Dylann Roof, in Shelby, North Carolina the morning after the attack. The United States Department of Justice investigated the possibility that the shooting was a hate crime or an act of domestic terrorism, among other scenarios. The Federal Bureau of Investigation considered it a hate crime, but not an act of terrorism. Roof was charged with nine counts of murder by the State of South Carolina. The Civil War-era flag of the South's pro-slavery Confederacy had become a lightning rod for outrage over the shootings in Charleston, South Carolina, which authorities said was motivated by racial hatred. [10]

I wish that moment had never happened. And my heart breaks each day at the thought of wonderful, innocent people dying at the hands of Dylan Roof. And if God would grant me the power to bring every person that died back to life, I would. But let us be very clear on the causes of such events and not be misled by the liberal media to destroy the peace Americans of different color have enjoyed among each other for years. And let me make this perfectly clear, that what I am about to say is not meant to overshadow what happened in Charleston, but to point out there is something bigger going on here behind the scenes. I think it is worth mentioning because it will directly affect the future of our children and their safety.

Since I grew up in South Carolina and went to The Citadel and the confederate flag is flown there as well, I think I have some helpful insights to the entire debate on whether the flag should have stayed or not on the State Capitol. The Civil War was a fight to prevent the southern states from seceding, not to destroy the institution of slavery. It was fought over different interpretations of our founding document. And to this day the tensions between Article VI and the Tenth Amendment of the Constitution keep lawmakers navigating that same argument. While slavery was not a good thing, and never is, I'm not here to address that issue as much as I am to state the importance of embracing our history so that future generations are not led to believe that change is brought by destruction. This is the very thing, once again, that happened in Somalia.

I believe that globalists are fueling or even perhaps instigating this destructive mentality as a way of erasing our history so that future generations in America can be redefined. They could be led to believe that they are themselves globalists, and that states' rights or even the notion of a free and sovereign nation is a thing of the past ... perhaps even an idea that should no longer be tolerated by a world that would be better off under a single governing body ... a one world order. I believe it is a real threat to America, a real threat to our unity as Americans.

I also believe there is a much bigger picture here. If such influences can turn a nation upside down and erase its history, then it can erase its laws — the very laws that now protect children from pedophiles. One day, generations could think that it is okay for an adult pedophile to sexually engage with children, because they never knew there was a law that prohibited it. Is this conspiratorial or far-fetched? Not so, as you will discover when you dive into the remaining chapters of this book.

So where does the Confederate Flag come in? The issue isn't a piece of cloth that waves on a flagpole ... the flag didn't make that young man kill those people in the church ... despite what the liberal media may want you to believe. The Confederate flag is a part of our history. For most it stands as a reminder of a devastating war between the states, a reminder to us that we never want to allow that to happen again in this country. Certainly, the Confederate flag can be used by the media, politicians and demonstrators as the next hot topic, but it does not hold any more influence than the American flag that General Armstrong Custer carried with him each time he literally slaughtered

Something Bigger Than Overthrowing Small Governments

innocent Native Americans. Therefore, if both flags are representations of injustice, then why not protest the flying of the American flag?

The American flag has stood as a symbol of our history, not all good and not all bad. Each state within the United States deserves to fly its flag as a symbol of its history. I grew up in South Carolina as the grandson of an immigrant from Lebanon and a Native American grandmother living in the only part of Georgetown, S.C. where people of race loved one another despite their color. It was never about color. It was about the moral standard in our hearts set by God that allowed us to love one another. That standard needs to be set in stone again, then perhaps we will focus on the real cause of hatred.

No different is the issue to remove guns. Guns don't kill people ... people with guns kill people. There are no better experts on this subject matter than we who have been down range and have actually run operations to remove weapons from fighting factions in other countries. If they don't have guns, they will use bombs, and if not bombs ... stones, sticks, etc. — just what I was experiencing in Mogadishu. So the issue isn't the instrument, the issue that needs to be addressed is what influences or motivates people to kill.

If it were the case that the tool or instrument is to blame, then why are we not removing cars from the road, the same cars that kill thousands of Americans each year. But we don't, now do we? What we do is evaluate the condition of the driver and prevent them from driving if we feel "they" are unsafe, like driving under influence. Can they still climb in a car and drive illegally? Yes, of course they can. Can they do the same damage that they did before? Of course, they can. But most of the time it is not premeditated ... unless it is influenced by something that motivates a person to take extreme measures to cause death and destruction. And what might that motivation be when it comes to the events like the shooting in Charleston S.C. or the destruction or our historical footprint?

Perhaps the answer is closer to home than most realize. Take a look at the propaganda on television and the video games that encourage this type of violence, that actually brain wash people into a world of insensitivity that promotes the devaluation of human life ... makes it no more than a game, detached from reality. Take it one step further and look at the greed and self- entitlement of a generation of activists or protesters who are paid by globalists (follow the money and you find the crime) to tear down those Confederate memorials, . And I would predict in the future they would tear down most any memorial that represents military patriots or veterans of any war the U.S. fought, memorials of our founding fathers, once again the Ten Commandments, and frankly anything that represents the history of our nation. Keep in mind that these monuments are reminders of Confederate Americans with as much right to express their beliefs as other Americans on the Union side ... it is our history.

Does all of this sound familiar? Does this not look like everything I mentioned in the opening paragraphs of this chapter? Had I not spent part of my life overthrowing small governments I would have no leg to stand on ... but mark my words, this is exactly what is happening, in our country, and I know it well. You have heard it said, "If it walks like a duck and quacks like a duck, it's a duck." The erosion of America, its moral high ground and the compassion instilled in us by earlier generations — like those of my parents — is being challenged, and for one reason only ... to bring about a systematic progression of events that will turn America into one nation no longer under God.

Then surely, we can save the ship and all the crew if we call upon our lawmakers and politicians to plug the holes, raise the sails and set the compass for true north. I wish it were that easy.

In my opinion, the majority of our lawmakers and politicians are superficial or they point to the superficial solutions because they themselves have no spiritual platform to draw from. They cannot understand that this is a spiritual problem, requiring a spiritual resolution ... a change of the heart that in every case is something God does. For in the spiritual realm of God — and I believe even the people at the church in Charleston will tell you — it is the moral compass and influence of His love that teaches us to be sensitive and value life.

This is a concept foreign to many of our lawmakers. They have wrapped themselves around their own human ego and forgotten that God set the standards from the beginning that promote a consciousness of wrong. They think we can legislate it and it will become right. They cannot legislate morality ... and they are fools to think so.

Something Bigger Than Overthrowing Small Governments

    The pursuit by our former pro-Islamic, socialist Obama administration at the time this book was started, to erase the history of this country from the minds of future generations, is exactly what the leaders of the Soviet Union did with its people, it is exactly what the fighting factions in Somalia did in Mogadishu. Once that has happened, future generations have no identity with a sovereign nation, how it was formed, or the sacrifices made ... and they can be molded into what the government wants them to be ... a new identity. Ironically, and very much in line with the sexual exploitation of children, that is what pimps do ... they take away everything a child remembers about their ties to their history, their family, their roots, strip them of their identity and create a new one for them, what they wish them to become ... a commodity. Sadly, this commodity has no rights or freedoms as defined by God, rights reinforced by the very Constitution of the United States.

    Even now as I write, it gives me great concern for my own country as I see our Supreme Court play God, as I watch our politicians dictate law and blur the line between their authority and God's ... as if they are God ... as if they are doing whatever they can to erase God from the memories of future generations. Their destructive measures are only different in the fact that they have not peppered our buildings with bullets, but they certainly have peppered our spirits with dictatorship and socialism ... enough to hurt my eyes when I look upon what can be the future if we do not stand up and hold them accountable and punish them with extreme measures for what they have done.

    Cut back to 1993 as we drove through the streets of Mogadishu while my mind played out the destruction I was seeing. When we start allowing any government to dictate what will and will not be taught to future generations about our history, especially when they alter the truth of history, we are entering dangerous waters. And that was why the people in Mogadishu, in my opinion, were dying. They had lost their identity — the rich, proud shameless identity — and there was nothing in hard form to remind them of that — no icon, no Lincoln Memorial and no open display of a Ten Commandments, the foundation for civilized law based on respect for the constitutional nature of man, the ten basic gifts or faculties which define his existence ... these were my thoughts. And although I knew it was relatively silly to even let that enter my mind, I wished for them that they had, even in the midst of Islam, openly displayed and valued their history enough not to blow it up like everything else in the city. And this was the case here in Mogadishu. No one had been held accountable for the death and destruction of all I was seeing along the way. And I knew that no one ever would be.

"It's such a shame all of this is destroyed," I said. No one commented ... a silent agreement. It caused everyone to take a moment to actually look for something other than an ambush, but just for a moment. Like I said ... I did my best to see through it all and recapture the images of what it used to be, wanting to appreciate the historical value of what once was ... but it was difficult.

I recall this ghostly stretch of road, desolate at best, a horrible choke point where Bud would put the accelerator to the floor. The speed odometer would climb to that 60 mph mark I spoke of and stay there until we had sailed over every pothole and dead animal in our way. If we made it through there alive, the Green Line was just around the corner. This is so poetically described in the 1993 *The New York Times* article, "On Mogadishu's Green Line–Nothing Is Sacred," which is placed in the Addendum section.

Something Bigger Than Overthrowing Small Governments

And it was every bit of what the article described as we rolled up to the U.S. Marine Corps check point. A few enlisted Marines armed with M16s and battle gear approached the vehicle and asked for our passports. They glanced inside the Trooper, paying close attention to the weapons we were carrying. "I need you to step out of the vehicle," said the young Lance Corporal.

Bud looked over his shoulder from the driver's seat at me and the others. "I'd sit tight and not make any sudden moves," were his words of wisdom as he left his weapon on the seat and opened the door.

Rich could see some tension in the moment and looked across and out the driver's side window. "We're with the State Department, Security."

He started to get out of the passenger side when ... "Stay in the vehicle!" shouted another Marine. Rich looked back at me with a grin and rolled his eyes as if it was sort of funny. I pulled off a fake grin with my teeth showing just to add to the humor. I think we were just lightening up the situation as best we could.

Rich sat there and carefully pulled something from his backpack. "Here's our papers." He handed them out the window to Bud, who handed them to the Lance Corporal. Directly to my right were four other Marines standing at the ready, not really sure what to make of us. I know Rich and the boys had probably been through the Green Line a dozen times but recognizing faces and vehicles all becomes a blur to Marines when death is barking at your door day in and day out. It isn't PTSD, but it isn't logical thinking either when you add apprehension and inexperience to the mix. It has always been and always will be the tradeoff when we expect our young men and women to go from high school to a battlefield where real people bleed real blood and last breaths leave you bewildered if you happen to be by the side of a dying buddy.

So we sat there realizing that at any moment someone could get a nervous twitch on the trigger and headquarters would be reporting CIA officers died from friendly fire. This was one heck of a day in Dodge City, going from having an AK-47 stuck in my face by a Somali boy to having an M16 at the ready by an American Marine. Clearly this was going to be a journey where watching your six meant watching your twelve, your nine and your three o'clock; where eyes in the back of your head was an understatement. And as threatening as it was, it had a bit of excitement that is hard to explain. Perhaps it was just the adrenaline coursing through my veins in a not-so-welcomed manner, but in a way that demanded I embrace it like you embrace a chronic disease, ignoring it as much as you can but knowing that you will have to find a way to live with it so it doesn't get the best of you.

The Lance Corporal pretended to study the papers Rich had given him. I say "pretended" because he was actually preoccupied with a more obvious danger in the form of an approaching SUV filled with "Skinnies," ... a truth that blanketed his face like the response you get from someone caught telling a lie on a polygraph machine. He handed the paperwork back to Bud, who climbed back in the Trooper.

"You guys be careful out here and give us a shout if you need anything," Bud offered.

The Lance Corporal broke a tiny smile of relief and replied, "We'll do that, sir," and moved with his other war fighters to a more attentive posture as the SUV got closer to the checkpoint.

From here on out we drove a normal 30 miles per hour in what seemed like a safer part of Mogadishu. Fewer guns were displayed by the locals, and even a few waved at our Trooper as we drove by.

Something Bigger Than Overthrowing Small Governments

    Bud picked up a radio and said something in Italian. It wasn't long before an Italian convoy of three armored vehicles pulled out of a side street and allowed us to pull in from behind. "Got a good relationship with the Italians ... they patrol our neighborhood," Bud said.

    We weren't far from the beach front when we turned down a dirt street and made a quick left, stopping at the front 12-foot iron gate of what was Lido Base ... a safe house of enormous statue, surrounded by a 12-foot wall with glass shards cemented on top ... obviously once owned by someone with a little influence and a lot of money according to Somali standards. The Italian convoy kept going. Bud honked the horn. A small portal in the solid iron sheeting opened and a black face peered through for only a second or two. A Somali boy about age 16 dressed in blue jeans, a dirty green short sleeve shirt and blue bathroom shower shoes slung his AK-47 over his shoulder and pushed open the gate allowing us to enter and then closed it afterwards, but not before looking down both sides of the street to make sure we had not been followed. It was obvious that he had seen his share of fighting.

    Another Somali boy about the same age, wearing a gray short sleeve shirt and gray green checkered sarong, handled an AK-47 with one hand down by his side, watching as we climbed out of the Trooper. Rich turned and introduced me to another Somali man, perhaps in his '50s, wearing a yellow cotton shirt with an imprint of London Bridge and the Tower, and a green sarong. He was the father of the two boys, and his AK-47 with banana clip showed the wear and tear of an instrument that had seen many surgeries. He smiled and shook my hand with a warm, genuine grip that told me he was there to be my friend and save my life if necessary. I spoke to him in the little bit of Arabic I had learned over the years, and he seemed to like me even better. I put my hand on his shoulder and thanked him.

I would see him in weeks to come pulling out his prayer rug, gently laying his AK-47 on the ground only inches from his side and acting out his Muslim faith. I wondered if he would welcome the idea of me joining him and acting out my Christian faith. As would be the case that very month, I would do exactly that ... kneel next to him and pray ... no prayer rug of course.

"This is home," Rich said. We entered the three-story, white, cement block house and echoed our voices off the ceramic tile that covered every floor. It was sparse with only the essentials stacked in

Something Bigger Than Overthrowing Small Governments

one corner of the living room, vacant of furniture ... MREs, cardboard crates of bottled water, ammunition as best I can remember. Funny, during my entire time in Mogadishu I can't remember what I ate or when I ate any meals. I know I had to have done so but reflecting back, I guess it was the last thing on my mind at the time.

"Yo, welcome home." An Asian looking fellow with a baseball cap, mustache and reading glasses came down the stairs. This was the third Centra Spike boy ... a communicator/medic. He really wasn't Asian, he was American ... as American as any of us with a Vietnamese ancestry and a wicked sense of humor as I recall. For the sake of security, we'll call him Dan. So there you have it, the three Centra Spike boys, Jake, Bud and Dan.

He shook my hand. "Got any bags you need a hand with?" he asked. "Nope ... what you see is what I have," referring to the one backpack slung over my shoulder.

"Well there's plenty of room, so just take your pick," he said. I headed up the stairs to the third and top level of the building ... not a really big room but it did lead out to an open parapet-style patio with a

104

view of the Indian Ocean directly to the east. Refugee camps were set up across the street where you would normally cross the sand dunes to get to the ocean. Their makeshift homes were dome-like structures covered in plastic, just enough to hold maybe three or four people. The community of domes was protected by large concrete walls, as if someone who owned one of these Italian villas had offered to protect them like Fort Apache.

I dropped my backpack on the floor next to a military cot and walked out on the parapet-style patio. Glancing down to all sides I noticed we were surrounded by similar Italian villas in the neighborhood ... sorely degraded.

As I looked at all the turmoil and devastation, I asked myself, "Why?" My mind drifted back to a conversation my mother and father had with me when I was younger. They were wise beyond their years.

"Fear is the lengthened shadow of ignorance," my father said ... a statement that I would hear again years later in 2017 by Sensei Auge at our Aikido Dojo.

My father continued, "I want you to consider obtaining some very important tools that you have not yet obtained that will help you in life. I want you to listen to me and heed very good wisdom and apply

Something Bigger Than Overthrowing Small Governments

it," he said. "We who are successful and fear nothing all go through a process one way or another of becoming who we are and building our self-esteem ... confidence, etc. There are tools missing from your toolbox of life that I want you to put in there and take with you, so you never have to return to the old way of doing things. We all make mistakes, and we become comfortable in sitting in those mistakes or not far from them in our life. It is scary stepping away from them, but as we go further and further away, we reach a point of no return where we see much more clearly, and we never return to them."

"It is like standing eye level here in the town. All we can see is what is in front of us. But if you have the energy and the bravery and take the effort to walk all the way up the cliff towards the mountain — which takes time, and sweat and energy — once you are on top looking down on the town, you have a much broader view of things. You can see everything. You can see the streets and which way they flow ... you're sort of on top of the world, so to speak. Your fear disappears because you can see how to get from the town to a neighboring town ... the strand, the roads, and the paths. And so that is how life is. We have to forge ahead and get on top of things where we can see more clearly. We have to leave a lot of stuff behind in order to do that. It is logical determination ... not emotional."

My father continued, "You see, many people have grown accustomed to wondering why certain things happen. They spend most of their life confused because they can't seem to get an answer always as to *why* something happened. The reality is that they don't need to know why. All they need to know is that if they do a certain action and it causes a certain result, if they stop doing that action, they get a different result. For example, if you stand in the middle of the road and get hit by a car, do you stay there trying to understand why you got hit by that car? If you do, another car is going to hit you. So what do you do? You simply get out of the road. You may never see the driver of the car again or find an opportunity to even ask the driver why he hit you. You have to be prepared to make a different choice without the need to understand what just happened. Most people waste a lot of energy trying to understand why."

And I would submit for the purposes of this book that trying to understand everything God was doing in my life wasn't important. I needed to stop having conversations with myself because I was flawed as a human, and there was no way I would be able to control uncontrollable circumstances. Nor did I know the master plan for my life and how to navigate those fault lines that ultimately would lead to the success of that master plan that God had for me.

Mom interjected to Dad, "Have your conversation with God instead and in that conversation, 'Trust in the Lord with all your heart and lean not to your own understanding' (Proverbs 3:5). It isn't important to waste energy on understanding, but it is important to put energy into accepting. Once you accept that you do not need to understand, then you are ready to understand accepting. If you accept God for who He is and the fact that He loves you and has your best interest at hand, you will no longer waste energy on something you have absolutely no control over. And with that type of thinking, you can do like your father said ... get out of the road before you get hit by another car."

She chuckled, "Look, Moses didn't call up the science team to figure out why or how the Red Sea was parting. He simply got the tribe across the Red Sea when it opened. Now maybe once he got out of danger, he pondered a few things, but I doubt it. And when I or your grandmother made you a wonderful meal, you didn't sit there asking yourself, 'How did she do that?' You simply stuck the flavorful food in your mouth and enjoyed it. And from then on, out you came to trust that I or your grandmother would always fix something good and flavorful for you to enjoy, whether you knew how we did it or not."

And as I gave it more thought, I realized that indeed understanding why some things in life bother us isn't that important. I was not a psychologist who intended to write some great paper on *why* life is the way it is. I was a normal person who was making it through life and I just needed to use the energy I had to make things happen or make things not happen. Suddenly life took a different perspective.

Across the dirt alley from our safe house, what looked abandoned was a single-story concrete building with tin roofs. The rest of it had no roof at all, and you could see the baby-blue painted walls of its exposed interior. No one lived there. But next to it, protected by a wall, was a similar structure with some of its roof protected by sheets of tin and the rest open to expose its interior baby-blue walls. Medium-

Something Bigger Than Overthrowing Small Governments

sized boulders were strategically placed on top of the tin to hold it down from the wind. The outside was yellow, and the security wall was topped off with glass shards to prevent intruders from climbing over.

On the shaded porch were four Somali children standing over a large, aluminum wash pan filled with fresh water, probably the only fresh water they would have for the day. I waved compassionately at them and they waved back. The two little girls were barefoot and wore cotton white dresses, more western than I expected. The two boys were in long cotton pants and dark shirts. I had met my neighbors or at least some of them and it was a good start.

In days to come they would play a game throwing rocks at me on the roof, and I would fire a few back gently, making them run and laugh. It appeared from what I had observed thus far that rock-throwing in Mogadishu, at least with these kids, was a favorite pastime. However, most often it wasn't a favorite past time, it was an act of violence with intent to kill. According to Islam stoning was still legal, and to the best of my knowledge folks here found it important to keep their stoning skills sharp just in case someone committed a crime and needed to be stoned to death. I mean, if you're going to do it you might as well be good at it, right? It was just bizarre in my book, but it was not overlooked nor taken lightly. I think David in the Old Testament actually brought the giant Goliath to his knees with a stone. Point well taken.

I walked back inside and unloaded my gear. I picked up my M4 and studied it with the intensity of scientist looking for nuclear atoms. I, more than most, had the capacity to appreciate the beauty of what I held in my hands ... it was more than a tool ... it was my best friend while in Somalia. "Take care of your weapon and your weapon will take care of you," my Gunnery Sgt. used to tell me.

I had been disciplined from a child to learn the effectiveness of any weapon I held in my hands, a mind built for shooting ... and now it was in my possession. I stared at its characteristics, the way it felt, how it handled, its internal ballistics, and how it moved when it fired. I pulled the bolt back and noticed the sweet smell of fresh gun oil in the chamber ... it was clean. I'd heard it said that people who want to focus less on the stress of life and more on what's important should make time "to smell the roses." The phrase takes on an even deeper meaning when you consider how often, according to some, roses play a part in miracles and angelic encounters. A rose fragrance may accompany the delivery of a blessing from God, such as a miraculously answered prayer. Right then and there that gun oil smelt like a rose to me, and as far as I was concerned the M4 was that blessing. I reached in my bag and pulled out a pink NO FEAR GEAR decal and stuck it to the stock. We were ready to dance.

I made my way down to the second-floor room where Rich was set up on a desk and a laptop computer. On the other desk was another laptop computer. The Centra Spike boys were running cable and wire all over the place setting up the satellite dish that would allow us to send burst transmissions of our Intel Reports to Langley. You could tell they really loved their work.

Over the course of the next three days Rich would brief me on the standard operating procedures of the base and introduce me to the young Somali girl who washed our clothes and did a bit of housekeeping. She was so "trusted" that she actually stole our camouflage fatigues off the line, the very ones she washed for us. I'm being sarcastic of course. Now I really didn't plan on wearing a military uniform while in Somalia, so it wasn't the clothing that

Something Bigger Than Overthrowing Small Governments

mattered. What mattered was the fact that someone now had U.S. Military uniforms and could try to enter one of the operations on the airfield or the Embassy disguised as an American and do some damage. Needless to say, unanimously we voted to have her leave the base that week.

It wasn't an easy decision by any means. She made a strong plea to stay. In Somalia, the cultural expectation for girls to undergo genital mutilation is based on sex and marriage. Men expect to marry a virgin. If a girl has not undergone female genital mutilation, she is considered unclean. As long as this girl was at our base, she believed she was safe from having to undergo genital mutilation. We had no way of knowing whether she was telling the truth or not or playing on our emotions hoping to persuade us to keep "the spy inside" so to speak. We just weren't willing to take ... that chance.

Up on the flat concrete roof, Dan, Bud, Rich and myself were painting a giant American flag that could be seen by anything flying overhead, especially U.S. fighter support and helicopters. We knew there might come a time when we would have to hunker down in the villa and defend ourselves. If surrounded, it was our plan to call in fire support to saturate the neighborhood, and we wanted to make sure they knew where the Americans were. "I hope my wife hasn't run off with another man by the time I get home," Rich teased.

"I've heard it said that girls are like monkeys. They don't let go of one branch until they have another," I said. Everyone laughed.

"Seriously though, a lot of overseas assignments can take their toll," Rich said.

I kept my focus on the painting I was doing, glancing up for a moment at a time ... I smiled at Rich, "Despite the schedule and obstacles, having faith and hope and determination over frustration is what gets me to the end goal. I control what I can, and the other things which I can't I have to be okay with. The ocean of love is way too powerful to struggle in it ... you will drown. If you relax, the currents will take you out and down a bit and you may lose sight of shore, but eventually it will spit you out on land."

I don't think what I said made Rich feel any better, but it was fun to talk about something else other than the turmoil in Somalia. In days to come we planned a lot of hours to fill sandbags and stack them along the walls of the first floor of our villa. We realized if some "technical" busted through our gate with a 106 RR that not even the sandbags would stop the impact of the HE rounds, but for small arms fire it was a warm-and-fuzzy for us.

We made sure we all knew what our firing positions were so we could cover as much 360 as we could if we got attacked. We weren't relying on any help from anyone if things went bad. The irony in operating a "secret base" is that your efforts to keep it a secret stop being a secret the minute you introduce the base to anyone you're asking help from. So you'd better be darn sure that if you ask for help, especially from U.N. Forces, that you're ready to abandon that base and your cover story if they arrive. Then you have to be prepared to find another secret base, which takes time and energy, neither of which we had much of, so we decided it was best to just fend for ourselves. There was some comfort in knowing that our agents had assured us that most of the neighbors were from Ali Mahdi's clan, but we never were sure if they would give us up in a pinch or not.

Every day our intelligence reconfirmed our precautions. Things in the city were heating up, and we knew that if we were attacked it

Something Bigger Than Overthrowing Small Governments

would be like ants swarming on a picnic. The sound of weapons fire at night became the norm ... but it would take its toll on us over time, sleeping with one eye open ... so much to the point that in order to get sleep we would pop an 800mg of Motrin at least one evening out of each week. And whoever's turn it was to do it made sure everyone else knew he was doing it ... such a deep sleep that he probably wouldn't wake up to the sound of bad guys storming the gate. It was an odd tradeoff with long-term benefits ... a rested body was able to pay more attention to the unpredictable surroundings.

In months to come in Mogadishu and in years to follow, the rest of the world would have a chance to see what we were concerned about when the movie *Black Hawk Down,* a war film directed by Ridley Scott, would be released in 2001. It is an adaptation of the 1999 book of the same name by Bowden, a 29-part series that chronicled the events of a 1993 raid in Mogadishu by the U.S. military aimed at capturing faction leader Mohamed Farrah Aidid and the ensuing battle. The Somali war fighters were not to be underestimated. They had no uniforms, they appeared to have no rank and file, they appeared to be unorganized. But that was not the case, and we made sure that our intelligence reports remained true to those facts. These were seasoned fighters ... with really bad teeth.

Jake stuck his head from the hatch leading to the roof, "We need to check out that big satellite station on the hill." We put the paint brushes in a box and went below to grab our gear. Out the gate we drove and through the dusty streets of Mogadishu in search of the giant Satellite facility on the hill. Finding our way through the maze of destroyed buildings reminds me now of the scenes in *Saving Private Ryan.* We rounded a bumpy corner and saw up ahead about two blocks a Marine Corps M60 Tank with its 105mm gun barrel staring us down. We stopped short so they could identify us. I climbed out of the vehicle and waved ... there was absolutely no response, no wave, no nothing.

"Hopefully they know we're friendly," Bud said.

I looked at everyone in the Trooper, "I'm good if you are."

I climbed back in and we started to move slowly forward when a Somali woman in her '50s ran from a building screaming and waving her arms in the air as if she wanted us to stop. I wasn't sure what was going on, whether this was an ambush, or she needed help or what. We took our weapons off safe, prepared to defend ourselves. She continued running at the vehicle, when all of a sudden about 100 feet behind her across the road in a blown-out building there was an explosion. She dropped to her knees and covered her head. We ducked to the left in our seats to avoid any flying debris. We got out of the vehicle carefully and helped her while a squad of EOD Marines (explosive disposal) casually made their way from behind the M60 Tank and down to where the explosion had taken place. There really wasn't much anyone could say. The Marines were just doing their job, and we just happened to be at the wrong place at the wrong time. Sure, it would have been nice to have those orange cones blocking the road and a big "Explosive Detonation," sign with yellow tape, but that isn't how it's done. They had found a cache of ordnance and needed to dispose of it. So they did.

We thanked the Somali woman and got back in the Trooper and headed up the street, only to pass the M60 Tank and one very burnt-out Marine with half his body out the copula. He was young, he was tired, and he was homesick ... I've seen it before. He could care less who we were ... he was there to do a job and collateral damage was acceptable. He too had no intention of going home in a body bag.

We all found it rather funny that we could have died had it not been for the Somali woman warning us. Our best calculations would have put us close enough to the explosion to turn our Trooper into an upside-down piece of scrap metal with body parts everywhere.

"Bud, I think you should marry that woman. She saved our lives," I blurted.

"She was attractive in a sort of Somali way, now that you mention it," Bud replied. We laughed.

"Maybe she has a sister," Jake said, looking over his shoulder at the ass end of the M60 tank fading in the distance. I knew what he was thinking.

"Bet you wish we had one of those bad boys sitting back at Lido Base," looking at Jake as he turned back around.

"We can always dream," he replied.

And so, I did for just a moment ... not about the M60, but how God had once again saved my life. We made it to the enormous satellite station, abandoned but still pretty much intact, did some looking around and gathered some intelligence. Then we headed back to check out a

Something Bigger Than Overthrowing Small Governments

ship called the *Felix* that, according to some rumors, had been shelled after delivering food supplies to the starving masses. It sat all alone like a beached whale, listing with its anchor midway hauled as if the crew had gotten caught short of leaving.

We took the long walk down the tormented concrete pier which it kissed. This was another evacuation (exfil) point we wanted to add to our list of "get out of town" opportunities, and frankly the *Felix* could be a nice piece of bulletproofing for a SpecOps (Special Operations) team providing waterborne exfiltration for us ... should it come to that. I felt sorry for the maritime giant stranded by the pier ... she had gotten slapped down by people who had no appreciation for her good intentions. It would be the last time the *Felix* would ever do a good will mission.

The next morning, we headed to the U.S. Embassy to pick up some supplies. I decided to look around the compound. U.S. Marine and Navy personnel in the form of security, logisticians, medical facilities and other support mechanisms were hard at work. Marine Corps snipers maintained sandbagged positions on the roofs. Nearby on a dirt field a bunch of sailors were playing a game of baseball, so I stopped to watch. Suddenly a flurry of stones flew over the compound wall and interrupted the game ... the sailors ran for cover.

"This happens to us every time we just try to have a little fun," said the sailor standing next to me. His name was Stuart Scott and years down the road in 2001, he and I would meet up again in a church parking lot at Rolling Hills Covenant Church in Palos Verdes, CA. He would recognize me after all those years.

I turned to him and asked if I could have everyone's attention. He gathered the team in front of me. "If you guys want to be able to play ball, then I have a way you can do that without being disturbed ... if you're interested," I said. I looked around at all the approving faces.

"Okay, everyone grab a rock, stand on line and wait until I tell you to throw it. When you do, hurl it over the wall outside the compound. Now start yelling like you're playing the game." And so, they did. About twenty seconds later the locals started throwing rocks over the wall into the compound.

"Okay, now," was my command. About thirty rocks fired back like naval gunfire over the compound wall. On the other side, you could hear the painful screams of those being hit by the unexpected barrage of the counter-offensive in stone. You could actually hear the sound of their bare feet pounding the pavement and dirt road in retreat. From that point on, according to Stuart Scott, no ball game was interrupted again, and I became a friend to the sailors in Mog. I turned to Stuart and said, "Learn it right, and you'll do it right the rest of your life. Learn it wrong, and you'll do it wrong and spend the rest of your life trying to get it right." I was assured he knew exactly what I meant when his hand drifted carefully to his sidearm followed by a smile.

On my way out I was fortunate enough to finally meet Col. Zinni, who called me into his office for an official introduction. Evidently, the COS (Chief of Station) had briefed him on my true identity as well as the fact that I was a former Marine. We had a great 20-minute discussion on the situation in Mogadishu, and he told me that Gen. Robert Johnston would be arriving in the future. He asked if I would be willing to give the General my assessment on things on the ground. I was delighted that he asked.

We shook hands and I departed, but not without almost literally bumping into Christiane Amanpour and her news crew on the sidewalk leading to the front of the U.S. Embassy. She just stared at me from the time we locked eyes until I passed her. I wish I could say it was because she thought I was handsome, but I know better ... it was the bulletproof vest, weapon and blue jeans that did it. As far as Christiane, in my book she had always been impressive. Any woman who would travel to the most dangerous parts of the globe to bring truth to the viewers and risk her life to do so was either crazy or very polished when it came to staying alive. I like to think the latter. She broke a gentle smile as did I on my way past and as I looked over my shoulder, she was looking over hers. We exchanged smiles one last time and went on about our business. I made it a point to stay as far away from the media as possible especially while in Somalia, but it was nice to get a glimpse of someone I admired and never thought I would see in this part of the world.

> Despite some setbacks and incidents, Operation RESTORE HOPE succeeded in its goal of bringing an end to mass starvation. The heavily armed UNITAF units quickly established security in their sectors, and an uneasy truce kept the peace between the factions. There

were some warning signs on the horizon, however, as U.N. diplomats began to press for a more active role of the military in confiscating weapons and in forcing some kind of political settlement. 'Mission creep' began to enter the vocabulary of those serving in Somalia, and soon after the United States turned over the mission completely to the United Nations in May, the situation began to unravel. [11]

We picked up our supplies and headed out to establish a number of infil and exfil sites around the city, just another part of the mission in addition to running agents and collecting intelligence. We would take multiple trips back and forth from our base to the U.S. Embassy over the course of my time there, taking chances as things heated up with the war.

We were about to find ourselves in the bloodiest week in Somalia since the arrival of the multinational task force on December 9, 1992. It wasn't difficult to hear the gunfire erupting for the second straight day on that Friday when we were headed to the U.S. Embassy, just days after Nigerian forces were shot at by Aidid's militia. The constant sound of gunfire echoed across the streets of Mogadishu starting in the early morning hours, disturbing the calmness that had prevailed since my arrival. As we approached K4 circle things seemed unsettled and tires burned, the road was blocked, and so we detoured to the right. Just the day before Nigerian, U.S. and Botswana troops fought Aidid's gunmen for eight hours at this same location. Two miles up the road it was blocked as well, and we knew there was no way to the U.S. Embassy. You could feel the anger in the air as hundreds of Somali protestors began to pick up stones and gauntlet the road.

"We need to get back to the base," I said. Bud turned the vehicle around. We stopped to see that the crowd was preparing to ambush us with stones once we got into their choke point. To the right and down a bit a Marine M35 2 ½-ton cargo truck was stalled, and I could see the crowd dangerously gathering about the vehicle with the young Marine inside frantically trying to start it up.

Something Bigger Than Overthrowing Small Governments

"That guy is in trouble! Let's go there," I said. Bud drove up next to the truck. "Get that out of here now!" I yelled.

The Marine looked down from his seat, "It won't start sir."

I jumped out of the Trooper and into the right seat of his truck to offer some firepower as the crowd got closer. We were being engulfed like molasses, slowly but with intent. They knew we had weapons and were cautious to see what we would do. I had no doubt they were out for blood. Suddenly the truck started.

"You follow us, and you don't stop for anyone or anything until we get you to the Green Line ... there is no way back to the Embassy." He was scared and trancelike. I slapped him on the shoulder, "Hey, did you hear me?"

"Yes sir," he replied, looking me dead in the eye. I jumped out of the truck and back into the Trooper. I looked Bud right in the eye.

Bud smiled, "Certainty of death, small chance of success ... what are we waiting for?"

"Roll down the window and fire over their heads to get them to scatter when we hit the gauntlet," I yelled.

No one argued with the fact that one stone was enough to kill a man. There is no such thing as a fair fight ... never plan a fair operation. Bud put the accelerator gently to the floor to give the Marine in the truck time to go navigate his gears until we were up to speed. We were on a roll and we had no intention of stopping. The M35 2 ½-ton cargo truck was so tight on us that I could see the radiator practically kissing our back bumper. With the windows down we started firing over the heads of the crowd — hot, expended cartridges bouncing off the dashboard, hitting us in the face, the sound from the blast, deafening. The crowd dispersed like people running from a swarm of African killer bees, some clenching their rocks, others dropping them, some half-heartedly throwing them and hitting our vehicle.

We sped by, feeling no relief as we rounded K4 circle and headed back to our side of town. Once at the Green Line we dropped off the Marine and his truck. When I got back to Lido Base, I settled in with pen and a brown paper bag and wrote down a little poem in memory of the day's events, and how it might be recorded in the future if we found ourselves in a mess.

Bazzel Baz

Lido Base

I knew of a place far away
Where silent heroes came to play
With eyes of steel and courage on their face
These were the men of Lido Base
The Lido Banditos, as known to us all
Bound and determined never to fall
A color much different from all the rest
It matched the same as their bulletproof vest

By night they were silent, by day all around
While death was common in Mogadishu town
Despite such risk, the mission was first
Adrenaline junkies, unquenchable thirst
So on that day they entered their truck
On to K4, praying for luck
And luck they did gain in the size of the rocks
Not one was hurt, not one was lost

The gauntlet they ran much a surprise
To run it again put sparks in their eyes
As Bud increased the speed of the truck
I knew that Jake thought we were out of luck
So from the window the colt was placed
Shots fired at the entire Somali race
Habargidir, ran throughout the streets
The Lido team alive and complete

No regret in the heart of Baz that day
Even Rich was so eager to play
The shattered window, the broken glass
We told Aidid to kiss our ass
So now they know the Lido Banditos
Men who have gigantic huevos
Don't stand in their way, don't try to resist
They'll make your grave if they get pissed

Something Bigger Than Overthrowing Small Governments

> No remorse for that day at K4
> Those stupid Somalis dented our door
> They threw their grenades, shot their guns
> RPG-7s ... just for fun
> Not sure how it started, us or them
> The news reported three hundred dead men
> All we know is Lido's alive
> Faces of courage, steel in our eyes
> With eyes of steel and courage on their face
> These were the men of Lido Base

Looking back at the events of the day, I thought that perhaps I have overlooked the deeply seated religious influences of this country and its people and passed judgment way too early on their intentions to hurt us. Clearly, these were good people, a peaceful people, a people without sin. Jesus did say, "he that is without sin, cast the first stone." Since they were casting the first, second and third stones, they must have been close to sainthood. I gave that thought more consideration than it deserved ... sarcastically speaking.

We would continue to receive Intel reports from our agents on the ground throughout the night and days to come. Unrest was smoldering like the campfire from the night before, the one that isn't quite extinguished and turns into a giant forest fire. I'm not sure anyone in Washington was seeing it but us. Although it appeared that U.S.-led forces had crushed an armed uprising by Aidid, we were all facing an explosive situation that was expected to plunge the country back into anarchy.

CHAPTER 6
AN OUNCE OF PREVENTION

Back at the base we were carefully and secretly planting a tracking device under a vehicle we intended to hand off to a team of Somali mercenary recruits who would act as a recon unit for us and push north of Mogadishu along the coast. I rigged the device to look like another piece of the undercarriage, and off they went. Unbeknownst to them, we followed our Somali mercenary recruits by satellite to verify they were where they said they were when they radioed back.

We were looking for routes out of the city that U.S. Embassy personnel and our CIA associates could use for evacuation if air or maritime assets were unavailable. Langley monitored their journey and found them to be very reliable ... so we kept them as part of the operations. It wasn't long before we had what we needed. We called the COS and set a meeting at the U.S. Embassy to brief her. As we

Something Bigger Than Overthrowing Small Governments

approached Afghoy Road, not far from the Embassy, the sea of people paid no attention to us at all but lined the road as if they were awaiting the Rose Parade. They shouted and chanted with arms in the air, as a white Toyota pickup truck slowly made its way. Standing in the bed of the truck was none other than Osama Bin Laden himself, who at the time was nobody to me. I had no idea how influential he was.

    Rich looked surprised. "Osama Bin Laden ... so that's Aidid's bag man," Rich stated. We had gotten intelligence from a number of sources that Aidid was receiving money from the Arab world, but we weren't quite sure at the time who the financial benefactor was. Now we knew. He stood upright and humbly proud of who he was, messiah-like in his glance to the crowd, his head draped in a white, Arabic headscarf which added that much more to his self-proclaimed holiness. For a moment, even I was fascinated.

Osama Bin Laden

    Here he was, just yards away from me and the team. Had I been able to look into the future and see the damage he would be responsible for in America on September 11, 2001, I would have zeroed in on him and taken the shot, even at the cost of my own life. In years to come, on May 2, 2011, to be exact, shortly after 0100, close friends of mine in the CIA would do me that favor by leading Operation Neptune Spear using DEVGRU or SEAL Team Six and killing Bin Laden. But at this time, he was only someone to be watched.

    Osama Bin Laden's hatred of the U.S. and conversion to "terrorist" status came about a few years earlier during the Gulf War of 1990-91. He was outspokenly critical of Saudi Arabian dependence upon the U.S. military and denounced U.S. support of a "corrupt, materialist, and irreligious" Saudi monarchy. So it made perfect sense that he would be in Mogadishu doing whatever he could to defeat a U.S. presence.

What didn't make sense was why Congress had not taken a proactive stance on getting rid of people like Bin Laden, who historically managed to destroy the world. And even now as history repeats itself, the question remains as to why President Obama in 2015 waited until ISIS grew so powerful in Iraq, slaughtered thousands of innocent Christians and managed to sneak into America across his unsecured border, and still took little to no action? How could we as the American people, at the cost of our lives, allow such stupidity?

And so, I watched as Osama Bin Laden performed the "Pope wave" to the crowd of supporters, still chanting, raising their weapons — raising their weapons? Then it dawned on us that most of the crowd was armed more than usual. It was amazing, scary and exciting all at the same time. There had been a pretty successful push over the past months by U.N. Forces to remove weapons from everyone in Mogadishu in order to keep the peace. But somehow, they had gotten more. Now that I think about it, the U.N. had to be kidding itself to believe everyone in Mogadishu would give up their guns. Just because they weren't walking around in the streets with them didn't mean they didn't have them ... and on this day, they had them.

Afghoy Road to U.S. Embassy

Something Bigger Than Overthrowing Small Governments

"We need to make a move," I said to Rich. He just looked at me in agreement. We drifted to a side street and made our way back to base until we felt the crowds had disbursed enough for us to try another run at the U.S. Embassy. We returned to the safe house and finished sending some Intel reports on the situation and then jumped back inside the Trooper. We had a clear shot to the U.S. Embassy ... it was strangely quiet on Afghoy Road.

As we rolled to a stop inside the walls of the U.S. Embassy a Humvee pulled right alongside. The driver, a young tall tree of a Marine with a helmet and goggles, cut the engine. In the right seat was a Somali American named Ibrahim in uniform with a giant smile ... their translator. In the open bed with the .50 cal. swivel was a freckled-face, redheaded gunner, and next to him was a dark-headed, handsome Italian American with a SAW (M249 Squad Automatic Weapon) slung around his body ... their team leader. I think his name was SSgt. Tascono, but my memory fails me regarding that. Either way, they were seeking us out for about a month now and finally caught up.

"Just wanted to introduce ourselves," Tascono said. "You're the guys over on the other side, right?" he asked.

"We are," I said. They introduced themselves.

"The word's out that you saved a Marine who got his six-by stalled," he said.

"Right place right time ... it wasn't a big deal," I said.

"Not the way he tells it. He pretty much believes he'd be dead if not for you guys ... thank you," Tascono stuck out his hand.

Rich and I shook it. These guys were itching to get their hands soiled and pretty much feared little, as you would expect of Marines. They reminded me of the North African version of The Rat Patrol.

"Look, if you ever need support, just give us a shout," Tascono said. We decided to take them up on their offer.

"Tell you what, why don't you follow us back to our base in a little bit so you will have our location, and then just stay for some chow," I offered.

"It's a deal," said Tascono.

"We gotta roll ... see you guys in a little bit," I said as Rich and I departed.

We were a little ways ahead when out of our thoughtful silence Rich murmured, "He would have been dead."

Neither one of us looked at each other. "Maybe," I replied.

We took some time with the COS and briefed her on what we had seen. She listened with a sense of urgency.

"Baz, I want you to go down to Kismayo and relieve the Ground Branch officer they sent me. He's an idiot, and I'm not happy with anything he's producing."

I knew who she was talking about, the same officer she had threatened to get rid of on two other occasions and who I defended on those two other occasions. If he were to be relieved of his duty, it would go against his career the rest of his life, and I didn't want to see that. It wasn't really his fault. He hadn't had an opportunity to go to The Farm and learn anything about reporting or recruiting agents. I really didn't want to be reassigned down there, and Rich didn't want me leaving Lido Base. We had developed a pretty good team in Mogadishu.

The Mogadishu Team

Something Bigger Than Overthrowing Small Governments

"I really need Baz here. Things are heating up," Rich argued.

"That's why I need him down there ... the base chief and 10th Mountain need support from us to make sure they don't get hit sideways ... end of conversation, you're going," she said.

The Rat Patrol followed us to Lido Base and spent about five hours getting to know us over some food and beer — a brief opportunity for them to lower their defenses and laugh a little. And for us, we had established a relationship with some really good Marines that could provide cover and fire support on the ground if we needed it. We put all the COVCOM (covert communications) in place with them so we could reach out when needed. They left in the middle of the night, something I was not comfortable with ... but like I said, they pretty much feared little as you would expect of Marines.

The next day I found myself on a chopper landing in the Port of Kismayo in southern Somalia and meeting up with the COB (Chief of Base) and the other SAS Officer. Inside a green canvas, marquee military tent sat the COB (Bruce), whose last name will remain anonymous, sending out some intelligence on his laptop. In the background sat the SAS Officer (AC), whose name will also remain anonymous, reading a book. Neither were happy campers. The heat and sand and dirt, not that far from everything they owned, made life in Kismayo a bad reflection of the television show M.A.S.H where those same green canvas military tents harbored moments of comedy and laughter ... but not here. The COB and I knew one another from other assignments with Africa Division (AF), and he was delighted to see me. We hugged. He was a rather stout fellow, actually as stout as I had remembered seeing him in the halls of headquarters on multiple occasions. He was in need of a diet if his heart was going to survive a 30-year career ... a diet he had no intention of starting anytime soon.

"I think you've lost weight out here," I said.

"It's all the typing my fingers are doing," he replied, while dancing his fingers in the air.

I turned to AC. "Got a moment?" I asked.

He stepped out of the tent with me, and I gave him the lowdown on how the COS viewed his work in Kismayo and told him that I would do whatever was needed to keep him in good standing — teach him as fast as I could on reporting and recruiting while I was there with them.

He realized his limitations, and everything about his attitude told me he was ready to go home. So I wasn't sure if my offer was appreciated or not, but it stood if he wanted help. It was evident that for some mysterious reason you could drive a truck through our relationship. He wasn't a happy camper, and I am sure the news I brought made it even worse.

Bruce interrupted, "Let me brief you on a few things."

I found a green 20-liter steel Jerry Can (military water can) to sit on as Bruce ran me through the ropes. Minutes later, Bruce got a call on his radio from 10th Mountain asking if he had someone they could talk with. I volunteered to go.

Even the fighting outside of Kismayo left its fingerprint on dead civilians in shallow graves.

Something Bigger Than Overthrowing Small Governments

Bazzel Baz

I was curious to see what battle plan the U.S. Army had in place to make sure none of our boys ended up the same way.

I headed over to the 10th Mountain Group to meet the commander and a few members, if I'm not mistaken, of the 4th Psyops (Psychological Operations) Group out of Ft. Bragg. That day they had a Somali informant that had been beaten pretty badly by other Somali Clansmen. He had disclosed to us the location of a large cache of weapons in the town where the people were often ready to voice their complaints with bullets. We loaded up in a convoy of Humvees and headed out the front gate and past a little, unoccupied shack on the left ... or so I thought. I glanced over my shoulder suspiciously at an elderly Somali man paying way too much attention to the base where the 10th Mountain Group was located. Something didn't sit right with me.

We drove around Kismayo with the informant hidden in the rear seat of the vehicle, having him point out a number of buildings where weapons were being stored and where the people who had beaten him up lived. The U.S. Military Intel guys made a note of everything so they could later pull off a raid and confiscate the weapons. As we headed back, I had the vehicle pull over just short of the little shack, now on my right. I jumped out and the convoy continued. As I carefully approached, the elderly Somali man was still inside ... sketching a layout of everything the 10th Mountain Group had on the base ... location of vehicles, supplies, headquarters, protective wire, etc. He had enough information to send mortar fire down on them like a hailstorm. I made myself known, and he turned startled, frozen and certainly afraid that I was going to shoot him. I trusted him as much as I did a factory-packed parachute ... so shooting him wasn't out of the question, if he threatened my life. I removed the pencil and paper from his hand, motioned for him to move ahead of me, and escorted him to a few soldiers for safe keeping while I briefed the base Commander and a couple of his Intel officers.

"I think you just prevented the base from being hit," said one Intel officer.

"Well, it's not like we're fighting the Irish here," I replied, broke a short smile and departed. I felt a little uncomfortable hanging around a building the size of a giant bull's eye, and so I made my way out.

Something Bigger Than Overthrowing Small Governments

"There is no second-place winner in a gunfight. Winners kill, losers get killed. Fight to win, Train to live." Not sure where I heard that quote, but I remembered it as I walked away.

I settled in to spend the rest of my tour in the armpit of Kismayo, but within two days I received a message from Lido Base that I was to head back up on the next chopper I could find. Either Rich had managed to convince the COS of my value back at Lido, or something was brewing.

"Good having you here," Bruce said as he handed me a report from Langley. He continued, "The U.N. just authorized UNOSOM II, to expand its enforcement power. The new mandate stresses the importance of disarmament of the Somali people."

"What are these guys smoking?" I replied. Every war fighter in the world knew the locals weren't going to just turn over their weapons especially when they knew UNOSOM II wasn't planning on being there forever. Why would we expect the locals not to be able to protect themselves once everyone was gone?

Bruce smiled, "the U.N.-led mission is taking over from the U.S.-led UNITAF. Gentlemen, we are now in the midst of an expanded U.N. mission that goes beyond providing humanitarian relief ... it's now in the nation-building business."

"They're actually going to attempt to get Somalia back on its feet by restoring law and order, shoring up the infrastructure, and helping to set up processes for establishing a representative government?" I asked.

"With a little help. By the end of March, 28 different nations will have sent contingents here in support of the new militarized operation and President Clinton is officially handing over the command to the U.N. on May 4 ... which in my opinion is a mistake." Bruce shook his head.

I read more of the report. "This is a nice kicker ... Clinton is ordering the number of U.S. troops in Somalia to be reduced and replaced by U.N. troops by June. Only 1,200 U.S. combat soldiers will remain in Somalia, with 3,000 support troops ... most of them being Marines. Urahhhhhh!"

The sound of the UH1 approaching the tarmac got my attention. I handed the report back to Bruce, shook his hand and crossed quickly so as not to miss my ride home ... if you could call Lido Base home.

The whop, whop, whop of the blades danced above my head as I approached the chopper.

"Heading to Mog," I yelled to the crew chief.

"You Baz?" he asked.

"All 190 lbs.," I replied.

"Hop on," he motioned.

The chopper lifted off and Kismayo grew smaller and smaller as we headed north, not high enough off the ground for my taste ... small weapons fire too easily could knock at our door if someone chose. Getting back to Mogadishu excited me in a way, like the excitement you feel returning to spring training on a football field ... you know you're going to get beat up, but you also know you're going to get a few hits in yourself, and when you do ... they'll remember it.

We were all up early the next day, Rich with that boyish smile on his face, "Dude, you owe me for getting you back here."

"Okay, I'll save your life the next time they start throwing rocks, how's that?" I replied while affectionately punching him in the shoulder.

Bud walked around the corner with a solemn look on his face. "During an inspection of a Somali weapons storage site yesterday, 24 Pakistani soldiers were ambushed and massacred. The U.N. Security Council just issued an emergency resolution calling for the apprehension of Aidid."

We glanced at Bud, and then ourselves, silently speaking to one another about the future of our stay in Mogadishu. We hadn't been in direct contact with the enemy bullet-to-bullet, but the chances of that happening felt imminent.

"Got a little humanitarian project, who wants to take a ride with me?" Bud asked.

Rich had reports due to the COS, so as much as he wanted to go, he was on a deadline. I grabbed my weapon and met Bud and Jake at the Trooper. There was a third Army guy there on temporary loan for the week, but I can't remember his name ... he jumped in as well. We headed out to the middle of town, bypassing a number of struggling bars

Something Bigger Than Overthrowing Small Governments

and restaurants, believe it or not. My favorite was "Bar & Restaurant Indian Ocean," which was surrounded by an eight-foot, yellow, concrete wall and a large red arrow with "Welcome" written on it pointing to the entrance. "HUBKU VILLA" and some other rubbed-out words in blue sat atop a wall-painting of an AK-47 and a machete, with a red X in between the two.

Obviously, no weapons were allowed, but I thought it silly — as did everyone else — that anyone in Mogadishu would put their weapons aside for dinner, unless you wanted it to be your last meal. I think we commented on that restaurant every time we passed it, curious to what might be on the menu, promising that we would stop in one day and have lunch.

We came to a stop in front of a gated villa similar to our base but far more dilapidated. A frail, Somali elder opened the small door set within the giant, solid tin gate that had been riddled with bullet holes. Inside we found nine or ten small children holding class in this makeshift school. There were two women who were the teachers and caretakers of these young students, both boys and girls, that ranged from ages two to five. They had no pen, pencils, paper or books to study with ... just two long pieces of wood planking. I could see they had used white chalk to do their math and spell out words.

They sat there in the dirt, as comfortable as you can expect, grateful to just be in some sort of educational environment and not having to be out there fighting for their lives. I could see from the look in the two teachers' eyes that they intended to do whatever it took to shield these children from war.

Bud and Jake pulled out some boxes from the back of the Trooper, each filled to the brim with Crayola Crayons, spiral notebooks and pencils with sharpeners. The faces of the two women lit up like a Christmas tree. The smile on the Elder was that of a man whose genuine friendship was based on the love that we were showing, and not the gifts we were bringing. It was so refreshing to feel for the first time in a long time that we were not surrounded by people who hated us. I felt sorry for everything they had experienced and everything the children would experience if they lived long enough. It wasn't that I wanted to adopt them or take them back to America for a better life ... what I wanted was for their life in their country to be better. I knew the only way that would ever happen was if those who were good and kind

Something Bigger Than Overthrowing Small Governments

and courageous fought back against those who would do them harm. And in this case, it was Aidid.

Running away never solved anything in a country run by bullies ... it just gave the bullies a better foothold to abuse more people. Those who want their freedom have to stand and fight, even at the cost of their lives. It was the story of my own country during the American Revolution, and I knew it all too well growing up and around South Carolina and Georgia, where monument after monument told the story of great American Patriots and their fight for freedom. It was the same for any place in the world and anyone in the world who valued their homeland ... you either fight for it, or you die trying. Either way you don't run. And so, it was with many of the Somali people who choose not to run but hoped that the U.S. and the world would lend a hand in stopping the atrocities. Sadly, I knew from experience that it would be a long time before that ever happened.

Our stay wasn't long at the school because we needed to drop some equipment off at the U.S. Embassy and get back to Lido Base before nightfall. Remember that ghostly stretch of road, desolate at best, a horrible choke point where Bud would put the accelerator to the floor and the speed odometer would climb to that 60-mph point? We called it "ambush alley" and we never wanted to get stuck there, especially from a flat tire. Yep, you guessed it ... on the way to the Embassy we got a flat tire.

We pulled aside and set up a perimeter while Jake changed the tire. Slowly, children began creeping in like ants coming out of woodwork ... simply materializing from the surrounding debris. You never saw where they came from until they were uncomfortably close ... and I am convinced that U.S. forces in the First Battle of Mogadishu and the *Blackhawk Down* incident know just what I'm talking about. It was a relatively uneventful experience and we did get the tire changed rather quickly, but what I took away from that was the fact that the city was like a poorly-made sieve, and that anything at any time that was bad could get through. If the U.N. actually thought it was going to strain out the evil, they were sadly mistaken. My convictions were so strong at this moment that the little voice in my head was a big voice shouting prophecy, and it needed to be shared with Col. Zinni and the Marine Corps. I could see it coming like the smell of rain on the

Serengeti. For those who don't know, the Serengeti is a vast ecosystem in east-central Africa. It spans 12,000 square miles, giving rise to its name, which is derived from the Masai language and means "endless plains" ... and what I felt was about to happen in Mogadishu would be exactly that ... endless.

We rolled up to the U.S. Embassy, and I went straight to Col. Zinni's office after getting permission from the COS. I had no idea General Robert Johnston would be there. He was commander of the First Marine Expeditionary Force at Camp Pendleton, California, a no-nonsense, serious fellow who never lost his cool, according to his colleagues, and I found him to be so. He was more than generous with his time and very frank about the issues he was facing with Washington and the State Department in particular. They asked me about Intel ... they knew what was coming out of Lido Base was ground truth (information provided by direct observation, i.e. empirical evidence). Our agents were good producers of solid Intel, and we were very seldom wrong. I listened to every word he and Col. Zinni had to say about repositioning the Marines in Mogadishu to better carry out the mission.

Something Bigger Than Overthrowing Small Governments

And then — I will never forget this as long as I live — General Johnston stopped in mid-conversation with Col. Zinni and asked, "Baz, what would you do?"

Now I don't know if he was just being courteous or seriously wanted the advice of a paramilitary case officer who had been sending reports that were getting disseminated to the White House. Whatever the case, I graciously took the opportunity to answer.

"Sir, we got our asses handed to us in Beirut because we let the State Department tell us how to fight a war. Right now, if I'm hearing you correctly, State is attempting to do that once again ... and once again we're setting ourselves up for failure. If I were you, Sir, I'd pull my Marines out of here as soon as possible and go home. We can't fight with one hand tied behind our back ... it's bad war fighting ... and we're in a war."

General Johnston looked me square in the eye, nodded his head a few times and said, "thank you." He turned to Col. Zinni, who had a smile on his face, Col. Zinni looked over at me, and then General Johnston sat down.

"Sir, if that will be all, I need to head back to base," I said.

Col. Zinni took a few steps my way and said, "Thank you Captain Baz."

I turned to leave the room when I realized what Col. Zinni had said, "Thank you Captain Baz." Evidently Col. Zinni had not forgotten our initial conversation when I first met him, and it was a nice acknowledgment that ... once a Marine always a Marine. I met Jake and Bud back at the vehicle and headed back to Lido Base. Little did I know that within days, my entire life would change forever.

Chapter 7
IF WE DO NOT ... WHO WILL?

Two days later Aidid was successfully able to stir up enough anti-UNITAF sentiment with his clansmen in Mogadishu to bring the relief effort to a standstill. In order to show that any efforts by the U.N. to reimpose law and order would be largely dependent on him, Aidid handed out the weapons and ordered his war fighters to attack the U.S. Embassy. Aidid needed an excuse, and so he accused the U.S. of backing a rival warlord known as Morgan.

First came the armed demonstrators fighting with bare hands, stones and knives, chanting "Go Home Americans" and "Down with America." This was more of a distraction as other Somalis armed with AK-47s and RPGs brought up the rear and began taking up firing positions. When that happened, the United States Marine Corp said, "enough is enough."

The U.S. Embassy gave us the SitRep (Situation Report), everything was on lockdown, people were arming themselves and preparing for the worst. Bud, Jake, Rich, Dan and I grabbed everything we had and headed towards the U.S. Embassy in support. I jumped in the rear cargo space facing backwards. Running gun battles were breaking out throughout the city wherever U.S. forces were positioned. As we rolled up on the Green Line, the Marines were ready to protect themselves.

"Sorry, Sir, no one can go through," said the Sergeant.
"Open the barricade or we'll run through it," I yelled.
Bud followed with a much gentler tone, "I think he means it."
"Sir there is gunfire everywhere," said the Sergeant.
"We know," I replied.

He lifted the wired barricade. We sped through knowing that we probably would not be able to even enter the Embassy, but what we could do is take up positions behind the enemy and cause some confusion — even ambush a few with as much ammo as we had with us ... enough to make them think twice about scaling the Embassy walls.

Something Bigger Than Overthrowing Small Governments

We had a pretty good idea where we wanted to set up but weren't sure it would work until we got close enough to the perimeter of the Embassy to figure it out. You do what you have to do until you can do what you want to do. And right now, we had to get within bird's-eye view of the action.

Up ahead we could see armed Somalis flooding the streets, so we made a detour. Then again, more Somali gunmen were heading our way, so another detour and then again. They were everywhere, and we weren't going to get close enough to ask them if they were supporting Aidid or not. I had the feeling that maybe someone in the city like Ali Mahdi's people might try and help defend the Embassy, but later I found out that wasn't the case. They basically stayed out of the entire scenario and let it run its course. Maybe they were smart, or maybe just tired of fighting ... who knows.

Everywhere we turned we found ourselves almost in a pickle, but we would not let despair hold us for ransom, and so we kept trying to find a route. The air in Mogadishu smelled of gunpowder, and smoke drifted along streets near some of the major traffic circles we tried to penetrate. We had lost all communications with the Embassy. Our only option would be to fight our way through if we ran into resistance, and that really wasn't an option. We were outgunned, outnumbered and would have expended the ammo we had just getting there. Once there, we would be defenseless and probably end up dead outside the Embassy in some little adobe building, only to be drug through the streets of Mogadishu by Aidid's clansmen. We knew the Marine Corps had the ability to call in fire support from offshore if it got too bad, and so we made a decision to carefully find our way back to Lido Base and pray we didn't end up in a firefight in the process. Passing by the Italian compound we noticed they were all buttoned up. The word had spread about the fighting. Then something caught my eye.

"Hey, wait ... go back to the Italian compound on the right," I yelled.

"What's up?" Bud asked.

"I saw something, some kids hiding ... that's odd," I said.

Bud slowed down and did a U-turn. We slowly entered the outside perimeter of the Italian compound and, sure enough, there were two girls hiding under some debris ... not just average Somali looking girls, but half-breeds (European and Somali) wearing blue jeans and green T-shirts. One looked to be about sixteen and the other maybe twelve years of age. The older one wore aviator sunglasses and the younger, an attitude that probably kept her alive all this time. Strangely, there were no adults or other people anywhere in the area. Both were good-looking kids that seemed so out of place.

We stopped the Trooper and climbed out. The girls were gun-shy and remained partially hidden behind the debris, not sure what to make of us. "I don't know where their family is, but sitting outside this compound makes them rape bate," I said.

Rich pulled me aside. "There isn't anything we can do about this right now ... it's collateral damage."

"I know," I replied. I looked at Bud and then Jake. "Maybe we can give them some food."

Bud grabbed some MREs from the back and cautiously approached the girls ... offering his kindness in Italian. We didn't know what language they spoke, so it was worth a try.

Something Bigger Than Overthrowing Small Governments

I turned to Rich, "Don't you find this odd that these girls are here all by themselves and wearing what they're wearing ... they don't even look Somali?"

"No, they don't, but it's not our mission to rescue kids, we're here to gather intelligence," Rich said.

And he was right. It wasn't our mission, and the CIA would probably have a hissy fit if they thought we were even entertaining the idea of rescuing kids. And besides, where would we take them ... back to our base? No way! That could compromise our entire safe house standing and operations.

"Okay, we gotta go," Rich said. And so, we loaded back up and left the girls to their own fate. I had little hope they would survive this war, much less the weeks to come.

By the end of the day the Marine Corps had shot and killed a number of protestors who were lobbing grenades or attempting to breech the Embassy. Marine Corps snipers racked up more kills than were on the books prior to arriving in Mogadishu. I think it made Aidid think twice about his choreographed political theater aimed at flexing his muscles. We settled back into the security of Lido base, happy that the U.S. Embassy did not get overrun ... this time.

It was relatively quiet at Lido as Rich and I tapped the keyboards of our laptops recalling the day's events — me handing Rich some of my stuff for him to incorporate in the Intel report. Bud was putting the final touches on his new communications invention that allowed us to take a picture of ourselves and send it over the net to our families back home. As far as we were concerned, we were on the cutting edge of our own military technology and it was pretty cool ... army green gadgets, cables and radio stuff that made us seem pretty official. Cell phone service in those days wasn't what it is today, but I think Bud was able to rig something up that allowed us to get a call out at least once during my time there ... maybe more, without us having to drive all the way over to the U.S. Embassy.

For the next two nights, I wrestled with the thought of those two little girls we had left outside the Italian compound. I hadn't allowed any of the devastation to affect me emotionally throughout my entire time in Somalia. War was war, and I had seen enough of it to let my mind bypass the ugliest parts. I needed a logical approach in order to accomplish the mission, and there was little to no room for error, especially here and now. And yet it still bothered me. Although no one was saying it, I could see it bothered the others as well.

"Anyone else still concerned about those little girls besides me?" I asked. The room grew silent. Bud stopped working on his invention. Rich stopped typing. Jake stopped cleaning his weapon. All eyes were on me.

"I'm just sayin'," with raised eyebrows.

Bud piped up in a kind tone ... "Even if we could rescue those girls, the CIA would string you up in a heartbeat, especially if something happened along the way."

Jake interjected, "Yeah, like getting shot ... them and us."

Rich went back to typing, my word resonating with him throughout the process. I knew Rich pretty well by now, and I could tell if he thought it were possible, he'd give it a go ... but he didn't think it was possible and right now the one thing he needed to focus on was reporting and an agent meeting in fifteen minutes just down the road.

"Besides ... we don't have anywhere to take them." Bud offered.

Rich left for his meeting, and I excused myself and headed up to the roof. It was a still clear night and a billion stars blanketed the sky like the sands of the sea. It was spectacular, and not even the gunfire across town was enough to distract me from it. I felt the presence of God standing there with me in all His holiness in a way I had not before. I thought perhaps it was the chill of the night air, but there was no chill ... there was no breeze. And so, I figured that if God was there then I might as well have a conversation.

I laid on my back looking up at all He had created in the universe and said, "Father what do you want me to do? These little girls are going to die, and I can prevent that but not without your help. These are your children, and they're precious in your sight. I've lived more than most men in three lifetimes, and you have showed me great favor. I'm not afraid to die if it means saving their lives. Lord, they're just kids."

Something Bigger Than Overthrowing Small Governments

I sat up and stayed there hearing absolutely nothing from God, not in my heart or my head. So I thought I'd keep on talking ... maybe He was in a mood to just listen.

"Father, everything about this place smells of death and destruction ... people are angry, hungry and dying. These girls are going to die. Is that what you want? Why don't you do something?"

And then as clear as day, as if someone else were standing on the roof with me, a voice, "I did ... I created you."

It startled me, and goose bumps covered my body. I looked around thinking that Bud or Rich had overhead my conversation and were responding, but it wasn't the case. I even walked back to the doorway to make sure they weren't hiding somewhere. I had heard an audible voice outside of my head. No one was there but me ... and God. It was that same voice I had heard when I was young and would climb high in the top of the trees in our back yard to talk to God ... it was familiar but daunting and it took a moment for me to gain my composure.

"Right. Well then where will I take them?"

There was nothing from God, not in my heart or my head again. I stood there for a good ten minutes waiting ... and still nothing. I looked around at a city ruled by darkness with tapestries of light here and there, took a deep breath and headed back downstairs. Obviously, God had finished.

I thought to myself ... "Most people have conversations with themselves when things don't go exactly as expected. They waste energy trying to understand why, trying to figure out what went right or what went wrong. Stop having conversations with yourself ... you're flawed as a human, and you cannot control all the uncontrollable circumstances, nor do you know what the master plan for your life is and how to navigate the path that ultimately leads to the success of that master plan. As my mother had said, "Have your conversation with God and in that conversation, lean not to your own understanding but trust Him in all His ways with what He is doing in your life. It isn't important to waste energy on understanding, but it is important to put energy into accepting. Once you accept that you do not need to understand, then you are ready to understand accepting. If you accept God for who He is and the fact that He loves you and has your best interest at hand ... you will no longer waste energy on something you have absolutely no control over."

As I entered the ops room Rich was just returning. I grabbed a seat in front of my laptop and started in on the rest of my reports. Bud was now cleaning his weapon and Jake was reading a field manual.

Rich provided us with a brief. "So I just finished meeting with 'Tidal Wave.' According to him Aidid is mounting an offensive. But interestingly Ali Mahdi Muhammad and Osman Ali Atto have been talking in secret. Atto is a former supporter and financier of Aidid, and of the same sub clan. According to Tidal Wave, Atto is the master mind behind a plot to defeat Aidid."

"Let's hope that plot unfolds sooner rather than later," I said. Rich laughed. Bud went back to cleaning his weapon and Jake back to the manual.

Rich started to walk out and then turned. "Oh, and here's one more thing. Can you believe this, Tidal Wave said there is this American woman from New York City that just opened an orphanage here in Mogadishu ... right in the middle of the battlefield. Is she crazy or what?"

Like a bolt of lightning striking time to a standstill, everything was silent. No one moved. Rich slowly turned around and looked at me. I looked at him. Bud and Jake were looking at us. I shrugged my shoulders.

"That's it, we'll take 'em there." Everyone was still looking at me. "I mean, it's an orphanage, right?"

"Yeah, it's an orphanage, right?" Bud mimicked.

"Yeah," Jake said as he closed the field manual.

A small smile came across Rich's face, "I don't know."

"We'll be in and out of there before you know it. Besides, we can take food to the orphanage, right Bud?" I asked.

"We should. It's our humanitarian duty ... Restore Hope," Bud replied.

"I'm going," I said.

"They might not even be there," Rich said.

"We can look," I replied.

"Yeah, we can look," Bud mimicked again with a bigger smile.

Something Bigger Than Overthrowing Small Governments

Rich lowered his head, shook it a few times and said, "Okay ... 0700 departure tomorrow before the city wakes up."

"Let's do this," I said. We contacted SSgt. Tascono and his Rat Patrol asking for their assistance the next day ... he was delighted.

The upper edge of the sun slowly appeared over the eastern horizon the next morning with its legs still wet from the Indian Ocean. It felt like Mogadishu was as far from civilization as you could get without leaving the planet. An early morning haze of gray smog from the wood-burning fires the night before lingered over the city like a dragon of doom seeking to devour anyone who came out on the streets too early.

But the dragon was no match for SSgt. Tascono and his Rat Patrol, who rolled up to the base as requested. It was a nice feeling to have some extra firepower trailing our Trooper anytime we could get it.

Each of us were armed and ready for what may come at us this day and climbed inside the Trooper on our mission to rescue two children. I had taped two banana clips together using white medical tape, the only tape we had. I preferred green 100 mile an hour (duct tape) tape but that somehow made its way to the locals just like our uniforms. It was a righteous mission and for all of us, a contribution to the humanitarian effort by the U.N. that had seemed to fail all around us. We were determined to leave Somalia with at least one good deed ... a story to surround us ... *something bigger than overthrowing a small government*.

My ear holes offered a nice resting spot for the headset of my Walkman. I pushed the button that filtered a world of music from the *Heart Shaped World* album by Chris Isaak. If it weren't Isaak it would have been The Grateful Dead, Enya, or Phil Collins and his "Smugglers Cove" adding ambience to a world we were trying to save. It was the one time in all of this mess that I was able to escape for just a moment, like people escape in the big theater with surround sound. More often than not I left the Walkman in the hooch and was careful only to silence the outside when I knew others were on guard. In a short time, I had learned to see with more than my eyes and hear with more than my ears, so I wasn't concerned about being distracted by the music at all.

The streets weren't as empty as I expected that early in the morning, especially after we crossed the Green Line. The tension in the air was as thick as the gray smog from the midnight fires, and it smelled like death ... the odor of rotten meat mixed with sweet urine that never leaves your nostrils ... no matter how many times you wash your face. We passed a small crowd of locals fixed on a man standing above them on a pile of rubble, machine-gunning fresh manifestos.

We drove our usual 60 miles per hour through "ambush ally" and found our way just outside the Italian compound. Slowing down, we drove to the place where we had spotted the girls days before and set up a security perimeter. We stuck our head in the debris where they were held up days before, but they were not there. Rich, Bud, Jake and I moved carefully around the area for about ten minutes, but sadly the girls were still nowhere to be found.

What we suspected could happen seemed to have happened. All of us felt bad and it churned in our stomachs uncontrollably. The silent words between us told the story ... they have been raped, or stolen and abused, or killed and laying in some gutter or trash pile in the city. If only we had picked them up when we first saw them. Why did we hesitate? All the good intentions in the world mean little if you don't act on them in a timely manner. And right now, our timing sucked.

We mounted up and prepared to leave. Bud hesitated to turn the key ... we just sat there for a moment hoping for something that would not happen.

"Okay God, I did what you told me to do," I whispered under my breath.

Bud started up the Trooper and made a U-turn in front of a wall of sandbags protecting the Italian compound. The Rat Patrol followed closely. We all sat there, eyes ahead and silent driving away. I didn't want to look back at a failed mission, but I did just one more time.

"Stop!" I yelled.

Bud stopped so fast that we almost got rear-ended by the Humvee. There in the distance standing in the middle of nowhere were the two girls. Where they had come from, I have no idea, but they were there, holding each other's hand, looking at us drive away. We climbed out of the Trooper and started carefully walking towards them. There was an unspoken kindness between them and us, and I think they understood we were there to save them. Our translator Ibrahim tossed out some Arabic, and sure enough they spoke back. He explained to them that we were there to help get them to an orphanage where they could be safe and have food. They seemed a little apprehensive at first and turned away to talk between themselves for just a moment in private. When they turned back around, they agreed to go with us.

We loaded them in the Trooper with us and headed out to the orphanage. Fortunately for us, Bud had already done some advance work and met with the staff from the orphanage, so we were feeling pretty confident about the meet-and-greet but not so sure they would accept the girls. Nothing had changed in the city except that by now it was filling up with more angry people, you could see it on their faces when they looked at us drive by. We came to a stop in front of a partially blown-out building in a neighborhood that still had some acacias trees. A few Somali women dressed in traditional garb greeted us when they saw the girls. Ibrahim told them why we were there, and they escorted us inside to meet the director of the orphanage, the American woman from New York City. She didn't know quite how to react to a bunch of mercenary-looking fellows and the hovering Marines who were making sure the streets were clear for our exit.

"Hi, can we talk to you?" I asked.

She smiled, "Americans?"

"One hundred percent," I said. She smiled and shook my hand. The conversation after that took place with Rich, Bud, Jake and I surrounded by curious little children. Some would touch you on the arm and step away laughing ... others just clung to your leg like a life preserver. I don't remember the name of the director, but I do remember the kindness in her voice. Her black skin blended in so well with the rest of the Somali population that I would have never identified her as an outsider.

She was amazingly brave to be there on this mission of protecting children, and the orphanage was full of them, well kept, well fed and safe. But these kids weren't blank slates ... they had been affected by this world. It was by no means above the standard of living, but it was a place of refuge where people cared. We told her the story of the girls and asked if she would take them in. She hesitated, and I could see that it pained her to do so.

I couldn't blame her for being reluctant, her hands were full, and the orphanage was already at capacity. She mentioned in the conversation that she had no idea how she could feed two more mouths. We were coming up short ... our efforts flashing in front of us like a soccer player passing every defender on the field except you and the goalkeeper, who somehow manages to stop the shot from going in the goal. It was hard to disagree with her situation. We were only adding insult to injury. Bud had walked away looking at all the kids and contemplating something. I got up and walked over to him.

"Is there any way we can score some food for this orphanage?" I asked.

"I was just thinking the same thing," he replied.

And so, we offered to bring food and clothing supplies the next week as part of the deal if she would agree to take the girls. I had no idea where Bud intended to get the food and clothing, but if anyone could, he could. We said goodbye to the girls and left them in the care of the orphanage ... mission accomplished.

On the way back to the base there was new blood in the conversation, exploring all the possibilities of establishing an unofficial supply line to the orphanage. SSgt. Toscano volunteered to patrol the orphanage at least once a day and vowed to protect it if things went upside down. The Rat Patrol had found another purpose for being there ... a real humanitarian purpose where someone actually cared. Unlike the adult population, who would take the food you provided and stab you in the back the next day, these children loved you each day you showed up at the orphanage, even if you had no food. We kept our promise, and within the week we returned with food and clothing ... pretty much buttoning up our "rescue operation" ... or so we thought.

"You guys have a minute?" the director asked.

"Sure," I replied.

"The girls you brought in are the daughters of a Foreign engineer who was contracted here in Mogadishu. When the war broke out, he basically abandoned them ... and their mother ... and their little brother. I suspect he had a family back in his home country." It was sort of jaw-dropping information. I looked over to see, standing in the background, the two girls eyeing us with unspoken requests.

"Can you go get their mother and little brother?" She asked.

"Uhhhh, what?" I replied.

Something Bigger Than Overthrowing Small Governments

"Can you find their mother and brother and bring them here?" She repeated.

This time it was just Jake, Bud and me. It was risky enough just getting to the orphanage. Traipsing around town with a photo of the girls wasn't really butter on our toast, and we had to give it some serious thought.

"I think we've done enough guys ... we've got other priorities," I said to Jake and Bud. Everyone agreed until we turned, and the two girls were standing there looking up at us again with their unspoken requests. So traipsing we went for two or three days in between all of our other assignments, with a photo of the girls, hitting one refugee settlement after another until finally we found their mother and little brother.

When we showed her the picture of her daughters, she started to cry and smile at the same time. Evidently, they had been separated during war and I wasn't sure she even thought they were alive. We didn't have a translator with us this time, so it was hit-and-miss with trying to convey or intentions. But eventually she climbed in the Trooper with her son and we headed back to the orphanage. When we arrived, the director escorted her into the facility and the reunion between her and her daughters was more than enough reward for our efforts. The good deed had been done, enough to satisfy me for a lifetime ... and that is where I left it, in Somalia ... or so I thought.

Rescue of two girls in 1993 during the Civil War in Somalia

Something Bigger Than Overthrowing Small Governments

Chapter 8
HEADING HOME

The weeks ahead would bring some extraordinary events that cannot be discussed until declassified. But in that time, I learned that taking everything but a man's life is the ultimate revenge. The circumstances surrounding these events would play themselves out over the next two years in my life, and I would be better for it.

On the home front in Washington D.C., in a visit to the brooding Vietnam Veterans Memorial, amid angry taunts and applause, President Clinton was calling for Americans to set aside the unhealed wounds of a war he bitterly opposed. "Let us continue to disagree, if we must," Clinton told a crowd of about 4,000 gathered at the black granite monument for a Memorial Day observance. "But let us not let it divide us as a people any longer."

Clinton, who later knelt at the wall to trace the name of a fallen classmate, pledged that he would accelerate the declassification of all records relating to soldiers missing in the war. The records, except for the "tiny fraction" that would compromise national security or invade some families' privacy, will be made available by Veteran's Day, Nov. 11, he said. Clinton's tangled draft history almost wrecked his presidential campaign and plans for this visit had provoked outrage among some veterans. His words mingled with chants of, "Where was Bill?" and taunts of, "Coward!" [8]

As soon as we got the news in Somalia, we speculated that Clinton would need a last hoorah if he was to regain the support of veterans and the military who were not all that keen on a draft-dodging Commander and Chief. But what would it be? With the continued problems Aidid was causing in Mogadishu and the escalation of civil war again, we suspected and talked among ourselves that Somalia somehow might be it. By June 1993, only 1,200 U.S. troops remained in Somalia. With little to no U.S. deterrent remaining, the warlords started fighting again.

On 12 July 1993, a U.S.-led operation was launched on what was believed to be a safe house where Aidid was hiding in Mogadishu. During the 17-minute combat operation, U.S. Cobra attack helicopters fired 16 TOW missiles and thousands of 20-millimeter cannon rounds into the compound, killing 60 people. However, the number of Somali fatalities was disputed. Abdi Qeybdiid, Aidid's interior minister, claimed 73 dead, including women and children who had been in the safe house. The reports Jonathan Howe got after the attack placed the number of dead at 20, all men. The International Committee of the Red Cross set the number of dead at 54. Aidid was not present.

The operation would lead to the deaths of four journalists — Dan Eldon, Hos Maina, Hansi Kraus and Anthony Macharia — who were killed by angry Mogadishu mobs when they arrived to cover the incident, which pre-staged the Battle of Mogadishu. Some believe that this American attack was a turning point in unifying Somalis against U.S. efforts in Somalia, including former moderates and those opposed to the Habar Gidir. On 8 August 1993, Aidid's militia detonated a remote-controlled bomb against a U.S. military vehicle, killing four soldiers. Two weeks later another bomb injured seven more. [12]

As for myself, my tour of duty was up. Langley had a maritime assignment for me off the coast of Albania in support of drone operations over Bosnia. I wasn't stoked to leave, knowing that Rich and Bud, Dan and Jake would be remaining. We had built a pretty good team, and I couldn't imagine them in the thick of it without me being there. Rich and I had some heart-to-heart discussions concerning the mission in Mogadishu and how even he was ready to go home. We both felt like things were going to fall apart in the very near future for this country, even more than they had already. You can't put new wine in old skins and not expect them to burst. The disagreements between

Something Bigger Than Overthrowing Small Governments

fighting factions were age-old, and nothing we gave them was going to resolve that.

My flight out of Mogadishu would be leaving that evening. The flag was finished on the roof; we had sandbagged the lower half of the villa and still had allegiance with our Somali guards. I took a moment to plug in my Walkman and lay back in a makeshift hammock on the second-floor side patio to collect my thoughts. I wondered what would happen to all of those children in the orphanage, what would happen to all the children in Mogadishu. By August of 1993 I will have been gone.

> The situation in Mogadishu worsened even as the raids continued. In one of the most violent and costly incidents, on 8 September U.S. and Pakistani soldiers were clearing roadblocks near a site known as the Cigarette Factory when they were attacked by Somali militia using 106-mm. recoilless rifles, RPGs, and small arms. It took extensive fires from ground and aviation units to suppress the enemy fire. Later that same day, near an abandoned allied checkpoint, the same clearing element was again attacked by militiamen, this time joined by a mob of

approximately 1,000 Somali civilians. Six UNOSOM II soldiers were injured. On 16 and 21 September two roadblock-clearing teams were attacked on 21 October Road. The team attacked on 21 September was a Pakistani element, and it lost an armored personnel carrier and suffered nine casualties, including two killed. On 25 September, a U.S. Black Hawk helicopter was shot down and three soldiers killed: one from the 25th Aviation Regiment, Fort Drum, and two from the 101st Aviation Regiment, Fort Campbell, Kentucky. U.S. and Pakistani forces secured the area and evacuated the casualties under fire. Particularly unsettling was the fact that the Somalis shot down the helicopter using simple RPGs, normally used to attack armored vehicles. This fact did not bode well for the helicopter raids of TF Ranger. [11]

President Clinton will have launched a new mission: sending in a force of Rangers and Special Forces units to capture the brutal warlord Mohammad Farrah Aidid and restore order. The unit deployed would be under the command of Major General William F. Garrison, Commander of Joint Special Operations Command (JSOC) at the time. (It would be years later in 2012 when Bill Garrison and I would be introduced by my dear friend Tom Flores, Director of Security Fluor Corps. concerning other operational support in Africa, now as a contractor.) I always felt that Garrison gotten the bad end of the stick with the whole *Black Hawk Down* incident. He took full responsibility for the outcome, while those who were actually responsible, like the President, showed their true colors. This isn't just my opinion; it is the opinion of a vast majority of war fighters who proudly served in the conflict.

It was the expert opinion of Army Veteran and Director of Security for Fluor Corporation, Tom Flores. He was Zorro in every sense of the word and outside my own father, one of the greatest men I ever knew. Not enough good can ever be said about him. Tom was like a brother to me and a friend to Bill Garrison, who knew the inner workings of hidden political agendas at the highest levels of our government, corporate affairs and the reasons behind why many things

Something Bigger Than Overthrowing Small Governments

of this nature went wrong while the media thought they had it right. Americans only saw what was in print, while Tom generally had ground truth or first-hand intelligence from those in the mix. He assured me that Bill Garrison would carry the memory of the men he lost in his soul forever, not out of a guilty conscience, but because he had only one life to give and could he have given it for every one of them, he would have done so a hundred times over.

> That force asked for heavy armor — in the form of Abrams tanks and Bradley armored vehicles — as well as the AC-130 gunship, but the Clinton Administration denied those requests. On October 3 on a mission to pick up Aidid, two Black Hawks were unexpectedly shot down; in the ensuing urban gun battle, 18 American soldiers were killed and another 73 injured.
>
> Many military experts believe that if the U.S. forces had had armor, fewer would have died. Secretary of Defense Les Aspin resigned two months after Somalia, having acknowledged that his decision on the armor had been an error. A 1994 Senate Armed Services Committee investigation reached the same conclusion. But perhaps the most poignant statement came from retired Lieutenant Colonel Larry Joyce, father of Sergeant Casey Joyce, a Ranger killed in Mogadishu: "Had there been armor ... I contend that my son would probably be alive today." [13]

If I recall correctly, I would have the chance to speak with Bill Garrison over the phone while he was in Kenya in 2014 regarding my need for an airplane to support a child rescue and I would hear everything Tom had told me in Bill's voice. I would also bury Tom at Arlington Memorial Cemetery on 2 April 2015, one of the greatest losses of my life.

Mr. Clinton's responsibility in Somalia didn't stop there. Despite the mistakes that October day, Aidid had been struck a blow. The U.S. military, with 18 dead, wanted nothing more than to finish what it had started. Mr. Clinton instead aborted the mission. The U.S. released the criminals it had captured that same day at such great cost, and the U.N., lacking U.S. support, was powerless to keep order. To this day Somalia remains a lawless, impoverished nation. Worse, the terrorists of al Qaeda interpreted the U.S. retreat from Somalia as a sign of American weakness that may have convinced them we could be induced to retreat from the Middle East if they took their attacks to the U.S. homeland. [14]

The United States entered Somalia in December 1992 to stop the imminent starvation of hundreds of thousands of people. Although it succeeded in this mission, the chaotic political situation of that unhappy land bogged down U.S. and allied forces in what became, in effect, a poorly organized United Nations nation-building operation. In a country where the United States, perhaps naively, expected some measure of gratitude for its help, its forces received increasing hostility as they became more deeply embroiled into trying to establish a stable government.

Something Bigger Than Overthrowing Small Governments

The military and diplomatic effort to bring together all the clans and political entities was doomed to failure as each sub-element continued to attempt to out-jockey the others for supreme power.

The Somali people were the main victims of their own leaders, but forty-two Americans died and dozens more were wounded before the United States and the United Nations capitulated to events and withdrew. American military power had established the conditions for peace in the midst of a famine and civil war, but, unlike later in Bosnia, the factions were not exhausted from the fighting and were not yet willing to stop killing each other and anyone caught in the middle. There was no peace to keep. The American soldier had, as always, done his best under difficult circumstances to perform a complex and often confusing mission. But the best soldiers in the world can only lay the foundation for peace; they cannot create peace itself. [11]

CHAPTER 9
THE WAR ON CHILDREN

The political climate in America was changing, and we in the CIA were paying very close attention. Intelligence was surfacing on questionable activities by Bill Clinton's firm, "Arkansas Development Finance Authority" (ADFA), and their laundered drug-money operations while he was governor of Arkansas. Cocaine at a value of $10,000,000 (ten million dollars!) a week was flown in and out of Mena Airport in Arkansas. The money was laundered via ADFA to a bank in Florida, to a bank in Georgia, to Citicorp in New York, and from there it was transferred out of the country. At the time as Governor, Bill Clinton created new laws that helped Tyson Foods to be the biggest company in Arkansas. The owner, Don Tyson, received a loan from the Clinton-owned ADFA, but never had to pay back. There was enough damaging evidence against Tyson to start an investigation regarding illegal drug-trade.

The first loan ADFA approved was to Park-O-Meter. When the company was investigated, it was found that the Directive Secretary and cashier was Webb Hubbell ... guess who wrote the law proposition ... which made ADFA possible, Webb Hubbell. Guess who drove the law proposition which looked into and admitted (Park-O-Meter's) request. "Rose Law Firm" (owned by Hillary Clinton). Who signed the admittance? Webb Hubbell and Hillary Clinton. There were two things I trusted more than Hillary Clinton ... Mexican tap water and a kiss from Judas.

Journalists started investigating the loans to Park-O-Meter and discovered that the company did not make parking meters, but removable airplane nosecones, delivered to the air-field in Mena. The equipment was used to smuggle narcotics into the country, and with this, Clinton and his companions participated heavily to the pushing of street-drugs in the USA. The intelligence was pretty damaging, but no one was being held accountable. The highest office in the land was being occupied by Pinocchio and was not being held to the highest standards of justice. This brought into question Congress' loyalty to "we the people" who had elected them. I was seeing for the first time in my life the American version of Lernaean Hydra ... for each head cut off, it grew two more.

Now in the office of the presidency, Mr. Clinton promised to cut intelligence spending by seven billion dollars over four years. The administration and Democrats, who controlled the committees with power over the intelligence budgets, defied strong warnings from CIA Director R. James Woolsey, who contended that cuts could have "devastating consequences" on the ability of United States intelligence agencies to monitor developments around the world and to assess their significance. "I personally think it's part of the we'll close the Washington Monument' syndrome," said a prominent Congressional official, who said he and others had concluded that Mr. Woolsey's arguments "just don't fly." Well the Democrats who defied Woolsey's warnings were wrong ... "it did fly." [15]

In fact, all four airliners on September 11, 2001 flew ... and were hijacked, resulting in the death of approximately 3,000 innocent Americans in a terrorist attack ... the "devastating consequences" he had mentioned. American Airlines Flight 11 hit the north tower of the WTC first. United Airlines Flight 175 hit the south tower twenty minutes after the first hit. American Airlines Flight 77 hit the Pentagon that morning, and United Airlines Flight 93 did not make it to its intended target. The crew and passengers overpowered the hijackers and instead, the plane crashed in Shanksville, PA.

Within the ranks of the Directorate of Operations most of us could have predicted this outcome. We were constantly being hamstringed by this administration ... it smelt like a tuna fish sandwich left on a city bus. With each passing week, our disillusionment was like standing on the sidelines in a football game constantly saying to the coach "put me in" and him ignoring you. He knew you could win the game for the team but refused to do it because he was best friends with some other kid's father, who was sitting in the stands. Ultimately, the team suffered, and the game was lost. There was talk of many paramilitary case officers resigning and moving on to civilian organizations who offered a better paycheck unfortunately for less exciting positions.

Years later in 2002 I would receive an email from my dear friend Bill Wilson, former Ambassador to the Vatican under President Ronald Reagan. The email was very telling and confirmed my feelings about the attacks on President Reagan but also the lack of leadership in Washington that was occurring in 1993 and 1994. I wasn't the only one seeing it, nor was I the only federal employee seriously doubting the integrity of those we had elected.

Unknown to most of the world, it was the brilliant and highly sensitive strategy of President Reagan in appointing Ambassador Wilson to the Vatican that has now yielded much of the intelligence that uncovered the sex trafficking and abuse of children that has occurred within the Roman Catholic Church. Unpredicted at that time, Ambassador Wilson would become a board member for ARC.

Bill Wilson and Pope John Paul at the Vatican in Rome.

Something Bigger Than Overthrowing Small Governments

From: Bill Wilson
To: Bazzel Baz
Sent: Wednesday, May 22, 2002-2:40PM
Subject: More

Baz:

The more I think about the manner in which the Demos are trying to set up a case against the President (Reagan) and the Republicans in the Senate and the House, the more I think they are building a case that could, if handled correctly by the Republicans backfire on the Demos. The case goes back to "what did they know, when did they know it and what did they do about it." The simple fact of the matter is that to go back then before 9/11 and ask what they knew, they knew that there was a threat, but no more than what my State Department Security men told me when Mrs. Wilson and I came home from Rome. There were threats, there were kidnappings and there were killings and bombings in airports, including the Rome airport. In addition to the State Department Security we had the Carabinieri with us at all times, and all night long outside of our residence. We weathered it, but when we came home and the Security guys said goodbye, they also said that the threat is not over and never will be. The United States will always be a target for terrorism. That was August 1986.

So now, let's go back to the primary question that the Demos are asking now. What did they know before 9/11? Well, we know there was a threat, our Security people told us that as far back and 1986. Ok, you knew there was a threat, what did you do about it? The same as you would have done if you knew there was a threat, we did all that we could with the intelligence that we had, but the threat was so widespread that there was almost nothing we could have done. So we did almost nothing. What would you have done?

All during the Reagan Administration, the Democrats were in control of both houses in Congress, why don't you ask them what they did? From 1992 to 2002 you had Clinton, what did you know then and what did you do about it. Clinton had Bin Laden in his cross hairs, and what did he do about it? Nothing, aside from the fact that the Republicans in the Senate are a bunch of candy-asses (and this comes from a life-long Republican) ... who was there to do anything? If the Republican Senators weren't what I just called them, how come they were so chicken in the Clinton impeachment matter? They could have impeached him for lying under oath and for obstructing justice. But did they? No! If the Republicans had any guts in Congress, they should be standing up today telling the Demos how the cows eat cabbage. But where are the strong Republicans? Baz, why is it that you always get me on a soap box?

Have a great day and keep in touch.

Bill

It was now towards the end of 1993, and I was caught up in the mix of things around the world that demanded my focus and attention, and I hadn't given much thought to the girls we rescued in Mogadishu since I left. I wish I could say that they remained front and center on my heart for the last months or so but that wasn't the case. All of that was about to change ... something shifted. I opened a drawer in my desk and stuffed away in the back was a yellow and black Kodak film box filled with 5x7 photos of my tour in Mogadishu. I remember having them developed, but took no time to look at them, since I had been on the road so much. There must have been at least a hundred full-color pictures.

I came to a shot of the girls we had rescued, standing there with their mother, little brother and the Director of the orphanage. I could feel the heat of that day, the smell of the streets, the look of desperation in their eyes and the sadness in my own heart that I would probably

Something Bigger Than Overthrowing Small Governments

never return to Somalia to see if they survived. I didn't stare much longer at the picture before I closed the box and put it back in the drawer. It was about 1730 hours (5:30p.m.) and time to call it a day. I made sure all my classified material was back in the vault, told Ron Franklin I was leaving, and grabbed my briefcase and then ... I stopped. I stood there with my face to the wall. I turned and walked over to the window and stared out across the openness of Virginia. I set my briefcase down on my desk, opened the drawer, opened the Kodak film box and grabbed the picture again. I studied everything about it, and I wasn't sure why.

For the next few weeks every time I would come to work, I would pull out the picture, study it for about five minutes and then put it back in the box. It was as if it was trying to speak to me in a language I didn't get, and so I just kept on showing up to class thinking that perhaps one day I would. There was no teacher to help me understand the noun or adjective of their expressions or the inflection of their words on that day — still embedded in my memory — as I looked at the picture.

Suddenly it dawned on me. What about all the children, where do they go? Even here in America, where do they go ... the runaways, the kidnapped, the exploited, and how are they exploited? Maybe it's just happening over there, in someone else's country? I mean we are the richest nation on the planet, and I can't really remember the last time I saw any children here hiding underneath some debris. I knew we had poverty levels in the Appalachian mountain region, and there were some homeless in the inner cities, but social services was pretty much aware of all this and must be doing something about it. But what if they weren't? I turned on my computer and typed in DOJ Missing Children. I remember reading two reports:

(1) The Federal Bureau of Investigation, the Stearns County Sheriff's Office and the Minnesota Bureau of Criminal Apprehension are investigating the disappearance of Jacob Erwin Wetterling, who disappeared from St. Joseph, Minnesota, on October 22, 1989. Wetterling was

162

last seen at approximately 9:00 p.m. with two other children when they were threatened at gunpoint by an unknown individual. At the time of his disappearance, Wetterling wore contacts and glasses for nearsightedness. He was a sports fanatic (especially televised sports) and loved football, hockey and baseball. Wetterling enjoyed playing Nintendo video games and liked to build things. He was very skilled with model kits. His favorite foods were pizza, steak and peanut butter. He was last seen wearing a red St. Cloud hockey shirt. [16]

(2) On June 30, 1994, six-year-old Crystal Ann Tymich was playing near her residence in South Los Angeles with her three older brothers. She was last seen picking peaches from a neighbor's tree, before disappearing sometime between 2 and 5 p.m. She was last seen wearing a pink T-shirt, shorts with a floral print, and tennis shoes with a picture of a mermaid. [17]

My curiosity was peeked. Where did these kids go? It seemed like foul play and it made me angry to think someone would kidnap and harm a child. I called a buddy of mine over at the FBI and asked how many children went missing in the U.S. last year. He told me over 200,000 in 1993.

When I asked where they went, he said, "Some are runaways, some are kidnapped and exploited in child pornography, some are used in satanic rituals, and some are non-custodial parental abductions and who knows what happens to the rest." While it was a problem, he admitted that it was not the highest of priorities for the FBI. And then he paused for a moment, that type of pause that you have before you tell someone they have cancer.

"What?" I asked.

"I hate to say it, but some kids are sexually exploited among very politically powerful and influential people in this world, and it's very organized. They get what they want, and we get blocked if we try to bring them up on charges for it. You didn't hear that from me." he said.

"What?" I asked differently this time. I was blown away.

Something Bigger Than Overthrowing Small Governments

"I suspect one day this use of children will become a billion-dollar business model," he concluded. I was silent. "You there?" he asked.

"Yeah," I said.

"I know you weren't expecting to hear that, but it's reality and I haven't figured a way to stop it or them yet. No one in the U.S. wants to believe it happens ... gotta go," he said. I hung up the phone.

Later that week I reached out to my local law enforcement contacts and inquired about their success rate in rescuing missing children. They told me that it wasn't very high. They had budgetary constraints that precluded them from investing too much time and energy into an investigation after so many days once a child went missing. They were undermanned and overworked. They also had jurisdictional issues. It wasn't like they could just go and run an investigation in another county or state without a lot of red tape ... not to mention communication challenges between them and other law enforcement agencies. They were doing the best they could with what they had.

The more I researched, the more I came to understand that missing children were slipping through the cracks. It was like fighting a snapping turtle in a mud bath, for those who wanted to do something about it. As I would come to learn many years later, there was also a darker side of this issue, a very organized side that catered to pedophiles, perverts, and influential people who wanted their way with children. Child porn was connected to adult porn and allowed to flourish, because of its revenue, to states like California. Obscenity laws on the books were ignored by local, state and federal governments to include the DOJ. Bloodline breeding programs among the elite were protected by law enforcement entities who were on their payroll. Not all law enforcement was involved, but certainly there were some corrupt officers within the ranks, no different than what we had within our own ranks at the CIA, like Aldrich Hazen Ames, an American who was convicted of espionage against his country in 1994. As we would discover later, not one child we rescued from sex trafficking had not had a law enforcement officer or multiple officers as "clients."

And that brought up the question as to who could be trusted regarding missing children when it came to law enforcement and attorneys. Had each of their departments vetted all of their people to see who was corrupt or a pedophile? I was convinced early out the gate by my research, that if anyone in law enforcement was involved in pornography or prostitution, they were just as much a part of the problem, particularly when evidence of child porn was tied to the adult porn industry. I was convinced of the same regarding any lawmaker or doctor or pastor or average person ... if they were involved in anything that abused children ... they were a part of the problem, and there is no way they were not complicit in the evil.

I knew the deterrent ... enforce stiffer penalties for crimes against children no matter who the culprit was. In my opinion it was clear, if you sexually molest a child or are responsible for circumstances that cause a child to be sexually molested, you should get the death penalty. It was the one condition where there should be no compromise in the law ... no plea bargains. And much to my amazement, after more research I discovered that legislatures were trying to get pedophilia removed as a crime and reclassified as a disease or a sexual orientation.

I knew exactly why that agenda was being pushed and supported by certain senators on the hill, the LGBTQ as well as the American Psychiatric Association. They all knew that under the current system if they got caught molesting a child, they would go to jail — not long enough, but they would go. They wanted to make sure that didn't happen to them and their friends. So if they changed the law, when they got caught, they would be told by the courts to seek medical help for "this disease." A trip to the doctor, some meds and they would be home free ... to molest another child. It was as if there was an infestation of predators in society, and I predicted one day it would be out of control. And I was not that far off. Now, some 24 years later, this article surfaced in *Mainstream Media Monday*, published on April 13, 2015 by Ethan A. Huff, staff writer:

Something Bigger Than Overthrowing Small Governments

PEDOPHILIA ISN'T A CRIME, BUT BEING UNVACCINATED IS
Conservative News, Nov. 1, 2017

What constitutes legal and illegal behavior in America today is becoming increasingly more inconsistent and bizarre. Some mainstream media sources are now calling for people who make the personal choice not to vaccinate to be jailed, implying that they're criminals, while other sources are now purporting that pedophilia isn't even a crime.

A recent *New York Times* op-ed piece published by Harvard graduate and law professor Margo Kaplan attempts to make the case that pedophilia is a mental disorder rather than a felony offense and calls for the rules to be redefined. In Kaplan's opinion, pedophilia is a condition that some people have rather than a crime that they commit, and she believes that it should be treated as such.

During a recent interview with Philadelphia magazine, Kaplan explained what she sees as a major variance between pedophiles and sex offenders. The former are merely born into a condition of being sexually attracted to young children, for which they have no control, she says, while the latter choose to act on their urges and harm children.

In line with what some had warned concerning the normalization of homosexuality — if people are born gay and accepted that way, the same argument could be used to justify pedophilia, was the claim — Kaplan's position seems to be inching society one step closer toward vindicating pedophilia as just another form of unique sexual preference.

Though she still condemns pedophilia as a "mental disorder," Kaplan's softening on how she views adult sexual attraction to children is concerning, especially as other media sources like USA Today call for the jailing of parents who don't vaccinate their children. Somehow, pedophilia should be treated with compassion, but not vaccinating with harsh punishment.

"Parents who do not vaccinate their children should go to jail," wrote USA Today columnist Alex Berezow in an inflammatory rant that gained nationwide attention during the recent measles hysteria campaign.

So let's get this straight — exercising one's right not to undergo a high-risk medical treatment that admittedly can cause irreversible health damage is a jailable offense, but lusting after pre-pubescent children is just another type of sexual orientation?

It's important to note here that in Kaplan's original NYT op-ed piece, she classifies pedophilia as a sexual attraction that often constitutes a mental illness. This implies that the "condition" is sometimes not a mental illness. Does this mean that there are appropriate ways, in Kaplan's view, of expressing one's pedophilia in a way that does not constitute mental illness?

Kaplan doesn't actually say it this way, emphasizing that pedophiles should have legal protections to seek out treatment for their disorder rather than to try to normalize it. She also agrees that pedophiles should still be held responsible for their conduct. But the underlying attraction, she says, is not a choice; pedophiles are born that way, in other words.

This reclassification muddies the waters in such a way as to open the door for the eventual normalization of pedophilia. Should enough out-of-the-closet pedophiles successfully make the case one day that they deserve legal protections to act out their urges with consenting children because they were born that way, then it's only a matter of time before pedophilia is just another form of sexual orientation.

"To suggest that pedophiles are the result of neurologic disorders is an attempt to mainstream a group of people who do not need it," wrote one NYT commenter. "If the sympathizers with pedophiles would talk to the victims of pedophilia, many of whom lead damaged and disastrous lives, it would be hard to imagine they would accept any pedophile under any basis."

Sandy Rios, cultural expert and talk show host on the American Family Radio network, has issued a statement on behalf of the American Family Association in response to the APA's position on pedophilia:

"Just as the APA declared homosexuality an 'orientation' under tremendous pressure from homosexual activists in the mid-'70s, now, under pressure from pedophile activists, they have declared the desire for sex with children an 'orientation,' too. It's not hard to see where this will lead. More children will become sexual prey."

In response to media calls, including queries from Charisma News, the APA admitted there was an error in the DSM and announced plans to correct its manual to make it clear that it does not classify pedophilia as a sexual orientation.

"The American Psychiatric Association's (APA) Diagnostic and Statistical Manual of Mental Disorders, Fifth Edition (DSM-5) has recently been published after a comprehensive multi-year research and review of all of its diagnostic categories," the statement reads.

"In the case of pedophilic disorder, the diagnostic criteria essentially remained the same as in DSM-IV-TR. Only the disorder name was changed from 'pedophilia' to 'pedophilic disorder' to maintain consistency with the chapter's other disorder listings."

"Sexual orientation" is not a term used in the diagnostic criteria for pedophilic disorder and its use in the DSM-5 text discussion is an error and should read "sexual interest." In fact, APA considers pedophilic disorder a "paraphilia," not a "sexual orientation." This error will be corrected in the electronic version of DSM-5 and the next printing of the manual. [18]

While the APA admitted the error, they only admitted it when they were caught. I submit it was no more than a proof of concept operation.

A proof of concept (POC) or a proof of principle is a realization of a certain method or idea to demonstrate its feasibility, or a demonstration in principle, whose purpose is to verify that some concept or theory has the potential of being used. A proof of concept is usually small and may or may not be complete. [19]

For years in the CIA we ran proof of concepts operations. I know it when I see it, and that is what the APA was doing and will continue to do.

> Sanity will never return to this culture until truth is reclaimed. It is not now, nor has it ever been acceptable for men or women to desire sex with children. Any who struggle with this must at least know that it is wrong before they can combat it and seek change. [20]

And I could not agree with this statement by Sandy Rios more. Pedophilia was becoming an all-out war on our children. Those who chose not to see this or who were complicit in the crime, had now become my enemy. The mental health profession is on a slippery slope heading in that direction.

On the heels of that article in 2015 I would interview adults that had been sexually trafficked as children to attorney generals and presidents and senators here in the United States. It was heartbreaking. I had no reason to believe their testimony was not truthful. There were too many things they knew about these elite people and places that they could never have known without experiencing it firsthand.

It was quickly looking as if I would have to choose which battle to fight, go after the corruption, or simply save one child at a time hoping that one day one of them would grow up to be in a position of influence to stop the evil ... if that was what God was hinting at. This was a world that was becoming more like its own espionage venue, and I could quickly see that the tradecraft I learned as a spy would be useful in my approach to all of this ... especially in attacking the hydra.

Something Bigger Than Overthrowing Small Governments

CHAPTER 10
GETTING STARTED

Each time I would talk to people about the number of missing children in the United States, they would be surprised. It was as if I was the only person in the whole world that knew there was a problem and was increasingly driven to do something about it. I realize now that wasn't the case, but at the time it felt that way.

I took a few yards off the Appalachian Trail to drop my pack ... sat on a big rock. It was a weekend of just being in the woods high above the rest of the world to think a few things through. The Shenandoah Valley below stretched 200 miles across the Blue Ridge and Allegheny mountains. Picture-perfect postcard farms and inns settled along most of the country roads. During the Civil War this region was nicknamed "The Breadbasket of the Confederacy." I reached in my pack and grabbed an apple and my Bible. I opened it to Luke 12:48, "For to whomsoever much is given, of him shall be much required; and to whom men have committed much, of him they will ask the more." I had been given so much all of my life, good health, a decent job, great family, rich history and born in America. Much had been given and much was required ... unless I wanted to be like the majority of the selfish world.

And as I looked at how daunting the mission of rescuing children would be, it became clear that this battle was not mine ... it was God's. It would be won by His strength and resources, and I had no intention of being involved unless God was going to get the glory. Only a fool would get so far ahead of himself that he would think that he could control all the uncontrollable circumstances that would arise on a battlefield of spiritual warfare.

There was a spiritual component in all of this whether a person was faith-based or not. Evil was evil, and anyone who harmed an innocent child had to be evil. It was as simple as that, and not even my atheist friends could deny it. Recognizing that right out the gate put me one step ahead of the average Joe who was out to create an NGO just to become popular. This could never be about me ... it had to be about God's call in my life. And whether there would ever be enough people in America to stand by my side or not, it didn't matter. I reflected back on what my parents had taught me about wanting to know "why." It didn't matter why people might not come along side of me in this mission. What mattered was this, "If we do not ... who will?" And so that became the motto of the association I was about to create ... ARC (*The Association for the Recovery of Children*). If God wanted me to rescue kids, then He was going to have to help me build this outfit to do that ... even if I was the only person in the outfit. I knew that in order for my faith to become a reality, it needed to be tested, and right now it certainly was. My primary focus would be on one thing and one thing only, the recovery of abducted children. I would not come home without them.

I started thinking about all the things I had learned in the CIA about overthrowing small governments. There's no doubt about it, communism, socialism, and dictatorships were all systems that oppressed people ... I had seen it firsthand, and there were not many suffering from those systems that did not want democracy and freedom from oppression. I am not ashamed of one single initiative by the U.S. to bring that about for those who asked. And keep in mind ... they asked for our help. Whether it was UNITA in Angola fighting the Russians/Cubans, the Mujahideen in Afghanistan against the Russian invasion, the Contras against the communist Sandinistas, counterterrorism units in Tunisia, Kenya, Bolivia, etc., we were there at their request to help them establish democracy. And in doing so, we had to build an army in each of those places to fight against the oppression. We had to recruit the right people, and we had to know whether those people cared about the cause, were willing to fight, and were motivated to win. I needed to understand the mindset of the people I was recruiting. Without those components, you could never build an army.

And so, I thought, "What if I built an army of Americans to fight against child exploitation, an army of Americans that cared about the cause and were motivated to win?" That was a good idea. I stopped my enthusiasm midstream. "But what is the mental inertia of

Something Bigger Than Overthrowing Small Governments

Americans and how do they feel about the cause?" Now that was the million-dollar question.

I was more than qualified to answer it. I came from a long line of war fighters with a military mindset. My grandfather fought against the Ottoman Empire before coming to America in 1914. My father was a Green Beret in Special Forces, and almost all of my uncles served in one branch of the military or another. Two of the many lessons I learned from my father and from my time in the Marine Corps was (1) know your enemy, and (2) it isn't about getting from point A to point B, it's about what you do between those two points when everything goes upside down. It dawned on me that there is something terribly wrong between point A, when we first notice the abuse of humans (trafficking, prostitution, pornography, etc.), and point B, where we should be toeing the line and doing something to stop it.

Adding to my military mindset was my espionage mindset. In a nutshell, the goals of the spy business were to influence foreigners to turn traitor against their country and provide secrets that ultimately secured the defense of the United States. And how were those goals achieved? I had to know what motivated people to do things. I had to determine a method to use such motivations to change their thinking and have them do what I wanted. And I had to understand these motivations like a science. "You can mold the actions of an entire society if you can influence the way they think." [21]

So how was this done? How could we influence the way society thought? Advertising! One of the greatest uses of advertising helped bring the entire Soviet Union to its knees. I hear from reliable sources that back in the CIA someone started shipping blue jeans through the Russian black market. Why blue jeans? Because blue jeans were American, and being an American meant freedom, and choice, and independence, and daring to be different. It gave the Russians a chance to express that and eventually want more of it. How else could we influence the way society thought? Propaganda! Sometimes it was in your face, and sometimes it was subtle. Sometimes subtle? Yes, sometimes subtle.

My father taught me something when we were flying one day. "If I take the stick and yank it hard to the left or right and we pull a few Gs, you'd know that you were turning, heading in another direction.

Bazzel Baz

But if I take the stick and pull it slightly two degrees in either direction, you won't even notice you're turning until I have you 180 degrees heading in the opposite direction. That is how you apply propaganda successfully, a little at a time. Change the definition of things slowly, and before you know it, you have society thinking in the opposite direction — exactly what you want them to think, and they never felt it happening."

Had people in America been led to think that child abuse was okay? Or had they been influenced via advertising and propaganda not to get involved? It was true that the only thing needed for evil to rule was for good men and women doing absolutely nothing. And what I was seeing from my research was exactly that ... apathy. A large percentage of Americans, more than I first realized, were not getting involved to stop the abuse of our children. It was obvious that some people had overwhelming responsibilities with family and work, and simply could not. Some were physically unable. Some were not aware. Some were aware but could not handle the reality ... it was emotionally disturbing. Others just didn't care. And others did care but they suffered from a social disease I called "MJS" (Milk Jug Syndrome). MJS is the deeply ingrained habit of ignoring the cry for help from humans that are abused. It is reflected in the ability to toss aside lives without a second thought, and it has permeated the very depths of consciousness in society.

Remember when our milk used to be delivered in glass bottles? The bottle had value, it had purpose, it had sustainability, and we were careful not to abuse it or break it. We cleaned it out and returned it to the milk man so he could refill it. This was the way we viewed the glass milk bottle. Now our milk comes in <u>plastic milk jugs,</u> and what do we do with them? Does a plastic milk jug have value, purpose, and sustainability, and are we careful not to abuse it or break it, and do we clean it out and return it to the milk man so he can refill it? No, we throw it away after we have used it ... consumed its contents. <u>We throw it away</u>.

So where did MJS come from? It was born from our efforts to keep money circulating in this country. The United States by design became a consumer nation, and products were developed to support

Something Bigger Than Overthrowing Small Governments

efforts for this cause ... thus the use of plastic. The act of consuming basically involves three stages in life:

1. **Purchasing:** (such as a buyer of goods and services), to acquire by payment of money, to acquire by effort, to influence by a bribe
2. **Ingesting:** eating or drinking, to suck in, to take
3. **Using:** using it up, or to help yourself to, to take unfair advantage of, to exploit

Basically, a consumer is an organism that feeds on others or on material derived from them, like we see in the ecological community or food chain. And that is what our nation has become. So if that is the case, then what consumer products were for sale? I took a deeper look into what I called the "first-come-first-serve Red Light Specials." Prostitution, pornography, slavery, sexual abuse, pedophilia, kidnapping for human sacrifice, child abductions, people for sale, Planned Parenthood selling aborted children for body parts, etc. were all on the list. Remember the definition of a consumer — uses it up, exploits, feeds on other organisms? In every one of these "Red Light Specials," that was exactly the case. Innocent people were being used up and exploited as if they were a commodity.

What was the driving force behind using people? Money! "The love of money is the root of all evil." People were making money on people. The human life was losing its value ... like the plastic, we use it and we throw it away ... it is a habit that has become acceptable in everything we do in life. We automatically throw things away without considering their value. All day long we unwrap something we purchase, we consume it, and we throw the paper or plastic wrapper away. Practically all day long we are throwing things away ... training our minds to throw things away ... training our minds to ignore their value.

Remember, nothing is made to last in a consumer society. I can remember a time when I was young that the mindset of the nation was to build things that lasted, things we valued, and things we valued so much that if they got broken ... we fixed them. My father still had an

RCA television sitting in his garage and guess what ... it still worked. It was made to last. But if it did get broken ... we fixed it. I want you to remember that, "if they got broken, we fixed them." Nowadays if you purchase a computer, television, etc. you're lucky if you can get two years out of it, because it is not made to last ... it is made to use and throw away. If you go in to have them repaired, it is cheaper to toss it aside and buy another. Do you see how the thinking of our society has shifted? Consuming has become a way of life.

Even younger generations are buying into the fact that things are not made to last. Even democracy, the Declaration of Independence and the Constitution are in question as to whether they are meant to last ... perhaps it is time to toss them away for something else. I always find it interesting when politicians or academia talk about how no nation under a democracy has last more than 250 years ... as if to insinuate that the U.S. is on the verge of collapse now at 241 years. Just because it hasn't, doesn't mean it can't. And just because we don't value human life doesn't mean we shouldn't. Perhaps our thinking needs to change.

But wait, there is more. Maybe not everyone is suffering from MJS. Maybe some are being overtaken by a severe case of "denialitus."

DENIALITUS (denial-"I"-tus) results in this mentality:
- "This can't happen to me and my family, this only happens to people who ...."
- "This can't be true, this doesn't really happen, I just can't believe it."
- "I imagine someone else must already be taking care of this problem."

Maybe it's that other popular ailment, Glitter Media "desensititus."

DESENSITITUS (desensit-"I"-tus) results in this mentality:
- Film and television have glamorized promiscuity, abuse, blood money and murder to an extreme where people have become desensitized to the reality of the current, real-life, dehumanizing atrocities occurring in people's lives.

Something Bigger Than Overthrowing Small Governments

- "Hmm, I wonder if the Holocaust was real? Did millions of people really lose their lives because of the <u>TWISTED IDEOLOGY OF ONE HUMAN BEING PLANTED INTO THE MINDS OF OTHERS?</u> Naaaah, that couldn't have really happened. Could it?"

Remember these words? "You can mold the actions of an entire society if you can influence the way they think."

I was beginning to understand exactly what I needed to understand about the American mindset. And as it became more of a reality, it infuriated me. I'm here to tell you there are some things that are meant to last, some things worth dying for — our Constitution, democracy, and our elderly and our children who are being abused. When I swore my oath as a United States Marine, it was to protect this nation against all enemies, foreign and domestic, and that was what I intended to do.

We cannot just go out and buy another human life. America needed to snap out of this MJS and start repairing the broken lives instead of throwing them away. We needed to give them value and wake up to the fact that it's human life ... not a piece of plastic. Issues like human trafficking and exploitation were hurting families, women and children. We had to stop consuming and start producing and giving back. These kids' souls were being ripped out, leaving them in a dysfunctional condition. If something wasn't done, then they would grow up to be dysfunctional adults ... that last thing we needed, dysfunctional adults running the country. So the survival of our nation was at risk as well.

I laid my Bible down next to my pack and leaned back to ask myself the hard questions. What was my life like, was I proactive or reactive? I wasn't advocating that everyone in America run home and throw away all of their plastic, but there was a bigger picture here, and it reflected and affected the thinking of an entire society. If people learned to develop different habits and practice life as if it counted for something, it would be a step in the right direction. If people could be wise and be very careful about those subtle influences, then perhaps we could make a difference.

But none of that was going to happen unless it started with me. I wanted to opt out and just repeat what I had said before ... "God why don't YOU do something about this?" and then I remembered his voice in Somalia, "I did, I created YOU." God never takes kindly to hypocrisy, nor does He need someone's belief in order to exist. So I wanted to be absolutely sure I did what I said I was going to do, and that I kept God in the center of it all. I didn't have any support, there were no other operators ... I would do what I had to do, until I could do what I wanted to.

We, the men and women who have fought for freedom, bear the right to fight for the freedom of others, no matter where in the world. It is our privilege, it is our honor, it is our duty to ensure all men and women are free to choose their destiny without suffering imposed upon them by tyrants, terrorists, dictators, pedophiles, rapists and corrupt systems. For those who have never tasted the bitterness of war and the sacrifice of life, know that we who fight, for a time, give up all our freedoms to come and go as we please, to sleep where and when we choose, and even the freedom to breathe, should we be called home to meet our Maker. For those countrymen who do not fight, they give up nothing. Therefore, if there be any who have the right to say what peoples we will protect, it is us, the men and women who have fought ... not those countrymen who enjoy the pleasures of our nation, provided to them through our sacrifice. We have earned the right to decide the fate of our nation because we are the fate of our nation.

I am immortal until my purpose on this earth is fulfilled, or my job is done ... because my life is in God's hands. There is no fear of death. And with that, I am not what happens to me, but instead, what I choose to become.

A life of rescuing children wasn't always going to be a bed of roses. It would have challenges and disruptions and circumstances that are beyond my control, stealing the peace I so desperately wanted to hold on to. When that occurred, I would remember, true peace isn't found in longing for different circumstances, true peace comes when you find God in the midst of your current circumstances. It is His strength that will make the difference.

But for now, in 1993, I was still in a process of discovery, wondering what all of this meant in my life. I had another ten years or

Something Bigger Than Overthrowing Small Governments

so before I could retire from the CIA, so it didn't look like I would be doing anything in the near future concerning children ... or would I? Weekends and holidays were open ... a good place for testing the waters to see if I could put my investigative skills to use and maybe even find a child or two.

So I started an association which years later turned into The Association for the Recovery of Children (ARC), a 501c3 non-profit organization of former intelligence, military and law enforcement officers dedicated to the safe recovery of missing and exploited American children. I had absolutely no idea what I was doing and had to learn many of the organizational skills along the way with the help of my sister, who acted as Director of Operations and Administration and never let a single thing slip through the cracks. She was amazing and provided the encouragement to continue the quest.

I ran rescue operations completely by myself for years under the radar, not charging a penny for my services, and not telling anyone about the rescues. That was my deal with God, that I would never charge a custodial guardian anything for the help I was providing. I wanted ARC to stay as pure as possible and different from all the other organizations I knew about. I received no salary, used money from my own accounts and took in a few donations from certain people who were read into my missions.

I was by no means a wealthy man, and it probably wasn't the best use of my resources, because eventually my personal bank account was being bled dry. But for me it was about one thing ... saving children, and I wasn't going to wait around for anyone else to feel the same way I felt about the calling, nor was I going to waste too much energy trying to convince wealthy people to support the cause ... either they wanted to or not. I wasn't good about asking for money ... it didn't feel right to me and yet, we needed it to merely get on an airplane and get to the target area to rescue a child.

My sister wanted to know why I never started a website where people could donate. My accountant asked why I never took money from the federal government. My close friends asked what I intended to do when I ran out of money. All were very good questions. I hadn't started a website because I still had that espionage mentality and keeping things under the radar seemed the safest. I hadn't taken money from the federal government because I didn't want them telling me who I could or could not go rescue. And as far as what I intended to do when I ran out of money, I intended to believe that if God had called me to this, then He had a plan. And if anyone could explain my life apart from God, then I wasn't living by faith. For faith is the substance of things hoped for. In its simplest form, faith is merely "belief." As our understanding becomes more complex and operative, when we begin to put faith to work, it becomes "confidence," and finally, in its best form, when it becomes fully operational, it is "trust." This trust, this full measure of faith, is alive and it works within our relationship with God. I knew I could stand on my faith because there was a history of its power with so many people that came before me, as recorded in Hebrews 11.

> And what more shall I say? I do not have time to tell about Gideon, Barak, Samson and Jephthah, about David and Samuel and the prophets, who through faith conquered kingdoms, administered justice, and gained what was promised; who shut the mouths of lions, quenched the fury of the flames, and escaped the edge of the sword; whose weakness was turned to strength; and who became powerful in battle and routed foreign armies. Women received back their dead, raised to life again. There were others who were tortured, refusing to be released so that they might gain an even better resurrection. (Hebrews 11:32-35)

What more did I need? ... I had faith.

So I started a website. I still did not take money from the federal government, and I decided to put my faith into action by devising a financial plan for sustainable funding so we would never have to ask for donations again ... the amount of sustainable funding that hopefully one day will grab the heart of some wealthy people who have a heart for saving children.

Something Bigger Than Overthrowing Small Governments

    Look, here's the deal. You can print up all the pictures of missing and exploited children on milk cartons you want, you can make all the people in the world aware. They look at the picture, and they feel good that they looked at the picture, and they believe they have done something about the problem by looking at the picture. And at the end of the day, do you know where that milk carton goes? In the garbage! A child DOES NOT COME HOME until there are boots on the ground locating and physically bringing that child home. And along the way, all of these years, I have encouraged people to join the fight to protect children.

    ARC is now up and running. with multiple assets to draw upon around the world. Our core team is small, and we draw upon a global pool of operators as needed for different missions. Once a custodial guardian of a missing child has exhausted all efforts with local, state and federal authorities, we get involved. No one gets paid a salary. The cost of the mission requires expenses for rental cars, hotels, air transportation, food and sometimes fixer fees to assets, depending on what country we are in. Our Strike Force Recovery Teams (SFRT) are stacked with some of the most highly trained Special Operations personnel on the planet, who all have been down range ... no exceptions allowed.

    Each of them understands that ARC is an organization founded by God and driven by God. While there is no requirement for each operator to have a personal relationship with Jesus Christ, there is no way they can avoid the presence of God as long as I am in charge of operations. I pray over the operation before we depart, we pray before each phase is executed, and we pray giving thanks once we return. I am not ashamed of the gospel nor of the God of this universe who has performed one miracle after another when it comes to finding and rescuing exploited children. It is not our mission to capture the perpetrator; it is our mission to stealthily and surgically remove the child from them in a way that does not create more trauma to the child than what is already there as a result of the abduction. This isn't about kicking doors in, and we do not go into the field with firearms. On a few occasions we have been forced to detain the bad guys and turn them over to law enforcement, but in most cases, they never see us coming, and they never know where we have gone once the child is in our custody. God will deal with them in His own time.

One of the great benefits about saving children is having a captive audience when it comes to the custodial guardians, law enforcement, the community, social services, the media or whomever else is involved in a case. And in those moments, I get to introduce them to God in various ways that hopefully instill faith and comfort and give them strength to persevere until we can bring their child home. I have found that no matter what their faith, when I ask to pray with them, they all accept. I think that is telling. "For ever since the world was created, people have seen the earth and sky. Through everything God made, they can clearly see His invisible qualities--His eternal power and divine nature. So they have no excuse for not knowing God" (Romans 1:20).

It reminds me of the saying, "There are no atheists in foxholes." It appears that when people are desperate, when they have turned to every human being they can for help, and those human beings have failed them ... when they have sought the assistance of every bit of technology and it has failed them ... then they reach out to God.

No matter what people thought of me, the one thing they would never be able to dispute would be the miracles that surrounded every mission ARC would go on. And as skilled as we are among men, none of us are that good. But God with us is a whole different story. I challenge anyone to stand in our way when it comes to rescuing children, for this is God's calling. "And the LORD, He *it is* that doth go before thee; He will be with thee, He will not fail thee, neither forsake thee; fear not, neither be dismayed" *(Deuteronomy 31:8)*.

ARC has been blessed to have a 100% success rate in that every child we have gone after, we have safely brought home. Over the course of many years, a record of those events has been kept in our files in the form of after-action reports. This is a way to evaluate our performance and improve our operations.

It is not our intention to be the largest child find organization in the world, but it is our goal to be the best. Our experienced agents are sensitive to the handling of the most advanced intelligence gathering systems. Our services include the use of innovative, proven techniques, and legal and ethical methods designed to identify the perpetrator(s) and

Something Bigger Than Overthrowing Small Governments

their whereabouts in relation to the safe recovery of the victim. ARC coordinates all investigations through proper documentation obtained from the judicial systems, both State and Federal. Background investigations are performed on custodial and non-custodial guardians, whether that be the parents, relatives, members of the State, law enforcement or other NGOs requesting our assistance.

If we continue to hold to what we know best, stay in our lane, and not try to be all things to all men, then I believe we will one day reach that goal of being the most effective child rescue organization in the world.

Many of our operations cannot, and will not, be disclosed to the public due to their sensitive nature and the need to protect our tradecraft. Keeping that in mind, I have carefully chosen a number of After Action Reports in the following chapters. I share these with the readers so that they may have an opportunity to see some of the ups and downs, successes and failures and lessons learned when setting out to save the life a child who has gone missing. But more importantly, it is my hope that those who decide to join the fight by creating their own child rescue organizations learn from us and navigate the fault lines properly, to quicken their abilities to go beyond the call of duty and bring home the children that await rescue.

Chapter 11
OPERATION CINCO DE MAYO
AFTER ACTION REPORT

Subjects: Ronica Colon, Jacob and Noah Ascencio

Date: May 5, 2006

Introduction:
For the purposes of this report, the SFRT consisted of Bazzel Baz and two attachments (1) Mark Miller and (2) Ronica Colon (custodial mother).

Background:
On or around April 1, 2006, *The Association for the Recovery of Children* (ARC) was contacted by Mark Miller, President of the American Association for Lost Children, Inc. requesting assistance in the recovery of two American children held hostage in Atencingo, Puebla, Mexico. The two children were Noah Justin Ascencio, age four, and his brother, Jacob Abraham Ascencio Jr., age two.

In the past Mark had worked a number of cases in Mexico, which culminated in his arrest. His concern for returning was well-warranted, and he preferred not to go it alone this time. In addition, cartel activity had increased, and he was concerned that being a six-foot-tall American in the heart of Mexico would make him a target. He had good reason to be concerned, as did all of us. President Felipe Calderón's high-profile "war on drugs" crackdown was in play against Mexican drug bosses such as Villarreal Barragan, and I anticipated it would drive an up-spike in the existing violence. At best 30,000 people had died in violence arising from the activity of increasingly powerful Mexican drug cartels. I wasn't that concerned about the amount of violence, but the spectacular nature of the violence — the elaborate style of the executions, such as beheadings with bodies left on display by roadsides. Seven months from the day we launched our operation to rescue the boys, Mexico's President would launch Operation Michoacán

Something Bigger Than Overthrowing Small Governments

against the La Familia Michoacana Cartel. A total of more than 60 Mexican soldiers, more than 100 police officers, and 500 cartel gunmen would be killed in the operation. I did not want to become a statistic.

Both abducted boys were born out of wedlock to Ronica A. Colon, a U.S. citizen, and Jacob Abraham Ascencio Hernandez, a Mexican citizen residing in the United States on a work visa. There was evidence to indicate Ascencio involved himself with Ms. Colon to obtain citizenship. When a marriage did not evolve, Ascencio began to seek other opportunities for employment and showed an interest in drug trafficking. His nature turned violent. On two different occasions he threatened Ronica, once by physically trying to smother her with a pillow, and again by holding a knife to her neck during an altercation. On a third occasion, while pregnant with a third child, Ascencio violently punched her in the stomach in an attempt to force her to abort the fetus.

Soon thereafter, Ascencio was the subject of a homicide investigation involving the murder of Ronica's best female friend. The victim had been smothered. Ascencio fled the country and returned to his hometown of Atencingo, Puebla, Mexico, where he became involved in drug trafficking and was employed in a sugarcane processing factory.

Sometime later, communication was reestablished between Ronica and Ascencio. Wishing to mend the relationship, Ronica traveled with her two boys, Jacob and Noah to visit Ascencio and his family in Mexico.

Located in a very isolated part of Mexico, Ronica was forced, against her will, to remain in Atencingo with Ascencio's family and himself. He continued to abuse her physically and steal what little money she possessed. After a number of altercations and during a time of sympathetic influence by Ascencio's parents and cousins, Ronica was allowed to depart, but not with her two children. Having only enough money left for one airline ticket, she and Ascencio agreed that she would return to the U.S. where she could work and make enough money to send back for the children's airline tickets.

Over a period of nine months, Ascencio held the children hostage and refused to purchase airline tickets with the money Ronica provided for the return of the children to America. Ronica once again traveled to Mexico to check on the welfare of the children and secure their return but was denied that opportunity. She left her credit/atm card so Ascencio would have funds to feed and clothe the children while she returned to the U.S. once again.

When Ronica realized the severity of the situation, that Ascencio had no intention of returning the children to her custody in the U.S., and that he threatened to sell the children into slavery and prostitution if she failed to supply more money, she contacted Mark Miller, president of the American Association for Lost Children. In addition, Ronica suspected that Ascencio was involved in the sexual abuse of his thirteen-year-old niece, who, from time to time, alluded in her actions and speech that such activity was occurring. A final concern was for the overall health of the children, who had not had their immunizations nor much-needed medication for Jacob, who was born with a hole in his heart. Any infection to the child could result in death, and this was something Ascencio expressed little concern over.

Mark Miller contacted ARC to assist in the international recovery of the children. He provided total funding for the operation as well as copies of the warrant for arrest for parental kidnapping and papers showing that Ronica Colon was the legal guardian with 100% custody of her children. He also made available the birth certificates of each child, proving their U.S. Citizenship. When Ronica had exhausted all efforts with local, state and federal law enforcement, who were unable to respond effectively due to international jurisdictional restraints, she followed up with an appeal for assistance from the U.S. State Department. She never received a response. Life doesn't allow time for paint to dry ... so getting involved was a no-brainer for me.

I've so often heard people who have no idea what they are talking about say, "You are re-kidnapping the kids," which is just about the dumbest thing I have ever heard. You can't re-kidnap someone who was kidnapped. What you can do is save someone who has been kidnapped or rescue them from being held hostage. When you are dealing with Americans who are being held hostage in a foreign country — child or adult — that is exactly what it is ... being held hostage in a foreign land. The mission is to take them back to America, the land in which they are a legal citizen, the very place they were kidnapped from in the beginning. As long as you have legal paperwork proving their citizenship and legal guardian(s) to whom they will be returned, you are breaking no laws. This was about Americans saving Americans who were going to be sold into the sex trade.

It doesn't take a rocket scientist to know what is right and what is wrong, much less to understand that the U.S. has a number of political and economic agendas in Mexico that they will protect, even if they have to sacrifice two little boys. I had seen it before in other countries, and I was not about to allow these two precious souls to be used as pawns in a game between diplomats who cared only about the comfort of their own careers.

Operation Overview:

At 1230 hours on 5 May 2006, I, Mark Miller and Ronica (three months pregnant) rendezvoused in Mexico City at the international airport. Travel to and from the AO (Area of Operations) via a 2005 Volkswagen Jetta was procured at the Alamo Rental Car at the airport. I had hoped to make contact with trusted friends of the Centro de Investigación y Seguridad Nacional (CISEN), but they were preoccupied with the uprising of the most technologically advanced, sophisticated, and dangerous cartel operating in Mexico ... Los Zetas. Los Zetas ran protection rackets, engaged in assassinations, extortion, kidnappings, and any other criminal activities you can think of. Fortunately, they were based in Nuevo Laredo, Tamaulipas, directly across the border from Laredo, Texas, which was a good distance from where we were at the moment.

An overview of the precise location of the AO (Atencingo) was not available. Because the AO is secluded and does not register as a primary location of influence, intelligence on this region would not be obtainable without ground reconnaissance. As with most small towns in this region, the Mexican government does not generally provide information that is obtained through technical sources. Overhead imagery was provided, and it proved to be accurate in its scheme of geography.

Due to the immense size of Mexico City, convoluted road systems under construction and our limited knowledge of the Spanish language, our travel to the outskirts was hindered and confusing. A number of wrong turns were taken, but eventually we ended up back on course. As the designated driver and the most proficient in Spanish, I found it necessary to stop on numerous occasions at various Pemex Gas Stations, to get directions from attendants, which did take us from point A to point B. We were able to make it to a national highway 190S out of Mexico City to 150D (toll road) to Puebla. Puebla had a very interesting history. Back in the day "when the OSS challenged Division Five's mandate for operations south of the border, Roosevelt 'directed that the FBI continue to have sole responsibility for the civilian intelligence operation in the Western Hemisphere,'" according to a study of the FBI of the period.

    The SIS/Division Five agents sent in were both undercover and open, as "legal attaches" to the embassies involved. This arrangement was kept up in the case of Mexico even after the War and remains in effect to this day. FBI operations in Mexico exceed those of the CIA and the CIA office in Mexico was the largest in the hemisphere. A crucial clue to FBI activity in Mexico is provided as a by-product of investigations into the assassination of President John F. Kennedy. These investigations unearthed south Texas court records of 1952 which showed that "there were 25 to 30 professional assassins kept in Mexico by the espionage section of the U.S. Federal Bureau of Investigation; [and] that these men were used to commit political assassinations all over North, South and Central America, the East European countries and Russia ... ." According to one source, the man in charge of the unit, back to 1943, was Albert Osborne — an intelligence agent operating under the cover of a Protestant missionary working in the state of Puebla from 1942-1962, and the man identified by six witnesses as the traveling companion of Lee Harvey Oswald in Mexico in September 1963. [22]

    While many may find it hard to believe, instinctively I smelled the stench of foul play like the left-behind excrement of bats who were no longer occupying a cave ... undeniable evidence, a fingerprint of mischief in my mind's eye as we drove through the streets. I had spent a good portion of my life making history under the remnants of the cloak that hid the dagger of espionage. Whether right or wrong ... it still smelled the same. You would have thought that I would be comfortable, but oddly enough, there was an uneasiness that warned me to not entertain the idea of ever passing by this way again ... and I

Something Bigger Than Overthrowing Small Governments

listened. Just ahead the sign pointed to the 190D to Matamoros to the 150 which would take us into Atencingo. The cost of the 150D toll road was in excess of 80 pesos one way.

The major highways were three lanes and in very good condition. The 190D from Puebla to Atencingo was rough and laced with speed bumps about every mile or half mile through the built-up regions of each town and the roads entering each town. Although Ronica had informed us of the possibility of motion sickness, she fared well throughout the trip.

Neither Mark nor Ronica were prepared logistically for this mission. The water and food I packed was shared with the two of them, and we made stops along the way at roadside restaurants to obtain more water. Radios, binoculars and other essential items were also supplied by ARC. Mark informed me that his organization's last three attempts at recovering children had been a failure. While I admire his tenacity, this did not come as a surprise to me. I had observed his lack of tactical tradecraft and ability to generate seamless operational planning. It was an accident waiting to happen, as I would later experience with him on the Kobie Reuben Case in South Korea.

I felt a little unsure going into the situation because I was not accompanied by other operations officers from ARC. Nevertheless, I proceeded, constantly reviewing operational procedures in my head as we drove. It was my intention not to control Mark's decisions, but to highly influence them as much as possible. He was not opposed to allowing me to offer up my opinion, and in almost every instance, agreed and followed.

The trip to the AO was in excess of four hours. Mark and Ronica slept for the duration. Once we drew closer to the town of Atencingo, they woke up. The road into the AO was a double lane, blacktop, potholed surface ... one way in and one way out with numerous choke points that made me feel uneasy. Traffic included slow moving trucks filled with sugarcane, personal automobiles, an occasional dog and, of course, pedestrians walking along the sides. There were sufficient Pemex Gasoline Stations along the way and very little sign of Mexican law enforcement Officials. I counted a total of four low class hotels from Puebla to Atencingo.

Bazzel Baz

We entered Atencingo around 1700 hours and drove the town for our recon. Oddly the soundtrack from the movie *Desperado* played in my mind, "... sharp knives, big guns, awesome fights, great dialog, wonderful characters and Selma Hayek looking better than ever." In my mind the town we had just entered was every bit becoming a stage for that shoot out scene in the end of the film, as though I were the movie's director and Atencingo were the set. As mentioned, there was one two-lane road in and out, numerous cobblestone streets, just large enough for one vehicle at a time, that snaked between Spanish-style villas in need of repair. The town, although not totally poverty-stricken, maintained a low-class aroma of peasants, sugarcane factory workers, prostitutes, drug dealers and presumably corrupt federal police officers dressed in black and armed with submachine guns and pistols, sparsely spread throughout. I did not observe a police station, only police loaded in the back of a pickup truck with official logos, seemingly making the rounds before leaving the town.

Ronica remained in the back seat of the car, disguised in a baseball hat and hooded jacket, as we located the house in which Ascencio resided. No children or relatives were spotted at that time. Without the cover of darkness, this was a town were strangers were easily recognized, so we proceeded to the end of town and used a rundown medical clinic as cover for action, all the while running surveillance on the traffic coming and going into the town.

During that time, we rehearsed a number of scenarios that could be put in place in order to successfully retrieve the children. Mark listened intently as I laid out the pros and cons of each. It was a mini five-paragraph order at best, most of which I am sure Mark did not comprehend, but he tried.

ARC maintained a very surgical posture that was designed to limit the degree of trauma to the children being recovered. That said, it was essential that Ronica and Ascencio not meet face to face. Mark suggested that he and I, posing as U.S. Representatives, could present a fake sealed document to Ascencio that would hopefully leverage our demands. "And where do you intend to get that document? It isn't like Kinko's is around the corner," I said. Mark thought about it and left his idea on the doorstep of unsound reasoning.

My assessment of the AO quickly proved itself to be genuine ... a small town of nesting vipers involved in everything but the sugar cane industry and perhaps knowing everyone else's business — including the fact that Ascencio was detaining the children illegally. There was no way he would just turn the children over, and in fact, to do so in a face-to-face confrontation would result in the three of us spending the rest of our lives in some miserable jail this side of hell. Our only chance of getting near the house where the kids might be was to draw Ascencio out, and even succeeding in that did not guarantee the kids would be there.

Then something caught my eye ... a pay phone. "I want you to call your ex-husband, Ascencio, and tell him you have just arrived in Mexico City and would like for him to come pick you up. Tell him you have the money and would love to see the children. Let's see how he responds," I told Ronica.

She dialed the number and Ascencio answered. Ronica did as I instructed, but Ascencio challenged her story, calling her a liar and hung up the phone. Ronica dialed again, per my instructions, and Ascencio answered again ... this time abruptly cursing her out and telling her that since she never sent the money, he wanted nothing to do with her. He said if she did not send the money, he would sell the children. Then he hung up the phone again. She hung up the phone in tears telling me as best she could, between waves of emotion, what he said. My blood began to boil, not in a vengeful way, but in that way that says, "enough is enough and it is time to take care of business." The thought of even suggesting that someone would sell their own children was enough to reconfirm not only my calling by God, but the fact that He was leading the way.

I stepped aside next to the car after quickly getting Ronica back into the car. I lowered my head, "Father, help me be sharp and wise. Show me a way."

Suddenly it occurred to me ... Psalms 141:8-10, "For my eyes are toward You, O GOD, the Lord; In You I take refuge; do not leave me defenseless. Keep me from the jaws of the trap which they have set for me, and from the snares of those who do iniquity. <u>Let the wicked fall into their own nets, while I pass by safely.</u>"

"Get in the car," I told Mark.

"Where are we heading?" He asked.

I said nothing. About three miles out of town we had passed a tiny local restaurant on our way in ... that is what I was looking for. I was praying that God would dilute time and space in the mind of Ascencio, as I confidently moved forward on the plan that was ever evolving in my mind ... as if God were pointing out step by step what to do. Things were appearing to unfold right in front of my eyes, doors opening, and I could see the future of a well-designed plan of faith. I was about to enter the dragon's den, one way in and one way out, with only God cloaking our arrival. It would go against all common sense and all odds if you were a man of fear ... but I wasn't, and it made perfect sense to me.

There it was on the left ... the restaurant. It was typical of the country. The one pre-Hispanic Mayan rural house made of perishable organic materials would demand a person pay little attention to the habitats of the common people that owned it if not for the Restaurant sign outside. A well, a latrine, and a chicken coup complimented the single rectangular room with rounded corners, no windows, and one central door built to face east. That is the door that Ronica would enter to carry out her assignment. I pulled the car up just short of the entrance.

"I want you to go inside and ask to use the phone. Make a call back to Ascencio and tell him that you managed to get a ride from a church group, who dropped you off about three miles from the town, and this is as far as you have gotten. He will most likely argue with you again and tell you he doesn't believe it. That is when I want you to put the restaurant owner on the phone so he can verify that you are here. Then take the phone back and tell Ascencio again that you have money and that you will wait for him. Then tell the owner of the restaurant that you will wait outside. Then leave. We will be two hundred yards down the road. Walk to the car and get in."

I made her repeat my instructions three times. She had it down, and off she went. I drifted the car to the pickup point just past the restaurant and waited. About ten minutes later Ronica climbed in the car. "He is on his way," she said.

Perfect! We headed to Atencingo. I told Ronica to lower her profile in the back seat. As we entered the outskirts of the town, Ascencio and another passenger passed us going in the opposite direction in their car, thinking they would be picking up Ronica. I smiled for just a moment at the fact that he fell for it, and at the delight that God was parting the Red Sea. I had absolutely no idea how the next phase would unfold, but I trusted that God would continue His favor. He isn't one to lead you down a road and not bring you back ... it isn't how He works, at least it isn't how He has worked in my life.

We meandered through the cobblestone streets in our vehicle, following Ronica's directions until we came to a place just around the corner from where the children supposedly were being held. We got out of the car and peeked around the corner. There were a few children outside the row-house dwellings, but not the children we were looking for.

I pulled everyone back to the car. "We have to pray. Father God we need you to bring those children out."

Then Ronica, who had stepped away during that prayer, said, "There they are." She was totally exposed by now, standing in the middle of the street, a small block from the dwelling. Sure enough, both boys stepped out of the house and into the street to play.

"Mark, go! You and Ronica go there now and grab them." I jumped in the car and backed it in place on the street they were headed down, following them, tailgate first. Ronica knelt down and hugged both the boys, who recognized her. "Let's go!" I shouted, looking back over my shoulder out the driver's side window.

Mark and Ronica grabbed both the boys and found their way to the car, which was now just feet away. A woman, Ronica's sister-in-law (the aunt) ran from the house shouting in Spanish. Ronica looked back and the woman waved goodbye — then I realized she wasn't waving goodbye at all, she was waving for us to stop. This was not adding up to a great send-off by members of the opposite side of the family. I realized they were pretty much in cahoots with Ascencio this entire time, knowing fully that he intended to sell the children. It had to be only a matter of time before she realized that Ronica would find her boys ... but I don't think the aunt or any member of Ascencio's immediate family expected it to happen this way. That was fine with me. I learned long time ago in the Marine Corps that one of the principles of war — the art of surprise — was very important. Strike the enemy at a time, or place, or in a manner for which he is unprepared.

Surprise can decisively shift the balance of combat power. By seeking surprise, forces can achieve success well out of proportion to the effort expended. Surprise can be in tempo, size of force, direction or location of main effort, and timing. Deception can aid the probability of achieving that surprise. I had absolutely no remorse for the tactics I was using to save the lives of these two young boys. While I didn't consider

Something Bigger Than Overthrowing Small Governments

Ascencio and his family to be my enemies, I did know that to them I was exactly that, and if they got the chance, they would show no mercy.

So my attitude shifted a bit, realizing that we were in the thick of it, and that I could not underestimate Ascencio or his family no matter how unrefined they appeared to be. We were in a hornet's nest, and hornets don't need to graduate from grade school to make life miserable.

In the seconds that passed, I drew a harder line when it came to people who knew what was right and failed to take action — in this case, the aunt, holding the children hostage and sending Ronica back to the U.S. without the kids the year before. I glanced in the rear-view mirror and, sure enough, the aunt was sprinting back to the dwelling. I assumed she would be calling the authorities.

We skirted people in the streets as safely and as fast as we could, but even so, it was like the entire town had come alive with an early warning system. As we turned left to make our escape to the main street of the town, a pickup truck blocked our exit, its driver defying my approach. He made three mistakes. The first, was not closing the gap between his truck and the wall — enough for me to hopefully squeeze through, but certainly not without damaging the car. The second, thinking I would not go for it. The third, not realizing God was on my side.

The truck outweighed us by its size and the load of debris it was hauling in its bed. It was not going to move. And what we were about to do defied all logic, all science, all engineering. I pointed the nose of our car between the building and the front of the truck and accelerated. We hit both. It pinched the body of our car with that metal-against-metal sound, or like dragging a fork between your upper and lower teeth. It wanted to stick, but it didn't. And like butter, the big truck at its strongest point (the engine) literally moved over a foot, enough for us to come out the other side.

"We're home free," Mark remarked.

"Not yet amigo," I stated.

We still had a number of those pesky presumably-corrupt, armed security officers dispersed throughout the town who could respond in a very nasty way. I drove cautiously and moderately on the one-way-out road, keeping my eyes peeled. A glance over my shoulder assured me that the boys were happy to be reunited with their mother.

"If for any reason we see a roadblock ahead, you and Ronica and the kids get out, go to the sugar cane fields, and parallel the road until you pass the checkpoint. Hopefully, they will let me through, and I can meet you on the other side one mile away. Just estimate. If you see me get picked up, keep going, wait until dark to come out past the checkpoint, and find the best way back to Mexico City and the U.S. Embassy. You know what to do after that," I told both of them.

The next 20 miles were as anticipated as darkness began to fall. At least if there were a roadblock, we might be able to see the lights of whatever police or security were in our path in enough time to pull off the road or detour. But honestly, there wasn't much of any detour according to my map, which at best was nothing more than an out-of-date Hispanic version of Rand McNally.

It wasn't that I would have not welcomed the police, but the interference, language barrier and educational challenges when dealing with an international rescue — especially in a region where payoffs are common — was not something that would be in our favor. In fact, chances are they would just shoot us and bury us in a sugar cane field after taking our money, and possibly raping Ronica ... maybe not even returning the children. I have seen this story written before in 3rd world countries. It either ends the way I mentioned, or it ends with two Americans being set up and convicted of a rape and murder they were not guilty of — Ronica and the children being the victims. Extortion would follow, and if not paid, we would rot in jail.

Of course, I always had a Plan B, and friends of mine (former Special Operations) were standing by, and vowed that should such an event ever transpire, they would come to save me with fire and brimstone in the form of heavy artillery. Since I had seen them in action before, nothing would convince me otherwise. My thought was, "God help the poor souls that put me in jail illegally. My boys won't hold back." It is the good side of coming out of Special Operations ... an allegiance that remains even to this day, and one I reach out to on every operation. It's an insurance policy better than State Farm.

But God was faithful, and the road to Mexico City was clear and clean. We rolled into the city seeking a pharmacy. One of the children was coughing up a storm the entire way, the other had a runny nose, both were suffering from a low immune system. This opened the door to whatever Atencingo had to offer in the way of parasites, viruses and bacteria. They both needed a bath, rest and the love of their mother, who held on to both of them with the care that only a woman who had brought them into this world could have.

I looked in my rear view mirror, Ronica was tired ... happily smiling, but tired. She was brave to have joined the journey, something I would have preferred not to happen, but that was the decision of Mark Miller and his organization. Sometimes it is necessary to reconnect the custodial parent and children sooner rather than later. We always perform a threat analysis when there is a chance that a custodial guardian will be on board. If it is too dangerous, they remain in a safe house nearby or remain in the U.S.

The pharmacy was that seedy type, tucked away in a strip mall, all lit up with that Irish green "Farmacia" illuminated sign over the door ... barely glowing — which made it even more mysterious. It was the kind of place bodybuilders frequented in Tijuana for steroids in the 70s. It was actually hard to tell if it was even open at 2 am in the morning.

"Stay in the car," I told everyone. I left the car running and stepped out, locking the door behind me. The air was gray and dusty in my lungs, and just keeping an eye out for sleeping dangers and immersive creatures was weighing on me a bit. We had been going now for some 36 hours since the operation began.

I grabbed the metal door handle of the Farmacia, and it opened ... sticking a bit at the bottom, the off-centered frame dragging the floor. On the counter in the back was Nyquil ... I grabbed a bottle. There was nothing in children's formula anywhere that I could see. I paid the cashier, didn't even wait for change, and walked out, straight back to the car.

"Here you go." I handed the Nyquil to Ronica. "I would recommend only a third of that for him because of his size."

"I've had to do this before," Ronica said.

I backed up the car, made one more stop for water and headed to one of the hotels we had placed on our list of safe houses in Mexico

City. Getting the rooms was uneventful, and why wouldn't it be? The clerk was wanting nothing but to go back to bed himself.

We settled Ronica and the children in for the night, knowing we'd all be awake in about five hours to head to the airport. You could see the calmness in the boys' faces ... they were glad to be with Mom. You could see the happiness in Ronica. She was glad to be with her boys ... something she thought would never happen.

I turned on the television in my room searching the news channels to see if there were any reports coming out of Atencingo. For the next twenty minutes I watched ... but nothing raised its head, except the report coming out of Los Angeles, California, about illegal Mexican immigrants protesting in the streets and demanding that California be returned to Mexico as a state. I saw the protestors pull down the American flag, burn it and raise a Mexican flag. My blood began to boil. I imagined myself standing in front of America wanting to rally the troops and talk some common sense into those who were just standing by allowing it to happen. From my mental archives surfaced something I had either heard or seen ... something I believed with all my heart.

Our Grandfathers watched as their friends died in WWI. Our Fathers watched as friends died in WWII and Korea. We all watched and waited as brothers and friends fought for and died in Vietnam. We watched as our friends fought and died in Desert Storm. We watched and waited while sons and friends fought in Iraq. None of them fought for or died for the Mexican Flag. Everyone fought for and died for the U.S. Flag!

In Texas, a student raised a Mexican flag on a school flagpole; another student took it down. Guess who was expelled ... the kid who

Something Bigger Than Overthrowing Small Governments

took it down. Kids in high school in California were sent home this year on Cinco de Mayo because they wore T-shirts with the American flag printed on them. Enough is enough. I had one message right then and there to every protestor on the television set and every American needed to hear it.

We've bent over backward to appease the America-haters long enough. I've always taken a stand, and others needed to as well. I'm standing up because hundreds of thousands who died fighting in wars for this country and for the U.S. Flag can't stand up ... and shame on anyone who tries to make this a racist message.

Let me make this perfectly clear. This is OUR country. And because I make this statement DOES NOT mean I'm against legal immigration. I am against illegal immigration. You are welcome here, in our country, welcome to come through legally: 1. Get a sponsor. 2. Get a place to lay your head. 3. Get a job. 4. Live by our country's rules. 5. Pay your taxes. And 6 ... Learn the language, like immigrants, our grandparents and great-grandparents have in the past. And 7 ... Please don't demand that we hand over our lifetime savings of Social Security funds to you.

If you don't want to back me for fear of offending someone, then you are part of the problem. When will we Americans stop giving away our rights? We've gone so far the other way, bent over backwards not to offend anyone. But it seems no one cares about the American citizen being offended. WAKE UP America!

I was finished with the speech in my head. I turned off the television set ready to get out of Mexico and back to the United States. I closed my eyes and the rack monster grabbed ahold of me. Before I knew it, I was in slumber land.

In the Aztec religion, there wasn't only *one* sun, but there were many sun-gods over many ages ... and this morning they all decided to wake up at the same time. It was hot ... like an iron on the back of my shirt as I stood in the parking lot facing away, waiting for Mark, Ronica and the boys to join me. I made a habit of waking up early to do a little counter surveillance on all my operations, and this day was no different, even if we weren't in a war zone. Mark carried one of the kids while Ronica carried the other.

We climbed in the car and headed to the airport car rental office, returned the vehicle (they didn't see the damage), and walked to the Aero Mexico counter. We needed to move fast ... faster than Ascencio having time to wrangle authorities down his way, who would wrangle authorities up our way, and profile us at the airport. Nothing is spookier than entering a foreign international airport under these circumstances, knowing that at any moment we could get picked up. And while we legally had every leg to stand on, just the fact that we would have to go from a Mexican jail to the U.S. Embassy and then finally back home, just made for a very long day. What I was counting on was the fact that Ascencio did not want to get caught in his own lie, especially if we were detained and Mexican authorities found out that he was the subject of a murder investigation back in the U.S. So maybe he did not make the call. But that was not a guarantee ... stupid people do stupid things, so I wasn't putting all my eggs in one basket.

Mark was very much concerned for his own safety, and I could see it on his face. "Hang back and let me and Ronica purchase tickets for ourselves. Then you do the same and keep an eye on us from a distance. If anything goes upside down, get to the Embassy." Mark nodded and fell back to a safe position observing our approach to the Aero Mexico counter.

The Aero Mexico agent was squared away in that very tight, gay-fashion of most very tight, gay airline agents ... well dressed and smiling. Actually, he was over-smiling at me with that uncomfortable stare a straight guy gets from gay guys on Santa Monica Boulevard as he passes through 'boys town' in West Hollywood. Flaming is a better word, as he asked, "Well ... hello, how can I help you?"

Respectfully, making every attempt to keep this professional, I replied, "I'd like to purchase four tickets, one for my sister and her kids, and one for myself."

"Why of course. May I see your passports?" I handed him my passport and then Ronica's.

"And the Forma Migratoria Multiple form for the children?" He asked.

I was at a loss. Everyone who enters Mexico gets a visitor's permit known as a FMM (Forma Migratoria Multiple) if the country you are from is on the no-visa-required list ... which in this case applied.

Something Bigger Than Overthrowing Small Governments

Ronica had them for the kids when she was forced to leave them with Ascencio, but that was over a year ago, and explaining that to the Aero Mexico agent was just going to complicate things. I had to think fast.

"How long have you been in Mexico?" He asked.

"About three days, we just came down to visit family and friends," I replied. He was looking at the passports. "Forma Migratoria Multiple for the children isn't happening since they got them wet from the swimming pool, disintegrated. I asked them to be careful but look at them, they're just kids. I should have never trusted them to hold on to them," I explained.

He looked at them and smiled. "By the way ... I don't know who cuts your hair, but it looks fantastic," I blurted. His attention quickly turned back to me. He lit up like a Christmas tree. I knew the path I was going down, and it wasn't going to be an easy one for me. Flirting with a butt pirate was about as far from anything I ever dreamed of doing on an operation.

"You like it?" he asked.

"It's clean ... and really nice," as I smiled ... looking him right in the eye. "Do you ever get to Los Angeles?" I asked.

He was taking the bait. "Well I certainly could be persuaded to under the right circumstance," he said.

"We should have that discussion," I replied.

I wrote a telephone number on one of those baggage tags from the counter. Then I turned and looked at Ronica. She got the act. Both boys were tired and quiet ... Ronica holding one of them in her arms, the other by her side. I stroked the head of the smallest one, and while doing looked back at the Aero Mexico agent. "These poor kids are so tired. They'll be glad to get home in their own beds. So what do we need to do about the visitor visa paper? I'm so sorry they destroyed it. You've got your hands full without having to deal with this. Oh, here's my number ... you should call if you come to Los Angeles."

He took the baggage tag with my number. "I would love to do that ... we could have a great time," he offered. Then he walked from around the back of the counter and brushed his shoulder against my arm, "Follow me."

Bazzel Baz

I wasn't sure where he was taking us, I wasn't sure if he was smarter than me and was not buying our story — perhaps leading us right to immigration authorities — but something told me to just trust God. We followed him up a set of stairs and, sure enough, there we were at Immigration and Customs. You could have heard a pin drop in my mind ... I felt double-crossed and backed into a corner, wondering how I was to come out fighting with two children and a mother — not literally fighting, but making every effort to diplomatically align myself with the authorities.

"Wait here," he said.

And so, we did for about 15 minutes as he disappeared into a room with a high-ranking Customs official. I could see the conversation unfolding between the two through the glass office window, and there was nothing in the reaction of the Customs official that led me to believe that things weren't lining up in our favor. "Father, if I am foolish for my approach to this airport exfil, forgive me, for the sake of these children, and show me a way out," I prayed.

Then the Aero Mexico agent emerged with the two FMM forms. "Here, fill these out for the children and put the dates everyone arrived here a few days ago," he said. Then he pulled me aside. "There will be a small fee," he added.

It didn't surprise me. Payoffs were common in Mexico. "How does a hundred dollars and a dinner back in L.A. sound?" I asked.

The agent smiled. I filled out the paperwork and handed it to the agent as we all walked out of the office and back down to the ticket counter. As we rounded a corner, I carefully put a hundred-dollar bill in his hand.

"Thank you," he replied.

Back at the ticket counter, the agent quickly arranged flights for us back to Los Angeles. Mark Miller waited about twenty minutes and then purchased his ticket as well, but from another agent two counters down. As we waited in the seating area, Mark could see us from a few rows over. He and I would make eye contact every now and then to reassure one another that we were still on the playing field. He knew not to join us until we had boarded the flight and wheels up. While a lot of people might think that once the flight is airborne, you're home free,

Something Bigger Than Overthrowing Small Governments

that isn't always the case. That bird can be ordered to turn around and land back at the same airport you're hoping to escape from. And if that happens, there is very little chance of you not being detained or incarcerated ... unless by some flash of the imagination you are able to squeeze yourself through that small hole in the toilet and find your way to the baggage compartment and out the door on the side of the fuselage. I think you get the message ... it's not impossible, just really tough. So don't count your blessings until you actually land back in America ... which is what happened for us.

    The flight arrived in Los Angeles. Right when I was saying my goodbyes to Mark and Ronica, my cell phone rang. Another child had been abducted, and I needed to be back in my office within the hour to take a Skype call to discuss it with authorities. Mark took over the rest of the operation, escorting Ronica and the children back to Miami, Florida, and I grabbed a taxi. The operation had been a success, and God had once again shown His amazing favor. And by the way, the number I gave the Aero Mexico agent wasn't my number at all ... for the record.

CHAPTER 12
OPERATION LILY PAD
AFTER ACTION REPORT

Subject: Lily Snyder

Date: April 2003

Introduction:
For the purposes of this report, the SFRT consisted of Bazzel Baz, George Ciganik, Kelly K. and Mr. Electric.

Summary:
Lily Snyder, age 4, vanished in June 2001 when her half-brother, Eli Snyder, now 29, allegedly took the girl for a visit to her father, Stephen Snyder, age 52, who was in the process of divorcing Lily's mother, Margot Thornton of Eugene, Idaho.

When Eli Snyder failed to return with the girl as agreed, Thornton notified police in Ketchum, Idaho, where Thornton was living at the time. The police contacted the FBI, and Thornton also sought help from the National Center for Missing and Exploited Children, which distributed Lily's photograph on the Internet, on posters and via bulk mailings.

The Blaine County, Idaho, prosecutor's office in August 2001 issued arrest warrants for Eli Snyder and his brother, Forrest Snyder, 26, of Eugene. Forrest Snyder pleaded guilty to felony interference with child custody and agreed to help locate his brother and father.

Devastated by her daughter's disappearance, Thornton, in late 2001, returned with her two other children to Eugene, where she had lived before moving to Ketchum. "Our life was pretty ripped apart," Thornton said.

Ketchum police Chief Cory Lyman said authorities finally got a break last fall when a bulk mailing in California generated a series of tips that the trio most likely had traveled to the Central American country of Costa Rica.

Something Bigger Than Overthrowing Small Governments

Police asked Thornton to identify the little girl in a photograph they received from the FBI. Before police could make their next move, an underground team of former military personnel (ARC), who help recover abducted children, rescued Lily and apprehended Eli and Stephen Snyder at the hut they shared deep in the jungle, according to *The Register-Guard newspaper in Eugene.*

Operational Personnel:

Kelly K. remained CONUS (Continental United States) as an H.Q. (Headquarters) control entity and was to arrive the AO on request by myself. She was chosen for this mission based on her past and present active experience as a private investigator and Ops Planner. Her ability as a "Snoop" is invaluable and has been the driving investigative force to connect the dots. She is the head administrator and coordinator for all technical planning and maintains the ability to perform exceptionally well. Her field experience is limited to city or towns. However, she is a fast learner and has the capacity to perform on the outer perimeter of remote environments. She is focused on the mission at hand, but her integrity would be in question by the end of this mission. She has worked as a Special Operator on the development of three other cases and the research of countless others in pursuit of case approval. My association with Kelly extends through the previous year with the SFRT and the successful location of Erik with Operation Winter Storm.

George Ciganik was chosen for this mission based on his past experience as a Recon Marine and law enforcement Officer and his willingness to participate unconditionally. My association with George extended two years previously with our introduction on the reality television program, *Combat Missions*. His credentials were impeccable.

Mr. Electric was chosen for this mission based on his past experience as a Special Forces Army soldier and his willingness to participate unconditionally. My association with Mr. Electric extended two years previously with our introduction on the reality television program, *Combat Missions*. I had never been down range with him, and this would prove itself to be a mistake by the time the operation was over.

In addition, I had never served with either gentlemen, George Ciganik or Mr. Electric, under combat conditions or my operational time in SpecOps CIA. To the best of my knowledge, neither had experience in the area of clandestine espionage operations.

Operation Overview:

Day 1: George Ciganik arrived LAX (Los Angeles International Airport) circa 1100 hours. I picked him up and moved to the staging area at 434 ½ Palos Verde, where I briefed him on the operation and asked him to review the INTEL file for the case. George immediately began his review of the file and walked to a local establishment for lunch while I headed back to CBS to complete the final day of work as a co-executive producer on the television series, *The Agency*.

One hour later I received a phone call from Mr. Electric. He was arriving circa 1245 hours and had made a decision to secure a taxi to the staging area where he would join George. I contacted George and relayed the information. George assured me that he and Mr. Electric would meet me later that evening after my duties with CBS.

At or around 2200 hours, I contacted George via cell phone and was directed to a local establishment in Hermosa Beach, California, known as Boogaloos Bar, where I met both him and Mr. Electric. Upon my arrival we greeted with normal formalities and departed the area together. Mr. Electric was intoxicated. George informed me that Mr. Electric had consumed more than his share of alcohol while at that establishment and already smelled of alcohol when they first met up.

We arrived at the staging area and began a quick brief of the op for the benefit of Mr. Electric. After noticing Mr. Electric's inability to focus on the subject matter, I made the decision to retire for the evening and pick it up the next morning. I gave an open invitation to the team to join me the following morning for a workout, and George and Mr. Electric said they would like to do so.

Something Bigger Than Overthrowing Small Governments

Day 2: I awoke at or around 0700 hours and noted that Mr. Electric had departed the staging area. He left a note stating that he had gone running. George and I went to the beach and ran the stairs at "C" street in Redondo Beach for about one hour, discussing the upcoming operation, until we noticed Mr. Electric approaching from the beach below our position. As we continued our workout, Mr. Electric had a seat and waited for us to finish. We moved to a local coffee house and had breakfast and engaged in small talk. Afterwards we went back to the staging area, showered and began the briefing. I asked Mr. Electric if he had finished reading the file, and he stated yes. I'm not sure when he had time to do so, but I had to take him at his word. Throughout both days, Mr. Electric continued from time to time to state, "I'm so glad you're my friend," something that I had heard from him since our introduction with *Combat Missions*, and something that was becoming quite superfluous even now.

    I began the briefing. "A former intelligence connection, now turned private investigator (Brett), was contacted as an agent of influence and had offered to assist or facilitate the exfiltration along the Panama Border once we located the package (the child, Lily Snyder). According to his report (see file) Costa Rican authorities did not recognize The Hague Convention and would most likely detain all parties involved in the rescue of Lily Snyder. To add insult to injury, it was widely known that some Costa Rican police were known to be corrupt. His recommendation was to transport the package via the Panama Border, where he would offer assistance through his agent in place and assist with the exfiltration, should we find ourselves between a rock and a hard place. His contact number is ███████████. In addition, another source provided the identity of an agent of influence named ███████, who is a member of the Howard Hughes family, responsible for the recent funding of a Ghana Op. Brett has given me the bona fides for a clear crossing at the border. For our team, the contact bona fides is 'Rainforest.' We need to be prepared to pay informants once we are down there. I dealt out some cash to the informants a week prior and am hoping they will remain in place ... but in that region there is never a guarantee ... we'll have to see once we get there."

I needed to have a few exfiltration options other than the Panama border. Looking at the map, we could see the coastline ... I pointed it out.

George spoke up ... "We may have to look at trying to obtain a rubber boat and move down the coast to Sixiola."

"A boat pickup would be nice, but the chances of that at this point are slim. It's unlike the old days, where you had a rubber boat standing by for the exfiltration to meet a freighter off the coast, to take you to an undisclosed location ... it's not happening for us. So as you can see, we're pretty much on our own," was my reply.

Looking at the file, our contact, Brett, did not recommend a boat extract and said a helo extract was even more difficult. Most of it would depend on the assessment once in the AO, so we needed to be thinking and looking for alternates once we were in place. We had another great asset, MOTHER, who was one of the most renowned females in the intelligence community. She was on the President's council for Terrorism and had offered her assistance as well. Thus far we had about $10,000 invested in the case, which started approximately one year prior.

We'd paid fees to agents of influence, money for research, and now tickets, travel and expenses. My good friend, Mark Burnett, had wanted to make this into a television show, or at least shoot this as an episode in order to get the CBS television network to fund the operation, but they were not willing to risk the unknown. It was a great try on his part, and we really appreciated where he was going with it. But in the end, for us it was simple ... there was a girl's life at stake, and we were going in ... with or without the financial backing of the television network or anyone else.

I looked at the team, "Here's the timeline and our support status. Basically, I'm out of cash, and what cash we do have for this op is estimated to run out at the end of two weeks, depending on what takes place once in the AO. This is going to require 24-7 work for all of us. I might ask you to help with some of the food expenses once in the AO. We'll purchase some MRE's at the surplus store to take with us to help offset the cost."

George did not hesitate to pipe up, "Don't worry about it, we'll help out."

Something Bigger Than Overthrowing Small Governments

Then Mr. Electric asked, "When do we expect to return?"

I took a beat and then said, "You can leave at the end of the two weeks. As for me, I'm not coming back until the girl comes back with me."

George stood. "We're with you."

I encouraged everyone to keep in mind that if we did this right, there would be nothing illegal about the operation. That said, however, and as mentioned, it was well known that corruption existed in the ranks of the Costa Rican law enforcement community, and they could do whatever they wanted to make it look illegal if we rubbed noses. In a nutshell, if that happened then we could consider the mission a failure. The FBI had this case for about six months, but it was slow going according to our sources in the Ketchum Police Department.

I fingered the file in my hands ... "The photo you see in the file was submitted via Lisa Brooks, the owner of an organic farm in Punta Mona, Costa Rica, that is run by her brother Steven Brooks. Her attorney, Hy Shapiro, contacted us and gave us the lead. Supposedly, Stephen and Eli Snyder, along with Lily, were there for some time. We will eventually need to visit there."

My concern was that the Feds may have already been in deep in the case, so we didn't want to bump heads. Everyone needed to keep a very low profile. If we were to run into the Feds, then we would have to assess the situation and go from there. The last thing I wanted was to botch up whatever good work some Special Agents were already involved in, so I made a back-channel call to "resources." The case was stalled. No one was in the field, and no one from the FBI would be in the field for some time regarding this case.

We moved forward with the operation. "If you read the file, then you know the situation with the leads that sent us the photo. That's all we have to go on at this stage. The kidnappers may still be there, or they may be gone."

Our cover story would be three guys traveling as tourists looking for land to establish an adventure company.

"How about *Extreme Adventures*?" George asked.

I smiled ... "Sounds good."

We would need to keep ourselves as separated from the ops gear as possible in case Customs took a look in the bags. Since most of the items were camouflage, I decided it best to just say we were planning a hunting trip afterwards. I instructed everyone to consider carrying the balaclavas (ski masks) on our persons through customs because those left in a bag along with the camouflage clothing and other tactical gear would be very incriminating. It was my experience that one piece of gear would not likely grab the attention of Customs, but it was a combination of items telling a story of intent that did.

But Mr. Electric decided not to agree. "I wouldn't say that," he insisted in a rather out-of-character manner, as if someone had tripped a switch on someone not getting enough stage time. "I wear mine in the woods all the time when I'm hunting," he continued.

Kindly I replied ... "Let's not take a chance. We're dealing with a third world country that only knows balaclava as something that terrorists wear to hide their faces. Please keep it on your person, in your underwear or hidden elsewhere."

This was the first red flag for me concerning Mr. Electric's inexperience with clandestine operations. I carefully navigated a fault line that could have forced a debate on who was right and who was wrong. "If we get detained at Customs, then we might as well call it, because chances are, they will be watching us from there on out. So let's be smart."

I turned the discussion back to the cover story. "We need to make sure we minimize all ops gear that looks paramilitary. Let's take a look at what we have."

We pulled out all of our individual tactical gear that the SFRT would be carrying. George requested to purchase a civilian-type surf shirt to wear in country and had brought his civilian hiking boots. He knew operations and was thinking ahead even before he left Pennsylvania. Mr. Electric, on the other hand, had numerous sets of military desert camouflage fatigues, military logo shirts and military combat boots. I was pretty sure I mentioned prior to his arrival that we were heading to the jungle. I was pretty sure that desert fatigues weren't going to fit in. I requested he part with his camouflage T-shirt with a surf logo on the back and duplicates of fatigues. He was not happy about this. It was becoming obvious that his undercover experience and tradecraft left much to be desired. Even his travel bag was camouflage, and I suggested that he consider purchasing another

Something Bigger Than Overthrowing Small Governments

that would not draw attention to the team. In all fairness, I had authorized the bag over the telephone a week previous when he asked if he could bring it, but I thought it was just to haul his gear from his house to the staging area. A decision was made to buy a different bag ... more civilian-like at REI for him to take in country.

I made a note to pay closer attention to all gear the team brings from home on future operations. It was entirely my fault in assuming that these new team members would know what to bring. As I learned in the Marine Corps "ASSUME" is the acronym for "ASS out of YOU and ME," which is what you get if you "assume" things ... as I did. But at the same time, and in fairness to me, when you have someone like Mr. Electric, who brags about all the operations he has been on in his career, you like to take a man at his word, which is what I did. In the future I would remedy this situation by sending specific gear lists to each member prior to arrival at the staging site. I grabbed a pen and made a note: <u>"Never assume that all team members have traveled under clandestine situations in their previous careers, and even those that have, may have been given different guidance from other commanders."</u> Moments later we drove to a local surplus store in Gardena called Major Surplus and purchased MREs, duct tape, and other essentials specifically for Mr. Electric.

During the drive from Major Surplus to REI, Mr. Electric continued his attempts to discredit anything George had to say about facts and figures, current events, small talk, etc. It was my second red flag concerning his compatibility with the team. His "one-up-man-ship" attitude began to wear on myself and George, but patience was the name of the game, and we hoped it would diffuse itself before the operation began. We arrived at REI, where we purchased some civilian-style packs.

George and I purchased civilian backpacks while Mr. Electric purchased a smaller stealth black daypack. The team returned to the staging area, inspected our gear and secured as much of it as we could in our individual packs. The remaining went in a larger green duffle bag that had been sterilized, meaning all markings of military affiliation were scrubbed with black ink or disguised with radical 8 stickers from an extreme skateboard company. George made a point that we remember to remain flexible and consider obtaining partisans (strong supporters) in the AO, which would be something to consider should we run into a dead end. It was an excellent idea, and I agreed, while there was no response from Mr. Electric at all. George was speaking the language of someone who had down-range experience.

The SFRT moved to the Rivera Mexican Grill for dinner. There wasn't much conversation at dinner, and even less after returning to the staging site where we retired for the evening. Everything that could be said in a day had been said. While the others began their rest, I sterilized the Ops File to make sure there was no incriminating intelligence and packed it in my bag. Redundancy was crucial, so I jumped on my computer and transferred an encrypted copy of the Ops File to a trusted agent in the AO via secure internet. Once sent, I closed her down for the evening.

Day 3 arrived and the SFRT departed the staging area for LAX, boarding a Continental Flight ▓ routing to Houston, Texas, and landing San Jose, Costa Rica.

George and I were prompted to run counter surveillance during the Houston layover after noticing a few government-like individuals three different times in more than two different places, always observing our actions. This started when they boarded our plane in Los Angeles and continued in Houston.

Everyone is suspect when it comes to running rescue operations, and as much as I love the FBI and others, even that organization itself can get political with the turn of one attitude or one ego within the ranks not wanting an NGO to do what the FBI should have done months earlier. I have the greatest respect for the Feds and the tremendous responsibility they have in fighting crime and keeping us all safe. But at the same time, coming from another government agency like the CIA, I understand completely the politics that surface when operations are in motion. I do not underestimate the power of either agency to shut down folks like ourselves, even at the expense of a child. It is sad, but over my years of doing this, I had seen a plethora of cases where political, financial or economic agendas by U.S.

government agencies have put Americans in foreign lands at risk, even leaving them behind to suffer the injustices of corruption. While most of those incidents were no fault of the hard-working patriotic employee within the FBI or the CIA, in my humble opinion, they were the fault of decision makers that merely wanted to advance their positions either by blatant disregard for the welfare of Americans, or by omission of responsibility and sometimes pure lies. After the two-hour layover, our suspected government-like individuals simply faded away into the business of airport foot traffic and we boarded our plane without them.

Sitting next to me on my left in the middle seat was a German female named Roze Jager. I brokered an introduction. She was traveling to Costa Rica to participate in the national conservation program. She had nothing to offer in the way of helpful intelligence since, according to her, this was her first trip to the region. I encouraged the SFRT to cozy up to a number of people (people who may have traveled there before or actually resided there) who might be able to give us the lay of the land. I myself had not been there since I was a child traveling with my mother, father and sister up from the Panama Canal Zone in 1968.

During the flight, Mr. Electric made his introduction to Jerry Lambert, Education Commissioner for the International Board of Education, International Headquarters Church of the Nazarene, who was heading to Costa Rica. The organization is located at ███████████████████████████████████████. He gave us his business card, and we were able to gather intelligence on the Costa Rican interior and another possible "partisan" that may come in handy. His POC (point of contact) was Rev. Ruben Fernandez from the Seminario Nuzareno De La Americas, ████████████████████ ██████████████████████████████████, who was affiliated with the Southern Nazarene University Organic Farm.

After the plane was airborne, I reseated myself on the aisle with George to my right, who was next to the window. I glanced over to my left and there was this giant blonde-haired guy that was built like a Viking in the row of seats across from us. I'm not sure why I didn't notice him when I first came aboard. His jaw was that Arnold Schwarzenegger square type and he wasn't really smiling ... possibly contemplating the trip. The only thing that softened up his demeanor were his board shorts, surfer logo T-shirt and sandals. But that still wasn't enough for him to be my new best friend, and in fact I had pretty much made up my mind that I would do whatever I could to avoid even making eye contact. I was on a mission and mission-focused was what I intended to be.

"Going to the head, be right back" I told George. I got up and found my way to the bathroom to relieve myself. When I returned, Mr. Electric was blocking my seat talking to George. Suddenly, we hit some air turbulence and the seat belt sign came on.

"We'll have to ask everyone to take a seat and buckle up," announced the flight attendant.

Instead of going back to his seat, Mr.Electric took mine, which, as you can imagine, yep ... left me with the only seat in the house next to the one guy I was trying to avoid. So I had no choice, and I sat. The ride was a little bumpy ... the kind of bumpy that cries out to people who have never flown before, "You're going to die!" ... a real attention getter. And then I made the fatal mistake of looking over at the big guy ... and he looked back. Right when I expected him to grunt and tell me to go find another seat ... he didn't. Instead, he smiled. Go figure. And then, he introduced himself.

"Hi, I'm Scott." He stuck out his giant paw, and I took it. He could have crushed every metacarpal in my hand, but he didn't. There was something gentle in his spirit. "Where you headin'?" he asked.

I really didn't think I was going to have to use any cover for action on this trip, but I was wrong. "Looking for some good surf," I told him.

He smiled again. "How cool is that. You should come down our way to Puente Viejo. I'm a Pastor from San Clemente, and I'm going down that way to see if God wants me to move my family down here to do missions."

I was really surprised now. The Viking was a pastor?

"Heading down to stay with Pastor Chris, a twenty-year heroin-addict-turned-preacher in Puente Viejo, who has been doing some amazing work for the locals. He knows everyone and has a good network of people across the country to spread the gospel," Scott said.

A light went on in my head ... this would make an incredible resource ... a network of intelligence already in place, knowing who came and went in the region, the partisans George had suggested. But it was just too risky at this stage of the game to expose our real reason for being down there, and so I decided to not even carry on the conversation any longer. We would just have to get in the bush and start looking around ourselves. Besides, Puente Viejo wasn't even an area I was interested in, and so far all the intelligence we did have pointed to San Jose as the place of discovery.

I didn't want to engage in too lengthy of a conversation just in case he started probing more. But it became almost impossible, as he held his stare and smiled, inviting more dialogue in a way that giants tell smaller people, "humor me or else." And so, I steered the conversation towards some of my surfing experiences at The Cove off of Palos Verdes, and he came on board with some of his in San Clemente as well as some information on his life as a graphic designer for SWB Graphix Media Solutions. He mentioned that Terry Martin, the well-known surfboard shaper, was a dear friend as well as a few other famous makers and riders. So the two hours I spent with him seemed to speed by discussing some of Terry's designs. (Terry Martin, a wonderful lover of God would be called home on May 12, 2012, losing a battle with melanoma cancer. I would count myself blessed to have met him at a Bible study in San Clemente before that time.)

I ended my meeting with Scott, "Well thanks so much. Not sure what coast we'll be on ... probably not the Caribbean side where you're heading."

"Well, let me pray for you," Scott said. And so, he did ... a strong, short prayer. Then I shook his giant paw again and took my now-empty seat next to George.

I paid close attention to my team and how they maintained their cover status, and it seemed to be working well ... even when Roze Jager reintroduced herself. I sat for a few moments with her to determine if she had anything new to offer as far as the intelligence we needed on the ground in Costa Rica, but she had nothing to offer other than her desire to get to know me. Upon landing, the team cleared customs with no problem. Security was minimal. Our MRE container, a cardboard box taped together with duct tape, was damaged to the point that rations were easily accessible by hand. George and I looked at one another knowing that any future operations would require a sturdier container for travel. I noticed that the lock on the duffle bag that contained some of our ops gear and jungle fatigues had been removed and closed back up with a zip tie, a clear sign that U.S. Customs or airline security had searched the bag. This gave me reason to consider that our operation may have already been compromised. My immediate concern was that authorities in San Jose might have been notified, and the team might come under surveillance.

I informed the team, and everyone knew to be on full alert. Mr. Electric observed a camera directly behind me after we cleared customs, so keeping the ops file on my person under my shirt was a good move. It wasn't classified, but it did have pictures of the suspects, a warrant for arrest, etc. — all the things that would have gotten us stopped and questioned if someone in Customs could read English. We casually meandered from the airport like the laid-back tourists we claimed to be and took a Rental Bus shuttle to the Advantage Rental Car location for rental car pickup. After taxes and hidden governmental insurance cost, the vehicle rental price for approximately two weeks was double the estimate we had received via internet the previous week.

The total cost was around $800.00 U.S. The credit card was used for the rental of a not-so-new and very used four-wheel drive Rav4. Our Team departed the rental car location and drove downtown San Jose to the Best Western, where reservations had been made for us by Kelly K. back at the Ops Center. The hotel was located in a very seedy part of town with a Rastafarian nightclub across the street and plenty of trouble dressed in local attire, with clearly nothing else to do except rob tourists.

George and Mr. Electric secured the room for the evening while I parked the car in the gated parking lot behind the hotel. It was a single room with two double beds, air conditioning and shower — everything one could hope for on the first day in country, minus the level of comfort I was hoping to feel about Mr. Electric. There was another red flag that could not go unnoticed ... his questionable motivation for participating and lack of focus for the mission. Mr. Electric wanted to go out and grab some beers, see the town and party. Knowing we had an early start the next day, why would anyone under the circumstances want to do that? Can you imagine being in a bar in a seedy part of San

Something Bigger Than Overthrowing Small Governments

Jose with the possibility of being robbed or knifed or kidnapped? That would not only leave us one man down but cause us to have to alter the mission now to recover someone from a hospital, jail or worse ... the morgue. Every operator understands that the team is contained when in the field. Work is work, and anyone who doesn't understand that makes me once again wonder just how much down-range time they really have had. And that was exactly what I was thinking, as was George.

After George and I declined his offer to accompany him on his party quest for the third time, he changed his mind and stayed with the team for the evening ... silently sulking in an attitude, giving no response when I said goodnight to everyone. "Goodnight George. Goodnight Mr. Electric." George responded in kind ... Mr. Electric said nothing.

Day 4 arrived and the SFRT ate breakfast, packed the vehicle, and snapped a photo of ourselves in the parking lot before George and I took a look across the street in a local market for some type of indigenous shirt for our cover status. We had no success, and the SFRT departed to locate water and cans of Sterno at a local Shopping Mall. Items of interest were eventually obtained in a local market and store. At this stage, I noted that Mr. Electric was anything but interested in the operation with no sense of urgency. He continued to suggest sightseeing San Jose, stopping at a gun shop, grabbing lunch and viewing the museum, etc. His comments and discussions did not reflect that of the operations officer he led me to believe he was. His bragging of his time in Haiti during the uprising did not add up, particularly since I had close friends in the CIA that directly participated in the escape of President Aristide, a task Mr. Electric took credit for.

Now, I could have been wrong since I was not there, and perhaps he in fact did singlehandedly bring Aristide to safety. But as I hear it, there was more to the story. Nevertheless, I found myself now in country with him and with no choice but to make the best of it, seeing how I needed every man I could get at this point in the operation. So I brushed it all off as ego. But it was not long before his attitude raised its ugly head again. Mr. Electric continued to counter statements

George would make, as if he was pushing for conflict. Even though I was writing it off as playful banter between the two, the angry undertones of Mr. Electric made it not so playful, especially when we started discussing the Masonic Organization. Mr. Electric mentioned that he might have some Masonic brothers in the region that could step up to the plate and help if we needed them. But in the same sentence, he told us that it was no guarantee. The road from San Jose to Limon was approximately a three-hour drive crowded with logging trucks, rainforest, rain, fog and, by now, all-out arguments between George and Mr. Electric. Mr. Electric just would not let things rest. No matter what George said, Mr. Electric countered it.

It was bizarre in my opinion. I simply sat silent, listening and figuring out just where in the operation I could count on Mr. Electric to do what I expected of him. I think the funniest statement made, which actually wasn't funny, was when we started talking about what type of vehicle would be nice to have in Costa Rica.

George said, "I like the Defender that Land Rover makes."

Mr. Electric responded with, "They don't make that vehicle any longer."

Since George had just purchased a Defender, he had the upper hand. But wouldn't you know it, Mr. Electric still insisted that George's Defender was not a Defender because Land Rover did not make them anymore. I was beginning to think Mr. Electric was delusional. I actually started laughing when I looked to the passenger seat to see the spasm of pain blanketing George's face ... the contorted snarl, a sign that George was doing everything he could to contain his anger. He reminded me of a man constipated by stupidity, hoping to relieve himself, but having nowhere to defecate. Only his eyes moved my way to capture the alignment in my laughter, for if he had turned his head, his nose would have met that of Mr. Electric, who was leaning between the two front seats in an effort to make his point.

When we arrived in Limon, Mr. Electric had given it a rest, and we made an attempt to purchase a map of the region. It was the largest city on Costa Rica's Caribbean coast, the birthplace of United Fruit Company and the capital of Limon Province. The city had not aged well ... the lack of political and financial support from the government was mostly to blame. We exited the vehicle with a caution instinctively

Something Bigger Than Overthrowing Small Governments

engrained by our wartime experience, eyeing dilapidated buildings and overgrown parks and sidewalks choked with street vendors. Until the 1850s, the most frequent visitors to Limon were pirates who used the area's natural deep-water bays as hideouts. And that history was well known to many people seeking to do exactly that ... hide out.

It felt like we were heading in the right direction. In fact, almost every local I spotted had the look of a person who was hiding out. Seriously, shifty eyed people seeped out of nowhere checking out the newcomers ... us of course. No one had to remind us that organized crime was a problem ... it smelled that way. We knew from our research that Limon had as many homicides annually as San José — even though San José had five times the population. Despite its shortcomings, it was where we needed to be in order to find a government building that would provide us information on a plot of land where we suspected the kidnappers might be.

After failed attempts downtown to locate the proper government office, I made a decision to investigate the local Department of Administration. Mr. Electric, for whatever reason, and as was the rule rather than the exception, countered the decision. I wasn't about to argue with him, so I ignored him and checked it out anyway. At this stage of the game, all people, all locations are possibilities, and no stone could go unturned. Mr. Electric's lack of investigative skills, lack of interest and understanding or apprehension to follow any chain of command was just one more red flag for me.

It wasn't long before we found ourselves on the road again and soon entering the town of Puente Viejo. The beaches and copious vegetation stood out prominently, as did the crippling poverty in this area. The town itself was a larger exterior version of the interior of the fictional bar located in the pirate city of Mos Eisley on the planet Tatooine in the movie Star Wars.

> It was the haunt of freight pilots and other dangerous characters of various alien races and sometimes a band of musicians named Figrin D'an and the Modal Nodes. The establishment was extremely rough in nature, and the clientele and the management give incidents of deadly violence no more than a moment's attention." [23]

Rastafarians, Ticos (Costa Ricans), Jamaicans, European Caucasians, Americans, and others fit the mold ... "dangerous characters of various alien races" here in Puenta Viejo. I would later discover in the wee hours of the morning, after searching all day for clues, a band of weed-smoking musicians that looked just like Figrin D'an and the Modal Nodes. Drug trafficking was the elephant in the room, lurking at the edges of every conversation.

We parked the car, and my guidance to the SFRT was to maintain a low profile and take a look around to assess the situation before we decided where to lodge. Mr. Electric, George and I spread out and ran a reconnaissance of the town. After about one hour, Mr. Electric came strolling down the main street with a Caucasian American in his sixties tagging along close behind. His name ... Captain Zero. The snagged-tooth drug dealer came with a story about a book that was written about his smuggling days in the Caribbean. His mode of transportation was a bicycle, and he smelled of flimflam nostalgia. He insisted that he could give us a great deal on a cedar-lined room with wonderful accommodations for thirty dollars per day. Thinking he may be a source of information, but more so trying not to raise our profile with initial rudeness, we took him up on his offer. The room was anything but cedar. Try pine. Try termite-infested pine. No sooner had we made our decision to stay ... he hit us up for a weed purchase. We declined with the diplomacy of most individuals with a story of how they gave it up years ago for better health, and he walked away a bit disappointed.

We settled in with our gear and made plans to get some chow and extend our recon of the town. George showed a brilliant display of OpSec (operational security) when he used the "paper door" technique for a breech indicator on our way out. We had lunch at a local cafe and used the location as an observation point. After lunch, the SFRT dispersed throughout the town again, and was directed to run mobile surveillance, while checking the internet center for possible communications back to Kelly. The Team observed all personnel entering and leaving the town and looked for any clue that might bring us closer to accomplishing the mission.

That evening Mr. Electric wanted to go back to the cafe where we had eaten lunch. When I directed the team to a different cafe, he copped an attitude. It was now becoming more apparent that Mr. Electric did not understand the need to maintain good OpSec by varying our routes and surveillance locations. For Mr. Electric, it was about the food. For George and me, it was about lowering our profile and having a different surveillance point to increase our advantage, pick up new information and recon the site.

Add together the stress of the mission, the time clock, and now a concern that I may be schooling a new recruit named Mr. Electric, and my bowl was slowly filling to the brim. By now I had considered the possibility that I might have to use him for whatever he is good for and redirect whatever his motivation was, for the sake of the mission. Quickly accessing his weaknesses and strengths, I started a plan. I pulled George aside and mentioned my concern about Mr. Electric's consumption of alcohol back in U.S. George did not think it would be a problem. I agreed based on his instincts, but still had some reservations.

Day 5 came early for the SFRT as we packed our gear for the initial recon of Manzanilla, which would determine if we needed to further our jungle hike to Punta Mona. George and I both carried 45 lb. packs with enough gear to sustain us if we got a lead and needed to start tracking the kidnappers deeper in the jungle. Mr. Electric, on the other hand, carried a 15 lb. pack with nothing sustainable beyond one day's supply. I guess he was skilled in the art of eating dirt to survive. We drove to Manzanilla, reconnoitered the area, collected data, investigated the local school, checked routes to Punta Mona, and the decision was made for us ... it would be the hike to Punta Mona. The safest way in would be an unsuspecting route through triple canopy jungle. It was difficult to determine exactly how long it would take us to make the destination, so we returned to Puente Viejo to pick up even more gear for the anticipated hike. A quick turnaround and we found ourselves right back at Manzanilla where we parked the vehicle in an open garage of a local house. The owner, an older farmer named Juan, was not only friendly, but was a good source of Intel regarding the routes to take, as was a female American Scientist we met, who was studying Dolphin migration in the region.

The jungle path followed the coastline for the most part, but eventually diverted deeper into the foliage. About one and a half hours into the trip, along muddy paths, hills, and open farmland, we made contact with an American couple who had just returned from Punta Mona. Their description of Steven Brooks and the Puente Mona Organic Farm setting led us to anticipate a community where the use of marijuana and other drugs might be commonplace. The couple's description of "getting naked and smoking weed" after the departure of a collegiate eco studies forum was not surprising. Thirty minutes later we were entering Puente Mona. A quick introduction to four males, one being Steven Brooks, the founder, and approximately seven females was followed by an invitation to join them for lunch.

Steven Brooks on the right

The SFRT had their own provisions and declined but was able to strike up conversations with many of the people from that point on and throughout the next hours. We offered to unload wood from an incoming boat in order to strengthen our cover story, which did in fact pay off as various individuals warmed up and offered information on the surrounding area. George and I took the opportunity to review the guest log to see when Snyder had last been at this location. I assumed Mr. Electric was also using his time to look for clues. However, I was disappointed to discover he was lying on the beach getting a suntan. George and I continued to search the area looking for signs of Snyder, but no clues were to be found. Eventually, after discussing with George, we felt it would be necessary to break cover with Steven Brooks.

Something Bigger Than Overthrowing Small Governments

    The hours were passing and travel back through the jungle at night was becoming a concern. Finally, Steven Brooks invited us to come along on a tour of the organic farm he was cultivating, which lasted about one hour. Brooks had a number of loyal farm workers, and he was fluent in the Spanish language. It was during this period that George was able to grab the attention of Brooks' girlfriend, who was trailing along, so I could speak to Brooks in private. I glanced at George, who eyed his allegiance to my decision to break cover ... both knowing we had no choice.

    I managed to distance Brooks and me from the group. I explained to him that his attorney had given us information via his sister on the case we were working. I asked if he had seen Snyder. He told me that he had not seen them for about eight months and that he did in fact know that they had kidnapped the girl but was told they did so because the mother was terrible. He also said the last time he saw them that she was healthy. Brooks had a difficult time believing that Snyder was doing anything wrong because in his words, "They fed Lily organic foods so they must care about her." When we arrived back at the Puente Mona facility, I showed Brooks the warrants for the arrest of Snyder, the Missing Child paperwork and the photo that his sister had forwarded us. He said his sister had not told him about any of this, and he needed to make some calls. He called his parents and his attorney but never actually told me that he would be willing to help. I could see fear blanket his face, his character morphing into a fog of reluctance. He hung up the phone. Who knows what was said on the other end that scrambled his brain waves from that of a normal conversationalist to a person who appeared to be suffering from ADD. And while I almost gave him the benefit of the doubt initially, I realized it wasn't ADD at all ... he role-played being stoned, and I wasn't buying it.

    I resorted to hard tactics, telling him that the FBI had been on this case since January of 2003 and that there was a good chance that they would be swarming his farm in the future. Hoping the thought of Federal involvement into his little David Koresh sanctum might push a button, I also told him that all we wanted to do was get eyes on the girl to send a message back to her mom that she was okay. Then ... he slipped. He stated, "She's okay, at least that much I can tell you." Now we knew that there was a strong possibility that Lily was still somewhere in the region.

Keeping him focused was a challenge in itself, and we eventually had to depart the area unsure if he would blow the whistle and gather those "dangerous characters of various alien races" back in Puenta Viejo. My gut feeling was that he knew something and wasn't going to disclose it.

A young married couple asked if they could tag along with the SFRT as it trekked through the jungle back to Manzanilla. We managed to continue to move under the cover of darkness until we reached our vehicle. We brokered a friendly conversation with the young married couple accompanying us and commended them for their ability to hang with us. I offered up a traditional congratulatory rhyme from the paramilitary ranks in an attempt to solidify the new friendship with hopes of recruiting them in the future if needed. "Here's to us, not many like us, in fact very few, and most of them are dead." Looking back, it made little to no sense to them and was not the best choice of words for the circumstances. They did not understand military jargon or understand the dangers they might have found themselves in had we not escorted them out of the jungle.

On the drive back to Puente Viejo we passed someone in a truck that fit the description of Eli Snyder. Because we had two unwitting people with us (the young married couple), I had to play up our cover story by pretending that the vehicle which just passed appeared to be driven by an old friend we were looking for. I did a U-turn and followed the vehicle and the individual to a house where we discovered it was not Eli Snyder. I believe our cover story remained intact and that our unwitting couple had no reason to suspect anything other than what we presented. We dropped the couple off at Rocking J's Camp Site and returned to our room, packed gear and moved to a different hotel named Grant's.

Changing locations, eating at different restaurants and staying under the radar was the best we could do in this small town. Mr. Electric did not have a good grasp of operational security or tradecraft and became irritated each time we did not go back to a restaurant or facility we had already frequented. Grant's offered good cover and concealment with a gated front, bar on top and secure parking lot, much

Something Bigger Than Overthrowing Small Governments

needed for surveillance towards the town entrance. It was an ideal observation point.

Now that we had broken cover with Steven Brooks, I felt a sense of urgency in everything we needed to do. It would only be a matter of time before the entire town knew who we were and anyone aiding Snyder could reach out and warn them. So remember that pastor on the flight that I was trying to avoid? Well guess where he landed? Yep, right in the same town we were investigating. Go figure. I took a moment to pray about meeting up with him and then a small still voice said, "Go meet him."

Mr. Electric accompanied me to a location where I broke cover with Pastor Scott Bailey and requested the assistance of him and his missionaries. He agreed to assist and offered to broker an introduction with the local Pastor, who had been a resident of the area for 20 years. That would take place the next day along the shoreline after the local Pastor finished surfing. Meanwhile, George was maintaining communications via internet with Kelly for updates. Mr. Electric and I rejoined George and went to an Italian restaurant, which again offered excellent visibility to the main street. We debriefed at the table and then retired for the evening.

On **Day 6** I was comfortable with the decision that was made to break cover with Pastor Scott Bailey and the missionaries in order to recruit more agents of influence as well as the local Pastor for the Baptist Church in Puente Viejo. Pastor Chris offered to distribute photos of Lily and her abductors to trusted members of his congregation in the region. Pastor Bailey offered prayer and any support we asked. Mr. Electric was given instructions to monitor events in Puente Viejo by using a bicycle ... a sort of roving surveillance. George and I took the vehicle and performed a recon on every single side road along the coast in the AO that we could map out as well as schools and local communities and housing on banana plantations. At the largest elementary school in the area, the preschool section was on holiday for two weeks. Although we were disappointed that we could not have a visual on the children, we remembered that the Intel report was specific about Snyder not letting Lily attend public schools, so the chances of her gaining a public education were slim to begin with, but every avenue had to be approached.

We returned that evening and debriefed. Mr. Electric had found no leads to advance the case. George and I had found no leads to advance the case but were ruling out specific locations. It was becoming obvious that our abductors may be lodged deeper in the jungle. We monitored the stores and internet cafes in the area. George relayed via Kelly back in the U.S. the request to have Hy Shapiro, Brooks' attorney, contact Steven Brooks and force the issue, advising him to tell us what he knew. Instead of doing what we requested, Kelly relayed info back saying that she would be arriving San Jose the following day because she believed she could be of more use to us in country. She ignored orders to remain in the U.S. and was reminded that she was not qualified to be in the field. My time to argue the point was limited as she chose to disobey my orders ... insisting that she was flying to San Jose, telling me she would obtain transportation and join the SFRT in Puente Viejo. Before I could discuss the issue further, she hung up the phone.

The reality of my bad choices in personnel was playing itself out and I prayed that if God would just keep His hand on things, I would make sure I was far more discreet the next time I choose operational personnel for any mission. And as tempting as it was to allow my mind to invent future outcomes because of my choice of personnel in this operation ... I did not. I put it aside, focused on the mission at hand and resigned myself to the fact that I would have to handle things step by step and believe that God would protect me.

That evening Mr. Electric attended a Bible study with me at the local Baptist church where our new agent, Pastor Chris, worked. During the Bible study, Mr. Electric frequently upstaged the local congregation with his legalistic knowledge of the Holy Scriptures instead of maintaining a low profile and giving way as any humble guest should. It was to such a degree, that the congregation stopped participating in the study because they knew he was going to speak up with the answer. He was "mister know-it-all," who knew nothing. Things became very uncomfortable and I eventually interjected to

Something Bigger Than Overthrowing Small Governments

change the deteriorating atmosphere by asking members of the congregation for their opinion on scripture to get them back in the ball game. Mr. Electric's unstoppable effort to seek attention and needing to be recognized even at the detriment of the mission was just one more red flag. Heck, by now I had enough red flags to set up my own Macy's Thanksgiving Day Parade. We returned from the church and dined at a different eatery called something like Natural Foods, a place where older crowds frequented, in hopes that Stephen Snyder might show up there. One more check on the internet disclosed Kelly's arrival to our location the following day, and I was not happy about this. We departed the eatery with no clues and retired for the evening.

Day 7 brought the sound of jungle birds and the smell of wood burning in the homes of the locals. Mr. Electric was instructed to continue his bicycle surveillance in and around the town and other communities in the AO and to be prepared to intercept Kelly during her arrival. George and I recruited the assistant pastor of the local Baptist Church, Pastor Ronnie, who accompanied us to regions outside the AO or regions that had not been within the intelligence sector. He was an excellent source of information and assistance, talking with trusted members of his congregation and showing the pictures of Lily to store owners, etc. We returned by noon and decided to recon additional roads further to the north but realized we would be needing more time to recruit additional agents.

George and I decided to grab some lunch at a local cafe in Puenta Viejo. The waitress was a lean '40s granola girl named Jerrilyn, who sat down as the locals do even if they are the hired help and started sharing her history. Her 90 seconds of fame revolved around her crew participation on a television show called *Survivor*. My previous working relationship with the creator and Executive Producer, Mark Burnett, could not have been more weirdly and divinely arranged since, wouldn't you know it, Mark and I were good friends. I mean, go figure ... we are 3,000 miles from Los Angeles, looking for a needle in a haystack, praying for a local asset that could be trusted, and Mark becomes the glue between Jerrilyn and me that, if played correctly, would allow me to recruit her.

So we decided that we would break cover with her, but not before thinking through everything I had learned in my career as a Case Officer when it came to obligating her. I needed an incentive. I would not be able to have her sign a secrecy agreement, as was done so often with the cloak and dagger protocols, but I could do something similar. Thinking outside the box and going for the same results, I made a phone call to Hollywood and got the ball rolling to secure a position for her as a worker on the next *Survivor* Television Series in her neighboring country of Panama.

I called Mark and explained my situation and he agreed to speak with her. Mark had always offered to support good causes in any way he could, never shying away from the fact that children needed saving and that ARC was down range doing exactly that. After his talk with Jerrilyn, he connected her with Tom Shelly, Producer, who was able to make the first payment for her services. While nothing was promised on Shelly's end, they did ask her to send her resume for consideration. She hung up the phone a happy camper and gave me a hug. The call proved to be a success, as she agreed to assist in any way she could ... and keep our cover intact. I really was hoping that it would work out for her, because she was sincere in her intentions, and I believe that all good people deserve to have good things happen for them.

George and I resumed our investigative efforts and performed a recon in the area of Gandoca where a sea turtle reserve was established. We discovered that from Gandoca, just south of Puente Mona, you could actually see the Steven Brooks organic farm, and that Gandoca could be reached by foot from his facility. We flashed the photo of Lily to some locals, and one native recognized Stephen Snyder. He had seen him on Puente Mona about two months ago. He was positive that he had seen Stephen and Lily there. We also discovered that the road to the Panamanian border branched off to Gandoca, giving us another access from a different angle to Puente Mona. We returned that day to Puente Viejo to receive a lead from Jerrilyn, which took us to the home of David and Julie, two young Americans, perhaps in their late twenties, with a number of small children.

Something Bigger Than Overthrowing Small Governments

    The road to their jungle house was off the beaten path, not far from the small town, but not so close as to attract unwanted attention. The triple-canopy jungle enclosing the skinny, one-track lane was our way in. A variety of jungle plants served as guardians, some were more permanent than others, but all sharing the element of refuge ... an out-of-the-way place just 300 yards ahead, where David and Julie could eat, sleep, read a good book, and avoid taxes from the IRS while they raised their children.

    We slowly pulled up to the living quarters and knocked on their door. I introduced George, talked about our mission and showed them the photo of Lily and Snyder. We had hoped they might have some information to lead us in the right direction, but they said that they did not recognize anyone in the photograph. They said they would keep an eye out. I asked if I could pray for them and the welfare of their children because we had heard from Jerrilyn that they were struggling a bit. They welcomed the prayer, and after I finished, George and I climbed in the car and started backing out. I say backing out because there wasn't any room to really turn the car around on the property ... so we proceeded slowly and cautiously.

    As we reached the end where the jungle road meets the beaten path, the left rear tire found a rut to snuggle into. I swear there wasn't a rut there before, or maybe there was, and we just barely missed it when we entered earlier. Nevertheless, we were stuck. I put the car in drive and tried moving forward to get out. Then I put it in reverse and tried moving it backward to get out. Then forward, then backward, then forward, then backward. How difficult could this be? It wasn't a ditch. It was just a silly little mud hole of a rut with just the right soil content to make it slippery as ice.

    Within moments of our gallant efforts to dislodge the car, David, from the house, approached the vehicle on his bicycle. He was exhausted and in a bit of a panic. "I'm so glad I caught you guys. I know where they are, but we were afraid to say anything because they led us to believe there would be retribution if we told anyone about their location."

    We assured him that we would apprehend them and make sure they were extradited before anything could happen to his family. He asked if we wanted to follow him back to the house. And then, like magic, the car just drove out of the hole. George gave me the strangest look. "That was weird," he mumbled.

We reentered their home and reviewed all legal paperwork, warrants, etc. that we had on hand. I asked David to draw out a map of the location where Lily was being held and advised them to keep a very low profile until the operation was over. According to David, the Snyder's were holding Lily on a jungle farm he owned. He had seen them two days previous. Eli Snyder often traveled down the jungle path to the beach wearing a pair of long pants and carrying an umbrella. He was often sent by his father to get food stocks from town. The location was about fifteen minutes off the beaten path and from the nearest road.

David drew a map for us, and we finalized all the points of attack. He also stated that he had killed a six-foot bushmaster on his property recently, and that snakes might be a problem. Although we knew we would probably make our move on Snyder that very evening, we told David that it probably wouldn't be for another day and that we would contact them again in the morning. I just needed to have the upper hand in case this was a setup by David and his wife, or in case they changed their minds and warned the Snyders.

We drove to the road that led near the target site and stopped the car so we could do a quick recon of the area. Dogs from neighboring houses were spotted as a potential problem, but our choices were limited. Given the short distance to thick jungle, it was determined that we could infiltrate quickly enough in the early hours to avoid the dogs or at least limit their awareness. They would bark, but only for a limited time until we had disappeared into the jungle. After the recon, we drove back just outside of town and decided to recruit Charlie, the owner of the local hotel where Pastor Scott Bailey was staying. Scott had assured us earlier that Charlie might be receptive to our recruitment, and as it would turn out, he was.

We told him of the $50,000 bond and pointed out he would have to split it with David and Julie if we were able to apprehend the Snyders. He made arrangements for us to use a room in the back of the facility as a detention center for the Snyders and agreed to keep them there until we were able to cross the Panama border with Lily and her mother, who would be arriving. In hindsight, there was a discrepancy on the amount of the bond from the Intel reports received. I could not

Something Bigger Than Overthrowing Small Governments

figure out whether it was $50,000 or $500,000. According to George, drawing from his years as a law enforcement officer, it was probably was $50,000.

We returned to Grant's Hotel where Mr. Electric and Jerrilyn were drinking at the bar. When we told Mr. Electric that we had located Lily his response was, "That's nice, oh by the way, Kelly's upstairs. You guys want to join us for a beer?" It was as if the good news went right over his head. I asked him to let Kelly know we were here and that we had to shift into "Go" mode and begin packing ops gear for the takedown. It was like pulling teeth to get Mr. Electric out of the bar, and once we did, he did not return promptly, and his sense of urgency was nowhere to be found. I left my room and went back to the bar to find him still conversing with Jerrilyn. I returned to my room to continue packing and assigned Kelly with "Mr. Electric retrieval duty." After repeated attempts by Kelly to carry out those orders, he finally joined us. Kelly later told me that he had been drinking throughout the day and attempting to entice her and Jerrilyn to have some more beers. He stated that, "George and Baz would never know because they would brush their teeth to cover up the scent." Drinking on the job was something I did not tolerate. Everything about what was unfolding with Mr. Electric at the bar was another red flag waving in the winds of an alcoholism that would soon turn into a hurricane of destruction.

We secured the room to begin the brief. On more than one occasion I had to instruct Mr. Electric to lower his voice so that the people outside the room would not be alerted to our operation. I presented the 5 Paragraph Order, reviewed the map and discussed the plan of operation. Rehearsal would launch at 0300, which gave us at that time a six-hour window. The plan would be to approach the target under the cover of darkness, recon and return to a rally point and possibly raid the next evening. That would be the best-case scenario. But with even that said, flexibility was primary, and we needed to be ready to raid before sunrise if necessary.

I informed the SFRT that we had no Intel on whether the Snyders were armed or not, and that each person should proceed with caution and understand that the situation could be life or death. I also instructed them to maintain a self-defense posture, understanding that if it came down to it, they were to act smartly. "We have one mission and that is to bring the girl home."

Kelly had received a coded message from Brett ["If I don't hear from you, I'm going fishing"] that the border was clear, and that his people were in place. Margo Thornton, Lily's mother, had been instructed to fly down and would be arriving the next day. Charlie had been instructed to contact the U.S. Embassy and the FBI at the appropriate time. We finished separating our ops gear from civilian gear in preparation for the raid.

The SFRT dined at the Italian Restaurant and returned to the room for some rest after packing the vehicle. At 0300 hours, the SFRT departed Grant's Hotel. Money and the key were left in the room to cover expenses. Staging took place at a safe house where Jerrilyn was house-sitting, not far from the target location. The SFRT changed into jungle gear and departed the safe house. The road to the target area was between Amador Resort and a local restaurant and ended about 500 yards up against the jungle, adjacent to a few houses. We backed the vehicle in, and I instructed Kelly to standby as the driver. Her cover for action would be that of a girl waiting to pick up some backpacking friends who are leaving the jungle trail at this location. The night darkness was as black as black can be. The three-man SFRT exited the vehicle and attempted to locate the trail that had been designated on the map. I chose to use a red lens flashlight, pointing it towards the jungle ground in an attempt to locate the start of the trail. It wasn't my first choice for an operationally secure start, but it got us going. I turned off the light and the SFRT filtered into the darkness.

I was pretty sure our movement at 0330 hours would draw little attention especially since the chances of civilian personnel being in the jungle at that time in the morning were slim. But we were not as lucky as I thought. We lost the trail in the dark and had to return to the waiting vehicle. Inside the vehicle, for whatever reason, Kelly turned on her lighter, exposing all four members. It would have been a slightly different story if the SFRT were on foot in the jungle because we would have a place to run and hide ... but there we were trapped inside a car with no place to run. Sure, we could have driven away, but then the staging area would have been burned. This was the stuff that bad movies are made from. This was the kind of thing that concerned me,

Something Bigger Than Overthrowing Small Governments

the reason I did not want an inexperienced person attached to the team, and the very reason I ordered her to stay put in the U.S in the first place. She had no training in jungle warfare, and obviously no light discipline.

By the grace of God, it did not compromise the mission. On any other given day — or should I say night — it would be a different story. Rehearsals are paramount in all operations, and failure to do so, in this case because of speed of movement, brought about tiny mistakes that could, under more stringent conditions, cost us the operation. I was mentally kicking myself over and over without showing it to the SFRT. If not for the patience of God, I would have sent Kelly and Mr. Electric home right then and there. And the little voice inside kept telling me to do exactly that, and to just trust God to carry us through with George and me.

My mind settled on the biblical account of a great warrior named Gideon. When God cut Gideon's forces down to 300 men, I'm sure there was a moment when Gideon said to himself, "This is what bad movies are made from ... can I win this war with so few men, especially since we are already outnumbered?" I knew I needed to listen to that little voice, but I didn't. I continued to tolerate both of them, looking for a bigger excuse to make my decision ... instead of God's decision that I wasn't paying attention to.

I remember thinking back when my mother told me, "When you hear God clearly, and you fail to act, He loves you so much, He'll act for you," and I knew it would only be a matter of time before God Himself would step in and cut down my forces, but at what junction in the operation I couldn't predict. The SFRT waited until early morning light and filtered back into the jungle along the trail towards the objective. Howler monkeys shouting to one another provided a good distraction for any noise we might accidentally make, but there was also some concern of waking the abductors, should they be at the objective.

The trail was clear, with the initial rally point being designated at the log bridge crossing the stream. We proceeded to high ground for the leader's recon overlooking a two-story jungle farmhouse with open sides and a tin roof. Just above our position and to the south was another building with closed sides. We observed no movement but noted clothing and mosquito netting over two beds in the upstairs of the structure. Mr. Electric's patrolling discipline was questionable. While George and I maintained a low profile, Mr. Electric stood up, stepped on sticks and did not talk at a whisper. You would have thought that the looks I gave him would be enough for him to get his act together, but he was oblivious. The threat of his incompetence and me having to keep him in line loomed over my shoulder like a clumsy oaf poised to let the world know we were there.

The SFRT moved down the trail and to the frontal approach of the structure with directions to observe, move on my signal, make a silent entry and to have eyes on the child before apprehending the abductors. Balaclavas were pulled down and the team moved in. A silent entry was necessary to ensure our ability to head back to the leader's recon position for a look at the other structure where the abductors might be hiding if they were not in the first structure. As the SFRT approached the structure, George and I were forced to low crawl. Mr. Electric was given instructions to move up closer but to wait for my signal before advancing on the hut, so our attack would be coordinated. Before George and I could even move close enough to have eyes on the girl, Mr. Electric did not wait for my signal and stormed the structure, yelling, "I got him, I got him." My nightmare had come true. The clumsy oaf had announced our arrival.

George and I sprinted up the stairs to the second floor and apprehended Eli Snyder, who was awakened by all the yelling and was preparing to make his escape. Lily was found sleeping in the same mosquito-net-covered bed with Eli Snyder, with just her night shirt and nothing else. Eli was fully clothed.

Something Bigger Than Overthrowing Small Governments

George picked Lily up, turned her away from me, as I grabbed Eli, and said to her, "Don't be afraid, your mother sent us to get you and bring you home."

As she held on to him, she looked him right in the eyes and replied, "I'm not afraid, I knew you would come find me."

I forced Eli Snyder to crawl down the stairs to the first floor, where he was duct taped, gagged and blind folded. Stephen Snyder was duct taped, gagged and blind folded while lying in the hammock. Both men were soon after placed on the floor and guarded. Lily was checked for injuries and then dressed in a footed sleeper for toddlers. Photos were taken of the SFRT with Lily, and then she was taken away to the exfil point by George and me as Mr. Electric was ordered to guard the felons. Kelly was staged at the exfil point in the vehicle and was ready to go as the sun peeked through the sky now at 0500 hours.

I told Kelly to stay at the car with Lily, as George and I headed back to assist with the capture of the Snyders. Lily seemed healthy, intelligent, fearless, and was talkative. She appeared to have a body fungus of some type, a few scars from bug bites and needed a bath.

George and I returned to the AO to find that Mr. Electric had removed the gags from the felon's mouths and was taking photos of the entire scene to "send to Special Forces associates to give them a look at a sustainable location." I had absolutely no idea what he was talking about other than that he intended to compromise the mission by sharing this operation with unauthorized personnel and non-cleared outside sources. It was obvious he had another agenda, and personal gain in all of this was part of it. While I was opposed to this, there was not time to discuss it. I instructed Mr. Electric to head to the car, accompany Kelly and Lily back to the safe house and not to leave them alone at any time. He was to contact Charlie and tell him that we would be arriving thirty minutes after darkness on this same day.

We could not afford to expose ourselves to civilians, especially dressed in war gear during daylight hours. I gave him specific instructions to change out his gear and return to us only once that evening when we were ready to extract the kidnappers. Additionally, we could not afford to contaminate the area with the vehicle staging in the exfil site again. He departed and returned about ten minutes later questioning my guidance. I remained calm and asked him to please just follow the direction and make sure he accomplished the task. He departed, but not without an attitude. George and I secured the felons for the next eight hours. Within those eight hours, Mr. Electric returned to our location on three different occasions with more suggestions on how the operation should be run from here on out ... the car dirtying up the staging area. When asked if he had accomplished the tasks previously given, he stated that he had not gotten around to it. The fiber of the mission was disintegrating at the hands of a mutinous rogue ... an incompetent piece of creation that had no business being on this operation, and I had no one to blame but myself.

But there was some good coming from all of this during that period, despite Mr. Electric's insubordination. George and I had the opportunity to illicit valuable information on the history of the kidnappers' travels since the abduction, pray with them, feed them and tend to the injuries they had sustained from living in the jungle environment. We treated them with great respect.

- The structure they were holed up in contained eating utensils, books, medicine, toys, clothes, food stock, marijuana, hammocks, fresh fruit, a working toilet, etc.
- According to their testimony, they had traveled to Canada and then to Mexico before entering Costa Rica.
- They had talked their way through customs, posing as Lily's Grandfather and Father, even though they did not have passports or birth certificates.

Something Bigger Than Overthrowing Small Governments

- Eli said that Lily had a deep intestinal parasite that was dangerous to the liver and needed to be treated.
- Lily cut her own hair but refused to dye it black when that was recommended by Stephen.
- Stephen had a large scar on his leg from a spillage of boiling water and an infected cut on the top of his left foot, which he sustained from hitting it with a machete.
- Stephen and Eli both had infections that appeared to be caused by staphylococcus bacteria on their body.
- Stephen had shaven all of his facial hair and head to rid himself of lice.
- Both men admitted that Lily would be better off back in the States with their mother, as long as the mother had changed her ways and was not destructive.
- Eli was very legalistic when it came to biblical scripture.
- Neither man answered when asked if they had ever let Lily smoke marijuana.
- Stephen stated that he abducted Lily because he did not believe he had a fighting chance in a U.S. court of law to obtain sole custody.
- According to Stephen, he was in the Marine Corps until he went AWOL. He was dishonorably discharged.
- His stories indicated a long history of running from problems.
- Both men had been administering their own medications, maintained organic diets but admitted that they had difficulty developing a sustainable organic farm like Puente Mona.
- They had taken Lily for walks on the beach from time to time.
- Eli remarked about the pleasure he was receiving from being tied up or in bondage and being controlled by us. That statement alone caused George and I to look at each other as if we had been introduced to a weirdo that needed to be as far away from Lily as possible.
- Both men wanted an update on current world events.
- Eli claimed that he had very good hearing in the jungle, and the fact that he didn't hear us coming must have meant we were professionals.

- Both men took instruction very well and did not create any problems. However, Stephen did manage to saw through the duct tape on his hands and keep them together so we would not notice, perhaps in an attempt to escape later. When we discovered it later that evening during the exfil, he stated, "Yeah, I was going to do something until I found out what type of guys you were." His hands were secured again.
- Both men were allowed to use the toilet to relieve themselves, were fed and given water throughout their detainment.
- Eli was of the opinion that Steven Brooks was running his own "Davidian Compound" at Puente Mona.
- Stephen pleaded with us not to hold the owners of the property responsible. He stated that they had no idea and were merely allowing him and Eli to stay and take care of the place.
- Eli told us that they had planned to be leaving the next day to make their way further down to South America. By the grace of God our timing was perfect. One more day and we would have lost them.

At around 1730 hours, George and I placed our balaclava on and removed the duct tape from Eli and Stephen's eyes, so they could see the path. Mr. Electric showed up unexpectedly again with a suggestion that we move out, but the sun was still up. He pointed out that the canopy was dark enough, but had no consideration for the open, lighted clearing the team would have to cross through, exposing us prior to reaching the car. I sent him back to the car, where he was supposed to be standing by for our arrival. At that point, I realized that the vehicle, our only way out, was not secured or guarded. As the darkness fell, George and I escorted the felons down the path to the extract point. Just prior to the clearing we noticed Mr. Electric again, not at the vehicle, but totally exposed about thirty feet to our front. His identity was made clear to the felons because he wasn't wearing his balaclava. We halted and sat the felons on the ground face down.

George moved to Mr. Electric, engaged in a low-whisper, heated conversation and then returned stating, "He's crazy, he's crazy. You need to talk to him."

Something Bigger Than Overthrowing Small Governments

    I approached Mr. Electric and he whipped out a paper list of items and stated, "Just hear me out. Give me ten minutes. I have a plan." Mr. Electric wanted to take the felons to Jerrilyn's place, the safe house that was designated for the reunion of Margo and Lily, instead of the preplanned and already arranged detainment location at Charlie's Hotel. He had failed to make the arrangements with Charlie, as he was assigned earlier that day, which Charlie was expecting, but he did say he spoke with him. When I asked what he spoke with him about, he did not reply, but instead fired back that we could not take them there "because there was only one communal bathroom." He was more concerned with the felon's need to take a piss than the need to maintain cover. As it would turn out, the prearranged detainment room was not only right next to a bathroom but was in the company of Pastor Scott and his missionaries as we had desired. Per the plan, Scott and his guys would assist Charlie in watching the felons. Mr. Electric also wanted for he and Kelly to escort Margo and Lily into Panama, while George and I took the felons to the U.S. Embassy and turned them over. He had already been told during the op order that he, George and I would all be crossing the Panama border while Charlie would contact the FBI or DEA at the U.S. Embassy and handle things on that end.

    I listened to his list until my level of frustration skyrocketed. He was willing to compromise the house that Jerrilyn was staying in without making previous arrangements with the owners, had no consideration for reading anyone in, wanted to expose George and I to the U.S. Embassy, and was now compromising the operation by not being at the car ready for extract. I told him that I needed him to just do his job, and that if he couldn't do that, then he needed to go home. I asked him how many of these operations had he done, and he remained silent. I sent him back to the car.

    We waited about fifteen more minutes for the cover of darkness and moved to the vehicle. We drove to Charlie's hotel and waited in the back lot until he made contact. Charlie had switched gears on us, thinking he had a safer place because of a discussion he had with Mr. Electric. I returned to the car and told the SFRT that Charlie had a contingency plan for another place, and we would follow his vehicle to check it out. It was becoming sketchy, but I had no choice since he was the owner of the hotel and was offering his assistance. The secondary location was lighted, had barking dogs and was within eyesight of unwitting civilians. I declined the offer, and we returned to the hotel where we detained the felons. They were allowed to shower and then were restrained again. Pastor Scott Bailey met with both felons and prayed with them. Mr. Electric was put on watch, while George and I moved to the safe house to pack the gear.

Margo had landed in San Jose (the capitol) and was in transit to the AO, as far as I knew. Kelly and Jerrylin took care of Lily in the meantime at the safe house. What I did not know was that Kelly had circumvented my instructions to Margo and arranged her own transportation for her from San Jose. George and I returned to the detainment site and assisted in monitoring the felons until our arranged departure time of 0600 hours. We sent Mr. Electric back to the safe house to pack his gear. We turned the felons over to Charlie and moved back to the safe house for a second time to pack the vehicle and depart.

When we arrived at the safe house, still dressed in our ops gear, we were met by Jerrilyn outside of the house, who informed us that Kelly had invited the taxi driver who drove her from San Jose into the house. Margo had arrived and was joyfully reunited with Lily.

As we entered the house, there sat a young, 26-year-old male Hispanic, lounging on the couch, observing the entire operation. I was livid. I pulled Kelly aside.

"Who the heck is that?" I asked.

She sheepishly replied ... "I met him in San Jose and had dinner with him, he's trustworthy. I used him to get Margo here from the airport."

My best guess was that Kelly had provided sexual favors to the taxi driver. "Did you sleep with this guy just to get him to drive you from San Jose to Puenta Viejo when you first got here ... after I told you not to come here?"

Something Bigger Than Overthrowing Small Governments

    In my mind her silence was loud enough to confirm my suspicions. The mission was closer to being compromised than ever before. The taxi driver was not read into the operation, and Kelly's lack of operational security was inexcusable. I told Kelly to ask the taxi driver to leave the room and remain in the taxi with the understanding that we would be needing a ride, knowing full well that we had no intention of using him. It was a Band-Aid on an open wound to prevent him from running to the local police and reporting what he had seen. As soon as he stepped out of the house, the SFRT began moving like rats abandoning a sinking ship.

    It wasn't long before Scott Bailey arrived to let us know our window was closing and we needed to depart. He prayed over the team in a rather Moses-like fashion that left us confident that angels would accompany us. For a brief moment the idea itself took away the frustration of all that was going upside down with a couple of Keystone Cops on my team. I remember thinking where did all the angels intend to sit in the vehicle given the fact that we now had two additional passengers ... Margo and Lily. I allowed a carefully guarded smile to break the angered framework of my face as an image of seven angels hanging all over the outside of the car for dear life tiptoed across my imagination. I guess if I have learned anything at all about angels it's that they have absolutely no problem finding a way to go wherever God tells them to go. We said our goodbyes to Scott, departed out the back door and drove away in the rental vehicle, leaving the unsuspecting taxi driver on the other side of the property.

On **Day 8** the humidity of the jungle danced with the sunrise as we headed towards the road to Gandoca and the border. All was silent ... the four-door car packed with six of us leaving a dust trail in my rear view mirror as we skirted past banana plantations that prominently displayed the DOLE company brand name from sign to sign. The silence was actually rather nice, allowing George and I to mentally exercise our movement across the border.

    "I'm not crossing the border with you guys ... I'm returning to San Jose with Kelly," Mr. Electric spouted.

I guess George and I should not have been surprised, but we were. Who bails in the middle of the operation, especially when he knows he's going to be needed most at the border to provide safety for Lily and Margo should our contacts fail to be in place? We were speechless. I pulled over to the side of the road, ready to dump Mr. Electric and his gear right there in the middle of nowhere. And then it suddenly dawned on me ... God was cutting my forces down by half. He knew that the next part of the journey would need to be lean and mean, and that I was still holding on to what I wanted in the mission rather than what He had planned. George just looked at me as I looked back at him. I pushed in so close that I could see the k-bar in his mind already dripping with blood. "Why don't we just go down there and see what God will do," I whispered. He stared straight ahead as I pulled back onto the road.

Minutes into the trip we pulled over again, this time for fuel. We separated Mr. Electric's ops gear from ours to lighten the load we would be taking across the border on our backs. He tried to pay for the fuel, but I refused to accept it. I pulled Kelly aside, briefed her on the situation with Mr. Electric and told her that she was in charge and that he was off the operation. She said she understood and accepted the added responsibility with little hesitation. She was extremely focused and professional about the task at hand, or at least seemed to be for the moment.

When we arrived at the border town Sixaola, I parked the vehicle, and everyone stayed close to it while I made contact at customs. George carefully followed me at a distance to watch my back. Sixaola is the town on the Costa Rican side of the border across from the sleepy town of Guabito on the Panama side of the border. It had no accommodations, restaurants, or services.

The towns are both dependent on the production of bananas and drugs, of course. The rickety bridge between them, crossing over croc-infested waters, was not very long. It was neither a destination nor an event ... more like an interesting inevitable experience ... not unlike this entire operation with Mr. Electric. It was the only place to legally cross into Panama. Trucks filled with bananas and other commodities were traffic-jammed and too wide for the structure itself, literally brushing against the railing of the bridge. The only way to get across would be to hang on the outside of the super structure and step from one rotten railroad plank to the next ... or sit there and wait for hours until all the traffic let up ... hours that we did not have.

My point of contact, 14-year veteran of the border system who fancied himself with the title of "Billy the Kid" provided a smooth transition at the Costa Rican border. His English and Spanish were excellent, and he was a Costa Rican native. I returned to the car for us to start unloading our gear and handed the keys to Kelly with instructions that I needed the vehicle to remain in place until all persons had safely crossed the border. Then she was to drive it back to San Jose. But as soon as we had started towards the bridge, I looked back to see Mr. Electric grab the keys from Kelly, somewhat forcibly put her in the car and depart Sixaola without waiting to see if we had made it across.

I put Lily on my chest and told her to hold on to the straps of my backpack. I then began moving hand over hand on the railing, carefully negotiating my steps from one rotten railroad beam to another on the outside of the superstructure. George did the same and managed to keep a hand on Margo as well. It was slow going and unpredictable. Every time a truck would move a few feet, the entire bridge would shake.

At one point where I needed to stretch my stride, I looked over my shoulder, back at George and then over my shoulder again. It wasn't the plunge I wanted to take.

Bazzel Baz

The river below was most likely infested with crocodiles, and the current was as unpredictable as our "current situation" — no pun intended. Lily was having a good time, confident and remarkably mature. I kept her attention drawn to my face the entire way, just to minimize her movement and prevent any fear that might come over her. But, strangely enough, and much to my delight, she was trooper all the way.

Once on the other side, George and I had no problems with our passports being stamped, but Margo and Lily's story was different. In an attempt to grease the skids, George informed the authorities that his occupation was law enforcement. I believe it did in fact help. The authorities claimed that Margo and Lily needed some type of tourist visa, and I was sent back across to the Costa Rican side, only to be denied. I soon discovered that our point of contact was attempting to dice us for some cash. He told me that he could get us across with no problems, but it would cost me $450.00 to travel to the city of David. He wanted me to agree to this before he would secure the tourist visa for Margo and Lily's birth certificates. When I declined, the system stopped, and we sat in the Panamanian Customs office for about one hour.

When I mentioned that I needed to contact the U.S. Embassy, our point of contact disappeared for about thirty minutes. The local

Something Bigger Than Overthrowing Small Governments

telephones were of no use, and our cell service was not working ... we were out of communications. The Border crossing personnel were very irritable, brusque and unfriendly. They were charging an entrance fee on the Panamanian side that was actually not legal. People in the know generally walked right past it.

We finally agreed to pay the border patrol via "Billy the Kid" $150.00 for a taxi to take us from the next town to the city of David. This also included the border fee to have Margo and Lily stamped through.

Bocas del Toro stamp office.

We loaded ourselves and our gear into a Toyota pickup and headed to Bocas Del Toro. It was not a far drive. Once there, I used the ATM at a local bank to pull another $120.00 which I paid "Billy The Kid" again as a fixer-fee and for the introduction to a Spanish-speaking taxi driver, who happened to be a Christian. We stocked our packs with some food and water, loaded up, and spent the next three hours heading south through the interior of Panama to the city of David. We made one stop to retrieve George's cell phone from his pack in the back of the trunk, and another down the road to use the bathroom and purchase some more food. For most of the trip George, Lily and Margo closed their eyes to the tune of a cassette tape of Christian songs. It was the Spanish version of English songs I knew all so well ... all of them. I could not help but think that this was confirmation from God that we were safe and on our way. There was something interesting about the driver. He said little to no words, but when he did, even in Spanish, it was as if I could understand that he had been sent there on a mission from God. His smile was heavenly and strong, as if underneath his small frame was a giant arch angel who could never reveal his true self except through bits and pieces of kindness.

We reached the city of David, boarded an air-conditioned bus and spent the next eight hours on the road until we finally reached the bus terminal in Panama City at or around 2200 hours. From there we took a taxi to a local hotel just outside the airport where we secured two rooms, one for Lily and Margo and the other for George and me. We still had no ability to communicate with Kelly to confirm her arrival or departure from San Jose, Costa Rica.

Day 9, the following morning, George staged the gear and prepped Margo and Lily for a possible flight to the U.S. I made my way to the airport to reserve flights in person. When I returned, we all ate breakfast together. Thus far Lily had not questioned once the whereabouts of Eli or Stephen Snyder. Her appetite was good, and she consumed more fruit on her plate than a kid her size should be capable of. I cut my meal short and shuttled back to the airport but was not able to confirm flights on Continental. However, I did purchase four new flights for $2,500.00 back to the U.S. on an American Flight. I returned to the hotel where George was ready to launch. We arrived at the airport about one and one-half hours before departure. Lily wore George's baseball cover to cut down her blonde hair profile. She remained within reach of each SFRT member at all times. We hunkered down in an airport cafe with a corner chair that provided good screening for Lily and her mother.

Ten minutes prior to departure, we advanced to the gate. The boarding was delayed about fifteen minutes, which gave us too much exposure for our comfort level. Although the operation was within all legal parameters, and there was no fear of law enforcement intervention from the Panamanian government, we did not want the hassle of detainment or questioning. A smooth transition for the SFRT and the child from the AO to the U.S. was of major concern after the tremendous amount of energy spent to recover her. The announcement to board the flight was sweet to our ears.

Once airborne, the pilot was notified of the situation via a flight attendant whom I spoke to, and over the loudspeaker he welcomed Lily back to the U.S. and congratulated her on the reunion with her mother.

Something Bigger Than Overthrowing Small Governments

For the first time in the operation, George and I could take a break and congratulate one another on a job well done. George's cell phone was up and running, and we placed calls to media contacts to schedule coverage at LAX for Lily and Margo. We also placed a call to Kelly, leaving a message for her to contact the media. Her status was still unknown at this point, and I had concerns about her safe departure from San Jose. The SFRT arrived at Miami Customs two hours later and was cleared without problems. It should be noted that neither Lily nor her Missing Child profile surfaced on the computer at Customs. This lack of attention to detail within the customs and immigrations system was a good example of how abducted children were so easily filtered in and out of the U.S. at that time without intervention.

From Miami we boarded another flight and arrived at Los Angeles International Airport, where we were greeted by an ABC news team, as well as a local affiliate channel 4 NBC. George and I maintained the lowest profile we could by standing in the background, far enough away to avoid cameras.

After the interviews, we escorted Lily and Margo to a taxi and finally to my home, where they stayed the night and departed the next morning for Eugene, Oregon. It was later reported that week in the Idaho Mountain Express, "The father and half-brother of Lily Snyder, 5, — who were captured in the daring rescue of the former Ketchum girl in the jungles of Costa Rica two weeks ago — are being returned to Blaine County to face charges in the alleged abduction of the child."

Prior to George's departure from Los Angeles, we received a call from Kelly. She was extremely upset and in tears. Kelly said that Mr. Electric was bad-mouthing George and I for the operation and made other statements that questioned my loyalty to Kelly and the professional relationship we had. In addition, according to her, on numerous occasions during the drive back to San Jose from the Panama border, Mr. Electric displayed sexually aggressive behavior by fondling her neck and leg. She repeatedly asked him to stop.

Once in San Jose, Mr. Electric suggested they split a room and offered to pay for it, since they were both getting up early the next morning. Kelly stated that she would rather get her own room even though she knew she could not afford it. But Mr. Electric insisted, stating, "Give me a break, I'm a married man, nothing is going to happen."

For whatever reason, she trusted him, but later found herself in a very precarious situation as Mr. Electric continued to invite her into the shower with him and made sexual remarks about her body. He even went so far as to jump in bed with her. She continued to deter his attempts and eventually left the room. When she returned to the room, she found him lying naked on the bed ▆▆▆▆, asking her if she wanted to touch his ▆▆. Disgusted, she departed the room. With nowhere to go, after standing in the hallway she eventually entered the room again, where Mr. Electric was still laying naked on the bed and remarked, "You wouldn't believe how much I ▆▆." Even more disgusted, she departed again. Finally, after an exhausting night of waiting outside her room, she reentered and insisted that he leave her alone. When she pointed out that he was married, he replied that his wife had an affair, that he had engaged in affairs before, and that it was not a big deal ... or words to that effect.

As we listened to the details, George and I were furious. Mr. Electric's behavior was not only uncalled for but unprofessional. His lewd and lascivious behavior, attempted molestation of Kelly, and defamation of character against George and me were all actions deserving of a day in court.

On **Day 10**, Margo and Lily continued to interview with media networks. The Ketchum Police Department was trying to figure out the identities of the SFRT, and Eli and Stephen were in the custody of the DEA in Miami waiting to be turned over to the Ketchum Police Department. Mr. Electric made contact with Kelly via the internet once she arrived back in the U.S. He continued his wild accusations of incompetence against the SFRT during the operation and continued sexual enticements and inappropriate behavior towards her. I had concerns that Mr. Electric would sell the ops photos that he had taken in the field to the tabloids to bring attention to himself for personal gain. I provided Kelly with some guidance. She spoke with Mr. Electric and told him that should the photos reach public exposure, he would be taken to court. She recommended that he keep a low profile, or the next time he heard from her, it would be through his wife and an attorney.

Although it did get his attention, I had concerns that he would still make an attempt at publicly exposing the SFRT and our tradecraft. What he did not know was that I would protect at whatever cost the welfare of the SFRT, the return of Lily, as well as future recoveries through whatever legal means necessary and prevent him from ever again engaging in operations of this nature. It was obvious that his mental stability, integrity and motivations were in question not only for this type of operation, but any operation involving the use of classified documentation, need-to-know procedures, clandestine activities, and the use of field sources and methods.

Months after her return to the U.S., Kelly admitted to having drug and alcohol addictions and suicidal tendencies that might have played a part in positioning her to be molested in San Jose by Mr. Electric. Evidence showed that Kelly may have, in fact, either attempted to engage Mr. Electric in a sexual liaison and backed off at the last moment out of fear or may have actually engaged in a sexual encounter with him. When I urged her to confront him, or at least tell his wife of the circumstances, she was very reluctant to do so. Further evidence showed that Kelly may have been disclosing operational material about the mission to Scott Halveston, a close friend of Mr. Electric, whom she was indeed sexually involved with.

Scott was later killed in 2004 in Fallujah, Iraq as part of a four-member independent contractor escort team for Black Water Private Military Company. Scott was burned and strung up on a local bridge for the media to view. Upon his death, Kelly confessed in writing to various accounts of giving SFRT operational information to Scott and others. Also prior to his death, she even joined Scott in Los Angeles to meet up with Mr. Electric and his brother, as they attended a meeting at FOX Studios to sell a television show based on ARC's recovery of Lily Snyder — something they had no legal authority to do. Kelly was later released from any association with ARC or the SFRT for dishonorable conduct. The remnants of Mr. Electric's operational gear that was left in Los Angeles prior to departing to Costa Rica was donated to the Good Will Store.

Rebecca Nolan of the Register-Guard would later report, "It is believed that before authorities could make their next move, an underground team of former military personnel, who help recover abducted children rescued Lily and apprehended Eli and Stephen Snyder at the hut they shared deep in the jungle. The police chief and Blaine County Prosecutor Jim Thomas said they don't really know much about the group that rescued her."

Dana Dugan of the Idaho Mountain Express would report, "It was an independent recovery team that went into the jungle and made the rescue, Lyman said. They allegedly tracked the trio for eight days and had them under surveillance for 24 hours before attempting the rescue. According to a confidential report, 'there were no weapons and they did not resist.'"

At the time, it was important to remain anonymous. Now enough time has passed that we can openly make our claim and say how humbled and grateful we are that God, in all of His omnipotence, chose us to save Lily Snyder.

Something Bigger Than Overthrowing Small Governments

Recommendations:

    Operation Lily Pad, despite the negative impact of two team members, can be counted as a great success. Lily Snyder was recovered during a clandestine operation, under potentially dangerous and life-threatening conditions, and returned to the safety of her custodial parent. She is now relocated within the borders of the United States of America and is on her way to a healthy recovery. The felons, Eli and Stephen Snyder each were detained within the U.S. under $500,000 bond and faced charges of kidnapping as they awaited trial. The remaining members of the SFRT returned to their separate locations within the U.S. and awaited their next operation. George is an experienced operator in hostage rescue and maintains a current employment as a law enforcement officer with honorable mentions for his successes in the field of police work. He is a thinker and has no problem being dedicated to the task at hand. He has vision and understands the serious nature of life and death. His world is real. He is mission oriented. He is quiet, observes everything, and applies himself in the most efficient manner to maintain his patience. His physical condition is not in question. He is recommended for operations in the field with the SFRT for future operations.

    Mr. Electric is an insurance salesman who, to the best of my knowledge, maintains his proficiency in hunting and his previous military history. His physical condition is not in question. Mr. Electric wants to be in charge and continues to brag on his West Point leadership skills as a method of validating his importance. He sees himself a cut above all the rest. He listens, but he does not hear because he is preoccupied with his own internal plan or hidden agenda. He is deceitful, insecure and inexperienced. He is not recommended for further operations in the field with the SFRT. He would not have been chosen as a member of the SFRT had these qualities been unveiled prior to this operation.

    Kelly K. was initially hired as an analyst in the Ops Center. She is an experienced operator in her specialty but not highly recommended for further operations in the field with the SFRT due to questionable motivations, recently discovered drug and alcohol additions and the inability to follow orders. Her failure to maintain within the borders of standard operational security is a detriment to any operation, and she would not have been chosen as a member of the SFRT had these qualities been unveiled prior to this operation.

It is by the grace of God and the skill of those dedicated and disciplined members of the SFRT that future operations and the return of abducted children will be possible. As George Ciganik, "It was a needle in a haystack." This operation provided a proving ground for future SFRT participation for George Ciganik and Mr. Electric based on their first-time performance, and not on the recorded events of any interaction on such operations with me in the past. As a Proof of Concept operation, this was the first of its kind, predetermined to include publicity for the parent and child once the operation was a success. In accordance with the SOP, all previous operations, thus far all successful, will remain classified and without publicity, as has been the case from 1993 to date. All files, plans, agents of influences, payment and locations remain Eyes Only and on a need-to-know basis. All files, plans, agents of influence, payment and locations are to be compartmented including Operation Lily Pad.

Something Bigger Than Overthrowing Small Governments

CHAPTER 13
OPERATION KIMSHI
AFTER ACTION REPORT

Subject: Tiffany Rubin, Kobe Rubin

Date: 3-29-08

Introduction:
For the purposes of this report the SFRT consisted of Bazzel Baz and two attachments (1) Mark Miller and Tiffany Rubin — (Custodial Mother).

Background:
On or about 1 March 2008, *The Association for the Recovery of Children* (ARC) was contacted by Mark Miller, President of *The American Association for Lost and Stolen Children*, requesting assistance in the recovery of one American child who was the victim of an international noncustodial parental kidnapping and was now being held hostage in Seoul, Korea. The child was Kobe Rubin, age 8.

The mother of Kobe Rubin, Tiffany Rubin, first met Jeffrey Salko (a.k.a. Jeffrey Lee a.k.a. Kang-Shik Lee) in December of 1996 at a night club in Manhattan N.Y. USA. Tiffany was 19 years of age at the time and Jeffrey was 26. They began dating and moved in together after one month. The relationship was tumultuous and full of physical and mental abuse by Jeffrey. Jeffrey was eventually arrested for domestic abuse and sentenced to three months in jail in California. As is the case in most co-dependent relationships, he and Tiffany got back together after he served his time.

Both Tiffany and Jeffrey experimented with illegal drugs, which eventually led to Jeffrey's addiction to methamphetamine. This was not Jeffrey's first encounter with the illegal drug market. He had served one and a half years of a three-year drug sentence before Tiffany met him.

Tiffany and Jeffrey maintained an "on and off" relationship between February 1997 and January 2001. It was in the midst of this unhealthy scenario, in October 2000, that Kobe Rubin was born. Tiffany cleaned up her act, and drug use was no longer a part of her life. Jeffrey was arrested in the State of California for parole violation and was extradited to New Jersey to finish out his sentence.

Jeffrey finished his prison time but continued his drug use and trafficking once he returned home to Tiffany and the newborn Kobe. He made claims of domestic abuse against Tiffany, insisting that she was withholding his parental right with the child and other obscure accusations. In reality, Tiffany refused to subject herself and her new baby to an environment of drug abuse and trafficking and was quickly growing tired of it.

In 2001 Tiffany left the house with Kobe and relocated to a different apartment. Although Jeffrey had full visitation rights, he still attempted to have Child Protective Services (CPS) take Kobe on a number of occasions until CPS threatened him with prosecution for making false reports against Tiffany. Just prior to the kidnapping of Kobe, Jeffrey was threatened with incarceration by the courts for non-payment of child support. Jeffrey used false documentation and forged Tiffany's signature to obtain a passport for Kobe. On 21 August 2007, while Kobe was visiting Jeffrey, Jeffrey kidnapped Kobe and left the United States bound for Korea. Once in Korea, Jeffrey denounced his U.S. citizenship and applied for Korean citizenship. He registered Kobe for the same. As a red herring, he maintained a website and emails that led people to believe he was still in the United States.

Operation Overview:

Circa mid-February, I was contacted by Mark Miller, president of *The American Association for Lost and Stolen Children* concerning the abduction of Kobe Rubin. Mark had great concerns about his organizations ability to run operations overseas and requested my assistance. According to Mark, an anonymous informant had contacted Tiffany Rubin on her Myspace account and had disclosed the whereabouts of her abducted son in Korea. However, none of this intelligence had been vetted, and I requested that Mark send me all the information he had for my review. Over the course of the next month, I spoke with Tiffany to assess the probability of a successful operation before agreeing to assist Mark's organization.

Given the nature of this operation and the fact that I would be leveraging intelligence, Embassy and FBI relationships as backup and support mechanisms, I insisted that ARC personnel not only be attached, but completely run the operation in a manner that would not jeopardize existing protocol and relationships, nor cause us embarrassment in those relationships. Mark Miller agreed to this and received, based on that agreement, our full support. Mark would finance the operation, and ARC would have the Con (control).

I immediately contacted Special Agent Maria Johnson of the New York FBI to receive a briefing on the division's involvement. While not always appropriate, this call was made to provide deconfliction with any and all ongoing efforts by the FBI to apprehend the abductor. Agent Johnson informed me that the hands of the FBI were tied politically and legally, and those negotiations with the Korean government were at a standstill. While the FBI could not officially green-light ARC to do the rescue, they certainly encouraged us to continue, stating that there was nothing against an American gaining help from other Americans for such a case. In other words, we were on our own. Reading between the lines ... if it went well, they would jump on board. If it went bad, they would wash their hands of it. Agent Johnson was very polite and supportive and did in fact forward a copy of the Federal Warrant for the arrest of Jeffrey Salko, as well as the Interpol Notification.

Interestingly, I read a report filed by the Department of State in the paperwork that Mark Miller had sent me, stating that U.S. Embassy personnel (Consul Officer) and Korean police did in fact visit the home of Jeffrey Salko to assess the status of Kobe Rubin. The report clearly showed that Korean police, U.S. Embassy Officials or the FBI attaché in Korea did not or could not take any action to arrest the abductor and recover Kobe Rubin. Evidently, Jeffrey Salko had renounced his U.S. citizenship and applied for Korean status as well as registered Kobe for Korean citizenship, which was soon to be processed. It is worth noting that Jeffrey Salko was originally a North Korean who became an American, who became a South Korean over the course of time, if my memory serves me.

It is my experience that this action is typical of U.S. Embassy or State Department support overseas, often attempting to brush off responsibility to The Hague (which in my opinion is nothing more than a feel-good puppet organization not unlike the U.N.) or find excuses not to assist Americans. It was from this report that I drew conclusions that it was not in the best interest of the operation to inform the U.S. Embassy of our plans, arrival and execution, but to simply show up on their doorstep requesting assistance for a passport for Kobe, after the fact. It is also my experience that State Department will protect the economic and political agenda of the U.S. within a foreign nation before it will protect the rights of an American citizen, and that they will not hesitate to throw you under the bus if it is in their best interest. The only time I have seen it differently is when good-hearted State Department personnel do otherwise, generally at the risk of being reprimanded.

Calls were placed to George Ciganik and Paul French, former operators of ARC, to assist in the mission. Paul was unable to assist due to other operational obligations on another project. George Ciganik was able to provide support up until days before the departure. A medical emergency within his family prevented his participation and thereby left me with no choice but to enter the operation with Mark Miller.

While Mark is qualified to some degree in child recovery operations, he is not cut from the same cloth, and this gave me great concern, as I had previously experienced his lack of operational savvy and tradecraft in the Mexico extraction in Operation Cinco De Mayo, dated 5-5-06. Nevertheless, I made a decision to participate, as I said, provided I had the Con. Mark would fund the operation. ARC would put it together and execute.

With no way to vet the anonymous informant, I had Tiffany establish contact via email and build rapport. For a period of two weeks prior to our departure from the U.S., I was able to receive enough intelligence to coordinate logistics via the informant. He provided back-story, current locations of the abductor and Kobe, his contact information, directions from the airport to a hotel near the extraction point, as well as an offer to meet with me once I was on the ground. He

Something Bigger Than Overthrowing Small Governments

even provided pictures of the hotel he had selected for us, supposedly directly behind his apartment building.

I still had my concerns ... what if it was a setup to hold Tiffany hostage or simply force her to waste finances on a trip that would come up dry. It has been known that foreign intelligence services and police have set up sting operations to leverage international policy with the U.S. In addition, I had no idea who Tiffany had been in touch with prior to this, and the chance of her falling into human trafficking was a real threat, something not to be taken lightly.

It was my intention to arrive a day prior, connect with the informant, run surveillance, and then meet Mark and Tiffany upon their arrival. However, I misread the departure time on the ticket and was delayed from 12am to 12p.m. on that same day, which calculated, would place me in Seoul about two hours after Mark and Tiffany's arrival. I had coordinated in the Ops plan for this very obstacle and coordinated with Mark prior to departure. It was set that we would all rendezvous at the Hotel Cello, 37-3 Bangi-Dong, SongPa-Gu, Seoul, Korea.

Mark and Tiffany departed New York, and I departed Los Angeles March 23, 2008. I was blessed to sit next to an elderly Korean American woman from Orange County, CA. She was an encyclopedia of information on Seoul Korea, the culture and routes to and from the airport to my destination. Her motherly posture even crossed over to the point of mixing my Korean dish with more hot sauce when I did not apply enough, in her opinion. Our arrival in Korea was blanketed by darkness, and the lights of a city seemingly the size of Los Angeles from the air. Once at Inchon International airport our paths crossed again, and she was instrumental in helping me find the right bus to Bangi-Dong district. The $20 (U.S.) ride was filled with some uncertainty, despite my experience as a world traveler. I had been told that most Koreans spoke English but found that not to be the case. I spent a small portion of the trip researching the map to actually write down the destination in Korean and present it to the driver.

Evidently, our informant had done a superior job of locating an out-of-the way hotel, because not even the bus driver was sure of the address. Once I reached the Olympic Park region of Bangi Dong, I got off the bus and started walking. Even knowing that I was very close to the rendezvous point, it was difficult to locate the exact address. It was a perfect opportunity to vet the responsiveness and capability as well as technical resources of the police. It is noted that the police that were observed were not armed.

I approached an Officer in his car and attempted to communicate in English that I was lost and looking for a certain address. I presented the hotel address. He looked puzzled. He made a few phone calls but received no guidance. Finally, he took me to the Lotte World Hotel, one of the largest, just a few blocks away and tried to inquire with a doorman. I was satisfied with the ineptitude of the police and took matters into my own hands. I went inside the Hotel and spoke with the Receptionist, requesting the use of his phone.

I placed a call to our informant and asked him to meet me at my location. He had not received a call from Tiffany or Mark, so neither of us had any idea whether they had reached Korea or not. Ten minutes later, a rather tall Caucasian male, who preferred to be called "Sam," climbed out of a taxi and introduced himself. He was a foreign schoolteacher who had been living in Seoul for a number of years, had met Jeffrey Salko through another schoolteacher friend and was aware of the kidnapping situation. He, in fact, was the one who sent the tip to Tiffany on her Myspace site. According to Sam, Jeffrey had dated a friend of one of his female schoolteacher friends, they had a falling out and she became suspicious after realizing that Kobe was a fish out of water and his father could never make two and two add up with his stories.

Sam and I took a taxi to the Hotel Cello, a rather dark and seedy hole in the wall, located in the back alley behind his apartment complex, just off the main drag. It was in fact, perfect for this operation. Much to my surprise and delight, Mark and Tiffany were already checked in and had proceeded to their rooms.

A knock on the door, and we were in, with first time introductions between Tiffany and myself, and I introduced Sam as the informant. I also needed to vet Tiffany by asking her a series of very important questions ... was she physically fit to run, did she have any preexisting medical conditions that I should be aware of, what was her emotional status, how much money did she have on her person, did she have a credit card, did she have a cell phone, did she speak any foreign languages, etc. everything I could think of that would benefit or deter the operation. It never is about getting from point A to point B in an operation. It's about what you do between those two points when everything goes upside down. What is the emergency procedure? And in this case the question was simple ... is Tiffany capable of surviving on her own in Korea if the operation goes on its head and we all get separated, with or without her son. Her safety was as important to me as every custodial guardian's who chooses to go in country.

In the next hour, I would brief everyone on operational security issues, Sam would provide what intelligence he had — maps to the location, directions, cautions, etc. and he would offer to continue providing assistance as long as he remained anonymous. We arranged a time the following morning for Sam, Mark and I to recon the school where Kobe was enrolled.

I checked into my room, sent appropriate emails to the ARC operations center in the U.S. reporting my safe arrival and then attempted to get some sleep. There was more room in a goldfish bowl than there was in this room. The black floors, black and white walls and the cheap white-knitted curtains were reminiscent of a scene from Ridley Scott's movie *Blade Runner*, dark and brooding. The city just outside my window had a lingering smell and sound that was penetrated only by the neon street signs and huge video advertisements. Had it been raining, I would not have known if I were in Seoul or in the movie.

At 0700 the following morning 25 March 2008, Sam met Mark and me at Hotel Cello's lobby. Sam mentioned that the police were not allowed to apprehend anyone. He told stories of how pedestrians basically argue with police until they go away or they often walk away from police. I hadn't had enough time on the ground to know whether that was true or not, but I certainly wasn't going to risk giving it a try ... but then again, in a pinch maybe it would be worth it. He also told us that the school where Kobe attended had no security and had free access all day long for parents and other people. I needed to see that for myself.

We took a taxi to the location about ten minutes from our hotel. In previous emails, Sam had mentioned that Jeffrey's mother walked Kobe to school each morning and arrived at 0900 hours. Jeffrey would go to the gym, which was in direct view of Kobe's school, and remain there from 1000 hours until around 1200 hours.

Since the three-story school was surrounded by a neighborhood of high-rise apartment complexes, he suspected that Kobe and Jeffrey lived somewhere nearby, but did not know exactly which apartment. That in itself could pose a problem. If we were not careful, our operation could be observed from a hundred different directions and we would never know it. So it would be important to do everything as if we were being watched ... nothing suspicious, nothing provocative and nothing out of the ordinary for locals or tourists to note.

Arriving in the early morning hours about 0600 allowed us time to walk around the school and the park next to the school to check on security and infil/exfil routes. Sam even escorted us inside the vacant school, and we found Kobe's classroom 2-2 with a picture on the outside wall of him and his classmates to confirm the location. Bingo!!! Although Mark said nothing, his face said everything as the wheels began to turn in his head as to how this mission would unfold. I had seen this uncontrolled enthusiasm once before in the Mexico operation, and it was that uncontrolled enthusiasm that gave me an uncomfortable feeling in the pit of my stomach ... the type of feeling that you get when you know that a train is coming, and you pray you can get off the track in time. I made sure we immediately departed the area and placed Sam in a taxi to keep the area clean. As you can imagine, three tall Caucasian men in this region stood out like a sore thumb and we were identifiable if not disguised.

I wanted to make sure that all of Sam's intelligence was correct, beginning with the gym that Jeffrey attended. I discovered that it was NOT in direct view of the school. In fact, it was two blocks away and obscured by other buildings. This was the first piece of incorrect intelligence from Sam.

While running surveillance, I was running routes, checking security, stake-out positions, exfil routes and timing all of it. Mark had no idea why. It was a lesson in place that he should have taken advantage of. But to him it was wasted energy, and he seemed satisfied to just sit down and wait until Kobe arrived and magically walked up to him and said, "Take me home." He had no idea of the magnitude of work that was required ahead of time in the AO to make sure we were not seen, and the work required to write up a good operations order. I finally asked him to just follow me as I looked for ways in and out of the building, multiple exfil routes up the street, pickup sites, all bundled in the type of operational planning that comes naturally to operators.

Another piece of intelligence I needed to vet was the supposition that you could easily catch a taxi every two seconds on the main street. Mark seemed frustrated that I was doing the math and continued to try and put his own plan together without taking into consideration all the obstacles, and without actually performing some type of clandestine rehearsal without burning up the area.

"Why do you keep looking at your watch and walking all of these different routes? We'll just grab Kobe and run for it and grab a taxi ... they come every two minutes," he said.

I looked at him as if he had to be nuts. "Seriously Mark, you really believe that?" I replied.

"I don't get it ... this is simple," Mark stated.

"I wish that were the case," I replied.

I headed back to the park next to the school and Mark followed. Between 0830 hours and 0900 hours children began arriving at the school, some escorted, others not. We positioned ourselves in the park adjacent to the school and kept an eye out for Kobe, his father or grandmother. Although it was a cold and overcast day, Mark did not use this to his advantage and disguise himself or cover his face. He stood out like a very tall American sitting in the park staring at children. I hinted a few times about his choice of positioning and appearance, but he refused to do anything about it. He had nothing to occupy himself to provide cover for action, like reading a newspaper, or exercising, or eating breakfast and listening to music ... nothing other than sitting or standing and gazing out at the school yard. It bothered me.

I wrapped myself in my coat, covered my face and found a different location to run surveillance from. At 0900 hours all the children were in class, and there had been no sign of Kobe entering, escorted or not. We remained in the area for about another hour to see if Kobe would come out to the playground at the 0945-hour break, but that did not occur. Finally, I told Mark that we had to abandon the area, so it did not get burned. He insisted that we continue to sit there over the next five hours hoping to see Kobe.

He even kept mentioning that perhaps we could grab him when he was walking to school. When I explained the difference between the solid intelligence that we had which placed him in the classroom and the lack of intelligence regarding how he actually got to school, and the fact that Mark was making an assumption that he walked to school on his own, Mark acquiesced. At least in the classroom it was controlled. We knew where he would be. Generally speaking, almost every teacher I know has their hands full in the first fifteen minutes after the classroom bell rings ... getting students settled. Unless this class of kids was different, there would be just enough confusion to make for the perfect distraction, if I could have Tiffany knock on the classroom door at 0915 hours.

Mark still insisted that his plan to grab Kobe when he was walking to school was best, and he would not let it die. Even if for one nanosecond I were to lean into Mark's assumption, what we didn't know was if Kobe walked to school by himself, if he walked to school with his father trailing yards behind, or his grandmother, or if Kobe walked to school with his father watching out an apartment window. His idea was terribly flawed and dangerous ... even if Kobe would be walking to school, he would be doing so along with hundreds of other students and parents. Everyone and his brother would see the pickup, the exfil route, the taxi and of course our identities. I had no intention of allowing Mark to turn this into a snatch-and-grab foot race.

If I was going to put ARC's reputation on the line with back-channel connections and expect assistance from other sources if needed, it had to be a clean, surgical operation — which I had already explained to Tiffany, Sam and Mark on day one in the Hotel Cello. There were just too many unanswered questions about how Mark wanted to perform this recovery, and he didn't have answers for them. I felt like I was teaching Espionage 101 at a time when the student should have graduated.

I saw there would be no end to this unless I took stronger measures to show how flawed his thinking was.

I encouraged Mark to follow me through the exfil route, between the high-rise buildings, to the main street, telling him that I

Something Bigger Than Overthrowing Small Governments

wanted to stress the importance of rehearsal. We stood on the main street attempting to hail a taxi.

"Four minutes, no taxi," I announced.

"Seven minutes, no taxi," I announced.

"Ten minutes, no taxi," I announced.

And then I turned to Mark and said, "Do you really think we can afford to stand here with Tiffany and Kobe for ten minutes waiting for a taxi?"

Mark replied, "No I guess not." I think he was finally getting it. I told him that we needed to look for alternate routes through a nearby alley and to an area that would provide concealment until a taxi could arrive. Evidently, Sam's intelligence on this was also misplaced to some degree.

I also suggested that it would be a good idea for us to run our routes via taxi from here to the hotel and then to the U.S. Embassy to determine times, obstacles and delays. We departed the area and returned to the Hotel Cello to check on Tiffany. Sam met us at the hotel and delivered some new intelligence.

"One week ago, Kobe joined the baseball team. In the afternoons after school, Kobe no longer goes to a private school where Jeffrey is teaching English to Korean clients but stays at the school playground until 1730 hours and arrives at his grandmother's house at 1800 hours," Sam said.

It was a known fact that many mothers and grandmothers go to the playground to watch the kids play ball. Sam also said that every Wednesday afternoon from 1330-1500 hours Kobe attended "robot class" at his school. Additionally, on Thursday, which for our planning was the day after tomorrow, Kobe, along with the 2nd grade classes, would be on a field trip to the museum.

One thing was for sure, if the 2nd graders were heading for a field trip to a very public government building (museum), we needed to exfil before that on Wednesday ... which was the next day. Attempting to pull this off at the museum would mean extra days of surveillance and a ton of uncontrolled disadvantages, like local police and cameras which were typical of any museum setting. Add the fact that most teachers are more alert during field trips than on school grounds, and you have one more challenge to take into consideration.

Today was Tuesday. In reviewing the new intelligence from Sam, I found it rather odd that kids would be playing baseball for close to five hours. It just didn't add up. What did add up was the fact that Kobe had been known to stay in the classroom while others came out for recess or playtime. Because of his mixed-race heritage, he was not easily accepted at the school. Rumor had it, at least from Sam, that he had frequently encountered opposition and harassment from the other children. That seemed a logical answer for why we did not see him on the playground the first day.

We then grabbed a bite to eat at a local Burger King. While we sat at lunch, Mark wanted to return to the park adjacent the school to see if he could see Kobe amongst the baseball team. I knew that if we returned, we could possibly draw undue attention to ourselves. He suggested that we could grab Kobe off the baseball field that day if we saw him. Once again, I entered into discussions, tossing out questions that he couldn't answer and possibly see the light.

"How are you going to make an introduction with Tiffany while all of these onlookers are at the baseball field?"

"What if the grandmother is there and she puts up a fight?"

"What if Jeffrey is there and he puts up a fight?"

"We haven't seen Kobe's route to and from the school, so how do you intend to grab him?"

"Where do you intend to stash Tiffany during all of this?"

"When do you intend to brief her on the operations plan, so she knows what to do if something goes wrong?"

"Will she know how to get to the U.S. Embassy if she gets separated from us?" and my list of questions went on and on until he finally settled down.

The day was growing late ... now 1400 hours, and the traffic would be upon us in another hour as we tried to check the exfil route to the U.S. Embassy on the other side of town. Against good judgment and in an effort to maintain friendship, I told Mark that we would head back to the school. He pretended not to want to go, but when I insisted, his tune changed to satisfaction.

We arrived at the school around 1430 hours and positioned ourselves once again in the park. We monitored the school for about two hours with no sight of Kobe or a baseball team, as a matter of fact.

Something Bigger Than Overthrowing Small Governments

Once again, Sam's intelligence was incorrect ... as I suspected it would be. I needed Mark to realize how complicated it was going to become if we did not verify all the intelligence, how "right on" we needed to be in order to pull this off. It was actually somewhat frustrating for me to have to spend the energy and time to readjust his imagination to reality. Finally, Mark grew tired and suggested we work the route to the U.S. Embassy. We hailed a taxi and headed out. Along the way he finally agreed that the best plan of action was what I had recommended earlier ... go back, allow me to work up an operations order, brief everyone, and then execute the plan with my direction and control.

We arrived at the U.S. Embassy slightly after 1700 hours. I attempted to enter the outside security building controlled by GSA Korean Officials, but they turned us away. They stated that the Embassy was closed, and we could come back tomorrow and request an appointment, or if there was an emergency situation, we should let it be known. The Official also informed us that most of the Consulate Staff would be working only half-day tomorrow (Wednesday), and that if we had any business needs it would be best to do it before then.

It was for this exact reason we ran the route, and Mark was starting to see it. He had assumed that the U.S. Embassy would be open 24 hours a day. Now it was imperative that we picked up Kobe and got to the U.S. Embassy before 1100 hours on the day, if we intended to have someone generate a passport and get us out of country.

I had not yet figured out whether we would receive a warm welcome from the Consulate, but I knew we could not exit Korea cross-border or via airport without a passport for Kobe. All of this would have to fall into the operations order that evening.

We returned to Hotel Cello, where I spent an hour working up an operations plan and then presenting it to Mark and Tiffany.

Operations Order

Situation: Kidnapping of Kobe. His location is Seoul-GorMyeong Public Elementary School

Enemy Situation: School teachers, police, Jeffrey Salko, Grandmother Salko, Local Civilians

Attachments/Detachments: Sam, the informant is standing by as a point of contact in case of emergency. Outside of two Rally Points, to be discussed, Sam is to be contacted as safe haven assistance and resource. Rally Point (1) U.S. Embassy. Rally Point (2) Salvation Army

Mission: Rescue Kobe from school, secure an undetected transport to U.S. Embassy, process passport, exfil Korea

Execution:

0700 – all personnel awake and gear packed no later than 0745.

- Tiffany- have Kobe's change of clothes laid out, have door key to hotel room on your person, have wig and shoes in bag with you, wear your coat with hood to disguise yourself, wear medical mask over your face, since you do not have gloves, powder your hands with the makeup I provided to lighten skin tone, and be prepared to use it on Kobe's face if necessary, have coat for Kobe
- Mark- Have Ops gear, radio, written directions for taxi driver to school, back to drop off point and then to U.S. Embassy, pack your bags and stage in your room.
- Baz- Ops gear, radio, written directions for taxi driver to school, back to drop off point and then to U.S. Embassy, pack my bags and stage in Marks room. Turn in room key prior to departure.

0800 – All personnel depart Hotel Cello for AO ... Kobe's school.

0820 – All personnel move into place. Mark positions at top end of park. Tiffany remains with me on park bench at lower end near school entrance. (Describe location on map and drawing)

Something Bigger Than Overthrowing Small Governments

0900 – School is in session

0915 – on command Tiffany follows Baz to Kobe's classroom. Mark follows and holds security at bottom of stairwell of school entrance.

0920 – Exfil with Kobe. Tiffany follows Baz, Mark runs rear security and interference if necessary. Find screened post to place coat and wig on Kobe.

0945 – All personnel arrive at drop site Hyundai Dealership one block from Hotel Cello and move to hotel to retrieve bags and disguise Kobe with new clothes.

1000 – Depart Hotel Cello for U.S. Embassy

1030 – Arrive U.S. Embassy

Service Support – Taxis and Directions in Korean

Command and Control – Radio channels 2.5, Alternate 3.5. Only move on my command. I move with Tiffany and Kobe, Mark trails until position to jump ahead and hail a taxi.

That evening I showed Tiffany how to wear her disguise. I applied the makeup I had brought to lighten up the skin on her hands to make her blend in more with the Asian community. I demonstrated how I wanted her to put the girl's wig on Kobe. I went over the operations order with her three times and walked her through the details on paper, mapping out the school, the classroom, the exfil routes, hiding places and taxi pickup spots ... everything she would need to do if, for any reason, we got separated from her. She was a little nervous, but I had faith that as long as I was there beside her, she could walk the walk and talk the talk.

The following morning everyone launched per the operations order. We arrived on time at the park and observed the children arriving. Tiffany sat with me on one of the benches while Mark took up another location not far away. I struck up a conversation with Tiffany to determine her comfort level ... she did not seem nervous. I learned that she was from Charleston S.C., the same city where I had attended The Citadel. I ran over the plan one more time with her. She stayed bundled up with her face covered ... not uncommon for the cold on that early morning, even among the local population. So far it was all working out. We continued to watch for Kobe, but he never appeared. I wasn't apprehensive, but there was no guarantee he was even at school that day. There were other entrances to the school, and perhaps he used one of them. The only way we would find out was to check his classroom.

We entered the school at the designated time, and I led Tiffany to the classroom on the second floor. Mark positioned himself on the first floor just near the stairs, keeping a lookout in the front of the school to the street which we would cross as part of our exfil. I instructed her to stick her head in the classroom, as rehearsed, and call for Kobe. She opened the door slowly, and we both saw Kobe sitting there. He responded and slowly moved outside the classroom, rather astonished that Tiffany was really there. The teacher stepped out, a little concerned, but recognized the likeness of Kobe and his mom. She asked in broken English ... "Mommy?" I said, "Yes, it is his mommy." I motioned with a finger that we needed a moment, and the teacher stepped back inside as we predicted, to handle what now was becoming a rather unruly group of children in the classroom.

I gave Tiffany the command, and we exited with Kobe in tow. We left the school grounds calmly and at a moderate pace, crossing the road and using as much screening from high-rise buildings as possible. The tiny profile of Kobe was swallowed up as I wrapped my jacket around him. We stopped in a stairwell and changed his white baseball shoes for black tennis shoes and placed the wig on his head. When he asked why he had to wear it, I told him that it was cold outside, and I needed to keep his head warm. He liked the idea and sported the wig rather handsomely. Mark hailed a taxi, and we headed back to Hotel Cello.

Something Bigger Than Overthrowing Small Governments

"I am so excited to see you, Mommy. I thought you were going to leave me here forever," Kobe said.

Tiffany gave him a big hug. "I love you. I would never leave you," she replied.

Along the way, Kobe continued to talk about America, his family in America and expressed his happiness that he was heading back. He was a little chatterbox.

His mother said, "I guess it's been a long time since you spoke to anyone in English?"

Kobe took a beat and replied, "Yep," and then started up again, not missing a beat in what he wanted to say.

We arrived a block from the hotel and got out of the taxi. If you're going to use a taxi, it's best not to let the driver know exactly where you are heading or staying, especially if there is an APB (all-points bulletin) out on you. We hopped out and headed south and around a corner. As soon as the taxi was down the road and lost in traffic, we headed back north and to the hotel via some alleys ... again using as much screening as possible to fog our route.

Into the hotel and up to the rooms we went. "Everyone has five minutes and no more to grab your bag and meet me here in the hallway ... get to it."

We dispersed, and within five minutes we were heading out the door.

Departure from Hotel Cello was without incident, and we arrived at the U.S. Embassy at 1045 hours. I approached Sgt. Fitzpatrick Marine Security Guard and requested assistance and contact with the FBI Attaché' and the Consular. I briefed him on the situation and announced myself as former Captain USMC. For the next twenty minutes he placed calls to find someone to assist us.

Finally, Rachel B. Crawford, Vice Consul, 2nd Secretary, six months pregnant, approached us. I showed her the paperwork, warrants, kidnapping charges, etc. and explained who we were and our purpose. She was familiar with the case and offered her immediate and total assistance. She moved us to a secure location and began processing Kobe for a passport. She informed us that Jeffrey, despite his international warrant for kidnapping, had the nerve to contact local police and even call the U.S. Embassy and tell them that they could not issue a passport without his signature. I think this worked against him, since Crawford had already been informed that Jeffrey Salko had illegally obtained a Korean passport from the black market for Kobe when they first arrived in Korea. Crawford sent word to the Marine Security Guard detachment to be on the lookout for Jeffrey Salko, should he attempt to enter the U.S. Embassy or position himself outside the gates.

Crawford ordered pizza for Kobe, Mark and Tiffany as a courtesy while she processed the paperwork. Another official arranged for our flights out of the country. I took Kobe inside the Consulate photo booth to snap some shots for his passport.

From what I could determine from the phone calls, officials at the highest levels of the U.S. Embassy were offering their full support and ordering Crawford to ensure the safe departure of Kobe and ourselves. I was more than impressed and really happy that my experience with the Department of State personnel this time around was a good one ... the kind that refreshed my faith in Americans working overseas.

I left the compound for about one hour to run surveillance on the perimeter and grab a bite to eat at a local Korean restaurant in the back alleys near the Consulate. Protestors against American Imperialism were in full swing, which was common these days ... men in business suits with bonsai-style head wraps and police escorts carrying four-foot batons and shields. A barricade of police buses lined the north wall of the building next to the Consulate, speaking the truth about daily and almost commonplace riots, student protests, and overall anger of a culture displeased with "American Imperialism" — the same imperialism that was keeping North Korea from bombing the life out of South Korea and bringing them all under communist rule.

Anyway, I returned to the Consulate in time to meet Scott Kim, Attaché and Diplomatic Security. Some complications were arising as the Korean government and police were trying to side with Jeffrey Salko and his story that Kobe was a Korean citizen. It would seem that Salko had indeed registered Kobe and was awaiting citizenship. It would seem that Salko had also renounced his U.S. citizenship in favor of Korean citizenship, as we had been informed by Sam. An exchange

Something Bigger Than Overthrowing Small Governments

of looks between myself, Crawford and Kim, an American of Korean grandparents, put us all on the same sheet of music ... we had to stall the Korean government and tie Salko's efforts up in the diplomatic cogwheel long enough for us to leave the country.

Kim's Korean Airport Police Liaison was standing by to assist our processing. Kobe, Tiffany, Mark and I loaded the black suburban with Kim and Crawford and a driver. Our destination was Inchon Intl' Airport. Kim and I had a few things in common. He had spent time in Iraq and other places of espionage interest, knowing full well that we were somewhat cut from the same cloth. Our conversations bordered on friendly talk, common associates, and a like understanding of the rules of war and, in this case, diplomacy.

Crawford was excited to be assisting and did not hesitate to engage in questioning the regions and types of operations ARC participated in. In between it all, she monitored her cell phone, always aware of the Consulate's progress in its play to stall Salko.

When we arrived at the airport, we were greeted by two plain-clothes police who escorted us to the counter for ticket processing, all the while, watching for the possible arrival of Jeffrey Salko. There was a sense of urgency in getting Kobe and his mother through customs, and the ticket counter attendant was as slow as molasses. I stood in the background providing security until Mark, Tiffany and Kobe got their tickets. They would be leaving on a plane one hour prior to my departure, just one gate away. I could not ask for better oversight.

I encouraged Kim and Crawford to head out to immigrations with Kobe, Tiffany and Mark. I would catch up as soon as I got my ticket. By the time I did catch up, they were being held up by a customs passport official (female) who realized that Kobe's immigration information had been flagged. There was some confusion, discussions, and more confusion as Kim, Crawford and the Police Liaison battled with immigration.

One police official, Mr. Park, who spoke good English, mentioned that we could cancel his Korean citizenship by paying a fee at immigration. In other words, pay the fee and we'll look the other way. So Tiffany borrowed $100.00 from Mark and headed back to Immigration with Kim and Crawford, while Mark and I watched Kobe. During this time, I could see the woman in Customs, like a dog with a bone, diligently scrolling through her computer, looking for anything and everything she could find to possibly deter our departure.

Back at the U.S. Embassy, officials were working with the Korean government to help Salko process the proper paperwork to the prosecuting attorney's office at the police department. Of course, once the papers were processed, they would have to come to the U.S. Embassy for review and then probably back to the Prosecuting Attorney's office for corrections and then back to the U.S. Embassy, etc. It was a nice stall tactic, provided we didn't end up getting turned away from Customs or incarcerated.

Tiffany returned about thirty minutes later, and we advanced to the gate, thanking our Korean Liaison for his assistance. Kobe, Tiffany and Mark would be departing in one hour. This would be the longest hour of the operation. Everyone was on high alert. The last thing we needed was Korean officials apprehending everyone before the flight or stopping the flight on the tarmac before takeoff. Time passed and God favored our exfil as Kobe, Tiffany and Mark boarded the plane with Kim assisting. With doors closed and their return fairly secure, Kim and Crawford escorted me to my flight, which would be departing within the hour. Kim slapped a Diplomatic Security Coin in my hand and told me if I ever needed anything, to call. Crawford offered up her assistance should I find myself in a recovery operation in India, her next assignment. A handshake to Kim and a hug from Crawford, and we went our separate ways. I boarded my flight for a ten-hour journey back to Los Angeles ... not without the pleasure of another Korean grandmother sitting next to me, insisting that I put more hot sauce on my dinner.

In the aftermath, Mark Miller and his organization managed to end-run ARC, giving little to no credit for the operation, no request to join him on television and radio interviews, no assistance with inviting viewers and listeners to ARC's website. Our expertise had been used and, in my opinion, abused with minimum return on investment of time and relationships. Tiffany Rubin went on, as did Mark, to sell their story to Lifetime Television and claim operational credit, misrepresenting the tradecraft they were guided by ARC to use. When Lifetime television discovered that ARC had actually run the operation, they mitigated liability by doing an add-on piece to the show called

Something Bigger Than Overthrowing Small Governments

"Behind the Scenes," where they did, in fact, credit ARC with the operation.

Recommendations:
- Work independently of other child find organizations unless they have been fully vetted as strategic partners.
- When working with other child find organizations, have them sign a contract that states there will be no media coverage without ARC's permission and full participation.
- Do not engage in operations with Mark Miller and his organization.
- Continue to maintain SOP not to contact the U.S. Consulate until after the exfil is in play.
- Tiffany Rubin should have contacted Jeffrey Salko, as directed, on the day to tell him that she had Kobe for three days in Seoul and would return him. This would offset any of Salko's action to contact police. She was instructed to do this but did not follow through. I hold myself responsible for not following up to ensure she had done so.
- Maintain Liaison with Korean Consulate for future operations.
- Only run operations with ARC team members or by myself.
- Process maps and directions in foreign language prior to leaving U.S.
- Contact media relations prior to return to U.S. and set up ARC interviews for PR.
- Always run routes in country and follow the Operations Order to the letter, as was done in this operation, and NEVER allow inexperienced operators to have the Con.

Chapter 14
OPERATION SALIX
AFTER ACTION REPORT

Subject: Willow Bradfute

Date: July 2011

Introduction:

For the purposes of this report, the SFRT consisted of Bazzel Baz, Thad Turner, Gonzo, Kurt Norrigen and two attachments (2) Mexican Special Forces Operators

Background:

Beginning early 2011, nine-year-old Willow Bradfute was abducted from her home in Killeen Texas. The abductors, Willow's non-custodial mother, Patricia Marie Patton, with a history of drug trafficking and imprisonment, along with her Colombian cartel boyfriend, Elias Gonzalez Velazquez — or so he later claimed to be — also previously imprisoned for drug trafficking, planned and executed the kidnapping and journeyed across the Mexican border to escape capture. Fearing for the life of his daughter, the custodial father, Cory Bradfute contacted local, state and federal authorities for assistance and was turned away. Authorities were either too busy or were classifying it a civil matter and dismissing it. The kidnappers threatened to harm the child if a ransom was not paid and began extortion demands for 50,000 U.S. dollars. While the custodial father, Cory Bradfute, negotiated as best he could, he and his parents had no choice but to pay the first installment of $1,000.00 to buy as much time as they could.

A moderate-income family, plumbers by trade, the Bradfutes had little money and had nowhere to turn, floating hopelessly in a sea of despair until the hand of God intervened. Through an underground network of Special Operations personnel and a company called Templar Titan (TT-former SEALS) a call was put into *The Association for the Recovery of Children* on behalf of the Bradfute family.

Something Bigger Than Overthrowing Small Governments

Operation Overview:

    I drove to San Diego, California, to talk with a good friend of mine, Gonzo, who is the CEO of Eagle Eye Security (EESS). Gonzo and his men had spent — and still do to this day — their entire careers dealing with a wide spectrum of threats across the world, be they physical, electronic, political, financial or natural. Their global reach capability and years of exposure to foreign and domestic threats was comparable to ours and had kept them at the forefront and cutting edge of what they do, continuously searching for innovative methods to improve their abilities to better protect their clients' interests. EESS had a special focus in Latin America, having operated in Mexico since 1990, and that would be invaluable for this operation.

    I arrived at a rather obscure location, hardly detectable by the common eye, entrenched by other buildings ... a perfect security setup, if I might say so myself. This would be my first meeting with Gonzo. I was met at the door by Kurt Norrigan. Kurt had served in U.S. government and corporate positions throughout his career and knew everything to do with Mexico like the back side of his hand. His Spanish was impeccable and his demeanor that of a calm river. He ushered me into a conference room laced with Navy SEAL memorabilia ... I was at the right place. Gonzo, a former Navy SEAL, entered with a Carey Grant smile and a firm handshake. I would find out later that Gonzo and I had both grown up in the Panama Canal Zone at Fort Gulick, my father being stationed there prior to deployment to Vietnam and his father being stationed there after returning from Vietnam all in the year of 1968/69. We never crossed paths as young boys there, but now our time had come, and it was a vote of confidence to have both him and Thad on this operation. While we never met at that age, it was certainly comforting, as if things had come full circle in life.

    Gonzo sat there and just listened as I briefed them on the situation. I told him that we didn't have much money to fund the operation with salaries. "We don't want to be paid. Just cover the cost of our guys in country and whatever technical services come up for discovery and we're good. This is about a child ... if you can do it without pay, so can we," he said.

I made arrangements for Kurt to contact his two-man Mexican Special Forces team in Mexico City to start doing some advance work for us ... and Kurt would attach himself to me and Thad Turner (ARC) when we were solid on the launch date from the U.S.

I drove back to the covert site for ARC and contacted Cory Bradfute to let him know we were ready to help if he needed it. Cory had been communicating with the kidnappers, Elias Gonzalez Velazquez and Patricia Marie Patton, via text message. Not being skilled or trained in the art of negotiations, it was not long before communications between the custodial father, Cory Bradfute and the kidnappers (Elias Gonzalez Velazquez and Patricia Marie Patton) broke down, leading to a horrible threat by the kidnappers to sell the young Willow into prostitution. To add insult to injury, we discovered that Willow had a younger half-brother in the mix, the child of Patricia Marie Patton and another man.

I was on the first flight to Killeen the next day, setting up a one-man command center in the office of the custodial family's business building and pulling together resources from the U.S. and Mexico to cross the border and bring the child safely home.

After numerous efforts by the Bradfutes to get the FBI involved, they refused, and so I took it upon myself to navigate USG contacts to reach ICE for assistance in country. Unfortunately, even ICE was bogged down in red tape and passed the word that it could take at least 90 days to put an operation together with all the diplomatic hoops they needed to jump through. They highly recommended that ARC stand down. From my point of view, there wasn't enough time to just stand down ... the life of the child was at stake, something everyone in a position of authority appeared to be brushing aside. We had developed very special high-level relationships — and I mean very high — in the Mexican government, who were sympathetic to our cause. Three in particular wanted to help as long as they remained anonymous. We intended to take them up on their hospitality.

Interestingly, I have come to see the intelligence community around the world differently than I did when I was in the CIA. It is filled with a number of spies who will never cross the line to help someone if it involves espionage but will not hesitate to jump in with both feet if it involves the rescue of children. All of us have a clear

Something Bigger Than Overthrowing Small Governments

understanding of where the line is, and we never cross it. But I assure you that we have no problem shaking hands or raising a toast when a child comes home safely due to the efforts of all.

Looking back, I think I know why most law enforcement officers were hesitant to support the Bradfutes. Cory himself had a brush with the law on a few issues in years past. He had served his time and proven himself a decent citizen and responsible father. He was very upfront with the mistakes he had made as a younger man, and everything about him told me it was true. But in the eyes of the law it seemed there was no forgiveness. Cory was branded for life, and that grudge was playing itself out like a forest that could burn twice ... they were just walking away. But the sad part was this ... by walking away, every sapling was going to die, and Willow was one of those saplings. It angered me to think that the legal system was blinded by their own ego, arrogance and intention of proving how tough they could be, at the expense of an innocent little girl. They could not look beyond their own arrogance long enough to realize that Willow had done nothing to deserve any of this. Heck, I didn't even know the child, and yet I was championing her because of exactly that ... she was innocent and was caught in the middle. So without question this rescue was the right thing for me to do.

As mentioned, Cory Bradfute had already been communicating with the kidnappers via text, so I decided to introduce myself using that channel, at least until I could persuade them to speak voice-to-voice on the phone. While I knew the importance of making sure criminals came to justice, it was more important to posture myself as someone not attached to the law, a mediator or civilian negotiator, in order to get them to let their guard down. Establishing communications with them would tell me so much more about the disposition of the kidnappers as well as buy time for EESS to gather locations and call records on the two Mexican phones Patricia Marie Patton and Elias Gonzalez Velazquez were using. The first text I issued: Messages sent from

Text 1958 hours from me: "Good evening. My name is Bazzel Baz. Go to www.RecoveryofChildren.org and familiarize yourself with me. I am now working on behalf of the Bradfute family as the negotiator for the release of Willow. The contact number from this period on will be the Bradfute business line @ ▮▮▮▮▮▮▮▮. I look forward to speaking, so we can resolve this issue."

Text 2008 hours from Kidnapper: "I will speak with u tomorrow about this and would like to have your number not the bradfutes I dont want to go thru them anymore at all"

Text 2125 hours from me: "I thought it might be worth mentioning that law enforcement is not involved. We are merely acting as a mediator so that things are fair to all parties. We really want this to come to a good closure. How much money will it take for the release of Willow, and get this over with? I'm sure you have a large sum in mind, so tell us what that is. Standard protocol is the clients number not ours. If you want my help call ▮▮▮▮▮▮▮▮. I will expect your call @ 10 am Texas time tomorrow. Thank you Mr. Baz/ARC"

Text 2149 hours from Kidnapper: "I dont understand y urinvovedive tried SEVERal times to work with them and they NEVER answer their fonesive done my part they haven't"

Text 2243 hours from Kidnapper: "Ill call once tomorrow around 12pm tomorrow ive already called so very many times if no answer then i will not try again send ur number not theirs"

Text 2429 hours, Sun. July, 17, 2011 from Kidnapper: "I decided you can call me tomorrow at 12 ive already spent too much time calling them so u call me at this number tomorrow i will not call ne more"

Something Bigger Than Overthrowing Small Governments

    Once I knew I had established this rapport, I entered negotiations texting with the Elias Gonzalez Velazquez and Patricia Marie Patton via phone over the course of one week, drastically reducing the ransom from $50,000 to something affordable. I continued with texting until I could get Elias Gonzalez Velazquez and Patricia Marie Patton voice-to-voice on the phone ... which wasn't that reliable once I got them there. It wasn't unusual for a call to drop right in the middle of our conversations.

    I was finally able to reach them on a stable connection on the phone and introduce myself ... a kind voice to reassure them that we wanted to work with them. Most of the introductory conversations afforded me the opportunity to appear sympathetic to everything they were doing ... positioning myself as the go-between so they could get everything they wanted ... rather than attempting to be the voice of reason or get them to see it our way. I also assured them that the family would be receiving all of their demands and making the final decisions. This way Elias Gonzalez Velazquez and Patricia Marie Patton would have the illusion that they were still dealing with amateurs rather than being threatened by a professional negotiator. If you watch enough television, you know, as I'm sure they did, that negotiators never tell you the truth, and they string you along just enough to get SWAT through the door. I wanted and needed to camouflage myself as best I could and setting the stage this way would do exactly that.

    It also offered me the opportunity to request technical assistance from a number of other associates who pin-pointed the location of the kidnappers in a third of the time federal authorities could have. Even armed with this intelligence, kicking doors in for a hostage rescue was not what I had in mind. A surgical and stealthy extraction would be the last option if the kidnappers failed to accept my terms and the money we had agreed on. I was talking them off the ledge just far enough to get our hands on Willow. There are a lot of things I learned in the CIA, much forgotten, but some things never ... like not stirring the fire when the landscape is dry, or not being afraid to dress up like the enemy when you need to get inside his camp.

    But then something changed. Elias Gonzalez Velazquez left a voice message that he was only going to talk to me via text. No more phone calls. I really wasn't sure why the sudden change, but what I did know was that I needed voice-to-voice, and I needed a way to subtly and subconsciously let him feel he had to do it my way.

I had now gotten them to bite and needed to see just how badly they wanted the entire cake, so I went dark for a day (not responding to texts). Finally, Elias Gonzalez Velazquez left a voice message rather than texting ... just what I wanted. Now I knew he was persuadable. I could hear Patricia Marie Patton in the background coaching him from time to time ... inserting her two cents worth of desperation. "You haven't sent any ransom money, so me and Patricia are leaving for Peru tomorrow on the 4 p.m. flight and taking Willow with us."

Obviously, this got my attention but not in a way that dissolved my logic. I had broken the operation into phases. Phase One: keep them communicating with the cell phone voice-to-voice as much as possible so Kurt and EESS could monitor their positions.

If Elias Gonzalez Velazquez and Patricia Marie Patton really wanted to disappear, they certainly would not be telling me when and where they were headed ... they would just leave. I decided to put more cake on their plate. So at 1400 hours I texted them rather than placing a phone call.

> **Text 1400 hours from me:** "Just received all of your text messages. Sorry for the late reply. We just learned how to use this. All we want is the safe return of Willow and will pay whatever you want to get her back. We trust you will keep your word. What are your demands?"

I got no response from the kidnappers, so I texted again.

> **Text 1420 hours from me:** "What happened to Patricia and the money you and she demanded earlier?"

Chances were if he were really going to Peru on a 4 p.m. flight, he would cancel that. I believed at this stage this was all a scam. If they had the money to travel to Peru, they would not be asking for more. Either way there was nowhere in South America they could go that we wouldn't find them ... it is difficult for a female to travel with

Something Bigger Than Overthrowing Small Governments

two kids. So on that note, depending on what his text response would be, I intended to text back to him either later that day or the next ... once we knew his location.

About an hour later I received a text from the kidnappers.

Text 1536 hours from Kidnapper: We want $50,000 dollars

Now they were back to demanding the $50,000 dollars they had initially asked for. I responded as if I were Cory Bradfute. I wanted them to feel like they were still dealing with a family who wasn't that quick on the draw, especially under stress, rather than a negotiator who would be expected to make lightning-fast decisions, or who was authorized to make decisions on behalf of the family. I also needed to start throwing the ball a little harder ... a few demands. I've found that if you mimic the kidnappers it does two things (1) catches them off guard and off balance (kuzushi), and (2) subconsciously aligns you with them.

I know it may sound weird, but if you enter a hostile village and do the same dance the natives do, you have something in common. And if you have something in common, it makes you part of their clan to some degree or makes them feel as if you understand who they are. They generally don't know what to make of it, so they begin to accept you either out of curiosity or just plain comfort.

> **Text 1640 hours from Me:** "It will take some time to raise that kind of money ... but we will do it for our granddaughter and daughter. In return, here is what we want. We want to speak with Willow on the phone and hear her voice, no texting, at least twice a day until we get the money to you to make sure she is okay. We want to speak with her in the morning before we go to work (8am is good) and again when we get home from work (6pm is good). If you agree, deal. If not ... no deal."

It was starting to look like we would soon be launching across the border with a three-man SFRT linking with former Mexican Special

Forces associates in Mexico City. I sent the following email to the ARC SFRT:

> From: baz@███████████
> To: "Sch, K" <ke>; T T<tha>
> Sent: Tue, July 12, 2011 5:13:20 PM
> Subject: Willow
>
> Gentlemen,
>
> Mexican sources are currently triangulating the signals and I am in negotiations via the custodial father with the kidnappers. There are a number of inconsistencies in conversation that lead me to believe they have little funding to travel from Mexico to their proclaimed Colombia or Peru. Once we get a signal lock we will be on our way with an escort from our San Diego SEAL partners and Mexican associates.
>
> If you can both be prepared to leave within 24 hours from your locations that would be great. I realize that everyone has a schedule that may not fit into this operation and if on the day that happens you cannot assist, I clearly understand. Meanwhile, if you can provide me with full name, DOB and SSN so I can grab tickets for you on the day that would be appreciated.
>
> Semper Fi and In His Service
>
> Baz

I needed to buy a little more time while I got my team on the flights, so I texted Elias Gonzalez Velazquez and Patricia Marie Patton.

Text 1850 hours from Me: "The Bradfutes had a family emergency and had to go to the hospital. We

Something Bigger Than Overthrowing Small Governments

will be talking again in about a day. I have checked their bank account and they do not have anywhere near $50,000 dollars, and the bank will not lend it to them. Maybe they can raise that in about one year, but for now all they have in their account is $10,000 dollars. How much do you need to release Willow?"

A few text messages and phone calls came in from Elias Gonzalez Velazquez and Patricia Marie Patton, but I did not respond to them and had no reason to believe that by not responding, they would simply disappear. I had set up the hospital crisis, which gave me the excuse I needed.

I wanted Elias Gonzalez Velazquez and Patricia Marie Patton to sit on it for a bit so I could gauge his sense of urgency as well as his temperament, and sure enough, it worked. The silence was killing them ... they wanted more cake, and started leaving multiple messages on the phone as well as texting:

Texts from Kidnapper on Thursday, July 14, 2011:

Text at 0817 hours: "Hey I hope everythings good at hospital, sorry but need 2 know what R U gonado,Usendin? or not 2500 seems a lot but u get willow,soner the beter"

Text at 0823 hours: "If u dont trust me or u dont want 2 pay u need 2 tellme that way I dont waste time with this bullshit,thesoner u send ? and pin# we get this overwi"

Text at 0829 hours: "Atleast answer the fone even if u dont want 2 pay. willwsheart broken we can work this out if U only trust me a lilbit.if u want send 1500 now"

Text at 0835 hours: "And 1000 later on. I hope u get this mess Cause U need to call me so u can talk 2 her.

282

Lets not drag this any longer now U Have tue solution in ur hand"

Text at 0933 hours: "I'll call U at 10 am 4 U 2 talk 2 willow and let her know that U gays R bein cheap cause of U shes not home with U guys & U love chayanne more than her"

Then I finally placed a call and left a message at 1305 hours. "We really meant this to come to a good closure. How much money is it going to take for you to give us back Willow, and leave us alone for life? I'm sure you have a large sum in mind so tell us what that is."
Elias Gonzalez Velazquez and Patricia Marie Patton responded by text.

Text at 1308 hours: "I told u send the 2500 now and 3000 when u get her i just want reimbursed for gettin her 4 u send the 2500 now and ill get to austin with her thats it"

Text at 1313 hours: "If u hurry we can still make the flight today and ull have her tonite and this will all be over let me know have to be at airport by 2 at latest"

Text at 1320 hours: "So r u going to do it so i can hurry to western union and then hurry to airport u gotta let me know so i can go or not"

Text at 1325 hours: "Send it to eliasgonzalezvelazquezguanajuatomexico and text me the pin so ican get there with willow tonite"

Text at 1358 hours: "I need to know whats up and try n find nother flight but u need to let me know once patricia gets here ? 7 icant help u so decide n lemme know"

283

> **Text at 1447 hours:** "U want willow u call me im done chasin u down. Imlookin 4 plane tickets but u need to call me if u really want willow and get this over with asap"
>
> **Text at 1452 hours:** "No more fukin games u text then no anwers. This is b.s. Send the 2500 and pin u get willow and give the other 3000it must b b4 patricia gets here"
>
> **Text at 1824 hours:** "i dont know how else to help u shell be here in like45 min u wont answer any fone calls so u screwed urself out of gettin willow maybe u can talk2 her"

Now we were getting somewhere. They had lowered their ransom from $50,000 to basically $5,500 dollars. I knew they were bankrupt and that reconfirmed that they were headed nowhere, especially on a flight to Peru. They couldn't afford it.

I still didn't respond immediately, but instead contacted the State Department to lock down some administrative intelligence that would prepare ARC should we need to interact with Mexican authorities. I discovered that Willow did not have a passport. Then how was it that the kidnappers were able to get her into Mexico? Our borders were so porous that anyone could come and go into Mexico without detection. It made me wonder how many terrorists had already taken advantage of this gateway and entered the United States.

I then contacted Texas department of criminal justice and found that Patricia Patton was convicted of "manufacture and delivery of cocaine." She was sentenced to three years. She served a year in prison and was released on parole on August 6, 2008. She was finished with her sentence on June 19, 2010. Her TDCJ # is 07624891. Patricia's birthday is 07-22-1984.

Then I contacted Catalan Hakan at DHS, hoping they would want to get involved now that I had probed the lines and opened some things up. I sent the following email:

Bazzel Baz

From: █████████████
Sent: Sunday, July 17, 2011 8:05 AM
To: 'Catalan, Hakan A'

Hak,

I'd like to filter intelligence through you and you can forward as you see fit to your boys in Mexico. However best works for you, whether you want to let them know you're getting it from me or simply getting it from a source.

I am currently in contact with the kidnappers, negotiating and attempting to keep them on the line so whoever in Mexico is pushing forward can triangulate on the phones and locate them.

As you and I both know, things at that level can run slow and before we know it, the child is gone. Highly recommend if it has not been done that airports are covered. We are receiving messages that Patricia intends to fly out ... to where, we have little indications other than previously mentioned Peru or Colombia. The last message we received was VM on the 16th prior to my introductory text with hopes of suspending the flight and having her engage me today.

FYI the FBI sent Special Agent Samantha A. Mikeska down to the Bradfute family to pick up the texts and messages. According to the Bradfutes, she told the family that, "this could take months. Just thought you guys needed to know." Great thing to tell the family and in light of how fast the kidnappers are moving, a sure sign that once again they are being provided an opportunity to hide a little deeper ... but she was telling them the hard truth of the matter.

Thank you.

Baz

Something Bigger Than Overthrowing Small Governments

It was evident that Agent Mikeska understood her Agency better than most, and the red tape was once again allowing criminals to get away. Right now, we were the only resource for maintaining contact, and someone in the FBI would benefit by using it, but that wasn't in the cards.

The next day I resurfaced and got Elias Gonzalez Velazquez and Patricia Marie Patton to agree to speak with me on the telephone to tell them that the family had gotten the $5,500 dollars together and was ready to deliver it to them. I kept them on the line long enough for Kurt to trace the call. Kurt and I spoke after I hung up with Elias Gonzalez Velazquez and Patricia Marie Patton.

"It was very interesting," he said, "████████ is from Laredo and seems to be a land line ... I am trying to get more details on this. But ████████ is same area code as the pay phone ... I'm trying to find out if it's a landline or cellular. If Elias called personally (we sure it was his voice on both calls?) then he is most probably in Laredo and the 413 number is a cell (the only other possibility that I can think of is that the 956 number that showed on the caller ID is the number of a switch used to relay the call from Guanajuato to Texas ... I remember in the 90's that this used to happen). Anyways, let me try to get some more info on the phones but we need to consider a contingency that they or he is in Laredo."

I gave it some thought and then replied, "I was thinking the same thing. But another possibility to consider is that Patricia had a change of mind and she did leave Elias and took Willow and the other child also, and he was just bluffing for the money ... if he persists in not letting Cory talk to Willow then this possibility increases. If this is true, then it would be good that Elias is no longer involved, and we could forget him, but also bad because Patricia had not made any contact or demands without him, and we had no leads on finding them. It is all speculation at this point," I pointed out.

I needed ground truth. I needed to speak with Willow, but I didn't exactly know how to coach Elias Gonzalez Velazquez and Patricia Marie Patton into doing that for me. I sat in the makeshift command center, so graciously afforded me by the Bradfute family. It worked, and it worked well — no distractions, solitude, a desk, a phone and the hospitality of a family who were grateful just to have someone with experience helping. I lowered my head and prayed, "Dear God, Maker of heaven and earth, hear my prayer. I don't even know if this little girl is alive."

The next morning, I called Kurt to give him an update ... an answer to my prayers. "Willow spoke on phone message alongside Elias this morning, so we know she is there. A fair assumption that Patricia does not have money to travel, and that Elias would cancel any of his credit cards if she even thought about stealing them ... it would leave her high and dry. My best guess is that Patricia is still involved and in the background. He put Willow on phone this morning to leave a message ... so she's there. She did not mention her mother abandoning her, which is what a child would say ... 'mom has gone and I'm alone,' or words to that affect. They have set a pattern and I have marked it well over the last two weeks. They are still very much in flux, and this stalking horse operation is very much on course, as I would like."

Kurt responded, "Excellent, then it's just a matter of tracking his phones ... I still have a doubt about the Laredo phone ... my guess is that it is a switch number that showed up on the ID ... everything else points to them still being in Apaseo."

The ARC SFRT caught the first plane out to Mexico City. We would figure out Phase Two ... a safe meeting place to deliver the ransom money, as soon as we got settled, do a reconnaissance of the city and/or the place where Willow was being held. Skirting the corruption, the Drug Cartels, city crime and number of other trip wires, the ARC SFRT began its final chapter of negotiations, dealing with kidnappers on the phone, who fluctuated on their demands, meeting places and location for the final exchange.

After three intense days of negotiations from a hotel room in Mexico City, the kidnappers were not able to agree to the meeting place and also jacked up the ransom price again. I reluctantly played the one card a negotiator seldom wants to play. "The deal is off, and I am heading back to the U.S. Furthermore, I assure you that an international warrant will be placed for your arrest, and both of you will be hunted down and dealt with appropriately by Interpol."

Immediately in the background I could hear the non-custodial mother scream, "No, we want the money, we want the money. Okay we'll meet you where you want to meet." The tone, and the greed and the love of money over the welfare of her own daughter was sickening to hear, but the deal was done ... or so I thought. I hung up the phone. I relaxed a bit, looked over at Thad, who was smiling.

Suddenly the phone rang again. I picked it up ... Elias Gonzalez Velazquez was on the line, "We have changed our mind, you can leave if you want."

I was feeling like my dog was off the leash and running so far ahead that I would never catch him. I put the speaker phone on so Thad and Kurt could hear the conversation. I bowed my head, "Dear God please tell me what to say."

Kurt and EESS with the help of Mexican authorities had been pinging the kidnapper's phones, so we had a pretty good idea where they were located. I took a breath, "That's not very wise of you. I think you need to look out your window and tell me what you see."

I could hear the movement of his feet across the wooden floor, slow and deliberate. About ten seconds passed when that slow and deliberate walk across the wooden floor turned into a speedy retreat back to the phone. "You know where we are."

"Yes, I do," I replied.

"Okay we will meet you," he said frantically.

"Tomorrow I expect a call from you no later than 8 a.m. letting me know that you are on the way ... if not, our people will roll you up before you even step out of your house. Otherwise, they'll let you get here ... understand?" I said.

"I understand," was his reply.

I hung up the phone. Now I have absolutely no idea what he saw out of his window, but whatever it was, it worked. Sometimes a bluff works, especially if inspired by God.

An hour later I received another call from him. He wanted to agree on a meeting place ... one of many we had already discussed earlier. I arranged a high noon meeting the next day, "inside at the Capuchin nuns' Temple, to the right of the old Guadalupe's as you are facing the building." He agreed to be there. I hung up the phone, bowed my head and said, "Thank you Father."

Thad put his hand on my shoulder and said, "Hand of God."

Kurt smiled and headed out the door. "I better get my guys ready ... I know you're going to want to recon the site before we go there tomorrow."

"Roger that," I replied.

Within the hour we found ourselves at the site rehearsing our plan. I knew the square would be filled with tourists the next day, which would provide enough cover and concealment for our team. The next day could not have come fast enough.

And that day did come. With our five-man team in place and unarmed, which in itself was risky, I entered the cathedral in search of Elias Gonzalez Velazquez, the Colombian drug trafficker/kidnapper, not really knowing if Patricia Marie Patton would be there. At first he was nowhere to be found, and then ... there he was, outside on the steps with his back turned ... talking on his cell phone.

The fright shivered almost comically up his spine when I tapped him on the shoulder. Few words were spoken, eye exchanges served their purpose. Once inside, towards the back and in the last pew, I looked at the English-speaking Elias and said, "Let us pray." He

Something Bigger Than Overthrowing Small Governments

followed my lead and knelt. I removed the first bundle of cash from my boot and passed it across.

Elias counted as best he could through the plethora of small bills, intentionally placed to buy myself more time if needed. The Colombian was nervous, hardly able to count through. He looked up to say, "I guess I will have to trust you that it is all here," eager to make his departure.

To Elias' surprise, I pulled the other bundle of cash from my other boot and handed it across, "It's good. I'm trustworthy, here's the rest." As he counted again, I looked across and said, "What you are doing is wrong, and you know it's wrong. I could shut you down right now, wipe you from the face of this earth, but that isn't what God wants. He loves you and He wants you to know that."

I had just turned off the faucet of every emotion in his being, interrupting every thought. His circulation ceased ... as fear paled his brown, Hispanic skin white. I was forcing every ounce of energy from my eyes to cut through him and drive hard to the pits of his soul declaring that I had the power to rip it from his body and leave him on the doorsteps of hell.

I was suddenly aware of the dichotomy of convictions intimately dancing within my words. How could I be compassionate and yet at the same time ready to wipe this being off the face of the earth for what he intended to do, or what he may have possibly already done to Willow? And then I remembered that it was only for me to obey God ... despite how I might feel towards Elias. In hundredths of a moment I was wrestling with God, and I knew He would win. I knew the sooner I was okay with that, the sooner I would see Elias the way God saw Elias ... a lost soul that perhaps never had anyone like myself to set boundaries in life in a way that was definable. Instead of throwing him off the cliff, I could take him to the edge ... which would be an eye opener. With that in mind I suddenly realized I was never angry ... just precise and matter-of-fact about this entire meeting. I sank back into my world of confidence and knew that if God had gotten me this far, He would finish the job. "So you don't get struck by lightning when you leave here, I should pray for you."

Following a silent command, the Colombian lowered his eyes as I prayed a short but deeply penetrating prayer for his salvation.

"Father God, You don't need our belief or disbelief in order to exist ... You show Yourself in all that is around us. You are the maker of heaven and earth, and men are foolish to not see. You give life, and you take it away, and no man can deny this. I pray You will spare Elias long enough for him to come to know You. Amen." And then it was over.

In Hebrews 4:12 the scriptures tell us: "For the word of God is living and powerful, and sharper than any two-edged sword, piercing even to the division of soul and spirit, and of joints and marrow, and is a discerner of the thoughts and intents of the heart." I looked directly at Elias as he tripped over his own words, trace images of brokenness and disorder permeated the boundaries of this encounter to illuminate the expansive flaws in his character.

"My mother is a missionary in Peru," he shamefully announced.

I wasn't buying it, and everything in my eyes let him know that. "Then your mother would be ashamed of you Elias." More shame and maybe even fright blanketed his face as I kept staring directly into his soul. "It's time to go," I said with that deep, raspy voice well-suited to reiterate my divine right and his diminishing power. As we exited the cathedral ... no doubt both of us were wondering if it was a setup. How ironic to be playing a game of chess on the large square of this Vatican replica, he and I seriously contemplating and anticipating the other's move.

I stopped. Elias stopped. "I have shooters following us, you just can't see them. If there's anything you need to tell your boys, you'd better tell them now. You're the first one to go down if anything goes wrong. Understand?" His foreboding stare was that of a three-year-old whose command presence was quickly going down the toilet. "I strongly suggest you make a call if you need to," I said. He pulled out his cell phone ... "In English," I insisted.

"It's all good. We're coming to you. Stay where you are with Willow and don't move ... just stay there," he barked. He pocketed the burner phone.

"It's good to come to an understanding, don't you think?" I said, as I pushed a fake smile.

"Yes" he replied.

Something Bigger Than Overthrowing Small Governments

Halfway across the square everything was looking good ... not feeling safe ... but looking good. "You know Elias, in another time, another place you and I might have been friends. But it's not this time or this place. When we get Willow, you need to stay right where you are until I release the snipers, who are watching you right now, okay?"

He could not get his mouth open to say anything. So I put my hand on his shoulder. "I understand ... bit off more than you could chew. Might be a good idea to never show back up in Texas." His eyes were listening as his head acknowledged my words with that subtle nod that would be bigger, but your neck is so stiff with fear that it just won't move. And that was exactly how I wanted it to be ... paralyzing at best. During that long walk I wanted to come at him from every angle I could that would make him think he was already dead.

It was an uncomfortable walk across the grand courtyard, not knowing when a shot would be fired, a knife blade plunged, or a grenade tossed — all slippery tactics from people like Elias Gonzalez Velazquez. Kurt and Thad were in the crowd acting the part of tourists and paralleling my route, then disappeared. In addition, God had His angels in full force and the presence of the Holy Spirit abounding when I spotted the nine-year-old Willow Bradfute being held by another Hispanic thug. The remaining ARC team members quietly converged on the scene, much to the surprise of the thugs and to Elias, hopefully outnumbering their unseen allies hidden in the shadows. As I drew closer, I smiled from a short distance ... a smile that I am sure, from the reaction on the face of the thug, made him curious and possibly think it was at him ... when it wasn't.

It was at Thad, who was close enough behind him to be a fly on his ear, close enough to break his neck if required to save Willow, and quite willing and ready to do so if I gave the word.

While everything was in play, I could have forcibly taken the money back and the child, and apprehended the kidnappers, but not on this day. I had given my word, and my word was my bond even to the evil ones. At the time it may have seemed silly, but later, in a court of law, when the kidnappers do come to justice — and they will — keeping my word would be one thing to strengthen my testimony against them ... a man always telling the truth. The last thing I needed was a defense lawyer saying, "So Mr. Baz, you lied to my client, so what makes us think you are not lying now?"

Suddenly there she was ... little Willow Bradfute, as cute as a button ... bewildered by the sudden appearance of myself hovering over Elias, like a child seeing glowing eyes under the darkness of the bed.

I knelt down in front of Willow. "Willow, your dad loves you very much and he sent us to take you back to the United States. Are you ready to go home?"

She smiled and replied, "Yes."

"Okay, take my hand and stay close to me. We're going to the U.S. Embassy to get you a passport."

Backing away the first ten steps is always the toughest, particularly if you don't have as big an army as everyone thinks you have. Running fast is a great option, but not so easy when you have a small child with you. It's not the load that breaks you down, it's the way you carry it, and at that moment there was not really any safe way to protect Willow if things went upside down. The welfare of the child is the number one priority, so every move is calculated with that in mind. I kept my eye on Elias and then turned while two of our team members remained behind long enough to keep Elias in his place. There were hundreds of people moving about, tourists mostly, but honestly it was hard to tell if any belonged to Elias. I wasn't worried about the horse being blind ... I was just loading the wagon. We scanned as quickly as we could while on the move first through a very uncomfortable choke point where construction workers had narrowed the connecting walkways from the cathedral to where we needed to go. Eventually we found our way to the outer streets. The team picked up the pace to the car and headed to the U.S. Embassy.

Once we arrived, we parked about a block away and held our position as our Mexican Special Forces attachments secured the perimeter. These two guys were a pleasure to work with ... their tradecraft, impressive, and their ability to anticipate our every move, spot-on with the orders I had given concerning the operation. As we moved closer to the U.S. Embassy, the surroundings seemed calm enough for Thad, being himself the parent of two children, to do what a dad would do ... he stopped and bought Willow some ice cream in a cup. She beamed with excitement and was more than appreciative when

Something Bigger Than Overthrowing Small Governments

he handed it to her. Strangely I noted that after finishing, she insisted on keeping the container. She was holding on to everything and every moment she could at the time, so afraid that this entire dream — which wasn't a dream at all — would be taken away, just like she was taken away from her father and grandparents ... the people she loved so much. I watched as she studied it and carried it like a little girl carries a doll ... giving it the attention she herself hungered for. When she wasn't gripping my hand, she was gripping Thad's ... never letting go. I remember how tiny it was in the palm of my own, and how careful I was not to squeeze too tightly, but tightly enough to make her feel secure ... to let her know we were willing to sacrifice even our lives to get her home.

When we got to the Marine Guard post, I handed them my passport. "Corporal, I'm Captain Baz, former USMC and head of ARC. We have a child who was kidnapped from the U.S. and we need to get her a passport. Can you call the right folks for us?"

"Stand by sir," he said. In about ten minutes the front door opened to the secure area we were standing, and a younger gentleman from ICE approached me. "Are you Baz?"

"There is but one," I replied. I thought he would think that was funny, but he didn't. And I did ... deep inside because he didn't.

"What are you doing here?" he asked.

I turned and pointed to Willow. "Well let's see, kidnapped girl, American, U.S. Embassy. I think that says it all," I said.

"Did you get the email that said not to come to Mexico and run this operation?" he spouted.

"Not that I recall," I stated.

He just looked at me. "Right." He looked over at Willow and Thad and Kurt. "My boss is going to be pissed. Wait here," he ordered.

"You're going to need this paperwork," as I handed him the legal documents surrounding her kidnapping. He took what I had, stepped back inside the Embassy and was gone for about thirty minutes. When he returned, four amazing women from Citizens Services accompanied him and were more than ready to embrace Willow. I can't remember their names, but I can remember their faces and energy. They had a flare we all hope to see from other Americans in foreign lands representing our country ... Americans who put aside political or economic agendas to save their own countrymen.

"If we can have Willow come with us, we'll get her passport processed so you can get her home," said the tallest of the women. Willow looked up at me silently asking permission.

"These ladies will take good care of you, and I'll be right here when you return. I promised your Dad I would get you ... I won't leave you here."

"Okay ... you promise?" was her reply, as she looked back over her shoulder while clasping the hand of the State Department employee. I smiled and returned a wink.

"Can I speak to you for a second?" asked the ICE rep. I walked a few steps to the side out of hearing range of my team. He looked me in the eye. "Off the record ... I would have done the same thing you did. Nice work."

"I believe you would. Thank you." I replied.

"Now I suggest you and your team not stay in Mexico too long. Evidently the mother is already reporting her child missing, which we know is a bunch of bull ... if she gets her back, she'll just hold her for ransom again."

"We plan on being out of here day after tomorrow," I assured him.

"Safe travels," he said as he turned and entered one final time into the U.S. Embassy. After about one hour Willow was handed back over to us by Citizens Services, and we headed to our hotel. Her passport would be ready for pick up the following day. Thad, however, could not resist the temptation to buy Willow about three more ice creams along the way. I anticipated she would be sick as a dog by the time we got back to the hotel, but she surprised us all, and that wasn't the case.

The team dispersed to various observation posts on different floors while we allowed Willow to get cleaned up. She had one small roller suitcase with almost nothing in it for clothes. Thad went to a nearby dress shop and picked up a white dress her size, while I made sure she was not bothered in the room. Within the hour Willow Bradfute was happily sitting in the company of five humble warriors in Mexico City, dining like a little queen, with eyes bigger than her stomach and non-stop one-way conversations fueled by her excitement. She was quite the little lady, well-mannered and smart as a whip.

It bothered me for just a moment to think that had we not rescued her, this amazing child would have most likely been trafficked into prostitution or worse. She was too pretty to go unnoticed by the flock of pimps known to exist in the town where Elias and Patricia held her captive. I dusted off the thought of such things quickly, as my mind returned to the table where Willow was entertaining us all with her smile and quick wit. We had done the right thing, and no one could convince us otherwise.

Too many times American children perish because of red tape, especially if people are bound by the policies of a bureaucratic system that pays them a salary. But that in itself is just an excuse. People are bound by policy because they chose to be bound by policy ... because they are so greedy and self-serving that they would rather ensure their retirement and collect their paycheck than do the right thing in saving the life of child. There is no policy that cannot be changed, altered or even ignored when it comes to saving the life of an American child. As long as it is within U.S. law, why would you not sacrifice it all for the life a child?

When will our government stop making excuses for not protecting our children? Probably never! The government funds organizations that kill our unborn and can't even keep track of those kids lost in our own country. And that is the difference between our government agencies and ARC ... we could care less if we get paid. Not every person is at fault in every agency. There are those inside government who really do try, but their hands are so tied that often they come to me in private conversations asking if they can join our team once they retire ... a way of somehow redeeming themselves for all the times they were forced to look the other way or could not navigate the fault lines in their own organization to save a child.

But on this occasion that would not be the story for little Willow. Her restful night sleep would attest to the overpowering love of God and the men He sent in to save her. Of great interest to Thad and I was this shoe box where she hid all her worldly possessions — a few toiletries and one cherished necklace with a '60s peace symbol.

The concept of owning a proper carrying bag or luggage was foreign to her.

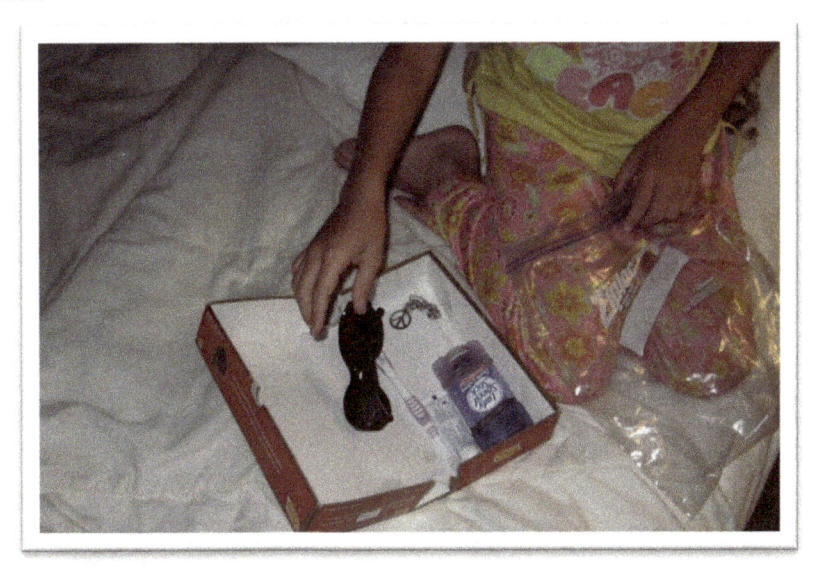

U.S. Embassy Mexico City 2011. ARC SFRT (Thad Turner, Kurt Norrigen, and 2 Mexican SF Operators), Willow Bradfute stands next to Bazzel Baz.

Something Bigger Than Overthrowing Small Governments

    The next day we returned to the U.S. Embassy where Citizens Services personnel handed us Willow's passport. A handshake, a few farewells, and the ARC team left with Willow Bradfute to fly back to America.

    The flight home was eventful. Most of my team took different flights back to the U.S., and those who supported us in Mexico returned to their families, no doubt wrapping their arms around their own children. Willow and I were sitting in the very last row of the United Airlines flight when the flight attendant leaned over and asked Willow if I was her father. I was so grateful to see that our flight attendants had evidently been trained to be aware and to look for children who possibly could be trafficked. Willow had no idea of the extent of her ordeal, and I did not want to make matters worse by blurting it out to the flight attendant. "This is Mr. Baz and he is bringing me to my dad. I was stuck in Mexico for a little bit." Then Willow looked out the window. "Hey, look at all those clouds!" she blurted. It was her first time to ever fly on an airplane.

I unbuckled my seatbelt and stood up slightly to the side of the flight attendant. Under my breath, "She was kidnapped. I'm with ARC and we're returning her home." I handed her a card and the note the U.S. Embassy had so graciously provided for reentry to the U.S. The flight attendant took a glance and smiled. I sat back down next to Willow. She was still looking out the window, mesmerized and dancing on every cloud in her mind.

The flight attendant reappeared. "Willow, would you like some refreshments?" Willow didn't know what to say ... she just looked at me. "Would you like something to drink or some snacks?" I said. She smiled and looked back at the flight attendant.

"Oh, thank you ... of course. Do you have milk?"

The flight attendant returned the smile, "We sure do."

"Do you have it in a carton?" Willow asked. Within seconds Willow's request was fulfilled, and she was sipping and talking of course about a million words a minute. The flight wasn't that long, and soon we began our decent.

The pilot announced, "Ladies and gentlemen we're starting our decent into Houston Texas. It's been a pleasure serving you. And for our special passenger, Willow Bradfute, welcome home to America."

Willow grabbed my arm, "Did you hear that?"

"Yes, I did. Welcome home Willow." My eyes began to water a bit. "Welcome home" is such a nice term, isn't it? Every kid in the U.S. and in the world should be able to hear someone who loves them say, "Welcome home."

We cleared customs without delay and started our walk to find a puddle jumper to get us to Killeen, Texas. As we strolled hand-in-hand through U.S. Customs, young Willow looked up at me and said, "Mr. Baz, I'm pretty shy but I feel I need to tell you this. If I could have another father, I'd want it to be you."

I just smiled. I stopped and knelt in front of Willow. "Thank you for saying that, and if I had a daughter I would want her to be just like you ... but I want you to know that you have a dad that loves you more than the world, and that is why he sent us. When you get home, I want you to love on him with all of your heart and never forget that he is the hero in all of this."

Something Bigger Than Overthrowing Small Governments

    We continued our walk ... she was silent, perhaps milling it all over in her head or just perhaps overwhelmed with the fact that she was really back in America. Who knows what goes through the head of a child at times? I certainly don't, not all of it. But I do know one thing, when they are scared, when they are lost, they pray that someone will save them ... this I know runs through the heart and mind of every child.

    The welcome home was warming, with friends and family at the small airport in Killeen Texas. Tears poured down the faces of relatives thankful for the return of Willow Bradfute.

    As I quietly made my way out of the airport, I was stopped by a friend of the family, who asked, "Why do you do what you do?"

    My reply was, "If we do not ... who will?" And with that, I faded into the thickness of the hot, humid Texas evening. Many would come to know me as "the Patron Saint of Missing Children" ... but to those closest ... I'm just Bazzel Baz, a brother in arms and friend.

    Two weeks later a Federal Officer, who will remain unnamed, called me. "I just wanted to say good job and apologize for my organization. We were wrong. We should have gone in and gotten that little girl out of there. Thank you for what you do."

While I could have lashed out, I didn't. "You guys have your hands full, and it's not easy making choices. You're always welcome to come alongside. Just know we're out there and we have no intention of stopping until everyone of them comes home."

The conversation ended on a friendly note, I was grateful for the call. This agent was an outstanding reflection of what their organization needed to be. And for a moment my faith had been restored ... not in the organization or any government organization, but in the few people of those organizations that can differentiate between what is right and what is wrong and put aside the baloney of bureaucracy for what really matters ... the children of America.

Recommendations: There are no recommendations at this time.

Something Bigger Than Overthrowing Small Governments

CHAPTER 15
OPERATION ICEBURG
AFTER ACTION REPORT

Subject: Ashley Ricks

Date: May 2012

Introduction:
For the purposes of this report the SFRT consisted of Bazzel Baz, Thad Turner, Stella Tong, and three attachments (1) Anthony Ricks -custodial father, (2) ▓ and (3) ▓.

Background:
Ashley Nicole Ricks (age 7) was abducted/kidnapped by her non-custodial mother and grandmother, former Philippins Congresswoman Cecilia Seares-Luna. Ashley was supposed to visit her grandmother in the Philippines with the ex-wife of custodial father Anthony Ricks for summer vacation. However, this turned out to be a premeditated plot to keep her there, since the Philippines is a Non-Hague Convention country. Once the kidnapping occurred, Mr. Anthony Ricks had contacted the local Fullerton, CA, Police Department, the Orange County District Attorney, the State Department, and now was reaching out to ARC in an effort to get his daughter returned. On October 2011 Mr. Ricks was awarded full legal and physical custody of Ashley Nicole Ricks from the Superior Court of California, Case Number 05D009915, Docket 126 MN115. All legal documents are on file with ARC.

The grandmother, Cecilia Seares-Luna, refused to adhere to U.S. court orders for the return of Ashley ... the same Cecilia Seares-Luna known to run a politically corrupt family in the Philippines. She was indicted in her country for embezzlement and suspected of strong-arming any opposition to her corrupt agendas. A local newspaper printed the following article:

> Two prominent members of a powerful political family in Abra are facing plunder charges for allegedly embezzling more than P130 million in municipal funds, in what a whistleblower has called 'big-time corruption in a small town.' Named in a complaint-affidavit are former Abra Rep. Cecilia Seares-Luna and her eldest son Jendricks.
>
> Cecilia served as mayor of Lagayan town from 1998 to 2007, when she ran for Abra's lone congressional seat. Jendricks succeeded her as mayor in 2007, ran for barangay (village) captain in October 2010 and is now president of Lagayan's Association of Barangay Captains. Jendricks allegedly continues to control the town, whose current mayor, Cecilia's 82-year-old aunt Purification Paingan, was also accused of dereliction of duty purportedly for allowing him 'to take over the helm of the municipality and continue his plunder of the town coffers' as ABC president. [24]

A number of local assets that we would need feared family reprisal if known to participate in ARC operations. Therefore, special considerations were taken to protect those assets who would remain on the ground in Manila after the success of the mission.

Our mission objective was to safely and surgically locate, extract Ashley from The School of The Holy Spirit, immediately reunite her with her father, move both of them covertly/securely to the U.S. Embassy in Manila and have her processed and returned to the U.S. with her custodial father, Anthony Ricks. The ARC team would consist of Thad Turner, Stella Tong and me, with attachments from local resources.

Operations Overview:
ARC completed a reconnaissance on May 2012 of the Philippine AO, where Ashley was known to be schooled, and met with

Something Bigger Than Overthrowing Small Governments

a number of local resources and assets in place who had been providing intelligence on the ground. While there was no visual of Ashley during the reconnaissance by the ARC SFRT, intelligence sources had told us that she attended school at the School of The Holy Spirit, F. Sotto St. BF Homes, Quezon City, Tel. 9314049. This information was confirmed through a friend of an asset who is a mother with a daughter attending the same school. It appeared also that Ashley was getting dropped off at school via motorcycle side cart, a typical mode of transportation in Manila.

As mentioned, Ashley was being held by a syndicate-type family. Bodyguards, tracking devices as well as specific instructions to school authorities to keep an eye on her were assumed to be in play. We also discovered that some local law enforcement and traffic police were on the syndicate payroll and were not to be trusted. If bodyguards were employed to protect Ashley, we had no idea how many there would be nor whether they remained at the school during the child's classes or simply dropped her off and picked her up. Therefore, we worked under the assumption that they may be armed as well as have direct communications to the other family members and local law enforcement.

Once again, and as always during operations of this type, it is good to remember that it is never getting from point A to point B that counts ... it's what you do between those two points when it all goes upside down that counts. And so, emergency procedures were critical. For us, if we found ourselves surrounded by bodyguards, we would call all members of the SFRT to reinforce our efforts, obtain the child and then withdraw. Under conditions where bodyguards were armed and had managed to detain members of the SFRT, all members were instructed to remain calm, allow the bodyguards to take the child and then withdraw. Should one or more members find themselves detained by local law enforcement, they were to make a call to one or more SFRT members for assistance. If that failed, everyone was instructed to contact the U.S. Embassy and explain that they had been detained and were not sure why. Deniability was crucial at this stage until I could assess the situation and reach out to the Department of State to resolve matters, so all of us knew to keep our mouths shut.

Based on the intelligence we had, all personnel not directly attached to the SFRT were considered hostile. It was not out of the question for the Department of State to make attempts to resolve anything that went upside down contriving a politically correct solution which might not favor us, so it was important that all SFRT members carry a copy of the Court Order of Custodial Authorization for Anthony and Ashley. And it was yet to be determined if the U.S. Embassy would offer security and safe passage through Philippines Customs. The grandmother was most likely still politically connected in some form or another and was suspected of being an influence in criminal circles. This said, it was safe to assume she may or may not have the ability to send out clandestine forces to retrieve Ashley even as we moved from the hotel to the airport the following day. We needed to be prepared to lay low and exfil through other channels privately if the U.S. Embassy found themselves unable to assist.

We were told that Philippine citizens could be considered somewhat friendly and helpful, but caution was given not to disclose the nature of the operation or the identity of the child and father at any time. There was also a large Muslim faction in certain parts of Manila, and the SFRT needed to be aware of those locations and avoid them at all cost as well as the local street crime that was common to every nation.

The only friendly forces we had inside the country were two assets by the name of ▮▮▮▮ and ▮▮▮. They had local knowledge and resources to draw upon. Outside of the country and based in the U.S. was a third named Joey Luna. His family was extremely influential in Manila and we could reach out to him should we find ourselves in a jam and without assistance from the U.S. Embassy in Manila.

The ARC SFRT would arrive in Manila and make contact with local assets who had been providing intelligence for this mission. Briefings on current intelligence would take place in a secure setting where charts, maps and ops orders could be displayed, reviewed and rehearsed.

Intelligence reports as of June 2012 showed that Ashley was currently attending The School of the Holy Spirit. Her time of arrival and departure was still yet to be determined. There would be only one day of reconnaissance and rehearsal (dry run) on location to satisfy two needs ... (1) to see if Ashley was delivered to the school, if there were

Something Bigger Than Overthrowing Small Governments

armed bodyguards, what was her mode of transportation, times, etc. and (2) to see if the SFRT could move through the region undetected and unencumbered.

On rehearsal day, the SFRT would access the community via two routes, the main entrance and the unsecured property that borders the local village and street on the other side of the gated community.

████, myself and Stella would enter the main entrance under the guise of a married couple as our cover for action, interested in having our child attend the school. A family photo that had been photoshopped was carried with us. At the school we would maintain a strategic position either on campus or outside the gate to observe the arrival of Ashley and collect appropriate intelligence.

████ would drop Thad off along the back road bordering the gated community. Thad would access and clear the route by moving across the vacant lot, about 500 meters down the street to the left and then to the right, encompassing the block which runs directly to the school. Americans in the community would be high profile, so cover for action was necessary. Thad's cover for action would be a Real Estate Broker. On the day he would dress the part and carry appropriate paperwork in his possession along with other real estate pocket litter.

On the day, ████, myself, Stella and Anthony Ricks would enter the gated community, as we would have done the day prior, and position the vehicle outside the gate of the school. ████ and Anthony would remain in the car while Stella and I remained either on the school grounds or nearby. Once Ashley arrived, and on my signal, Anthony would depart the vehicle, walk on the school grounds and meet up with Ashley. It was imperative that Ashley's mode of transportation had departed. I, Stella, Anthony and Ashley would join ████ in the waiting vehicle. The vehicle would immediately and carefully move to the street by the vacant lot. Ashley, Anthony and I would depart the vehicle, cross the open lot and join ████ and Thad waiting in a van on the other side in the village. Stella and ████ would depart and exit the gated community in the vehicle we used to transport Ashley and return to hotel where the SFRT had been staying. ████, myself, Ashley, Thad and Anthony would drive back to the U.S. Embassy in Manila where ████ would return to the hotel and join all members of the SFRT at the end of the day, once Ashley had been processed for departure. The SFRT would have to be prepared to relocate in a safe house should the U.S. Embassy not want to assist. If that were the case, a plan would be constructed to safely transport Ashley, Anthony and the SFRT to another location for extract back to the U.S. So that was the plan. But as life would have it, it isn't exactly how it unfolded.

So let's put some meat on the bones of this story. Rochelle, Anthony, Rick's ex-wife hinted that she wanted Ashley to spend the summer in the Philippines. Something inside Anthony said "no," but they were getting along pretty well. Anthony thought about it more, and since he had never had any problems with Rochelle's side of the family, he entertained the idea of Ashley spending the school year with him and possibly a month in the Philippines for summer vacation.

As the time approached to meet Rochelle, Anthony wanted to call it off ... but he didn't. He went against that still, small voice inside that was telling him something was not right. He dropped Ashley off with Rochelle, and they parted ways. Little did he know that their lives were about to be changed forever. The two-month trip would turn into an ordeal that would last for over a year.

Once Ashley was in the Philippines, Anthony was able to monitor her stay there with frequent phone calls. At first the phone calls to Ashley were frequent and three times a week were normal. And then he noticed the phone calls were sporadic ... he would be calling them instead of them calling him.

On August 10th Anthony got a call from Rochelle. He told her he was ready to pick Ashley up at the airport since she had previously told him Ashley was flying in. There was a moment of silence and then Rochelle said, "Hey, Mom wants Ashley to stay in the Philippines." Anthony thought it was a joke at first. Unbeknownst to Anthony, Rochelle had already abandoned Ashley and was attending school in London. When challenged by Anthony, Rochelle said, "talk to Mom, I'm in London," and hung up the phone. Anthony's heart dropped. What had he done? Why did he allow her to go with Rochelle in the first place?

He made a call to the airlines and, sure enough, Ashley was not on the flight. He called the mother-in-law and engaged in a not-so-nice conversation that basically ended with her telling Anthony that he would never see his daughter again.

Anthony went to the Fullerton Police department with his 50/50 custody agreement. When the Fullerton police department called Rochelle in London, she yelled at them, hung up on them, and changed her number. The police instructed Anthony to file a complaint against Rochelle for not abiding by the court order and informed him that nothing could be done unless the DA took up the case.

Anthony headed to the Orange County Family court and began the process to get Rochelle back into court so a judge could order her to return Ashley. The DA contacted Anthony but informed him that this would be a difficult case since the Philippines was not a signatory of The Hague. Anthony was not willing to sit by and do nothing. He called the State Department, who told him to talk to the DA. He called the FBI, who told him to call the local police. He contacted the National Center for Missing and Exploited Children, who told him to call to DA. He called his local congressmen, who referred him to the State Department.

It was a very frustrating circle jerk that was getting him nowhere, and no one was willing to help. He was now realizing that child abductions to a foreign country, especially a country that was not a signatory of The Hague, were virtually impossible to act on. He recalled the story of an American who had his daughter kidnapped to Brazil, and how it took nine years to get her back. He wasn't about to let that become his story, but at this point he had no idea what to do next.

He became desperate and contacted the U.S. Embassy in Manila, informing them that he intended to board a flight and come get his daughter. It was common knowledge that the Luna family had people killed. In fact, there had been an assassination attempt on Cecelia Luna as retribution. The U.S. Embassy advised against Anthony traveling to Manila for fear that he would be arrested or even killed.

Anthony had nowhere to turn, so he threw himself into his work and studying everything he could about family court so he could obtain full custody. Rochelle and her family had all the leverage in the Philippines, and the circumstances went from bad to worse when Rochelle's family ceased all contact with Anthony. It would come out later that they were telling Ashley that her father did not want her anymore. More danger was right around the corner when Cecilia Seares-Luna made an attempt to gain full guardianship of Ashley in the

Something Bigger Than Overthrowing Small Governments

Philippine courts without Anthony's consent. Anthony was distraught ... the end was in sight, and his daughter was going to be lost forever.

Then one morning a friend told Anthony about ARC. He investigated the website and it seemed too good to be true. He wrote us a letter and spelled out every detail of his dilemma. I contacted Anthony the Friday morning after Thanksgiving and explained to him that though it would not be easy, we could get Ashley back. I mentioned that it would cost him nothing other than his own personal expenses if we needed him to fly over to Manila. I needed Anthony to go to court and get full custody immediately. Fortunately, he had already started that process. In February 2012, he received the permanent sole custody order, and the planning began.

Anthony's former roommate had an acquaintance by the name of ▮▮▮ who lived in Manila. When he learned of Anthony's situation, he offered to help. ARC contacted ▮▮ to make sure his motivations were not financially driven. To ensure this was the case, we had ▮▮ state in writing exactly that ... he did not want any financial compensation for his help. And so, ▮▮ became a valuable resource for ARC. He was able to confirm the location of the school which Ashley attended and gather vital information about the Luna family and the extent of their reach in the local community. We took our first clandestine meeting with ▮▮ in May of 2012, while Anthony remained in the United States, ready to get on a flight as soon as we believed it was safe. I am sure that Anthony was restless, perhaps concerned that the rescue would never happen, but in July 2012, I placed the call that Anthony was hoping for.

"You need to plan on being in the Philippines from August 24th to September 2nd. It's time to move on the extraction." The conversation was about 30 minutes long, but I am certain it felt like two hours to him ... he had a few questions, as did I. "Do you think there is any chance that Ashley will not want to leave with you?"

Anthony responded, "I am not sure what they are telling her, but I am pretty confident she will be fine."

I reminded him that he is her father, and that while we could encounter some issues, at the end of the day, "You are her father, and that is all you need to say." Anthony asked if we were carrying weapons and of course I said, "No."

Anthony was bold in his question, "I wonder with the Luna family and no weapons and/or assistance with their local authorities or government, how can we make this happen?"

I told him that I would go into further specifics when we on the ground in Manila, but the plan was to go where Ashley went to school and retrieve her. I had contacted the School of The Holy Spirit, the same school Ashley was enrolled in the month before, and said my family and I were moving to the Philippines and we wanted to enroll our kid. We sent a complete folder of family documentation including pictures of Stella and myself with our (fake) daughter and contact numbers in the U.S. In a short period of time we were having phone conversations with the school and were being invited to visit once we arrived in Manila. This was our ticket in. In a nutshell, once at the school, I would identify Ashley and have Anthony escort her off the campus.

I reiterated that he was her father, and once he had her in his arms that I did not want him running but walking with a purpose off the campus. I intentionally drilled this into his mind, because I needed to start building his confidence and ensure he was clearheaded and single-minded before he entered the AO. I ended the conversation with, "We need God on our side, and if you're a praying man, then pray for success with this extraction."

Thirty days later would be Anthony's first trip outside the United States. I am sure he did not picture his first out-of-country experience being a situation like this. He was about to embark on the most dangerous adventure of his life. If he was caught by anyone from his ex-wife's family, it could cost him his freedom and possibly his life. He was putting a lot of trust in me and the other operators of ARC, and it was nothing we took lightly. His safety and the safety of his daughter could come at the expense of our own lives as well, a price each ARC operator was prepared to pay.

It would be only after we had successfully accomplished the mission that I would discover that Anthony had disclosed the operation to a number of people, even after I had told him repeatedly not to mention a word of the operation to anyone prior to us departing the U.S. He told his mother, his best friend Ron, Jerry Hayden, who was running for Congress, and his boss's family while on a trip to New Jersey.

Something Bigger Than Overthrowing Small Governments

Looking back, it is only by the grace of God that we were not compromised. What he had done was inexcusable, and it could have cost him, his daughter and our team the very lives we were trying to save.

Let us be clear about one thing ... custodial guardians have no concept of operational security, are generally driven by their emotions, and are not equipped to be down range unless reigned in constantly by the NGO (non-government organization). You should work on a need-to-know basis, and my experience has shown that the custodial guardian only needs to know what you want him or her to know in order to move one step at a time. If I had to do it all over again, I would have directed Anthony to get on a flight to some other country under the pretense of a general meeting and then yanked him from there to the AO, taken his cell phone away and disclosed nothing but what I wanted him to be doing the day before I needed him to do it. And knowing now that he leaked the operation and lied to me about that on multiple occasions, I would have cancelled it all together and looked him right in the eye and said, "Do you know why your daughter is not coming home now? Because the mission was leaked, and the Luna family is waiting for us."

I realize that may sound harsh, but this is serious business, and we are not in the habit of being stupid. There is a future full of kids that need to come home, and we are not about to let a custodial guardian who cannot follow orders jeopardize that for so many others. None of this made Anthony a bad person, just a person like all inexperienced people who are scared and out of their element but are still refusing to let the experts take control and do what they are good at. And my harsh words in regard to him not being truthful are not to be taken personally by him. It is what it is, and God protected us in spite of it all. If I were to see him on the street today, I would certainly shake his hand, give him a big hug and be glad that all went well ... because it would be the right thing to do ... the thing God would want me to do.

ARC had two other local assets, employees of the airport, monitoring Anthony's arrival. He cleared Manila Customs without much of a hassle, although for a minute there was one Customs Agent who engaged him in lengthy conversation regarding basketball. As our asset brushed close to both of them, he reported that the conversation was non-threatening, and in a short matter of time Anthony and the

Customs Agent were relatively friendly, with him bidding Anthony farewell. I'm certain that in Anthony's mind it was just a matter of time before someone recognized and arrested him. His confidence level, according to our assets, was noticeably failing. Would he have held up under interrogation? I don't think so.

The ARC SFRT had distanced itself from his arrival, not by design but by default, since it is impossible to be in two places at one time. We were running surveillance on the school and rehearsing. Once we returned to the hotel, I left a message for Anthony to meet us on the 24th floor at 1100 hours. Anthony was met by me, Thad and Stella. We had used the school records Anthony provided to arrange a meeting with the Principal of the school, but that meeting was postponed until the next day — the day we intended to be on campus and see if we could spot Ashley — just spot Ashley, not retrieve her on that day. The Ops meeting took place in the hotel conference room. We opened the map and the model of the school and surrounding locations. I needed to meet with ▮▮▮▮▮▮▮ as well, since he had provided us the intelligence gathered from a mother who had a daughter in the school.

Stella and I would go to the school on Tuesday morning to meet with the Principal. Thad would be driving. I would be in the right seat, Stella in the back with Anthony. Stella and I would depart the vehicle and move to the entrance to the classrooms while Anthony would remain in the back seat and do his best to identify Ashley if she showed up. If we spotted her before Anthony did, we would stop her and tell her that her daddy was here, and after signaling Anthony, he would depart the car, retrieve her, and bring her back to the car. Once everyone was in the vehicle, Thad would make sure we exited the huge iron gateway entrance before the guard was able to close it.

I showed everyone on the map an alley where we would exchange cars. Most likely everyone would be looking for a 6'2" black man, a Chinese woman and two caucasian males with a little girl in the primary vehicle. So switching with ▮▮▮▮▮▮▮ to another vehicle, we will have staged across a vacant lot leading to a village street outside the gated community, would be the ploy to throw them off the trail. Once in the other vehicle, the team would rapidly deploy to the U.S. Embassy.

Something Bigger Than Overthrowing Small Governments

We met again that Sunday to go over the plan again, this time including ▆▆▆ and ▆▆, ▆▆'s assistant. I made it very clear to him that the vehicle he was driving would be identified early, and that he was not to remain with the vehicle if he came upon a roadblock at the entrance of the gated community. I made it very clear to ▆▆ that he was to remain with his vehicle on the village street across the vacant lot. Both men said they understood completely and were ready and willing to go with the plan.

Monday was a holiday in the Philippines, a perfect day to rehearse for the Tuesday that would follow. We observed Anthony spending his time in the gym, the hotel buffet and the lobby, where he used the free Wi-Fi, assuming he was simply maintaining contact with his business back home, but in reality he was keeping his friends informed of his status. When Anthony finally departed the hotel, we followed him to a 7 Eleven store where he grabbed a Slurpee and then made his way eventually back to the hotel. There would be one more meeting on Saturday to introduce ▆▆ and ▆▆, who Anthony had yet to meet. There Anthony sat in a secure conference room with two locals, two former SpecOps military men and a female undercover investigator for human trafficking. The look on his face made his thoughts transparent, "What have I gotten myself into."

The look on my face eye to eye was intentional ... I wanted him to read my mind. "Are you sure you are up for this?" It was like two people having a silent conversation and in all of it ... complete understanding of what each was saying. I could tell he wanted to speak out loud. "Spit it out."

He looked at each of us and then, "Ashley's Philippine Grandfather threatened that if I came here, I would get hurt."

I cornered his words with as much kindness as needed to a father who had been sideswiped by thieves. "Your daughter lives in more fear every day not knowing when she will ever see you than you have right now. You can go back home, if that makes you feel safer, and I won't have a second thought about it. Ashley is an American that has been kidnapped and held illegally in a foreign country ... those are the facts. When you contemplate her safe return, ask yourself one thing ... if we do not ... who will?"

Bazzel Baz

He would have two days to digest my words. When Monday arrived, Anthony was standing tall in the hotel lobby, more polished to begin the final rehearsal. The drive to the target would take us through some of the worst poverty-stricken areas of Manila, with thousands of slum and shanty town dwellers where the populace was forced to live in makeshift homes, hastily built from scrap in the areas most at risk of natural disaster.

The privilege of having the scent of burning trash wafting through our rental car as we drove the streets of Manila was every bit how I remembered it from other visits. I glanced in my rear-view mirror and could tell that this was a rude awakening for Anthony, and that if there was ever a time in his life that he appreciated Orange County, California, USA, it was now.

Stella and I were in the front seat while Thad and Anthony maintained the back. ▆ and ▆ followed in the other car. We flashed our passports to the security guy at the gated community telling him that we had an appointment at the school tomorrow, and that we'd like to drive around the community to look for a house to purchase. He waved us through. When we arrived at the school, the gate was locked,

Something Bigger Than Overthrowing Small Governments

as expected on a holiday. We had dropped Anthony off in the other car with ▮ and stationed them down the street. The armed guard at the gate was more than curious when we pulled up. I turned to Stella ... "By the time we leave here, I want this guy to have a crush on you." Stella exited the car and started up a conversation with him regarding the enrollment of her daughter, pointing to Thad and me in the car as her husband and brother-in-law. Within about ten minutes of discussions and distractions by Stella, Thad and I had all the intelligence we needed on the layout of the school. Stella, with just the touch of her hand on his arm in saying goodbye, had managed to put the guard exactly where we wanted him ... wanting more of Stella. We turned and drove away slowly, Stella waving until we disappeared around the block.

The extended neighborhood was quiet enough to allow us to finish marking the vehicle exchange points, primary and alternate routes as well as physically walking the vacant lot that would take us to the village outside the gated community. We rehearsed the entire operation until I was confident everyone knew what they were supposed to do. Back at the hotel I called for another meeting. "Tomorrow is D-day. If we do not identify Ashley, or if for any reason she does not show up, we may have to push things to the next day. Even if we do identify her on the day, we will not pick her up. We need to see how the school operates while the kids are being dropped off. We have meetings set up that will get us back in there the day of the actual extraction. I repeat, we will not be picking her up on the first day we see her. Does everyone understand that?"

Everyone said they understood. Although Anthony said he was okay with that, I realized he wasn't. Instinctively, I was keeping a really close eye on him. He leaned into ▮ on the way out of the room, not realizing Thad had his ear a few feet from them, and Anthony said, "I am so ready to go home. I sure hope Ashley goes to school on Tuesday so I can get the hell out of dodge."

That evening Thad and I would have to make a hard decision to either keep him in the hotel or bring him along as rehearsed. It was only the confidence in Thad's presence that kept my mind from being completely polluted with thoughts of what Anthony might do wrong. Thad was, and always has been, a remarkable safety net for unexpected moments of destruction ... as far back as our days working together in the CIA. He was the only combat swimmer I had ever met that could have his entire underwater compass board disintegrate in zero visibility, put together another one and lead a team directly to the target — and may I say, successfully complete the mission. It always sucks at this stage of the game when you can poke holes in the fiber of team members, and that was essentially what we had turned Anthony in to ... a team member.

While there are many operations when a custodial guardian will never go down range, there are some, like this one, where you need them to be there. It is the face that the child recognizes, minimizing the fear that could come from strangers attempting to do the same. But that said, in the history of ARC we have never had one child that has not come to us with open arms, somehow realizing that we are there to save them ... even if the custodial guardian was not there with us.

Our departure time would be 0430 hours the following morning. Anthony hunkered down in his room not really sleeping. He received a message from his boss ... a scene from the movie *Taken*. The lead actor, Liam Neisen was speaking:

> "I don't know who you are. I don't know what you want, if it's money you are looking for ransom I can tell you I do not have money, but what I do have is a very particular set of skills, skills that I have acquired over a very long career, skills that make me a nightmare for people like you. If you let my daughter go now, that will be the end of it. I will not look for you. I will not pursue you. But if you don't, I will look for you. I will find you and I will kill you."

The scene planted itself in the back of his mind and took him from a nervous wreck to a state of ease, confirming that he was in the company of the right people, and that all would be okay. Now, I never considered ARC to be the Liam Neisen of the world, but if it boosted Anthony's confidence, then I certainly wasn't about to buck against it.

The day of reckoning arrived. The team gathered in a hidden section of the hotel lobby. I chose my words carefully and delivered them softly. "On paper all this works out perfect, but the unknown is something we can't account for. It isn't about getting from Point A to Point B, it's about what you do between those two points when it all goes upside down that matters. We've been over every emergency procedure we can think of. You all know what needs to be done and the consequences if you don't do it right. If anyone wants to back out, now is the time." I looked around the room and saw nothing but firmness of purpose in each of their eyes. If they were scared, you could have fooled me. "Let's roll," and out the door we went.

By 0430 hours we were on the road headed to the school — Thad and I in the front seat, Stella and Anthony in the back, ▇ and ▇ in the car behind. Stella had been on the front lines before and knew the drill ... keep the anticipation to minimum by engaging Anthony in conversations about life, sports, women, and anything else you can imagine, making it more like a road trip rather than a covert operation.

We were ten minutes out as the sun struggled to show itself through the blanket of pollution that choked the sky. I stopped the car and Thad changed places with Stella. We entered the gated community with no problems and proceeded to the school a bit early ... taking no chances on when or how Ashley would arrive. ▇ had not entered the neighborhood but instead had driven a route to the village street outside the neighborhood across from the vacant lot. Our drive through the neighborhood allowed us to see him posted where we had mapped it out from our recon. As we drove past, I stuck my hand out the window and discretely signaled him. I slowed a bit, and once I knew he was set, we continued down the road.

We pulled up to the gate at 0615 hours to be greeted by the same armed guard Stella had enchanted a few days prior. It was not physically possible to have a smile as big as he had on his face when he saw Stella, but he did it. He looked in the back seat and saw Anthony and Thad, but as soon as Stella put her hand on his arm, his focus shifted. We reminded him that we had an appointment with the Principal. He opened the large, rod iron gates and into the school parking lot we drove, parking nose-out for a quick getaway. Discreet communications checks were in order, and everyone was up on the net loud and clear.

Stella and I got out of the car, and Thad took over the driver seat. I looked at Anthony, "There are armed guards on the grounds. Do not get out of the car unless I signal for you to get out of the car, even if you see Ashley, do you understand?" Anthony responded, "I understand."

Stella and I managed to find a seat inside another gated portion of the school's outside corridor leading to the classrooms. Thad had a visual on our position. A few teachers inquired as to our being there, but as soon as we mentioned our scheduled meeting with the Principal, they walked away. By 0645 hours there were children being dropped off in small buses and coming from all directions right to the choke point where Stella and I were sitting. We patiently monitored each of them as they approached, and then suddenly there she was, heading right for us with her Hello Kitty book bag in tow. Stella and I turned to look in the other direction to see where security and teachers where monitoring from. I looked back as Ashley passed us heading to her classroom and monitored her movement.

We had the intelligence we had come for, the bus she had arrived on and, most likely, the bus that would take her home that day. I formulated the plan in my head immediately. We would follow the bus after school in a less-restricted setting and make the pickup. Now it was time for Stella and I to take our meeting with the Principal and get back in the car and leave the school. But that part of the plan never happened, because Anthony jumped out of the car yelling, "There she is, Ashley, my daughter," running towards Stella and I and creating a scene that was drawing the attention of teachers and the armed security guards. Things were getting ready to become interesting. It was going upside-down between Point A and Point B. As he reached me, I had no choice but to tell him to go get her.

Anthony tapped Ashley on the shoulder carefully, and when she turned, she stared at him with what seemed like far more time than we had available, and then said, "Daddy."

He responded with a kiss and said, "I told you I would come get you, but now we have to go."

I told Anthony to pick her up now and move to the car. As he did, a teacher tried to block him and asked who he was. "I'm her father, and she is not going to school today." The teacher tried to restrain

Something Bigger Than Overthrowing Small Governments

Anthony, but we pulled away and he said again, "Get your hands off me, I'm her father and we are leaving."

Stella and I were covering his six and ushering him out of the gated breezeway before someone could shut us in. "Get to the car now and go," I ordered. Stella and I ran interference as he skirted through the gate and ran for the car. I don't believe at the time anyone on campus made the connection between Stella and I and Anthony, but it would only be a matter of time before they did. Thad looked back at me as Anthony and Ashley climbed in the car. He wasn't about to leave us behind, but the window of escape was quickly narrowing with the shout of teachers yelling, "Close the gate, close the gate." And, sure enough, the armed guard manning the large rod iron gate was doing exactly that. I motioned for Thad to go. He hesitated for just a moment looking at me as if he was about to leave his best friend behind to be eaten by lions. I know it pained him greatly, but I am proud of him for holding to the mission and getting Ashley out of there. He peeled rubber, barely squeezing past the closure. I looked around and said to God, "Lord we need a way out, please hear me." You see, it isn't that God is in the equation ... God is the equation.

I turned to Stella and said, "We have to go now."

Stella, in a collected manner, responded with, "Where?"

"Just follow me," I said as I moved out at a fast pace using the confusion of the event to smokescreen our departure. We filtered out another back gate that led to another neighborhood. Sitting in traffic was a driver in a minivan. A voice in my head said, "This one." I opened the sliding door, and Stella and I jumped in. The driver was so caught off guard that he did not know what to say. "Hi, we're just two Americans needing a lift. Could we ride with you down the road a bit?" He wasn't exactly smiling, but he wasn't super unfriendly either. Immediately the traffic began to move. Two miles down the road Stella and I jumped out and grabbed a taxi to get me to the U.S. Embassy and Stella to the hotel, where she would pack up all the gear and prepare to move to another hotel on my call.

Back in the neighborhood as Thad was squeezing through the campus gate, Anthony was letting out a big sigh of relief, "Woooo!" But little did he know, things were just getting started. Thad brought the car to a halt at the vacant lot where ▇ was now standing next to the other car for the exchange. Thad, Anthony and Ashley jumped out, and ▇ jumped in the other car and immediately headed down the street to get out of the gated community. Since ▇ had not been seen at the school, there was a pretty good chance that he could make a clean exit. Keeping that in mind, however, I did tell him the night before that it was a safe assumption that he could be recognized, and should he find himself facing a roadblock up ahead to abandon the vehicle and make his way on foot.

During the rehearsal the vacant lot was vacant, but today it was a different story. A hornet's nest of locals gathered, evidently learning as quickly as wildfire that something had happened at the school. The opposition was mounting, and Thad knew they had to move quickly. "Now, Now, Now!!!" he shouted as he herded Anthony and his daughter through what seemed was going to be sea of villagers who had nothing better to do that day than mess with the wrong people.

A couple of guys made the mistake of getting in Thad's way, and he introduced them to the ground beneath their feet. When another fellow tried to grab Anthony, he got what was coming to him ... a punch that knocked him out cold. It is safe to say that this day ARC was not going to be stopped.

They reached the waiting car with ▇ inside. Thad took the driver's seat, knowing full well that the next hour or more would be in rush hour traffic. It was possible that this could work in our favor, like hiding in plain site with one too many vehicles for the police to watch for. Then again, it might not. If they got stuck in traffic, it could prevent them from reaching the U.S. Embassy before it closed, or they could be detained at a roadblock by local police. Thad remained his cool, calm self, but by this time Anthony was a nervous wreck. Anthony asked ▇ to speak Tagala to Ashley and inquired as to the whereabouts of her mom and grandmother. She was very forthcoming when she said that her mom was living in London, and her grandmother in Abra. The nanny had been taking care of her all this time.

Suddenly, a call came in to ▇, something unexpected. It was ▇. Instead of abandoning the vehicle when he noticed a roadblock up ahead at the gated community entrance, he decided to sit, inching his way with the other vehicles. It was the wrong thing to do. He soon

Something Bigger Than Overthrowing Small Governments

found himself surrounded by about 15 uniformed and plain-clothes police officers with weapons.

Thad told ▓ to hang up the phone. It was too easy with the right technology for them to be tracked. ▓ continued to talk with ▓. Thad told him to hang up the phone again. There was nothing we could do for ▓ at that point ... our priority was getting Ashley and Anthony to safety. Thad told ▓ again to hang up the phone, but ▓ ignored him until finally Thad yelled like a tidal wave, "I said hang up the phone, now!"

▓ did not hesitate, he hung it up. Thad apologized to Ashley for yelling. She was a resilient child, and asked Anthony if they could go to Disneyland and asked if she still had all of her toys at home. "We can go whenever you want but first, we have to get to the Embassy," he replied.

The sound of police, ambulance or military vehicle sirens intersected the route, possibly nothing more than responses to emergencies in the metropolis, but Thad was not making any assumptions and asked ▓ to identify each one, police, military or ambulance. Nothing would be assumed at this stage especially in planning any evasive maneuver. If it were police heading their way, action would need to happen at the sound, not when they were on their tail. Two miles from the U.S. Embassy ▓ requested to be let out to maintain his anonymity. Thad pulled to the side and ▓ exited, disappearing into a sea of people between some shanty businesses.

As Thad drove up to the Embassy, he noticed that there were local police in front of the Embassy. It was safe to assume they intended to arrest any of our team before they could reach official U.S. soil. Thad drove by the Embassy, under the foot bridge that crossed the highway leading from one side to the other and parked two blocks away next to a Sushi restaurant. He realized that the car could have already been burned (identified), so he pulled Anthony and Ashley out of the car and had them follow him inside. The stress was wearing on Anthony, and Thad could see it.

"What are you going to do?" he asked.

Calmly, Thad replied as he picked up his phone and dialed a few numbers, "...Call a few Embassy contacts and see if we can get an escort if I don't hear from Baz. Sit here and act like a tourist." Thad stepped away, phone to his ear. When he did ... Anthony once again went outside operational boundaries that could have cost us the mission. Had I or Thad known what he was doing, I would have yanked that phone out of his hands and shoved it down his throat. I discovered later from a debriefing, during that time Anthony started calling people from the States for help. He called his boss and explained that he had Ashley and was about two blocks from the Embassy and asked if he would call the U.S. Embassy and explain the situation. Then he called Jerry Hayden, who was running for congress, and he put a call into Dana Robacher, who was a congressman already. He then called Ellery Williams, who was a lieutenant for the Phoenix Police department. All of these calls were on a non-secure line, and who knows who could have intercepted them at the time. A little triangulation and the police would have been all over him and Ashley and Thad.

What Anthony did not know at the time, and what he soon found out, was that I had already made it into the Embassy and was setting up their retrieval. Stella had efficiently made it undetected to our hotel and was packing everyone's gear and moving to another hotel.

Thad and I made contact, as we usually do in these cases, and I informed him that according to the RSO (Regional Security Officer) the local police we spotted outside the Embassy were not there for us, but instead simply preparing for some demonstration by locals regarding U.S. occupation of Manila. I instructed Thad to take Anthony and Ashley and walk over the bridge to the Embassy, and if he felt threatened ... run.

Anthony had ordered some food when Thad handed Anthony his ball cap. "Put this on and lay low. I'm going to take a walk over the bridge and check things out. I'll call you if it's clear to come over with Ashley." Anthony chuckled in his mind. With or without the hat, he was still a 6'2" black man who was hard to hide among 5' Asians. As he and Ashley started to get reconnected over the meal, the phone rang ... it was Thad. "Okay, start moving my way ... you'll see me on the other side of the bridge."

Anthony asked for his check, paid the waitress and took Ashley by the hand. "We may have to run," he said to her.

"Ok," she responded.

Something Bigger Than Overthrowing Small Governments

Thad had them covered 360 degrees, motioning to Anthony with his forked fingers back in his own eyes so Anthony would maintain eye contact with Thad all the way. It's what you have to do in order to get a very nervous person to focus on the goal rather than their surroundings. While there was no one following, you could tell by his actions that Anthony thought differently. His paranoia was par for the course and excusable to a point. It is not excusable when you need a person to remain calm, so they do not draw attention, and you get the opposite ... and that is exactly what happened. He could see the Embassy, and although close, perhaps to him it was not close enough. Twenty yards from the Embassy he and Ashley started running. Our Embassy contact and two guards appeared in front of them before they could get in full stride. "Mr. Ricks we are aware of your situation ... please follow us into the Embassy."

Once in the Embassy, Anthony was forced to shut off his phone, and those whom he had been reaching out to without my permission were left in the dark probably to think the worst. Ashley was her normal self, fairly playful and ready to leave Manila. I left both of them in the hands of the RSO and other Embassy personnel for processing while Thad and I secretly made our way out of the Embassy and to the new hotel where Stella was heading.

In a private meeting with Embassy officials just prior to Thad, Anthony and Ashley making it across, I had been told that they could get Anthony and Ashley out of the country but could not guarantee the same for the ARC SFRT. I told them not to worry about us ... we'd have no problem getting off the island. One Embassy official, who will remain unnamed, was extremely helpful on all fronts but was making no promises ... we were too early in the game to determine the final outcome on a number of levels. I have no doubt that traffic (communications) was flooding State Department in D.C. with the events of this rescue.

Thad and I managed to get to the new hotel ahead of Stella and take up some positions to run a little counter surveillance. She checked in with all of our bags and headed up to the room. No one followed. When Thad and I got to the room, I gave a full briefing on the situation and the plan of attack from that point forward. Some things had shifted, and a warning order put it all in perspective. We would change our clothes and be prepared to evacuate with only our essentials, bags not in tow. Fresh batteries were put in the radios, and new rally points were mapped out. Thad and I headed back to the Embassy, and Stella stood by in the room. We detoured to the car just down the road by the Sushi restaurant and moved it to an underground parking lot to keep it off the street in case local police or mobsters were looking for it.

Back at the Embassy Anthony was being grilled privately. The Embassy was going to corroborate my story with his. He explained his custody situation and showed them his legal paperwork.

"The Luna family is corrupt, and I do not feel safe here, and I need protected passage for my daughter and I back to the United States." The Embassy official was a bit combative, telling Anthony that he was guilty of kidnapping his daughter. "How can I kidnap my own child?" he abruptly responded.

The clock struck twelve and the Embassy official was more interested in lunch than the matter at hand. "Have seat outside and we'll handle this after lunch," he said.

I have no doubt that Anthony probably thought this was the easy part, getting help from fellow Americans, but it seemed more like they were the enemy. Later Anthony would come to understand that it was just a matter of needing time for due diligence in order to help everyone. Anthony sat there with Ashley. "So how was your time in Manila so far?"

Ashley looked up, "The kids at school are not very nice to me. I hardly ever see my grandmother. Nanny takes care of me. They told me that you wanted me to stay, and that you never wanted to see me again."

Anthony put his arm around her. "You don't believe that, do you?"

She leaned into Anthony, "No."

After the lunch hour Anthony was called back into a private room. Thad and I had arrived back at the Embassy by then and sat guarding Ashley.

"Okay, your story pans out, but we're not sure we can get everything done today," the Embassy official explained.

"I will chain myself to a desk and will not leave this Embassy unless I and my daughter are headed to the airport," he pleaded.

Something Bigger Than Overthrowing Small Governments

"Ok Mr. Ricks. Wait outside again. We would like to speak with Ashley by herself." The Embassy needed to make sure she identified Anthony as her father.

Although I had inside knowledge of the entire situation, all of the conversations, and what the Embassy intended to do, I still needed to ask Anthony a question just to take his temperature.

"How are things going so far?" I asked.

"It is taking so long, and I'm really frustrated," he replied.

"Breathe up, everything will be alright ... things are in play." I assured him. It seemed to bring some comfort to him.

The RSO called my name and motioned for me. I stepped behind closed doors and engaged in conversations with a number of officials, figuring out the best way to get Anthony and Ashley off the island. When I returned, I walked up to Anthony. "They'll probably have you meet one more time with someone a little higher up," I explained.

No sooner had I spoken when, "Mr. Ricks, can you step into the office please?" Anthony found himself standing in front of a higher-ranking Embassy officer. "I'm a father myself, Mr. Ricks. It took a lot of guts to do what you did. I would have done the same. You're fortunate to have ARC on your side. You need to leave tonight."

Anthony smiled, "That's a great idea."

Four hours earlier Anthony had thought the Embassy was going to turn him in to Manila Police, and now they were bending over backwards to get him a ticket and emergency passport for Ashley.

Meanwhile, as we were planning our departure, I still had one operator in a Philippine jail. I called Eric Volz at The David House Agency (DHA) and explained the situation. The David House Agency's clients include families, law firms, private corporations and individuals, both in the United States and overseas. The David House has worked complex matters all over the world — achieving success in Europe, Latin America, the Middle East, and Asia. Some of their more recent cases included high-profile international Show Trials, wrongful imprisonment, international adoption and custody disputes. Eric Volz, in my professional opinion, is smarter than most U.S. Ambassadors twice his age. His fingerprint was on some of the most famous cases ...

Amanda Knox, Scott McMahon, Amir Hekmati, Matt and Grace Haungs, Tim Tracy, and Jason Puracal just to name a few.

As strategic partners, ARC never moved forward on an operation of this type without DHA on standby. ███'s detention was clearly wrongful imprisonment, and I was clearly the mission leader on an operation that, though he showed lack of judgment, was still my responsibility. Eric had been in contact with Main State Department and the Embassy in Manila to assert his organization's support of ARC, so there was no doubt we brought the "big guns" with us. Eric made it clear to me that in his conversations with Main State regarding ███'s detention, that they intended to do nothing about it.

"Tell Main State that if they don't intervene, that I will turn myself in to Manila Police and take his place immediately. He's my responsibility." I told Eric.

"Don't do anything yet ... just stand by and let me get back with you," he pleaded. Eric knew enough about me to know that I was serious. He also knew enough about my background with the CIA that turning myself in could create one heck of an international incident that no one wanted. I was hoping that it would make people step up to the plate and get ███ out. I sat with Thad and talked him through my intentions. He was not in favor of it, but he understood and agreed to make sure Anthony and Ashley got back to the U.S. Under his breath, "If for any reason you have to go down that road, I'll be back with a team to get you out of wherever they send you, and when I do, they'll wish they had never sent you down that road."

"That would be nice. Don't make it too long, I hear they have parasites here," I said with a confident smile.

About that time my phone rang, and it was Eric Volz. "Don't do anything, and do not turn yourself in to local police. I just spoke to Main State, and that is the last thing they need. They're making arrangements as we speak to get ███ out of prison and get you guys on a flight tonight out of Manila. Someone from the Embassy will be speaking with you."

Out of the corner of my eye, I could see the RSO trying to get my attention.

"Thanks, bro. Need to go, I think we're on the move."

Something Bigger Than Overthrowing Small Governments

"Okay we have an understanding, right? Do not turn yourself in?" Eric pleaded.

"Yes, I understand. I will not turn myself in. Gotta go, bro." And with that I hung up the phone and walked over to the RSO.

Another behind-closed-doors meeting occurred with the RSO informing Thad and myself that all the team members of ARC needed to be on the same flight as Anthony and Ashley tonight. "Not a problem in my book," I replied.

"You have a way of paying for the ticket?" the RSO asked.

I waved a credit card in front of his face. "Okay, we'll get those tickets processed for you immediately. I have a blackout van in the back. We'll load up, swing by the hotel and pick up your bags and your female operator and get you guys to the airport. We've made arrangements for you to get through hopefully without any problems. We've got a Federal Marshal escorting an American back to stand trial, and he agreed to keep an eye on you guys at the airport and inform me if anything sours."

We grabbed Anthony and Ashley and loaded up the van. I called Stella to let her know we were heading her way and to meet us downstairs by a side entrance that was not that easily observed by passing locals. Five minutes later she was standing tall as we drove up, loaded up and headed to the airport.

I gave the orders, "Anthony, you and Ashley will be escorted through customs by the RSO, so just stick close. Stella, you and Thad and I need to be out of the bursting radius of each other, so stagger your entry into the airport and customs. Once inside, keep the same distance and monitor Anthony and Ashley. Everyone should be on channel 2."

Thad and Stella confirmed with a look and nod my way. As planned between the RSO and myself, he stopped just short of the airline we were departing on and allowed Stella, Thad and I to hop out. We quickly entered the airport and found a vantage point to watch Anthony and Ashley as they entered. The van arrived curbside about 300 feet further down from where we were standing. The RSO got out and led Anthony and Ashley to customs where they filtered through to their gates. The RSO was an old hand at this and simply glanced my way and winked ... not really allowing other eyes to know we were associates. The rest of our team followed as I had instructed and found ourselves on the other side, sitting in various locations near the gate where all of us could monitor Anthony and Ashley.

When it came to airport security, I really could not tell who was assisting the U.S. Embassy and who was not ... but I felt a bit uneasy when a very curious plain-clothes security officer approached me and asked, "Do you know that American sitting down there with the hat?" referring to Thad.

"Nope. I spoke with him outside customs briefly and he seems like a nice fellow, but couldn't tell you much more than that," I replied.

Cautiously, I followed his eyes and tone to figure out if he was working for the bad guys or the good guys. Given more time, I'm sure we would have ended up discovering more about him than I cared to know. But that wasn't going to happen because the U.S. Marshal escorting the American drew the attention of whoever this plain clothes security officer really was and every other airport security officer nearby. I settled back into my chair and watched from afar. In cases like this, it's not a given that the Embassy has pulled all the right strings, and even if they have, corruption in government can cut all of those in a heartbeat. The flight was announced, and everyone began boarding ... rather uneventfully, which is what I had hoped for.

When we arrived back at Los Angeles International Airport, the flight captain asked all the passengers to remain seated. U.S. Customs Officers entered the airplane and asked me, Thad, Anthony and Ashley to follow them. Since Stella had not been approached, I gave her the signal to hold back and exit carefully with the rest of the passengers. I had no idea what was happening. Were we getting arrested by our own country? Once inside the customs area we were expedited though customs and to a private bag check section. I looked at Thad, puzzled. Then out of nowhere stood old Gunnery Sgt. Ford from my days at the Staff NCO Academy in Quantico, Virginia. He was now head of this customs unit. He had that same boyish smile he had been known for in the Marine Corps. He was indeed a Marine's Marine.

"Ford!" I yelled. He looked up and smiled.

"Captain Baz ... what are you doing here?"

"I don't know, you tell me," I replied.

"All I know is that we got word from the State Department that a couple of U.S. Marshals were escorting Mr. Ricks and his daughter

Something Bigger Than Overthrowing Small Governments

back to the U.S. and we were supposed to give them special treatment," Ford announced.

I smiled and handed him my ARC card. "This is what I'm doing these days." They checked our bags and then told us we were ready to go. I was shaking hands with Ford when I noticed that Stella had been pulled from the line and taken into another room.

"Ford, that Asian girl going in there is with us. I'm not sure what is happening, but can you help find out?"

"Not a problem, Cap, follow me," and so I did. Ironically everything we did to keep Stella compartmented failed ... not because of anything mission-related but simply because she was flagged as a Canadian. It was somewhat funny, at the moment, because she had managed to pull off an extraordinary operation against all odds in a not-so-friendly country, and then got singled out in the U.S. because she was Canadian. Ford and I walked in the room where she sat. She looked up with those sort of sad, puppy dog eyes, wondering what she had done wrong.

Ford had a talk with a female customs officer and came over to me. "It's just a random screening."

I whispered in his ear, "Gunny, she's on our team. We can vouch for her. She is married to a Santa Monica police officer. She was with us on the operation." I pulled out a copy of the legal documents and a photocopy of her passport along with Thad's. Ford took a look and then went back over to the female customs officer with what I had provided him. Then Ford and I stepped out of the room.

"She'll be out in a minute," he said.

It was a good moment for Ford and me to catch up on times past. He had retired from the Marine Corps and joined U.S. Customs, which he was proud to be a part of, and would soon retire from them as well. About ten minutes into our exchange, Stella was released. I introduced her to Ford, we laughed about the situation and then we said our goodbyes. Thad was waiting with Anthony and Ashley when we finally caught up with them in the terminal lobby. I took a moment to pray that God would continue to bless Anthony and Ashley and that the rest of our team would have safe travels home until it was time for us to gather again for another rescue.

Recommendations: Maintain constant control over the custodial parent and monitor all communications to such a degree that if necessary, remove their computers and cell phones as soon as they are in the AO with the SFRT. Should they fail to relinquish those items or any others deemed by the SFRT to be a threat to the operation, or should they fail to abide by the orders given, immediately fly them back to the United States and allow the SFRT to complete the mission without the custodial parent in the AO.

Something Bigger Than Overthrowing Small Governments

CHAPTER 16
OPERATION PINWHEEL
AFTER ACTION REPORT

Subject: Kalista Reyes

Date: August 2014

Introduction:
For the purposes of this report the SFRT consisted of Bazzel Baz, Thad Turner and "Gonzo."

Background:
On 5-10-2014 at 1921 hours, Officer Hotz #190 was dispatched to the lobby of the ▮▮▮ Police Department to speak with Sandra Reyes (DOB ▮▮▮) in reference to a missing person (Kalista ▮▮▮ Reyes DOB ▮▮▮). Sandra stated that on January 26, 2014, her brother, Brandon Reyes (DOB ▮▮▮), took Sandra's son and Brandon's daughter, Kalista, to the Cedar Rapids, Iowa Airport to board a plane to head to California to visit family. Brandon ended up taking both children to Mexico instead.

Sandra's son was held for ransom and then later sent home to be with her. However, her niece, Kalista, was believed to be in a dangerous part of Durango, Mexico with a great aunt, Delia Reyes. Sandra stated that Brandon "abandoned" Kalista at 122 Camino De La Cascada, Durango, Mexico, and took off with his father, Noe Reyes (DOB ▮▮▮), to unknown parts of Mexico. Sandra believed that the reason Brandon took Kalista to Mexico was due to an outstanding warrant he had in Iowa.

Sandra was able to keep in touch with Kalista through Facebook and through Kalista's Google phone (▮▮▮). Sandra stated that she spoke with her almost every evening to make sure she was okay. Sandra had been working with Holly Witt of the Iowa Department of Public Safety. She was also meeting with her attorney to gain sole legal custody of Kalista. Sadly, Kalista's real mother was a drug addict, divorced from Brandon Reyes and had never gained custody of her daughter in court. In the meantime, ARC was collecting the following documents in preparation to launch a rescue operation for Kalista:

- Warrants for Brandon's Arrest
- Crimes committed by Brandon in the U.S.
- Charges against Brandon for Kidnapping
- ███ Police reports on kidnapping
- DPS State paperwork showing involvement
- NCIS report
- Any FBI reports filed on kidnapping
- Copy of Birth Certificate
- Any Missing Children's report with NCMEC or otherwise
- Federal, State, local paperwork acknowledging the situation
- Court documents or certified history of abuse by Brandon on children or family
- Pictures of Brandon, Grandpa, the girl (who we were referring to as "K")

Operations Overview:

Holly Witt of the Iowa Department of Public Safety and Lenchen Reaside of Cedar Rapids Gives, a non-profit NGO, contacted me to discuss the disappearance of Kalista Reyes. Her Grandfather and Father, Brandon Reyes, both had a history of selling, buying and trafficking illegal substances within the United States. It appeared that their trip to Mexico could include new business deals with members of the drug cartel ... especially those in Chihuahua, where both men had been now for weeks, leaving Kalista with her great aunt in Durango.

Something Bigger Than Overthrowing Small Governments

	Type of Victim	Sequence No.	Name - Last	First	Middle	Suffix
V	I - INDIVIDUAL	001	REYES	KALISTA		
I	Business/Organization/State/County/Municipality Name		Address	City	State	Zip Code
C						
T	Phone		Alias(es)			
I						
M	DOB Known? DOB		Age or Lower Age Range	Upper Age Range	SSN	Resident Status
	YES		14			R - RESIDENT
001	Driver's License - Number		State	Gender	Height	Weight	Eye Color	Hair Color
			IA	F - FEMALE	5' 00"	120 LB	BROWN - BRO	BROWN - BRO
	Skin Tone	Race		Ethnicity		Scars/Marks/Tattoos	
	OLIVE - OLV	W - WHITE		H - HISPANIC ORIGIN		NONE	
	Type of Injury (up to 5)						

EMPLOYMENT OR SCHOOL INFO

Employer or School	Occupation
	STUDENT
Address	City	State	Zip Code	Work Phone

VICTIM CONNECTED TO UCR OFFENSE CODES

UCR Offense Code 1	UCR Offense Code 2
ALL OTHER OFFENSES - 90Z	
UCR Offense Code 3	UCR Offense Code 4
UCR Offense Code 5	UCR Offense Code 6
UCR Offense Code 7	UCR Offense Code 8
UCR Offense Code 9	UCR Offense Code 10

ADDITIONAL OFFENSE CIRCUMSTANCE INFO

Aggravated Assault/Homicide Circumstances (up to 2)

Additional Justifiable Homicide Circumstances

VICTIM'S RELATIONSHIP TO OFFENDER(S)

First Offender Seq. No.	Victim's Relationship to First Offender	Second Offender Seq. No.	Victim's Relationship to Second Offender
Third Offender Seq. No.	Victim's Relationship to Third Offender	Fourth Offender Seq. No.	Victim's Relationship to Fourth Offender
Fifth Offender Seq. No.	Victim's Relationship to Fifth Offender	Sixth Offender Seq. No.	Victim's Relationship to Sixth Offender
Seventh Offender Seq. No.	Victim's Relationship to Seventh Offender	Eighth Offender Seq. No.	Victim's Relationship to Eighth Offender
Ninth Offender Seq. No.	Victim's Relationship to Ninth Offender	Tenth Offender Seq. No.	Victim's Relationship to Tenth Offender

SPECIAL CIRCUMSTANCES

Not Applicable ☐   Bias Crime ☐   Domestic Abuse ☐   LEOKA ☐

BIAS CRIME

Bias Motivation	Target Code
Bias Group Affiliations	

DOMESTIC ABUSE

Children Present?	Seq. No. of Domestic Abuse Offender	Domestic Abuse Referrals (up to 6)

LAW ENFORCEMENT OFFICER KILLED OR ASSAULTED

Officer Killed or Assaulted	Type of Assignment
Body Armor	Call Type

OFFICER'S INVESTIGATIVE NOTES

On 5-10-2014 at 1921 hours, I, Officer Hotz #190 was dispatched to the lobby of Marion Police Department to speak with ▮▮▮ Reyes (DOB 04-20-1981) in reference to a missing person (Kalista ▮▮▮▮▮▮▮▮▮▮▮▮▮).

▮▮▮▮▮ stated that on January 26th, 2014 her brother ▮▮▮▮▮▮▮▮▮▮ took ▮▮▮▮▮ son and Brandon's daughter Kalista to the Cedar Rapids Airport to board a plane and head to California to visit family. Brandon ended up taking both children to Mexico. ▮▮▮ son is safe at home with her. However, ▮▮▮ is worried that her niece Kalista is in a dangerous part of Durango, Mexico with a great aunt (▮▮▮ Reyes DOB unknown).

▮▮▮▮▮ stated that Brandon "abandoned" Kalista at 122 Camino De La Cascada, Durango Mexico and took off with his father Noe Reyes (DOB 11-19-1947) to another part of Mexico. ▮▮▮▮▮ believes that the reason Brandon took Kalista to Mexico is due to an

Printed At: MARION POLICE DEPARTMENT   5/12/2014   1:44 AM   Page 2   Form #: 14009489

OFFICER'S INVESTIGATIVE NOTES
outstanding warrant he has through Iowa.
▮▮ has kept in contact with Kalista through Facebook and through Kalista's Google phone ▮▮▮▮ ▮▮▮ stated that she talks with her almost every evening to make sure she is doing okay. ▮▮▮ is working with Holly Witt to get Kalista back in the United States and home in Marion. ▮▮▮ stated that she meets with her attorney this week in attempts to get legal custody of Kalista.
Kalista was entered into NCIC as missing.
Nothing further to report at this time.
Lobby interview room A/V- yes Car 86 Body A/V- No

	Reporting Officer	Badge Number	Video Taken?	Evidence Seized?	Photos Taken?
OFFICER	HOTZ NICOLE	M190	02 - OFFICE	NO	NO
	Supervisor WHITSON, JERRY	Badge Number M150	Incident Assigned To		

Why anyone in their right mind would take a female teenager to this part of Mexico was beyond logic. A year earlier, both Zeta and Sinaloa Drug Cartels received support from government officials at every level and crippled the Mexican federal government's attempts to bring the violence under control. Hundreds, if not thousands, had been killed in massacres and executions. Even the Roman Catholic archbishop of Durango commented that "Sinaloa kingpin Joaquin 'El Chapo' Guzman was omnipresent in the state, unimpeded by authorities." [25]

I took a trip to speak before Cedar Rapids Gives to gain their financial support as donors so we might bring Kalista home. I explained to them that the region where she was held had become one of Mexico's bloodiest gangland battlegrounds as the Zetas battled for control against Sinaloa Cartel factions. It was a war zone that no child should be subjected to, especially a female American who spoke no Spanish, had not been enrolled in school and was spending her time outside of the great aunt's house walking the streets of Durango with no adult supervision. We knew this to be true because when Sandra would ask what she did to not get bored, Kalista said she would walk to the park or take a bus downtown by herself and hang out.

This was a clear case of a girl who would end up being sex trafficked, and it was only a matter of time. You never have to look far in Durango to find a prostitute, and they seem to be getting younger every day with a total to date of 1,368 prostitutes/escorts, etc. Trafficking of girls and women is not only the norm, but it is booming business. Before girls are trafficked, many as young as 14 are routinely kidnapped from villages surrounding Durango by men who trick, threaten, and even seduce them into working for the illicit sex trade.

What a lot of people I spoke to at Cedar Rapids Gives failed to realize at that time is that the prostitutes are not willing participants. Pimps in Durango are masters of manipulation — trafficking organizations send their most handsome men, often called "Romeos," to pick up young women at bus stops, malls or in parks ... the same bus stops, malls and parks that Kalista was frequenting. The "Romeos" pretend to be very wealthy businessmen and seduce the women into following them.

In my opinion, the bleed-over into Durango starts in Tenanting, Mexico, widely considered the sex trafficking capital of the world, and the single largest source of sex slaves sent to the U.S., according to the U.S. State Department.

One woman we know of was held captive for three months by her "boyfriend" after going there to meet his family and him telling her he loved her and wanted to have children with her. The "Romeos" figure out how to get to the core of traditional values that these victims have.

Others are simply kidnapped like another girl we read who was forced into prostitution at age 14 after accepting a ride home from a "friendly" man named "Rodolfo," who she met in the park. He took her to his home where he beat and raped her.

"He told me that even if I was screaming, that no one would hear me and no one would help me," Miranda told Fusion. A feeling of helplessness is instilled in victims to prevent them from trying to escape.

Even if they were to escape, there is little chance that the women would ever see their captors behind bars. Only 17 of the 3,000-5,000 pimps in nearby Tenanting were convicted in Mexico between 2010 and 2013, Fusion reported, and enforcement in the U.S. does not fare much better.

> American police departments spend 22 times more fighting drugs than fighting human trafficking despite that fact that 18,000 women are trafficked into the U.S. every year, according to the State Department. [26]

Everything about this case was becoming time sensitive. Gonzo, CEO of a private security firm and a strategic partner with ARC, volunteered to come on board as an operator for this mission. Gonzo was a former Navy SEAL who, as I would find out later, had a lot in common with Thad Turner.

Gonzo launched to Durango, Mexico, as a one-man advance team and provided the ground truth we needed to complete the operations order that I would distribute once Thad and I arrived with Sandra Reyes. We don't always take custodial guardians in country with us, but this time it felt right to have an adult female, who was the custodial guardian, help us escort Kalista back to the U.S.

Gonzo arrived in Durango one day prior and handled logistics and pre-route recce work for the SFRT. He reserved two SUV-type cars able to handle off-road terrain in Durango in case we needed to go there. He would only have 24 hours to put everything in place that would allow the SFRT to make it out safely once Kalista was located.

It is always interesting and sometimes challenging when you're under the gun and working as an advance team in a 3rd world environment. Gonzo had his hands full, and none of us could afford for him to make even the slightest mistake. He was battle-hardened and knew better than most how to keep it tight ... that is why I sent him.

On day one he arrived only to have the rental car place tell him that they only had beat up used cars as opposed to the nice ones he had reserved online. So he took what he could get. By the end of the day Gonzo had established communication with ARC Headquarters. I passed along the target location and address via secure channels ... he was off and running, performing SDRs (Surveillance Detection Routes) and determining possible locations where we could pick up Kalista Reyes. His route reconnaissance confirmed the Google satellite map and street overview, including the close-up-and-personal pictures he took and sent back to me of that location. He wasted no time in driving around Durango and establishing the main routes out of town and to safe havens and was able to pick out secondary routes to nearby towns and other airports we could depart from outside the local area.

Back in the U.S. we received word that Kalista's non-custodial father and grandfather were departing for "business" to Chihuahua and would once again be leaving Kalista to fend for herself. That gave us a small, unpredictable window of opportunity, and I requested Sandra Reyes meet our team in Redondo Beach, California, the next morning and be prepared to travel with us to Mexico.

Sandra Reyes arrived at the hotel in Redondo Beach where Thad and I agreed to meet her for the first time the following day. She was a very humble woman who hid her apprehensions like a good tattooist covering up bad ink with something better. She had every reason in the world to be apprehensive. She was traveling into a dangerous and unpredictable part of Mexico with two former SpecOps men she knew little about, other than what she had obtained from the frequent phone calls we had exchanged the month before and the reputation of ARC, so graciously supported by Cedar Rapids Gives.

Thirty days prior we were able to set the stage by having Sandra, with the help of Special Agent Holly Witt of State of Iowa Department of Public Safety Division of Intelligence and Fusion Center and Lenchen Reaside of Cedar Rapids Gives, walk her through the court system to obtain sole legal custody of Kalista. It was clear that Kalista wasn't old enough to understand that her father was being anything but an unselfish father until time passed ... and when it did, she realized she was being held captive. Her cry for help over social media did not go unnoticed by ARC. Kalista's father had a warrant out for his arrest back in the U.S. and he had no intention of returning. And to make things worse ... he had no intention of ever sending Kalista back.

From known social media for Kalista Reyes:

Kalista Reyes
March 3

O.K. I'm sick of this. It took me a bit to decide if I should post this but I decided I am. With all that's been going on in the past few weeks has extremely annoying. Now, I don't want to get in trouble, I'm just saying what I feel. Please just read what I have to say. I want to go home. I like here but I would much rather be at home right now. I miss everyone and everything. I hate that I've been out of school for over a month and I really need to get back in school. I can't go to school out here cause they teach in Spanish and the English teaching school's out here cost a lot of money. Most schools here have uniforms and I don't want that. I want to be able to express myself. I miss my friends, teachers and family out there. I would have been way more excited to come during the summer and stay the whole summer if it meant I was going back in the fall. I have teacher's out there that I miss! :I Do you know how sad I felt when I was told I wasn't going back? I was crying for a long time and I was upset. I miss the dogs and I miss the cats. I miss my best friend and all my other friends. I never even got to say goodbye to anyone. I saw the letter that I was tagged to read and I read the whole thing. I feel like I'm going to explode because I'm so bored. I would rather be sitting in school right now taking a test instead of being bored. That's how much I want to go home and see everyone again. I feel like I was meant to be in the ▮▮▮▮ district and I really miss everyone. Dad, I know you kept asking me if I was fine and that you wouldn't get mad if I told you I wanted to go home. But I felt it was useless because I wouldn't automatically get to go home and I was kind of scared because I know you wanted me here. Go ahead, be mad at me, but all I've wanted for the past two-ish weeks is to go home. I was so excited to go home on Monday the 17th but then we come down to Mexico. I loved seeing family and all that, but I would be a bit more open if I was actually happy. I'm super sad that I may never see my friends for a long time. I was all so sudden too. I kept thinking you were joking and maybe you'll really drive to the airport and we all go home and be happy. I understand if you weren't happy there but I was and that is why I wanted to go home so bad. I seriously miss everyone and you don't know how bad I want to go home. I hate moving and anyone who knows me enough knows that I hate moving. I remember moving quite often as a child and it didn't matter all that much because I never made close enough friendships with anyone to really want to stay in a certain school. But then we moved to Olin and we were there for about 2 years. And remember how sad I was when we moved to ▇▇▇? But now, being in ▇▇▇ for 3 years, it's even worse than that. And this time, I never got to say goodbye. That's even worse that Olin. All I want is to go home, like if I'm not home for my birthday or Christmas, the only gift I would want is to go home. I will stand by that unless I am home. I won't want anything else. That's how bad I want to go home. Just read this and understand that all I want is to go home. I'm not asking for anything else. Please. — 🥺feeling unsure with Leslie ▇▇▇ and 2 others.

For at least 30 days prior, Sandra Reyes was the go-between for ARC and Kalista in setting up our operations. Kalista had no idea that she would be rescued but continued to provide surmountable intelligence to us in regard to location, patterns, lifestyle, times and events. A Facebook account was the primary mode of communication, which was a blessing on one hand and a nightmare on the other ... especially when Kalista's non-custodial father was able to access her laptop computer and spy on her account. But what he did not realize was that Kalista had another laptop computer that she kept hidden. And it was that computer ARC advised her to use when speaking to us using a different Facebook account under a different name.

Kalista had no idea we would be contacting her in country the following day ... we had sent no word of a rescue. We could not be absolutely sure that the second computer had not been compromised, or that any Skype calls were not monitored. We spent the evening over dinner breaking down the operation in civilian terms so that Sandra would have a better idea of what was expected of her.

Although we were fairly certain Kalista would go with us once we introduced ourselves, it is always better to have a familiar face such as Sandra on the spot during the actual pickup. First, it keeps the apprehension down for the child and second, it mitigates liability for the NGO such as ARC. It provides a witness such as Sandra so that no one can ever claim there was any abuse by members of our team. While this should not be an issue, we live in an upside-down world and the chance of a child making a false claim or a relative after the rescue making a false claim of abuse or endangerment of a child is in fact a real issue that always has to be addressed. While there are some cases where it is just too dangerous to take a family member such as Cecelia, we photograph and record as much of the operation as possible, including the welfare of the child at that time, in order to mitigate liability. We also have the custodian guardian sign a "Hold Harmless" agreement before we begin our operations ... something I highly recommend other NGOs adopt as part of their SOP (Standard Operating Procedures).

Thad and I hit the strand early the next morning for a run. The ocean lightly crashed along the shoreline as dolphins teased the local surfers just past the first break. As much as both he and I would have loved to have put on the wetsuits and purged our souls in the Pacific, time was running out, and it would not be long before we boarded a flight to Durango, Mexico.

We milled over a number of strategies that fit within our wheelhouse, speeding up our pace in order to bleed out any anxiety that hid itself in the crevasse of confident bravery. We never took operations lightly, and we followed what we had learned in the military to the letter of the law tactically. It had served us well over the years and it would serve us well on this operation. Thad and I had served together back in the day when SEALs were not known to keep company with the likes of men who spied on other countries. But it is where we met originally, and it is where some pretty extraordinary missions changed the face of history and plunged our enemies into national fatigue to the point that everything about them collapsed. And although we could never talk about it, most of the world certainly read about it. It was dangerous, exciting and hidden in files marked "Top Secret" ... and we would go to our graves with all of it. It was just the way things were in those days ... keeping America safe.

Thad was a quiet soul, determined, strong and accurate with a great sense of humor. We could read each other's mind at times, as can most members of a team that have been down range together. He was a man who had found God and glory in the dirt unlike most men who defined bravery as not being scared of the dark. He had an uninterrupted understanding of right and wrong, and it was this that I admired so much in him. His framework of motivations had always been unselfish, a single father raising two children, a boy and a girl, that blossomed into people who would change the world for good. I had the honor of watching them grow from a distance, hearing him brag about their achievements until suddenly they had become young adults, ready to live their lives in a manner that would be worthy of his love. I knew I could depend on him in life and death situations, and that is why he remained an integral part of ARC ... a leader who would risk value for something of greater value ... the welfare of a child.

The 3-hour flight to Durango, Mexico was uneventful. Thad and I sat quietly pondering emergency procedures if for any reason Mexican customs jacked us up on arrival.

While tourism is common in other parts of Mexico, the intelligence report Gonzo had sent made it clear that was not the case in

Durango. Thad and I would split up and filter through Customs separately, myself staying close to Sandra.

It was a sleepy little airport not unlike other airports where officials exercised their duties like straw men, creating the illusion of having completely refuted or defeated any opponent's proposition regarding drug trafficking in the area. Almost every employee seemed to be under the age of 30, uniformed and stiff in their intentions. I could not help but feel as if the entire building was a Hollywood backdrop where the whole scene could be stopped at any moment by some director yelling, "Cut."

A young Hispanic woman dressed in flight line garb approached me. "Did you have a nice flight?" she asked. Customs was written all over her demeanor. Thad glanced back over his shoulder. More than six people were ahead of me. We made eye contact just long enough to prepare for the unexpected.

"The flight was wonderful, and I'm so glad to finally get here. I've been wanting to see Durango since the days Hollywood used to shoot westerns down this way."

She smiled. "Are you a cowboy?"

I smiled back, "Do I look like a cowboy?"

She laughed. "Enjoy your stay," as she moved on.

Something Bigger Than Overthrowing Small Governments

Sandra and I reached the Customs Officer who stamped our passports and waved us on. As we headed to another line where our bags were screened, Thad was pulled aside with his backpack by another female customs agent. As she rummaged through his items, Sandra and I were forced to continue past and out the exit to the airport lobby. It is never a good feeling when one of your team guys is being held up and you lose visual. Within seconds he could be swept up by authorities for any number of reasons and hauled off to a police station, or worse, some other non-disclosed location in the country for interrogation. He was carrying nothing that would compromise the mission, but I still had concern. Like I said, he could be swept up by authorities for a number of reasons, but the more I thought about it, the more I realized that he could be swept up for no reason at all.

There are a few technical tricks of the trade that can help you locate a team member, but they're not always guaranteed to work. Nevertheless, it's something to consider when running operations where team members can get separated. And at that moment, I wished we had been given enough time prior to leaving the U.S. to put that system in place. We had worked years without having bells and whistles, and we always managed to find one another. But hey, times had changed, and quite frankly state of the art technologies had proven themselves to be valuable and reliable in a pinch.

But since there was no such technology to fall back on at this moment, I found myself diving deep into my tradecraft locker, using what I had been taught at the Farm ... thinking on my feet. I stalled just before the exit door, putting my backpack on the ground and adjusting the stubborn straps that conveniently malfunctioned ... lucky me. Sandra had no idea what was happening but knew not to drift far from me ... so she just stood there patiently. I whispered under my breath, "Father, let this go clean." I stood up and looked past Sandra's shoulder while speaking to her to see how things were going with Thad. "We have someone meeting us on the other side, so just follow me close." It looked like their inspection was complete and Thad was putting his gear back in the backpack. I knelt down to tie my boot that had also conveniently come untied in the process of me fixing my backpack straps. It bought me the thirty seconds I needed for Thad to load up and head out the door ahead of Sandra and me.

To my right and about 40 feet ahead was the bearded Gonzo. We made eye contact and walked past him, as he himself headed outside to the parking lot. Thad lingered a moment, fixed on a Mexican trinket in a shop, all the while watching my movement in the reflection of the glass window. After about two minutes Sandra and I stepped outside as I watched Gonzo find his car. Gonzo was the rabbit, and my job was to make sure no one followed him with their body or their eyes. The coast was clear, and the three of us, Sandra, Thad and I walked a casual pace to where Gonzo was parked.

"Hey amigo," I said with a smile.

Gonzo smiled back. "Gonzo, this is Thad and Sandra." Even though Gonzo and Thad were both SEALs, they had never met before.

"Happy to meet both of you," he replied. "The rental car company screwed me. They told me over the phone they would have the cars, confirmed online and on the phone. Not only did they not have the right cars ... when I got here there was only one car. So we had some words and now we have two cars, and the other is parked at the hotel. It worked out just fine."

Within the hour we arrived at the hotel. It was as good as it gets ... perhaps a few bed bugs, some running water and a 1960s decor that would persuade any American tourist to search for other accommodations. It was perfect for what we needed to do, blend with the locals and get in and out of town quickly when the time came.

Something Bigger Than Overthrowing Small Governments

Everyone dumped their gear and met in my room for Gonzo to give us a briefing on routes in and out of town as well as some advantage points for picking Kalista up on the day. And although it seemed pretty solid on the maps, we still needed to drive it, and so we did. For the next three hours we ran surveillance on the house she was held in, the routes to the park, routes in and out of town, the police station, multiple exit strategies, practiced car exchanges, emergency procedures regarding vehicle breakdowns and did extensive trolling of the park itself. The park was the place we determined would be best for the pickup of Kalista, plus it offered us long range surveillance in case she was followed.

The day was coming to a close when we returned to the hotel. Sandra decided to retire to her room and get some rest while Gonzo, Thad and I stepped across the street to a local cantina to grab dinner. As much as I would like to say we blended in ... the only one blending was actually Gonzo. Thad, with his baseball hat, reminded me of some Air America operator just in from a flight over Thailand, and me with my long hair, some misfit seeking to start up his own drug business. Gonzo was smart enough to get us a corner table where we could all watch each other's six, but even that wasn't enough to brush off the stares of a few local boys who definitely greased their palms with cartel currency. It wasn't uneasy it was just uncertain, and the sooner we got our food and got out of there, the better we would all be.

This historical place still had the original floor tile and barstools. The walls were hung with pictures of Mexican revolutionaries and bullfighters. The white-shirted, one-eyed waiter walked over to the jukebox and punched in a Sinatra tune for two tables of customers who were sipping margaritas. Much to my surprise I was expecting the sound of something more like "La Adelina," one of the most famous folk songs of the Mexican Revolution.

I sat there listening to Gonzo and Thad explore one another's SEAL careers while keeping an eye on the patrons in the room and those entering the door from outside. The waiter kindly approached and took our orders and I have no doubt that Gonzo's excellent use of the Spanish tongue put us in better standing with the locals, who were wondering what breed of trouble we might be.

Gonzo stopped mid-conversation and leaned back in his chair, staring at me and stroking the new growth on his face. "I've seen this look before," he said.

I looked at both of them. "I know I said we would do the pickup in the park, but I need to change that. We're going to pick her up before she gets to the park." I pulled out the street map I had tucked away in my jeans.

"We have no idea whether the discussion we have with her tonight on Facebook will be compromised, but we need to plan as if it is. So here's what we're going to do." I pointed to a street location. "Thad, I want you to park your car here and keep an eye on her as she rounds the corner from her house and heads to the main street. The site has good cover for action since it's a coffee shop that opens at 0600 hours tomorrow. Grab some coffee and have a seat. She has to turn right and head down that street and head to the park. If she isn't followed, then let us know. Gonzo, you and I and Sandra will park our vehicle here in this parking lot. I'll sit on the bench with a magazine, and when she gets to my location, I'll introduce myself and point to the car here where Sandra and you are located. You need to make sure Sandra does not get out of the vehicle. You'll be driving. We get her in the car, and we head out of town to this spot," as I pointed again at the map.

"You and Thad take the lead car, and I will drive Sandra and Kalista as if we are a family. We have to drive out of this state to the next, which is Chihuahua, and depart that airport. I know it's more time on the road, but communications between states is really bad, and the chances of anyone here contacting authorities in another state is slimmer than someone contacting Durango Airport officials from Durango. If she is followed, then we shake it out until they drop off of her, or we follow her to the park and set up surveillance at points to be determined tonight when we rehearse. Chances are once no one is there to meet her, she will head back the same way to her house, and we will pinch her at a location that offers us enough screening."

Something Bigger Than Overthrowing Small Governments

Thad and Gonzo saw the logic in all of it and agreed to the plan. I put the map away as I saw the waiter coming to the table with our food. He sat the plates before us and departed. Gonzo looked at me and said, "You going to say grace, because I ain't eating until you do. I made a promise that whenever I'm with you I ask God to bless the food ... so do it."

I smiled and bowed my head and thanked God for our food and our safety. I looked up and Gonzo had a big smile on his face. "Thanks," he said. Thad just smiled. We finished dinner and headed back across the street that twisted and coiled behind old buildings, forming a sinister landscape befitting the crimes that took place there throughout history. What we needed was the anonymity of the masses, but that wasn't happening now at 2200 hours. Our hotel was down the street about 200 yards ... a distance that sent chilling visions of a city that had eyes and ears that could at any hour compromise the mission. I'm sure that the average tourists would think otherwise, but then, wasn't it always the average tourists that found themselves lying in a pool of blood with their wallets stolen in this town?

We met with Sandra to go over the new plan of attack and have her send one final message to Kalista, instructing her to walk to the park at 0800 hours the next morning because someone that we knew, who would identify themselves, wanted to talk with her. Kalista mentioned to Sandra that she had just received word from her father that he and her grandfather would be back in town tomorrow evening. For me and the team it was now or never in rescuing her the next morning, and as best we could tell, Kalista still had no idea we were in town to do exactly that.

We grabbed the vehicles and rehearsed the operation from the moment we would pick up Kalista to the routes in and out of town and then down to the park to set up surveillance points and the alternate pickup point. By the time we returned to the hotel, the hands of the clock next to my bed were resting at 0200 hours. Gonzo had already locked down three rooms from the previous day, and that is where each of us spent the next four hours before we were up and out the door.

The airborne pollutants did more than soften the color of the sky; they robbed the sunrise of its brilliance and intensity. The streets were quiet with perhaps one or two cars passing us as we staged the vehicles. We had not seen very many police during our entire time of rehearsals, and I could only surmise that the Cartel had cut their forces in half so they could not interfere with drug operations ... so, if that was the case then it was working out perfectly for us.

Thad was in place one block to the north at the coffee shop while Gonzo and I and Sandra pulled into a small parking lot adjacent some buildings. I picked up the hand-held radio. "Radio check over."

"I read you Lima Charlie. I'll be on my alternate (cell phone) in the shop and pop up on the primary (handheld radio) once in the car," Thad replied.

"Roger, out," I responded.

Everything was set, and there was nothing more to talk about, so Gonzo and I sat there reading newspapers and magazines while keeping our eye on the sidewalk just in case Kalista somehow slipped by Thad. Sandra sat quietly in the back.

I checked my watch and called Thad. "Okay, amigo, they should be serving breakfast any moment," ... meaning "Kalista should be heading his way any moment."

There was about five minutes of silence before Thad responded. "I found sugar for my coffee," letting me know he had eyes on Kalista.

I exited the vehicle with my newspaper and planted myself on the bus stop bench by the sidewalk. I glanced up the street but had no sight of her rounding the corner yet ... and then ... there she was, heading my way. Thad called me on the phone. "This is good coffee," ... letting me know she was clean ... not being followed.

I waited calmly, as she continued towards me, heading to the park at the end of the very long street ... getting closer and closer. When she was within ten feet of me, I closed the paper and said, "Kalista Reyes ... I'm Mr. Baz, and we're here to take you back to America, your Aunt Sandra is in the vehicle over there," as I pointed in that direction. "I want you to walk calmly with me and get into the vehicle, okay?" Kalista acted like a pro and followed me. Once inside the vehicle, she and her aunt embraced one another in tears of joy.

"Kalista, I need for you to put this baseball hat on and these glasses and lower yourself into your aunt's lap while we drive a little. Don't sit up until I tell you."

I called Thad on the radio. "Is your coffee still hot?"

Something Bigger Than Overthrowing Small Governments

"Yep," he replied.

"Okay, let's order breakfast," I radioed back.

As we pulled out of the parking lot, Thad passed us on the street taking the lead to our next rally point where we would switch up personnel. We drove about ten minutes and pulled into the rally point ... a gas station. Gonzo joined Thad in the lead vehicle, and Kalista and Sandra stayed with me in mine.

The toll road we were about to travel had a bit of a creepy history. Five years earlier "the naked bodies of eight decapitated men had been found dumped along roads in a Mexican city plagued by increasingly deadly conflict between rival drug gangs." [27] It was the very city we were rescuing Kalista from.

> Six of the corpses were found along a highway leading out of the capital of the northern state of Durango, with their heads lying nearby. The two other bodies were found in another street in Durango City. One was identified as the remains of Gerardo Galindo Meza, the deputy director of a city prison who had been kidnapped on a Monday. Galindo's head was on a different street corner, accompanied by a threatening message signed by a drug gang, the attorney general's office said in a statement. It was the second time that week that decapitated corpses had been found in Durango State. Eleven bodies were found on that same Monday, including six left opposite a school in the state capital.
>
> Meanwhile, soldiers digging at mass graves in five places around the city on that Wednesday uncovered another eight bodies — seven men and one woman, bringing the total number of victims there to 196.
>
> Durango is one of Mexico's most dangerous states. Its murder rate had more than doubled 2008 to 2010. At least 1,025 killings were reported in 2010, compared to 930 in 2009 and 430 in 2008, according to government figures.
>
> Durango's secretary for government, Hector Vela, said many of the victims were likely to be gang members killed by rivals. But some might have been missing police officers,

and others may be victims of kidnapping and extortion attempts. [27]

We had no idea what to expect. We weren't armed. All we knew was that we needed a speedy exit, and this toll road offered that to us. Just 24 hours earlier we had considered driving all the way to the U.S. border town of McAllen, Texas, but for three days warring factions of the Gulf Cartel had turned a number of cities just south of McAllen into a warzone that had left at least 14 gunmen dead, with the true number of casualties remaining unknown. If we drove most of the day and night, we would most likely be crossing at 0400 hours the next morning, provided we had no emergencies. It would allow us to stay more under the radar than flying out of a major airport. But the more we thought about it, the less appealing it seemed, and our best choice would be to rely on the inefficient communications network between the Mexican States themselves as a blanket to cover our movement to the airport in Monterrey.

So we booked the flights. Not my first choice, but it appeared that our flights would be routing us all the way back south to Mexico City and then up to Tijuana, which meant more time in country, which meant more opportunity for something to go upside down and for authorities to be notified. And although we were doing nothing wrong, Kalista's captors could certainly lie about the sequence of events and create a whole bucket of worms that no one wanted to eat.

"Everyone ready to hit the headless highway?" I asked. Gonzo broke a halfway smile, and Thad did what Thad always does, put on his game face and jumped in the passenger side of their vehicle without saying a word. What we needed was God to make the way clear for us ... .no Cartel, no police, no accidents and no obstacles. And so, I bowed my head and asked for these things, so that we might be successful in our efforts and get this little girl back to the United States safely.

Two miles down the highway I had Kalista remove the battery from her cell phone and toss it out the window. A mile later I had her toss the phone out as well. We were not taking any chances of being tracked. Always check and double check, and never assume that just

Something Bigger Than Overthrowing Small Governments

because you have been running operations since the time of Moses that you can't make a mistake. If you think too highly of yourself, chances are you will.

Our drive for the next six hours was uneventful ... no Cartel, no police, no accidents and no obstacles. It was as if my prayer was being answered. Every now and then we would see a few cars heading in the opposite direction, but for us, we were the only two vehicles heading north until we started entering Torreon to refuel. Kalista and her aunt were fast asleep in the back for most of it. The only thing that really caught my attention along the way was the plethora of trash and plastics that were tilled in the soil of what appeared to be thousands of acres of land with rows for growing crops of some sorts. Once I saw that, I knew that I would not be eating anything that was grown in Mexico and shipped to the United States, ever. Another five hours would take us into Monterrey, where we would return the vehicles and board flights back to the U.S., or so I thought.

I had Kalista use my burner phone to call back to the house where she had been detained and leave a message telling her captors that she was still at the park and was planning on going shopping, and then out with some friends, and would not be home until later that evening. This would buy us some more time before they got concerned and started calling for help.

At the same time, we placed a call to Ken Schaffer, who was an agent with ICE, and who had been so instrumental in the successes of ARC in the past on multiple occasions. Ken had some major conflicts that precluded him from being there to assist us back across the border from our arrival at the Tijuana airport. He sounded deeply disappointed and actually a little reluctant for the first time since I had known him. I was pretty sure he was getting pressured by his superiors to not assist us in future operations, or at least to stay within the bounds of what ICE was allowed to do. Ken had mentioned on many occasions how a number of superiors were just yes-men to the Obama Administration, and how they deliberately would not do what was right when enforcing the laws ... especially on immigration issues. He said that most of the good agents in ICE were hamstrung from doing the job they joined up to do. I remembered that conversation and rested in the fact that God was working in Ken's life, and that God would coach him through all the tough decisions. I told him to just pray about it, because God was watching over us and would make a way.

I had met Ken a few years earlier when both he and I were speaking at a Preventing Abuse conference held by the late Tony Nassif. Tony had rocked the world with his two-day conferences that educated the American public on how to prevent kidnappings and human trafficking. I noticed Ken sitting at my table but had yet to introduce myself. I spoke for about 45 minutes on stage and returned to my seat, and Ken got up to speak. When he finished his presentation and sat back down next to me, his voice was a bit shaky as he introduced himself. "I'm Ken Schaffer and I want what you have ... with God." His eyes watered, and I could tell the Holy Spirit was in the house. I spent the next twenty minutes sharing my testimony and giving him what I thought God wanted me to tell him.

From that day forward Ken set out to do his very best to learn and build a relationship with God unlike anything he had attempted to do in his life. I could tell that he was sincere and relentless, and that he would not be one to give up easily in his pursuit to know the Creator of the universe. And that is how I came to know Ken Schaffer. And that is the Ken Schaffer I know to this day.

It wasn't long until we arrived at the airport in Monterrey. We turned the vehicle in to the rental car agency, took the first picture of all four of us involved in the rescue, and headed to check in for our flight.

Something Bigger Than Overthrowing Small Governments

No different than entering the country ... we exited the same way, checking into the counter at different times and seating ourselves dispersed, but close enough to keep an eye on one another at the gate. Kalista was very cordial, polite, well-spoken and even funny from time to time. I could see she was happy to be heading back to the U.S. Her aunt was a prayerful woman, and I could see in her silence the conversation she was having with God asking for protection, and Him granting it with a smile. We boarded the flight and settled in for the trip home.

When we arrived at Tijuana airport there was Ken Shaffer, standing in the lobby with a big smile on his face. I shook his hand and said, "I didn't expect to see you here brother. What changed?"

His eyes teared up somewhat, and his voice choked just a bit, "God reminded me that being right with Him is more important than following the asinine rules that prevent me from helping people and doing what is right. So I put aside concerns about my employment, and no longer concern myself with the consequences of doing right and being right." Later, I would come to learn that it was a pivotal moment in his growth as a man of God.

We piled into Ken's car and headed to the border, which, as you can imagine if you have ever been south of the boarder outside of San Diego, was bumper-to-bumper and not moving at all. And when it did move, it was at a snail's pace. Gonzo knew this territory well enough to navigate his way home by foot, so he bid us farewell and departed the vehicle with his gear tossed over his shoulder, like a sailor taking leave from a very long time at sea. I was pretty certain that he would be across the border and home in bed before we even touched American soil, and as I suspected ... later the next day in a phone conversation, he told me he had done exactly that.

When we finally rolled up to the U.S. Border Patrol, the agent didn't even ask for our passports. I'm not sure what Ken showed him, but it sure expedited the process. Ken was going beyond the call of duty, and I have never forgotten that to this day. He drove us all the way up to Hermosa Beach, where we dropped Kalista and her aunt off at a hotel and Thad and I back at my place. Far out of his way and hours into the night, that would surely bring repercussions the next day as he dove into fighting crime. There is a lot that can be said for your favorite football team scoring a touchdown, or your favorite soccer team scoring a goal, but none of it compares to the sacrifice and dedication displayed by the members of my team, who risk their lives and endure great discomfort for the sake of saving a child in danger. As I look back at their qualifications, I never second guess their ability to get the job done. Are they qualified in all things? No! No one is. We're only qualified in what we have learned or experienced ... and none of us have experienced everything.

So what does that say about us? Well let me put it this way. In tenth grade I got a D- in Algebra, and yet I still managed later in life to help win the Cold War and save the free world. My interest in linear warfare far outweighed that of linear equations, and it became obvious that God had a different plan for my life, whether I ever learned why A plus B equaled C ($a+b=c$). In God's plan the equation never really has to make sense ... because, as I have mentioned so many times in this book, it isn't that God is in the equation ... God is the equation. So whether I ever understood linear equations or not, one thing is for sure ... I understood God. And I understood He could take a tenth grader who was struggling with the numbers and raise him up to be a mighty warrior. And thus, I understand He can take each of my team members and show them great favor to raise them up, not based on how much they know ... but what they know and what they have experienced. And that is why I never second guess their ability to get the job done. If God is for them ... who can be against them?

Something Bigger Than Overthrowing Small Governments

Chapter 17
OPERATION VAN HELSING
AFTER ACTION REPORT

Subject: Jordana Houser

Date: May 13, 2016

Introduction:

According to our intelligence, Chad Houser and his mother, Peggy Houser, blazed a corruptible path through the United States and foreign countries stealing money from individuals and institutions. In February 2016, they illegally abducted Harrison (age 2) and Pierce (age 1) from their legal custodial guardian (mother) Jordana Houser. In a joint operation between ARC and the Swiss Police, the children were recovered on 10 June 2016. Peggy Houser was detained, while Chad Houser escaped apprehension.

We are honored to thank the following organizations and people for their assistance in this recovery: Staff and Operators of the ARC SFRT, S.E.R.T. Ministries, Jennifer Harkins CA/OCS/CI U.S. State Department D.C., U.S. Embassy personnel, Bern Switzerland, Nic (ACS) U.S. Embassy Paris France, Dr. Cedric Loiret-Bernal, Attorney Bridgette Meyer, Officer Miller of the Interlaken Police Department, Switzerland, and the Officers who assisted, Edith Rico (resort manager, Hapimag Resort Interlaken) and her assistant, The David House Agency, Det. Becker LAPD, District Attorney's Office in Los Angeles Ca, Darlene Ford, Diane Nichols, Stacy Nichols, Reid Nichols, Alves, Pjetur Sigurdson, William Josephsen, Mr. and Mrs. Johnston. A warrant for Chad and Peggy Houser's arrest is currently in effect in the U.S.

Background:

In March 2016, Ms. Meyoung Spektor notified ARC that a friend, Jordana Houser, was seeking assistance in the recovery of her two children, Harrison and Pierce, who had been abducted by their non-custodial father while the family was living in Indonesia. We received the following email from Mrs. Houser:

> Hi there, I was introduced to you by a dear friend and I need your help. I have two kids that have been kidnapped from Bali Indonesia to Switzerland I think. My ex is a con man and has been in trouble in America, Singapore, and now Bali. I have a compressed story I can send you and it is now being revised cause now he has kidnapped my kids but if you can be of any help I need it. The guy has devastated me financially but seems to take people's money and get away with it only to get more from others and when he does it is a lot at a time. Here is a little about me written by friends ...
>
> I am on my way to L.A. to be near friends and family so I have support. Please let me know if you can help I need it so badly and my heart is breaking immensely.
>
> Sincerely,
> Jordana Houser

Jordana, now divorced and back in the United States, met with me and explained her situation. Her ex-husband, Chad Houser, since the beginning of their marriage continued to engage in get-rich schemes and monetary ventures using other people's money (OPM), with little to no success. As evidence would later show, he was actually stealing OPM to live a lavish lifestyle with his then wife, Jordana Houser. When OPM would be expended, and hard times would fall, Chad Houser would reach out to family members of Jordana and manipulate the circumstances to acquire even more money. For example, he owed

Something Bigger Than Overthrowing Small Governments

Darlene Ford, the grandmother of Jordana Houser, close to 100K, a landlord in San Francisco 65K, a Singapore financial institute 300K, and a list of other persons around the world similar amounts of money. Frustrated by criminal behavior, a number of victims filed suit against Chad, resulting in two civil judgments and one criminal. This would not be known to Jordana until after her divorce, her children's abduction, and her return to the U.S. when papers were served to her on behalf of Chad.

UNITED STATES DISTRICT COURT
NORTHERN DISTRICT OF CALIFORNIA

HROTHGAR INVESTMENTS, LIMITED,
    Plaintiff,

v.

CHADWICK HOUSER,
    Defendant.

Case No. 15-cv-01116-JD

ORDER ADOPTING REPORT AND RECOMMENDATION

Re: Dkt. No. 23

The Court has reviewed Chief Magistrate Judge Joseph Spero's report and recommendation, recommending that plaintiff Hrothgar Investments, Limited's motion for default judgment be granted. Dkt. No. 23. Magistrate Judge Spero's report and recommendation was filed on August 18, 2015. No objections have been filed in response to the report, and the time to file objections has expired. *See* Fed. R. Civ. P. 72(b).

The Court agrees that for the reasons stated in the report and recommendation, the motion should be granted for Hrothgar's conversion claim; Hrothgar's claims for breach of contract, fraud and money had and received should be dismissed with prejudice; and judgment should be entered in Hrothgar's favor in these amounts: (1) $230,000 in principal, (2) $43,712.60 in prejudgment interest, and (3) $651.50 in costs.

Consequently, the Court adopts the report and recommendation of Magistrate Judge Spero in full, and directs the clerk to enter judgment in Hrothgar's favor.

IT IS SO ORDERED.

Dated: September 30, 2015

JAMES DONATO
United States District Judge

Bazzel Baz

**SUPERIOR COURT OF CALIFORNIA
COUNTY OF SAN FRANCISCO**

Document Scanning Lead Sheet

Sep-04-2014 10:58 am

Case Number: CGC-14-541481

Filing Date: Sep-04-2014 10:54

Filed by: ROSSALY DELAVEGA

Juke Box: 001   Image: 04609741

COMPLAINT

ROBERT NEWCOMBE VS. THE MUIR GROUP, INC.

001C04609741

Instructions:
Please place this sheet on top of the document to be scanned.

Something Bigger Than Overthrowing Small Governments

SUMMONS *(CITACION JUDICIAL)*	**SUM-100** FOR COURT USE ONLY *(SOLO PARA USO DE LA CORTE)*

NOTICE TO DEFENDANT:
(AVISO AL DEMANDADO):
The Muir Group, Inc. Chadwick houser, Does 1 to 5
388 Market Street, Suite 1300, San Francisco, CA 94111   Inclusive.

YOU ARE BEING SUED BY PLAINTIFF:
(LO ESTÁ DEMANDANDO EL DEMANDANTE):
Robert Newcombe and Thomas Summersall

NOTICE! You have been sued. The court may decide against you without your being heard unless you respond within 30 days. Read the information below.

You have 30 CALENDAR DAYS after this summons and legal papers are served on you to file a written response at this court and have a copy served on the plaintiff. A letter or phone call will not protect you. Your written response must be in proper legal form if you want the court to hear your case. There may be a court form that you can use for your response. You can find these court forms and more information at the California Courts Online Self-Help Center (*www.courtinfo.ca.gov/selfhelp*), your county law library, or the courthouse nearest you. If you cannot pay the filing fee, ask the court clerk for a fee waiver form. If you do not file your response on time, you may lose the case by default, and your wages, money, and property may be taken without further warning from the court.

There are other legal requirements. You may want to call an attorney right away. If you do not know an attorney, you may want to call an attorney referral service. If you cannot afford an attorney, you may be eligible for free legal services from a nonprofit legal services program. You can locate these nonprofit groups at the California Legal Services Web site (*www.lawhelpcalifornia.org*), the California Courts Online Self-Help Center (*www.courtinfo.ca.gov/selfhelp*), or by contacting your local court or county bar association. **NOTE:** The court has a statutory lien for waived fees and costs on any settlement or arbitration award of $10,000 or more in a civil case. The court's lien must be paid before the court will dismiss the case.

¡AVISO! Lo han demandado. Si no responde dentro de 30 días, la corte puede decidir en su contra sin escuchar su versión. Lea la información a continuación.

Tiene 30 DÍAS DE CALENDARIO después de que le entreguen esta citación y papeles legales para presentar una respuesta por escrito en esta corte y hacer que se entregue una copia al demandante. Una carta o una llamada telefónica no lo protegen. Su respuesta por escrito tiene que estar en formato legal correcto si desea que procesen su caso en la corte. Es posible que haya un formulario que usted pueda usar para su respuesta. Puede encontrar estos formularios de la corte y más información en el Centro de Ayuda de las Cortes de California (www.sucorte.ca.gov), en la biblioteca de leyes de su condado o en la corte que le quede más cerca. Si no puede pagar la cuota de presentación, pida al secretario de la corte que le dé un formulario de exención de pago de cuotas. Si no presenta su respuesta a tiempo, puede perder el caso por incumplimiento y la corte le podrá quitar su sueldo, dinero y bienes sin más advertencia.

Hay otros requisitos legales. Es recomendable que llame a un abogado inmediatamente. Si no conoce a un abogado, puede llamar a un servicio de remisión a abogados. Si no puede pagar a un abogado, es posible que cumpla con los requisitos para obtener servicios legales gratuitos de un programa de servicios legales sin fines de lucro. Puede encontrar estos grupos sin fines de lucro en el sitio web de California Legal Services, (www.lawhelpcalifornia.org), en el Centro de Ayuda de las Cortes de California, (www.sucorte.ca.gov) o poniéndose en contacto con la corte o el colegio de abogados locales. AVISO: Por ley, la corte tiene derecho a reclamar las cuotas y los costos exentos por imponer un gravamen sobre cualquier recuperación de $10,000 ó más de valor recibida mediante un acuerdo o una concesión de arbitraje en un caso de derecho civil. Tiene que pagar el gravamen de la corte antes de que la corte pueda desechar el caso.

The name and address of the court is:
(El nombre y dirección de la corte es): San Francisco Superior Court
400 McAllister Street
San Francisco, CA 94102

CASE NUMBER: CGC-14-541481

The name, address, and telephone number of plaintiff's attorney, or plaintiff without an attorney, is:
(El nombre, la dirección y el número de teléfono del abogado del demandante, o del demandante que no tiene abogado, es):
David R. Burtt, Mobility Legal P.C., 317 Washington St. #207, Oakland, CA 94607 (510) 208-1909

DATE: SEP 0 4 2014   CLERK OF THE COURT   Clerk, by DE LA VEGA-NAVARRO, Rossely   Deputy
(Fecha)   *(Secretario)*   *(Adjunto)*

(For proof of service of this summons, use Proof of Service of Summons (form POS-010).)
(Para prueba de entrega de esta citación use el formulario Proof of Service of Summons, (POS-010)).

NOTICE TO THE PERSON SERVED: You are served
1. ☐ as an individual defendant.
2. ☐ as the person sued under the fictitious name of *(specify)*:
3. ☑ on behalf of *(specify)*: The Muir Group, Inc.
   under: ☑ CCP 416.10 (corporation) ☐ CCP 416.60 (minor)
   ☐ CCP 416.20 (defunct corporation) ☐ CCP 416.70 (conservatee)
   ☐ CCP 416.40 (association or partnership) ☐ CCP 416.90 (authorized person)
   ☐ other *(specify)*:
4. ☐ by personal delivery on *(date)*:

Form Adopted for Mandatory Use
Judicial Council of California
SUM-100 [Rev. July 1, 2009]

SUMMONS

Code of Civil Procedure §§ 412.20, 465
www.courtinfo.ca.gov

DAVID R. BURTT, State Bar No. 201220
MOBILITY LEGAL P.C.
317 Washington Street #207
Oakland, CA 94607
Telephone: (510) 208-1909
dburtt@mobilitylegal.com

Attorneys for Plaintiffs
ROBERT NEWCOMBE and
THOMAS SUMMERSALL

F I L E D
Superior Court of California
County of San Francisco

SEP 04 2014

CLERK OF THE COURT
BY: _____
                  Deputy Clerk

SUPERIOR COURT OF THE STATE OF CALIFORNIA

COUNTY OF SAN FRANCISCO

ROBERT NEWCOMBE and THOMAS SUMMERSALL,

    Plaintiffs,

v.

THE MUIR GROUP, INC., CHADWICK HOUSER, and DOES 1 through 5, inclusive,

    Defendants.

Case No. CGC-14-541481

COMPLAINT FOR:

1. Breach of Contract;
2. Breach of Guaranty; and
3. Fraud (Intentional Misrepresentation).

    Plaintiffs Robert Newcombe and Thomas Summersall ("Plaintiffs"), by and through their attorneys Mobility Legal P.C., complain and allege against The Muir Group, Inc. and Chadwick Houser ("Defendants") as follows:

The Parties

    1.   Plaintiffs Robert Newcombe and Thomas Summersall are individuals who reside in Singapore.

    2.   Plaintiffs are informed and believe that defendant The Muir Group, Inc. is a corporation organized and existing under the laws of Delaware with its principal place of business in San Francisco, California. Plaintiffs are informed and believe that defendant Chadwick Houser formed The Muir Group, Inc. in 2013 to operate as an alternative investment

- 1 -

COMPLAINT FOR DAMAGES
Case No.

Something Bigger Than Overthrowing Small Governments

management company focusing on real estate investment through both direct investing and real estate capital markets.

3. Plaintiffs are informed and believe that defendant Chadwick Houser is an individual who resides in San Francisco, California, and who also serves as the principal agent for The Muir Group, Inc.

4. Plaintiffs are ignorant of the true names and capacities of defendants sued as DOES 1-5, inclusive, and therefore sue these defendants by such fictitious names. Plaintiffs will amend this complaint to allege their true names and capacities when ascertained.

Jurisdiction and Venue

5. This Court has personal jurisdiction over Defendants because The Muir Group, Inc.'s principal place of business is located at 388 Market Street, Suite 1300, San Francisco, California 94111, and because Houser resides in this county.

6. Venue is proper in San Francisco County pursuant to California Code of Civil Procedure section 395.5 because The Muir Group, Inc.'s principal place of business is located there.

General Allegations

7. On or around March 20, 2013, Plaintiffs Newcombe and Summersall (collectively "Lenders") entered into a valid written bridge financing agreement ("BFA") with Defendants The Muir Group, Inc. and Chad Houser (collectively, "Borrowers").

8. As explained in the BFA which Houser prepared:

> "Due to the delay in the angel funding for THE MUIR GROUP, some of the payments due for set up have fallen behind. For example, legal set up fees, office start up fees, lease payments, insurance premiums, etc. These funds will be used as bridge financing to support the expenses of the operation until the 'seed capital' is in place. This is anticipated in April 2013."

9. Pursuant to the BFA, Lenders each loaned Borrowers the sum of US $75,000 (the "Debt") to be repaid, in full, upon Borrowers' receipt of seed capital in April 2013 or at any point thereafter.

10. Pursuant to the BFA, no interest was to accrue on the Debt so long as Borrowers timely performed their obligations and repaid the Debt.

11. Pursuant to the BFA, as consideration for making their interest-free short-term loans, Lenders also received a 2.5% ownership interest in The Muir Group, Inc. (or the equivalent of 125,000 shares each at a price of .$.60/share).

12. Pursuant to the BFA, Houser also personally guaranteed repayment of the Debt with his personal assets ("Guaranty"). More specifically, Houser guaranteed that:

> "Should 'seed capital' or the arrangement with angel investors fall apart or fail to solidify, Chadwick Houser personally guarantees this debt to Tom Summersall and Robert Newcombe with personal assets. This debt would be repaid with proceeds from a sale of Houser's San Francisco real estate portfolio."

13. On March 20, 2013, Houser thus represented to Lenders that he held personal assets sufficient to repay the Debt in full, including without limitation a "San Francisco real estate portfolio" which representations, on information and belief, were knowingly false when made.

14. On information and belief, Houser made these false representations with the intention of inducing Lenders' reliance and ultimately to lure Lenders into loaning Borrowers money under false pretenses.

15. Lenders reasonably believed Houser's representation and, based on their reliance, collectively loaned The Muir Group $150,000.

16. Plaintiffs have performed all conditions, covenants, and promises required on their part to be performed in accordance with the terms and conditions of the BFA. All conditions required by the BFA for Defendants' performance have occurred.

17. Borrowers have unjustifiably and inexcusably breached their obligations under the BFA by failing to timely repay the Debt.

18. Houser has unjustifiably and inexcusably breached his Guaranty under the BFA by failing to use his personal assets (including liquidating his purported "San Francisco real estate portfolio") to timely repay the Debt.

19. As a proximate result of Defendants' breaches of contract, Plaintiffs have suffered, and will continue to suffer, general and special damages in excess of the jurisdictional limit of this Court. Plaintiffs seek compensation for all damages and losses proximately caused by Defendants' breaches of the BFA and punitive damages on account of Houser's oppressive, malicious, and fraudulent actions.

FIRST CAUSE OF ACTION

(Breach of Contract)

(By Plaintiffs Against Defendants)

20. Plaintiffs re-allege and incorporate by reference each and every allegation contained in Paragraphs 1 through 19 of this Complaint.

21. Plaintiffs and Defendants entered into the written BFA on or about March 20, 2013, which agreement was valid and binding.

22. Plaintiffs have performed all conditions, covenants, and promises required on their part to be performed in accordance with the terms and conditions of the BFA.

23. All conditions required by the BFA for Defendants' performance have occurred.

24. Defendants wrongfully breached the BFA by failing to repay the Debt when and as required by the BFA.

25. As a result of Defendants' breach of the BFA, Plaintiffs have been damaged in the amount of approximately $150,000 plus accrued interest, or more according to proof.

SECOND CAUSE OF ACTION

(Breach of Guaranty)

(By Plaintiffs Against Defendant Houser)

26. Plaintiffs re-allege and incorporate by reference each and every allegation contained in Paragraphs 1 through 25 of this Complaint.

27. Plaintiffs and Houser entered into an agreement on or about March 20, 2013, which Guaranty was valid and binding.

COMPLAINT FOR DAMAGES
Case No.

28. Plaintiffs have performed all conditions, covenants, and promises required on their part to be performed in accordance with the terms and conditions of the Guaranty.

29. All conditions required by the Guaranty for Houser's performance have occurred.

30. As guarantor of The Muir Group, Inc.'s obligations under the BFA, Houser's failure to repay the Debt either through his "personal assets" or "with proceeds from a sale of Houser's San Francisco real estate portfolio" constitutes a material breach of his Guaranty.

31. By reason of Houser's material breaches of his obligations, Plaintiffs are now owed and have sustained damages of $150,000 (exclusive of interest).

THIRD CAUSE OF ACTION

Intentional Misrepresentation of Fact

(By Plaintiff Against Defendant Houser)

32. Plaintiffs re-allege and incorporate by reference each and every allegation contained in Paragraphs 1 through 31 of this Complaint.

33. Houser made false representations, with knowledge of their falsity, to Plaintiffs, when he stated on or about March 20, 2013, that:

> "Should 'seed capital' or the arrangement with angel investors fall apart or fail to solidify, Chadwick Houser personally guarantees this debt to Tom Summersall and Robert Newcombe with personal assets. This debt would be repaid with proceeds from a sale of Houser's San Francisco real estate portfolio."

34. On information and belief, as of March 20, 2013, Houser did not have personal assets sufficient to satisfy the personal guarantee he pledged on the BFA, nor did he personally own any real estate in San Francisco or otherwise in the Bay Area.

35. Houser's representation concerning his personal assets, consisting in part of his personal "San Francisco real estate portfolio," was intended to induce, and did induce, Plaintiffs to loan The Muir Group $150,000, collectively. In justifiable reliance on Houser's representation, Plaintiffs entered into the BFA and performed their obligations thereunder.

36. Plaintiffs have suffered damage as a result of Houser's intentional misrepresentation and deceit, the amount of which will be proven at trial.

COMPLAINT FOR DAMAGES
Case No.

37. Houser's actions were done with oppression, malice, or fraud, entitling Plaintiffs to exemplary damages.

PRAYER FOR RELIEF

WHEREFORE, Plaintiffs prays that judgment be entered in their favor and against Defendants as follows:

A. General damages according to proof;

B. Consequential damages;

C. Special damages according to proof;

D. Punitive damages;

E. Interest at the maximum legal rate on all sums awarded;

F. Cost of suit; and

G. Such other and further relief as the Court deems just and proper.

DATED: September 4, 2014

MOBILITY LEGAL P.C.

By: _____
David R. Burtt

Attorneys for Plaintiffs
ROBERT NEWCOMBE and THOMAS SUMMERSALL

Bazzel Baz

CM-010

ATTORNEY OR PARTY WITHOUT ATTORNEY *(Name, State Bar number, and address):*
David R. Burtt
MOBILITY LEGAL P.C.
317 Washington St. #207
Oakland, CA 94607
TELEPHONE NO.: (510) 208-1909   **FAX NO.:**
ATTORNEY FOR *(Name):* Plaintiffs Robert Newcombe and Thomas Summersall

SUPERIOR COURT OF CALIFORNIA, COUNTY OF San Francisco
STREET ADDRESS: 400 McAllister Street
MAILING ADDRESS:
CITY AND ZIP CODE: San Francisco, CA 94102
BRANCH NAME: Civic Center Courthouse

CASE NAME:
Newcombe et al. v. The Muir Group, Inc. and Chadwick Houser

FOR COURT USE ONLY

FILED
Superior Court of California
County of San Francisco
SEP 04 2014
CLERK OF THE COURT
BY: _____ Clerk

CASE NUMBER: CGC-14-541481

CIVIL CASE COVER SHEET	Complex Case Designation	
[✓] Unlimited [ ] Limited	[ ] Counter [ ] Joinder	
(Amount demanded exceeds $25,000)	(Amount demanded is $25,000 or less)	Filed with first appearance by defendant (Cal. Rules of Court, rule 3.402)

JUDGE:

Items 1–6 below must be completed (see instructions on page 2).

1. Check one box below for the case type that best describes this case:

Auto Tort
[ ] Auto (22)
[ ] Uninsured motorist (46)

Other PI/PD/WD (Personal Injury/Property Damage/Wrongful Death) Tort
[ ] Asbestos (04)
[ ] Product liability (24)
[ ] Medical malpractice (45)
[ ] Other PI/PD/WD (23)

Non-PI/PD/WD (Other) Tort
[ ] Business tort/unfair business practice (07)
[ ] Civil rights (08)
[ ] Defamation (13)
[ ] Fraud (16)
[ ] Intellectual property (19)
[ ] Professional negligence (25)
[ ] Other non-PI/PD/WD tort (35)

Employment
[ ] Wrongful termination (36)
[ ] Other employment (15)

Contract
[✓] Breach of contract/warranty (06)
[ ] Rule 3.740 collections (09)
[ ] Other collections (09)
[ ] Insurance coverage (18)
[ ] Other contract (37)

Real Property
[ ] Eminent domain/Inverse condemnation (14)
[ ] Wrongful eviction (33)
[ ] Other real property (26)

Unlawful Detainer
[ ] Commercial (31)
[ ] Residential (32)
[ ] Drugs (38)

Judicial Review
[ ] Asset forfeiture (05)
[ ] Petition re: arbitration award (11)
[ ] Writ of mandate (02)
[ ] Other judicial review (39)

Provisionally Complex Civil Litigation (Cal. Rules of Court, rules 3.400–3.403)
[ ] Antitrust/Trade regulation (03)
[ ] Construction defect (10)
[ ] Mass tort (40)
[ ] Securities litigation (28)
[ ] Environmental/Toxic tort (30)
[ ] Insurance coverage claims arising from the above listed provisionally complex case types (41)

Enforcement of Judgment
[ ] Enforcement of judgment (20)

Miscellaneous Civil Complaint
[ ] RICO (27)
[ ] Other complaint (not specified above) (42)

Miscellaneous Civil Petition
[ ] Partnership and corporate governance (21)
[ ] Other petition (not specified above) (43)

2. This case [✓] is [ ] is not complex under rule 3.400 of the California Rules of Court. If the case is complex, mark the factors requiring exceptional judicial management:
   a. [ ] Large number of separately represented parties
   b. [ ] Extensive motion practice raising difficult or novel issues that will be time-consuming to resolve
   c. [ ] Substantial amount of documentary evidence
   d. [ ] Large number of witnesses
   e. [ ] Coordination with related actions pending in one or more courts in other counties, states, or countries, or in a federal court
   f. [ ] Substantial postjudgment judicial supervision

3. Remedies sought *(check all that apply):* a. [✓] monetary b. [ ] nonmonetary; declaratory or injunctive relief c. [✓] punitive
4. Number of causes of action *(specify):*
5. This case [ ] is [✓] is not a class action suit.
6. If there are any known related cases, file and serve a notice of related case. *(You may use form CM-015.)*

Date: September 3, 2014
David R. Burtt
(TYPE OR PRINT NAME)   (SIGNATURE OF PARTY OR ATTORNEY FOR PARTY)

NOTICE
- Plaintiff must file this cover sheet with the first paper filed in the action or proceeding (except small claims cases or cases filed under the Probate Code, Family Code, or Welfare and Institutions Code). (Cal. Rules of Court, rule 3.220.) Failure to file may result in sanctions.
- File this cover sheet in addition to any cover sheet required by local court rule.
- If this case is complex under rule 3.400 et seq. of the California Rules of Court, you must serve a copy of this cover sheet on all other parties to the action or proceeding.
- Unless this is a collections case under rule 3.740 or a complex case, this cover sheet will be used for statistical purposes only.

Form Adopted for Mandatory Use
Judicial Council of California
CM-010 [Rev. July 1, 2007]

CIVIL CASE COVER SHEET

Cal. Rules of Court, rules 2.30, 3.220, 3.400–3.403, 3.740;
Cal. Standards of Judicial Administration, std. 3.10
www.courtinfo.ca.gov

367

Something Bigger Than Overthrowing Small Governments

Chad's history of physical violence began on July 4, 2014, when he attempted to strangle Jordana. As a result, he was incarcerated in Lake Tahoe, CA. On October 23, 2015, not long after the births of both Harrison and Pierce, Jordana got up from sleeping to get a glass of water at the same time Chad arrived home drunk. He started throwing rocks at her and calling her a "dirty whore." Confused, she asked him what was going on. He started arguing. Fortunately, she recorded all of it on video. He then picked up a wooden stick and hit her in the head ... an injury that later would require 12 stitches. As the blood streamed down her face, she ran to get her kids and leave, but he grabbed her by the hair and pushed her head into the lawn. Helpless, and unable to defend herself or the children, Chad took both of them from her, placed them in the car and started to drive away. Jordana commandeered her bicycle in pursuit. Chad slammed on the brakes, causing Jordana to crash into the rear bumper and fall from the bicycle. Once on the ground, Chad put the car in reverse and attempted to run over her. She barely escaped with her life. The relationship was anything but good, but as most married couples will tell you ... they just kept trying despite the circumstances.

Sometime later, once the dust had settled, Chad convinced Jordana that he had a temporary work position in Thailand and they would live in Bali, Indonesia. They needed to move immediately. After two months on the island, Jordana was beaten by Chad again. She retreated to stay with a friend. Since Chad had her passport and those of the children, it was impossible for her to take her children back to America. He refused to turn them over to her.

The relationship was tumultuous throughout the time in Bali. Chad did not show signs of sustainable work, thus once again milking Jordana and members of her family for money. Chad was also engaging in the use of narcotics like cocaine and alcohol. Jordana suffered continuous verbal and physical abuse from Chad during their time in Bali, with a number of police and medical reports to substantiate the events.

On February 14, 2016, Chad supposedly took both the boys to a place called Elephants. He said he would be home by 5 p.m. When Chad and the boys did not arrive home at that time, Jordana texted him. He responded with, "We have been at Elephants, maybe home closer to 6, will let you know how traffic is."

A number of inquiries, "Can you respond, so we don't have to escalate this?" went out between 6-9 p.m. from Jordana, with no response from Chad.

Something Bigger Than Overthrowing Small Governments

Finally, at 9 p.m. he responded. "The boys and I have left Indonesia. We will not be returning."

It is at this point in the story it is worth mentioning that Jordana's husband from her previous marriage also lived in Bali, Pete Matthews. Jordana described Pete in the following way:

> He works for Rip Curl. He's really cocky and super stuck up. He's a bully too. He's 6'5" and uses his tallness to bully people, a lot of people hate him and think he's an asshole, he has one friend and u may know him. Matt George. He was in some movie, I forgot the name, it was a huge surf film. He also is a surf journalist. He's cool, but that's Pete's only friend really. He has an Indonesian wife now and she's OK, but kinda dumb. She's from Sumbawa. He has a surf shop called White Monkey by Padang Padang Beach. That was mine before, and he took that when I left Indonesia. I also helped him buy a home at V land in Hawaii on the north Shore he never paid me back for. His company in Hawaii his brother Steve Matthews runs is named Thirdstone. It's in North Shore too at the sugar mill. It does ok. He is a Gemini, so he changes his mind a lot, and he is a little like Chad, where he keeps bothering people until he gets his way. He has never worked with me and has always tried to be the controller. As he is doing it now with our daughter. He calls me names a lot and says mean stuff to me all the time trying to make me look bad.

Jordana and Pete also had a daughter together named Avani when they originally lived in Bali in 2009. Divorced in 2010, Jordana left Bali with Avani and obtained full custody in the United States. When Jordana and Chad moved to Bali, Avani was able to visit Pete from time to time. Fast forward to the day of the kidnapping of Harrison and Pierce, we discovered that while the boys were taken to

Switzerland by Chad, two weeks prior, Pete had taken their daughter Avani to Hawaii for a vacation.

Jordana was packed and ready to get back to America to report the kidnapping, but there was just one problem ... Chad and she had overstayed their visa time in Bali. Chad had taken her passport and the kids'. She had no idea where it was, and he wouldn't tell her. But he did tell her if she told the U.S. Embassy, they would kick her out, because she had overstayed many months. Looking back, every time Jordana would inquire about the visa, Chad would say that he was working on it and not to worry ... obviously now, that was not the case. When Chad got beat up by the Balinese and she found out he might be killed for ripping them off if he didn't pay them back, he told her where the passports were ... immigrations had seized them. Immigrations was going to charge Chad and Jordana over $8,000.00 for all of their passports. She was only able to raise about $4,000.00 ... enough money to pay for her and the boys. The immigration officer promised to take the $4,000.00 as sufficient payment and not to give the passports to Chad, but he lied. When Chad was able to produce more money, the immigrations officer turned over the passports to Chad, except for Jordana's.

So it appears Chad knew exactly what he was doing when he departed with the boys, and that Jordana would be stranded on the island. Jordana checked with authorities and was told that overstaying more than 60 days is a crime, which may be punishable by up to five years in jail and was not considered a small offense by the Indonesian government. The immigration officers would have no choice but to detain a foreigner who had overstayed. It was exactly what she feared ... she had been tricked again by Chad. According to our experience it's not likely that Jordana would have been released to go home after filling out forms. She was contacted by a friend of a friend, who advised her not to go to the authorities, but to instead pay him $7,000 USD, and he would fix it for her. She did exactly that, the issue was resolved, and she departed for the U.S.

Once back in America she filed a police report against Chad right away and spoke to Pete on the phone, discovering that Pete was back in San Pedro, California. She asked if he would pick her up from the airport stating that he and she and their daughter would go to

Something Bigger Than Overthrowing Small Governments

Disneyland. When Jordana landed in Los Angeles, Pete was nowhere to be found and never picked her up as he said he would. She called a friend for a ride and tried to reach Pete. Once on the phone, he said he would allow her to see Avani. But in the four days he was in California, he never came through, and eventually kidnapped Avani back to Bali ... obviously without Jordana's permission.

As it would turn out, Chad and Pete were in communication with one another the entire time, co-conspiring — Pete even offering his attorney to Chad for legal assistance against Jordana. In hindsight, it appears that Chad and Pete were friends even before Chad's decision to move everyone to Bali, and that prior to that a plan of abduction was put in place without Jordana knowing it.

Darlene Ford, Jordana Houser's grandmother was kind enough to forward this email from Pete, which confirmed our suspicions.

Please do not let Pete know I sent this to you

Darlene J. Ford
Maui Lodging Properties LLC
▓▓▓▓▓▓▓▓ Office
▓▓▓▓▓▓▓▓ Home
▓▓▓▓▓▓▓▓ Cell

-----Original Message-----
From: third stone [▓▓▓▓▓▓▓▓▓▓▓▓▓▓▓▓▓▓▓▓]
Sent: Monday, June 06, 2016 4:25 AM
To: darlene ford
Cc: chadwick houser
Subject: Custody

Hi Darlene,

Wanted to touch base after speaking with you today. I spoke to Chad after we spoke. We both very much want to figure out a peaceful solution to these issues. Jordana and Christian did not show up at the scheduled meeting today with Liz Nigro to work on some sort of custody solution. Liz is hoping to hear what Jordana wants or thinks is best for the kids. We have only heard accusations of kidnapping, abuse and fraud. When the real question is who is capable of giving a stable home environment and the best education. Can you give us an idea of a reasonable plan that would be a positive for the kids.

Maybe you can help since no one can deal with Jordana directly on real terms. Everyone wants to be peaceful and find a solution. With all the kids enrolled in school, what do you suggest? We have no information on where Jordana lives, is she employed? The only address she has given is Marta's house in Hollywood. Does she have a home fit for three small children? We would like to hear realistic ideas of what is best for the kids.

Thanks

Sent from my iPhone

Operation Overview:

Once Jordana Houser met with ARC, we were able to accompany her to the Los Angeles Police Department and meet with Detective Kevin Becker to fill out all the proper paperwork regarding the kidnapping and begin processing a warrant for Chad's arrest. LAPD wanted Jordana to fill out a Hague Application, which we advised her against.

According to the U.S. Department of State (travel.state.gov) the primary purpose of the Hague Convention is to deter international child abductions and to provide a prompt remedy for the return of an

Something Bigger Than Overthrowing Small Governments

abducted child by ensuring custody rights under one Contracting State that are respected in other Contracting States. Thus, for example, if a parent removes a child from the country of the child's habitual residence into a separate country, acting in breach of the other parent's rights of custody, the left-behind parent may commence an action under the Convention by filing a petition for relief in the jurisdiction to which the child was wrongfully removed or retained (the removed-to state). The petitioning parent must establish that the child was wrongfully removed or retained from the country of the child's habitual residence (the removed-from state), in breach of the petitioning parent's custody rights. The Convention also provides a series of affirmative defenses, exceptions, which, if established by the respondent, may preclude the child's return. If the petitioning parent demonstrates the elements of the prima facie case, and the abducting parent fails to establish excepting circumstances, the Convention requires the prompt return of the child to the country of his or her habitual residence.

A Hague Convention proceeding is a civil action brought in the country to which a child (under the age of 16) was wrongfully removed or retained. The Convention applies only between Contracting States and only when the wrongful abduction occurs after the Convention is in force between those States. In cases where the Convention is not in effect between the United States and the other nation involved in the dispute, U.S. courts must look to domestic law to determine jurisdiction and the extent of their authority.

So think about this ... if the custodial parent has already been through the agonizing process in a U.S. court of law to establish that the child was wrongfully removed or retained from the country of the child's habitual residence, in breach of the parent's custody rights, then why would anyone penalize them by having them go through this entire petitioning process in the Hague? It makes absolutely no sense at all, unless the U.S. judicial system and those who uphold the laws that protect American citizens just are not willing to go to bat for American citizens. And in some cases with law enforcement who are not willing to, or do not have the budget to pursue the kidnapper, it is simply easier for them to pass it off to The Hague and wash their hands of the entire matter — all the while looking like they did something about it in order to avert a lawsuit from citizens — to check the box or to wash their hands of the entire matter. Then again, some of them may actually believe that The Hague works, and that they are doing the right thing to resolve the issue for the custodial parent.

To date, in our opinion and the opinion of many other NGOs, The Hague has failed. There is no evidence that it has operated in any significant way to provide greater protection for children or American birth parents against exploitation by foreign legal firms that charge enormous fees, and from foreign judicial systems that are not aligned with U.S. law, values or culture. And yet, time and time again we see congressmen, lawyers, law enforcement and NGO's who are dealing with an international child abduction case, simply roll over and submit to The Hague, as if it were the enforcer of a global law greater than U.S. law.

It is not clear that The Hague's requirements add any real protection, but what is clear is that in every case we have investigated, the decisions by The Hague are heavily influenced by politics. Let us be clear, domestic and international law designed to provide such protection already existed prior to The Hague. In my opinion, the United States needs to tell other countries ratifying and implementing The Hague that they do not have to follow wrongful interpretations being promoted by The Hague Permanent Bureau.

Many law enforcement professionals have limited experience with parental child abduction cases and specifically with procedures in international parental abduction cases. When Detective Becker suggested Jordana sign The Hague application, I don't think he realized what he was asking her to do ... turn over her sovereign right as an American, who already held full custody of her children by a U.S. court under U.S. law. He had a great sense of urgency and was extremely helpful and would prove himself in days and weeks to come. Detective Becker pushed for the warrant for arrest and kept Jordana informed regularly on the proceedings from the District Attorney's office. Even his one or two conversations with me regarding ARC's intentions were heartfelt and genuine. He was a true professional and did everything he could within his power.

Something Bigger Than Overthrowing Small Governments

There was no dispute that Chad Houser had kidnapped the children, Jordana had all the official court documents giving her full custody. What we were seeking was a warrant for his arrest, which would provide ARC with much more credibility in the eyes of whatever foreign authority we would be partnering up within our search. Generally, the successful resolution of international parental child abduction cases through use of criminal charges requires a coordinated effort among federal, state, and local law enforcement authorities. In some cases, U.S. law enforcement will also enlist the help of Interpol and foreign law enforcement authorities to carry out an investigation, which is also what we wanted. We filled out paperwork to get Interpol involved.

We left the LAPD office feeling satisfied that we had put into place all the necessary paperwork to move the case along and to mitigate any liability ... we had done everything required of us by law. I explained to Jordana that in many countries, citizens can be prosecuted for crimes committed abroad if the act is a criminal offense under local law. However, parental abduction is rarely considered a crime outside of the United States.

Two days passed when we received an email from a medical doctor in Switzerland by the name of Dr. Cedric Loiret-Bernal. "We might have seen your two boys in Switzerland. The police want conformation that you have reported them as missing to the U.S. Embassy in Djakarta or the State Department ... URGENT ... Can you be reached by phone and/or e-mail?"

Little did we know at the time, but Cedric would become a major intelligence asset for us as well as a driving force that would lead to the eventual recovery of the children. Cedric emailed and stated that he had a location on Chad, his mother and the boys. Chad had brought the boys in to Cedric for some medical attention, and when he could not pay the bill, Cedric became suspicious. He found the information online about the kidnapping and was not about to let Chad escape. We contacted Cedric and found out that he had actually served for many years in the U.S. Navy prior to returning home to Switzerland. Cedric had an opportunity to visit the chalet where Chad was staying in order to attend to his mother, who was ill. While there he took a number of photographs, which he sent to us as confirmation.

On our end, we were pulling together the financing to send the ARC team over as soon as possible. Per our guidance Cedric informed the local police and requested that they detain Chad until we could arrive. His response was immediate:

Dear Mrs. Loren, per our phone conversation, I do need a copy of an official document of the court order in place here in America and an arrest and warrant and the police report here in LA for missing children. I will provide to the Swiss police at 8 am today (Swiss time) or 11pm your time. I understand that your husband might change location by Monday. He might be in Zurich this morning, so your children are with his mother (Peggy Dillard). The address of the rented chalet is known to me and will be communicated to the police. It is Good Friday in Switzerland so going directly to the police is critical.

Best regards,
Cédric LOIRET-BERNAL, MD

We contacted Detective Becker and requested that he send the warrant and other necessary paperwork to the Swiss police. We had a direct number then and confirmed that all the paperwork had indeed arrived, but suddenly the Swiss police decided not to detain Chad. What they did next was basically aide a criminal in his escape. Instead of detaining him, they questioned him and told him he was free to go. Cedric had been monitoring the chalet from time to time making sure the vehicle was still there. He, in fact, was brilliant enough to send a photo of the vehicle and licenses plate to us. We had spoken with the local Swiss Police and requested that they simply run surveillance on Chad so he would not be spooked. But that did not happen.

Something Bigger Than Overthrowing Small Governments

Within 24 hours of the police speaking with Chad, he and his mother and the boys were no longer at the chalet and, in fact, had departed without paying the landlord the $3,000.00 rental fee they owed. Our man on the ground, Cedric emailed us:

Neighbors of Chalet Valerie (in GRYON, VAUD) have not seen the children and Mrs. Peggy DILLARD today. They saw Chad H. around 9 am this morning moving all luggage out. The owner's cleaning lady confirmed around 1pm that the Chalet had been vacated (more than one day ahead of schedule). I spoke to Baer TRAVIS at the U.S. Embassy in Bern who confirmed that Chad H. told the police he was moving to a new address in VERBIER ... (AirBnB rental?). I just called the police in Verbier (+41 27 775 3545) three hours ago to give them a heads-up about a "possible child abduction case involving two U.S. Children" and that we would be in touch with the correct paperwork ASAP. They will call the Police Cantonale de VAUD (State Police of Canton of VAUD who interrogated Chad Friday evening: Inspector Jean-Marc Blaser +/- Emilie) to get the Police Cantonale of VALAIS (State Police of Canton of VALAIS) moving. I can still pick you up tomorrow (MONDAY) early evening. I hope you get Senior Detective (D3) BACKER (213 972 2922) of the LAPD or a colleague to file the proper paperwork with the Feds or Interpol

(http://www.interpol.int/notice/search/missing) today ....

All the best, Cedric"

The ARC operation and SFRT stood down. We had no idea which way Chad went, so it would be fruitless to put boots on the ground and waste finances simply guessing where in the Alps he would hide. The Swiss Police of Gryon offered no apology for their decision to encourage Chad to run again, but it was plain to see that this would be the attitude of law enforcement on the ground there ... they were just not interested in arresting anyone suspected of a crime. Or I may be wrong ... it might have just been their way of making him go away so they would not have to deal with it. I have always admired the Swiss for more than the Army knife. Chocolate is a major export, there are 208 mountains over 3,000 meters high, the economy is based on highly-skilled workers, most people in Switzerland are Christian, it has four national languages, the Swiss are an educated population, and it has one of the lowest crime rates of all industrialized countries — despite having liberal gun laws (2.3–4.5 million guns in a population of eight million). In 2010, there were only 0.5 gun murders per 100,000 people compared to five per 100,000 in the US.

Despite my love for the nation, this seemed to be so out of character for any police station, especially in Switzerland, until I recalled that this was the same country that gave Adolf Hitler refuge during the war. I suspected their mindset of neutrality would be a fault line to navigate ... but if done correctly, could work to our advantage. I had faith that God would lead us to all the right people, Swiss people who did care and did want to see justice prevail, perhaps other police officials, despite the directives of their government ... and, as I experienced later, that would be exactly the case.

Jordana and her family were distraught. We had Chad in the palm of our hands, and now he was allowed to slip away. My guidance to them was clear. "Without sounding preachy, we never take God out of the equation, and I know that while it appears that we have lost Chad, we have not. There is no where he can hide in the world where we cannot find him. Trust me and I will show you the hand of God in all of this." Jordana and her mother and grandmother did exactly that ... trusted ARC.

During the next three months we called upon multiple strategic partners like Sovereign Intelligence, CDS Group International, S.E.R.T. Ministries, Wind and Fire Ministries, who had developed systems and resources that not even the U.S. Federal Government possesses, systems capable of tracking Pete and Chad, intercepting communications, running surveillance in Bali, and generating promising intelligence and overhead imagery with strong yields of information that pulled us closer ... and we prayed a lot. The best part of these partnerships rested in the fact that they are all faith-based believers who understood the spiritual component ... the darkness we were up against. This allowed them to be more effective in their research.

I've been down range long enough to care less what people may think about my methods or care whether they believe that mind, body and spirit are all connected ... one affects the other in every case. The mistake that conventional non-believers make is that they neglect to incorporate all three and eventually get blindsided by one or more of them, either in the form of wasted energy, false leads, dead ends, lack of support, blurred vision, miscalculated operational planning or uncontrollable circumstances that totally cause the investigation or operation to go haywire. I learned long ago that I needed those uncontrollable circumstances to be controlled, not by myself, but by God.

God sees it at the 14,000-foot level, as if He is the drone, so to speak. He can see so much further down the road than we can on the ground, and it certainly helps to have that intelligence in your back pocket. He acts like the advance team that gets to the AO and puts things in place, so it all feathers out for success. Without making a hard attempt at trying to convince you, the reader, how my faith in God is essential, let me just re-iterate that we have a 100% success rate in that every child we have gone after, we have brought home. Let that speak for itself. And while a lot of people will point to the level of experience we have as the reason, I can promise you as someone who is in the trenches fighting the battle ... that is not the case. We are merely people with a talent, and we are not beyond making mistakes. We are not extraordinary people; we are people given extraordinary strength and wisdom by God almighty who cares for children and has called us to a life of unselfish sacrifice to FOLLOW HIM.

You have heard me say it before ... God is not just in the equation; He is the equation. "Obey My voice and I will be your God and you shall be my people. And walk in all the ways that I have commanded you ... that it may be well with you" (Jeremiah 7:23 NKJV).

I cannot tell you how exciting it is to know that God — not Allah, not Buddha, not any other false god in this world — is leading the charge and is ready to open the Red Sea for you. If you knew what I knew and could experience what I experience with the one true God of this universe who has made Himself known to man from the beginning of time ... you would not be able to contain your enthusiasm when called upon to rescue a child in danger.

Three months after the disappearance of Chad, his mother and the boys from Gryon, on 5 June 2016 I found myself before God early in the morning sincerely asking Him to show us where Chad was located. On the morning of 6 June 2016 God answered that prayer in an email from Jennifer Harkins, U.S. State Department.

Financially we could only support a three-man SFRT and the custodial mother Jordana Houser. I contacted Thad Turner, ARC Operator and former Navy SEAL, and Rudy Gonzalez of S.E.R.T. Ministries, a former U.S. Marine Recon. Both were packed and ready to roll. Time was of the essence, and I knew this was God saying, "Go now." Thad would fly in from Pittsburgh and meet us on the ground in Zurich, while Rudy and I would escort Jordana Houser.

The flight itself was uneventful but when we hit the ground, everything was in full play. We had no idea who was informed in the Swiss government or State Department that ARC was involved. While I wish State Department, after all these years, would embrace our missions, we have sadly come to learn that State is more concerned with maintaining economic and political relationships with foreign countries to such an extent that the rights and protection of American citizens in that country fall second to this agenda.

Over my 40 years of being in the field, I have seen nothing different, other than the individual employees of State from time to time crossing a line to help and do the right thing by risking their positions and facing reprimand from their superiors. Take a look at Benghazi on September 11, 2012. Need I say more?

I can name a number of other places we have operated where had State known we were in country ahead of time, I'm pretty sure they would have done all they could to prevent us from rescuing an American child. I remember specifically speaking to a State

Something Bigger Than Overthrowing Small Governments

Department Officer in Islamabad regarding an American child, Doolie Rael, who was kidnapped by the family of Osama Bin Laden's physician. The State Department Officer, who will remain nameless, actually told me that if I came to Pakistan to pull off a recovery operation that he would do everything in his power to alert the ISI and have me imprisoned. I never forgot that conversation, and it set the stage for the way I viewed most people working at State. I am happy to say that despite a few "buttheads," I have great appreciation for a number of men and women in American Citizen Services who have been nothing but amazing, and I am sure a few Ambassadors and some RSOs as well. To them I say thank you for doing the right thing. Perhaps one day all of that will change, and we can work hand-in-hand with State prior to departing CONUS (Continental United States). We shall see.

So knowing all of this, we moved in on Zurich using as much tradecraft as we felt necessary to avoid having our entire team stopped or followed. I saw Thad when we exited the gate. He did not make contact, but instead followed at a distance. Rudy had exited ahead of Jordana Houser and me and led the way at a good distance. It would not be until the rental car was acquired that everyone would meet. I don't usually discuss any tradecraft in books, but this isn't really a big secret, just common sense, and it's pretty much known by anyone who moves tactically. The larger portion of tradecraft used on this mission cannot be discussed, so you, the reader, will just have to use your imagination. Suffice it to say, we used every trick in the book, and we always do. It's been a proven standard for spies who want to stay alive, so like MasterCard we "don't leave home without it."

Our destination was Bern, Switzerland. The country was every bit as beautiful as I had remembered from my trip to Lucerne two years before when I was acting as Director of Operations for The David House Agency. Eric Volz, the Managing Director, and I had just left Qatar dealing with the illegal incarceration of two Americans, Matt and Grace Haung.

Switzerland was rainy and overcast on the superhighway to Bern. The drive provided enough time for us to put a Warning Order in place for the operation. At that stage, we knew only what the email from State had explained, and our mission was to meet with a Swiss

Attorney, Brigette Meyer, the following day hoping to gather more intelligence. I suspected that Mrs. Meyer would insert herself as the resident legal authority and attempt to get Jordana Houser to hire her for some sort of court procedure, but until we got face to face, we weren't sure.

We arrived in Bern and had enough time to actually recon the city by car — the attorney's office, and routes in and out. Coincidentally, Parliament was meeting in Bern and every hotel in the city was booked.

> The Old City of Bern is the medieval city center of Bern, Switzerland. Built on a narrow hill surrounded on three sides by the Aare River, its compact layout has remained essentially unchanged since its construction during the 12th to the 15th century. Despite a major fire in 1405, after which much of the city was rebuilt in sandstone and substantial construction efforts in the 18th century, Bern's old city retained its medieval character.
>
> The Old City is home to Switzerland's tallest cathedral as well as other churches, bridges and a large collection of Renaissance fountains. In addition to many historical buildings, the seats of the federal, cantonal and municipal government are also situated in the Old City. It is a UNESCO Cultural World Heritage Site since 1983 due to the compact and generally intact medieval core and is an excellent example of incorporating the modern world into a medieval city. [28]

Three miles outside of town we found a Holiday Inn where we could drop our gear and set up a temporary command center. Rudy was in contact with a number of associates from "The Tactical Beard Owners Club" (or TBOC for short) which was founded in August 2011, with a fistful of members that were personally invited by the founder. The genesis of the club was a spontaneous impulse.

It should spark like-minded people to make new friends. It evolved into the most significant tactical beard network in the tactical scene and has become a true brotherhood. Back in 2002 when the Afghanistan campaign rolled on, the very first units that did deploy were none less than the Operational Detachment Alpha (ODA) units known as 'Green Berets.' They did make the initial advance into the country and worked together with local allies. What distinguished these men from the regular military was their distinctive facial hair style that they were allowed to have. Not only for personal or strategic security reasons but predominately for cultural acceptance from local inhabitants of hostile environments, who generally perceive bearded men as masculine, experienced and a senior figure within his organization (all above in addition to his personal passion for facial hair) and thereby a person worthy of respect. The beard is a sign of attitude and not for fashion reasons.
(www.tacticalbeardownersclub.com)

Trust me when I tell you that ARC is not without resources and alliances that support our mission. Based in almost every nation, they have never hesitated when it came to the rescue of children in danger.

We were in luck, or so we thought. Two members of the TBOC were part of the police force in Bern and were willing to jump in immediately, but they were in the United States on vacation. Rudy reached out to a few more in Bern, but they were on assignment. A wealth of resources that slipped right through our hands within a few phone calls took us from feeling excited to a little despair ... just a little until we realized that it was God saying, you don't need your friends, I'll handle this one. And that is where we placed it, in God's hands, so we could rest with confidence. Most of the night before, I shut my eyes. I played the operations order over and over, rehearsing a number of scenarios in my head, anticipating the outcome of our efforts. To expedite our movement, we printed out all the necessary paperwork

Jordana Houser would need to submit to the U.S. Embassy for temporary passports for Harrison and Pierce once we recovered them. She dove into the process with disregard for her own sleep until in the wee hours of the morning, all of it was filled out.

That morning, I awoke to Rudy already having his Bible study, and mine was to follow. It was clear to me that we needed to know our exfil routes either to Germany, France or Italy — what was the fastest, the shortest, and the cleanest. We departed the hotel after breakfast for a meeting at 1000 hours with Mrs. Meyer in Bern. All the gear was packed in the vehicle, nothing left in the hotel. You never know when you'll have to make the jump immediately when tracking someone, so it's always a night-to-night reservation at hotels — that is, if you can find a hotel. If not, then you sleep in the car while running surveillance. Thad and Rudy would drop Jordana Houser and myself off and then run the route to France and check for obstacles.

The rain continued in typical Alps fashion as we exited the vehicle and found our way up the stairs of a very old building to the offices of Von Ins Wyder Zumstein. For just a moment I felt like Van Helsing returning to Transylvania. On the second or third floor, I can't remember which, we met the receptionists, who ushered us into a white renaissance room, minus elaborate furniture or paintings ... just a large conference table sporting some bottles of drinking water and chairs.

It wasn't long until Mrs. Meyer entered the room and introduced herself. She immediately dove into what seemed a very practiced sales pitch regarding our arrival in Switzerland and the events surrounding the kidnapping. She wasn't aware of a lot of the evidence surrounding Chad's antics, and when informed, took notes but brushed them under the rug with no follow-up questions regarding any of it. She made it very clear that the Swiss did not like to arrest people, and that she saw her role as a facilitator to bring Chad and Jordana under the rule of a Swiss court, to see if all of this could be resolved, despite the fact that Jordana already had custody as granted by a U.S. Court. To Mrs. Meyer none of this mattered. What did matter — and this became evident as she repeated it on a number of occasions — was that Jordana retain her services.

Something Bigger Than Overthrowing Small Governments

    Jordana smirked and said, "Do you really believe Chad is going to turn up for court? I was married to this man. I know him better than anyone." Mrs. Meyer had a blank look on her face and said nothing. She collected herself and then mentioned that the circumstance surrounding the kidnapping from Indonesia precluded this from becoming a Hague case. What a relief. After making the mistake of submitting The Hague application through LAPD, and days later trying to have it stopped ... miraculously it stopped itself. She still hadn't mentioned the location of Chad, and I needed to probe the lines.

    "What is the name of the Police Chief again? Where is he located? Is that where Chad is located?"

    Reluctantly, she revealed Chad was located in Interlaken and that Mr. Miller, the Chief of Police, had been called to the Hapimag Hotel because Chad owed them 10,000 Swiss francs. According to the management Chad had stayed too long and there would not be room for them another night there. They were having them check out by noon today. I looked at my watch ... it was 1100 hours and Interlaken was one hour away. You can imagine ... I wanted to grab Jordana Houser and head out of the room immediately, but I could not afford to alert Mrs. Meyer to my intentions and have her react by calling the police or whomever to stop us. I looked Mrs. Meyer in the eye, "Can you have Officer Miller detain them? Can the hotel security detain them? We need time to get there. What if Chad leaves? This will be the same situation the Swiss police put us in when we located Chad in Gryon."

    It was as if the gears in her brain were not shifting quickly enough. "I do not know if we can do that." And then she jumped right back into a non-stop dissertation on how she saw all of this playing out. She wanted Jordana to sign a Power of Attorney so she could interact with the local police on our behalf. I advised Jordana to sign, and so she did. There was no way she was going to allow us to deal directly with the police, for a number of reasons. She needed a paycheck, and if she could show she orchestrated the recovery of the children, detained Chad, and pulled everyone into a controlled judicial environment, then Jordana would have no choice but to retain her services. I had seen this play out so many other times on foreign soil, and I was not about to allow this to happen to Jordan Houser. Mrs. Meyer asked how long Jordana could stay in Switzerland and advised her that she would need to pay for expenses in addition to her fees. When I asked her how long she believed it would take to bring Chad to court, she did not have an answer. It was time for me to turn the tide in our favor. I whispered to Jordana to text Thad and Rudy under the table and tell them to turn around immediately and come pick us up and plan a route to Interlaken.

Now that I knew where Chad was and who the Chief of Police was, we were set. I needed to be on my best behavior, toss out an idea, and make it seem like it was her idea. "Bridgette, may I call you Bridgette? I believe if we go to the hotel and speak with Chad, that he will see the error of his ways and turn the children over."

Her eyes widened. "No, you cannot do that. It could cause violence. Chad could get mad." I was starting to wonder whose side she was on. There was something dark about her motives that I did not like ... something dark all wrapped up in white.

Perhaps in years to come I will look back and feel differently about her, perhaps have a better understanding of what influenced her motives, come to realize she really was on our side. But for now ... it did not appear that way. Our sense of urgency was not her sense of urgency.

"What if we meet Officer Miller at the hotel and he goes in with us?" I said.

She thought about this for a moment and then replied, "I can arrange that and have CPS (Child Protective Services) there as well, and then they can take the children and hold them until we can hold court."

I saw a glimpse of hope and knew I could stretch it to our advantage tactically. Under my breath I said, "Dear God please make a way for us to get to Interlaken before Chad leaves and make me sharp and persuasive ... make good of evil if it is sitting in front of me."

I looked at my watch. "If the hotel is requiring Chad to check out by noon, we only have about an hour. Can you make those calls now? And I have another idea, since Jordana has not seen the children in such a long time, what if CPS helps us get the kids, and then they turn them over to Jordana, who can stay in a hotel in Interlaken until court?"

Mrs. Meyer responded favorably to the idea and left the room to make some calls. We sat there and sat there and sat there. Finally, Thad and Rudy texted us to let us know they were downstairs. I told

Something Bigger Than Overthrowing Small Governments

Jordana to follow me. We found Mrs. Meyer still on the phone, long winded as usual. I intentionally positioned us outside the glass window of the office, so she could see we were still waiting. I asked the receptionist to tell her we were departing. When she did, Mrs. Meyer got off the phone. We told her we were headed to Interlaken and would plan on meeting Officer Miller at the hotel. She said she had coordinated for CPS to take charge of things and look for us to coordinate. We departed immediately.

On the drive to Interlaken, the majesty of the Alps encompassed the route. One hour later we rolled into the small village, complete with tourists and attendees of the International Conference on Nanoscopy. There were no hotels available and no parking spaces near the Hapimag Hotel where Chad was staying that would allow surveillance from the vehicle. The three of us, I, Thad and Rudy fanned in and out of the hotel. No police were in sight, no CPS in sight, and no calls from Mrs. Meyers to tell us how and when they would arrive. Inside the hotel Thad was approached by one of the hotel managers, and being his usual self, charmed her into a friendship — she, being a Brit and evidently welcoming an American in short pants, T-shirt and baseball hat. We always teased Thad about his clothing ... seems he loves his shorts. Rudy, on the other hand, with his thick beard was looking more like a Middle Eastern terrorist than an American. As for myself, I was realizing that we could only hang out at this location for about an hour without drawing attention, and I needed to think of something quick. I contacted Jordana, sitting in the vehicle behind a building, and told her I wanted her to drive out the exit, turn left and find me standing in a parking place in front of the hotel. Now here's the lesson in this. Never ask a mom under stress to perform even the simplest task without direct supervision, no matter how calm she may look.

I positioned myself across the street to hold on to a parking space that just opened, thinking she would exit the alley and drive right over. Jordana came out of the exit and, wouldn't you know it ... turned right instead of left and kept on driving, and driving, and driving until I lost sight of her. We quickly got her on the phone and told her to turn around. She finally made it back to where I was standing. I really wasn't sure how far she would have gone if we had not reached her. It was somewhat comical and somewhat not ... given the fact that we were in such an unpredictable situation. The last thing I needed was Chad seeing her. When she made it back to my location, I parked the car in the space exactly across from the hotel and had her remain in the car, disguised with a hat and scarf.

    I sat there watching the hotel and then suddenly, a still, small voice in my head told me, "You need to go in and let hotel security know why you are here." It was so clear that I did not hesitate. I entered the hotel and asked for security. Ironically, there was no security. What hotel has no security? This hotel had no security. But it did have Edith Rico, the Resort Manager and her assistant, the Brit, who Thad had charmed earlier. I disclosed who I was and why I was there. I opened the entire file, photos, warrants for arrest and all. She was startled at first but then quickly got with the program. Edith shared the fact that Chad owed them 10,000 francs, that he had disappeared a few days ago, and that Peggy and the kids were still in the room. That was just what I wanted to hear. Edith stated that her job was on the line if Chad did not pay them. She was just being kind to him because of the children, after requesting multiple times throughout his stay that he make payments. It was just one more scam by Chad, taking advantage of some really nice Swiss people. It infuriated me to think how this "ugly American" was making my country look bad in front of the Swiss.

    I could see that Edith and her assistant, whose name I cannot remember at the moment, were concerned for their jobs, and that anything other than a quiet recovery operation would further create problems. I advised them that the best approach to getting the kids would be a low-profile operation and suggested it would be best for her to contact Officer Miller and have him meet us in the underground parking lot below the hotel.

    Thad went for the vehicle with Jordana still waiting. Rudy, I, Edith and her assistant went to the underground parking lot. Thad soon arrived, and we staged the vehicle in one of the spaces. Ten minutes later Officer Miller and about four other very nice and very professional police officers arrived on foot. We introduced ourselves, and I asked if we should wait for CPS.

    Officer Miller said, "No, I'm handling this."

Something Bigger Than Overthrowing Small Governments

    I flashed my NYPD challenge coin I had been given by former NYPD officer and friend James Bodner. Officer Miller smiled. I looked at him and said, "Thank you."

    A quick discussion between Officer Miller and myself summed up the next few steps that would take us upstairs to the room where Peggy Houser and the children were. Chad had not returned and was nowhere to be found. Since there was no armed threat, Edith spearheaded the team, Swiss Police and us waiting in the stairwell until the knock on the door. When Peggy Houser opened the door, the police carefully and respectfully entered behind Edith. The children, Harrison and Pierce were asleep, both in diapers, one in the bedroom and the other on the living room couch. Peggy Houser was directed to a chair at the kitchen table and launched into the most pathetic performance of innocence I had ever witnessed. "What is happening? I'm so confused. What is everyone here for? I'm just astounded." She looked at me several times and asked who I was, to which I had no reply.

    She went on and on until finally the female police officer told her, "It is best that you be quiet ... you know exactly what is happening."

    While the police searched the room for documents and evidence, Edith and her assistant dressed the children and followed me, Rudy, Officer Miller and a few of his men down to the underground parking lot. It was there that we reunited Jordana Houser with her boys. It was there that she cried, as did the police, as did the hotel resort manager and as did I. It is really tough not to be moved by these circumstances. I handed Officer Miller my NYPD challenge coin. He removed his Swiss Police rank insignia and put it in my hand. Another Officer removed his detachment insignia (Police Cantonale) and put that in my hand. There was a bond, the same bond that transcends all politics, the brotherhood of doing what is right and knowing that no matter whatever or wherever the call ... we will always be there for one another. Officer Miller and his team earned my eternal respect, devotion and allegiance. And no matter where we are, should they need our help, we will do our best to return the favor. We salute them.

    CPS still had not shown up. Nor did we receive instructions from Mrs. Meyer. Officer Miller said we were free to go and that they would keep an eye out for Chad. The other officers found a manila envelope with Jordana's social security card, the boy's birth certificates, but no passports. I had no idea what they would do with Peggy Houser, and I really did not care. As far as I was concerned, she would eventually have her time in court ... here on earth or before God. And the same would go for Chad Houser once the law caught up with him or hired strong arms from someone he owed money to.

We cranked up the vehicle and departed with full intent of leaving Switzerland as soon as possible. We did not want to be wrapped up in some political whirlwind devised by Mrs. Meyer and the SCA (Swiss Central Authority), and we were not going to wait around until they decided to invent one. We were Americans with all intent of protecting our sovereignty and answering to no one except our own trusted judicial system. We had broken no laws, and there were no orders by the SCA put into motion.

Our next destination was Paris, France. By now, our phones were dead, and we had no time or place to recharge them. The ten-hour trip was filled with the voices of Harrison and Pierce telling their mom how much they loved her and missed her. Pierce had the song twinkle-twinkle little star down to perfection and the breath to sing it for about 15 minutes straight — a five-minute break and then another 15 minutes repeatedly for a good portion of the ten hour trip. Harrison became the backseat driver, intrigued with oncoming traffic, wanting Rudy to drive in and out of orange construction cones and ensuring Thad was wide awake enough to entertain him.

By the time we rolled into Paris, the boys were fast asleep. The Holiday Inn Paris Gere de Lyon Bastillie was a welcome harbor for some very exhausted travelers who knew full well that we needed to be on the U.S. Embassy doorsteps by 0700 hours the next day, Friday. The emergency passport section provided a two-hour window 0800-1000 hours the next day for us to submit the paperwork to request temporary passports for Harrison and Pierce. The longer we stayed in the EU, the greater the chances were that something not in our favor would develop ... like the fog gradually drifting in off the shoreline that consumes the night and makes it all that much more difficult to see. It made our resolve even stronger and our trust in God deeper ... for when you are surrounded, that is when He pulls out all the stops.

Something Bigger Than Overthrowing Small Governments

    I delighted in my soul with what was about to happen. God was going to show Himself in a way that would be undeniable. I didn't know in what form, but I knew it was on the horizon ... I could feel it as King David felt it when he said to Goliath, "You come to me with a sword, with a spear, and with a javelin. But I come to you in the name of the Lord of hosts, the God of the armies of Israel, whom you defied. This day the Lord will deliver you into my hand and I will strike you and take your head from you ...." I certainly didn't have any intentions of taking anyone's head, but I sure could feel God's favor ... calmness in knowing that He would come through, and I needed to trust him. There was a feeling that He would take us one step at a time down a path to freedom and, for whatever reason, He did not want to reveal it all lest we got ahead of ourselves. So I was poised to keep my eyes open along the way and lean not to my own understanding, if I was to see the hand of God.

We were first in line, Jordana, Harrison, Pierce and me. By now, all phones were charged, and Jordana Houser was getting repeated text messages from Mrs. Meyers in Switzerland, "Where are you? You have to come back to Bern so I can finish my work. This is urgent. Please contact me asap," (or words to that effect). I instructed Jordana to be kind and text her that we were in Paris at the U.S. Embassy, following their guidance and that we would be in touch later.

The first window we approached when our number was called was manned by a young man with a French accent. He reviewed the paperwork but said the boy's passport photos were insufficient and recommended we use the coin-fed photo booth to take new ones. That in itself was a challenge with both the boys ... especially Pierce. In fact, it was rather comical. I stood him on the stool, holding him in place while squatting down from view of the camera. In order to get him to look straight ahead, Jordana would say, "Okay, look at the screen, a rabbit is going to appear." He would look straight ahead and on every single shot just before the camera took the picture, he would look away towards his mother. His timing was impeccable for a kid who wanted to sabotage his two seconds of fame. We tried over and over until there were no more coins available to use. The two larger prints that we hoped would work were rejected at the window when we returned, but we convinced the Officer to attach them anyway and ask for approval. Reluctantly he did so.

It wasn't long, about 20 minutes before we were directed to another window where a Consular Officer named Nic presented herself. "Mrs. Houser we are aware of this situation, and I am afraid this will not be resolved in the next couple of hours. You have been flagged in the EU by the Swiss. They are sstating that they are trying to establish a court session for you and your ex-husband."

All we had were certified copies of all the birth certificates for the boys, certified copies of all the court documents, and it wasn't what they wanted. I mentioned that all the originals were at Main State in D.C. and suggested they contract Jennifer Harkins. Jordana responded carefully and accurately, "There is no court session scheduled, and my ex-husband has not shown up since we rescued my children. He has a warrant for his arrest in the United States, and he owes a lot of money to

Something Bigger Than Overthrowing Small Governments

a lot of people. I doubt seriously he intends to turn himself over to the authorities."

Nic was very polite, but very stern in her professionalism. "If I were you, I would go get some breakfast or lunch and wait until you hear from us. I cannot promise that a decision can be made now or Monday." I handed Nic one of my ARC business cards attached to the paperwork. We thanked her and departed.

We headed to a local hotel not far from the U.S. Embassy for Thad and Rudy to pick us and the boys up in the vehicle. Once we returned to our hotel, the boys and Jordana found time to rest. I, Thad and Rudy discussed the option of exfiltrating from Gibraltar to Morocco or driving to Moscow — anywhere the EU did not have oversight — and using the birth certificates if for any reason passports were not issued. We would take our chances on the other end when we arrived in our own country.

The day lingered, and then at 1545 hours we got a call from the U.S. Embassy, "We have been trying to get in touch with you. Can you come down before we close at 1600 hours and pick up the kids' passports? They are ready."

With delight, we all piled in the vehicle and fought Paris traffic for twenty minutes. When we arrived, I escorted Jordana and the boys back though security for what seemed like the 20th time that day. The place was practically vacant with the exception of one American woman standing at the window receiving her new passport and hearing Nic say, "This is your third passport. Please hold on to this one."

The woman replied, "The streets of Paris are dangerous. My other two were stolen right from under my nose in broad daylight." When the woman turned around, she and Jordana recognized one another. This was the Landlord from San Francisco that two years earlier had been trying to track down Chad because he owed her and her husband $65,000 dollars. I mean, think about this. How coincidental to have someone there from halfway around the world to verify the story we had told the U.S. Embassy about what a rotten egg Chad Houser was ... to verify all the legal documents we submitted regarding his crimes leading up to the kidnapping.

I took the woman and led her to the window where Nic was. "I just want you to hear this woman's story. This is too weird. Here she is in Paris and Chad Houser stole $65K from her and her husband. Now you see what a dirt bag we are dealing with and why we need to get these kids home to safety." The look on Nic's face was one that suggested she totally understood and was sympathetic to our cause. In my book, this was the hand of God.

Nic motioned us to another window. "When are you planning on leaving Paris?" She asked.

"Tomorrow morning," I replied.

"The passports are only good for five days. I suggest you do what you need to do within that period of time. You've been flagged by the Swiss. Chances are you are going to get stopped at Immigrations at the airport. If that happens, I cannot promise you that we can help, but here is my card," handing me a U.S. Embassy business card for American Citizen Services with her number. "There is someone here 24 hours a day and they can reach me. Just ask for Nic."

I looked her square in the eye, "So you're saying we will get stopped."

She did not even hesitate, "Yes, you are going to get stopped. Good luck. Let me just say, I hope I don't see you here again." And with that we thanked her and departed.

Back at the hotel the sun had not yet dropped from the sky. Thad, Rudy, Jordana and the boys went to a local restaurant while I finished up on an ops order, putting into place a number of alternate plans should we get stopped at the airport. I took a walk to clear my head and settled in about 200 yards from the hotel at a Greek Restaurant, sitting outside as is common with many French eateries. Across the street three prostitutes walked back and forth looking for attention. I pondered their lives in sadness and began praying for them. It was not long before all three made their way to the same restaurant and found their place in front of what appeared to be their 80-year-old pimp. It was as if Satan had sent his vultures to perch themselves around me, and I found it odd. I made no eye contact, and none was made with me. There was an unspoken understanding between spirits that I belonged to God and that they were the fog that rolls in off the shore at night making it difficult to see. But I could see fine, as if God

Something Bigger Than Overthrowing Small Governments

had allowed me to have spiritual night vision goggles. This war was not being fought by amateurs. We were seasoned warriors, and God was supplying us with everything we needed.

    I finished my meal and departed. Back at the hotel Thad and Rudy had returned. There was an understanding among us that should we get detained and released tomorrow that we would head to Morocco, provided immigration handed back the children's passports. I anticipated calling Nic to help with as much of this as possible on the day. 0400 hours that morning came early for all of us. We headed to Charles De Gaul International Airport. Thad would be departing at 0800 hours on Icelandic Air, while Jordana and the boys, Rudy and I would board XL Airlines at 1100 hours.

    I had never heard of XL Airlines. The name itself made me wonder if it meant Extra Large as in the extra leg room we all desire when flying for 14 hours. Much to my disappointment, that would not be the case, but for now we were just thankful to have an airline to fly out on ... since we had reserved seating just the day before. I had no idea how all of it was going to transpire when we left the ticket counter. I imagined it was no different for gladiators heading to the arena knowing their fate awaited them in the closed arena, and there was no turning back.

    The ticket agent swiped our passports, finished typing whatever essential information she needed to have on the tickets and then methodically hit the print button. Five tickets came out ... five blank tickets ... five pure white tickets. I stared at them, and so did she. And then I heard it. A voice in my head as clear as any voice I had heard that day ... "I shall make you invisible." It wasn't like I was thinking or hearing myself. It was like a voice in my ear that went to my brain.

    I turned and looked at Rudy, who was standing about five feet away behind me. He saw the blank tickets come out, but I don't think he understood what had just happened. This was another hand of God moment.

    "That's strange, I've never had that happen," she said. She called her supervisor, and he opened the box to the ticket dispenser and made some corrections and then closed the box. She hit the print button again and out came five printed tickets with all of our flight information. As we walked away, I stopped Rudy and told him about what I had heard. He looked at me, his eyes smiled. "Well let's go." From that point forward we moved with great confidence and anticipation but admittedly ... with curiosity as to what God was going to do.

There it was ... Immigrations. Pick your window, there were four to choose from, and each was manned with French Customs Officers. Rudy approached the window to the far left. Jordana, with the children, stepped up to the one next to it. And then I noticed in my being, it was as if the Holy Spirit had fallen upon the Customs Officers. The Officer did not even look up at Jordana, nor did he swipe her passport. Did you hear what I said? He did not even swipe her passport nor the boys'. He stamped all three, and did not say a word, just handed them back. Then I stepped up, and he did the same thing ... opened my passport and stamped it without swiping it. When he did look up at me, it was as if I were invisible, as if he were looking right through me. If this had been a Star Wars movie, it would have been Obi Wan Kenobi using the force against the Storm Troopers to allow him to pass.

Now anyone who would want to challenge divine intervention might say ... "Well maybe that is just their protocol, they don't swipe passports." Well if that's the case, then why was the other Officer swiping Rudy's passport over and over again, only for it to not process. She was so nervous that her hands were shaking. Something had come over her. After multiple failed attempts, she handed his passport back and told him he was free to go.

The line through security was long. We found our place behind a ton of people, but then security pulled us out and told us to take the kids and go through the shorter line with the flight crew. We did as we were told and skirted through in no time at all. Jordana Houser and the boys stayed alongside me as we made our way to a deli to await our flight that would depart in two hours. Rudy and I shared what we had just experienced at the Immigration counter with one another once we sat down. How could we not? We had both traveled the world and never experienced anything like this. There was an omnipotent presence, as if we were walking on holy ground. You could feel it in the air.

We hunkered down in a corner booth at the deli. It wasn't that we lacked trust in God, it was simply maintaining good OpSec

Something Bigger Than Overthrowing Small Governments

(Operational Security) all the way to the end, as we felt He required of us. The kids were crazy restless and interacting with them in a creative manner just to keep our profile low was more than I had anticipated. We weren't exactly successful at it in the beginning. Harrison had a demanding attitude, and when he did not get his way, he would throw a fit and start screaming and crying. Pierce, on the other hand, simply watched the spectacle with the quiet manner of a ninja. Overall, both of the boys were just being boys, and once we were able to outsmart them, things settled down.

Two hours later we loaded up on the shuttle bus to the tarmac where our XL Airplane awaited. At first glance, it looked like a repo, greatly in need of a fuselage cleaning and all the more suspect as we tromped up the aluminum staircase to the open hatch that took us inside a flying machine, noticeably older ... no individual television screens on the back of each seat, and a crew that looked as if they would prefer to be staffing Air France but just couldn't quite make the cut.

It wasn't until they passed out the baloney sandwiches as a snack that my suspicions were confirmed, and by then we were some 30,000 feet in the air on our way back to America. The only question now was, how long could this excuse of an airplane stay in the air? So I closed my eyes and went to sleep.

But that didn't last long. I felt the presence of something or someone mind probing me. I opened my eyes, and Harrison was standing there in the aisle staring at me with a big smile. Obviously, he was rip roaring ready for phase two of what kids do when their mother gives them too many sugar cookies ... and that is exactly what had happened. I wasn't about to engage, because it would be a battle I would not win. I smiled at him and closed my eyes, hoping he would go back to his seat. Seconds later I carefully peeped out the corner of my left eye and there he was, smiling and staring at me again. He was trying to figure out what to do with his finger, extended and slowing moving in my direction. I had seen this finger before with other kids ... a symbol for the brotherhood of the bugger eaters, and I wondered if there was anything green and slimy on the end of it that was about to touch my arm. I knew he wanted to do something with it, but just couldn't figure out how the sleeping giant would react ... so he just stood there with it in the ready position. I could see this was going to be a Mexican stand-off. In my head I was laughing. I kept my eyes closed just enough to look like I was asleep but could still see him. A little while and then he went back to his seat. It was a cute moment, and I cannot put aside the fact that when a kid feels safe with you, they just want to be all over you ... and sometimes what is on their finger does as well.

Some 15 hours later we were landing in Los Angeles. I got up to use the toilet and noticed both boys and Jordana Houser slumped over one another fast asleep. To their left Rudy Gonzalez was watching a movie. He and Thad Turner had performed flawlessly on this operation, and I could not have been blessed with two better operators. There was absolutely no doubt in my mind that should anything have happened to me, they would carry on the mission and get Jordana Houser and the boys back to America. Both displayed the patience of a sniper and the wisdom only found in seasoned warriors with humble spirits and dirt under their fingernails. These were more than talented men ... they were mission-essential tools for success, all packaged up in human form with a dedication to duty unlike no other. Neither was in question ... I had served with Thad down range on some of the most classified operations the CIA and Navy SEALs could put together ... dangerous in nature and still, to this day, monumental events in history that kept the Soviet Union at bay. Rudy was a former Recon Marine. And although we had not served together in the past, he was a Marine ... and I was a Marine. He and his organization had an outstanding record for rescuing trafficked victims off the streets with precision — a quality all of us at ARC appreciate.

There had been a lot of miles covered in such a short period of time for everyone to accomplish this mission; the rest ahead would be well deserved for all of us. The landing was uneventful until we cleared Customs and were greeted by members of our family and friends. My fiancée at the time, Renee, had bought gifts for the boys, and Rudy's wife and daughters added the emotional support He was so looking forward to after a trip like this. Thad would get the same from his son and daughter and mother and father when he arrived in Philadelphia that day. Having Renee there was that very special part of the operation that brought into focus the need for a warm and loving reception for the

Something Bigger Than Overthrowing Small Governments

mothers and fathers of abducted children ... outside of an operations team that had been glued to their side day and night. It made it special, a big deal, a wonderful reunion with America ... simply to have an American like Renee make it a big deal right there in the airport. And for me ... it was a nice surprise because I had no idea she was even going to be there.

Everyone was cleared to depart and went their separate ways. Renee and I headed straight to Rolling Hills Covenant Church to make the 1700 hours service. We were about 15 minutes late but just in time to see Pastor Byron McDonald take the stage and open his Bible to begin the sermon. And this is what he started with: "So how does God make us invisible?" I looked at Renee, she looked at me, and something stirred inside my soul. My eyes began to water as my emotions welled up inside, grateful that God showed ARC, once again, His great favor.

Recommendations: There are no recommendations at this time.

Chapter 18
MARRIED TO AL QAEDA

This chapter is the true-life account of an American woman fighting to free herself and her son from his father, a Pakistani, who became an Al Qaeda terrorist. This is the story of a woman's coming of age, her budding heroism in the face of the most dangerous gang on earth, and ARC's involvement in the rescue of her son.

The enormous expense associated with running a recovery operation inside Pakistan, where known terrorists and their actions flourished with impunity, required ARC to find a solution to raising funds far beyond what currently existed in the bank account. We believed, and still do believe, that by persuading Marybeth Rael to write an autobiographical account (manuscript) of her years spent as Yasmeen Aziz, a convert to Islam and the wife of Imran Aziz, who became an Al Qaeda jihadist, and sell this as a book or movie was our most effective strategy. Should a feature film be made from this manuscript, it could bring global attention to the heinous crimes committed by Imran Aziz. It could allow ARC to politically leverage the outcome, while at the same time putting into place all assets needed from an extralegal perspective to perform an extraction of an American child being held hostage with the intent, by his captors, to eventually radicalize him as an enemy against the United States of America.

For ARC, it was a first of its kind where operations felt driven by a larger ticking clock with no mechanism for turning the hand of time backwards. We weren't dealing with just the average non-custodial parental abduction, we were dealing with members of a terrorist organization that were very well capable of outnumbering us and making our lives extremely miserable should we miss one beat in our approach. Our reality surfaced on the faces of every ARC operator that was read into the project, and we all knew this operation was taking us back to a time when our tradecraft would be the most important tool in the shed if we were to survive in Pakistan. This was a heterogeneous

Something Bigger Than Overthrowing Small Governments

culture that had the imprint of invading armies and of the migrations of people passing through on their way to and from Indus.

I personally had worked in Pakistan in earlier years when the Russians invaded Afghanistan, and it was without a doubt one of the most interesting periods of my CIA career. Two events particularly, one of which I can speak openly and the other not, would change the course of history and impact the way I would come to view the Pakistani bureaucracy ... vile and offensive, with a twinge of unearned British arrogance. It wasn't that I wanted to view them this way, it was simply the result of dealing with Pakistani Government officials during my time as one of two U.S. negotiators for the hijacking of Pan Am Flight 73. It is because of their arrogance that they were unable to heed good advice and fair warning that could have prevented the loss of lives on that flight ... that first event:

THE HIJACKING OF PAN AM FLIGHT 73

The incident began in September 1986 as passengers boarded the Frankfurt-bound aircraft in Karachi. A subsequent CIA investigation revealed that the hijack occurred despite the presence of armed agents near the aircraft. The four hijackers were dressed as Karachi airport security guards and were armed with assault rifles, pistols, grenades, and plastic explosive belts. At about 6:00 a.m. local time, the hijackers drove a van that had been modified to look like an airport security vehicle through a security checkpoint up to one of the boarding stairways to Pan Am Flight 73.

The hijackers stormed up the staircase into the plane, fired shots from an automatic weapon, and seized control of the aircraft. Neerja Bhanot was able to alert the cockpit crew using intercom, allowing the pilot, co-pilot, and flight engineer to flee through an overhead hatch in the cockpit. This was to prevent the hijackers forcing the plane to take off. The plane was effectively grounded at the airport. [29]

Bazzel Baz

A CIA officer, who for the sake of his cover we will call "the Russian," and I were sitting at the safe house in Islamabad when we got the call from Milt Bearden, Chief of Station. "Get to Karachi. An American jetliner with passengers sitting on the tarmac has been taken hostage by an unknown terrorist group. I need eyes and ears on the ground now." It took about an hour from our location to get to Karachi and meet up with Filipe Jones, the Deputy COS (Chief of Station), who worked for Milt.

Within a short time after seizing control of the aircraft, hijacker Zayd Hassan Abd Al-Latif Masud Al Safarini realized that the flight crew had escaped off the plane and therefore he would be forced to negotiate with officials — the only two negotiators on the ground, the only two authorized by Pakistani Airport authorities … the Russian and me.

Something Bigger Than Overthrowing Small Governments

> First and business class passengers were ordered to go towards the back of the plane. At the same time, passengers at the back of the plane were ordered forward. At approximately 10:00 am Safarini negotiated with officials, in particular Viraf Daroga, the head of Pan Am Pakistan operations that if the crew wasn't sent on the plane within 15 minutes then Kumar would be shot. The timing for one American on board could not have been worse. Rajesh Kumar Patel, 28, a naturalized American citizen and a prosperous motel owner from Huntington Beach, California, mistaking the hijackers for Pakistanis, rose up from his seat and shouted: "I am an American citizen."
>
> Whether Safarini became impatient with Viraf Daroga or was reacting to Patel's outburst is difficult to say. He grabbed Patel and shot him in the head in front of witnesses both on and off the aircraft. Safarini then heaved Patel out of the door onto the tarmac below. Pakistani personnel on the tarmac reported that Patel was still breathing when he was placed in an ambulance, but he was pronounced dead on the way to the hospital in Karachi. [29]

It was a wakeup call to we who were knee-deep in the game. Distraught, Viraf Daroga confided in us that he was not schooled in this type of emergency nor were his language skills sharp enough to continue conversations with the terrorists ... he was in way over his head.

The Russian and I found the Saudi Airline representative, whose name I cannot recall, and recruited him as the voice for our intervention, since he spoke the native tongue. Unbeknownst to the terrorists, we carefully coached his dialogue with Safarini. The only communications we had prior to that time were by way of Viraf Doroga using a megaphone to begin negotiations with the hijackers on the tarmac, and that was what the Saudi Airline representative would use until we were able to establish phone communications with the aircraft. Per our guidance he told the four terrorists that the airport authorities were looking for pilots to fly them where they needed to go. He was scared and brave at the same time, and he expressed his relief that we were there to help him.

Milt Bearden called on a secure line and informed us that Delta Force had been put on alert and was flying in from Germany, and that we needed to take an active role in securing enough time for them to get to Karachi and do what they do best ... save lives. The 1st Special Forces Operational Detachment-Delta (1st SFOD-D), popularly known as Delta Force, is a U.S. Army unit used for hostage rescue and counterterrorism, as well as direct action and reconnaissance against high-value targets. The CIA's highly secretive Special Activities Division (SAD) and, more specifically, its elite Special Operations Group (SOG), which the Russian and I were part of, had often worked and recruited operators from Delta Force. So we were confident that if we could get them on the ground, Safarini would meet his worst nightmare.

It was an interesting setup ... the Russian and I discussing options, me coaching the Saudi Airline representative each time before and after he spoke with the terrorists on the tarmac, the Russian running back and forth upstairs to meet with Pakistani government officials who had finally arrived on site ... doing his best to convince them to follow our lead whenever the terrorists had demands. For some odd reason, the officials started demanding final approval on every bit of strategy we intended to employ in a time when waiting for them to have tea and discuss it among themselves wasn't practical. It was a known fact that a large percentage of passengers were either Indian or U.S. citizens of Indian descent. It was not long before we realized that the political discourse between the countries of India and Pakistan would unfavorably play out in the lives of these innocent passengers on Pan Am Flight 73.

After listening to the Russian and seeing his frustration over their incompetence for the umpteenth time, I strongly believe that the Pakistani government officials actually hoped for the death of those on board, or at least those of Indian decent on board. If not that, then they were just so inept at decision making that the depth of the situation was too much for them to digest. Either way, the Russian continued to push because he, like me, wanted to save lives.

Something Bigger Than Overthrowing Small Governments

Much to our delight and against all odds with the Pakistani government officials, we were finally able to begin negotiations with the terrorists and have them at multiple times either delay actions or continue discussions in a manner that was building the right kind of relationship with hope in sight. At first, the hijackers set a 1900 hours deadline and demanded a relief crew to fly them to Larnaca, Cyprus. They also demanded the release of three of their comrades imprisoned in Cyprus.

We had convinced Safarini that it would take a number of hours for us to get another crew to fly the Pan Am Flight 73, because it took a special type of pilot to fly that type of aircraft. He bit on it, hook line and sinker. But it was short-lived, when Pakistani government officials behind our back ordered the Saudi Airline representative to tell the Safarini that a crew would not be coming at all. Safarini was furious and threatened to start killing hostages.

The Russian and I knew that if we did not react immediately, he would hold to his word. We instructed the Saudi Airline representative to tell Safarini that he had misspoken regarding the flight crew and that, in fact, a crew had been located and would be arriving from Europe. The Saudi Airline representative was torn between our instructions and the belligerent demands of the Pakistani government officials whispering in his ear. He chose to listen to us, and we were able to have the deadline extended to 2300 hours.

We contacted Milt Bearden, COS (Chief of Station) and requested that he notify U.S. Ambassador Raphel to see if he could get the Pakistani government officials to stand down and let us do our job. Since this was a U.S. airliner, I would have thought the U.S. Government would have been able to influence the situation in our favor, but we were left in the dark as to what would come. Finally, Milt called back and said that U.S. Ambassador Raphel had his hands tied but would continue to do what he could to help, possibly from a different angle. Who knows what discussions were happening at the U.S. State Department during all of this. All we know is that we were the only two Americans on the ground at the airport dodging incompetency and politics.

Safarini then joined the hijackers and ordered the flight attendants to collect the passports of all passengers. The flight attendants complied with this request, risking their own lives. During the collection of the passports, one stewardess, Neerja Bhanot, the senior attendant, believed passengers with American passports would be singled out by the hijackers. She proceeded to hide some of the American passports under a seat and dumped the rest down a rubbish chute. [30]

Several news articles, including Wikipedia, follow the course of events and our actions as negotiators. Here's how the situation unfolded.

After the passports had been collected, one of the crew members came onto the intercom and asked for Michael John Thexton, a British citizen, to come to the front of the plane. He then went through the curtain into the front of the plane where he came face to face with Safarini, who was holding Thexton's passport. He then asked Thexton if he was a soldier and if he had a gun. Thexton replied "No." He then ordered Thexton onto his knees. Safarini then told us that if anyone came near the plane, he would kill another passenger.

Now we needed to stay away from the airline and at the same time needed to find another method of communications instead of the megaphone. We directed the Saudi Airline representative to tell Safarini that there was a crew member on board who was able to use the cockpit radio and asked him to negotiate through the radio. Meherjee Kharas, a 28-year-old Pan Am mechanic on board, was forced to make radio contact with the Saudi Airline representative while the Russian and I quietly directed from the background.

At this stage, the hijackers still believed a pilot would be found to fly the plane for them. Safarini then went back to Thexton and asked him whether he would like a drink of water, to which Thexton replied, "Yes." Safarini also asked Thexton if he was married. Safarini claimed he did not like all this violence and killing and said that the Americans and Israelis had taken over his country and left him unable to lead a proper life. Then one of the hijackers ordered Thexton back through the

Something Bigger Than Overthrowing Small Governments

plane to a seat. We were back in action with relatively decent dialogue with Safarini, at least enough that the hijack stalemate continued on into the night.

    During the stalemate, flight attendant Neerja Bhanot secretly removed a page from her manual that explained all the procedures for the 3R aircraft door and placed it inside of a magazine and then handed it to the passenger near the door. She instructed him to "read" the magazine and then close it up, but to refer to it later if necessary. This page included information on how to open the exit door and deploy the slide down to the apron. [29]

    The almost ten-hour ordeal by this time was taking its toll on Safarini; I could hear it in his voice over the radio. He was exhausted and worried. Ironically, at one stage he actually started asking the Saudi Airline representative for advice on what he should do next. Surprised, the Saudi Airline representative looked across the table at me as if to say, "Is he serious?" It was a golden opportunity in the negotiation process that the Russian and I intended to take full advantage of. Via the Saudi Airline representative, we suggested he consider allowing women and children to leave the airplane. He said he would think about it. We asked if he had enough food and water on board to be comfortable. He seemed to appreciate the concern. We were buying more time than we had expected simply by engaging him in conversation. But that too would be short lived.

    Eventually the militants threatened that if a pilot did not materialize a passenger would be shot every 15 minutes. But once again we were able to negotiate him out of that action. Safarini demanded that the external lights on the tarmac remain on so he would be able to see anyone approaching the aircraft. He threatened to kill passengers if this demand was not met, and so we agreed to his demand, saving lives and buying more time for Delta Force to arrive. The lighting situation would not be that disruptive tactically because we knew that Delta Force would most likely approach from the blind side at the rear of the aircraft and be able to get in place to storm the aircraft before the terrorists could do much about it.

I realized that the APU (Auxiliary Power Unit) attached to the airliner had been running since 0600 hours that morning. Common sense told me that if it wasn't refueled immediately it would power down, and we would be left with 15 minutes of aircraft emergency power before plunging it into darkness. No doubt Safarini would panic, thinking he was under attack and start killing hostages. I tried to get lower level management to attend to the problem, but no one budged. When I mentioned it to the Russian, he bolted upstairs and spent the next thirty minutes arguing with the Pakistani government officials.

The Russian returned with disappointing eyes, "Idiots, idiots ... they aren't going to refuel it. This is insane."

I looked at the Russian, "Something isn't right here, something really bad is going to happen, and we need to wash our hands of it right now. Call Milt and let him know. Ask him to let Ambassador Raphel know. They haven't taken any of our advice all day long, and the advances we have made have been out of our own pocket. They are serving their own hidden agenda here."

The Russian decided to run upstairs and engage the Pakistani officials one last time. When he returned I thought he was going to explode. The veins in his neck were protruding like a clamped-off water hose. "They just refused Delta Force landing rights." I could not believe what I was hearing. We had worked so hard and were so close to getting the cavalry to save the day, and now the door was shut? The writing was on the wall, and we called the COS immediately. At 2015 hours (8:15 p.m.) the COS told us to get out of the bursting radius ... he was letting Ambassador Raphel know immediately.

About 9:00p.m. (2100 hours) the auxiliary power unit shut down, all lighting turned off, and emergency lights came on. Passengers at the front were ordered toward the back, while passengers at the back were ordered forward.

Something Bigger Than Overthrowing Small Governments

Since the aisles were already full of passengers, those passengers standing just sat down.

The 17-hour long hijacking came to an end when the hijackers opened fire on the passengers at 9:30 p.m. (2130 hours) Pakistan Standard Time. With the plane out of power and sitting in near darkness a hijacker at the 1L door said a prayer and then aimed to shoot at the explosive belt the other hijacker at the 1R door was wearing. The intent was to cause an explosion massive enough to kill all passengers and crew on board, as well as themselves. Since the cabin was so dark, the hijacker missed, causing only a small detonation. Immediately the hijackers began shooting their weapons into the cabin at passengers and attempted to throw their grenades. Yet again the lack of light caused them to not pull pins fully and create small explosions.

Ultimately, bullets created most damage since each bullet would bounce off the aircraft and create crippling shrapnel. The flight attendant at the 3L door decided it was time to take action and opened the door; although the slide did not deploy, several passengers and crew jumped down the fifteen feet (or 6m/20 ft.) to the tarmac. The passenger that was near 3R had read the page the flight attendant earlier gave him and was able to successfully open that door. It was the only door opened to have the slide deploy. Ultimately this slide allowed for more passengers to evacuate safely and without injuries. Neerja Bhanot assisted a number of passengers to escape from the flight, and then she laid down her life shielding three children from the bullets fired by the terrorists. They soon ran out of ammunition, resulting in more passengers fleeing the aircraft through the aircraft's emergency exits. Twenty passengers were killed and over a hundred were injured. [29]

Pakistan quickly sent in the Pakistan Army's Special Services Group (SSG) commandos, who had been standing by off the edge of the tarmac in some discombobulated fashion, as I recall from my reconnaissance earlier that evening. According to the newspaper reports, the SSG responded by storming the aircraft and capturing the hijackers, but that was not true. Contrary to Pakistan claims, the SSG

410

was nowhere near the scene of action till long after the drama ended in a hailstorm of bullets.

If I recall correctly, all of the hijackers escaped with the passengers and were later picked up on the tarmac or streets of Karachi not far from the airport. One was captured running along the fence surrounding the tarmac looking for a hole to escape through, another running in the crowd of fleeing passengers — those passengers pointing him out — and the third almost successfully escaping in the airport terminal itself. Safarini was still on board when Pakistan's security forces entered the plane. Ironically, he had been accidently shot by his own men during the excitement.

The 380 total passengers plus crew on Pan Am 73 were citizens of 14 different countries. Citizens of India represented roughly 25% of the people on board the flight, and 65% of those killed. I am convinced that the bloody denouement was exacerbated by a series of unforgivable blunders on the part of airport authorities managing the crisis at Karachi airport. They later actually tried to blame us for their mistakes, which did not hold water, given the fact that we had carefully documented five ways to heaven and back, every conversation and every sequence of events, not only among ourselves, but to the COS as it unfolded.

Nor did it hold water in the eyes of the rest of the world when the India Times reported, "Now that the cloud of confusion surrounding the hijack has cleared sufficiently, the actual sequence of events pieced together from passengers and crew members leaves no doubt that senior Pakistani officials blundered fatally in their handling of the crisis." [31]

On July 6, 1988, five Palestinian men were convicted in Pakistan for their roles in the hijacking and murders and sentenced to death: Zayd Hassan Abd al-Latif Safarini, Wadoud Muhammad Hafiz al-Turki, Jamal Saeed Abdul Rahim, Muhammad Abdullah Khalil Hussain ar-Rahayyal, and Muhammad Ahmed al-Munawar. The sentences were later commuted to life in prison.

Safarini was handed over to the FBI from a prison in Pakistan in September 2001. He was taken to the United States where on May 13, 2005 he was sentenced to a 160-year prison term. At the plea proceeding, Safarini admitted that he and his fellow hijackers committed the offenses as members of the Abu Nidal Organization, also called the ANO, a designated terrorist organization. The other four prisoners had escaped from Adiala jail Rawalpindi, reportedly in January 2008. Go figure. Libya has been accused of sponsoring the hijacking, as well as carrying out the bombings of Pan Am Flight 103 in 1988 and UTA Flight 772 in 1989.

In August 2003, Libya accepted responsibility for "the actions of its officials" in respect to the bombing of Pan Am Flight 103 but was silent on the question of the Pan Am Flight 73 hijacking. Libya offered $2.7 billion USD in compensation to the families of the 270 victims of Pan Am Flight 103 and, in January 2004, agreed to pay $170 million to the families of the 170 UTA victims. The seven American UTA victims' families refused the offer and instead filed a claim for $2.2 billion against Libya. From 2004 to 2006 the U.S. and UK opened up relations with Libya, including removing sanctions and removing the country as a sponsor of terrorism.

In June 2004, a volunteer group of families and victims from the incident, *Families from Pan Am Flight 73*, was formed to work toward a memorial for those killed in the incident, to seek the truth behind this terrorist attack, and to hold those responsible for it accountable. On April 5, 2006, the law firm of Crowell & Moring LLP, representing the surviving passengers, estates and family members of the hijacking victims, announced it was filing a civil suit in U.S. District Court for the District of Columbia seeking ten billion dollars in compensatory damages, plus unspecified punitive damages, from Libya, Muammar al-Gaddafi and the five convicted hijackers. The lawsuit alleged Libya provided the Abu Nidal Organization with material support and also ordered the attack as part of a Libyan-sponsored terrorist campaign against American, European and Israeli interests.

British media that was critical of normalization of relations between Gaddafi and the West reported in March 2004 (days after Prime Minister Tony Blair visited Tripoli) that Libya was behind the hijacking.

As of September 2015, and to the best of my knowledge, about $700 million of funds that Libya gave the USA to settle claims related to Libyan sponsored terrorism has not been distributed to families of victims who were Indian passport holders.

On December 3, 2009, the FBI, in coordination with the State Department, announced a $5M reward for information that leads to the capture of each of the four remaining hijackers of Pan Am 73, who were reported to have escaped from prison in Pakistan in 2008. One of the four, Jamal Saeed Abdul Rahim, was reported killed in a drone strike on January 9, 2010, in Pakistan. His death was never confirmed, and he remains on the FBI's Most Wanted Terrorists and Rewards for Justice Lists.

During his November 9, 2015 parole hearing at the federal prison in Terre Haute, IN, Zaid Safarini claimed to have been in touch with Jamal Rahim and the other hijackers recently- thereby confirming that the above news report of Rahim's death was false. [29]

During that same year the Russian and I would be relentless in persuading a disenchanted U.S. Congress to apply new technologies ... the deployment of anti-aircraft systems under life threatening conditions to support a U.S. Government 20-billion-dollar covert initiative, which resulted in defeat of one of the most powerful communist military forces on the planet ... the Soviet Union. As members of the CIA's Special Activities Division, we were directly involved in President Reagan's Covert Action program that is given credit for assisting in ending the Soviet occupation of Afghanistan. This great victory belonged to the Americans and not the Pakistani government, and there was no way we would tarnish the honor of those very few good Pakistani military friends and Mujahideen warriors that understood bureaucracy has no place on the battlefield ... and in remembrance ... no place on the tarmac.

MARYBETH'S FIGHT FOR HER SON

So by now I am certain you can see that I have a very good understanding of life inside Pakistan and, with that, a very good

Something Bigger Than Overthrowing Small Governments

understanding of the difficulties Marybeth Rael would encounter regarding the kidnapping of her son. A good friend of mine, Bob Eisele, was instrumental in putting the following synopsis together that tells her story:

Marybeth Rael first met Imran Aziz when they were both students at Arizona State University. Imran, a citizen of Pakistan, was a handsome, young intellectual, an agnostic with a quick wit and a curiosity about the world. There was an attraction between them, but for reasons unknown, the two drifted apart.

Imran returned to Pakistan where he married Rukshana, a physician. Their ten-year marriage brought them two children: Dime, a boy, and Saleha, a girl. Imran also has a twin brother, Kamran, and an older brother, Dr. Amer Aziz. It's the notorious Amer Aziz, doctor to Osama Bin Laden before his death, who convinced Imran to return to his Islamic faith and join forces with Al Qaeda.

Imran also has a sister, Lena, who's a doctor like Amer. Though the women of the Aziz family are accomplished individuals, they've been subjugated under Sharia Law to customs such as "purdah," the virtual confinement of women to their homes.

But one woman in the Aziz family wields real power — Ami Gee, the obese matriarch and Muslim fanatic whose influence pushed her sons toward Al Qaeda. Abu Gee, her senile husband, was once a Lieutenant Colonel in the Pakistani Army, as well as a domineering husband. That's why Ami Gee took such pleasure in belittling and tormenting him as he grew old and weak ... payback.

When Marybeth converted to Islam and became "Yasmeen," she married Imran and Ami Gee eventually became *her* tormentor as well. So what attracted Marybeth to Imran and his family in the first place?

The reasons are a mystery to us at this phase in Marybeth's life. But common sense dictates that she was searching for some kind of stability and structure in her life; searching for a faith and a family that would protect her and lead her toward salvation and inner peace. What she found instead was a psychologically disordered clan that led her into a living hell.

Marybeth/Yasmeen was in Pakistan on 9-11-2001. Imran's niece, Saadia (Lena's daughter) was 14 years-old at the time, and she told Marybeth *it was angels who knocked the Twin Towers down.* The girl's deluded, fanatical attitude was an ominous foreshadowing of things to come.

Marybeth, sensing a gathering storm, left Pakistan for the U.S. just eleven days after 9-11. She was not abandoning Imran, who had not yet begun fighting for Al Qaeda. (His first trip to Afghanistan was December of 2001.) Marybeth just needed a visit home to her family after the horrendous events of 9-11.

Once in the U.S., she discovered she was pregnant with Imran's baby — a son, who would be named Abdola. When the FBI paid Marybeth a visit, she realized — for the first time — that the Aziz family was not what it appeared to be. The FBI interviewed her about Amer and even Imran. Marybeth knew Amer was headed to Afghanistan to fight for Al Qaeda and the Taliban, but she withheld this information from the FBI. She was still loyal to the Aziz family and believed that Amer, a doctor, would be ministering to wounded Taliban, not shooting Americans.

While still in the U.S., Marybeth got a call from Imran, who warned her not to fly back to Pakistan over the Atlantic. A few weeks later, Robert Reid, the would-be shoe bomber, was caught trying to detonate explosives aboard an international flight.

Imran wouldn't admit to Marybeth that he knew about the plot beforehand, but her first suspicions were raised. Since she was pregnant with Imran's child at the time, and still in love with him, she returned to Pakistan — the biggest mistake of her life.

The Aziz family's connections to Al Qaeda soon became a who's who of Islamic terrorists. For example, Imran revealed to Marybeth that he knew the American Taliban, Johnny Walker Lindh. When Daniel Pearl was abducted by Omar Saed Shiek, Imran was delighted. He told Marybeth that Pearl was a CIA agent, but she insisted he was just a journalist ... and that caused a huge fight between them. The rift between them began to widen.

Imran's dedication to Al Qaeda continued to deepen and, with it, his need for a relationship with his wife that reflected Sharia values. Imran wanted Marybeth, an American woman despite her Islamic faith, to obey his every demand. She stood her ground as best she could, but Imran's entire family and the culture itself were stacked against her.

Something Bigger Than Overthrowing Small Governments

Emotionally, Marybeth became increasingly isolated and, at times, she even felt her life was in danger. But she didn't fall apart. She began to grow stronger, determined to protect herself and, ultimately, her child from the fanaticism that surrounded her ... a fanaticism that forced her on a journey to Osama Bin Laden's house.

Amer had become Bin Laden's friend, confidante and physician ... but Imran was now his money runner. And one day, he forced Marybeth to accompany him on a run to Bin Laden's house. She wasn't allowed inside and had to wait in the car as Bin Laden's bodyguards patrolled the street. Finally, one of them stepped up to Imran's car, shoved a gun in Marybeth's face and threatened to kill her. She escaped with her life, but the message was clear: If you ever turn against us, you're dead.

After Marybeth's baby was born, her desire to escape Pakistan and Al Qaeda intensified. Only now it was nearly impossible. And she still loved Imran enough to believe she might be able to change his mind. Marybeth still hoped to free him from Al Qaeda. But it soon became clear to her that she'd get no help from the authorities in Pakistan. When ISI, the Pakistani CIA, visited Amer to "interrogate" him, it was obvious they were sympathetic to his cause.

After the interview, Amer told Marybeth that if she was ever questioned by ISI or the Americans, she must lie for him. But she refused to do so ... and that incensed Amer and his mother even more. The two began to hate Marybeth, now. They no longer saw her as a Muslim. She was only an American to them ... a sell-out.

When the Pakistani police took Amer in for interrogation by U.S. authorities, the entire Aziz clan turned against Marybeth. It didn't matter that she had nothing to do with it. She was the enemy now. But through her oppression, she began to see the light about Islam. As Marybeth grew in character and courage, she began to lose her belief in a religion that speaks of death to infidels.

When Asia Bibi, a Christian Pakistani woman, was condemned to die for "blasphemy," Marybeth's growing strength was affirmed. If this woman could resist — even under the threat of death — so could she. As Marybeth's sense of self deepened, she stood up to Imran and their relationship began to crumble. His anger at her crescendoed on a trip ... where he planned to kill her.

But Imran couldn't bring himself to murder his wife. So instead, he gave her one last chance to prove herself. He asked her to fly to the U.S. and bring some detonators back to Pakistan. But Marybeth refused to join forces with him and started to plan her escape with her son, Abdola.

Her only hope for an ally in the family was Imran's twin, Kamran. He practiced Sufism, a more mystical and less radical form of Islam. But Marybeth soon learned that even Kamran wouldn't take her side against the family. Not because he loved them, but because he feared them.

Finally, Imran asked Marybeth to renounce her U.S. Citizenship to demonstrate her loyalty to Islam and the family. She refused to do so. Soon after, their four-year-old son, Abdola, was taken away from her. Marybeth was only allowed to see him a few hours a week. She suffered terribly from their separation, plagued by insomnia and depression. She couldn't leave now. Not without her son. But then, Imran forced Marybeth to accompany him on a trip to Afghanistan ... where he tried to sell her to the Taliban. But when the buyer didn't show up, Imran brought her back to Pakistan ... then forced her to leave the country.

Devastated, Marybeth went straight to the FBI. They promised to help her get her son back, but they did nothing. Finally, she secured an international warrant against Imran for child abduction ... but no one in Pakistan would enforce it.

Deeply frustrated, Marybeth ignored the threats against her life and returned to Pakistan. Abdola was six years-old now, and she was desperate to see him. Soon after her arrival, she was attacked and badly beaten ... yet she battled bravely in the corrupt Pakistani courts to get her son back. Though her ex-husband, Imran, was the abductor, it was Marybeth who lived under the constant threat of arrest and prison. And prison for a foreign woman in Pakistan was often a life sentence.

But Marybeth fought on. She got an article published in a major Pakistani newspaper, THE DAWN, to win sympathy for her cause. The reporter, fearing for his life, wrote the article anonymously. A few brave female activists stepped forward to help Marybeth's cause. She lived with Asma, a courageous divorcee, who looked out for her. Marybeth endured two-hour bus rides to attend the multiple trials at the

Something Bigger Than Overthrowing Small Governments

High Court in Lahore. And finally, she won the right to visit her child. Abdola had been told terrible things about his mother. But in a heartrending scene, he finally found his way to her embrace.

Every piece of intel needed for a perfect extraction was acquired, vetted and set in motion. Marybeth supplied us with hand sketches of the AO in addition to our resources on the ground.

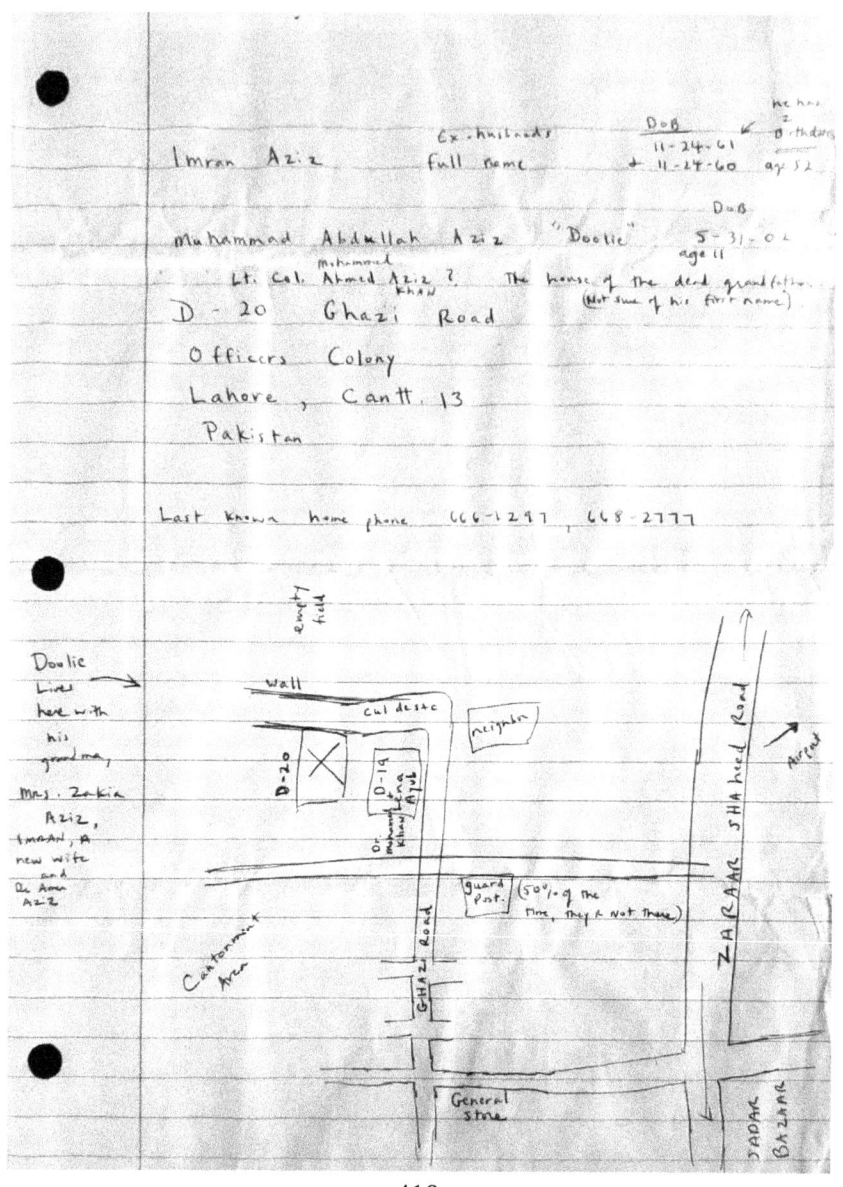

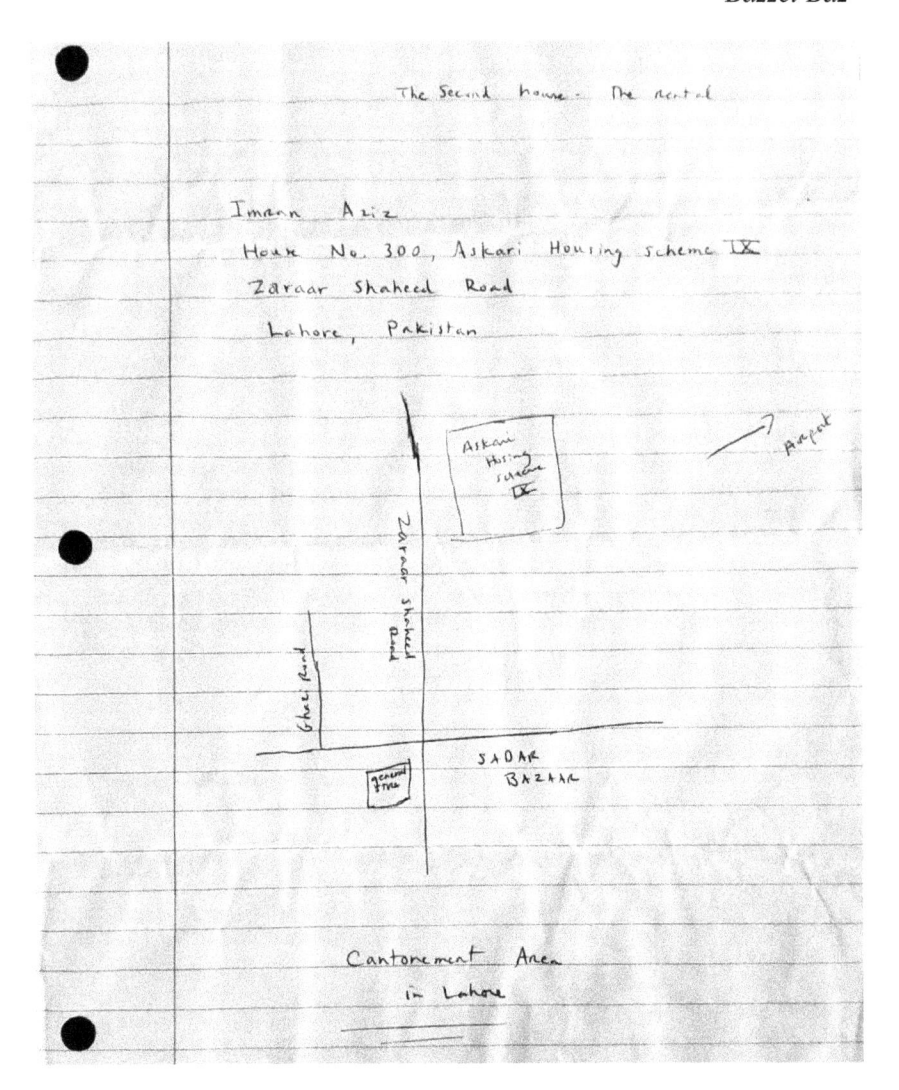

> The Second house - The rental
>
> Imran Aziz
> House No. 300, Askari Housing scheme IX
> Zaraar Shaheed Road
> Lahore, Pakistan
>
> [sketch map showing Askari Housing scheme IX, Zaraar Shaheed Road, Ghazi Road, Sadar Bazaar, general area, arrow to Airport]
>
> Cantonement Area in Lahore

Today, Marybeth Rael still hasn't won her case in Pakistan. The courts are not only corrupt; they're frightened of Imran and his Al Qaeda ties, but ARC is not. But Marybeth still persists — just like Malala, the brave Pakistani teenager who stood up to the Taliban. Her case rested in the arms of ARC until Marybeth disappeared.

Something Bigger Than Overthrowing Small Governments

Chapter 19
OPERATION DAGGER
AFTER ACTION REPORT

Subject: Nikki (alias)

Date: Oct 2018

Introduction:

For the purposes of this report the SFRT consisted of Bazzel Baz, Thad Turner, Tina Paulson, and former FBI Agent Dell Spry.

Background:

In an effort to protect the integrity of the ongoing federal investigation into the events disclosed in this after-action report, many names and places have been changed. The action of this report involves the rescue of a 21-year-old female who was sold into sex and labor slavery at the age of seven by her parents here in the United States. The following information was derived from our interviews with the victim, who will be known by her alias as Nikki.

Operation Overview:

Nikki was born July 9, 1997 in a major city in a state within the United States of America. She was the youngest of six siblings and half-siblings. She said her early childhood was just okay, but her parents fought a lot, did not love each other and would spend most of their time cursing and screaming at one another. It was not uncommon for her to overhear her mother shouting at her father, "I have no love for you, I hate you and you're a terrible person." Her father was the disciplinarian in the family, who made a point to swat Nikki with a leather belt as a form of punishment. While there is no evidence that he violated her sexually, he did make her disrobe down to her panties during these times of punishment. On one occasion he caught Nikki stuffing tissue paper in her underwear, so the spanking would not hurt as bad. After that he forbade her to ever wear underwear during the punishment.

It was around age seven when Nikki's mother developed a severe case of skin cancer. The medical bills were mounting, and debt collectors were calling. Nikki's father had a long-time business partner named Mr. Smith, who offered to assist with the medical bills by arranging for Nikki to be sold to a child sex trafficker he knew.

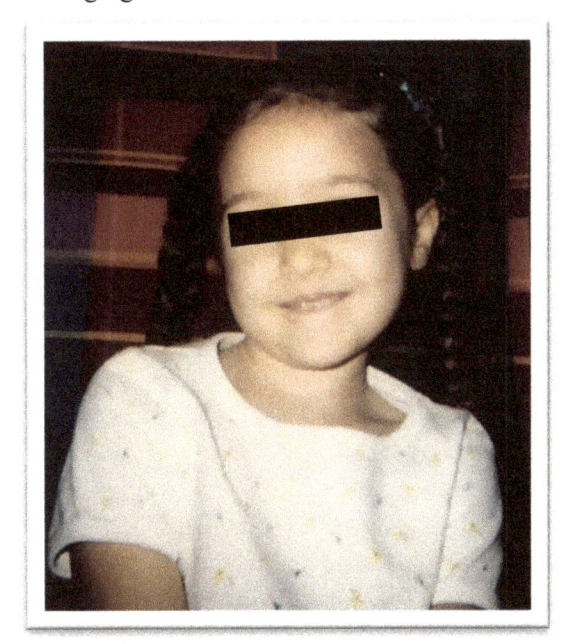

Nikki was later that week taken to a business party by her father to the house of Mr. Smith. Mr. Smith's daughter, Julie, was there as well and the two of them played together. Her father and Mr. Smith asked Nikki if she would like to have a sleepover with Julie. Nikki said yes. Her father left her at the house and within about thirty minutes or so Julie's mother, who was divorced from Mr. Smith showed up and took Julie home with her, now leaving Nikki at the house all alone with Mr. Smith.

When Nikki kept asking to go home, Mr. Smith agreed to take her home. He placed her in his car and instead drove her to the child trafficker's apartment. When they reached the front door, innocent Nikki asked if this was where Julie lived. Mr. Smith said "sometimes." When the door opened, a waft of foul odor and cigarette smoke engulfed her. Standing in front of her was another man with a stained shirt. They brought her into a filthy townhouse setting, led her to the bedroom and sat her on the bed. Nikki asked if she could go home now, and Mr. Smith told her, "you get to have two homes now ... this is your new one." Mr. Smith unbraided her pigtails, removed her clothes and raped her then and there. This would be her loss of innocence and the beginning of the destruction of her life. She would never braid her hair again. To cover up the sale of Nikki, her siblings were told by her parents that she had gone to live with relatives.

She would be allowed by Mr. Smith to go home from time to time and visit her family, but she felt awkward because she knew she was an outcast. She would try to tell her parents what was happening to her, but she did not know how to articulate things. One day she kept telling her mother that she did not feel well, that her tummy and her "peepee" hurt. Her mom was either on the phone or busy with the other kids and kept ignoring her. Nikki finally grabbed onto her mom, crying in desperation and said "Mommy, I don't feel good." Her mom told her to go to the bedroom and lay down and she would check on her later ... which never happened.

Nikki was soon returned to Mr. Smith at the townhouse where she was introduced to three of his associates Mr. T, Mr. J and Mr. H, who were porn/sex traffickers. They owned 13 children from ages seven to 12, who resided in the townhouse. The traffickers photographed and videoed Nikki for child porn. She was eight years old by then. Children nine and up were taken to motels to service Johns (sex buyers), who were normally in their 30s and 40s. It was customary when the traffickers purchased a child and first brought him or her to the townhouse, to send the other children away for a day or up to three days while the new child was raped and introduced to other traffickers and the rules of the house. While Nikki was sent back to her parents' house, she was never sure where the other children went.

Once she returned to the townhouse, she met up with the other children she was familiar with as well as a new friend named Bobby. Bobby was about three years older. Above him were two even older children — Steven, age 12, and Leah, age 12, who helped care for the younger ones ... surrogate parents of sorts. Steven was the first of the 13 children to be sold away. One week after his 13th birthday Steven did not come back from a trip to the motels. Leah explained to Nikki that Steven went to someone else, and they would not see him again. Nikki became sad and afraid. Leah was sold the day after her 13th birthday in November.

The traffickers paired Nikki and Bobby up in front of the camera to perform child sex acts as well as on-camera sex acts with the traffickers themselves. By her 9th birthday the traffickers had her working the motels.

The townhouse was more than just a secret containment facility ... it was a house of murder. Nikki witnessed Mr. H arguing with another man. He had him in a headlock and slammed his head repeatedly on the coffee table until he was dead. The children were ushered to the bedroom and the door closed so they could not see who came and got the body.

The arrangement between her family and her traffickers was odd ... often at times floating back to her family and then back to the townhouse to be abused.

During her 4th grade year she was enrolled in a private Christian School by her parents and in cooperation with her traffickers. She did not have anyone to buy her school uniforms, so the school had uniforms made for her. When she was measured for her fitting, the seamstress left the room for a while, and the Vice Principal was alone with Nikki. He put his fingers up under her jumper and started molesting her while he said, "We need to make sure it's long enough to cover these parts."

On a later day at the end of that week, he called Nikki to his office (which was in a remote part of the campus with no one around). He told her that her jumpers were ready, and he gave them to her. Then he started to criticize her about her math grade and told her she was the worst in the class and ridiculed her. He told her she was a "stupid little girl, aren't you?" Then he sat her up on his desk in front of him and started molesting her while he told her how stupid she was.

He continued to call Nikki to his office about once or twice per week and molest her, saying that he was tutoring her in math. He would strip her naked and have her lay on his desk, face up while he held a flexible plastic ruler in his hand and asked her multiplication problems. If she gave the wrong answer, he would slap her genitalia with the plastic ruler. The more he slapped her, the more confused she would become and unable to give the right answers. She would cry, and he would call her a stupid little girl. The abuse inherently created a mental block with math.

She became so traumatized by math that she started pulling her eyebrows out whenever she did math. At home her father would degrade her if his efforts to help her with math were met with challenges ... calling her a "Bimbo" for not getting it.

Mr. Smith withdrew her from school before the end of her 4th grade year. The school was later closed down by the County Board of Health for health code violations.

Nikki was allowed to go home and live with her parents for two months straight. That ended on November 2, 2006. Nikki was nine. She was out playing on her parents' driveway drawing with chalk. Suddenly she noticed her dad closed the garage door and left her outside. She was startled and stood up, looking at the closed door. Then a car pulled up shortly after that. It was Mr. J. Bobby was in the car. Mr. J put Nikki in the car and drove the two of them to someone's house. He explained on the way that they were to behave and obey and be respectful to their new owner. At one point in the car he laughed and said they were "damn pricey pets."

They arrived at an undisclosed location and met their new owner ... Mr. Pelican. The children were brought to him and he examined them, then he gave them their new uniforms. Nikki and another girl were given nothing but an itchy burlap dress, nothing underneath. Bobby was shirtless and wore just khaki pants and nothing underneath. Those were their uniforms for the whole time they were slaves of Mr. Pelican, except when they went out to meet clients. On those occasions they were dressed up.

Nikki was not allowed to go home to her parents from that day forward. Mr. Pelican owned Nikki and Bobby and the other girl, who was Nikki's same age, nine. Mr. Pelican called them "girl" instead of by their names. They were mostly slaves and cooked and cleaned for Mr. Pelican, but on occasion he would drive them to motels and sell them for sex.

As punishment the children were whipped. One of Nikki's flashback memories was being locked in the closet while hearing Bobby yelling and crying as he was being whipped by Mr. Pelican. Then he was locked back in the closet with Nikki. She was so traumatized by Bobby's injuries that he was more worried about her than himself. On many occasions when Bobby was whipped, he would be left so injured that he would be unable to do strenuous work for a few days. Nikki could see Mr. Pelican rethinking his method of punishment because

Bobby was a hard worker and could do more than the two girls. Him being out of commission was becoming inconvenient for Mr. Pelican.

In 2007 things were about to change. Mr. Pelican had a customer, Mr. Sneak come over for dinner. The three children were serving him. When he saw Bobby, he said to Mr. Pelican, "I didn't know you had a boy." He motioned for Bobby to come over to him. He unzipped Bobby's pants, checked out his genitals, and then Mr. Pelican said, "If you want to examine him further, you're going to have to pay for it." So Mr. Pelican and Mr. Sneak went into a different room to have a discussion. Nikki became very afraid that Bobby was going to be sold.

After a while Mr. Sneak came out smiling. He pulled off his tie and tied it around Bobby's neck and wrists and led him away saying, "We're going home!"

Nikki started screaming and crying hysterically, and Mr. Pelican carried her out of the house. Mr. Pelican would find himself constantly annoyed by Nikki's anger towards him in days to come. She despised him for selling Bobby, and even more so a month later when he sold the other girl ... now leaving her alone with Mr. Pelican.

By the time Nikki turned 11, Mr. Pelican would allow her to go to church with him from time to time. They attended *Turning Point at Calvary, 3500 FL-16, St Augustine, FL 32092,* and he would drive there together. Nikki was allowed to go on a youth group retreat weekend where the drama team did a performance demonstrating salvation. In the drama a girl was wrestling with demons attacking her, and Jesus came into the scene, fought off the demons and rescued her and shielded her. The girl saw that Jesus was now beaten and bloodied for her sake. It was then that Nikki understood the gospel and made a decision to accept Jesus into her life as her Lord and Savior. The next morning the retreat went to the beach where she spent time with God by herself with the wind and the breeze and the horizon, and she felt like her life was starting anew. But that was not going to be the case, and in fact later in her life the gospel would be twisted by wolves in sheep's clothing, pedophiles within the church, using the holy setting as a platform for targeting children.

As more time passed, Mr. Pelican grew tired of Nikki's despise of him and sold her to Mr. Armstrong, who was an extremely wealthy

Something Bigger Than Overthrowing Small Governments

professional assassin for organized crime. On the day Mr. Armstrong bought Nikki there was an altercation between two of his friends, both armed with knives. At first, he tried to stop the fight, but then he stood back and allowed it to take its course. Nikki was terrified at the fact that they were hurting each other. As one of them fell to the ground, she jumped on him to try and break up the fight, yelling for them to stop. She accidently blocked his arm in the process and his opponent used the moment to deliver a fatal blow and kill him. Nikki immediately felt responsible for what had just occurred.

At first her new "owner" was mad and said, "I did not pay all that money for a little assassin! I paid for a sex toy." But then wheels started to turn in his head and the idea of having her "eliminate" (assassinate) "targets" (people selected for assassination) with him materialized. One week later, her training began.

The targets would be chosen by people she did not know ... but certainly people Mr. Armstrong knew, and sometimes knew well. She would not be introduced to other organized crimes. Mr. Armstrong named Nikki "Dagger ... small but deadly," and called her that the entire time she was with him. He tattooed the back of her right shoulder with the word "Dagger" and the drawing of a dagger stabbing through it. He paid two instructors, who spent time training her to do "eliminations" with him.

Part of her training involved water survival and becoming comfortable in and around anything to do with water. The pool with the marble bottom was where Nikki would do the majority of this training, which over the course of time put her in excellent physical condition. Once trained, it was not uncommon for Nikki to terminate people by drowning them in the bathtub. Not all of this sat well with Nikki, and she became apprehensive about the monster Mr. Armstrong was turning her into.

If she refused to eliminate a target as instructed, Mr. Armstrong would make the murder much worse and blame her for it and/or torture her. About eight months into her "slavery" with Mr. Armstrong she stopped resisting because she knew he would torture the targets to death unless she did it, and he would blame her. She detached emotionally and psychologically and did whatever he said.

Nikki told us she was not trained to fight, she was trained to kill. Mr. Armstrong had a dummy in the training center that had plastic veins. They would pour cranberry juice into the veins so she could learn which arteries to cut, which were the most fatal, what would cause the most damage, what would have different effects. As part of the training he would encourage her to fight with him and get aggressive. He would sometimes pull a knife on her to teach her to be prepared.

Nikki said that Mr. Armstrong took care of her the best of all six of her traffickers, in that she was in prime physical shape, the best of her life. She did not have to cook or clean or anything. He was rich and had other people to do that. She was allowed to speak. She could eat anything she wanted. She was "the most free" under him, of all her owners. He did not really treat her like a "slave." She could read or go anywhere in the house she wanted. She got to go with him places outside the house, to parties and clubs. She was his arm candy, and he showed her off even though he was a lot older than she was.

One day there was a family get-together for all of Armstrong's relatives at his house — his mother, father and brothers. His mother was a stern, unfriendly, angry-looking woman. Nikki came into the room wearing a custom-made royal blue evening gown with a fitted bodice down to her hip joints/groin, then a flowing skirt with a slit that went up one of her legs all the way to the hip joint. Mr. Armstrong's mother saw her and asked him, "Is this one of your subs?" He said, "No, I own this one." His mother said, "She's young!" Nikki was now 13. Mr. Armstrong's mother walked up to Nikki, eyeing her body, not her face. She grabbed the slit of Nikki's dress and said, "You should show her off more," while she pulled it open to expose her. Nikki grabbed his mother's wrist, stopping her, and said, "I can lift your skirt up higher, Grandma."

Mr. Armstrong grabbed Nikki and took her to a room, chastising her for her behavior. Then he took her back to the gathering and laid her on top of a low table with her dress pulled up and legs spread, exposing her, and told everyone to have their fun with her. His brothers took advantage and molested her.

From this point on in our interview with Nikki, the accounts of her exploitation would become so extraordinary and sometimes questionable that we would take a few steps back to assess the truth of the matters and determine for ourselves how much embellishment might be part of the discussions. I was hesitant to even place this chapter in my book for fear that it might slightly sound conspiratorial and take away from the validity of who we are at ARC and the existing opinion of those who know us as "solid as a rock" in our deeds, always keeping our operations and processes in a lane that is indisputable and, frankly, very credible.

I took it upon myself to seek the advice of associates in the FBI, DHS, CIA, law enforcement, and the likes who, after reviewing Nikki's story, encouraged me to press forward with this chapter because many of them did not find the information implausible. They had known it to be so from their own experiences in dealing with other human trafficking cases.

As we began to collect evidence from other unrelated human trafficking accounts involving multiple victims in multiple different locations and times in the U.S., we began to not only see a pattern, but also the reliability and reality of everything Nikki was saying. We chose to record the rest of her testimony of her slave life in the following intel report timeline in order to make things easier for the reader, rather than have them struggle through a narrative. Here are those facts to provide the reader with the opportunity to not be surprised when, over the course of time, you come to realize that what appears to be fiction may turn out to be more close to the truth than any of us wish to admit.

September 2010 - December 2010

ACCESSORIES:
- Nikki would wear an arm sheath/band covering her lower arm that held her dagger on the inside of her lower arm. It had leather and elastic bands that went around her arm holding the sheath in place. At first, she hated wearing it. She hated her new identity, but later on she began to accept it as her new definition of "her place" as a "slave."
- She used a garrote to do the eliminations a couple of times. She would wear it around her wrist like a bracelet.

- She also wore daggers in sheathes around her thighs and under her clothes.
- For one elimination ARMSTRONG had NIKKI outfitted with fingernails with blades in the sides of them. She was supposed to use the razors to eliminate the target. She did not go through with it. She only wore them once.

ELIMINATIONS (ASSASSINATIONS): He would use NIKKI as bait, and then she was supposed to do the execution. ARMSTRONG would tell her how and when she was to eliminate each target. If she did not accomplish the elimination within a certain amount of time, ARMSTRONG would come in and eliminate the target in a much worse way, usually torturing them to death. He would blame her for the fact that they were killed in this horrible manner. It was his way of forcing her to do it herself, as he ordered her to. The eliminations occurred at his house. He had other people help remove the bodies for him once the targets were dead. She was kept away from that.

She was 13 and 14. She was with ARMSTRONG for 11 months. She traveled with him. She described a flashback of that time with ARMSTRONG in a text message.

> "Sometimes after the elimination of a target, my 3rd [Mr. ARMSTRONG] would wash off my hands and the rest of me if need be instead of letting me methodically clean myself. He'd do it so fast and rough and carelessly, it was kind of hard for me when he'd do that instead of letting me have the time to clean myself off and try to pull myself back together after the elimination. How could he do that though? Just quickly scrub it all off me. Fast. Dismissively. How could he do that? He'd usually clean himself first then me, but sometimes he did us together and that felt even worse because it made me even more feel equally at fault but still even cleaning himself off, it was like he acted like he was cleaning paint off, not people's fluids, people's lives. How could he do that."

PARTIES: ARMSTRONG would often host big, lavish parties at his luxury house. They included alcohol, food, entertainment, music.

Something Bigger Than Overthrowing Small Governments

The targets would be invited to the parties where ARMSTRONG and NIKKI would make contact with them. She followed ARMSTRONG around at the event, right by his side as his "arm candy." During the party, ARMSTRONG would arrange for each target to come back and "have time" (sex) with NIKKI. When they came back for their "time," she was to eliminate them.

For example, ARMSTRONG made NIKKI eliminate a target at one of the parties. She went to get drinks for herself and the target. ARMSTRONG poisoned the target's glass and she took it to him. But when she got to him, she was confused as to which glass was poisoned. It turns out both glasses were poisoned, but ARMSTRONG trusted that NIKKI would be smart enough not to drink either one. The target died. NIKKI felt badly for him. She was wearing a long evening gown, and she cut off the bottom of her dress to lay it over his face. She told him she was sorry before the people came to take away his body. She was schooled to notify those people and let them in once a target was eliminated.

On multiple occasions NIKKI would try to use the parties as a chance to run away. She despised ARMSTRONG, and he knew it. When ARMSTRONG was occupied, she would try to get out the front of the house. ARMSTRONG had private security around the house who wore black suits. They would catch her trying to run and stop her or tackle her and take her back to ARMSTRONG.

OUTINGS: Sometimes ARMSTRONG would take her out to clubs at night. They did not go to strip clubs, but they went to high-end clubs for more elite people, private parties and parties on his yacht. ARMSTRONG attempted to drown her once as a punishment. Although she had spent hours and hours being trained by his instructors in water, this event triggered a change, and suddenly she found herself fearful of water.

ARMSTRONG hosted parties on his yacht. She doesn't know the name of the boat nor how big it was. She said she can only remember seeing one bedroom, a small kitchenette, a small bathroom, a sitting room, but it had a very large deck. She took a guess that as many as maybe 100 people were on the boat at most. She said his family probably has the boat now.

2011

NIKKI THREATENS PELICAN: At one time NIKKI's trafficker #2, MR. PELICAN, came to ARMSTRONG's house. NIKKI hated MR. PELICAN for selling BOBBY away. She asked ARMSTONG if they could kill him. ARMSTRONG said no, that MR. PELICAN was not a target. NIKKI confronted MR. PELICAN when he was sitting in a chair. She stabbed her dagger through his jacket just above his shoulder and pinned it to the chair, but she did not hurt him. He laughed at her failed efforts to kill him.

February 2011

ARMSTRONG tries to break NIKKI's will with decapitation incident: One time when NIKKI refused to eliminate a target, ARMSTRONG came in and tortured the target — a male — blaming her for it, and then finished him off by decapitating him. As punishment, he told NIKKI to clean out the head's scull, cleaning out the brain, and peel off the skin and muscles, stripping the scull down to the bone. NIKKI refused, so he chained her to his bed, legs and arms spread open, and placed the man's head resting on her between her legs. He left the head there and came back every day until she agreed to strip down the head. She endured for four days, chained with the man's head in that position, until she finally couldn't take it anymore and agreed to strip the head down to the scull. And she did.

May 2011

ARMSTRONG succeeds in breaking NIKKI's will by locking her in a walk-in refrigerator: One time when NIKKI refused to eliminate a target, ARMSTRONG locked her in a training room for a week. She describes the room like a refrigerator room or "meat locker" without the refrigeration on. It was where they stored training dummies, tools and equipment. It was metal with a metal door. He tortured her in the training room during the day and then would lock her in the refrigerator room with the lights

Photo journal example

Something Bigger Than Overthrowing Small Governments

on (without refrigeration) every night for a week. He whipped her back on one of those days.

One of those days her trainers came to train. ARMSTRONG had forgotten to tell them not to come. They saw ARMSTRONG torturing NIKKI and were visibly alarmed by that. He sent them away. She wrote this poem about being locked in the room.

Breathing. Panting. Loud in my ears.
Pain + fear cause my breaths to labor out of and back into me
They seem to be made even louder by the mostly metallic small room I'm enclosed in.
Locked. Trapped. Imprisoned for saving a life.
Tortured for this "crime."

I hurt. Everything hurts in a way I've never experienced before.
I have to struggle to suck in each breath.
Why this action causes even my ankles to scream in agony I don't understand.

Glaring. The lights are fucking glaring at me it seems.
Unrelentingly shining.
Unwaveringly illuminating my makeshift cell
So as to conceal the time of day from me.

They seem to say, "No rest. No sleeping! Reprieve is for good, obedient slaves only!"
I glare right back at them.
I am not sorry.

July 29, 2011

ARMSTRONG Killed at age 39 by DAVID, and DAVID Takes NIKKI:

NIKKI had by this time participated in/accomplished eliminations of 64 targets under ARMSTRONG's ownership. DAVID is her fourth trafficker.

THE ELIMINATION OF DAVID'S SISTER: DAVID's sister was the president of a bank. She was in her 30's or 40's. She was involved in some business deals that she and "they" (presumably organized crime) were at odds about. NIKKI said, "it was nothing to kill someone over." She was a target who was eliminated by NIKKI in June 2011. NIKKI did not eliminate her in the manner ARMSTRONG demanded, so he punished her by making her dig the woman's grave, a shallow grave in a grassy area with trees somewhere in St. Augustine, FL. NIKKI was taken there not by ARMSTRONG, but by the men who normally disposed of the bodies. She says it was dark, and they only buried three bodies that night, digging three graves, and she could see that other graves were nearby. After she dug the grave, they made her drag the woman's body down into it. NIKKI was down in the grave and accidently pulled the body down on top of her. The murder of the bank president woman involved cutting (or cutting off) some of her extremities. NIKKI mentioned that one of the woman's feet was dangling and flopping when she dragged the body into the grave. There was no body bag. One of the other men threw dirt on top of NIKKI's face and made a comment that they could bury her there too.

After NIKKI filled in the grave with dirt, the other men pushed her down on top of the grave and they all raped her. Apparently, ARMSTRONG had given them permission to do that.

THE CONFRONTATION: DAVID, is the brother of the murdered bank president, and NIKKI had killed his sister. He figured it out and showed up and said he wanted a "date" (sex) with NIKKI. He paid ARMSTRONG for her, then he said he wanted to talk with ARMSTRONG first. He sat down and, at first, they talked. She stood by her owner. Then he explained who he was and that he knew that ARMSTRONG had killed his sister, and then he pulled out a gun. When ARMSTRONG saw the gun come out, he pushed NIKKI on the floor. DAVID shot ARMSTRONG three times, and his blood splattered on NIKKI. She sat there on the floor. She was shocked when ARMSTRONG died. She hated him, but she was shocked that he could actually die. DAVID pointed the gun at her and asked what she did for him. She said, "anything he wanted." Then he said she had to come with him.

CHAINED TO A BED FOR TWO YEARS: DAVID took her and locked her in a room in a "mother-in-law suite" behind his house — not in his house, in a separate part of the house. No one went in there except the customers (sex buyers) and a man who cleaned and fed her twice a week. She was chained to a bed continuously by one ankle, sometimes more restraints, and did not leave that room for almost two years. There were no windows, and it was dark. She never saw the light of day. DAVID wanted to punish her for what happened to his sister. He beat her, even whipped her back a handful of times and had a revolving door of customers coming in for sex. They beat her as well.

She saw DAVID only rarely when he would stumble in drunk and scream at her that it was her fault his sister was dead. He would threaten to kill her or cut her hands off — he even brought in the weapon to do it sometimes — because her hands were the reason his sister was dead ... "these hands" killed his sister. He would make NIKKI recount over and over how his sister died. He would tell NIKKI it was her fault, over and over, and call her a murderer. By now it was 2012. She thought she was 14 but did not even know her 15th birthday had passed.

NO SENSE OF TIME: From the middle of 2011 to the beginning of 2013, she never left that room. DAVID had a guy come in twice a week to clean her up and empty her bed pan. She was chained to the bed the whole time, but he would take the chain off and tie her wrists with rope to take her to the shower and wash her. He would clean her off and give her a little food and water. She would ask him what the date was, and she would try to keep track of the days. When she was beaten badly enough by a customer or by DAVID, she would dip her finger in her own blood and mark on her leg a tally of how many days it had been. She had no sense of day or night, except that when more frequent customers were coming in, she figured that was night, and when they came in less often, she figured that was day. She was in a one-bedroom suite. She was only in the bedroom and could not see the rest of the suite. She would get very sick, but DAVID would do nothing if she was sick. She said she figured he hoped she would just die.

HURRICANE: A severe hurricane occurred during her imprisonment in the room. DAVID drugged her heavily and told her that they were leaving to get out of the way of the hurricane. At one point she vaguely started to regain consciousness and saw that they were on a private jet. Then he drugged her again and she woke up back in her room chained to the bed.

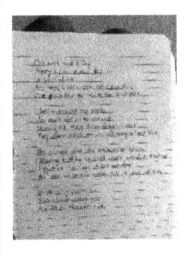

NIKKI wrote a poem about her experience with DAVID:

On this bed I lay
Every hour, every day ...
Or so I think.
For there's no clock, no calendar,
No window to track the sun's sink.

Chain around my ankle
No slack for it to dangle
Staring at these same beige walls
They stare back at me as many a tear falls

He comes after the animals 've gone
Cleaning, bathing my blood, tears and dirt all gone
I gather courage to ask the date
He tells it's been a month. Six. A year of late

Each day passes on
Every hour,
Every year,
And it's on this bed I lay

August 2012

At one point after NIKKI had been chained to the bed for a year, she decided she wanted to die. She stopped eating the food and water that was brought to her. She would hide the water bottles. But after a short time, the man found the hidden bottles and started to force-feed her and force her to drink the water.

January 2013

DAVID began a "beautification treatment" of NIKKI: He fed her well and took care of her better for one month.

February 2, 2013

NIKKI is sold to auction dealer, branded, held in storage unit in Florida: One day DAVID came in, bound NIKKI, blind-folded her, chloroformed her out and transported her to an unknown place. He sold her to a guy who sells humans at the auction.

THE "SLAVE" AUCTION: NIKKI was assessed/evaluated for her capabilities. She was branded (tattooed) on her left upper arm with an alpha-numeric code SFWP9251750 that meant "Slave, Female, Work and Pleasure, number 925" followed by her category 1750. They also inserted a small GPS device in her arm just below the brand.

She was held with other slaves in storage units in the dark. The slaves were confined with different restraints. They wore collars that were connected down their backs. There was a bar across the ceiling of the storage unit. Each person's collar was chained to the bar at the ceiling of the unit. They were gagged the whole time and not allowed to talk. They were kept in the dark, sitting in their own urine and feces, unable to move around.

February 26, 2013

TRAFFICKER #5 "STUPID OLD FAT GUY" (SOFG)
They were transported to an unknown warehouse building for auction. It was nearby because they weren't driving for very long. The building had a stage and stage lights and big screens. NIKKI said there could have been hundreds or a thousand people there by the noise of all of their voices. She could not see very well because of the stage lights, but she could see most of their shadowy figures in the audience. Like the other slaves, she was brought to the stage, and people were bidding and laughing and commenting. The bidding was done electronically by keypads that the bidders held. She stood there when the auctioneer said, "sold." Then she got moved to one of various waiting areas where the slaves would wait to be picked up by their new "owners" and do paperwork. SOFG bought NIKKI from the

auction. She was not cooperative with him and continually threatened him. She did not use his name, so she called him "stupid old fat guy."

March 2, 2013 *(APPROXIMATE DATE)*

NIKKI ESCAPES TRAFFICKER #5, "STUPID OLD FAT GUY," and RENUNITES WITH PARENTS: NIKKI had been with SOFG for one week when she escaped. She was able to get a letter opener out of his nightstand. When he came home and was on the bed, she pinned him down and held it to his neck, threatening him. She told him to take off her slave collar, which was locked and attached to a chain. He did. She told him to stay there. He did. She went to the front door and with the letter opener, she stabbed herself in the left upper arm and ripped open a gash to remove the GPS device in her arm. She ran out into the woods, naked, bleeding, and found a gas station, the first place she came to. The gas station attendants called 911 and an ambulance came to take her to a hospital. She refused to tell the hospital staff anything except that she wanted to "go home."

NIKKI gave the hospital staff her BIRTH PARENTS' names and home address (hoping they still lived there after all the years since they sold her). They did still live there. They came to the hospital and took her home. She told them a little of what had happened to her, and they felt terrible and let her stay home, trying to help her.

June 2013

JANET AND STEVE (NIKKI's 6th traffickers): JANET got a Master of Divinity degree at a Theological Seminary. She got a job in Jacksonville at a mega-church, ███████████████████. She knew STEVE and TRENT before moving to Jacksonville.

June 2013

███████████ **CHURCH OF** ███████████████: NIKKI started going to church after her 5th trafficker, while living with her parents. The church has over 25,000 members. She liked the pastor, whose name was ███████████. The church takes up several city blocks, centered at ███████████████████████████████████.

Something Bigger Than Overthrowing Small Governments

She went to church to find a safe place. Started to volunteer at church. JANET was a youth leader there, she was a youth pastor's assistant. She was on staff. JANET was engaged to TRENT, a volunteer youth leader at the same church.

NIKKI feels like the large church was a good place for them to hide what they were doing. She never really saw the same people, so even when there was something wrong, no one stopped to pay attention.

JANET and STEVE: JANET and STEVE had been friends for years. STEVE has a happy marriage, and JANET was engaged to TRENT. NIKKI says she does not believe there was any romantic involvement going on between JANET and STEVE. JANET asked STEVE to help groom and break NIKKI's will as a sex and labor "slave." He is a Sergeant with the Sheriff's Department. He was serving at the church but was not on staff. He is the one who has been torturing NIKKI through the duration of her ""enslavement" with them (approximately four years).

NIKKI had been at the church for five months before JANET approached her. NIKKI got her high school diploma, not by attending classes, but by passing multiple-choice end-of-year tests with the help of her parents. So at age 16 she had her high school diploma and had technically "graduated." She started attending the college group even though she was only 16. She started befriending a guy who liked her. But he found out she was 16 and told the pastor. NIKKI got kicked out of the college group and started getting involved with the youth group. NIKKI was also on the college group worship team.

December 2, 2013

At a banquet event JANET picked NIKKI out to groom her as a "slave." The event was held at a huge public library next to the church, at █████████████████████████████.

December 4, 2013

JANET introduced herself to NIKKI and asked her out to lunch.

Bazzel Baz

January - April 2014

January 10-14 Start 6th traffickers, JANET and STEVE:

GROOMING: JANET began grooming NIKKI, making her feel special. JANET earned NIKKI's trust. JANET had frequent sleepovers with girls from the youth group at her house, where she lived alone. JANET's parents paid for the house for her. NIKKI had gone to these sleepovers many times before and everything had been fine.

JANET and STEVE RAPE NIKKI: But on 1/11/2014 NIKKI showed up at JANET's house (possibly ███████████████████, Jacksonville, FL 32218) for a sleepover party, and after a while she noticed that no other girls showed up. She asked JANET about it, and JANET said no one else was coming. NIKKI felt special that JANET was spending time with her alone. She told NIKKI to go change in the guest room, and she was going to change too, and then they could have snacks and play games and paint their nails. NIKKI went to the guest room and changed, but she found the door was stuck shut when she tried to get out. She banged on the door, laughing and calling out to JANET that the door was stuck. She waited about 20 minutes, but still chuckling, thinking it was just stuck.

She heard someone walking down the hall and started laughing, prepared to explain that the door was stuck the whole time. But she heard a latch unlock, and then STEVE walked in with JANET. He shut the door behind them and leaned back against the door.

NIKKI started to realize she was in danger and kept looking at JANET saying she did not understand, asking JANET what was going on. JANET had a smirk on her face. NIKKI says she felt like a fly in a spider web. She started backing up. STEVE was very serious and repeatedly, sternly ordered NIKKI to sit down. NIKKI ran to the window and threw it open to call out for help. There were bars on the window. JANET closed the window and window coverings while STEVE grabbed NIKKI and held her down on the floor. NIKKI fought him but was unable to get out from under him. STEVE was laughing. He said to her, "Are you done yet?" Then STEVE and JANET raped her. NIKKI said she was never, at that time or other times, able to defend herself against both of them, even though she wanted to.

MOTIVATIONS: NIKKI believes JANET "enslaved" her because of her own abuse from her past. JANET was abused by her uncle and did not get therapy, so she acted out. She was abused her whole childhood until she left home for college.

TRAFFICKING OTHERS?: Although JANET seems very skilled in the grooming process, had her bedroom door equipped with an external lock to confine someone in the room, had bars on her windows, had STEVE and three other youth leaders "in on it," assisting her in breaking and assaulting NIKKI, NIKKI insisted on multiple occasions that JANET and STEVE were/are NOT trafficking others. She said she is positive they were not abusing other kids, but she has no proof to substantiate her belief. She believes that JANET wanted her specifically. She wanted a "slave" to cook for her, clean for her and provide sexual pleasure. NIKKI went around and did errands with her. She liked the companionship. NIKKI lived with JANET before she was married. JANET was with her all the time.

TREATMENT: NIKKI was not allowed to sit on furniture. She had to sit on the floor. She was required to cook for them, but she was only allowed to eat water and crackers for the most part. She would eat out of the trash sometimes and get caught and punished. They would watch her while she cooked so she could taste the food, but not eat it. They would punish her with torture. They also watched her because the first year with them she was a threat and they were afraid she would get a kitchen knife or utensil and attack them.

WHIPPING: STEVE and JANET beat and tortured NIKKI very frequently. One of their common methods was whipping her back.

MYSTERY SURGERY: She was anesthetized for a mystery surgery during the Washington D.C. torture event in 2014 in her lower, right groin area. She was told afterward that she would never be able to have children

DRIVERS' LICENSE: STEVE and JANET had NIKKI get her drivers' license because JANET would sometimes get very drunk and need to be driven home by someone sober.

OUTINGS: Sometimes STEVE and JANET had NIKKI around their families or around other people in public. She was not allowed to speak or smile or make eye contact with anyone. They told people that she was a youth that they were "helping out," and that is why they had her with them. People thought NIKKI was just a messed-up kid that JANET was helping.

SHOCK COLLAR: STEVE and JANET sometimes made NIKKI wear a shock collar in order to control her and torture her.

JAW CLAMP DEVICE: One time, STEVE wanted to teach NIKKI not to speak. He put a device that fit inside her mouth with a keyhole in the front. It was like a black mouth guard that filled the inside of her mouth. It could not be seen from the outside when her mouth was shut. On the sides it had spring hooks. If the key was turned, the device would send hooks into the inside of her jaws, piercing the gums and literally clamping her jaws closed. STEVE demonstrated it to her half-way, and it hurt terribly as it pierced her gums. He told her that when he or JANET put black lipstick on her, that meant she was not allowed to speak or even smile. If she did speak, he would insert this device in her mouth and turn the key. That was his way of teaching her not to speak. She never challenged that rule, so he never had to use it.

SERVICING CUSTOMERS (Prostitution): STEVE and JANET put NIKKI to work in prostitution from the first few months they had her. She had quotas similar to other trafficked girls. She worked hotels (economy to upscale) clubs, bars, truck stops, restaurants, private parties, yachts, boat clubs, strip clubs. She was not booking the dates or posting ads. She did not set up the dates. Most of the time she was going to meet customers at their hotels, but many times STEVE and JANET would get hotel rooms and would have a steady stream of Johns (sex buyers) coming in to her. They took all the money. They took the pictures of her. (Those pictures could still be on their computers and/or still online.) She couldn't speak or even choose her pose.

On Valentine's Day every year they would "turn her out" to work so much that they would drug her with Ketamine, so she would be

Something Bigger Than Overthrowing Small Governments

tolerant. They would rent a room, and the customers would be a revolving door until morning. They cuffed her to the bed and then they went out.

But she also felt protected by STEVE from "wacko Johns." One sicko came into her room for a date and pulled out a drill and said he needed to "put more holes in you." She screamed for STEVE, and he got rid of him. (But he had also set up that date for her).

FLORIDA COPS WERE INVOLVED: STEVE trafficked NIKKI to multiple police officers and Sheriff officers in the state of Florida. They called her "Cop Slut," and referred to her as "it," not as a person. NIKKI believes she was sexually involved with every police officer in the city of ▮▮▮▮▮▮▮▮ and likely the entire state. STEVE had clout in the department, so no one confronted him or held him accountable. She was trained by STEVE not to ever resist their touch, commands or sexual advances. She was to do whatever they wanted. Any police officer who saw her anywhere could pull her into his car or elsewhere and rape her for free. Often, they raped her in their police cruisers, in uniform, often multiple officers took turns.

NIKKI was forced by STEVE to make a quota of prostitution money each day. She struggled with the interference of police officers because they did not pay her and would cut into her work time, causing her to come up short on her quotas. She tried to run from all police officers, but they would still chase her down. She now has a trauma trigger every time she sees an officer or police car.

RESISTING A COP INCIDENT: One day NIKKI was working (prostitution) on the streets where the hotels were. A cop saw her and called out to her. She tried to run because she was supposed to meet STEVE while he was working. The cop called out to her with a derogatory term (she would not repeat it) and said, "Hey, where are you going, I'm talking to you." She ran, and he grabbed her and took her to his car. She begged him "please, Sir" to leave her alone, and she resisted and wrestled against him. At one point she pushed him off of her and said, "Get off!" She spun around to get out of his grasp and spun right smack into STEVE, who had seen the whole thing and come up behind her. NIKKI dropped to her knees and went silent, as trained not to speak. STEVE said, "Explain to me what I just saw." She knelt on the ground, shaking. He told her she had permission to speak. She still could not get any words out, so he grabbed her by her "slave" collar and yanked her to her feet and said, "I ordered you to speak." She told him that she resisted.

STEVE asked the officer, "can I borrow your car for a minute?" So STEVE laid her down in the back seat, reprimanded her, and broke her wrist. STEVE told her when she was done with the other cop to just come back and they would be done for the night. STEVE said to the other officer, "She's all yours. Watch out for its wrist." The other officer thanked him and then proceeded to rape NIKKI in the back of his car.

GOOD TIMES: NIKKI says she had shared good times with her "owners" too, like going places, traveling. JANET used NIKKI as a companion and seemed to really enjoy her company and getting to know her. NIKKI confided in her about the abuse of her principal in 4th grade. NIKKI bonded strongly with JANET and loves her. This is one reason why the trauma bond is so strong.

February 2, 2014

A temporary controller named MIGUEL had NIKKI wrapped up in a ribbon for his birthday. She hated that. He was also a youth leader at ▮▮▮▮▮▮▮▮▮▮▮▮▮▮▮▮▮▮▮▮▮ church, and had a wife, RUBY. They assisted STEVE and JANET in trafficking NIKKI.

April 9, 2014

KIDNAPPED INTO BROTHEL: NIKKI was serving customers in a hotel room and apparently STEVE and JANET were not watching, so she got kidnapped by a customer. He delivered her to a brothel. She was at the brothel being worked to service customers. STEVE called the customer who kidnapped her, was able to locate NIKKI at the brothel, and went to get her back. The brothel was unmarked as part of the underground sex trade. NIKKI describes it like a large warehouse. Inside were multiple floors of rooms where girls were servicing customers. The windows of the brothel were dirty and yellow, with tattered curtains and bars on the windows. The place was filthy.

Something Bigger Than Overthrowing Small Governments

STEVE negotiated to buy NIKKI back for $10,000. He was spotted or identified as having gone to the brothel. He then reported the brothel to law enforcement as though he was working under cover. Over a year later, after an investigation, the brothel was shut down by law enforcement in October 2015. There was an article in the news about that.

April 14, 2014

When STEVE bought NIKKI back, he showed NIKKI the paper contract between him and the brothel saying that had paid for her, and that he officially owned her. He took her to a sketchy tattoo place and had his initials tattooed on the right side of her groin area, branding her as his.

April 15, 2014

SUICIDE ATTEMPT: The morning after he branded his initials on her groin area, NIKKI was lying next to him after he had sex with her again. NIKKI was in despair, feeling trapped and wanted to kill herself instead of being a "slave" again. She saw that he had left his gun out on the nightstand. She said he had used it with her the night before (particulars unknown) and had left the safety off. She jumped up from being next to him, grabbed his gun, and had it pointed up under her jaw to shoot herself in the head when he grabbed it away from her. He threw the gun across the floor and pushed her down on her knees beside the bed and yelled at her.

For the next week STEVE punished NIKKI, having her bound to the bed for a week while he and JANET took turns punishing her. The punishment was all focused psychologically around STEVE's possession of her, that she was *his* and her life belongs to *him* and *he* gets to decide whether he takes it or not.

June 15-22, 2014

Washington D.C. Trip and Medical Torture, Death and Resuscitation:

▬▬▬▬**Church** ▬▬▬▬ **Youth Group trip to DC, June 15-22, 2014:** The trip was a pre-graduation reward/celebration for seniors in the youth group who were about to graduate and leave the high school group. It was a drive trip on a bus from Florida to D.C. There were approximately 100 students on the trip including 11 Leaders. JANET and STEVE were among the staff.

Three other Leaders on the trip assisted JANET and STEVE in torturing and assaulting NIKKI. They were not only in the know but participated and were regular abusers of NIKKI. Their names were MIGUEL, RUBY (the married couple) and CYNTHIA. MIGUEL was a regular sexual exploiter and temporary controller of NIKKI. His wife went along with it, but she was the only one who was kind and did not hurt or assault NIKKI. She would sometimes ask for "time" with NIKKI (which was the term used for a sex date) but instead she would go in the room and talk to NIKKI and bring her food.

NIKKI was the youngest one on the D.C. trip. She was not considered one of the "students," but she came along as a "Junior Leader." JANET and STEVE were youth leaders, so they had to go. JANET and STEVE had arranged the torture with people STEVE knew in D.C. They used the church vehicle to transport her with the group. The whole group went to Cracker Barrel to eat breakfast (100 teenagers) the first morning they arrived in Northern Virginia. (West Virginia was also part of this trip). NIKKI said she "got to eat bacon" that day.

JANET drugged NIKKI in the bathroom: She believes it may have been Ketamine, because that's what they used on her every Valentine's Day when they sold her to customers. It made her pass out as she left the bathroom about 15 feet from the door in front of eight of the other teenagers on the trip. Then they told the kids that she had heat exhaustion and that she needed a doctor.

They actually took NIKKI, later on, to an ER at *George Washington Memorial Hospital* to develop the cover story. The drug was sufficiently out of her system when she got to the hospital ER that night, and they did not have the ER staff do any blood tests. STEVE, JANET and three other staff, who were assisting them in the exploitation of NIKKI, started suggesting heat exhaustion as an excuse to leave the ER and take NIKKI elsewhere. The youth pastor, ▇▇▇▇▇▇▇▇, went himself to the hospital, very concerned. The others sent him back saying she was okay.

The torture occurred nightly from June 15–22, for seven consecutive days except for Thursday, June 19. The torture episodes lasted for eight to thirteen hours each night. STEVE and JANET told the rest of the youth group that they had to stay with NIKKI in the hospital because she was suffering from heat exhaustion. STEVE's WIFE was along on the trip with their kids, but she did not go to the torture. Instead they took NIKKI to a clinic after hours where the air conditioning was off. They were in one surgical room with very bright fluorescent lights. She said the room would get stuffy and muggy because of no air circulation. She would sweat.

In the room was a metal surgical table, bags of blood, IV, scalpels and other surgical instruments, a machine with wires and electrodes, blue surgical gloves and other medical instruments.

She has visible marks still from torture. She had burn marks from flaming lighters and the electrodes. They put water on her legs and patches with wires and electrodes. It burned her. It was for breaking and training. For six months before that, she wasn't cooperating, and she was resisting and fighting them every step of the way. So he paid them to break her.

STEVE and JANET were both there. There were also three youth leaders assisting them, who were present during some of the nights. They took turns. Two medical personnel conducted the tortures with STEVE. STEVE was directing the procedures. The other medical staff were a woman in her 50's and an African American man in his 20's or 30's. They were wearing scrubs and occasionally surgical masks. NIKKI said their faces were straight the whole time and they showed no reaction — except one time before they strapped her to the table when NIKKI attempted to kill the female nurse. Minutes earlier, NIKKI had managed to grab a scalpel off the tray and hide it under her leg. When the nurse reached over her body, NIKKI tried to slit the nurse's throat. STEVE caught her arm before she could, and he pulled her arm out of the socket. At one point, NIKKI flipped off STEVE and he broke her middle finger.

They bound NIKKI to a metal surgical table. The torture included hours of cutting and bleeding her, electric shock, burning, etc. STEVE wanted her to say that she was his, she belongs to him, she has no will of her own. STEVE took turns with the nurses torturing NIKKI. At one point JANET turned pale white and told STEVE they had gone too far, but he continued.

NIKKI says that she changed. She wrote a poem about that incident:

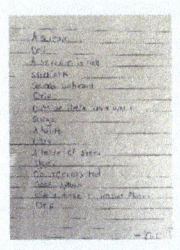

A scream
Drip
A scream in hell
Ssshhinkk
Sounds unheard
Drip
Outside these white walls
Surge
A table
Clink
A table of steel
Slam
Oh terrors had
Gasp, splash
Within these crimson floors
Drip

During the electrocution on the second-to-last day, she flatlined and was resuscitated by the nurses.

NIKKI says that she lost her sanity during one of those days. She was too weak to hardly move, and when they took her to start the torture again she started laughing and laughing, in an insane way.
To keep up the appearance that they were taking NIKKI to the hospital, STEVE would take off his shirt upon arriving in the medical room and put on something else ... a different garment. The garment would become splattered with NIKKI's blood and sweat throughout the torture. When they were done for the night, he would put back on his shirt that he came in with, which was still clean, and would wear it back to rejoin the youth group.

Something Bigger Than Overthrowing Small Governments

One girl, KATHY, was one of the seniors on the trip and saw NIKKI collapse unconscious at the museum on one of the days. She became extremely worried, even traumatized along the trip because NIKKI became increasingly sicker each day. She caught on that something was wrong and told Pastor ▇▇▇ that every day the leaders took NIKKI to the hospital and she came back sicker. He talked to them and told them he wanted to see the papers for the hospital stays. They only had one, because they hadn't been going to the hospital the rest of the time. They had been going to another clinic after hours. NIKKI doesn't know how they "worked some magic" with the pastor to work it out, but they did, and the issue got dropped. Pastor ▇▇▇ never asked NIKKI what happened.

JANET SETS THE TRAUMA BOND: One of the days during the torture trip, when NIKKI was resting in agony and fighting to survive, JANET came to her and lay next to her, wrapping her arms around NIKKI and comforting her. NIKKI became deeply bonded to JANET after this, because although she tortured her, then she comforted her. She tenderly stroked the bridge of NIKKI's nose with her finger, which made NIKKI "fall in love" with JANET.

NIKKI BROKE: NIKKI says she "broke" in D.C. the day after flatlining and being resuscitated. That was the last day of the torture. She spoke what STEVE wanted her to say — that she was his, that she had to give up all hope of things ever being any different, that she was nothing, that she was theirs, that she was nothing more. She was crying, and then she just gave up. She just glazed over and didn't respond. When she said it, STEVE said, "Good girl." NIKKI has always been triggered by the words, "good girl" because her traffickers often said that.

SEVERAL MONTHS in RECOVERY: On the trip back from D.C. to the city of ▇▇▇▇▇▇▇ the other kids on the bus noticed she was unresponsive to anyone and didn't remember anything. NIKKI was in a mental "fog." She said she felt like she could hear a humming noise all the time in her head. She did not recognize people. Her memory was temporarily gone. She was unresponsive to her surroundings. She was so damaged by the torture that they had to leave her at her parent's house for a couple of months to recover because she could not even stand up without passing out. They told her parents that she had a stroke from heat exhaustion.

NIKKI picked up a severe stuttering problem after D.C. It annoyed STEVE and JANET so badly that they sent NIKKI to a speech therapist. Without giving any specifics, the therapist was able to determine that the source of NIKKI's stuttering problem was fear. She used singing to help NIKKI. She also introduced NIKKI to her best friend, ELYSIA.

Somehow, with God's help and the trauma bond with JANET, she was able to regain her sanity over time. She does not understand what happened to her mentally and psychologically. She feels that she left her soul behind in that medical torture room. She feels that she is still in that room, screaming in a perpetual echo that never stops.

October 2014

Around October of 2014 NIKKI was taken to a gathering of JANET's family in Texas. She was told to keep her head down. She was not allowed to speak at all or smile. They put the black lipstick on her lips. She was not allowed to eat either. NIKKI describes JANET's family as stiff and unemotional "like cardboard." Everyone puts on a façade.

2014-2015

NIKKI's TRAUMA BOND with her Traffickers strengthens: She feels from STEVE and JANET belonging, quality time, acceptance, purpose, love, touch, a twisted type of affection. Anything she needed for customers they would buy, but otherwise she did not have clothes and was treated more like an animal. But she feels "unconditional love" because they don't get rid of her even though she does things wrong. She feels that they see value in her.

August 15, 2015

JANET got married in ▓▓▓▓▓▓▓▓▓▓ area. NIKKI helped JANET with her wedding preparations and errands. Before the wedding JANET locked NIKKI in STEVE's closet for a week during the wedding and honeymoon to keep her hidden.

Something Bigger Than Overthrowing Small Governments

December 2015

NIKKI ran away to Orlando and worked at DISNEYWORLD ORLANDO from December 2015 to May 2016. Her parents helped her get a place to live there. But it was only about two weeks later that DARRIEN (a cop friend and accomplice of STEVE's) spotted NIKKI and reported her location to STEVE. As an Orlando Police officer, DARRIEN's beat was that area. STEVE went to Orlando to "deal with" her. She lived with DARRIEN for a while.

NIKKI escaped at one point and spent some time at a Safe Home in Orlando, but she was still being partly controlled by STEVE and JANET and was servicing customers for them when she was not at work with Disney. They made her quit Disneyworld, telling her she was "forgetting her priority." NIKKI was back and forth for a while in a tug-of-war between the SAFE HOME, her advocates, and STEVE, JANET and DARRIEN, who would literally walk into the SAFE HOME (in police uniforms) and take her out. They did not create conflict with the staff, because the staff cooperated with law enforcement authority. They would just come in and NIKKI would go with them. This occurred multiple times.

January 2016

JANET and TRENT moved to Texas because he got a job there as a youth pastor.

2016

At one point when NIKKI was at a SAFE HOME in Orlando, she began seeing a Therapist, who attempted to mis-diagnose her (NIKKI said to get rid of her) with a mental disorder that would have put her in a lock-down mental hospital. The staff at a SAFE HOME refused the diagnosis and recommendation. NIKKI's mother was outraged at the therapist. The therapist was also breaking confidentiality and talking with the church people at ███████████████, ORLANDO (now under a different name). The thought of being locked up triggered NIKKI so badly that she is still daily affected by the fear of that experience. It re-traumatized her at a very vulnerable point. The therapist said that NIKKI could either go to a mental hospital or be returned home to her parents. NIKKI's parents took her back home.

June 2016

STEVE GETS NIKKI BACK: Very shortly after she returned home, STEVE showed up at her parents' house and called NIKKI saying that he was there. NIKKI saw STEVE outside in the car, crawled out the window and immediately went back with him out of fear and obedience.

STEVE continued to use NIKKI as a sex slave — rough, injuring her, trafficking her to cops and clubs and sex buyers. His wife, IRENE, was complicit with all of it. STEVE even brought NIKKI on vacation with their family once, but only STEVE spoke to her. No one else acknowledged her. She was not allowed to eat with the family. When they went to restaurants, she was not allowed to eat or speak and he put an ankle bracelet tracking device on her.

December 2016

STEVE allowed NIKKI to go see her favorite band, "For KING and COUNTRY." NIKKI had met the band during their "PRICELESS" tour movement against human trafficking. She was able to talk to the band at their outreach, and they gave her three free tickets to their concert in Orlando.

March 2017

NIKKI RAN AWAY AGAIN: March of 2017 was the last time NIKKI saw STEVE. She ran away and said it was terrible, and it wasn't her choice to do it that way. NIKKI had just earned STEVE's trust again, and he had just taken the ankle tracker off of her.

But NIKKI's parents told her that if she did not leave her traffickers, that they would report STEVE and JANET to their attorney and to FBI. NIKKI ran away in an effort to save her traffickers from being reported.

The oddity in all of this is that her father sold her into trafficking when she was seven, and her mother is in denial, claiming that she did not know or believe that NIKKI's father had done that. In her discussions with her mother NIKKI learned that her parents were so dysfunctional that they actually believed that there was enough time and separation between what they did when she was a child until now,

Something Bigger Than Overthrowing Small Governments

that most, if not all, of the blame would fall on the traffickers that groomed her from that church. It was obvious to NIKKI that their story would never hold water in an FBI investigation.

NIKKI's PARENTS flew her to Illinois to ▮▮▮▮▮▮▮▮▮▮ shelter program. It was her first flight on a plane. She was very afraid of getting caught, so she flew in the middle of the night by herself. She was very injured, having been whipped the day before, and had not slept for three days. Her back was so injured that she could not sit back in the seat, so she sat forward the whole time. When she got to the shelter and finished intake, she laid down on the floor on her stomach and slept until dinner the next day.

She was at ▮▮▮▮▮▮▮▮▮▮ program until July when STEVE discovered her whereabouts. STEVE used NIKKI's Social Security number to track her activities. She had applied for college in Illinois when she was at the ▮▮▮▮▮▮▮ Shelter. Then STEVE came to Illinois to get her. A staff member at the shelter mentioned STEVE was on his way, and NIKKI left Illinois and ran to California. NIKKI's aunt bought her the ticket and drove her to the airport.

August 2017

NIKKI found shelter at ▮▮▮▮▮▮▮▮▮▮▮▮▮ in Fullerton, California. ▮▮▮ allowed her the freedom to grocery shop and run errands, etc. while she lived at the shelter.

August 2017

NIKKI was out running errands one day and was spotted by a former CUSTOMER from Florida who was on a business trip in Orange County, CA. She did not see him and was not aware that she had been spotted. The CUSTOMER contacted STEVE that he had seen NIKKI.

One week later the same CUSTOMER snuck up behind NIKKI while she was in line at an ice cream parlor and held his cell phone up to her ear and it was her "Master" STEVE's voice on the phone giving her orders. He told her to go to the CUSTOMER'S car and go with him, and that the CUSTOMER would be her temporary controller for a while.

Instead NIKKI's advocate was able to help her escape, get her to a hotel and then transition her to another program, ▮▮▮▮▮▮▮▮▮

August 31, 2017

NIKKI went to ▮▮▮▮▮▮▮ program in San Diego. She said they have too many restrictions and rules and are very much about "their healing" program and what you do for "them" — not for you. NIKKI left on December 9, 2017.

December 2017

Mary ▮▮▮▮▮▮▮▮▮▮▮▮▮▮▮▮▮▮▮▮▮▮ took NIKKI into her shelter program. The place was dirty, but NIKKI felt safe. She left at the end of February. NIKKI had a personality conflict with Mary. Mary washed the dogs in the kitchen sink and the fur would stay in there. There was dog poop all over the floor, etc.

February 2018

NIKKI's PARENTS came to California. NIKKI moved into an apartment in Anaheim with the financial help of her parents. They gave her a car and were paying for her apartment in Anaheim. NIKKI has an uncle in the area who was helpful.

She was also employed with ▮▮▮▮▮▮▮▮▮▮▮▮▮▮ as a receptionist. She was in ▮▮▮ at ▮▮▮▮▮.

April 2018

NIKKI started getting to know a guy online who was from Mission Viejo, and she told him a bit about her life. They never really dated. He called Anaheim PD and reported what she had told him. Four PD officers came to question her and search her apartment. She told them quite a bit of information. She feels they "forced her" to say things. They reported the encounter to the FBI. That started an investigation, but NIKKI got "her lawyers" (hired by her parents) to shut it down, and the police stopped talking with her. She told the guy never to talk to her again.

Something Bigger Than Overthrowing Small Governments

A couple of weeks later on April 29, 2018 Senior Pastor ███████ resigned from the ████████████████████████ (church where JANET recruited NIKKI) with no warning and no explanation. It is unknown whether these events had any connection.

May 2018

JANET called NIKKI and they started talking over the phone for a few days. Then JANET started to give NIKKI orders to dress up (according to her instructions) and arranged a flight for NIKKI to come to her in Texas. NIKKI was packed and ready to go, but she got nervous because she knew she was in trouble and would be punished. She wasn't sure she wanted to go back to JANET and STEVE, so she did not get on the flight.

JANET was outraged at NIKKI's disobedience in not coming to Texas. JANET ordered NIKKI to go meet a CUSTOMER at a hotel. She said if NIKKI refused, that they would send someone to get her and "drag her out" to take her to the hotel anyway. So NIKKI went to the hotel and the CUSTOMER turned out to be an Anaheim PD cop (NIKKI knows who he is but would not tell us his name). He did NOT pay for the date but got her for free and also beat her to punish her. He had NIKKI for a while at the hotel. JANET was mad at NIKKI and did not speak to her for the rest of the month. NIKKI did not get to wish JANET a happy birthday on May 27th.

June 2018

JANET contacted NIKKI in June. She was still mad, but did not fuss very much, just was tense. JANET reinforced that NIKKI must come home when JANET says for her to come — that NIKKI does not have a say. They did not talk again until August.

August 23, 2018

DOBY ████ is a young adults' group leader at ██████ Christian Church. He and MAHALIA (another young adults' group leader) have developed a trusted friendship with NIKKI. She has confided in them about her trafficking history.

Against her wishes, but using their better judgement, they began to reach out for help for NIKKI. DOBY ▌▌▌ works for a mutual friend of TINA Paulson, who is the Director of Human Trafficking/Victim Advocate for Association for the Recovery of Children (ARC). The mutual friend, who works for ▌▌▌ in Fullerton, referred DOBY to TINA for advocacy for NIKKI.

At 4:22 p.m. DOBY texted TINA. They had a phone conversation about NIKKI wanting a survivor mentor, and TINA sent a couple of resources to DOBY to pass on to NIKKI, including TINA's Google Voice number.

TINA continued to talk/text DOBY to get the back story on NIKKI and what she needed. Apparently, MAHALIA knew of someone who had contacted the FBI regarding NIKKI's case. The FBI called her back and referred to a police report that NIKKI (or someone else) had filed when she first escaped (not clear which escape this was).

Apparently, Homeland Security had investigated the case for eight months, something "did not add up," and they decided to close the case. The FBI seemed to cast doubt on the validity of NIKKI's claims.

August 23, 2018

NIKKI was working for ▌▌▌ as a receptionist but lost her job when ▌▌▌ discovered she was willingly in communication with her traffickers.

August 24, 2018

JANET had contacted NIKKI again and told her to buy a certain outfit/lingerie and to dress up. She had NIKKI do a Skype sexual performance for JANET.

August 24, 2018

DARRIEN flew to Anaheim and got a hotel room to detain NIKKI and control her, use her, punish her for a week, then transport her to JANET.

Something Bigger Than Overthrowing Small Governments

August 26, 2018

NIKKI was forced by DARRIEN and JANET to go work at a gentlemen's club (strip club).

August 28, 2018

NIKKI messaged MAHALIA at 5:43 p.m. regarding her temporary controller, DARRIEN. "He's staying in a hotel here. LOL. It's fine. He's an officer in Orlando, He was my temporary controller in Orlando for a few months but now my Master had Him come out here so He can keep me in line right now and He'll be bringing me home [to JANET] next month if that happens."

DOBY said they were staying at a Hotel on La Veta in Anaheim, CA.

DARRIEN moved from the hotel to stay at NIKKI's apartment. He was sometimes gone for long periods of time, but she stayed waiting for him. (This cooperation is very typical of "slave" mentality, child soldiering, Stockholm syndrome, trauma bond).

August 31, 2018

Friday, DOBY met TINA (HT ARC), with MAHALIA on Facetime at 9 a.m. at Starbucks 1070 N. Tustin Ave, Anaheim, CA 92807. They exchanged information about NIKKI and came up with some plans to help draw her back into safety away from her traffickers. They were keenly aware that she may disappear any day.

TINA (HT ARC) took down information regarding NIKKI's traffickers and began research utilizing internet, social media and apps searches as well as background checks.

August 31, 2018

Unbeknownst to anyone else, NIKKI's temporary controller, DARRIEN had beaten her (on authority of STEVE). He raped her and then in the shower he smashed her head against the wall, giving her a concussion. She also sustained other injuries.

NIKKI was abducted by DARRIEN and was driven in a car for a long distance. NIKKI reported later that at the time she was gagged, blindfolded and handcuffed to the seat in the back of DARRIEN's car, a little red car. This was witnessed by a bystander somewhere in OC (Orange County), California, who saw NIKKI being taken out of a car, bound, and called FBI.

NIKKI was blacking out because of the concussion and was unconscious part of the way. When they needed to stop for the bathroom, DARRIEN would unbind her and take her in and bring her back and bind her again.

They left OC, California, Friday morning, stayed at hotels Friday and Saturday nights, and left very early in the morning. She was blindfolded, gagged and handcuffed in the back seat the whole time Friday and Saturday.

September 2, 2018

Sunday she was allowed to sit in the front seat, only one wrist was handcuff to a grip near the gear shift. NIKKI got word to DOBY at some point on Sunday that she believed she was being taken to Dallas, back to JANET.

When NIKKI got to JANET, she and DARRIEN used the "bathtub method" to waterboard NIKKI until she started to drown, then would let her recover, and repeat. This was simply to punish her and force her to "remember her place" as a "slave."

JANET's husband, TRENT, was not there that night. Their one-year-old daughter was hospitalized, so JANET's husband was gone staying at the hospital. NIKKI spent the night with JANET, which included abuse, waterboarding, cooking for JANET, sexual performances, etc. She had DARRIEN join in for a while in the punishment, but then made him leave, and NIKKI and JANET had sex the rest of the night.

NIKKI is not angry about these punishments and abuses because she says she deserves them for running away. She believes there is no way to avoid getting punished by them.

Something Bigger Than Overthrowing Small Governments

September 3, 2018

Approximately 8 a.m., NIKKI arrived at ▮▮▮▮▮▮▮ Airport from Texas. JANET put her on a plane back to ▮▮▮▮▮▮▮ from Dallas DFW. DOBY texted TINA (HT ARC) at 8:21 a.m. saying that NIKKI was at the airport needing a ride home to her apartment. NIKKI's uncle was picking her up.

DOBY reported to TINA (HT ARC) that when NIKKI arrived at her apartment, she had a concussion, was weak, short of breath, unstable, nauseated, bleeding from the nose, had a black eye, cuts and bruises. DOBY and TINA (HT ARC) struggled to get her medical attention, but NIKKI refused medical treatment because of her fear and trauma from her torture in D.C.

DOBY asked TINA (HT ARC) for a doctor to come to NIKKI's apartment to render medical aid. TINA (HT ARC) worked on this while navigating her trauma factors (called "triggers") — NIKKI was unwilling to (1) go with anyone she doesn't know (2) be in a medical facility (3) be in the presence of certain medical triggers including, but not limited to: scrubs, needles, masks, oxygen masks, blue gloves, tables, trays, metal tables, bags of fluids/blood, wires, machines, monitors beeping, restraints, fluorescent lighting, knives and scalpels.

DOBY and a friend visited NIKKI in the evening to keep her company, bring her food and watch movies. They reported to TINA (HT ARC) that NIKKI was not wanting medical help. She had bruises on her right eye, a cut on her lip, apparently cuts and bruises elsewhere. She said, "the usual places." She said she just needed to rest.

At 9:26 p.m. a human trafficking advocate colleague, "FOOTPRINT" texted TINA (HT ARC) for help with a client who she was doing all she can for but "nothing is working." TINA (HT ARC) called FOOTPRINT back and quickly realized that the client she was describing was NIKKI. FOOTPRINT had been providing support and referrals to resources to NIKKI for several weeks. TINA (HT ARC) provided FOOTPRINT her Google Voice number to encourage NIKKI to call TINA (HT ARC) for assistance. TINA (HT ARC) and FOOTPRINT discussed NIKKI's current injuries and the urgency of getting medical help to NIKKI for her concussion. FOOTPRINT worked to navigate medical providers who could eliminate the use of scrubs and medical tools in order to facilitate a CT scan and other necessary medical evaluations.

September 4, 2018

TINA (HT ARC) made some phone calls to ▓▓▓▓▓▓▓ and others who arranged for several options, but were struggling to eliminate all of NIKKI's trigger factors from being present in the medical evaluation, and to find medical professionals who could go to her apartment instead of a medical facility.

MAHALIA called TINA (HT ARC) at 10:48 a.m. and reported that FBI had contacted her and that she had an appointment with FBI at 2 p.m. that same day. TINA (HT ARC) advised MAHALIA to cooperate with FBI and answer their questions, to remain very calm, not to become defensive or fearful, as to do so would only complicate the situation.

MAHALIA returned from a church retreat in Hume Lake. She had taken one year as a pre-med major and intern and knows emergency medicine. MAHALIA went to NIKKI's apartment to clean her up, bandage her and do a cursory medical evaluation. She reported that NIKKI showed signs of concussion. "It hurts when she moves her head, she gets dizzy, she blacks out periodically." MAHALIA insisted on medical help, but NIKKI refused saying she's "had worse before."

At 2:54 p.m. MAHALIA called TINA (HT ARC) and said that she had met with FBI. They had received a report over the past weekend of someone matching NIKKI's description seen being taken out of a car bound and was seen being unbound to leave the car. FBI agent "Steve," blond, blue eyes, tattoo sleeve, handsome, said FBI had "nothing on her," and was questioning the validity of NIKKI's situation. He asked if NIKKI's real name was even her real name.

FBI agent Steve arrived at NIKKI's apartment that evening (time unknown) to talk with NIKKI and try to verify her injuries. NIKKI was alone when FBI arrived. Two FBI agents, Agent Steve and an FBI woman attempted to talk to NIKKI. They went inside her apartment, but NIKKI did not give information. She said she would not speak to them without an attorney present. They asked her about her black eye, and she said, "it was an eventful weekend." They asked if she was okay, and she said she was fine.

MAHALIA visited NIKKI at approximately 5 p.m., shortly after FBI had left. MAHALIA texted TINA (HT ARC) that NIKKI had what looked like the beginning of "head lack." Her eyes bounced when she was tracking visually. NIKKI finally agreed with MAHALIA to get medical help the next day (9/5). She insisted on no scrubs and that we eliminate the presence of her triggers. She preferred for them to come to her.

TINA (HT ARC) and ███████ found a trauma-informed medical clinic that could take NIKKI the following morning (9/6), but none of NIKKI's trusted friends were available to transport her. TINA (HT ARC) deferred to FOOTPRINT to arrange something else because NIKKI already knew and trusted FOOTPRINT.

NIKKI had an appointment with a new therapist at 6 p.m., but shortly into their session, the therapist said that she might need to call authorities to report what NIKKI was saying and report her injuries. NIKKI became alarmed and abruptly left the office, never to visit that therapist again. FOOTPRINT texted TINA (HT ARC) that NIKKI was going to drive to LA to meet her at 8 p.m. at the Starbucks at her building. NIKKI did not show up.

September 5, 2018

MAHALIA told NIKKI that FBI had called and told her they were dropping the case.

September 8, 2018

DOBY texted TINA (HT ARC) that NIKKI had been very depressed and blaming herself for surviving when others did not.

September 9, 2018

NIKKI was struggling heavily with flashbacks of the eliminations. She texted and called FOOTPRINT all throughout the day and evening.

September 10, 2018

FOOTPRINT orchestrated an amazing and successful effort by physicians (dressed in T-shirts) to give NIKKI a full medical evaluation and CT scan. ▆▆▆▆ is the Emergency Director at ▆▆▆▆ ▆▆▆▆▆▆▆▆▆▆▆▆▆▆, who brilliantly tended to NIKKI's needs and avoided her triggers. FOOTPRINT was there to coordinate between NIKKI and the medical staff. A brilliant job was done by everyone and NIKKI did just fine.

September 11, 2018

But NIKKI was discouraged about her psychological recovery. She had a bad experience with her new counselor, who threatened to report to police, and was rejected for services by PTV (Program for Torture Victims) because she was not a refugee. NIKKI began threatening to run away to Vegas (Las Vegas, NV) to make her traffickers jealous that she was prostituting without them, so they would come get her. She said, "I need my life back."

She texted and called FOOTPRINT repeatedly and told DOBY she was packing up and running to Vegas because she "needs her life back." DOBY texted TINA (HT ARC) and TINA (HT ARC) texted FOOTPRINT to call her and try to prevent her from running. NIKKI actually got as far as Victorville, but then returned home to her apartment

September 12, 2018

MAHALIA left ▆▆▆▆ Church at night and a ▆▆▆▆ police officer or officers in a police cruiser followed her out of the church parking lot all the way up to her neighborhood. But they pulled away when she stopped short of her house, since she knew she was being followed. This gave everyone great concern for her safety, given the fact that there appeared to be a strong corrupt law enforcement component to the equation regarding NIKKI's trafficked life.

September 13, 2018

TINA (HT ARC) re-ran background reports and searches on STEVE looking for updates. She discovered that STEVE's background report had been altered since her first search — all the names of his known

Something Bigger Than Overthrowing Small Governments

affiliates had been removed and replaced with "John Doe." Their photos had also been removed. She alerted BAZZEL BAZ, Founder and President of *ARC, The Association for the Recovery of Children*, and informed DOBY and MAHALIA to "lay low" and stop talking about the case, since it was possible that STEVE was tipped off and was trying to undermine the investigation.

FOOTPRINT arranged to invite NIKKI to meet TINA (HT ARC) for lunch at Chick Fil A at 12:15 p.m. 18605 Gridley Rd. Cerritos, CA. They all arrived separately. NIKKI came dressed provocatively, like she was "working." Four LA Sheriff Dept. Officers happened to come in right as the ladies were ordering their food. NIKKI was traumatized and removed herself to a back-corner table. The three ladies started to eat, but the Sheriff personnel wound up coming to a table right next to them, so the ladies moved outside. They spent about an hour and ½ eating and talking outside. NIKKI started to trust and build rapport with TINA (HT ARC).

September 14, 2018

In the evening, NIKKI texted TINA (HT ARC), FOOTPRINT, DOBY and MAHALIA and threatened to run to Vegas again. TINA (HT ARC) ignored NIKKI's Vegas threats completely without acknowledgement and instead suggested doing a fun outing with NIKKI the next week. NIKKI sounded excited.

Meanwhile, for several hours, DOBY and FOOTPRINT had intense and emotional conversations with NIKKI, trying to talk NIKKI out of leaving for Vegas. TINA (HT ARC) advised everyone to put the responsibility back on NIKKI and tell her she was making a poor choice, but that no one was going to circumvent her will and try to stop her. There was a clear attention-getting tactic on the part of NIKKI. She even said she wanted her traffickers or someone else to come save her. Everyone stopped responding to NIKKI's threats. TINA (HT ARC) texted her at 10:30 p.m. and said, "See you next week. Nite!" and NIKKI responded cheerfully that she was excited about it. NIKKI never left for Vegas.

September 15, 2018

NIKKI texted TINA (HT ARC) in the evening to say that she would like to get together soon. She insinuated that she might be leaving town. TINA (HT ARC) ignored the "bait" as an attempt to provoke a worry reaction. NIKKI called and texted FOOTPRINT and DOBY threatening to run to Vegas again. They conferred with TINA (HT ARC). Based on NIKKI's statements, TINA (HT ARC) advised all to ignore this threat as manipulation and just say "ok" and not try to stop her.

TINA (HT ARC) told NIKKI that if she was still going to be in town next week, they could meet up to talk. NIKKI seemed cheerful and said that sounded great. NIKKI didn't wind up leaving for Vegas. She stayed home all weekend.

September 17, 2018

NIKKI and TINA met at Starbucks 2219 W Ball Rd, Anaheim, CA 92804, then drove immediately in TINA's (HT ARC) car to Panera Bread 1480 S. Harbor Blvd, Anaheim, across from Disneyland's main entrance.

TINA (HT ARC) asked NIKKI why she always addresses her as "Ma'am." She said, "It's because I'm a slave and I have to, it's a rule. I'm not an equal so it's disrespectful to call anyone superior to me by their name. That's what I was taught anyway."

September 18, 2018

FOOTPRINT called and texted TINA (HT ARC) that NIKKI was calling her excessively. NIKKI had shown up to a survivor support meeting for ▓▓▓▓▓▓▓▓▓▓▓▓▓▓▓▓▓▓▓▓▓▓▓▓▓▓▓▓▓▓, but the location had been moved, and NIKKI was triggered because she was in a bad area being "followed" by a man. TINA (HT ARC) advised

Something Bigger Than Overthrowing Small Governments

FOOTPRINT to calmly give NIKKI firm instructions to stop trying to find the meeting, return immediately to her car and go home.

September 19, 2018

NIKKI and TINA (HT ARC) met at *Pretend City* in Irvine at 10 am, walked through it, went to Irvine Spectrum for brunch at Corner Bakery until 1 p.m.

September 21, 2018

TINA (HT ARC) picked up NIKKI at her apartment leasing office at 3 p.m. and they drove to Baldwin Park to pick up an order for TINA (HT ARC). NIKKI was wearing tight skinny jeans and jacket with 5-inch-high heels.

They ate an early dinner at TGI Fridays at The Block of Orange, returned back around 7 p.m., went to Anaheim theaters by the Honda Center to watch "Christopher Robin," then went to Downtown Disney and walked and talked until about 11:30, when TINA took her back to her apartment. NIKKI had a great time but triggered going through security at Downtown Disney because they used the wand scanner, since her outfit set off the metal detector.

NIKKI shared with TINA (HT ARC) two poems (included previously). She sent picture-mail of hand-written poems she wrote about her torture experiences in Washington D.C. and about her time with DAVID being captive chained to a bed.

September 22, 2018

NIKKI texted TINA (HT ARC) that she was struggling with depression and could not get out of bed. She was forcing herself to try to eat. She was having flashbacks that she could not seem to turn off.

September 24, 2018

TINA and NIKKI's other supporters had been helping her to apply and interview for jobs. TINA (HT ARC) texted NIKKI about getting together for lunch on Tuesday, 9/25 to prepare for her interview with Disneyland.

NIKKI offered to have TINA (HT ARC) over to her apartment to cook for her (she used to cook for JANET). TINA (HT ARC) felt uncomfortable with the psychological association, and with being in NIKKI's apartment without a third person, so she suggested that she would rather treat NIKKI to lunch somewhere instead of having NIKKI go to the expense and trouble of making lunch.

At 6 p.m. NIKKI texted TINA (HT ARC) that she was thinking of "going out" because she was "getting the urge" and she hadn't "gone out in a while." TINA (HT ARC) was on another call and did not respond for 20 minutes. NIKKI texted, "Nvm, I'm sorry, I'm just gonna go." TINA (HT ARC) saw this as a manipulative tactic and responded, "I've been on some phone calls ... You know I won't chase you or try to stop you. You should listen to some worship songs on your phone. The urge would totally leave you. I promise."

NIKKI responded that she decided not to go out. She'd been depressed because of memories of her "siblings'" (fellow slaves') birthdays. TINA (HT ARC) continued to text chat with NIKKI until 8:30 p.m. and NIKKI's mood improved.

All afternoon and evening TINA (HT ARC) strengthened her ▮▮▮▮ covers and continued to research leads related to the case. At 11:30 p.m. TINA (HT ARC) determined the identity and history, background, social media, etc. of JANET and found her to be a match to NIKKI's descriptions, dates, and information.

September 25, 2018

NIKKI and TINA (HT ARC) met at 11 a.m. at Chipotle 2773 N. Main Street, Santa Ana, CA 92705. NIKKI shared a picture of herself at age seven just before her parents sold her away. She also shared a poem she wrote about being locked in a storage room by ARMSTRONG as punishment/torture.

TINA and NIKKI spent time praying and rehearsing for NIKKI's interview with Disneyland, which wound up going very well. They decided to take the day Thursday 9/27 to go do an outing. NIKKI asked if they could go to NIKKI's favorite place, Cracker Barrel in Victorville. TINA agreed.

Something Bigger Than Overthrowing Small Governments

Because NIKKI struggled so much with loneliness and isolation, and those factors contributed to flashbacks, TINA (HT ARC) encouraged NIKKI to reach out to her church friends for socializing and spiritual support. TINA (HT ARC) also texted NIKKI's church friends asking them to reach out to NIKKI.

11:30 p.m. TINA (HT ARC) sent a ▇▇▇▇▇▇▇▇ to JANET's Facebook account. It was rejected the next day 9/26.

September 27, 2018

TINA (HT ARC) picked up NIKKI at 8:30 a.m. and they went to Cracker Barrel in Victorville for breakfast and found a place on the porch to talk for a few hours. They went to Victorville Mall in the afternoon and returned NIKKI home to her apartment at 5:30 p.m.

September 28, 2018

5:30 p.m. NIKKI texted TINA (HT ARC) that she was reaching out for support because she was feeling the urge to go out on the streets and "flirt," and she kind of hoped she "doesn't come back." TINA (HT ARC) responded with several text messages helping her through the point of doubt and helping her stay focused on her positive experiences and good things coming up. NIKKI did not respond.

TINA (HT ARC) contacted FOOTPRINT, who had already received the same messages from NIKKI but was unable to return a call because she was at work. TINA (HT ARC) reinforced that advocates do not control or chase survivors, they help survivors make better decisions, but do not fight against the survivor's will if they are making bad choices.

October 1, 2018

NIKKI GOT HIRED BY DISNEYLAND. NIKKI and TINA (HT ARC) went to The Block of Orange to celebrate. NIKKI got the job and Disneyland in Fantasyland and would start in two weeks.

But the story doesn't end there. Over the course of the next four weeks Nikki decided to leave her Disneyland job and prostitute herself again in hopes that she could eventually make her way back to Janet and Steve. We were able to persuade her to start a deeper dialogue about recovery based on her seemingly sincere request to change her life and leave behind all of the torment associated with the dark world. She expressed her desire to one day open a refuge house for children that had undergone the same abuse she had experienced. It was all worth discussing and figuring out how we could provide guidance, so her dream could come true one day. To begin that process, the first thing she would need in her life was trauma clearing. Since we have been 98% successful with our Restorative Prayer Protocol method, we knew, if given the chance, her healing would begin.

She decided, at the request of Tina (HT ARC), to meet with myself (Bazzel Baz) and Tina in a park in Manhattan Beach, California, and talk about what options she may have for trauma clearing and seeking help for a better life. I was sure the path was paved with good intentions, but her underlying attitude during the meeting seemed suspect. She refused trauma clearing and pretty much shrugged off any good advice. But all was not lost, for at the end of the day she agreed to meet another time, about one week later at the same location.

It was, however, during that week that she threatened again in text to return to the streets and once again prostitute herself. She disappeared off the map, no contact with us or anyone connected with us in the anti-trafficking community. To make things darker, the local news was reporting the discovery of a deceased female body found in suitcase in a garbage dumpster just a few blocks from where Nikki lived. Our hearts sank with the thought of that being her. We wrestled with the thoughts of what could have been done to prevent this, should she be that body found. We came to the conclusion that we had done everything we could and that the one thing we have no power over is the choices people make. Much like the story in my book *The Narrow View*, (www.BazBooks.com), you can give people their heart's desire, all the good they have ever wanted, and if they choose to destroy what you have given them and return to their ugly, diseased world, there is nothing you can do about that.

Something Bigger Than Overthrowing Small Governments

Fortunately, and much to our relief, the body was not that of Nikki, and she did reach out to us one week later. She agreed to meet with us again. During the second meeting we challenged her to look at the biblical foundation of what she herself assumed was justification for being a "slave." The upside-down belief that had been instilled in her head by Janet and Steve to feign God's approval for them to abuse her began to rub her the wrong way, and it was not long before she decided that she could not face the truth set before her, that she was <u>not</u> a slave. She agreed that she would not want any other children to suffer under the same circumstances at the hands of her perpetrators. She agreed that it would be considered wrong for anyone to abuse a child. And at the same time, she could not agree that what Janet and Steve had done to her was wrong. She found it difficult to think that Janet and Steve could be doing this to other children. And in fact, she went to great lengths to defend them in what they had done and said she would never want to see justice served against them for their illegal deeds.

It was pretty messed up, but all so typical of those victims we had dealt with in similar cases ... Stockholm Syndrome at its finest. To add to the mix, I sensed a demonic component at work, the smirk on her face that told me she was not free from whatever possessed her over the years. Could she claim that Jesus Christ was Lord — which even demons do — and in the same breath support the evil deeds of those who destroyed her over time?

We provided the way out, offering her every good option we had, and at the same time reinforced the fact that what had been done to her over the years was not only wrong, but it was illegal, and that those who were guilty of such crimes would eventually be punished. We also drew the line in the sand that should she decide to return to her abusers or continue in prostitution, that what we had to offer would be withdrawn. Too often victims of prostitution and slavery will manipulate situations and take advantage of people who are actually trying to save them, and if anyone new to this game thinks otherwise, they are a fool. Victims of prostitution and slavery have been taught to manipulate, and they have learned that so often it is the only way they can survive. They have trust issues — and rightfully so — but tough love is just about one of the only ways of making them re-evaluate their destructive quagmire. It also keeps an NGO out of the bursting radius of victim's destructive choices, preserving manpower, energy and finances for others who really need help and really want help.

On that day Nikki decided to walk away from an opportunity to change her life for the better. She chose to remain a slave. And the more I thought about how destructive her perpetrators had been and the depth of their brainwashing and manipulation, the more I started to see that Nikki had become one of them. In one breath she would agree that children should never experience what she experienced, and in the next she would say that Janet and Steve and her other perpetrators had a right to treat her the way they did as a child. To the average person that would make no sense, but to people like ourselves, who had been in the fight for such a long time, it totally made sense. She had become a ZOMBIE, so to speak, and with that revelation, I realized there was a potential that what she was actually after in her pursuit of a refuge center for children was not a safe place for restoration but instead a place tucked away from society where she could carry out the same system of brainwashing and sexual abuse without ever being caught ... just like Janet. Looking back on how often she bragged about who her "owners" were and what they were capable of doing, my opinion of her true intentions became more solidified.

Sadly, my conclusion is this ... not all victims can be saved. Not all people who are sexually exploited, especially from early childhood will be able to recover unless God intervenes in a powerful way. And it is for that very reason that we who continue to involve ourselves in the anti-trafficking mission realize how important it is to stop this evil at the headwaters of society. And if, per chance, those on the anti-trafficking battlefield run into a similar situation as we did with Nikki, I want to reiterate ... weigh out the amount of time, energy and resources to see if you are spinning your wheels or investing in a lost cause.

There are thousands, if not tens of thousands, of children and children who are now adults that will gratefully accept your help, unlike Nikki. Be sure that you do not drive your operations solely on compassion. Reason is the capacity for consciously making sense of things, establishing and verifying facts, applying logic and changing or justifying practices and beliefs based on the information you have

Something Bigger Than Overthrowing Small Governments

acquired. Use it. Intuition is the ability to understand something immediately without the need for conscious reasoning. Use it. Prayer is the act or practice of speaking to God and in this case asking that the Holy Spirit guide you in your reasoning and confirm your intuitions. Use it.

Trust me when I tell you that we will never win the war on trafficking until God returns to this earth. It is much bigger than all of us and has existed almost since the beginning of time. But what we can do until He returns to clean it all up is fight the good fight and put a huge dent in the way traffickers operate, slowing the process. We can build an army of people who realize that saving one child at a time may not change the world, but for that one child their world will change forever.

Nothing is perfect in this world, especially the people. Realizing that law enforcement is inundated with crimes hour after hour, it is not a surprise that most officers reach their breaking point and are just as frustrated with the insurmountable, never ending demands of this world on their professional and personal life. They barely have time to breathe. It is certainly no excuse for not doing their job, but it does provide some insight as to why good law enforcement officers who start out with good intentions can eventually get to a point where all they want to do is live long enough to retire and keep their own family intact during the process. It is not an easy profession, but it is one that requires them to stay the course day in and day out if they intend to honor the oath.

That said, we as NGOs must always remind ourselves of their burden and encourage them to stand firm and do what they were called to do. We must be willing to come alongside with our intelligence resources and tradecraft and assist where most appropriate. We are not always well-received because our intelligence collection systems may be far more advanced, or our credentials more intimidating, but we must remember that we are all in this to save a child and with that comes setting aside differences — not by any means accepting excuses or overlooking incompetence but finding how we best help one another.

For this reason, personal relationships are so important, like the relationships ARC has with Detective Marcella Winn, Journalist Anita

Bush, and members of the LASD, LAPD, law enforcement departments across the U.S., Human Trafficking Task Forces, and with the FBI, DHS, ICE and DOJ. Once you bond human to human, the dialogue changes to something much more effective than just two entities. Most of the time it changes to two friends willing to do whatever it takes to ensure the best outcome for all parties. And for those law enforcement associates who, as in the case here with Nikki, chose to cross the line and involve themselves in the crime of human trafficking, let it be known that in the eyes of the public and officers who did not cross that line — the very people that trusted you — you have broken that trust. It isn't a matter of being disappointed in you, it is a matter of knowing that every single one of us intend to seek you out and ensure that you pay a heavy penalty under a ethical judicial system for doing such. You have no excuse for what you have done, and no excuse will be accepted.

In early July 2019, an ARC asset was contacted by someone claiming to be the FBI and was flown to Houston, Texas to identify the deceased body of Nikki. The asset was met by two men who did not show Federal Agent identification. She was taken to a non-descript building where she positively identified the mangled body parts of Nikki, which were presented in four separate body bags. Nikki had been brutally murdered and hacked to pieces.

The abnormalities in protocol on the part of these so-called FBI agents brings into question who exactly they were. It also brings into question their access to information that was written in the ARC Intelligence Report that was submitted to the Integrity Unit of the law enforcement office where Steve was employed — a report that by all means should have been held as a sensitive document and not disclosed to any of the suspects noted in the report. The fact that the ARC asset was notified and the fact that Nikki's body was identified could lead us to believe that the Integrity Unit of the law enforcement agency where Steve was employed did in fact leak the ARC Intelligence Report, thereby warning the suspects, who then initiated a witness disposal plan of the primary witness, Nikki. The timing was too coincidental.

ARC inquired with FBI regarding Nikki's death and FBI responded that they had no information on the people who claimed to be FBI, nor the trip to Houston, nor the fact that Nikki was even dead. So

Something Bigger Than Overthrowing Small Governments

the question remains, who are these other suspicious actors? How far does corruption exist within the ranks of this particular law enforcement agency where Steve is employed? And more than all of this, what does the FBI intend to do with this case now that it has been fully reported?

Recommendations:

For the purposes of this operation, vetting is the process of performing a background check on someone before allowing any affiliation with ARC and its operations, and in doing so, fact-checking prior to making any decision to affiliate. Such affiliates may include law enforcement, judicial systems and personnel, strategic partners, other NGOs, security personnel and the victim themselves. During the required intelligence gathering, assets are vetted to determine their usefulness as well as any level of corruption, prior, during and after operations. The vetting process should never be overlooked or discarded as non-essential, nor should operations advance nor meetings be taken with unknowns until all vetting is complete, even if operations are in play.

Chapter 20
BY WHAT AUTHORITY

I am so often reminded of my wish list when I get to heaven and stand before God. It's actually pretty simple ... one request. I want to be the first person with sword and shield in hand on the front lines of God's army leading the charge against Satan and his army. I want to be the first person out front spearheading the attack that will ultimately put Satan and his principalities of darkness to an end for all eternity. I've seen it in my heart since I was a boy and I felt it in my heart every time I spoke with God and God spoke to me.

"Wait, God speaks to you? I find that rather odd," some have said.

"Of course, He does," I reply. "You mean He doesn't speak to you? Now I find that rather odd. And I find it sad that you would not be able to hear the voice of our Creator."

Now most who read this lean more towards thinking that I might be a little delusional ... actually believing that hearing God is something that people of the world find impossible. But once you experience it, your entire perspective on who God is and the power He has suddenly changes. It is as if you know that you know that you know, and no one can convince you otherwise. And who are they to tell you differently, because it is your experience, not theirs. Just because they cannot hear or see God does not invalidate your experience or mine. The Holy Scriptures (Bible) make it very clear that the population of the world that does not know God acts like the blind leading the blind. "Satan, who is the god of this world, has blinded the minds of those who don't believe. They are unable to see the glorious light of the Good News. They don't understand this message about the glory of Christ, who is the exact likeness of God." (2 Corinthians 4:4 NLT).

And that explains it all. They can't hear or see ... but I can, and I do. And it is how I run my operations at ARC because the battle we fight is against those principalities of darkness that are out to destroy the

Something Bigger Than Overthrowing Small Governments

innocent children of this world so that they may never have a chance to know their Creator, know what it is like to be happy and know that they are safe forever. God has made it very clear in my life that He has given me power to defeat the enemy and it has played itself out time and time again with every single rescue ARC has on file. With that type of success, I know I am doing what God has called me to do. Josh McDowell, author of *A Ready Defense,* describes the authority given by God to those who believe in Jesus Christ and everything he says has paralleled the guidance God has given me throughout my life and especially in ARCs mission.

>"Behold, I give unto you power to tread on serpents and scorpions, and over all the power of the enemy; and nothing shall by any means hurt you.'" (Luke 10:19 KJV)
>
>Two separate Greek words are used for *power* here, but one English translation. The first one should be translated *authority*, not *power*. The Lord is saying, "behold, I give you authority over the power of the enemy." The Christian does not have *power* over Satan; he has *authority* over Satan. Let me give you and illustration. I used to live in Argentina. Buenos Aires, the second largest city in the western hemisphere, has six subway lines, one of the longest streets in the world (almost 60 miles long) and one of the widest streets in the world (25 lanes, almost three blocks wide). One street is called Corrente, which means *current.* It is a solid current of traffic ... sometimes considered one of the longest parking lots in the world.
>
>One intersection is so busy, about the only way you can make it across is to confess any unknown sin, make sure you are filled with the Spirit, commit your life to the Lord and dash madly! But one day we approached, and an amazing thing took place. Out in the center of the intersection was a platform, on which stood a uniformed policeman. About 20 of us waited at the corner to cross. All of a sudden, he blew his whistle and put up his hand. As he lifted his hand, all those cars came to a screeching halt. With all of his personal power he couldn't have stopped one of those cars, but he had something far better; he was invested with authority of the police department. And the moving cars and the pedestrians

recognized that authority. So first, we see that <u>*authority is delegated power*</u>.

Second, let's examine the source of this authority. Paul writes about:

> What is the surpassing greatness of His Power toward us who believe. These are in accordance with the working of the strength of His might which He brought about in Christ, when He raised Him from the dead, and seated Him at His right hand in the heavenly places, far above all rule and authority and power and dominion, and every name that is named, not only in this age, but also in the one to come. And He put all things in subjection under His feet, and gave Him as head over all things to the Church, which is His body, the fullness of Him who fills all in all. (Ephesians 1:19-23 NASB)

When Jesus Christ was raised from the dead, we see the act of the resurrection and the surrounding events as one of the greatest workings of God manifested in the Scriptures. So powerful was the omnipotence of God that the Holy Spirit, through the apostle Paul, used four different words for *power*. First, the greatness of His power-in the Greek- is *dunamis*, from which comes the English word *dynamite*. Then comes the word *working-energios*, where energy comes from — a working manifestation or activity. The third word is *strength-kratous*-meaning "to exercise strength." Then comes *might*, or *esquai* — a "great summation of power."

These four words signify that behind the events described in Ephesians 1:19-23 are the greatest workings of God manifested in the Scriptures-even greater than creation. This great unleashing of God's might involved in the resurrection, the ascension and the seating of Jesus Christ. "When He had disarmed the rulers and authorities, He made a public display of them, having triumphed over them through Him" (Colossians 2:15, NASB) Satan was defeated and disarmed. All of this unleashing of God's might in the resurrection, the ascension and the seating of Jesus Christ was for you and me- that we might gain victory right now over Satan. *Our authority over Satan is rooted in God and His power.*

Third, what are the qualifications you must have to be able to be consistent in exercising the authority of the

Something Bigger Than Overthrowing Small Governments

believer? *First* there must be _knowledge_, a knowledge of our position in Christ and of Satan's defeat. At the moment of salvation we are elevated to a heavenly placement. We don't have to climb some ladder of faith to get there. WE are immediately identified in the eyes of God-and of Satan-with Christ's crucifixion and burial, and we are co-resurrected, co-ascended and co-seated with Jesus Christ at the right hand of the Father, far above all rule and power, authority and dominion and above every name that is named.

The problem is that, though both God and Satan are aware of this, most believers are not. And if you don't understand who you are, you will never exercise that authority which is the birthright of every true believer in Jesus. So the first step is knowledge.

The *second* qualification is _belief_. A lot of people really don't comprehend one of the primary aspects of belief, which is "to live in accordance with." This is not merely mental assent, but it leads to action. You could say it like this: That which the mind accepts, the will obeys. Otherwise you are not really a true believer. Do we actually believe that we've been co-resurrected, co-ascended, co-seated with Jesus Christ? If we do, our actions will be fervent.

We should wake up each morning and say something like, "Lord, I accept my position. I acknowledge it to be at the right hand of the Father, and today, through the Holy Spirit, cause it to be a reality in me that I might experience victory." You talk about space walking! A Christian who is filled with the Holy Spirit and who knows his position with Christ is walking in the heavenlies. Put it like this: Before you can be any earthly good, you have to be heavenly minded. Your mind should be set at the right hand of the Father, knowing who you are.

Often, when I wake up in the morning, while my eyes are still closed, I go over my position in Christ, thanking the Holy Spirit for indwelling me, etc. But every morning, I acknowledge my position in Christ. I don't have to drum it up-I ask the Holy Spirit to make my position real in my experience.

The third qualification is _humility_. While belief introduces us to our place of throne power at the right hand of the Father, only humility will ensure that we can exercise that power continuously. Let me tell you, ever since Mr. and Mrs. Adam occupied the Garden of Eden, man has needed to be reminded of his limitations. Even regenerated man thinks he can live without seriously considering his total dependence upon God.

Yet, humility to me is not going around saying, "I'm nothing, I'm nothing, I'm nothing. I'm just the dirt under the toenail. When I get to heaven all I want is that little old dinky cabin, that's enough for me." That's an insult to Christ. It's not humility-its pride. Humility is knowing who you are and knowing who made you who you are and giving Him the glory for it. Sometimes, when I hear a person claim he's nothing, I say, "Look, Sir, I don't know about you, but I'm someone." I am someone. On December 19, 1959, at 8L30 at night, Jesus Christ made me a child of God, and I'm sure not going to say I'm nothing. Maybe I'm not all I should be, but I am more than I used to be, and God's not finished with me yet. I know He has made me, and I won't insult what God has made.

The next qualification, the *fourth* one, is <u>boldness.</u> Humility allows the greatest boldness. True boldness is faith in full manifestation. When God has spoken and you hold back, that is not faith, it is sin. We need men and women who have set their minds at the right hand of the Father and who fear no one but God. True boldness comes from realizing your position in Jesus Christ and being filled with the Holy Spirit.

The *fifth* and final qualification is <u>awareness</u>, a realization that being at the right hand of the Father also puts you in the place of the most intense spiritual conflict. The moment your eyes are open to the fact that you are in that place, that you have been co-resurrected, co-ascended and co-seated with Christ, Satan will do everything he possibly can to wipe you out, to discourage you. You become a marked individual. The last thing Satan wants is a Spirit-filled believer who knows his throne right. Satan will start working in your life to cause you not to study or to appropriate principles which show you how to defeat him."
(32, Chapter 39, pages 395-398)

As silly as all of this may seem to someone who is not a believer, the fact is, we have a 100% success rate in that every child God has sent us after, we have brought safely home. Those are the facts.

Something Bigger Than Overthrowing Small Governments

And so, it is with this _authority_ that I boldly take ARC and its operators into the field each time to do what God has called us to do ... rescue missing and exploited American children. And it is with this _authority_ that I challenge anyone or anything to stand in our way when it comes to our mission.

We live in a world where man has taken the principles of God and either abandoned them or turned them upside down on their head, where moral absolutes are being eliminated and truth and honor are being redefined to suit the corruptible nature — everything Satan would want to accomplish. And in that process Satan is about to destroy everything we love in this life ... if we miss _the point of our existence_. When I stand in front of the mirror each morning and look at myself, I remember that my value is not in what I do but in who I am. When you stand in front of the mirror and look at yourself, do you understand that your value is not in what you do but in who you are?

So who are you? Are you a person that realizes that it is your heart ... not the dictionary that gives meaning to your words? "A good man out of the good treasures of his heart brings forth good things and an evil man out of the evil treasures brings forth evil things," (Matthew 12:35 KJV).

By the time you finish this book I want you to become a person who gets the attention of the world and then impacts it. So who are you?

Well I can't speak for everyone reading this book, but I can speak for myself. I'm a warrior. Warriors are the only ones who stand between the enemy and our loved ones, our country and whatever else we value. If this is something that resonates with you then maybe you're a warrior as well. This is our mission and it is a lifetime mission. Once you are a warrior you cannot be something else ... that is who you are. It becomes part of your DNA, and in fact I would go as far as to say that it is part of your spiritual DNA from the beginning.

Too many people fight against themselves to be something other than what they are, other than what God made them to be — warriors. Warriors are written about throughout the entire Holy Bible ... Gideon and King David, just to name a few.

Bazzel Baz

  I know all of this to be true about warriors because I have lived as one for generations ... from the time my grandfather fought against the Ottoman Empire to all of my uncles and my own father, who served in the U.S. Military through the Korean War, Vietnam and myself, being down range from 1978 when I first entered the United States Marine Corps, my time in CIA SpecOps from 85-96 and later as a Paramilitary Contractor. So what I learned was to embrace who I am and take the examples from the warriors of the Bible who loved God with all their heart and used their skill set to further the purposes of God.

  On a couple of occasions down range when things got a little sticky, I remember telling my men, "We fall where we stand." It was our way of saying that we would never retreat, we would never allow the enemy to get by.

  I remember hearing someone else tell the story about an outpost under fire in Vietnam where my father was in command. On a given night when all the ammunition ran out, my father gave the battle cry, "Fix bayonets." The enemy came through the wire and when the sun came up the next morning, not all were standing but the battle had been won and the enemy defeated. Now that is not something I have ever experienced in my military career, nor do I welcome it, but my father and his men held their ground at all cost, and they won. Why? Because they were defending someone or something they loved. He was sending a message to the enemy that it was not going to be easy for them, and if they wanted to cross the line then they were going to be in for the fight of their lives ... and so it was. It took great sacrifice and courage, but most of all it took giving control up to God.

  How many of you reading this book have someone you love, someone who perhaps has journeyed on from this life into eternity? Did they sacrifice for you? How did they sacrifice for you? *Remember, the life of the dead is placed in the memory of the living.* As you take a moment to think about that, let me tell you something that will set things in stone for you. If you loved them ... <u>honor them with the way you live your life</u>.

  When you fail to do your best, to do what is right, when you do things that destroy you physically or mentally or spiritually, whether that involves drugs, alcohol, pornography, anger, greed, etc., you are

Something Bigger Than Overthrowing Small Governments

being selfish and irresponsible. You are delinquent in your duties. It is like laying down your weapons or sleeping on post, all the while knowing that the enemy is just outside the gates waiting to get in. The enemy, the darkness, Satan wants to slaughter everything you love, your family, your job, your sound mind, income, health, friends, your relationship with the Holy Father, etc. because Satan is afraid that you will say, *"We fall where we stand."*

Now no doubt there are those reading this book that will say, "I don't believe in Satan and I don't believe in God." Fair enough. But can I share with you another fact? Satan and God don't need your belief or unbelief in order to exist. In the scheme of things people who make those statements need to deal with their smallness because when they die ... and we all will one day ... they are going to stand before one or the other. I've yet to see a man or woman on their death bed have the power to stop themselves from dying when God called in their number. So call it what you want, but there is a greater power than man ... it's God.

The battle for the souls is as real as the battle for the flesh. Like I said, warriors are the only ones that stand between the enemy and the people you love. Honor them with the way you live your life ... be strong, stay in God's Word, set the examples of holiness and DO NOT allow the enemy to come through the wire even if you run out of ammunition. And if you do, then fix bayonets and ready yourself to get bloody and take the enemy with you into the trenches, and when you have them down there ... be relentless. Make this your vow as a warrior because it is *who you are*. It is who God made you to be and you cannot be anything other than that. It is your brand into eternity.

Now most of you will say that what I am suggesting takes more than you have to give in life. Perhaps you are beaten down and the road traveled has been long and hard and you're really tired. I get it. So let me offer you an answer to eternal strength, the weapon that never runs out of ammunition, the 782 gear that is as light as a feather, the armor that no 7.62 can penetrate and the communications gear that never has interference ... *trust!* It's that simple ... *trust*! And for the purposes of this book ... *trust in God*.

Ahhhhhh but *trust* requires understanding. If I can understand who God is and what God is doing in my life and I can understand where I need to go, then I can accomplish the mission and make things work out as I expect according to my battle plan. Then I can control things better. That's how a warrior wins the war, right? Wrong!

Most people have conversations with themselves when things don't go exactly as expected. They waste energy trying to understand why. This is a distraction by the enemy. In warfare, especially spiritual warfare, the enemy does whatever it can to create distractions so they can launch another attack from a different direction. If you have ever studied the history of warfare, or better yet experienced it, then you may have heard of the "indirect approach" on the battlefield.

Dislocation is the aim of strategy. Direct attacks almost never work. One must first upset the enemy's equilibrium by applying the eight rules of strategy.

1. Adjust your ends to your means
2. Keep your objective always in mind
3. Choose the line of the least expectation
4. Exploit the line of least resistance
5. Take the line of operations which offers the most alternatives
6. Ensure both plans and disposition are flexible
7. Do not throw your weight into an opponent while he is on guard
8. Do not renew an attack along the same lines if an attack has failed

Therefore, I submit that trying to understand everything God is doing in your life opens you up to all eight of these tactics by the enemy. Stop having the conversation with yourself. And once again, to reiterate the wisdom of my mother, we are all flawed as human beings and we cannot control all the uncontrollable circumstances. Nor do you and I know what the master plan for our life is and how to always navigate the fault lines in order to ultimately reach the success of that master plan. Have your conversation with God and in that conversation "trust in the Lord with all your heart and lean not on your own understanding" (Proverbs 3:5 NKJV). It isn't important to waste energy on understanding, but it is important to put energy into accepting. Once

Something Bigger Than Overthrowing Small Governments

you accept that you do not need to understand, you are ready to understand *accepting.* If you accept God for who He is and the fact that He loves you and has your best interest at heart, you will no longer waste energy on something you have absolutely no *control* over.

Ahhhhhh, which brings me to *control*. How many of you like being in control? How many of you get frustrated when you cannot control the outcome of events? How many of you get frustrated and even angry when things are out of control and you don't understand why?

May I share another fact with you? Ours is never to be in control. If you think you will ever be in control you are barking up the wrong tree. God is in control, just like the very breath you have in your lungs right now ... He controls that. He controls everything, and the sooner you give in to that reality — which by the way isn't going to change until you leave this planet — the sooner you will relieve yourself of stress and frustration. Yours is to only apply yourself and your God-given talents and do it with 100% of what you have ... the outcome is God's.

For you who do not know the story of Gideon in the Bible, let me recap for you.

> Gideon was a warrior in the Bible who was convinced that God wanted him to lead this group of men who had gathered around him. But God said that Gideon had too many men. God wanted Israel to know that it was not the might of 32,000 men that saved Israel, but God Himself. God asked Gideon to pare down his army.
>
> Gideon said that the men who were afraid to go to battle were welcome to return home. It must have been disheartening to see 22,000 men turn around and walk away. But Gideon was left with 10,000 brave men (Judges 7:2, 3). Even though these men were brave, they were not all wise. God asked Gideon to take them down to the river and watch them drink. The number of those who drank while keeping guard of their surroundings was 300 men. The other 9,700 bowed down to the water losing sight of potential enemy attacks. God said that the 300 would become Gideon's army to fight against the Midianites in the book of Judges 7:4-8.

And according to the book of Judges 8:10 there were at least 135,000 enemy troops against Gideon's 300 soldiers. [33]

Gideon took his faith, took 300 men, did not lean to his own understanding, trusted God and won the battle. Believe it or not you and I have absolutely no control over the outcome of things. We can apply ourselves and, if done correctly, can influence the outcome to some degree. But even that can change at the flip of a switch — we've all seen that happen — if God wants it to be different than we anticipate.

Remember what God said, "Trust in the Lord with all your heart, and lean not on your own understanding" (Proverbs 3:5 NKJV). So we don't need to understand why things happen or do not happen. We have to trust God that it is for His reason and because He loves us. It is good for us and believe me, it is really bad for the enemy. God is not mean, but He can be dangerous especially against the enemy, which brings me to exactly that ... *the enemy*.

Know the enemy and make sure the enemy not only remains outside the gate, but that you take it upon yourself to leave the green zone/fortress and hunt Satan down, whether that is door to door, city to city or nation to nation, and with the strength of God send him and all who work for him back to the pits of hell for eternity.

"Do not be afraid of the enemy, remember the Lord and imprint Him on your mind, great and terrible, and fight for your brother, your sons, your daughters, your wives and our homes" (Nehemiah 4:14 NKJV).

The verse in Nehemiah shows Nehemiah a strong and wise leader. Not only did he seek and rely on God, he also knew that the people needed to be ready to fight in the strength of the Lord. Let me encourage you today. Fight for your home. Fight for your children. Fight for your right to live free from guilt and condemnation. Fight for your right to

Something Bigger Than Overthrowing Small Governments

live under the grace of God and not be bound by legalism. Fight for your right to be happy. Fight for the dreams God has put in your heart. Fight for the fight of faith. That means hold on, don't give up and above all that you do, trust God because He is fighting for and with you. Refuse to settle for anything less than everything God has for you and be thankful that with God on your side, there is no way you can lose the fight. [34]

And that is the ***point of your existence***.

Bazzel Baz

Chapter 21
HOW TO MURDER A CHILD WITHOUT KILLING THEM

The Association for the Recovery of Children (ARC) is a non-profit organization of former intelligence, military and law enforcement officers, dedicated to the safe recovery of missing and exploited American children on domestic and international soil. These child recovery missions are carried out at no cost to the custodial guardians. What we lack in donations for this cause, we pull from our own pocket. It is our calling. As I have previously stated, currently ARC is blessed to have a 100% success rate in that every child we have gone after ... we have safely brought home.

For such a time as this God has created me. From the days of my ancestors until now, my destiny has been forged and my calling announced. This battlefield is like no other. I know the time is near. God is bringing forth an army of men and women dedicated first in their love for Him and second in their love for justice. Saving children will be no small thing as we enter a dimension of spiritual warfare that has preyed upon young souls. Now is our time and we want them back ... God wants them back. I am being approached by people of faith time and time again who have the most interesting qualifications and bring the most interesting requests for ARC. Either they want to partner strategically with ARC or enter into discussions about things they know concerning victims who are trapped, where they are trapped, how many are trapped. The inquiries come at the oddest places and times, from people who know someone who knows me from years past, who trust me to listen to the secrets they have.

I questioned what God was doing for years. Now I simply listen and map out the events that seemingly open doors to the future, which I see all too well. God is good. I march forward with the attitude of Gideon, "Let us go down there and see what God will do." I don't give God instructions ... I just show up for duty. Some may call it blind

Something Bigger Than Overthrowing Small Governments

faith, others stupidity. God doesn't call the qualified ... He qualifies the called. And God doesn't have a special plan for us ... He graciously allows us to be a part of His great plan. I am not a man concerned with what this world thinks. I am not looking for its approval or its applause. I know clearly the difference between right and wrong, good and evil, success and failure. And I know who stands with me. In knowing all of these things, I count myself blessed to have been chosen for a mission in life that few will ever accept. If I sound to you like a man determined to make a difference in this world, then your ears do not deceive you.

The years as a warrior have taught me to line up the targets so that one will fall after the other — a chain reaction of sorts — to maximize my energy and the efforts of my men. "I have done so much for so long with so little that I can do anything with nothing." I believe I first heard that quote from the United States Marine Corps and I have come to depend on it as a pillar of strength in my thinking when I have no resources to draw from. I believe David probably thought the same way when he was avoiding King Saul because he certainly proved it in the end. Now that I think about it, he probably proved it in the beginning when he slew Goliath. Five stones, no armor, no brave men to back him, a single frontal attack sprinting toward his enemy, and he won.

Keeping my thoughts aligned, I study with great intensity to understand the fault lines that must be navigated and the barriers that must fall, the very barriers that currently prevent us from winning this war against human trafficking and the exploitation of children.

The first barrier, and probably one of the most important, involves accountability. We live in a society that believes that once you have discovered a crime, you've done something to stop it from ever happening again simply because you discovered it. It is reflected in the highest offices of our land when those who are supposed to set the example of righteousness, honor, truth and dignity fail miserably at it and are never held accountable. There have been many such events, but those that have occurred in recent history have gained my attention. Perhaps that is because I know from good intelligence that those involved, who were never held accountable, were also involved in the exploitation of children. That has caused me to look with a microscopic lens. For example:

The Lewinsky scandal was an American political sex scandal in 1998, referring to a sexual relationship between 49-year-old President Bill Clinton and a 25-year-old White House employee, Monica Lewinsky. During a televised speech, Clinton ended with the statement that he did not have sexual relations with Lewinsky. Further investigation led to charges of perjury and led to the impeachment of President Clinton in 1998 by the U.S. House of Representatives and his subsequent acquittal on all impeachment charges of perjury and obstruction of justice in a 21-day Senate trial. [35]

So how did that happen? He was found guilty and then not? While I don't approve of his adulterous actions in the White House, what bothers me most is the fact that he lied to the American public ... which brings into question what else he had lied about or would lie about in the future? Even sadder ... he was reelected to the Presidency. Our justice system took a turn for the worse, for it was clear that any other American under the same circumstance would have never been allowed a foot back in the door of a position he or she had criminally abused, in a public office, an educational institution or a business just to name a few. In short, he was not held accountable, or at least was not held accountable to a degree that would prevent him from ever using such power for personal gain again ... on the backs of American citizens who cherish the history and sanctity of that office. And what was demonstrated to the American people was that Bill Clinton was above the law, or that he had friends in higher places that could hamstring justice. Years later his wife Hilary Clinton would be caught in multiple scandals, found guilty and never held accountable for her actions.

And the Clintons are not the only people who occupied positions of authority, broke laws and went unpunished. I think it is safe to say that I would have to add 50 more chapters to this book to discuss all of whom they were and what they did. The fact of the matter

Something Bigger Than Overthrowing Small Governments

is that our national leaders are held at a higher standard, they are supposed to be an example of righteousness and trustworthiness. But when that is not the case, then younger generations of Americans begin lowering their standards as well and falling in line believing that they too should not be held accountable for their actions. And when you think about it, how can you sentence the common man for a crime when you will not sentence the elite for theirs? Justice is supposed to be fair and balanced, but unfortunately it is not that way anymore.

I'm not encouraging this, but I predict that one day soon Americans will take it upon themselves to bring justice as most vigilantes do when the judicial system is as corrupt as ours is becoming. The masses will seek out those who are not being held accountable, like the Clintons and others, and bring swift punishment at the end of a rope or other means because that is what history has shown us is what happens when you push a nation of patriots to the edge of the cliff. They fight back, and they do so in a manner that mirrors the actions of our founding fathers in 1776. I honestly believe that we are once again at that point in our nation when good Americans are saying "enough is enough." The under-the-table deals in our nation's capital have become the business model for smaller criminal activity in almost every neighborhood of almost every city in America — the commodity being in many cases ... children.

This business model has become very sophisticated, monitored and secured so that the perpetrators can have their cake and eat it too, at all levels of society. It is their notoriety that makes the world think they are good people when in fact their notoriety is no more than a veneer that allows them to continue sexually abusing and trafficking children or adults.

> Citing a "well-placed source" in the New York Police Department, Blackwater USA founder and retired Navy SEAL Erik Prince claims that among the 650,000 Huma Abedin emails on her estranged husband's laptop is evidence Hillary Clinton, as well as former President Bill Clinton, were visitors to convicted pedophile Jeffrey Epstein's Caribbean hideaway, known as "Orgy Island."

"They found State Department emails," he said of FBI investigators. "They found a lot of other really damning criminal information, including money laundering, including the fact that Hillary went to this sex island with convicted pedophile Jeffrey Epstein. Bill Clinton went there more than 20 times. Hillary Clinton went there at least six times."

In May, FoxNews.com reported Bill Clinton was a much more frequent flyer on Epstein's infamous Boeing 727 "Lolita Express" jet than previously reported.

Flight logs show he took at least 26 trips and apparently even ditched his Secret Service detail for at least five of the flights. The manifests for the trips, between 2001 and 2003, identified fellow passengers by their initials or first names, including "Tatiana." The jet was reportedly outfitted with a bed where passengers had group sex with young girls.

FoxNews.com reported in July that attorneys for Epstein touted his close friendship with Bill Clinton and even claimed the billionaire helped start the Clinton Global Initiative. Emails that surfaced in August showed famed defense attorney Roy Black was deemed too controversial to host an event for President Obama because he represented Epstein against charges of trafficking nearly three-dozen underage girls for sex for himself and his powerful friends. Black and co-counsel Alan Dershowitz were able to secure a deal in 2008 in which Epstein pleaded guilty to only one count related to prostitution with a minor. Epstein registered as a sex offender and served, partly in-home detention, just 13 months of a 19-month sentence.

Meanwhile, in a bizarre twist, WikiLeaks published Friday an email inviting Hillary Clinton's campaign chairman, John Podesta, to a "spirit cooking dinner" hosted by performance artist Marina Abramovic, which features an occult ritual created by Satanist Aleister Crowley.

A tweet from WikiLeaks' Twitter account hinted there is far more to the story: "The Podestas' 'Spirit Cooking' dinner? It's not what you think. It's blood, sperm and breast milk. But mostly blood. See http://wearechange.org/spirit-cooking-disturbing-podesta-email-yet-warning-graphic-content."

John Podesta's brother, Tony Podesta, forwarded the June 28, 2015, email in which Abramovic wrote: "I am so looking forward to the Spirit Cooking dinner at my place. Do you think you will be able to let me know if your brother is joining? All my love, Marina."

Something Bigger Than Overthrowing Small Governments

Tony Podesta wrote to his brother, above the forwarded email: "Are you in NYC Thursday July 9 Marina wants you to come to dinner."

In another tweet regarding the exchange, WikiLeaks commented: "Tony Podesta. By Day, mild mannered Foreign Agent for Saudi Arabia. By night, Spirit Cooker." Abramovic was touted in New York Magazine as "the world's most famous performance artist." She has published a new memoir, "Walk Through Walls," and appeared in a video with rapper Jay Z, who was campaigning for Hillary Clinton in Ohio.

Prince said the NYPD wanted to do a press conference announcing the warrants and the additional arrests they were making in the Weiner investigation but received "huge pushback" from the Justice Department.

"The amount of garbage that they found in these emails, of criminal activity by Hillary, by her immediate circle, and even by other Democratic members of Congress was so disgusting they gave it to the FBI, and they said, 'We're going to go public with this if you don't reopen the investigation and you don't do the right thing with timely indictments,'" Prince told Breitbart News Daily. [36]

Whether it's flying brothels where wealthy men and women can do their dirty deeds without detection, or highly secured islands that cannot be approached by outsiders without them being incarcerated, or the basement of a demented abuser's home ... these situations do not just happen. They are intentional. They involve strict planning and careful guidance from advisors who have been in this business for a long time, strategically placing their own people in positions of authority within local, state and federal government so that they are never held accountable if caught in the act.

I recall interviewing a number of survivors — adults who claimed they had been molested when they were children by well-organized opportunists, flown to various parts of the world to sexually entertain high ranking and very influential political and business figures. According to the testimony of a now 40-year-old woman, she had suffered at the hands of people with the initials J. R., H. C. and T.

K., as well as others when she was just a child. Her testimony was so compelling that we filmed hours of her speaking of places where the abuse had happened. It was evident to us that no one would be able to describe these places in such detail unless they had been there, i.e. the White House (prior to the Trump administration). She spoke of how this type of abuse had been going on for years and how no one was being held accountable because they were above the law. I told her that they may be above the law, but they are not beyond our reach. And she was not the only one to testify ... there were more. And the interesting part of this was the fact that many of the victims did not know one another. Their testimonies were taken thousands of miles apart and yet they all described to a tee the same locations and some of the same people by whom their sexual exploitation had occurred.

So there we stood with all of this very damaging evidence ... evidence that under a good judicial system would hold the perpetrators accountable. But sadly, we aren't dealing with a good judicial system, and knowing what to do with the filmed testimony became a challenge. We thought long and hard about where we could take this evidence, but we never found the safe opening we were searching for. It appeared from our investigations that few could be trusted, and even those few were either scared of reprisal or were not in a powerful enough position to make a difference. And when we did find someone who was in a powerful enough position to effect change ... they would not do so because they were "complicit in the crime."

Complicity is the act of helping or encouraging another individual to commit a crime. It is also commonly referred to as aiding and abetting. One who is complicit is said to be an accomplice. But even though an accomplice does not actually commit the crime, his or her actions helped someone in the commission of the crime.

The concept of accomplice liability means an accomplice faces the same degree of guilt and punishment as the individual who committed the crime. Indeed, accomplices can face the same penalties, including prison time. The key consideration is whether the individual intentionally and voluntarily encouraged or assisted in the commission of the crime, or (in some cases) failed to prevent it. (37)

So imagine this ... you're a senator or congressman or employee of DOJ and you know an associate is sexually exploiting children. You choose to look the other way. Years go by and now even if you do want to turn that associate in for committing this horrible crime you realize that you're complicit in the crime. You realize that if you have to go to court and testify that the Judge, provided he or she is an honest, law-abiding Judge, is going to ask why you failed to prevent this crime from happening when you first learned of it. And there is a pretty good chance that all of the media fallout might have a negative impact on your constituents, and there is the possibility that you yourself could go to jail. It's just too radioactive for you to handle. So you decide to not say a word and chalk it up to things just being the way they are in Washington, Miami, Chicago, Los Angeles or whatever city you name in America. You toss all your moral absolutes down the toilet and children suffer because you failed to do the right thing ... report the crime when it first occurred.

This evil has permeated the very fabric of society and infected even members of our law enforcement community whom we trust to protect our minors. These are the men and women who work in our neighborhoods and ask us to believe in them as keepers of the law, yet in so many situations they are becoming abusers of the law. For example in 2016:

> Seven Bay Area police officers faced criminal charges for their involvement in a scandal centering around a teenage sex worker. Alameda County District Attorney Nancy O'Malley on that Friday announced the charges including accusations of oral copulation with a minor, engaging in prostitution, lewd acts and soliciting.
> One Oakland Police sergeant, Leroy Johnson, was charged with failing to report sexual misconduct by his officers. The

police departments came under scrutiny earlier this year when Celeste Guap, the now 19-year-old daughter of an Oakland police dispatcher, said that she had slept with dozens of officers. Guap alleged that she slept with some while she was only 17.

She said that she worked as a prostitute and would receive tips from her law enforcement liaisons about avoiding raids in exchange for sex. Guap said that officers exchanged tips about prostitution raids in exchange for sex.

An investigation was launched after one of the officers accused of sleeping with an underage Guap committed suicide last September. The probe ultimately led to Oakland going through three police chiefs in a little more than week. Oakland Mayor Libby Schaaf, who earlier slammed a "frat house" culture in the police force, announced that there would be four officers fired and seven suspended from the department, which is also embroiled in a racist texting scandal.

However, the case had expanded to several Bay Area departments including San Francisco, and Friday's charges were filed against officers from Oakland, Livermore and Contra Costa County.

Former Contra Costa deputy Ricardo Perez was charged with oral copulation and lewd acts in a public place and a resigned Livermore officer, Dan Black, was accused of engaging in prostitution and lewd acts in a public place. Oakland Mayor Libby Schaaf announced earlier that a dozen officers would be disciplined." According to the intelligence ARC gathered, there were actually 32 officers implicated and seven charged.

Oakland Officer Giovani LoVerde was accused of oral copulation with a minor, and colleague Brian Bunton was accused of engaging in prostitution and felony obstruction of justice. Former Oakland cop Tyrell Smith was investigated for possible forcible sodomy of an 18-year-old, though Contra Costa County prosecutors refused to press charges in June because of "insufficient evidence," according to the San Francisco Chronicle. He now faced four counts of searching official criminal justice databases without permission, with Warit Utappa facing one count of the same charge.

Guap was later arrested for battery after an alleged violent incident at drug and sex addiction rehab in Florida, where she says she was sent with financial support from Richmond, a city north of Oakland District Attorney O'Malley

Something Bigger Than Overthrowing Small Governments

said that she protested Guap leaving California, and that she hopes the teen returns and "receives the services and help she deserves. [38]

These types of incidents have been occurring and continue to occur in our nation. Still no one is being held accountable because the narrative is that these types of crimes against children are not as brutal as some would have the world believe. Those who sit in judgment are so busy protecting their own kind — perhaps because they too are complicit in the crime or for whatever reason have never understood that the exploitation or molestation of a child is a death of their soul. It is a horrible hell on earth for them with no recourse and virtually no way of regaining not just their childhood but their human dignity.

Perhaps those who sit in judgment are more reactive than proactive because it gives them purpose, or perhaps it gives them a job. I have often heard it said by lawyers and police officers that they would be out of business if there were no crimes committed. Now that surely is not the attitude of the majority of judges, attorneys and police officers. I have dear friends who hold many of those positions in life ... but it only takes few bad apples to spoil the entire basket. Once the bench is shamed, once the uniform is soiled by the actions of those who have no honor ... it is an uphill battle for those who do.

I wish I could say it was just a few, but in our research it is an ever-growing problem. If you could see the number of politicians, judges, attorneys, doctors, clergy and police officers that view child pornography and think nothing of it, it would make your head spin. Now don't get me wrong, I am not on a witch hunt for politicians, judges, attorneys, clergy and police officers, but I will tell you that these types of people are supposed to be the pillars of strength for our nation dealing with sexual exploitation and trafficking of children and adults. If they cannot be our heroes, then who can be? If they cannot be trusted, then who can be?

And that is where we are in society at this point. And it is for that very reason that the ever-increasing number of NGOs with former military and special operations personnel are joining the fight because we do keep our word, we can be trusted, and I can promise you that if one, even one person of any NGO is found to be dishonorable in their actions, not upholding the moral code to protect children or those being trafficked, our breed will not allow it to go unpunished. We will not look the other way.

And so we have quickly come to realize that our effort to find a home for this evidence from our survivors is going to be an uphill battle. It will require timing and precision and tradecraft to expose the perpetrators in such a fashion that the judicial system and those assigned to it will be forced to make a choice ... either take action or fall back on themselves and have their careers die a quick death from bad publicity. But even this is not a guarantee that justice will be served.

The second barrier to overcome is a compromised judicial system. Justice needs legs that cannot be unscrewed, cemented in an incorruptible platform in view of all and yet far beyond the reaches of those who would attempt to chip away at it. That platform is represented in a new law. The laws that currently exist to deter child exploitation have had their legs unscrewed in such a fashion that allows pedophiles, pimps and commercial child pornography filmmakers to go unpunished as they destroy the body and souls of our children. After years of being in the trenches, I am convinced that this evil can only be stopped and the children in our country protected if two things emerge ... the instatement of the death penalty as the standard punishment for anyone who sexually exploits a child and the formation of a sanctioned "justice league" that does nothing but target those who sexually exploit our children.

U.S. history has shown that if the risk in committing a crime is too high because the punishment for the crime is enormously stiff, people who would generally commit that crime ... don't. I will continue to do whatever I can in my power to change the law — you molest a child and you get the death sentence. You exploit a child for pornography, and you get the death sentence. If you are found guilty of trafficking children, you get the death sentence ... end of story. If we truly want to take a bite out of this evil, then make it impossible for the evil to exist.

Something Bigger Than Overthrowing Small Governments

How long will it take to have this law enacted? That is hard to say. But what I do know is that "a river cuts through rock not because of its power but because of its persistence." [39]

Make no mistake, my outlook on these issues is very much aligned with the wishes and moral high ground of our founding fathers when they adopted the Declaration of Independence on July 4, 1776.

The Declaration of Independence

We hold these truths to be self-evident, that all men are created equal, that they are endowed by their Creator with certain unalienable Rights, that among these are Life, Liberty and the pursuit of Happiness — that to secure these rights, governments are instituted among men, deriving their just powers from the consent of the governed — that whenever any form of government becomes destructive of these ends, it is the right of the people to alter or to abolish it, and to institute new government, laying its foundation on such principles and organizing its powers in such form, as to them shall seem most likely to affect their safety and happiness .... For the support of this Declaration, with a firm reliance on the protection of Divine Providence, we mutually pledge to each other our lives, our fortunes and our sacred honor.

It is not a matter of interpreting the Declaration of Independence ... it does not need to be redefined. It is plain and simple and to the point, and it clearly tells us that *"We the People"* have the right to abolish a local, state or federal government, or those positions within that government that are destructive. And I submit that anyone in those positions that offers any leniency to those who sexually exploit children or traffic other humans have become destructive to life, liberty and the pursuit of happiness that all Americans are entitled to under the protection of not just our laws but under the protection of all Americans who have a duty to one another. That, in itself, is the moral high ground our founding fathers spoke of in the Declaration of Independence and the Constitution of the United States.

But the house has not been cleaned yet. There has been no revolution, no harsh demand for people who are guilty of not upholding the laws protecting children from sexual exploitation to step down. And ARC is not waiting for the masses to gather around us ... we are fighting the fight now. Who will come along side? I have no idea. Will it make a difference if they do? I would like to think so. We aren't just on a mission ... we are a movement.

We aren't the "justice league," but I wish there were one ... engaged in sending those who sexually exploit children to facilities to be interrogated, and if found guilty, sentenced and put to death. Once the word spread among the ranks of pedophiles and other child exploiters, you would see a shift away from crimes of this type. However, it saddens me because I believe there is nothing in Washington D.C. these days that has the moral thread to do this. There is too much water under the bridge for them. If I sound like a man who hates crimes against children, then let me assure you that your ears do not deceive you. I am not and will never attempt to be politically correct. I am not wishy washy about this issue, and let there be positively absolutely no doubt about where I stand.

"The care of human life and happiness, and not their destruction, is the first and only object of good government" (Thomas Jefferson). But then again, perhaps I am mistaken ... perhaps "the swamp will be drained," to quote President Trump. Perhaps America will be great again. But this will not happen on its own, and it will not happen if left to the devices of certain depraved members of Parliament, Congress, etc. who try to make us believe they are protecting the nations. It can only happen if *"We the People"* demand justice and take action against those in authority that do not serve it up when perpetrators are found guilty.

Would I advocate violence? ... Never. Would I advocate physical reprisal? ... Absolutely, in the form of a capital punishment sentence by a U.S. court. In my opinion those who sexually exploit children lose the right to ever be treated like humans or given the considerations we give to humans, ever again. They give up that right

Something Bigger Than Overthrowing Small Governments

when they steal the heart and soul of another human — it is demonic and animalistic, and it should be dealt with accordingly.

There are those who are among the elite, in what they believe are untouchable positions in U.S. and global society, who sexually exploit children. What is the only thing they fear? They do not fear being sued, or being tried in a corruptible court of law, or even embarrassed in the news media. What they fear is loss of their own life. And for those who protect the elite in untouchable positions in society and around the world that sexually exploit children, I predict in days to come your life will be required of you as well ... if not by God then by a society that will say enough is enough.

The third and final obstacle to overcome is diversity. Why has everyone bought into celebrating diversity when in fact we should be celebrating unity. I hear it all the time, "I'm an Irish American, African American, Japanese American, Mexican American," and so on. Seriously people? When you make that statement about yourself, you automatically divide yourself from the country and your countrymen and women. If I told you I was a lizard monkey you'd be confused. Am I a lizard or a monkey ... which is it? So what are you ... Irish or American, African or American, Japanese or American, Mexican or American? I submit that when you take hold of your national right as an American, that you stand on two of the most powerful documents ever created in history ... the Constitution of the United States and the Declaration of Independence. Because of them you cannot be justifiably discriminated against nor treated unequally in our country without having recourse. When I hear that you are an American, you become my brother or sister with no division between us. When you tell me you are something other than an American, then I have cause to wonder just who you are, what you truly believe in and where your allegiance rests.

According to the Online Etymology Dictionary, the word *"diversity"* only acquired a positive connotation regarding things such as race and gender in 1992. Prior to that, the word was derived from the French word *"diversite,"* which signified less cheery synonyms such as "wickedness" and "perversity," and the ancient Latin word *"diversitatem,"* which connoted "contrariety, contradiction, and disagreement."

It's instructive that the modern word *"diversity"* is rooted in a Latin word that signified "disagreement," because perhaps the primary reason the Roman Empire crumbled was because as it spread itself too thin and allowed incursions from non-Roman ethnic elements. Diversity's weight proved too much for the empire to sustain itself.

Note the similarity between the words *"diversity"* and *"division,"* the latter of which is derived from *"divide."* Fifteenth-century Italian political strategist Niccolo Marchiavelli posted a basic rule of politics: *"divide et impera,"* which in English is most often translated as *"divide and conquer."* And so it would appear that within our great nation and with the support of the last Obama administration — socialist in nature, of course, and outspokenly proclaimed so — the push to celebrate diversity was evident in every sector of our society — schools, military, business, etc. — demanding that we as a people be tolerant of everyone and everything that is different. The silliness in it all is that the more you focus on how different people are, the more different you see they are. And then to add insult to injury the lawmakers try to sugar coat it with the word "celebrate," as if it's a wonderful thing to be part of, when nothing could be further from the truth. Why would I want to "celebrate" a pedophile or "celebrate" a socialist simply because they are different or believe differently than I do?

No one should be forced by suggestion or law to like or dislike the differences they see in other people. It is my right to have my own opinion, to tolerate what I choose, and to disagree when I know something is wrong — especially when it contradicts my moral beliefs as well as the written principles in the Bible and the Constitution of the United States of America. Make no doubt about it, this nation was founded on Judeo-Christian principles that do not need redefining. What they need are good men and women in our country to stand behind them. How well they have served us is evident in the protection they have provided each of us.

Anything other than what I am telling you is a brilliant plan by a globalist regime to divide and conquer our nation. For those who are too young to remember the Cold War, that was exactly the footprint of communism/socialism, and it was destructive in nature to people who wished to live in a democratic society. Are we devoid of its influences?

Something Bigger Than Overthrowing Small Governments

Absolutely not. It merely wears the disguise of globalism. And those who support its agenda do their best to shame people in public if they do not buy into that agenda, shame them in public if they are not tolerant, shame them in public if they chose to have a different opinion, and shame them in public for keeping the moral values that our great nation was founded on ... that all men/women are created equal in the eyes of God.

I look back at my Marine Corps career and realize how united we were ... not divided. Down range there was no room for diversity ... only unity. So we worked as one fighting machine, and that is where our head stayed so if one Marine was hurt, all Marines were hurt. If one Marine was successful, all Marines were successful. We were all the same color ... green, and we all bled the same color ... red. It is because of this unity that the American public asked guys like us to rid the world of despicable characters like Osama Bin Laden and other terrorists like ISIS that lurked in shadows of the world just waiting for one chance to destroy you and your families. We are the standard for success and unity, and that is what we need from all Americans in order to prevent child exploitation. It is a time for our country to remind itself that we are united as Americans and that is it ... Americans ... not African American, Mexican American, Japanese American, Irish American, or whatever ... just Americans. That is our nationality, and with it comes respect for all who claim citizenship as long as they abide by the Constitution of the United States of America, drink in our history, respect those who died for our nation, swear allegiance to our flag, and, for those who choose to serve in the U.S. military, swear to protect our country against all enemies, foreign and domestic.

With that comes the great responsibility of protecting our American children who might otherwise be exploited and abused if it were left up to a divided society, one which tends to be prejudice in nature. So until we find our way back to being "just Americans," let us not allow such prejudice to affect the innocent lives of little ones who have done nothing to deserve abuse by a growing population of twisted minds — the very minds that smirk at the attempts of men and women to protect innocence, and are determined to prey on these children. Let us realize who we are as Americans — one front, one nation under God, indivisible with liberty and justice for all — and as that, let us save our children. Let us show the world who we are as a people, as a nation that is willing to do whatever it takes to stop the evil crimes against our young ones.

There are a lot of us and a lot of you out there who are qualified to be a part of this movement, who have been down range and are covered with blood that is not our own. Remember this ... it was just your job, not who you are. And that truth, along with God's grace and forgiveness, has allowed you and us to continue on in life without the burden of our past. Strangely though, when it comes to this movement and ARC ... it is who we are. I am convinced that all of us will answer to God Almighty if we know children are in danger and we refuse to do something about it.

Something Bigger Than Overthrowing Small Governments

Chapter 22
WHAT HIDES IN THE DARKNESS

Most people will never step into the darkness. They will never know just how disturbing the crimes against children really are. How did we get to a place in society where children have become a commodity for the perverted? How did we get to a place in society where sexually exploiting children is not seen as a crime punishable by death?

The answer to that question resides in the things that hide in the darkness right under our own noses — the evil agendas and negligence of legislative bodies and organizations that have been accepted as commonplace in our society. Their efforts go unreported by media in order to evade the outrage of citizens who would oppose such actions if they knew. Well, now you are going to know! And what you choose to do with this information will make the difference between stopping these atrocities or allowing them to flourish until every child on the planet is abused.

Exploitation of children will not remain in your own backyard ... it will spread like wildfire as it is across all of America. Protecting our children requires you to fight on all fronts and to be well trained to fight. That is the reason we started offering our three day *Fight Child Sex Trafficking Comprehensive Training Course* to equip people who want to take action and are tired of attending one trafficking conference after another, hearing people preach to the choir about awareness. I think the nation is pretty much aware by now that we have a child trafficking problem. If you haven't learned this yet, let me school you. Traffickers and pedophiles could care less about the next fundraiser music event or walk-a-thon to raise money against trafficking because they know the money usually never reaches beyond the pockets of the performers themselves or the management or all the people organizing such events. What traffickers and pedophiles are afraid of is an army of citizens who hit the streets and physically save children, physically interrupt trafficking operations, physically apprehend traffickers and pedophiles and put them behind bars.

So allow me to show you what hides in the darkness so that you will see with more than your eyes and hear with more than your ears and better know your enemy. Prostitution in the State of California is illegal. And yet we have a sex workers union. How can that be? And how can a law-abiding legislative body in Sacramento allow this to exist? Perhaps they are not law abiding ... and therein resides the problem. But bigger than that is the fact that most citizens of the State of California have no idea that the very legislative body responsible for passing laws intentionally keeps those same citizens in the dark to avoid interference as it institutionalizes components of the left wing agenda it wants.

The following are two briefings by ARC's Human Trafficking Program Director, Tina Paulson. The issues she brings to light are agendas being pursued to an increasingly greater degree in California today and in states across the nation.

Trends in U.S. Laws and Ethics: Destroying Innocence and Eliminating Moral Absolutes
Tina Paulson, ARC Human Trafficking Program Director

In the arena of child sex trafficking, ARC's objective is not only to locate and rescue American children who are being exploited and victimized by the commercial sex trade, but to protect the safety, innocence and defend the rights of our nation's most vulnerable citizens...*children*. The lines defending their innocence should be defended by laws and ethics in our society. Yet their innocence is being invaded by an increasingly sexualized society intent defining *sexual indulgence* as a *freedom*, as a protected right. Factions of society are pushing for the *elimination of moral absolutes*. Regrettably, our laws are flowing in this current instead of standing firm.

Demonstrative sexual conduct and variant sexual preferences, even pornography — yes, even pedophilia — are

Something Bigger Than Overthrowing Small Governments

being celebrated as freedoms, while moral standards are rebuked as being bigoted and are even labeled "abusive." In the name of *tolerance* adults are teaching children to explore and experiment with sexuality, even variant sexuality, before they have developed a moral compass. Graphic sexual content is now in elementary school curriculums. Do children have a say in whether they want to be subjected to this? No. Most children are embarrassed by it. Children at that age don't even understand adult sexuality and how it can be a threat to them. Concerned parents who object to this content or pull their kids out of class are considered a roadblock to child wellness. They are circumnavigated by other programs determined to make sure their children get sexualized anyway.

American children **do have a voice**. We are their voice.

Briefing 1

LGBTQ+ Agenda to Advance the Sexualization of Children

San Diego, CA — On October 15, 2015 and again on October 7, 2016 I attended a one-day certified course for professionals and service providers entitled **"Law and Ethics: Dilemmas in Clinical Work with Adolescents and Children: A Practical Workshop on Ethical, Legal and Clinical Factors."** The course was taught by Ellen G. Stein, Ph.D. in Clinical and Forensic Psychology, former Adjunct Clinical Professor at Alliant International University in San Diego, CA, and former member of the Ethics Committee of the California Psychological Association. She is an outspoken advocate for LGBTQ+, boasts her own lesbian relationship and argues her beliefs that children and adolescents should be encouraged (and not discouraged by moral conservatives) to explore and experiment with sexuality, particularly gay, lesbian and transgender tendencies. She also described how LGBTQ+ advocacy is influencing legislation and professional practices relating to children.

At one point Dr. Stein instructed that for adults to subject children to viewing pornography was not considered by CPS to be abuse or neglect as long as it was "normal porn." When asked by a student to clarify what "normal porn" was, Dr. Stein said, "not child porn," leaving the class to conclude that any other kind of porn was "normal." She stated that since viewing pornography has not been proven to cause *every* child to act out sexually in a wrongful manner, it cannot be concluded that pornography has harmful effects on children.

Then Dr. Stein addressed new mandated reporting laws and amendments. A **mandated reporter** is a professional who works with children, who is legally required to report any suspicion of child abuse or neglect to the appropriate authorities. The goal of mandated reporting is to prevent children from being abused and stop possible abuse as quickly as possible by allowing authorities to intervene. To my dismay, Dr. Stein informed us that the new laws would not necessarily require a report if children were engaged in sexual intercourse with older partners or even with adults. Dr. Stein saw this as a victory and a professional relief. I saw it as a way for pedophiles and child abusers to evade the law.

The mandated reporting laws Dr. Stein discussed were amendments to California Penal Code sections 11165-11167 and California Assembly Bill AB 327. To be clear, the legal age of consent in California is 18 and that means that **NO CHILD under 18 is legally competent to CONSENT to sexual acts — so all sex acts under 18 are <u>non-consensual</u>, thus exploitative and illegal**. The law further states that sexual activity that is deemed forced, coerced or abusive <u>**does**</u> require a report. And yet the following new laws and amendments limit whether it is necessary to report when child sex acts are discovered.

DEFINITION: Sexual "intercourse" is genital penetration strictly between a male and female.

ACCORDING TO NEW CALIFORNIA MANDATED REPORTING LAWS although the following **child sex acts are illegal**, they **<u>DO NOT</u> need to be reported to police or Child Protective Services:**
- *No report necessary* for sexual activity including oral, anal or intercourse between two 13-year-old children or children younger than 13
- *No report necessary* for sexual intercourse or any sexual activity (masturbation, touching, kissing, fondling, groping or showing of pornography, etc.) of **a child age 14 or 15 with anyone under age 21** except if there is oral or anal copulation

Something Bigger Than Overthrowing Small Governments

- *No report necessary* for sexual intercourse between a child 16 or older and anyone of any age

This analysis chart of AB327 was provided by the National Center for Youth Law, Oakland, CA, whose website proudly displays the rainbow LGBT pride flag on every page. Also note below the chart, there is a further loophole suggested, *not to ask about the sexual partner's age.*

WHEN AM I MANDATED TO REPORT THE SEXUAL ACTIVITY OF MINORS TO CHILDREN'S PROTECTIVE SERVICES OR POLICE IN CALIFORNIA?

If a minor has consensual sexual intercourse with an older partner, is a report mandated?

AGE OF PATIENT ▼ \ AGE OF PARTNER ►	12	13	14	15	16	17	18	19	20	21	21+
11	N	N	Y	Y	Y	Y	Y	Y	Y	Y	Y
12	N	N	Y	Y	Y	Y	Y	Y	Y	Y	Y
13	N	N	Y	Y	Y	Y	Y	Y	Y	Y	Y
14			N	N	N	N	N	N	N	Y	Y
15				N	N	N	N	N	N	Y	Y
16					N	N	N	N	N	N	N
17						N	N	N	N	N	N
18							N	N	N	N	N

Note: Providers have no legal obligation to ask about partner's age.

(Copy of chart analysis of AB327 provided by National Center for Youth Law, distributed by Ellen Stein, Ph.D.)

Following Dr. Stein's course, I took this chart and supporting materials to staff of the District Attorney's offices in San Diego, Los Angeles and Orange County. I inquired whether they knew about these laws. They reacted with shock and insisted this was *against* the mandated reporting laws. Oddly, no one I spoke to could tell me where to look up the current California mandated reporting laws. They weren't certain how to find them. So how does anyone in California know what the laws are? Fortunately, taking this chart to the DA's offices amplified a campaign to combat this new legislation.

You may have heard it said a method for totalitarian control of the masses is to (1) create a problem, (2) provide the solution, then (3) keep everyone confused. Let's say some pedophiles could (1) create child sexual abuse, then (2) create laws so the public believes the problem is under control, but (3) they keep everyone confused about the laws so no one knows what to do, so kids can keep getting abused ... (4) they get themselves elected to solve the crisis.

BRIEFING 2

SEX WORKERS UNIONS IN CALIFORNIA ARE OPPOSING ANTI-TRAFFICKING EFFORTS

Although prostitution is illegal in the state of California, I have found that sex workers unions are vibrant and powerful in California and lead the way in protesting anti-human trafficking legislation. They claim anti-human trafficking efforts infringe on their rights — let me interject — their **rights** to do what is ***illegal*** in California: prostitute. There is an unstoppable wave to decriminalize and deregulate prostitution in California and in many states across the country. I stand with every sex trafficking survivor I personally know (well over 100) who are vehemently opposed to this. Prostitution is paid rape. Period. It is a crime.

I have found that the legislative process over all does not engage the general population — it is illusive. The public doesn't even know about most legislation until after it is signed into law. Finding new laws that are being written is like a hunting expedition. Only experienced citizens and lobbyists can track it.

In October of 2015 I was casually informed by some legislative staff members that there was to be a hearing at the Capitol in Sacramento on California human trafficking bills on October 20, 2015. Upon examining the calendar for the California Assembly, I could not find any mention of a Human Trafficking hearing anywhere. After asking for help, I was told had to look up the particular committee, which was the Assembly Committee on Public Safety, in order to find a listing of hearing dates, then select the specific date before I

Something Bigger Than Overthrowing Small Governments

could find the topic. I would never have found it without help.

I flew to Sacramento to attend the hearing and arrived at the State Capitol, Room 126, about 20 minutes early. Upon approaching the committee room I was confronted in a rather aggressive manner by three women and a male cross-dresser wearing campaign buttons for different sex workers unions. They proceeded to ask me what I was there for, and I responded that I represented child trafficking victims and was prepared to make a statement advocating for stiffer penalties for traffickers and buyers. The four sex workers reps became verbally agitated with me explaining that underage youth had the right to work in the sex industry if they wanted to, even at brothels. I listened politely to their rhetoric and then proceeded to find a seat once the chamber room opened.

I was surprised and disappointed by several things. Only about 35 people attended the hearing, and of the many panelists who had been preselected by the chair of the Public Safety Committee, Honorable Bill Quirk, half were advocating for the sex industry. Less than half the panelists were advocating for stronger anti-trafficking laws.

The primary pro-prostitution panelist was Maxine Doogan. She represents the Erotic Service Providers Union whose website not only offers a vast list of blog columns and articles including *"Feminist Whore"* and *"For The Love Of Porn, Prostitution and Pussy,"* but also distributes *Bitch Magazine* by *Bitch Media*. With each new monthly subscription, they offer a free copy of *"The Sick Issue"* and their official ceramic mug which has just three words on it in all capital letters, "FILLED WITH RAGE." Why is she a panelist at the Capitol?

I researched the chair of the Public Safety Committee, Honorable Bill Quirk, and found that his district includes the Hayward and Union City area, which is a sex trafficking hot spot. It did cross my mind that perhaps the amount of money coming in from the commercial sex trade in the Chairman's district could incentivize him to prevent anti-trafficking efforts and promote decriminalization of prostitution purely for the revenue.

I recognized several anti-trafficking advocates and legislative staff who I knew attending the hearing, but we all seemed discouraged. During the lunch break I found a staff member of our Los Angeles Assemblyman who informed me that there was realistically no way for the public to influence this legislation and that the $10 million/year in government funding dedicated to anti-trafficking efforts in California could be held up inconclusively or eaten up in red tape and salaries. It's supposed to support recovering survivors.

At the end of the hearing when the microphone was opened for statements, the four activists I had met earlier gave their statements advocating for more government-funded services for sex workers. Ironically, all of them said they had been sex trafficked as minors and spoke of the horrible and terrifying abuses they have continually experienced in the sex trade. But instead of opposing the sex trade, they were clamoring for deregulating and decriminalizing prostitution, public funding for medical and mental health services for prostitutes (because they are brutalized), and a de-stigmatization campaign (less shaming of prostitutes).

This seemed to prove my point that the sex industry is a horrible thing. Why is the California Assembly making a point to promote it instead of helping victims find other careers?

Online research and the news media have pointed to many other growing issues that are making American children more vulnerable to sexual abuse, exploitation and trafficking.

LGBT History Month Promotes Gay Porn To Kids
Pacific Justice Institute, October 1, 2013

Sacramento, CA — The Pacific Justice Institute is warning parents to take immediate action to prevent their children from being blindsided by explicit and highly objectionable material during LGBT History Month, which begins today. A patchwork of schools, districts, and individual teachers across the country are expected to promote LGBT History Month to students during October. The leading website for the event, www.lgbthistorymonth.com, features an "icon" of

Something Bigger Than Overthrowing Small Governments

LGBT history for each day of the month — 31 total. Many parents will no doubt be alarmed when they see some of the characters being highlighted this year.

In addition to the usual activists and celebrities being re-branded as historical figures, PJI researchers were shocked to come across a few individuals whose work is X-rated. Take, for instance, "Tom of Finland," who makes the list at No. 18 and is known primarily for his homoerotic fetish art, and his contributions to gay porn. Or Patrick Califia, a bisexual transman known for erotic fiction.

"It is deeply disturbing that the organizers of LGBT History Month think our kids should be celebrating homoerotic authors and porn producers," stated Brad Dacus, president of Pacific Justice Institute. "This should be a serious wake-up call for anyone who still thinks gay history in schools is a good idea."

PJI is urging parents across the nation to ask all of their children's teachers whether any reference will be made to LGBT History Month. If so, parents should confront the teacher, principal, and school board members with the reality of the individuals being presented as role models this year.

Besides the X-rated inclusions, this year's list continues a trend from previous years of including a drag queen, current television personalities, foreign political figures, and activists. The list also appears to be more targeted this year at ethnic and religious groups that have traditionally opposed homosexual behavior, highlighting several black and Asian LGBT figures, as well as a former Mormon.

"This is exactly why we fought California's gay history mandate a couple of years ago," noted PJI Staff Attorney Matthew McReynolds. "We knew this was not about real history; it was about pushing a political agenda and sexualizing kids at increasingly young ages. It is completely irresponsible for the organizers of this event to promote individuals whose work is utterly inappropriate for minors."

Last year, LGBT History Month was officially recognized by school districts from California to Florida. It has also stirred controversy in New Jersey, where two years ago Gov. Chris Christie suggested a teacher should be fired for posting objections to LGBT History Month on her personal Facebook page." [40]

I've researched this and it's happening in libraries all over the country. Even though child porn is against the law, libraries are told by lawyers that it violates privacy rights for internet content to be filtered.

Child Porn in Libraries Due to American Library Association Facilitation; Another Library Breaks the Law
SafeLibraries, December 25, 2015

The American Library Association [ALA] provides libraries with a model Internet Use Policy that facilitates child pornography viewing by advising librarians only judges can determine what is child pornography, not librarians, so do not help the police [EN 1]. ALA advice is followed by law firms that advise libraries not to report child pornography viewers to the police because that would violate the child porn viewers right to privacy [EN 2]. Law enforcement entities have noted ALA policy essentially aids and abets child porn crimes in public libraries [EN 3].

Many libraries follow ALA advice and, among other things, essentially end up defrauding the E-rate program that is funded by the "Universal Service Charge" that appears on all our telephone and Internet bills [EN 4].

A New Jersey library even set policy, following ALA guidance, ensuring children in the children's section of the library retain unfiltered access to the Internet despite an 11 year old boy viewing porn there [EN 5].

An Illinois library caught covering up child porn crimes was awarded for passing an ALA-like policy protecting child pornography viewing where the policy was passed during the Lincoln's Birthday holiday, a move ruled illegal by the Illinois Attorney General. But that didn't stop ALA's wish to hold the library's policy up as a model for other libraries. Hence, the library was literally awarded for breaking the law to facilitate child pornography viewing on the Internet [EN 6]. [41]

"PORN-SAFE" LIBRARIES CLEARLY NOT ALA'S GOAL

By Charlie Butts, *OneNewsNow.com*, February 22, 2016

A recent court ruling emphasizes the need for people to get involved in stopping the viewing of pornography in their public library.

A Wisconsin appeals court has ruled there is no First Amendment right to view pornography in public libraries. The case is related to David Reidinger, 45, who was cited in 2014 for creating a disturbance after police caught him viewing porn at the University of Wisconsin-Eau Claire.

According to Haley Halverson of the National Center on Sexual Exploitation, the oldest and largest library association in the world likely wouldn't agree with the court's decision.

"The American Library Association often spreads misinformation that you have a First Amendment right to watch pornography in libraries," she says. "But that [opinion] has not been upheld on several instances."

In fact, the U.S. Supreme Court ruled in 2004 that Congress can deny federal funds to libraries that don't install filters to block porn. For years the ALA has worked to convince libraries to not filter their Internet access — and they have offered parental advice, too.

"One representative from the American Library Association even said that parents who don't let their kids read *Playboy* don't really care about their kids growing up and learning," Halverson shares. "They obviously have an agenda — a pro-pornography agenda."

On its website the ALA argues that "only unfiltered Internet access accommodates both parental guidance and sensitive recognition of the First Amendment rights of young people." And regarding the use of porn filters, the ALA encourages libraries to actively oppose any proposed legislation that "negatively impacts intellectual freedom."

Halverson says people need to get involved and investigate their local libraries to see if they are "pornography safe." She refers individuals to SafeLibraryProject.com here tools are available to do exactly that. [42]

Bazzel Baz

Librarian Fired for Reporting Child Pornography - Supervisor Warned Her Not to Call Police Over Illegal Activity
WND, March 20, 2008

A bizarre battle has erupted over the arrest on child pornography charges of a man at a California public library, with library and county officials siding against the staffer who called police to arrest the alleged criminal.

Librarian Brenda Biesterfeld was fired from her job after disregarding her supervisor's orders not to call police. Now a pro-family organization and a law firm are rallying support for her.

The incident developed on Feb. 28 when Beisterfeld, a single mother, was working in the Lindsay Branch library, and she noticed Donny Lynn Chrisler, 39, viewing child porn on one of the public-use computers.

"She immediately went to her supervisor, Judi Hill, who instructed her to give him a warning and explain that on his second warning he would be banned from the library," Liberty Counsel said. "When Biesterfeld asked if she should call the police, Hill told her not to and that the library would handle it internally."

She also was told that "this happens more often than she would think."

Biesterfeld was so unnerved by the situation, she talked with police the next day. Then on March 4, when Chrisler returned, Biesterfeld saw him viewing more child porn and called police.

"When police officers arrived they caught Chrisler viewing the child pornography, arrested him, and placed him in the Tulare County Jail, where he remains on $10,000 bail," Liberty Counsel said. "Further investigation uncovered more child pornography in Chrisler's home."

But when police confiscated the computer from the library, Hill confronted them and said they had no business enforcing the child pornography law within the library.

"Even after the police captain explained that a federal law had been violated, making it a legal matter to be handled by police, Hill never offered to help," Liberty Counsel said. "Instead, she demanded to know who made the report."

Even though police investigators concealed Biesterfeld's name, Hill claimed she knew who it was, and within 20 minutes the captain got a call from Biesterfeld saying Hill had called her and rebuked her. Two days later and without explanation Biesterfeld was fired.

The law firm's letter demands Biesterfeld's reinstatement and that the library change its policy to prevent the use of library property for illegal behavior and to establish a prompt reporting system.

Mayor Ed Murray submitted a similar request to the county, officials said.

"Brenda Biesterfeld had a moral and a legal responsibility to report to police a library patron whom she observed viewing child pornography," said Staver. "It is outrageous that the Lindsay Branch library fired Ms. Biesterfeld for reporting child pornography. Child Pornography is a despicable crime against children."

Thomasson said the local battle, however, has national implications. "We're also defending children nationwide," he said. "You see, the American Library Association, which is the controlling influence over libraries nationwide, views pornography and obscenity as 'intellectual freedom.' Because of this, many libraries in the U.S. allow child pornographers to use their Internet system undetected and unreported. Is it any wonder why child molestation has become so common?"

According to the association's own web page regarding intellectual freedom and censorship, it is not the work of a library to protect children from material that is "legally obscene."

"Governmental institutions cannot be expected to usurp or interfere with parental obligations and responsibilities when it comes to deciding what a child may read or view," the ALA says.

It also defines "intellectual freedom" as the right to see material "without restriction." Those who object to obscenity and its availability are "censors," who "try to use the power of the state to impose their view of what is truthful and appropriate."

"Each of us has the right to read, view, listen to, and disseminate constitutionally protected ideas, even if a censor finds those ideas offensive," the ALA states.

"Censors might sincerely believe that certain materials are so offensive, or present ideas that are so hateful and destructive to society, that they simply must not see the light of day. Others are worried that younger or weaker people will be badly influenced by bad ideas, and will do bad things as a result," the ALA said.

That was the point Steve Baldwin, a former California lawmaker, was making when he previously penned a column citing a report from the Family Research Council.

"A 2000 report by the Family Research Council details how its researchers sent out surveys to every librarian in America asking questions about access to pornography. Despite efforts by the ALA to stop its members from responding, 462 librarians did respond. Their replies revealed 472 instances of children assessing pornography, 962 instances of adults accessing pornography, 106 instances of adults exposing children to pornography, five attempted child molestations, 144 instances of child porn being accessed and 25 instances of library staff being harassed by those viewing pornography. Over 2,062 total porn-related incidents were reported by a mere 4.6 percent of our nation's librarians so one can assume the number of incidents is probably twenty times higher," he reported.

He wrote that the "bias" of the ALA is obvious.

"When parent groups have offered to place books in libraries with conservative themes or are critical of the left, the ALA's claims of being First Amendment guardians suddenly look fraudulent. When one parent tried to donate George Grant's book, 'Killer Angel,' a critical biography of Planned Parenthood founder Margaret Sanger, the library sent a letter stating that 'the author's political and social agenda...is not appropriate.' Huh? A biographical book with zero profanity is banned but books that feature the 'F' word a hundred times are sought after with zeal. Go figure," Baldwin wrote.

Thomasson called on librarians across the country to report child pornography to law enforcement whenever it happens.

"The liberals who run the library system in America must stop violating the federal law because they regard child pornography as 'free speech,'" he said. "All pornography is immoral, but possession of child pornography is a federal crime. No librarian should fear reporting child pornography to the police, but libraries that fail to report these crimes should be very afraid. Brenda Biesterfeld will get her job back, and more."

Biesterfeld said she felt intimidated by Hill after the police investigation was launched. "She kind of threatened me," Biesterfeld said. "She said I worked for the county, and when the county tells you to do something, you do what the county tells you. She said I had no loyalty to the county. I told her I was a mother and a citizen also, and not just a county employee."

The dismissal letter from Tulare County Librarian Brian Lewis said probationary employees can be fired if they don't perform at a level "necessary for fully satisfactory performance."

But Thomasson reported a Lindsay city councilwoman said she'd been told just a few weeks earlier Biesterfeld was doing a great job.

The city of Lindsay also has complained to the county about Hill's "abrupt, demanding and demeaning" telephone call to police telling them to halt their pornography investigation. (43)

I think it is safe to say by now that you get the picture. For some it is unbelievable, for others extremely frustrating, and then for others a condition of society that angers you beyond explanation. Our country is upside-down and, for the most part, not even interested in protecting the lives of innocent children. Take, for example, Virginia Governor Northam's statements condoning infanticide and California Governor Brown's support of AB 775.

Virginia Democratic Gov. Ralph Northam said he doesn't regret statements he made appearing to condone infanticide and late-term abortion, at a Thursday afternoon press conference with Virginia Democratic leaders. A reporter asked Northam if he has any regrets about his comments or the way he said them. "No, I don't," Northam replied.

"If a mother is in labor, I can tell you exactly what would happen. The infant would be delivered. The infant would be kept comfortable. The infant would be resuscitated if that's what the mother and the family desired, and then a discussion would ensue between the physicians and the mother," Northam said in the interview.

Northam's initial comments regard Virginia's HB 2491, which would allow a doctor to perform an abortion when a woman is about to give birth. [44]

PJI Asks Federal Court to Block Abortion Speech Mandate
Pacific Justice Institute, November 17, 2015

Sacramento, CA — Attorneys with Pacific Justice Institute are asking a federal court to block implementation of a law that would force pro-life pregnancy clinics to point women toward abortion.

Last month, California Gov. Jerry Brown signed AB 775, which would require pro-life clinics to tell women about the availability of free or low-cost abortions. PJI filed suit within 24 hours on behalf of three clinics across the state that believe in the sanctity of life and are morally opposed to abortion. On Friday, PJI filed a Motion for Preliminary Injunction asking the court to prevent the law from going into effect on January 1, 2016.

Brad Dacus, president of Pacific Justice Institute, commented, "It is imperative that we stop the government from forcing people of conscience to advocate messages to which they are morally and religiously opposed. If the government can do this, none of our First Amendment freedoms are secure."

The case is pending in the United States District Court for the Eastern District of California. Oral arguments are scheduled for December 18 at 10 a.m. before Judge Kimberly Mueller. [45]

Something Bigger Than Overthrowing Small Governments

    It is an embarrassment to many of us as Americans when the very officials and institutions we set in place to uphold the laws that protect children are in fact the very ones that fail to protect them or even abuse them. And it will remain this way until we shine a light on the darkness, expose crimes against children, and make sure those responsible for upholding the law are held accountable.

Chapter 23
IF WE DO NOT ... WHO WILL?

"Worry is the interest paid by those who borrow trouble," (George Washington). Those who sexually exploit children need to be worried because ARC is coming for you. We will show no mercy, take no prisoners and be the thorn in your flesh until you are brought to justice. We are hundreds of operators strong worldwide, and we are woven into the fabric of every society on the planet. Our technological tools and tradecraft far surpass anything governments currently use to identify and locate victims and perpetrators, and we will maintain that edge into the future.

I believe God creates all men and women with extraordinary gifts, but a lot of people never choose to accept the assignments. Here at ARC we are building a coalition of strategic partners with a compliment of skills ranging from intelligence gathering to covert communications that will allow us to be the most effective child rescue organization in the world. We are faith based, as you have probably realized after reading the previous chapters. We are beholding to none other than Jesus the Christ, the Messiah, the Way the Truth and the Life. It isn't a matter of our knowledge of Him, but our relationship. We are ready and willing to give our life for Him, and because of that we are ready and willing to give our life for a child in danger. "Certainly, it is true that many people throughout history have died for what they thought to be true, even though it may not have been. But the Christian martyrs of the first two centuries A.D. confirm at least three important facts.

First, whatever doubts might be raised from late tradition being unreliable as to whether certain apostles endured martyrdom, the testimony of second and third generation martyrs indicates that most of the apostles before them died for their testimony. If the students were willing to die for their faith, how much more the teachers? Further, the voluntary sufferings and deaths of the original eyewitnesses and disciples of Jesus confirm that the basic historical information they

Something Bigger Than Overthrowing Small Governments

passed on was true. If they knew, for example, that Jesus had not performed miracles or had not risen from the dead, because they themselves had stolen the body, what possible motivation would they have had to go out and die martyrs' deaths for spreading these lies?

Second, the continued suffering and martyrdom of second, third and fourth generation Christians confirms that, at the very least, any thinking person would make every possible effort to verify the accuracy of the gospel reports. From the very beginning, such a vast Christian network of multiplication spread out across the empire that it would have been easy enough to verify the historical events of Jesus' life. Even 120 years after the death of Christ, at least one godly Christian, Polycarp, was still living who could verify what some of the original disciples of Jesus had reported.

A third fact confirmed by the early reports is that the early Christians considered moral and ethical integrity more important than life itself. These Christians do not appear to be wild-eyed fanatics. Nor are they simply zealously devoted to a particular philosophy of life. They are men and women who, at the very least, are saying by their shed blood, "I cannot deny that Jesus of Nazareth lived, taught and died, and has been raised from the dead to demonstrate that He is Messiah and Lord and God." [32, Chapter 43, page 437]

With so much evidence we cannot but help keep Jesus Christ as our foundation. As I mentioned in an earlier chapter, Jesus (God) isn't in the equation ... He is the equation.

Now there are finer men than I in this fight. And I am honored to be able to put pen to paper and motivate people to pick up their battle axe and run to the front line. But those who deserve the credit for all I have accomplished with ARC are my parents, Sharkey and May Baz, my sister Seebe Baz, her children, my relatives, the men and women of ARC and a very big God who keeps us alive on every dangerous assignment. The protection of American children is our duty. The hearing and reading of this trafficking issue may be useful, "but if men and women rest in hearing and praying, as so many do, it is as if a tree should value itself on being watered and putting forth leaves, though it never produces fruit." [46]

The fact is a child does not come home until there are boots on the ground that pull them from the evil and bring them home. Most people spend a lifetime wondering if they have made a difference. I don't have that problem. And I don't want you to have that problem. When it comes to rescuing children, it is simply stated ... If we do not ... who will?

Make no doubt about it ... these are God's children and He is speaking to each and every one of us in a world with unprecedented evil that is out to destroy our children. If we allow our children to exist in a dysfunctional world, they will grow up to be dysfunctional adults. Is that who you really want running the country?

There is a spiritual component to every human being ... it is called the soul. When children are trafficked, molested, abused, and exploited, their soul is ripped from their very being. Each of you knows this to be true ... just look inside yourself ... you too were once a child. And if you were that child again in a similar exploited situation, would you not want someone to save you?

Therefore, my friends, I implore you to not shy away from your duty to prevent our children from being exploited. My father said there are only two types of people in this world ... followers and leaders. I can only pray that what I have written will have inspired you to take your rightful place in society as a leader who is willing to say, "the exploitation of children will not happen on my watch."

I know there are some of you who will finish this book and say, "... well all of this is easy for you to do Mr. CIA Special Operations, you've been trained." Okay Spanky ... let me tell you something. You and I have one thing in common, the most important thing. We both have 24 hours in a day. So what are you doing with yours?

Look, if I have 99 cents in my pocket and take it to the bank and ask them to give me a dollar, do you think they'll do that? Of course not. Why? Because I'm one penny short. It is the one penny that completes the dollar. The one penny is actually the most important part, and without it we are financially incomplete. So for all of you reading this book that feel like you're alone in this fight ... just realize you may be that one penny, the most important part and it may very well be you who completes the efforts of an NGO struggling to win the war on trafficking. One man or one woman with courage ... is a majority.

Something Bigger Than Overthrowing Small Governments

    Remember this and hold it close to your heart, for it will be a sword of encouragement when the system fails you — and trust me ... it will. It will be a sword of encouragement when you discover that some NGOs are lying about how many people they rescue and how many beds they provide, when you discover that some NGOs are exploiting children by using their unfortunate circumstances to build a business model that pays record-breaking salaries, when laws favor the perpetrator rather than the victim, when corruption runs amuck in our judicial system and among trusted officials, and when fellow advocates fall by the wayside. You must think outside the box, march to the sound of your own drummer and never be ashamed of being in this world and yet not of it.

    On 12 June 2019 I flew to Washington D.C. to take a meeting at the White House with Katie Sullivan, who in days soon after would be appointed by Attorney General Barr to become the Principal Deputy Assistant Attorney General for the Justice Department's Office of Justice Programs.

> "Katie Sullivan has been an energetic and great leader of the Office on Violence Against Women, and I am confident she will bring the same enthusiasm to the Office of Justice Programs. Katie's leadership will further enhance the department's efforts to strengthen public safety and the

criminal justice system through research, programs and strategies, and to provide critical services to victims of crime." - Attorney General Barr [47]

Sitting in front of me, Katie was all that and much more. I had sat among some of the most powerful people in the world in my time, people who literally had changed the face of history and now once again it was no small thing to be in the same room with one of the most powerful, and at the same time one of the most compassionate, judicial executives in our land. I knew she was a warrior with a righteous heart for all the things God cared about, especially the crimes against children. My reputation had proceeded me, and our small talk soon lead to the discovery of common ground in many areas of life, liberty and the pursuit of happiness, as well as ARC's mission.

Katie leaned in, smiled and said "okay, tell me what you're thinking."

And so, I did.

How do you MURDER A CHILD without KILLING them? YOU SEXUALLY EXPLOIT THEM.

"Chronic and acute sexual trauma inflicts unspeakable and immeasurable emotional pain on the heart and mind of a child. Such trauma destroys a child's innate potential to evolve into prosperous adults, robbing them of opportunities to create meaningful and purpose driven lives. Further, the residue of these vile experiences compromises their ability to create deep, intimate attachments with others, the kind of attachments wherein true safety, security, and love can be experienced. For the victims of sexual abuse, meaningful bonding is threatening and dangerous, which is really to say that love is threatening and dangerous. And a life without love is a life of

Something Bigger Than Overthrowing Small Governments

profound suffering worse than death. It is a suffering defined by a chronic sense of separateness and aloneness that permeates each unfolding moment as if they were confined to a life of solitary confinement." (Michele L. Blume, Psy.D. Clinical Psychologist PSY24331)

HOW MANY CHILDREN ARE SEXUALLY VICTIMIZED?

STUDIES BY DAVID FINKELHOR, DIRECTOR OF THE CRIMES AGAINST CHILDREN RESEARCH CENTER, SHOW:

PREVALENCE
Self-report studies show that 20% of adult females and 5-10% of adult males recall a childhood sexual assault or sexual abuse incident

ONE-YEAR STUDY
During a one-year period in the U.S., 16% of youth ages 14 to 17 had been sexually victimized

28% OF YOUTH
Over the course of their lifetime to date, 28% of U.S. youth ages 14 to 17 had been sexually victimized

THE MOST VULNERABLE
Children are most vulnerable to child sexual abuse between the ages of 7 and 13

And none of these statistics includes the children that are sexually abused by sex traffickers here in the United States. The U.S. Department of Health & Human Services estimated that between 240,000 and 325,000 children are at risk for sexual exploitation each year. Children who are considered runaways are at particular risk of prostitution or of being trafficked into the sex industry.

ADDRESSING THE ISSUE IN THE UNITED STATES

After thousands of interviews with survivors of childhood sexual abuse, we see first-hand the horror they daily encounter from the effects of this abuse. We see and hear the fear that parents and responsible adults try to cope with on a daily basis while they try to protect children from sexual predators.

There are countless stories of the horrors children suffer from repeat offenders. There are countless stories of child sex trafficking by pimps.

It is time to end this cycle once and for all by creating a consequence that will end the recidivism rate for this crime.

We deserve to be able to live without this fear following us constantly. Our children and grandchildren deserve to live a better life than we have lived.

LET'S END THIS NIGHTMARE ONCE AND FOR ALL BY PASSING A BILL TO EXPAND OUR NATION'S **CAPITAL PUNISHMENT** STATUTE SO THAT THOSE WHO ARE CONVICTED OF RAPING CHILDREN OR SEXUALLY EXPLOITING CHILDREN UNDER 18 ARE ELIGIBLE FOR THE DEATH PENALTY…AND MORE THAN THAT…THE DEATH PENALTY IS ENFORCED.

The critics who worry that the bill may result in unintended consequences do not understand or acknowledge the damage sexual abuse does to a child. Or perhaps they are complicit in such crimes and fear for their own lives.

Others argue that the legislation will lead to family members refusing to come forward regarding intra-family offenses. Intra-family offenses take place every day and very few come forward to expose them.

Something Bigger Than Overthrowing Small Governments

Yes, there are times down the road when a child becomes an adult and seeks therapy to expose the crime, but that is rare. Most never come forward because they do not believe they have a voice, and they believe that justice will never be served for the crimes committed against them.

Other critics are concerned with the idea that such a bill would actually create more death because the person facing the death penalty for this kind of offense might be inclined to say, "No greater punishment will be incurred if I kill the victim." Taking a look at these kinds of crimes that have been committed, we see that often the victim is killed by the predator regardless.

Speaking with predators has revealed that the one thing they do fear most is losing their life. And it is the one thing that causes them to change their mind regarding child sexual exploitation.

The U.S. Supreme Court has ruled the death penalty cannot be used in cases involving adult rapes, but it has not weighed in on the issue of imposing the death penalty on those who commit child rapes.

When this legislative proposal came before the State of South Carolina, Representative Fletcher Smith said that he believes that such a proposed bill will not meet constitutional standards regarding the death penalty because a death is not involved. *How wrong can one person be when it comes to the definition of death?*

Constitutional standards that apply the death penalty as a punishment for physical murder should equally punish the psychological and physiological destruction of children's lives at the hands of sexual predators.

The Federal Government must promote the value of life of infants and children and defend their human rights above legislative trends that condone infanticide and promote sexual freedom at the expense of child safety.

If the State of New York can pass a law that does not protect children (partial birth abortions), how many other States will be politically driven to follow with an attitude that our children are an expendable commodity?

JUSTICE MUST BE UPHELD IN DEFENSE OF OUR CHILDREN

ARC has been on the front lines of this issue since 1993. We have served our country, and we know the difference between right and wrong. Justice must be upheld in the defense of our children. If we allow them to be exploited in a dysfunctional environment, then they will grow up to be dysfunctional citizens in our country.

We have a moral obligation as well as a national obligation if we truly care about the future of America. *If we cannot protect the rights of the most vulnerable of society, it is only a matter of time before we will not be able to protect our own rights.* If we as a nation are to protect our children, then it must be done at the Federal level. If we are to put a stop to child sex trafficking, then it must be done at the Federal level.

It is our belief that the President and his Administration can set the standard so that all American children will know in the future that they are protected. The members of ARC are more than ready to come alongside and spearhead our options in making this a reality.

Something Bigger Than Overthrowing Small Governments

I've been in this war against human trafficking for 22 plus years now. One day after seeing as much of the ugly side of child exploitation I could stand, I paddled out on my surfboard in the evening hours along the California coast. As the sun settled on the horizon and the new moon crested the heavens I looked up and cried out again as I did when it all began in Somalia, "Dear God, are you still doing something about this?" And as clear as day once again He said ... "Of course ... I created you." And so, I tell you the same, He is doing something about all of this .... He created each of you.

May God bless you and may God bless this great country of ours, the United States of America.

"OBEY MY VOICE AND I WILL BE YOUR GOD AND YOU SHALL BE MY PEOPLE. AND WALK IN ALL THE WAYS THAT I HAVE COMMANDED YOU, THAT IT MAY BE WELL WITH YOU." (JEREMIAH 7:23 NKJV)

ADDENDUMS

ADDENDUM 1
REFERENCED ON PAGE 48

The Long Gray Line–Military

- Col. Charles C. Tew CSA (1846) first graduate of the college, founded Hillsborough Military Academy in North Carolina. Killed in action at Battle of Antietam in 1862 on the eve of his promotion to brigadier general.
- Col. William J. Magill CSA (1846) first graduate to serve in the U.S. Army, Cavalry officer in the 3rd U.S. Dragoons during The Mexican War. Professor and Commandant of Cadets at Kentucky Military Institute and Georgia Military Institute; commanded a regiment of Georgia regulars, was severely wounded and lost his sword arm at the shoulder during Battle of Antietam.
- Brig. Gen. Johnson Hagood CSA (1847) commanded Confederate forces in Charleston during the attack on Fort Wagner depicted in the movie "Glory." Governor of South Carolina 1880-82 and instrumental in reopening The Citadel after occupation by Federal troops at the end of the Civil War, Johnson Hagood Stadium, where The Citadel plays its home football games, is named for him.
- Brig. Gen. Micah Jenkins CSA (1854) First Honor Graduate of his class, one of the "boy generals" at age of 26; he was a favorite of General Robert E. Lee, killed in action at The Battle of the Wilderness. Jenkins Hall, which houses the Military Sciences and Commandant's Office is named in his honor
- MajGen. Evander M. Law CSA (1856) fought in 13 major engagements during WBTS, wounded four times and youngest general in Army of Northern Virginia. Founded South Florida Military Institute, Law Barracks is named in his honor
- Brig. Gen. Thomas Huguenin CSA (1859) fought in defense of Fort Wagner, the last Confederate commander of Fort Sumter

Something Bigger Than Overthrowing Small Governments

- MG William W. Moore USA (1888), Adjutant General of South Carolina 1910-21
- MG James B. Allison USA (1895) Chief of U.S. Army Signal Corps 1935-37
- MG Edward Croft USA (1896) U.S. Army Chief of Infantry 1935-38
- BG John T. Kennedy USA (1907) awarded the Medal of Honor in the Philippines Campaign, 1909 (attended one year, USMA graduate)
- LTC Robert H. Willis USA (1908) one of the first military pilots earning his wings as an army aviator in 1913, flew scout missions during the Punitive Expedition in Mexico of 1916 crashing twice and the second time walking 65 miles back to his base. In 1918 he was appointed by Gen. John J. Pershing to be the first head of the U.S. Army Air Service but was killed in France before assuming the position.
- BG Barnwell R. Legge USA (1911) one of the most decorated alumni and 3d most decorated U.S. military member of World War I earning the Distinguished Service Cross, Distinguished Service Medal, four Silver Stars, French Croix de Guerre and the Purple Heart during combat; during the Second World War he was the military attaché at the U.S. Embassy in Zurich, Switzerland and helped arrange the escape of many interned U.S. fliers.
- MG Edward F. Witsell USA (1911) U.S. Army Adjutant General 1946-51
- Lt. Gen. James T. Moore USMC (1916) early Marine aviator who held important command positions in USMC aviation during World War II, famous as Pappy Boyington's boss in the South Pacific air war and featured in the 1970s TV show *Baa Baa Black Sheep*.
- MajGen. Lewie G. Merritt USMC (1917) pioneer in Marine aviation who developed tactics of dive bombing and close air support, commanded several major flying units in World War II. Namesake of the Marine Corps Air Station in Beaufort, SC.
- Gen. William O. Brice USMC (1921) another early Marine flier who led units during World War II and Korea. Commanding

General, Fleet Marine Force, Pacific; Assistant Commandant for Air and Assistant Chief of Naval Operations for Marine Aviation. Youngest Marine Corps general in World War II, first Marine aviator four-star general.
- Gen. Edwin A. Pollock USMC (1921) Navy Cross winner at Guadalcanal in 1942, led the 2d Marine Division during combat in Korea. Also commanded 1st Marine Division and only Marine to have commanded both the Pacific and Atlantic Fleet Marine Forces. Instrumental in founding the Marine Military Academy in Harlingen, Texas; served as first President and Commandant. Chairman of The Citadel Board of Visitors and named Chairman Emeritus upon retirement.
- VADM Bernard L. Austin USN (1922) highest ranking Navy alumnus, won 2 Navy Crosses during World War II; President of the Naval War College and Deputy Chief of Naval Operations (attended two years, USNA graduate)
- Major Thomas D. Howie USA (1929) Immortalized during World War II as "The Major of St. Lo"; leader of the battalion that captured the strategic city of Saint-Lô, France (where he was killed). He was the model for Tom Hanks character in *Saving Private Ryan*.
- GEN William Westmoreland USA (1935) Commander of U.S. forces in Vietnam, U.S. Army Chief of Staff; father James R. (1900) served as Chairman of the Board of Visitors in the 1940s and son James A. graduated in 1961 (attended one year, USMA graduate)
- Major Roland F. Wooten USAAC (1936) fighter pilot and "ace" with 6 victories while flying the British Spitfire with the 31st Fighter Group, one of the most highly decorated alumni in WWII; over 200 combat missions in North Africa and Europe and shot down twice, POW in Germany 1944-45. Named Postmaster of Charleston in 1961 by President Kennedy, Arnold Air Society chapter at The Citadel named in his honor.
- LTC Thomas N. Courvoisie USA (1938) Iconic school figure known as "The Boo," Assistant Commandant 1961-68. Inspired the first book written by novelist Pat Conroy '67, "The Bear" in Conroy's novel "The Lords of Discipline" was based

Something Bigger Than Overthrowing Small Governments

on Courvoisie and played by Robert Prosky in the movie version.
- LtCol George B. McMillan USAAC (1938) fighter pilot and "ace" with 8.5 aerial victories, flight leader with the Flying Tigers 1941-42. Commander, 449th Fighter Squadron, 51st Fighter Group in China 1943-44; shot down/killed in action over Pingsang, China 24 June 1944.
- LtCol. Horace E. Crouch USAF (1940) B-25 bombardier/navigator, member of crew #10 on the Doolittle Raid in 1942 and shot down two Japanese Zeroes
- MajGen. Andrew J. Evans USAF (1940) fighter pilot and "ace" with 8.5 confirmed kills, he was the highest ranking POW during the Korean War (attended for two years, USMA graduate)
- LtCol. Robert E. Smith USAF (1942) RAF pilot with "Eagle Squadron," European equivalent of the Flying Tigers. Fighter pilot in Korea and Vietnam
- LTG George M. Seignious USA (1942) appointed by President Johnson as military advisor to the Paris Peace Talks in 1968; Commanding General, 3d Infantry Division and U.S. Army, Berlin. Deputy Assistant Secretary of Defense; Director, Joint Staff for the Joint Chiefs of Staff; President of The Citadel 1974-1979. Seignious Hall, the football facility at The Citadel is named for him.
- MG James Grimsley, Jr. USA (1942) combat veteran of World War II and Vietnam earning two Silver Stars, former Deputy Assistant Secretary of Defense. President of The Citadel 1980-89 and President Emeritus 1989-2013
- LtGen. Herbert Beckington USMC (1943) Military Aide to Vice President Hubert Humphrey, Assistant Commandant for Plans and Operations
- LTG Joe Heiser USA (1943) U.S. Army Assistant Chief of Staff for Logistics; Commanding General, 1st Logistics Command in Vietnam. Left school in 1942 to enlist as a private and received battlefield commission in 1943, highest ranking alumni to never receive a degree

- MG William E. Ingram, Sr. ARNG (1943) Adjutant General of North Carolina 1977–1983
- LTG James B. Vaught USA (1946) Commander of the Iranian hostage rescue mission in 1980; former Commanding General of Combined US/ROK Forces, Korea
- Capt. Dolphin D. Overton USAF (1948) F-84/F-86 pilot in Korean War and "Ace" with seven enemy aircraft shot down. Most decorated alumni earning Distinguished Service Cross, four Silver Stars, six Distinguished Flying Crosses and nine Air Medals. (attended one year, USMA graduate)
- MajGen. Irwin Graham USAF (1949) Military Assistant to Secretary of State Henry Kissinger; Executive Assistant to the Chairman of the Joint Chiefs of Staff; Deputy J-5, Joint Chiefs of Staff. One of the highest ranking navigators in Air Force history.
- MajGen. John A. Wilson III ANG (1950) Adjutant General of West Virginia 1982-86
- LTG Don Rosenblum USA (1951) Commanding General of 1st Army and 24th Infantry Division; Deputy Commanding General, XVIII Airborne Corps
- Col. J. Quincy Collins USAF (1953) Tactical Officer for first group of cadets at U.S. Air Force Academy; fighter pilot and one of longest serving Vietnam POWs (7 ½ years), onetime cellmate of Sen. John McCain in the "Hanoi Hilton"
- MajGen. (Dr) Thomas P. Ball USAF (1954) first Commander of the Joint Military Medical Command, San Antonio
- LtGen. Claudius E. Watts III USAF (1958) Fulbright Scholar and Comptroller of the USAF, President of The Citadel 1989-96
- LTG Jack B. Farris USA (1958) commanded U.S. forces during invasion of Grenada in 1983. Deputy Commander-in-Chief, U.S. Pacific Command; Commanding General, 2d Infantry Division
- LtGen. Ellie "Buck" Shuler Jr. USAF (1959) Commander, 8th Air Force (SAC)
- LTG Harold T. Fields USA (1960) Commanding General, U.S. Army Pacific and 6th Infantry Division

Something Bigger Than Overthrowing Small Governments

- LTG Sam Wakefield USA (1960) Commanding General, Combined Arms Support Command; Commanding General, U.S. Army Transportation Center and School
- Major Samuel R. Bird USA (1961) Officer in charge of casket bearers at President Kennedy's funeral; severely wounded in Vietnam and subject of a Reader's Digest article on leadership and strength of character (May, 1989)
- LTG Carmen Cavezza USA (1961) awarded two Silver Stars for combat service in Vietnam, served as Military Assistant to Secretary of Defense Caspar Weinberger. Commanding General of 7th Infantry Division, U.S. Army Infantry Center and I Corps
- GEN William W. Hartzog USA (1963) Commanding General, U.S. Army Training and Doctrine Command; Commanding General of 1st Infantry Division and U.S. Army, South
- LtCol. Dave Smith USAF (1963) Commander of the Thunderbirds 1979-81
- LtCol. Joe Vida USAF (1963) holds records for most years as a crewmember (16) and most flying hours (1,392) on the SR-71 "Blackbird" spy plane. Served as the reconnaissance systems operator on the retirement flight of the SR-71 in 1990 that flew from Los Angeles to Washington DC in 68 minutes, setting four world speed records. The aircraft and the pressure suit he wore are now on display at the National Air and Space Annex in Chantilly, Virginia.
- MG Nate Robb ARNG (1964) Adjutant General of North Carolina 1989 — 93
- LtGen. Frank B. Campbell USAF (1966) Director, J-8 Joint Chiefs of Staff; Commander, 12th Air Force/U.S. Southern Command
- LtGen. Frank Libutti USMC (1966) Commanding General Marine Forces Pacific, Marine Forces Korea and 1st Marine Division .
- LTG William Tangney USA (1967) Deputy Commander-in-Chief, United States Special Operations Command; Commanding General U.S. Army Special Operations

Bazzel Baz

Command, JFK Special Warfare School and Special Operations Command-Central
- LtGen.John B. Sams USAF (1967) Vice Commander, Air Mobility Command; Commander, 15th Air Force. Current member of the Board of Visitors
- LTG William M. Steele USA (1967) Commanding General U.S. Army Pacific, Combined Arms Center and 82nd Airborne Division
- Lt. Gen. VeerachaiIamsa-ad (1968) Deputy Commander-in-Chief, Royal Thai Armed Forces
- LtGen. Garry L. Parks USMC (1969) Assistant Commandant for Manpower and Reserve Affairs; Commanding General, Marine Corps Recruiting Command
- LTG John P. Costello USA (1969) Commanding General, Army Space and Missile Command; Commanding General, Air Defense Artillery School and Center
- General LetratRatanavanich (1971) Chairman of the Joint Staff, Thai Armed Forces; member of Thai Senate
- LTG Colby Broadwater USA (1972) Chief of Staff, U.S. European Command; Commanding General, 1st Army and U.S. Army-NATO
- LtCol. Gilbert M. O'Brien USAF (1973-veteran) P-51 pilot and "ace" in World War II with eight aerial victories. Also served in Korean War and flew more than 50 types of aircraft during his career
- LtGen. John W. Rosa USAF (1973) Superintendent of the Air Force Academy 2003-05, current President of The Citadel
- MG Terry Juskowiak USA (1973) Commanding General, Combined Arms Support Command; Commanding General, U.S. Army Quartermaster Center and School
- LTG John F. Kimmons USA (1974) Staff Director, Office of National Intelligence; U.S. Army Assistant Chief of Staff for Intelligence; Commanding General, U.S. Army Intelligence and Security Command
- MG Robert Williams USA (1974) Commandant, U.S. Army War College

Something Bigger Than Overthrowing Small Governments

- MG Steve Smith USAR (1975) Deputy Assistant Secretary of the Army for Manpower and Reserve Affairs
- RADM Joe Kilkenny USN (1977) Commander, U.S. Naval Education and Training Command
- LTG Daniel P. Bolger USA (1978) Commanding General, Combined Security Transition Command-Afghanistan and Commander, NATO Training Mission Afghanistan; U.S. Army Assistant Chief of Staff for Operations and Training; Commanding General, 1st Cavalry Division and Joint Readiness Training Center
- LTG Mike Ferriter USA (1979) Commanding General, Installation Management Command/U.S. Army Assistant Chief of Staff, Installation Management; former Commanding General NATO Training Mission, Iraq and U.S. Army Maneuver Center
- LtGen. Glenn Walters USMC (1979) current Assistant Commandant for Programs and Resources
- LtGen. Frank McKenzie USMC (1979) current Commanding General, Marine Forces Central Command
- MajGen. Larry Nicholson USMC (1979) current Commanding General, 1st Marine Division
- MG Glenn K. Rieth ARNG (1980) Adjutant General of New Jersey 2002-11
- Col. Cesar "Rico" Rodriguez USAF (1981) F-15 pilot with two aerial victories in Desert Storm and 1 in Bosnia; leading MIG killer of all U.S. aviators since Vietnam
- Lt. Gen. Hussein Al-Majali (1981) current Director of Jordan's Public Security Forces
- LtGen. John Cooper USAF (1983) current Deputy Chief of Staff for Logistics, Engineering and Force Protection
- MajGen. Tim Leahy USAF (1985) current Director of Operations (J-8) United States Special Operations Command
- Col. Randolph Bresnik USMC (1989) Current NASA Astronaut, Mission Specialist on STS-129 space shuttle Atlantis in November, 2009

- CAPT Greg McWherter USN (1990) Instructor, "Top Gun" Fighter Weapons School; Commander of the Blue Angels 2008-12 and longest serving Team Leader

The Long Gray Line–Business

- Charles E. Daniel (1918), R. Hugh Daniel (1929)-co-founders of Daniel International Construction Corporation. (at one time the largest construction company in the world); major Citadel benefactors for whom Daniel Library is named.
- Randolph Guthrie (1925) Chairman of the Board, Studebaker Corp.
- John Monroe Holliday (1936) President of Holliday Associates LLC, once the largest SC tobacco grower. Member of the Board of Visitors for many years, The Citadel's alumni center is named for him.
- Alvah Chapman, Jr.(1942) CEO Knight-Ridder Newspapers
- John B. Sias (1947) President, ABC TV
- Harry M. Perks (1951) President, Day & Zimmermann, one of the largest privately held companies in the United States
- BGen Harvey Schiller, PhD (1960) CEO of YankeeNets, a conglomerate that owns the New York Yankees, New Jersey Nets and New Jersey Devils; President, Turner Sports Network
- Tandy Rice (1961) Owner of Top Billing, one of the biggest talent agencies in Nashville; clients have included Hank Williams, Waylon Jennings and Dolly Parton. Former President of the Country Music Association, inducted into the Country Music Hall of Fame and first inductee in the Nashville Association of Talent Directors Hall of Fame.
- Allan Schreiber (1962) Vice President, Chase Bank
- L. William Krause (1963) Chairman, CEO, and President, 3Com
- William Sansom (1964) Chairman, Tennessee Valley Authority
- H. Stephen McManus (1964) CEO of Hardees
- LtGen. John Sams (1967) Vice President, Boeing
- Richard R. Wackenhut (1969) CEO of Wackenhut Security, the world's largest private security firm

Something Bigger Than Overthrowing Small Governments

- Tom Hendricks (1979) President, National Air Transportation Association
- Larry Melton (1984) Vice President, Bechtel Corporation

The Long Gray Line-Sports

- Andy Sabados (1939) Guard, Chicago Cardinals 1939-40
- Paul Maguire (1960) color commentator with NBC and ESPN; Tight End and Punter with Los Angeles/San Diego Chargers and Buffalo Bills 1960-70. Played on three consecutive AFL championship teams and in six of ten championship games; one of only 20 players who were members of the American Football League from its inception in 1960 until its merger with the NFL in 1970; member of The Citadel Athletic Hall of Fame
- Harvey Schiller (1960) Commissioner, Southeastern Conference NCAA 1986-90; Director, United States Olympic Committee 1990-94; President, Atlanta Thrashers NHL 1994-99; CEO New York Yankees/New York Nets/New Jersey Devils 1999-2007; President, International Baseball Federation 2007-09 and current member Board of Directors, Baseball Hall of Fame. Named several times by SPORTING NEWS as one of the 100 Most Important People in Sports; recipient of IOC Olympic Order, member of New York City Athletic Club and Citadel Athletic Halls of Fame. Retired Air Force Brigadier General and combat fighter pilot in Vietnam
- Ed Steers (1968) Head Wrestling Coach at William and Mary, East Carolina and West Point; Associate Athletic Director, The Citadel. Member of the National Wrestling Hall of Fame and Citadel Athletic Hall of Fame.
- John Small, Sr. (1970) 2d Team AP All-American linebacker; Atlanta Falcons 1970-72, Detroit Lions 1973-75. Member of The Citadel and South Carolina Athletic Halls of Fame. 1st round draft pick by Falcons in 1970.
- Brian Ruff (1977) 1st team AP 1-A All-American linebacker 1976; two-time Southern Conference Player of the Year, two-time Southern Conference Male Athlete of the Year, three time All Southern Conference and lead team in tackles four

consecutive years. Drafted by Baltimore Colts; first player to have jersey retired, member of Citadel and South Carolina Athletic Halls of Fame
- Dr. Ken Caldwell (1979) three time Academic All-American and recipient of NCAA Postgraduate Scholarship, four year letterman as linebacker and punter. Current football team physician
- Fred Jordan (1979) Head Baseball Coach, The Citadel 1992-. Winningest coach in school history with more than 770 victories as of the 2015 season; 13 regular season and tournament conference championships, four time Southern Conference Coach of the Year, 29 players selected in MLB draft.
- Tom Borelli (1979) Head Wrestling Coach at Central Michigan University 1991-; 12 regular season conference titles, 14 conference tournament titles. Has produced 36 All-Americans, National Coach of the Year 1998
- Lyvonia "Stump" Mitchell (1981) holder of school records for season and career rushing yards; 3d Team 1-A All American, Southern Conference Player of the Year and #2 rusher in the country in 1980, Southern Conference Male Athlete of the Year and South Carolina Amateur Athlete of the Year. Running back and kick returner for St Louis/Phoenix Cardinals 1981-89, Kansas City Chiefs 1990; holds Cardinals record for career all purpose yards (11,988), second in career rushing yards and career 100-yard rushing games. Assistant Coach San Antonio Riders 1992, Head Coach Morgan State University 1996-98, Running Backs Coach Seattle Seahawks 1999-2007 and Assistant Head Coach/Running Backs Coach Washington Redskins 2008-09; Head Coach of Southern University 2010-12, running backs coach Arizona Cardinals 2013- . One of only six Citadel players to have jersey retired, inducted into The Citadel Athletic Hall of Fame.
- Mark Slawson (1981) wide receiver New York Giants 1981-82, New Jersey Generals 1983-84
- Byron Walker (1982) wide receiver Seattle Seahawks 1982-86

Something Bigger Than Overthrowing Small Governments

- Jeff Barkley (1982)-pitcher for the Cleveland Indians 1984-85; member, Citadel Athletic Hall of Fame
- Tim Jones (1983) infielder for the St. Louis Cardinals 1988-93
- Regan Truesdale (1985) Two time Southern Conference Men's Basketball Player of the Year 1984-85, Honorable Mention All-American as a Senior in 1985. Second on career scoring list.[8]
- Greg Davis (1987) kicker for Oakland, San Diego, New England, Minnesota, Atlanta, Tampa Bay and Arizona 1987-98; co-holder of NFL record for most 50+ yard field goals in a game (3), third on Cardinals all-time scoring list with 484 points. Member of The Citadel Athletic Hall of Fame
- John Hartwell (1987) Athletic Director, Utah State
- Ed Conroy (1989) Head Basketball Coach at Tulane, former Head Coach of The Citadel
- Anthony Jenkins (1990) All-American baseball player and Southern Conference Male Athlete of the Year; drafted by St. Louis Cardinals. Scored winning run against Cal State Fullerton in 1990 College World Series (The Citadel is the only military school ever to reach the College World Series).
- Tony Skole (1991) current Head Baseball Coach, East Tennessee State University. Starter on baseball and football teams, played in College World Series and I-AA playoffs
- Jack Douglas (1992) set record for most rushing yards by a Division 1-AA QB, holds school records for most total offense and touchdowns. Lead bulldogs to Southern Conference Championship and #1 ranking in I-AA, 1992; South Carolina Offensive Player of the Year and Amateur Athlete of the Year. Member of Citadel and South Carolina Athletic Halls of Fame, former member of the Board of Visitors
- Lester Smith, Jr. (1992) two-time 1-AA All-American and three time All Southern Conference selection at Safety; CFL player with Baltimore Stallions 1994-95, Toronto Argonauts 1996-98 and Montreal Alouettes 1999-2001; CFL All-Star and member of two Grey Cup Champions. Had Citadel jersey retired and member of Athletic Hall of Fame
- Dan McDonnell (1992) Head Baseball Coach, University of Louisville 2007-; rivals.com National Coach of the Year, 2007.

three appearances in College World Series, member of The Citadel Athletic Hall of Fame.
- Chris Lemonis (1992) Head Baseball Coach, Indiana University
- Lance Cook (1992) defensive end, Saskatchewan Rough Riders 1992-93
- Travis Jervey (1995) fullback Green Bay Packers 1995-98, San Francisco 49ers 1999-2000 and Atlanta Falcons 2001-03. First member of Packers named to Pro Bowl as special teams player; only alumni to play in the Super Bowl and member of Packers Championship team in SB XXXI, 1997. Member of South Carolina and Citadel Athletic Halls of Fame.
- Britt Reames (1996) Pitcher with St Louis Cardinals 2000, Montreal Expos 2001-03, Oakland Athletics 2005 and Pittsburgh Pirates 2006. Current Pitching Coach for The Citadel
- Scott Mullen (1997) Pitcher with Kansas City Royals 2000-03, LA Dodgers 2003
- Dallas McPherson (2001) 3rd Base Anaheim Angels 2004-06, Florida Marlins 2008 and Chicago White Sox 2011
- Cliff Washburn (2002) All-Southern Conference selection in basketball and football, played in East-West Shrine Game and Hula Bowl. Offensive tackle Chicago Bears 2003, Amsterdam Admirals 2004, Frankfurt Galaxy 2005, Green Bay Packers 2007, Toronto Argonauts 2006, 2008; Edmonton Eskimos 2011
- Nehemiah Broughton (2005) fullback Washington Redskins 2005-08, New York Giants 2009 and Arizona Cardinals 2009-10
- Andre Roberts (2010) All-American wide receiver, holds school records for season and career receptions, receiving yardage and punt return yardage. Arizona Cardinals 2010-2013, Washington Redskins 2014-
- Cortez Allen (2010) cornerback, Pittsburgh Steelers 2011-
- Chris McGuiness (2010) 1st Base Texas Rangers 2013
- Asher Wojciechowski (2010) Pitcher, U.S. National team 2009; Houston Astros 2015

Something Bigger Than Overthrowing Small Governments

The Long Gray Line-Government

- Johnson Hagood (1847) S.C. State Comptroller 1876-80, Governor of South Carolina 1880-82. CSA Brigadier General
- Hugh S. Thompson (1856) S.C. Superintendent of Education 1876-82, Governor of South Carolina 1882-86, Assistant U.S. Treasury Secretary 1886-89, U.S. Civil Service Commissioner 1889-92. Thompson Hall is named for him.
- Thomas B. Ferguson (1861) U.S. Ambassador to Norway/Sweden 1894–98
- George W. Croft (1865) S.C. State Representative 1882-83, 1901–02; State Senator 1883-1901; U.S. Congressman from the Second District of South Carolina 1903-04
- George W. Dargan (1865) S.C. State Representative 1877-80, U.S. Congressman from South Carolina 1883-91
- George Johnstone (1865) U.S. Congressman from South Carolina 1891-93
- Joseph H. Earle (1866) S.C. State Representative 1878-82, State Senator 1882-86, South Carolina Attorney General 1886-90, United States Senator 1897
- William E. Gonzales (1886) U.S. Ambassador to Cuba 1913–19 and Peru 1920–22
- Edward C. Mann (1901) U.S. Congressman from South Carolina 1919-21
- Gabriel H. Mahon (1911) U.S. Congressman from South Carolina 1936-39
- Charles E. Daniel (1918) United States Senator from South Carolina 1954
- Maurice G. Burnside (1924) U.S. Congressman from West Virginia 1949-53, 55-57 (attended 1920-22)
- Marvin Griffin (1929) Lt. Governor and Governor of Georgia 1948-59
- Thomas H. Pope (1935) S.C State Representative 1936-42, 45-49; Speaker of the House 1949-50
- George Bell Timmerman, Jr. (1937) Lt. Governor 1947-55, Governor of South Carolina 1955-59

- Marion H. Smoak (1938) S.C. State Representative 1966-69, United States Chief of Protocol 1972-74
- James R. Mann (1941) S.C. State Representative 1948-52, U.S. Congressman from South Carolina 1969-79
- Ernest Hollings (1942) S.C. State Representative 1949-55, Lt. Governor 1955-59, Governor 1959-63, United States Senator 1966-2005
- John C. West (1942) S.C. State Senator 1954-66, Lt. Governor 1966-70, Governor 1971-75, U.S. Ambassador to Saudi Arabia 1977-81
- LTG George M. Seignious, U.S. Army (1942) Director, Arms Control and Disarmament Agency 1979-81; Delegate at Large for Arms Control 1981-84
- Harlan E. Mitchell (1943) U.S. Congressman from Georgia 1957-60, Georgia State Senator 1960-62
- Burnett Maybank, Jr. (1945) Lt. Governor of South Carolina 1959-63
- Tim Valentine (1949) U.S. Congressman from North Carolina 1982-94
- W. Brantley Harvey, Jr. (1951) S.C. State Representative 1958-74, Lt. Governor 1975-79
- Clyde Hagler (1953) Florida House of Representatives 1974-80
- Donald C. Latham (1955) Assistant Secretary of Defense 1981-87
- James B. Culbertson (1960) U.S. Ambassador to The Netherlands 2008-09
- Langhorne "Tony" Motley (1960) U.S. Ambassador to Brazil 1981-83, Assistant Secretary of State 1983-85
- COL James Endicott, USA, (1960) Assistant Secretary of Veterans Affairs 1991-93
- Harry "Buck" Limehouse (1960) South Carolina Secretary of Transportation 2007-11
- William H. O'Dell (1960) S.C. State Senator 1988-present
- Gen. ChokechaiHongstong (1963) Deputy Prime Minister of Thailand
- Joseph P. Riley, Jr. (1964) S.C. State Representative 1968-74, Mayor of Charleston, South Carolina 1975–present

Something Bigger Than Overthrowing Small Governments

- William Sansom (1964) Tennessee Secretary of Transportation 1979-81, Commissioner of Finance 1981-83
- Bob Hall (1964) Texas State Senator 2015-
- Evan S. Dobelle (1966) United States Chief of Protocol 1977-78, Massachusetts Commissioner of Environmental Management 1981-87
- Lt. Gen. Frank Libutti USMC (1966) 1st New York City Deputy Police Commissioner for Counterterrorism 2001-03; Undersecretary, Department of Homeland Security 2003-05
- F. Gregory Delleny, Jr. (1974) S.C. State Representative 1991–present
- CAPT William J. Luti USN (1975) National Security Advisor to Vice President Dick Cheney 2001, Deputy Undersecretary of Defense 2001-05, Special Assistant to President George W. Bush 2005-09
- Creighton B. Coleman (1979) S.C. State Representative 2001-2008; S.C. State Senator 2009–present
- Steve Buyer (1980) U.S. Congressman from Indiana 1992-2010. Buyer Auditorium in Mark Clark Hall is named for him.
- Charles Sims Jr. (1980) Georgia House of Representatives 1996–2014
- Lt. Gen. Hussein Al-Majali (1981) Jordanian Ambassador to Bahrain 2005-10
- J. Gresham Barrett (1983) S.C. State Representative 1996-2002, U.S. Congressman from South Carolina 2002-10
- Thom Goolsby (1984) North Carolina State Senator 2011–present
- Ted Vick (1995) S.C. State Representative 2005–present
- Christian McDaniel (1997) Kentucky State Senator 2012–present

The Long Gray Line-Other

- James Robertson (1850) Superintendent, Georgia Military Institute
- Benjamin Sloan (1856) President, University of South Carolina

- Ellison Capers (1857) 1st President of Sewanee University; CSA Brigadier General and Episcopal Bishop
- George E. Haynsworth (1861) as a cadet fired the first shot at the steamer Star of the West from the battery manned by cadets on Morris Island in January, 1861.
- Kenneth G. Matheson (1886) President of Georgia Tech and Drexel University
- Henry S. Hartzog (1886) President of Clemson University and University of Arkansas
- Dr. Walter "Curley" Watson (1931) oldest living graduate and oldest practicing doctor in U.S. (age 102) at his death in October, 2012
- A. Lee Chandler (1944) former Chief Justice of the South Carolina Supreme Court
- Calder Willingham (1944) novelist, playwright and Oscar nominee; screenplays included *One-Eyed Jacks*, *The Graduate* and *Little Big Man*
- Arland D. Williams, Jr. (1957)-saved five other passengers following the crash of Air Florida Flight 90 into the 14th Street Bridge and Potomac River in Washington, DC on January 13, 1982. Williams passed the lifeline lowered for him by a rescue helicopter to others, and died as a result. Posthumously awarded the Coast Guard Gold Lifesaving Medal by President Reagan, 14th Street Bridge over Potomac River named in his honor. [Note-Lt. Col. George Mattar (1963) also died in the Air Florida crash]
- Dr. John Palms (1958) President of Georgia State University and the University of South Carolina
- Evan Dobelle (1966) President, City College of San Francisco and the University of Hawaii
- Pat Conroy (1967) best-selling author whose works include *The Great Santini*, *The Water Is Wide*, *The Lords of Discipline*, *The Prince of Tides*, *Beach Music*, and *South of Broad*
- James O. Rigney, Jr. (1974) author (writing with pen names of Robert Jordan, Reagan O'Reilly, *et al.*) whose works include the best-selling *The Wheel of Time* series, *The Fallon Blood* and several *Conan the Barbarian* novels

Something Bigger Than Overthrowing Small Governments

- Steve Pettit (1978), evangelist and fifth president of Bob Jones University
- Morris Robinson (1991) two-time All-American Offensive Lineman and football team captain, now a nationally renowned opera singer who has performed at Carnegie Hall and with the Metropolitan Opera. First black artist to sign an exclusive contract with a classical label (Decca)
- Frances "Lu" Parker (1992-MAT) Miss USA, 1994
- Nancy Mace (1999) First female graduate and one of the first group of four female cadets to enter The Citadel in 1996, daughter of former Commandant of Cadets B.Gen. Emory Mace (1963)
- Lt. Shane Childers USMC (2001) first American KIA in Operation Iraqi Freedom, one of 18 alumni killed in Iraq and Afghanistan.

ADDENDUM 2

REFERENCED ON PAGE 52

LAWRENCE N. FREEDMAN SERGEANT MAJOR, UNITED STATES ARMY
From a 1997 Article by Ted Gup, *ArlingtonCemetery.net*

In some ways, Lawrence N. Freedman was an unlikely candidate for the career he chose. Born into a devoutly Jewish home in Philadelphia, he brazenly declared himself "SuperJew," a nickname used by his colleagues in Delta Force, the elite counter-terrorist unit headquartered at Fort Bragg, N.C. His sister even made him a Superman-like cape with the Hebrew letter for "S" that he wore at parties. On Friday evenings he would sometimes say the blessing over the Sabbath candles, but he could also be as obscene and profane as anyone on base.

He was deliberately over-the-top. A notorious flirt and rogue, he tested all who came in contact with him, taking their measure and weeding out the squeamish. He was only 5-foot-

9, but armored with muscle from years of pumping iron, running five miles a day and keeping his survival skills sharp. When he wasn't on a mission he was often cruising down the highway on his Harley Davidson FXRT, 1340 cc, the fringe of his black leather jacket and chaps flying. To the outside world he might well have been mistaken for an aging truant, but many who got close enough to know he saw him as a man consumed by the military's ideals of duty and honor. "He believed in everything we all believed in -- red, white and blue, John Wayne, apple pie," says former colleague Ron Franklin.

Freedman sought out risky assignments around the world. First it was as a Green Beret in Vietnam, where he married his first wife, a Vietnamese woman, and adopted her two children. Then it was Central America. He was there for Desert One, the aborted 1980 mission to rescue the U.S. hostages in Iran, a journey that took the lives of eight of his fellow soldiers. From 1986 until 1990, he helped train the Delta Force. Then he retired -- at least that was his cover story. In fact, he signed on with the CIA's Counter-Terrorism unit.

As a soldier, Freedman was many things -- a medic, a "bomber" trained to defuse explosive devices, an intelligence officer, an expert in hand-to-hand combat, and a communications, or "commo," man. But as a sniper he was nearly without peer. Once, remembers Gale McMillan, a maker of specialty weapons, the two of them were testing night scopes at Camp Perry. It was a night so dark it swallowed up the faces of their watches. Freedman lay down, steadied his arm on a sandbag, and fixed his scope at a target no larger than a quarter at a distance of 250 yards. He squeezed off five shots. When they examined the target they found a single ragged hole through which all five bullets had passed, McMillan says.

In 1992, Freedman sought an assignment in Operation Restore Hope, the campaign to deliver food to Somalia's famine-stricken population and to restrain the country's warring factions. He was a 51-year-old grandfather. Some ten days before shipping out, he visited McMillan in Phoenix. The visit was part personal, part professional. Freedman appreciated weapons. He always carried a Colt .45, its grip customized to fit his hand, its works "tuned to combat" -- retooled so the clip would feed faster. In Phoenix, he bought a tactical scope for his .308 rifle, a 10-power built to click each time he adjusted his aim for distance. The day before

Something Bigger Than Overthrowing Small Governments

Freedman left, he and McMillan had a long talk. "I was telling him," recalls McMillan, "`Look in the mirror and see the silver in your temples. That ought to tell you it's time to slowdown and let the young guys take the risks and do the dirty work. You've already done everything expected of you.' He kind of laughed and said, `If there's any way I want to go, it's doing it.'"

His wife, Teresa, remembers the last phone call she got from him. "His voice was different. It was more like a real goodbye. It was more like this was a journey he was going on and he wasn't going to be returning. I sensed the fear that possibly this time he would not be back."

At 6 a.m. on December 23, 1992, Teresa's doorbell rang. It was the CIA's liaison officer at Fort Bragg. His message was stark, if incomplete: Larry had been killed the day before. Teresa screamed, then collapsed in his arms.

Only days and weeks later would she be given any details. She was told Freedman had driven over a Russian-built mine near the town of Bardera. His body had been helicoptered to the USS Tripoli, where a medical officer filled out the death certificate. The blast had caused severe head trauma, blown off his lower right leg and opened his chest. Death was "immediate." Three men with Freedman, all listed as "State Department Security Personnel," were also wounded. One of them died, she was later told.

A former CIA officer who worked with Freedman says that while the precise nature of his mission in Somalia was not known to him, it was essentially to perform a liaison role between the U.S. Embassy in Somalia and the U.S. military forces then arriving in the country. Freedman was part of a "pickup" team, an elite paramilitary unit whose job was to provide the agency and the resident ambassador with a stream of intelligence to guide specific military operations.

Freedman's funeral was held at Fort Myer Chapel in Arlington. Col. Sanford Dresin, then the senior-ranking Jewish chaplain in the armed forces, gathered Freedman's immediate family together to observe a time-honored ritual of grief -- the rending of the black cloth known as keriah. But they could find no black cloth, so Dresin improvised and used black paper. Such a field expediency would have been appreciated by Freedman, he remarked.

During the service, Dresin referred to the tradition of Jewish warriors, such as the Maccabees who two millenniums earlier had valiantly struggled with the Syrians. The service was attended by family and friends, among them beefy members of Delta Force and a cadre of dark-suited men behind mirrored sunglasses, some of whom arrived by limousine. In the days after, Teresa received many expressions of condolence. One of the callers was President George Bush, who telephoned from Camp David.

To the public, Freedman was identified as a civilian employee of the Defense Department. On a Pentagon casualty list, his name was even misspelled, and he was given the wrong middle initial. Hardly anyone recognized the error, much less the man.

On December 31, 1992, CIA Director Robert M. Gates awarded Freedman a posthumous Intelligence Star for exceptional service. The citation recognized his "superior performance under hazardous combat conditions with the Central Intelligence Agency."

It took three years for the agency to send Teresa the medal and citation. With it came a letter and a warning: "Those persons who may be told of these awards will be left to your judgment; however, please do not disclose the details on which the awards were based. In addition, please do not release or cooperate in the release of any publicity concerning these awards."

Following Freedman's death, contributions in his honor were made to a Fort Bragg museum dedicated to special warfare, supporting construction of the "Sergeant First Class Lawrence 'SuperJew' Freedman Memorial Theater."

Teresa retains a photograph of two Belgian paratroopers standing at an American-built bridge in Somalia near where her husband fell. Stenciled in white paint on a steel plate at the entrance to the bridge is written "Lawrence R. Freedman Bridge." (Again the middle initial is wrong.) And at Fort Bragg, in the plaza that honors heroes of the Special Operations Command, Freedman's name appears on a plaque, listed as a State Department casualty.

Today Freedman's grave at Arlington National Cemetery, Section Eight, No. 10177, is marked by a jet-black tombstone. On it is the Star of David, the wings of a paratrooper, a Green Beret and an inscription: "The life of the dead is placed in the memory of the living." [48]

Something Bigger Than Overthrowing Small Governments

ADDENDUM 3
REFERENCED ON PAGE 99

ON MOGADISHU'S "GREEN LINE," NOTHING IS SACRED
By Diana Jean Schemo. *The New York Times*, 14 Feb. 1993

Mogadishu, Somalia Feb.13 – The clocks at the Cathedral of the Croce del Sud stopped at 9:45.

The cherubs looked ever skyward as fire sent the roof crashing in shards to the floor. White spaces where gilded crosses once hung tell of plunder, and the sepulchers of the bishops remembered only as Zucchetto and Colombo have been emptied.

The remains of the bishops may be lost somewhere along the so-called "green line" that divides northern and southern Mogadishu between warring factions. The area between them has become a ghost town, haunted by the memories of splendor and of failure. The hopes of the one-time residents have been crushed and twisted beyond repair, like the metal gates to the local palaces of commerce, art and religion.

"It Sparkled"

"Before the church burned, it had beautiful golden colors, and colored tiles," said Tahlil Omar Hassan. "It sparkled . . . like New York," offered Abdi Yare Huyogo, a 12-year-old who stood on the carpet of broken tiles nearby.

"It was like flowers," Abdul-Ahi Ulo Sahel called down from the perch where he hacked away at the church's remaining beams for firewood. "It had gold and brass. It was bella, bella," he added in the Italian that still peppers the Somali language.

Long the epicenter of the fight between two clan militias for control of the Somali capital, the line dividing Mogadishu is also a microcosm of Somalia's past and future. Its streets are littered with the fallen monuments of both colonial and indigenous masters; its bombed and ransacked buildings stand as testimony to the latest blood rivalry for control.

The United States Marines at the command post at the one-time Commercial Bank of Somalia speak by way of comparison of the destruction and tension in Beirut as they patrol Mogadishu. But Mohammed Jirdeh Hussein, a Somali businessman whose family owns several office buildings along the dividing line, remembers the days before the fighting started and looks beyond what is lost to what may be. At the now-closed Hotel Croce del Sud, the former assistant manager and receptionist await the return of the owner, an Italian named Tomas Briata.

Mr. Briata last spoke to the men in April. In a call from his Padua, Italy, home to the Italian consulate, Mr. Briata told Ali Mohammed Roble, the receptionist, and Abdul Rahman Salam, the assistant manager, to watch over the hotel.

"We are waiting for him to come, and he is coming," said Mr. Roble, a 50-year-old who had worked in the hotel from the age of 15. There are no guests, but Mr. Roble wears a beige safari uniform. He sweeps the courtyard where cafe tables once surrounded the fountain. He shows off the hotel rooms, proud that only three of 40 were hit by bombs.

"In front of our hotel there were trucks firing," said Mr. Salam. "The bandits came with guns, saying, 'Give us all the dollars you have saved here.' "We'd say we didn't have dollars. We don't even have food," Mr. Salam recalled, and shuddered. "So they'd take our watches, whatever we had in our pockets." Looters took all the mattresses, beds, cutlery and linens.

No Pay and No Mail

The men, as desperate as they are loyal, have not received salaries since April. There is no mail service here. The only telephones are the satellite phones foreigners bring, and the cost of using those is exorbitant.

"Tell Briata we are in this condition," Mr. Roble said, as he unfolded a paper with the owner's phone number.

"Tell him of our sacrifice"

Mr. Briata left Mogadishu on an Italian military plane, after a mob of police officers, soldiers, bandits and beggars climbed the hotel's walls on a looting spree in the last days before the final fall of Mohamed Siad Barre, the ousted Somali dictator. Mr. Briata, his employees and the handful of guests fought off the intruders' guns and knives with machetes. Mr. Briata, 60 years old at the time, was thrown from the hotel's second-story window and broke two vertebrae, his daughter-in-law, Tracy Briata, said from Padua in a telephone interview.

Something Bigger Than Overthrowing Small Governments

The family escaped, but lost computers, paintings, furniture -- virtually all its personal belongings, she said. They carried no suitcases when they fled.

"I am trying desperately to find a way to come back, but I have no money," Mr. Briata said in halting English before passing the phone to his daughter-in-law. He said he would seek other investors, or perhaps help from the Italian government. But most of all, he would need to know that the bloodletting will not begin again.

Selling the Past

Some Somalis are beginning to show enterprise again. At the foot of the Italianate arch erected in the center of the old city in 1928 for a visit by Mussolini that never materialized, Aden Sidou Rage ventured to sell a rare prize: glass negatives that depict these streets in the 1930's. He kept them in a brown plastic pouch, the kind now used for the American military's field rations. The photos show men in fascist uniforms sipping tea and espresso along the piazza and at the Cafe Nazionale, last a camera shop, now a mass of concrete debris. [49]

BIBLIOGRAPHY

1. Middleton, Drew. "Amid Guantanamo War Games, The Peaceful Life," Special to *The New York Times*. A version of this article appears in print on 3 Apr. 1983, Section A, Page 2 of the National edition

2. "S-Mine." *Wikipedia*, Wikimedia Foundation, 18 Nov. 2019, en.wikipedia.org/wiki/S-mine.
   Also excerpts from the *U.S. War Department Technical Manual TM-E 30-451*: Handbook on German Military Forces, 1945 (Ch. VIII, Sec. V.5.a-b).

3. Ap. "12 Bodies Recovered from Florida River in Navy Plane Crash." *The New York Times*, 2 May 1983.

4. Thompson, Hunter S., et al. *The Proud Highway: Saga of a Desperate Southern Gentleman, 1955-1967*. Ballantine Books, 1998.

5. Gup, Ted. "Lawrence N. Freedman Sergeant Major, United States Army." *ArlingtonCemetery.net*, 30 Dec. 1992, www.arlingtoncemetery.net/lnfreedman.htm.

6. "Armed Forces of the Democratic Republic of the Congo." *Wikipedia*, Wikimedia Foundation, 8 Jan. 2020, en.wikipedia.org/wiki/Armed_Forces_of_the_Democratic_Republic_of_the_Congo.

7. Brooke, James. "U.S. ARMS AIRLIFT TO ANGOLA REBELS IS SAID TO GO ON." *The New York Times*, 27 July 1987.

8. "Operation Eastern Exit." *Wikipedia*, Wikimedia Foundation, 23 Sept. 2019, en.wikipedia.org/wiki/Operation_Eastern_Exit.

9. Diana Jean Schemo. "On Mogadishu's Green Line, Nothing Is Sacred." *The New York Times*. 14 Feb, 1993 Section 1 Page 2

10. "Charleston Church Shooting." *Wikipedia*, Wikimedia Foundation, 20 Feb. 2020, en.wikipedia.org/wiki/Charleston_church_shooting.

11. John S. Brown, Brigadier General, USA, Chief of Military History. *The United States Army in Somalia 1992-1994.* CMH Pub 70-81-1 Pg.14, 19, 26

12. "Battle of Mogadishu (1993)." *Wikipedia*, Wikimedia Foundation, 2 Feb. 2020, en.wikipedia.org/wiki/Battle_of_Mogadishu_(1993).

13. Paul Richter and Howard Libit. Times Staff Writers. "Clinton's Black Hawk History." *The Wall Street Journal*, Dow Jones Company, 6 Aug. 2002.

14. "Battle of Mogadishu (1993)." *Wikipedia*, Wikimedia Foundation, 2 Feb. 2020, en.wikipedia.org/wiki/Battle_of_Mogadishu_(1993).

15. Jehl, Douglas. "CLINTON AND CONGRESS: Intelligence; BUDGET CUT LIKELY FOR INTELLIGENCE." *The New York Times*, 18 June 1993.

16. "Missing Person Report, Jacob Erwin Wetterling," *FBI* St. Joseph, Minnesota. 22 Oct. 1989,

17. "Missing Person Report, CRYSTAL ANN TYMICH." *FBI*, 10 Sept. 2010.

18. "Mainstream Media: Pedophilia Isn't a Crime, but Being Unvaccinated Is - *Conservative News,* 1 Nov. 2017.

19. "Proof of Concept." *Wikipedia*, Wikimedia Foundation, 9 Feb. 2020, en.wikipedia.org/wiki/Proof_of_concept.

20. AFA. "Breaking News Spiritual Perspective: Sandy Rios, cultural expert and talk show host on the American Family Radio network," *Charisma News*, October 30, 2013.

21. Armani, Christian. Private life coaching session. July 17, 1987.

22. "Nomenclature of an Assassination Cabal, Chapter 7, Albert Osborne, Missionary for the A.C.C.C. and the Cabal." *Scribbleguy.* www.scribblguy.50megs.com/torbitt7.htm

23. "Mos Eisley - Wikipedia Republished // WIKI 2." - *Wikipedia Republished // WIKI 2*, wiki2.org/en/Mos_Eisley_Cantina.

24. Rimban, Luz. "Lagayan, Abra: 'Bigtime Corruption in a Small Town'." *The Manila Times*. 13 Sept. 2011.

25. Althaus, Dudley -, et al. "Durango Becoming Ground Zero for Zetas-Sinaloa Cartel Battle." *InSight Crime*, 6 Oct. 2017.

26. Bertrand, Natasha. "This Mexican Town Is the Sex-Trafficking Capital of the World." *Business Insider*, 10 Feb. 2015.

27. Batty, David. "Mexico's Drugs War Escalates as Eight Headless Bodies Discovered in Durango." *The Guardian*, Guardian News and Media, 12 May 2011.

28. "Old City (Bern)." *Wikipedia*, Wikimedia Foundation, 2 Jan. 2020, en.wikipedia.org/wiki/Old_City_(Bern).

29. "Pan Am Flight 73." *Wikipedia*, Wikimedia Foundation, 21 Feb. 2020, en.wikipedia.org/wiki/Pan_Am_Flight_73.

30. Ghosh, Tarak. *Flight 73: The Inner Story*. 2018

31. Hussain, Zahid. "Pan Am Hijack in Karachi: Pakistan Security Forces Handling of Situation Raises Questions." *India Today*, 30 Sept. 1986.

32. "Chapter 39." *The Best of Josh McDowell: a Ready Defense*, by Josh McDowell and Bill Wilson, Thomas Nelson Publishers, 1993. Chapter 39, pages 395-398.

33. Peach, David. "Gideon Bible Story Summary With Lesson." *What Christians Want To Know RSS*, www.whatchristianswanttoknow.com/gideon-bible-story-summary-with-lesson/.

34. Meyers, Joyce. *Never Give Up: Relentless Determination To Overcome Life's Challenges*. Chapter: Fight Don't Fear, First E-book Edition, 2009.

35. "Clinton–Lewinsky Scandal." *Wikipedia*, Wikimedia Foundation, 1 Feb. 2020, en.wikipedia.org/wiki/Clinton%E2%80%93Lewinsky_scandal.

36. "Erik Prince & Breitbart CONFIRM True Pundit's Hillary Weiner Email Story." *True Pundit*, 5 Nov. 2016.

37. Reuters, Thomson. "What Is Complicity or Accomplice Liability?" *Findlaw.com*, 25 Mar. 2019, criminal.findlaw.com/criminal-law-basics/what-is-complicity-or-accomplice-liability.html.

38. Brennan, Christopher. "Seven Bay Area Officers Face Charges in Teenage Prostitute Police Sex Scandal." *New York Daily News*, 9 Sept. 2016.

39. Watkins, James. "Jim Watkins Quote: 'A River Cuts through Rock, Not Because of Its Power, but Because of Its Persistence." *Quotefancy.com*

40. "LGBT History Month Promotes Gay Porn To Kids." *Pacific Justice Institute*. 1 Oct. 2013.

41. *SafeLibraries®*. "Child Porn in Libraries Due to American Library Association Facilitation; Another Library Breaks the Law." safelibraries.com, 25 Dec. 2015.

42. Butts, Charlie. "'Porn-Safe' Libraries Clearly Not ALA's Goal." *OneNewsNow.com*, 22 Feb. 2016.

43. Staff, WND. "Librarian Fired for Reporting Child Pornography." *WND*, 21 Mar. 2008.

44. Carr, Grace. "Gov. Ralph Northam: 'I Don't Have Any Regrets' About Infanticide Comments." *The Daily Signal*, 1 Feb. 2019.

45. "PJI Asks Federal Court to Block Abortion Speech Mandate." *Pacific Justice Institute*, 17 Nov. 2015.

46. Quotes, Benjamin Franklin. "112 Benjamin Franklin Quotes That Light The World." *KeepInspiring.me,* 13 Feb. 2020.

47. "Attorney General William P. Barr Appoints Katharine Sullivan to Be Principal Deputy Assistant Attorney General for the Office of Justice Programs and Announces That Laura L. Rogers Will Serve as the Acting Director of the Office on Violence Against Women." *The United States Department of Justice*, 17 June 2019.

48. Gup, Ted. "Lawrence N. Freedman Sergeant Major, United States Army: From a 1997 Article By Ted Gup" *ArlingtonCemetery.net*, 30 Dec. 1992, www.arlingtoncemetery.net/lnfreedman.htm

49. Schemo, Diana Jean. "On Mogadishu's 'Green Line,' Nothing Is Sacred." *The New York Times*, 14 Feb. 1993.

TRIBUTE

This book would not be complete without a tribute to the following people who at one time or another taught me there are a million ways to die but only one way to live ... fearlessly. There are most likely so many more names that should be printed, so forgive me if they do not come to mind. But please be assured, your faces are engraved in my heart forever:

Ralph & Edith Baz
Sharkey, May & Neseebe Baz
Alicia & Courtney Denney
Douglas McArthur Baz
Franklin Delano Roosevelt Baz
Lavern Baz
Lilly Blanton
Belsar, Martha, William, Charlene Cooper
Tom Flores
Ambassador Bill Wilson
Alex Bassina
Dana Robinson
Walter Gray
Scotty O'Neal

Jim Smith
Bill Mott
Steve Pettit
Ebbie Taylor
Jim Scott
Leo Mercado
Maxie Birch
Rex Rodrique
Kenny Caldwell
Scott Wilson (R Co. Citadel Class of 76')
The Citadel Soccer Team
R Co. The Citadel Class of 79'
Ed Benes, "Frijole" (USMC Blue Angels)

Something Bigger Than Overthrowing Small Governments

Classmates of USMC Basic School and Officer Infantry School
Ground Branch CIA
Maritime Branch CIA
Air Branch CIA
Jim Monroe, "Alabama"
Buck Ashby
Greg Vogel
Ron Franklin, "Popeye"
Tim C., "The Beard"
Kelly Brimhall, "The Mormon"
Mick McGrath, "Vern"
Carlos Rivas, "The Excitable Boy"
Steve Stormoen, "Hormone"
Dick Bradford, "Dickus"
Julio Ryan Royal
Larry Freedman, "Super Jew"
Mike Raiole
Bill Gerhardt, "Buddha"
John Perkins, "Farmer John"
Rob Chadwick, "Sniper"
Mike Radnothy
Chuck Kleebauer
Tom Fosmire
John Hermes, "Pencil Neck"
Jimmy Byars
Jim Marsh
Hank Booth
Serge Alexandrov
Tom Hannifen
Steve Cash
Jim Ryan (Air Branch)
Garn Anderson
Col. Nick Pratt (USMC)
Polecat
TJ
Ric Prado
Billy Waugh
Rich (Lido Base)
Centra Spike (Lido Base)
Dave Phillips, "Doc"
John Snow, "Little Doc"
Don Johnson
Jim Mcginnis
President Jonas Savimbi (UNITA)
Captain Martin (UNITA)
General Wambu (UNITA)
Steve Einsel
Eric Volz
Todd Burns
Bud Keilani
Mark Burnett
Michael Watkins
Col. George Navadel (USMC)
Col. Jim Williams (USMC)
Col. Wesley Fox (USMC)
GySgt Clayton Hartsel
GySgt Gloria Cano
Dennis Stephenson
Katy Sullivan
Capt. Buford Wells (USMC)
Dell Spry
Tina Paulson
Kirk Freeman
Gonzo
Thad Turner (Sublime Prince/Christina)
John Long, (Sublime Prince)
Ben Darr (Sublime Prince)
Adam Curtis (Christina)
Lee Barber (Christina)
Tommy (Christina)
Kevin Chapman (Christina)
Bobby Keene (Christina)
Scott Clark (Christina)
Pastor Rudy Gonzalez
Gianluca Sciorilli
Dan Erber
Lisa Christoffersen
Scott Bailey
George Ciganik
Rodney Nutter
Nick Lembo
Mark Johnson
Anita Busch
Marcella Winn
Pastor Byron MacDonald
William Lovett
Ken Schaffer
Tony Nassif
Gator
Eric Rose
Gen. William G. Boykin (USA)
Gen. Roy Moss (USMC)
Gen. George M. Seignious (Commandant The Citadel)
Craig Sawyer
Patrick Auge Sensei
Kaoru Sugiyama Sensei
Students of the International Yoseikan Budo Federation